The Play Therapy Primer

The Play Therapy Primer

Second Edition

Kevin J. O'Connor

John Wiley & Sons, Inc.

New York • Chichester • Weinheim • Brisbane • Singapore • Toronto

ISBN 0-471-24873-8

Printed in the United States of America.

Preface

The first edition of this primer was entitled *The Play Therapy Primer: An Integration of Theories and Techniques.* As the subtitle reflected, the bulk of that edition contained a description of play therapy that integrated elements of several existing theories and techniques using cognitive developmental theory as an organizing framework. Further, the integrated model that was presented maintained a broadly systemic or ecosystemic perspective. The organization of the material reflected a widespread trend in the field of psychology toward the integration of divergent theories and techniques. Such integration has been lauded by many for emphasizing the similarities among different models as opposed to their differences. Thus, integrated models create the opportunity for dialogue between professionals who might otherwise see their views as having virtually no common ground. Instead of arguing the differences between interpretation (a psychoanalytic concept) and reframing (a cognitive behavioral concept), theorists and clinicians might integrate the concepts and emphasize the similarity between the two techniques.

While many continue to develop and to value integrated models, others have begun to emphasize the importance of differentiating between two types or degrees of integration. One type or level of integration involves finding and articulating similarities between existing theories and techniques. In so doing, the authors do not make substantive changes to either the elements or structure of the original models. The other type or level of integration involves making significant changes to the elements or structure of the models from which the integrative model was derived. Let's use the preceding example to note the difference between these variations on the process of integration. One way to integrate the concepts of interpretation and reframing without necessarily changing their meaning or the structure of the theories from which they are drawn would be to suggest that the difference between the two is largely semantic. Both actually mean the same thing. That is, both mean that the therapist conveys to the client an alternative understanding of his or her situation. Let us call this *simple integration*. Alternatively, the concepts could be integrated by introducing a new concept, change processes, to link the two. For example, both interpretation and reframing are similar because they are designed to promote change in the client's thinking. The concept of change processes could then be used to link ever more divergent events in psychotherapy on the premise that each promotes change. This latter integration strategy, which we will call *complex integration* actually creates a new, third model.

Why is it important to differentiate between these two strategies or levels of interpretation? The issue is one of scientific clarity in the conceptualization, communication, and implementation of ideas. Simple integration is important and serves to eliminate conceptual redundancy in the field. It promotes the exchange of ideas and facilitates cross-fertilization in theory and technique. Complex integration is important because it creates new ideas and practices in the field while building on the strengths of what has gone before. The goal of any form of integration should be to maintain an ongoing dialogue between theories by looking for points of differentiation while conducting judicious integration (Safran & Messer, 1997). The model presented in the first edition of this Primer was an attempt at writing a simple integration of many of the ideas and techniques found in the field of play therapy. Over the past 10 years, the ideas presented in the first Primer crystallized (O'Connor & Braverman, 1997) and, with the help of Dr. Sue Ammen, became Ecosystemic Play Therapy (O'Connor & Ammen, 1997). Ecosystemic Play Therapy is a complex integration and, indeed, a new free-standing model.

The model continues to maintain a broadly *ecosystemic* perspective. Thus, the type of play therapy described in this volume is somewhat less than traditional in that it is characterized by a shift in the therapist's thinking away from an exclusively individual approach. Historically, play therapists, regardless of their theoretical orientation, have focused on the individual child when conceptualizing everything from the pathology of the child they were treating to the therapy they were implementing. Ecosystemic Play Therapy focuses on the totality or pattern of relations between organisms and their environment. This emphasis is unique to the extent that the play therapist is forced to consider the multiple systems of which the child is a part from the point of intake until termination. The focus is similar to, but broader than, the family systems approach. The model most closely resembles community psychology in the breadth of its conceptual focus and should be familiar to many of those who were trained within a traditional social work model.

Since the publication of the first edition, all those in the mental health field have felt the impact of managed care with respect to the delivery of client services. The rise of managed care programs reflects a shift in the administration of most people's medical insurance. This shift was triggered by the continuous upward spiral of medical costs over the past few decades. Traditional, private medical insurance paid for an insured's care as long as a physician indicated the treatment was medically necessary. As a result, mental health care tended to be dominated or at least administered by psychiatrists and to allow for very long-term treatment. As managed care companies took over for private insurance and attempted to control costs, there were some significant changes. On the positive side, managed care organizations sought out nonmedical therapists such as psychologists, social workers, and counselors who provided mental health services at a lower cost than did psychiatrists. Cost control also meant a reduction in the number of sessions for which managed care companies would agree to pay. This is probably the most controversial aspect of the plan. On the one hand, it forced mental health practitioners to seek out more effective, short-term intervention strategies and to evaluate the efficacy of the interventions they used. This tended to mean more clients got better treatment faster. On the other hand, the refusal of managed care companies to provide long-term treatment in all but the most extreme circumstances meant that persons with ongoing life problems or serious, chronic mental illness were often denied the kind of care they needed. As a result, many such patients became the responsibility of various governmental agencies including community mental health centers. These centers soon found themselves overwhelmed and unable to provide the services clients needed. Slow to respond to the needs of their constituents, politicians are only now beginning to advocate for mental health services that will genuinely meet the needs of young and old alike.

The increased emphasis that managed care placed and continues to place on short-term treatment is discussed throughout this edition. Issues of the populations and types of problems to which it is best suited are addressed. Conversely, the fact that not all children's mental health problems can reasonably be managed in 4 to 12 sessions is also addressed. The pendulum set in motion by managed care is beginning to swing back and it seems clear that it will settle at a place where a broad range of client needs are recognized and an equally broad array of services are available to address those needs.

As with the first edition, this edition is geared to the novice practitioner. Part I presents a history of play therapy as well as a review of the major theories of play therapy in use today. Additionally, material is presented on the importance of cultural awareness, knowledge, and skills to the effective practice of play therapy in the twenty-first century. All of this information applies equally, irrespective of the theoretical orientation finally adopted by the reader. In Part II, both Ecosystemic Play Therapy and the basic assumptions underlying the model are presented. In Part III, Ecosystemic Play Therapy is described in detail. Part IV describes the practice of structured group play therapy consistent with Ecosystemic Theory. Parts II through IV are extensively illustrated with case material. All the identifying information in each case was altered to protect the confidentiality of the clients. While most of the material was derived from actual clinical cases, certain details and in some instances entire cases may have been fabricated to optimally illustrate the concepts being presented.

While this edition was written with the student or novice therapist in mind, psychologists, psychiatrists, social workers, nurses, counselors, and child life specialists at all levels of training and experience will find this book stimulating, pragmatic, and clinically indispensable.

KEVIN J. O'CONNOR

Fresno, California

Acknowledgments

I would like to acknowledge the contributions a number of persons made to the development of the ideas presented in this volume and to the production of the final text.

First, I would like to thank the various clients with whom I have had the privilege of working over the years. My struggle to understand the nature of your experience pales in comparison to your struggles to meet the challenges of everyday life. Second, I must also thank the students and professionals I have trained. Your questions and interest have forced me to continue to organize my thoughts and develop my ideas and create a niche suited to ecosystemic thinking as it is presented in this text. Last, I would like to extend my sincere thanks to Sue Ammen whose insights and continual willingness to engage in an exchange of ideas has helped refine Ecosystemic Play Therapy to its present level of sophistication.

I would also like to thank all of those who made a personal contribution to this book. Again, I must thank those clients who have shared their lives with me so that we both might learn. I would like to thank my family of origin for their ongoing love and support. I would like to thank my nuclear family. The support of my partner Robert kept me going and prevented me from being overwhelmed by the many demands of day-to-day life none of which seem to include writing. And, I must thank my children, Ryan and Matthew, for the joy they bring to my life and for all they have taught me about children.

K.O.

Contents

PART I

Introduction

In keeping with the ecosystemic perspective of this book, the first three chapters provide the reader with a broad context for understanding and practicing play therapy. Chapter One establishes a common vocabulary for all readers by defining play and play therapy. Next, the functions of the play behavior in human life are delineated. Finally, a brief history of play therapy is provided.

Chapter Two reviews the most widely used models of play therapy as well as several other theoretical models of psychotherapy that were used to develop the Ecosystemic Play Therapy model presented in Part II. The widely used models that are reviewed are psychoanalytic play therapy, humanistic play therapy, and behavioral play therapy. Each theory is presented somewhat uncritically by describing it from the perspective of its practitioners.

Chapter Three discusses the importance of play therapists' awareness and management of the interaction of their complete ecosystem, their personal philosophy, values, background, language, religion, family experience, and culture with the ecosystem of their child clients.

CHAPTER ONE

Definition and History of Play Therapy

It is necessary to begin by defining the term *play therapy* as it is used in this text. It is logical to first define the term play by itself while examining the implications of these definitions for defining play therapy.

DEFINING PLAY

No single, comprehensive definition of the term *play* has been developed. The most often quoted definition was developed by Erikson (1950), who stated that "play is a function of the ego, an attempt to synchronize the bodily and social processes with the self" (p. 214). Play is generally thought to be the antithesis of work; it is fun. "It is free from compulsions of a conscience and from impulsions of irrationality" (p. 214). Play is also defined as (1) intrinsically motivated, (2) freely chosen, (3) nonliteral, (4) actively engaged in, and (5) pleasurable (Hughes, 1995). Many others agree that play is pleasurable (Beach, 1945; Csikszentmihalyi, 1976; Dohlinow & Bishop, 1970; Hutt, 1970; Plant, 1979; Weisler & McCall, 1976). However, if one considers the occurrence of play essential to the definition of play therapy, this way of defining play proves quite problematic. Much of what disturbed children do in play therapy is far from fun; it is compulsive, impulsive, and irrational—in other words, the opposite of everything Erikson said it should be. The traumatized child who replays a variation of the traumatizing event for the fortieth or fiftieth time in session can hardly be said to be having fun. Two questions arise: Is this child playing? And, is this play

---

This chapter was adapted from the Introduction to Part One of the *Handbook of Play Therapy* (Schaefer & O'Connor, 1983).

therapy? The answer to the first question seems to be a tentative "No"; the answer to the second question appears to be "Yes."

A further review of the literature on play reveals that certain elements are generally considered as typifying play behavior. These elements are generally consistent with what children do in their play therapy sessions.

Play is intrinsically complete; it does not depend on external rewards or other people (Csikszentmihalyi, 1976; Plant, 1979). This element is consistent with most of the behavior in which children engage during play therapy. Most children's play behavior does not require external rewards; children continue to act whether or not the adult is present. This is not to minimize the impact of the therapist's presence, only to say that it is not needed for most children to engage in play behavior.

Probably because it is intrinsically motivated, play tends to be person-dominated rather than object-dominated; that is, it is aimed not at acquiring new information about an object but at making use of the object (Hutt, 1970; Weisler & McCall, 1976). Furthermore, intrinsic motivation and object independence tend to make play highly variable across both situations and children (Weisler & McCall, 1976). Again, this seems consistent with most children's behavior during play therapy. Once the child has initially explored an object, the child tends to switch her focus to the use of the object rather than continuing to explore it. However, one notable exception comes to mind: The in-session behavior of the autistic child tends to be object-focused. Is it therefore really play? Here one would probably have to answer "No." Can one then say they do play therapy with such an autistic child? If play therapy requires that the child be able to engage in play behavior, then the answer, it seems, is "No."

Play is noninstrumental: It has no goal, either intrapersonal or interpersonal, no purpose, and no task orientation (Berlyne, 1960; Bettelheim, 1972; Goldberg & Lewis, 1969; Huizinga, 1950; Hutt, 1970; Plant, 1979; Weisler & McCall, 1976). This element is also consistent with most children's play behavior in play therapy sessions. Rarely does the child engage in play with a conscious goal in mind. Even when the child says, "Let's build a castle out of blocks," rarely has the end point, or even the process, been consciously planned.

Csikszentmihalyi (1975, 1976) talked about the concept of "flow" as it relates to play: Flow, among other things, involves a centering of attention in which action and awareness merge and a loss of self-consciousness occurs in the sense that the child is paying more attention to the task than to her own body state. These last two points are evidenced when an adult walks in on a child who is playing. Initially the child remains oblivious to the adult's presence, but when her attention is finally broken, she may seem suddenly embarrassed and then, just as suddenly and quite genuinely, realize that she has needed to go to the bathroom for quite some time. Flow is characteristic of children's play behavior in play therapy sessions.

Several authors noted that play behavior does not occur in novel or frightening situations (Beach, 1945; Berlyne, 1960; Hutt, 1970; Mason, 1965; Piaget, 1962; Switsky, Haywood, & Isett, 1974; Weisler & McCall, 1976). Most play therapists find that children do very little that resembles play when they first enter treatment. In fact, much of a play therapist's training is geared toward the development of a style and techniques that will help the child feel safe and relaxed enough in the playroom so that play will ensue.

Many writers identify variations on the general concept of play behavior, including pretending, fantasy, and games with rules.

Pretend play is characterized by certain types of communication:

1. *Negation:* The means, often abrupt, by which the state is broken or terminated.
   a. "I stealed your cake."
   b. "I don't care. It's not cake any more."
2. *Enactment:* The gestures, tone, statements, or attitudes that the actor puts forth to establish or support the pretend situation or character, for example, crying like a baby, speaking sternly like a parent, making noises like a motor.
3. *Signals:* These support pretense by tipping off the partner and urging him to go along with the play. They include winking, grinning, and giggling.
4. The preparatory gestures set the stage, supply terms and conditions, and get the ball rolling at the beginning of the pretense: "That green telephone is the kind that policemen have in their cars." "Do you want to play with me?"
5. The final behavior is one that involves explicit mention of transformations in or out of the pretend situation or defines the terms or roles. "I'm a work lady at work." "Pretend you hated baby fish." "This is the train" (while pointing to the sofa) (Krasner, 1976, p. 20)

One type of pretend play, sometimes labeled fantasy play, is characterized by secret contents. It is the type of play that creates wish-fulfilling situations that allow instinctual discharge that would not be allowed within the framework of existing reality and that modify and correct that reality (Sandler & Nagera, 1963). Fantasy play also allows for the gratification of impulses that would not be allowed in reality, such as pretending to follow through on killing a hated sibling.

Games with rules do not generally fit within the standard definition of play, because there is some sense of implied task or goal. Games are, however, viewed as an intermediate phase between the unregulated play of young children and the often over-regulated play behavior of adults. In examining children's behavior in play therapy, one finds examples of all these play subtypes.

In spite of the consistency of this description of play, it is not entirely consistent with the types of play seen among children in play therapy. Their play includes:

1. *Connecting play,* where the child simply and literally makes contact with the toys, materials, environment, and the therapist.
2. *Safe play,* which is engaged in when the child is in control of either the toys or the therapist.
3. *Unsafe play,* involving the uncontrolled expression of emotions; this includes the child pretending actions that cannot be stopped by the characters in the play such as a tornado or an earthquake.
4. *Resolution play* where the child or the character in the child's play finds a way to cope with or contain unsafe play (Fall, 1997).

Again, a critical difference between the play behavior of normal children and those seen in a clinical context is that the play behavior of the latter is not always fun. In spite of this, it still seems to meet most of the other requirements of the definition and so it will continue to be included under the general heading of play for the purposes of this discussion.

DEFINING PLAY THERAPY

Defining play therapy is not as simple as saying "It is a treatment modality in which the child engages primarily in play." Some of the behaviors in which children engage in the course of their treatment cannot be defined as play, yet that does not seem to obviate the rationale for labeling the treatment modality *play therapy.*

It is also not easy to define play therapy by focusing on its therapeutic aspects. Many individuals are capable of creating an environment that maximizes the naturally therapeutic aspects of play as they are described next; however, this situation seems best described as therapeutic play. Play therapy makes use of these therapeutic aspects of play, but it is distinct from therapeutic play in its reliance on a given theoretical orientation in directing the thinking and behavior of the play therapist. The play therapist has the training to work within a given theoretical model to help the child move systematically toward mental health. It is this incorporation of a system that qualifies what play therapists do as "therapy" comparable to any other clinical intervention.

In 1997, the board of directors of the International Association for Play Therapy developed a definition of play therapy that seems to address a number of issues in the field. The definition is inclusive of both a variety of definitions of play itself and of the wide variety of theoretical orientations represented by those who practice play therapy.

> Play therapy is the systematic use of a theoretical model to establish an interpersonal process wherein trained play therapists use the therapeutic powers of play to help clients prevent or resolve psychosocial difficulties and achieve optimal growth and development. (Association for Play Therapy, 1997, p. 7).

For the purposes of this book, that definition has been expanded only slightly:

> Play therapy consists of a cluster of treatment modalities that involve the systematic use of a theoretical model to establish an interpersonal process wherein trained play therapists use the therapeutic powers of play to help clients prevent or resolve psychosocial difficulties and achieve optimal growth and development and the re-establishment of the child's ability to engage in play behavior as it is classically defined.

This means that the play therapist seeks to maximize the child's ability to engage in behavior that is fun, intrinsically complete, person-oriented, variable/flexible, noninstrumental, and characterized by a natural flow. High-quality play therapy as practiced by a given play therapist represents an integration of the therapist's specific theoretical orientation, personality, and background with the child's needs in working toward this goal. That both the child and the play therapist may engage in behavior that might be called anything but play along their way to this ultimate goal is irrelevant. Play therapists universally recognize that treatment has been successfully completed when the child demonstrates an ability to play with joyous abandon—this is what makes play therapy unique.

FUNCTIONS OF PLAY AND THEIR IMPLICATIONS FOR CONDUCTING PLAY THERAPY

Having accepted this compiled definition of play and, subsequently, the definition of play therapy, one may examine the various functions of play behavior in the lives of children and the possible value of these functions within the conduct of play therapy.

Biological

Play has several functions that can be loosely construed as biological. First, play is the medium through which the child learns many basic skills (Boll, 1957; Chateau, 1954; Dohlinow & Bishop, 1970; Druker, 1975; Frank, 1968;

Slobin, 1964). An infant first learns to coordinate hand-and-eye movements by reaching for desired objects as she playfully explores her environment. In play therapy, most of the basic skills that the child learns are incidental to the overall focus of the treatment. However, one cannot ignore the therapeutic impact that learning to catch a ball might have on a child's self-esteem. Second, play allows the child to expend energy and relax (Schiller, 1875; Slobin, 1964). What pleasure children take in running themselves ragged in a game of tag, only to collapse in a giggling pile when it is over. Third, the process of playing is one of the ways in which children become aware of their own affect as well as the affect of others. Play itself stimulates a variety of internal sensations that children gradually learn to associate with a variety of positive and negative feelings. As they learn to differentiate these states in their own functioning, they also gradually learn to perceive and empathize with those feelings in others. Last, play gives the child kinesthetic stimulation (Plant, 1979; Slobin, 1964), another function that is especially important in infancy when the child is totally involved with her sensory intake. An infant lying in her crib wiggles and sets her mobile in motion. The mobile's movement causes the infant to wriggle more, and a cycle is created. Soon the infant is a wriggling, giggling ball of fire with every body part in motion. Play therapists rarely use the kinesthetic aspects of play, but they can be of great benefit in helping a child develop body awareness sufficient to allow for self-regulation.

Intrapersonal

Play serves three types of intrapersonal functions. First, play meets a need for "functionlust" (Slobin, 1964; Walder, 1933). That is, all human beings have a need to do something. Most of us find it almost painful, if not impossible, to do nothing. Even when kept perfectly still and sensorially deprived, we will do things in our minds. For children, play is something to do. When one takes this function of play into consideration, it is a little difficult for the play therapist to dismiss a session as a failure because "the child did not do anything." Barring the possibility that the child was comatose or catatonic, she did something, and whatever that was, it met at least this one intrapersonal function.

Second, play allows a child to gain mastery of situations (Erikson, 1950; Slobin, 1964). Play lets the child explore her environment (Druker, 1975; Frank, 1955). In playing hide-and-seek, the child explores the environment in a somewhat novel way as she looks for places to hide. Play also allows the child to learn about the functions of the mind, body, and world (Cramer, 1975; Frank, 1955). A child running around the room pretending to be an airplane learns about the ability of her mind to create the sense of flying, the ability of her body to imitate the sounds of an airplane, and the fact that planes obviously do not fly by making noises and running around. In this sense, play fosters the child's overall cognitive development (Frank,

1968; Piaget, 1962; Pulaski, 1974). It is through play that children learn to recognize, label, understand, and express emotions. In play therapy, these situational mastery aspects of play can be used to help the child develop competence relative to things with which she will never come in contact during the actual session. A play therapy session need not occur in the dentist's office for the child to learn not to fear the situation by playing it out in the playroom.

Finally, play lets the child master conflicts (Cramer, 1975; Druker, 1975; Erikson, 1950; Frank, 1955; Walder, 1933) through symbolism and wish fulfillment (Pulaski, 1974). This function of pretend play is probably the most widely used in the context of play therapy. A child may never actually experience her parents' remarriage after a long and bitter divorce, but she may play out just such an event over and over until she can eventually allow the bride and groom in the play not to marry but to be friends. Similarly, other traumatic events can be replayed until more satisfactory outcomes in terms of the child's thoughts and feelings can be effected.

Interpersonal

Play serves two primary interpersonal functions. Initially, play is one of the main vehicles through which the child practices and achieves separation/individuation from the primary caretaker. At home, the caretaker plays peek-a-boo, making a game of temporary separations from the infant. Later on, the toddler will delight in games of running away and being chased. These and many other games allow the child to experience separation, not as an overwhelming and terrifying thing but as a pleasurable and controllable game. In therapy, many of these same separation themes are played out relative to both the child's life outside the sessions and her experience of the sessions. After all, every session has a beginning and an ending, during which the child must learn first to engage and then to separate. Unfortunately, many play therapists do not make full use of the play rituals most children develop to contain these stressful realities. For example, some children will attempt to hide in the waiting room prior to the session. The therapist can either respond to this as an avoidant behavior or as a play behavior through which the child is attempting to initiate a game of hide-and-seek with the therapist. The child is beginning to play before even reaching the playroom. The therapist who makes an exaggerated effort to find the hidden child uses play to make the transition as well as communicating to the child that she is worth searching for.

Later in the child's development, play helps the child learn myriad social skills. Children learn how to share both toys and ideas in play. They learn to take turns and cooperate. They learn what is expected of them in school by playing with older peers. Essentially, they learn about human interactions simply by being with others. In individual play therapy, the child learns what it is like to be with an adult in a very special kind of interaction.

Fortunately, or unfortunately, this interaction is not always very realistic, and the degree to which the child is able to generalize from it to the outside world varies considerably. On the other hand, in group or family play therapy this interpersonal function of play can be used to its full advantage.

Sociocultural

Finally, one must consider the sociocultural functions of play. It is the medium through which children learn about their culture and the roles of those around them. In play, children learn games that are culturally and, often, historically specific. These games may convey a great deal about society's values. Although ring-around-a-rosy has lost a lot of meaning over time, it once conveyed a powerful message to children. Originally, the game was ring, a ring, a rosey, first played during the Black Plague of the Middle Ages. It went as follows: Ring, A Ring, A Rosey; A pocketful of posies; Achoo, Achoo; We all fall down. The poem describes the round red blotches that first appeared on those stricken with the plague, then the practice of stuffing the victim's pocket's with flowers to cover the smell of both the illness and death because quick burial often was not possible, and finally the respiratory complications that caused the victim to fall down and die. One can imagine a group of children surrounded by the certainty of death playing a game that, if only in some bizarre way, helped to make death less frightening. In retrospect, one can certainly extract a sense of the social atmosphere of the time.

It is important for the play therapist to remember that "the play of children tells us much about the values of the culture they live in" (Hughes, 1995, p. 15). Their spontaneous play is a reflection of their culture. For example, the more complex a culture the more complex the competitive games in which children engage. Games of physical skill are found in simple cultures. Games of chance are found more often in cultures whose fate is more dependent on chance such as agricultural or nomadic cultures. And, lastly, games that involve the use of strategy tend to be emphasized in technical and complex cultures (Hughes, 1995). An excellent resource for therapists interested in learning about children's play in other cultures is Roopnarine, Johnson, and Hooper (1994), *Children's Play in Diverse Cultures* (Albany, NY: State University of New York Press). The book presents detailed descriptions of the play behavior of East Indians, Taiwanese, Japanese, Polynesian, Puerto Rican, Italian, African, and Eskimo children in nonclinical contexts. The degree to which children's play is both a result and reflection of these very diverse cultures makes for very interesting reading and helps attune one to the cultural variability in what is considered normative behavior among children.

Children use the sociocultural aspects of play to rehearse desired adult roles. They pretend to be mommy and daddy. They pretend to be the teacher or a policeman. And in so doing they learn many of the thoughts, behaviors, and values associated with these roles. This is thought to be one of the primary ways in which children learn about and rehearse gender role behavior as it is manifested in their culture. That is, children learn and rehearse those behaviors typically associated with being a boy or a girl. In therapy, this process continues as children act out the roles of both desired and feared people in their lives.

HISTORY OF CHILD PSYCHOTHERAPY
AND PLAY THERAPY*

Psychotherapy with children was first attempted by Freud (1909) in an attempt to alleviate the phobic reaction of his now historic patient Little Hans. Freud did not treat Hans directly but advised the child's father of ways to resolve Hans' underlying conflicts and fears. Although it was many years before therapists again attempted to work through a child patient's parents, it was this first therapeutic case that laid the necessary foundation for such interventions as filial therapy.

Play was not directly incorporated into the therapy of children until 1919, when Hug-Hellmuth (1919) used it, feeling it was an essential part of child analysis. However, Anna Freud and Melanie Klein wrote extensively on how they adapted traditional psychoanalytic technique for use with children by incorporating play into their sessions. Both theorists, as well as many who followed them in applying psychoanalysis to children, began to modify not only the techniques involved but the underlying theoretical model as well. Generally, all of these modified versions of psychoanalytic treatment are grouped under the heading of psychodynamic therapies. The primary goal of their approach was to help children work through difficulties or trauma by helping them gain insight. Although both women relied on play as part of treatment, they used it in very different ways.

In 1928, Anna Freud began using play as a way of luring children into therapy. The rationale behind this technique involved the concept of a therapeutic alliance. Traditional psychoanalysis held that the majority of the work of analysis was accomplished once the healthy aspects of the patient's personality joined forces with the analyst to work against the patient's unhealthy self. This joining of forces was termed the therapeutic alliance. Freud was aware that most children do not come to therapy voluntarily; they are brought by their parents, and it is the parents, not the child, who have the complaint. In addition, she realized that the therapeutic techniques of free association and dream analysis were foreign to most children's means of relating. Therefore, to maximize the child's ability to form an alliance with the therapist, Freud used play—the child's natural

---

* Portions of this section are direct extracts used with permission from the Introduction to Part One of the *Handbook of Play Therapy* (Schaefer & O'Connor, 1983).

medium—with which to build a relationship with her child patients. She used games and toys to interest the child in therapy and the therapist. She made particular use of magic tricks as a way of engaging the child (A. Freud, 1928, 1965). Many therapists continue to find these very helpful in engaging even the most resistant child.

Dr. Diane Frey makes extensive use of magic tricks in her work with clients of all ages. She has plans to publish a compendium of these in an upcoming book. Gilroy (1997) writes about the value of using magic tricks to build rapport in play therapy. He indicates that magic tricks can be used to build the therapeutic alliance, as positive reinforcement, as diagnostic tools, as a way of enhancing the social skills of withdrawn children, and as a way of bypassing the defenses of resistant adolescents.

As the child developed a satisfactory relationship, the emphasis of the sessions was slowly shifted from a focus on play to a focus on more verbal interactions. Since most children were unable to make use of the technique of free association, Freud concentrated on the analysis of dreams and daydreams. She found that children were often as able and interested in the work of dream analysis as their adult counterparts; further, the children were often able to create mental images, and while visualizing their fantasies they were able to verbalize them.

Whereas Freud advocated using play mainly to build a strong, positive relationship between a child patient and the therapist, Klein (1932) proposed using it as a direct substitute for verbalizations. Klein considered play the child's natural medium of expression. She felt that children's verbal skills were insufficiently developed to express satisfactorily the complex thoughts and affects they were capable of experiencing. Kleinian play therapy has no introductory phase; the therapist simply starts out making direct interpretations of the child's play behavior. And, whereas A. Freud thought that analysis was most appropriate for neurotic children whose disorders were primarily anxiety-based, Klein thought that any child, from the most normal to the most disturbed, could benefit from her style of "play analysis."

The modifications of classic psychoanalytic theory and technique begun by A. Freud and Klein led to the development of a variety of theoretical models all loosely grouped under the heading of psychodynamic psychotherapies. One of the most important developments relative to work with children was an increasing emphasis on the role of the environment in the development of the child's personality and, related to this, the importance of attachment. The vast majority of psychoanalytically oriented play therapy practiced in the United States is based on psychodynamic rather than psychoanalytic theory and technique.

Between the 1930s and the 1950s, the number of child therapy theories and techniques grew rapidly. Not only were new theoretical models developed, existing models were modified to treat those children who were not suitable candidates for traditional psychoanalytic play therapy. In addition, a number of models and techniques were developed as reactions against various aspects of psychoanalysis.

In the late 1930s, a technique of play therapy, now known as structured therapy, was developed, using psychoanalytic theory as a basis for a more goal-oriented approach. Common to all the therapies in this category are (1) a psychoanalytic framework, (2) at least a partial belief in the cathartic value of play, and (3) the active role of the therapist in determining the course and focus of the therapy. Levy (1938) developed a technique called "release therapy" to treat children who had experienced a specific traumatic event. Levy provided the child with materials and toys aimed at helping the child recreate the traumatic event through play. The child was not forced into a set play pattern, but very few toys were made available to her other than those that the therapist thought might be best used to cathect the emotionally loaded event. The concept of this type of therapy was derived from Sigmund Freud's notion of the repetition compulsion. The idea here is that given security, support, and the right materials, a child could replay a traumatic event over and over until she was able to assimilate its associated negative thoughts and feelings.

Solomon (1938) developed a technique called active play therapy, that was to be used with impulsive/acting-out children. Solomon thought that helping a child express rage and fear through the medium of play would have an abreactive effect because a child could act out without experiencing the negative consequences she feared. Throughout interaction with the therapist, the child learns to redirect the energy previously used in acting out toward more socially appropriate play-oriented behaviors. Solomon also heavily emphasized building children's concept of time by helping them separate anxiety over past traumas and future consequences from the reality of their present life situations.

Hambridge (1955) set up play sessions in much the same way that Levy did, however, he was even more directive in setting up the specifics of the play situation. While Levy made available materials that would facilitate re-enactment of a traumatic event, Hambridge directly re-created the event or anxiety-producing life situation in play to aid the child's abreaction. This technique was not used in isolation but was introduced as a middle phase in an already established therapeutic relationship with a child; that is, when Hambridge was sure the child had sufficient ego resources to be able to manage such a direct and intrusive procedure. After the situation was played out, Hambridge let the child play freely for a time to recoup before leaving the safety of the playroom.

"Adler (1927), one of Freud's early students and colleagues, was the first to rebel against orthodox psychoanalytic thought. He was followed by Karen Horney (1937), Eric Fromm (1947), and Harry Stack Sullivan (1953). These four theorists often are grouped together because of their mutual concern for the role of the self and the importance of interpersonal and social dynamics in the development of personality and psychopathology. Each theorist, however, placed a different emphasis on the self (Adler, Horney), the role of the individual in society and culture (Fromm), and interpersonal dynamics (Sullivan). Although these theorists provided the basis for variations in psychoanalytic treatment, many common elements remained. In general, though, their treatment methods involved more active interaction with the patient, less interest in unconscious processes, more concern with the patient's present than past situation, and interpretation based on their particular theoretical focus" (Johnson et al., 1986, p. 127). As was previously mentioned, those treatment models that use traditional psychoanalysis as their base while modifying either the theory or technique are referred to as *psychodynamic.*

Also in the 1930s, a number of play techniques generally grouped together under the heading of *relationship therapies* developed. The original philosophical basis for relationship therapy came from the work of Rank (1936), who stressed the importance of the birth trauma in development. He believed that the stress of birth causes persons to fear individuation and thus leads them to cling to their past. He de-emphasized the importance of transference and the examination of past events in therapy and instead focused on the realities of the patient/therapist relationship and the patient's life in the here and now.

Taft (1933), Allen (1942), and Moustakas (1959) adapted Rank's ideas to work with children in play therapy. These theorists emphasized the negative role of the birth trauma on the child's ability to form deep positive relationships. Because of this trauma, susceptible children may have difficulty separating from their primary caretaker by becoming either clinging and dependent or isolated and unable to relate sufficiently to others. Through therapy, the child is given a chance to establish a deep, concerned relationship with a therapist in a setting that, simply because of the basic therapeutic agreement, is safer than any he or she will ever experience again. Taft adopted an existential approach and focused on the interaction between the child and therapist and the child's ability to learn to use that relationship effectively. Moustakas focused on helping the child to individuate, to explore interpersonal situations while using the secure relationship with the therapist as a safe base. Despite the tendency to emphasize the child/therapist relationship and to de-emphasize the significance of past events, the relationship therapists still maintain a strong tie to psychoanalytic theory. Rather than completely discarding this theoretical framework, they seem to have relaxed the "rules" of analysis while retaining the essential element, the therapeutic relationship.

In the 1940s, Carl Rogers (1942, 1951, 1957, 1959, 1961) developed the client-centered approach to therapy with adults; Axline (1947) modified it into a play therapy technique. This approach is based on the philosophy that children naturally strive for growth and that this natural striving has been subverted in the emotionally disturbed child. Client-centered play therapy aims to resolve the imbalance between the child and her environment so as to facilitate natural, self-improving growth. The therapist and child develop a warm and accepting relationship in which the therapist reflects back the child's feelings so that the child gains insight that allows her to solve her own problems and institute change as she desires.

In 1949, Bixler wrote an article titled "Limits Are Therapy" and, in a sense, ushered in a movement in which the development and enforcement of limits were considered the primary vehicles of change in therapy sessions. Bixler suggested that the therapist set limits with which she is comfortable, including:

1. The child should not be allowed to destroy any property or facilities in the room other than play equipment.
2. The child should not be allowed to physically attack the therapist.
3. The child should not be allowed to stay beyond the time limit of the interview.
4. The child should not be allowed to remove toys from the playroom.
5. The child should not be allowed to throw toys or other material out of the window. (Bixler, 1949, p. 2)

Ginott (1959, 1961) felt that the therapist, by properly enforcing limits, can re-establish the child's view of herself as a child who is protected by adults. To say that this technique stresses limits is not to say that other techniques do not use limits. Many other therapists and therapy techniques use limits explicitly, but they are not seen as the major effective element of the therapy. The rationale in limit-setting therapy is that children who manifest specific acting-out behavior can no longer trust adults to react in consistent ways and therefore must constantly test their relation to adults. Limits allow the child to express negative feelings without hurting others and subsequently fearing retaliation. Further, limits allow the therapist to maintain a positive attitude toward the child because she does not feel compelled to tolerate the child's aggressive acting out.

The role of parents or caretakers has been emphasized from early in the play therapy movement. As was mentioned, Freud's treatment of Little Hans (1909) was the first example of what later came to be known as Filial Therapy, in which parents act as the primary therapeutic agents with their own children. As early as 1949, Baruch was advocating planned play sessions to enhance parent-child relationships. In 1959, Moustakas talked about play therapy sessions conducted in the child's home by the parents. The term, *Filial Therapy,* was applied to the technique by Bernard Guerney in 1964. While the method has been around for some time its use has become a growing trend over the past 10 years (Landreth, 1991). Other strategies for involving parents in play therapy can be clustered under the heading of developmental play therapy. Brody (1978) developed a technique she specifically called *Developmental Play Therapy,* that emphasizes the use of physical contact and somewhat structured sessions. Deriving from her work and the earlier work of Des Lauriers (1962), Jernberg (1979) developed one of the most succinct theoretical and technical models of developmentally oriented play therapy, *Theraplay®*. The technique is based on the notion that normal caretaker/child interactions in the first few years of life are essential to establishing the basis for the child's future mental health and that these types of interaction may be instituted later in the child's life with the same health-producing effects. Each of these is important for the degree to which they include parents. The developmentally based therapies are important for the degree to which they advocate for a high level of therapist-child interaction in session.

The last four decades have witnessed a burgeoning number of new theories and techniques of child psychotherapy in general and play therapy in particular, some of which are described in such texts as:

Johnson, J., Rasbury, W., & Siegel, L. (1986). *Approaches to child treatment.* New York: Pergamon Press.

Kazdin, A. (1988). *Child psychotherapy: Developing and identifying effective treatments.* New York: Pergamon Press.

Morris, R., & Kratochwill, T. (Eds.). (1983). *The practice of child therapy.* New York: Pergamon Press.

O'Connor, K. & Braverman, L. (1997). *Play therapy theory and practice: A comparative presentation.* New York: Wiley.

O'Connor, K. & Schaefer, C. (1994). *The handbook of play therapy* (Vol. 2.) New York: Wiley.

Schaefer, C. (1979). *Therapeutic use of child's play.* New York: Aronson.

Schaefer, C. & O'Connor K. (Eds.). (1983). *Handbook of play therapy.* New York: Wiley.

Schaefer, C. & Kottman, T. (Eds.). (1993). *Play therapy in action a casebook for practitioners.* Northvale, NJ: Aronson.

A great deal of the credit for the growth of the field of play therapy over the past decade or more must go to the International Association for Play Therapy (IAPT). This association was founded in 1982 by Dr. Charles Schaefer and Dr. Kevin O'Connor. The IAPT began with approximately 50 members and, as of this writing, has over 3600. Besides the parent organization, branches now exist in 33 out of the 50 United States as well as Canada and South Africa. The IAPT promotes theoretical development, research, and clinical work through its annual conference and its publication of the *International Journal of Play Therapy.* Additionally, the IAPT developed standards for registering individuals as play therapists (Registered Play Therapist; RPT) and as play therapy supervisors (Registered Play

Therapist—Supervisor; RPT-S). The work of the association has led to a steady increase in both the quantity and quality of work done in the field of play therapy. You may contact the International Association for Play Therapy at 2050 N. Winery, Suite 101, Fresno, CA, 93703.

As discussed in the Preface to this volume, the first edition of this text focused on the need to integrate ideas from a number of different theoretical models of play therapy in order to provide optimal treatment to the widest range of child clients. In this edition that integration is taken to the next level and elaborated into a freestanding model called *Ecosystemic Play Therapy.* In spite of this shift in emphasis, the effective practice of play therapy requires the practitioner to understand a broad range of theoretical and technical models of play therapy. To this end Chapter Two of this edition presents the major existing theories of play therapy as well as some additional theories that contributed significantly to the development of Ecosystemic Play Therapy. In Part II, Chapters Four to Fifteen current information on the theory and practice of Ecosystemic Play Therapy is presented.

CHAPTER TWO

Theories of Play Therapy

Although three theoretical models of play therapy, psychoanalytic, humanistic, and cognitive-behavioral, tend to dominate both the literature and clinical practice, the number of theoretical models of play therapy has grown dramatically in the past few decades. In *Play Therapy Theory and Practice: A Comparative Presentation,* O'Connor and Braverman (1997) present information on 13 distinct models of play therapy. While not all of these theories are as well developed as the original core models, these represent an ever-broadening way of thinking about children's personalities, problems, and suitable treatment strategies. A number of theories have become more explicit about their ties to a phenomenologic philosophy (Knell, 1997; Kottman, 1997; Landreth & Sweeney, 1997). This reflects an increased interest in understanding and intervening in the child's world from the child's perspective. Each child is recognized as viewing the world in a unique way, therefore, requiring treatment that takes that view into consideration throughout its course.

Further, while each of the three core models originally represented a single, rather narrowly defined theory and set of techniques, each has grown to include a wide variety of related models as well as techniques. The phrase "psychoanalytic play therapy," for example, is now often used to refer to everything from the original work of Anna Freud (1928) and Klein (1932), two radically different approaches, to the ego analytic, neoanalytic, and psychodynamic variants of play therapy being practiced today. Similarly, behaviorally oriented child psychotherapy has come to be modified and is now best represented by Cognitive Behavioral Play Therapy as described by Knell (1993, 1994, 1997, 1998). A fourth model referred to in the literature as "developmental play therapy" has appeared to follow a similar process in its evolution in that it has grown primarily out of the work of Des Lauriers (1962) and now is used to group a number of models and

18

techniques that emphasize the developmental process in play therapy. For the sake of simplicity, no attempt to review the numerous theoretical and technical variations of each of these general categories of play therapy is made here. Where possible, readers are referred to other texts containing such detailed histories of these topics.

This chapter briefly reviews the three major theory clusters and, to some extent, the significant modifications of those theories. In addition, brief discussions of four theories that played a significant role in the development of Ecosystemic Play Therapy, namely, Theraplay (Jernberg, 1979; Jernberg & Booth, 1999), Filial Therapy (Guerney, B., 1964a; Guerney, L., 1983, 1991, 1997; and VanFleet, 1994), Adlerian Play Therapy (Kottman, 1995), and Reality Therapy (Glasser, 1975), are presented. Each theory is presented somewhat uncritically by describing it from the perspective of its practitioners. The focus of all seven reviews is the presentation of those elements of each theory used in the description of Ecosystemic Play Therapy presented in Part II.

PSYCHOANALYTIC

Theory

The practice of high-quality psychoanalytic play therapy and all its variants must be based on a thorough understanding of the psychoanalytic theory of personality. To review very briefly, the psychoanalytic theory of personality is developmental and assumes a tripartite personality structure (S. Freud, 1933) consisting of the id, ego, and superego. The id is that portion of the personality that seeks to gratify basic needs. It is driven by biological forces, including sexual energies—that are referred to as libido—and it acts on impulse. Freud also struggled with the notion of an opposing intrapsychic force he labeled Thanatos or the death instinct. Unlike libido that motivated the person to survive and prosper, Thanatos pushed the person toward chaos and destruction. In most of his writing, however, the overwhelming emphasis is placed on the libido as the primary driving force. The superego is comprised of those parental and social rules that a person internalizes over time. It is the part of the personality that attempts to restrict the id and force conformity to its perception of right and wrong. The ego is the portion of the personality that mediates between the id and superego and operates out of reality. The system is thought to be closed and hydraulic in that the more energy an individual channels into one of the three structures, the less energy is available to the other structures. Thus, the stronger an id impulse is allowed to become, the less energy the superego will have to prevent it from spilling over into action and the less energy the ego will have to try to find a way to gratify the impulse within realistic constraints.

Only the id is present at birth; the ego and superego evolve over time. When infants are very young, they exist only to get their needs met in whatever way they can. They act, without restraint, on their impulses. As an infant begins to differentiate from his caretaker, he begins to learn that there are certain reality constraints to getting his needs met. He gradually learns that some impulses must be delayed, with the toileting process being one of the most universal examples. According to more traditional Freudian theory, the child does not develop a superego until after the resolution of the Oedipal conflict between the ages of 4 and 6. Other analytic theories postulate the development of a primitive superego during toddlerhood (Klein, 1932). This latter view postulates that to emotionally tolerate separations from the primary caretaker (the mother), children introject an image of her they rely on when she is not physically present. But since this image has been introjected, that is, taken in without any filtering or processing, it brings with it all the child's perceptions of harshness as well as those perceptions of nurturance. This harsh introject is thought to be the precursor of the superego in that it can act to punish the child when the primary caretaker is not present. According to the more Freudian model, it is the child's identification with the same-sex parent in an attempt to resolve the Oedipal conflict that causes the child to internalize parental prohibitions and social rules. In either case, it is agreed that by the age of 5, most healthy children have developed all three personality structures.

Not only does the psychoanalytic model present a developmental sequence for the acquisition of personality structure, it also organizes the child's psychosexual development from birth through adolescence. Let us briefly review the stages as proposed by Freud (1905).

The infant is born into the oral stage, in which all his libidinal energy is focused on the mouth and the process of incorporation. This is a biologically functional orientation in that it focuses the infant on obtaining life-sustaining nurturance. During this time, the infant develops a powerful attachment to his primary caretaker while establishing his sense of self through the process of separation and individuation.

More recent psychodynamic literature has placed an ever-increasing emphasis on the importance of the oral stage and on the attachment that develops between the child and his caretaker during this stage. Specifically, it is hypothesized that children develop internal working models of the self in relation to their caretakers during this stage (Bowlby, 1973, 1982, 1988). Working models are internal representations formed through repeated interactions with caretakers that include expectations of how one will be treated. These models are used to evaluate and predict other's behavior. Because of this they become self-fulfilling prophesies that stabilize over time (Bowlby, 1973).

All of the child's later interpersonal functioning is derived from these working models. Therefore:

1. Current interpersonal functioning must be viewed in the context of past interpersonal relationships.
2. The link between past interpersonal experience and current interpersonal functioning is through cognitive representations derived from recurrent or salient interpersonal episodes.
3. Interpersonal schemata are not static representations but play a functional role in the organization of experience and behavior (Shirk, 1998, pp. 5–6).

As used here, interpersonal schema are made up of one's understanding of the relationship between one's representations of one's own behavior and one's representations of other's prototypical response to that behavior (Teasdale, Taylor, Cooper, Hahurst, & Paykel, 1995). This becomes a critical factor in treatment as therapy is thought to modify and correct the child's interpersonal schema primarily as a result of his pattern of interactions with the therapist.

As the child acquires language, he makes the transition into the anal stage, during which his libidinal energies focus on the processes of elimination. During the anal stage, the child is preoccupied with issues of control of both his own body and the environment. During this stage, he learns how to mediate impulses to some degree and how to more actively work to get his needs met.

At about the age of 3, the child moves into the phallic stage, during which libidinal energies focus on the penis: its presence for boys, its absence for girls. The existence and nature of the phallic stage of development is one of the most controversial aspects to psychoanalytic theory. Both analytic and nonanalytic writers reject it as a male-dominated and sexist conceptualization of development. However, it is essential to understand this phase as Freud conceptualized it to understand Freud's thinking with regard to many aspects of psychopathology and its development.

During the phallic stage, according to Freud, boys develop an awareness of the social power associated with having a penis and become preoccupied with the possession of such power. This preoccupation culminates with the boy's desire to possess the most valuable female in his environment, namely, his mother. Unfortunately, for the little boy, the father is a major obstacle to the realization of this fantasy. At first, the young boy fights with his father and experiences feelings of rivalry, but he soon realizes that he is outmatched and fears losing this contest with the father. According to the theory, he becomes more fearful that the father will castrate him if he does not give up his quest for the mother. Fearing the loss of this valuable organ and symbol of male social power, the little boy relents and identifies with the father to avoid retaliation as well as to possess the mother vicariously. This powerful threat to the boy's safety causes the complete termination of his desire for the mother and an intense identification with the father. Freud saw the absolute resolution of this Oedipal conflict as forming the very strong and well-developed superegos that he attributed to males. Men who successfully negotiated this stage of development were thought to rarely act on impulse and to keep their emotions under rather strict cognitive control.

The young girl in the phallic stage becomes envious of the little boy's possession of a penis and wishes to have one for herself. She looks to her father, as the most powerful male in her environment, to provide her with one or, failing that, to provide her with a penis substitute in the form of an infant. Note that the young girl does not have the same motivation to give up her fantasied possession of her father as does the young boy to give up his fantasied possession of his mother. After all, the young girl views both her mother and herself as having been castrated already and therefore having nothing to lose. Only because the fantasy of possessing her father never comes to pass does the young girl give up her desire and identify with her mother. Because this process of resolution is more passive in women, Freud postulated that women's superegos were not as strong as those of men. Consequently, women were seen as more prone to act on their impulses and to allow their emotions free reign. Women were also seen as more susceptible to neurotic conditions.

It was theorized that young boys and girls, having differentially resolved their Oedipal issues, returned to rather parallel development as they entered the latency period, a phase that was thought to last from the resolution of the Oedipal conflict at around the age of 5 or 6 to the onset of puberty at about 12 or 13. During this stage, Freud postulated that very little psychosexual development occurred; instead, the child's primary development during this period was thought to be cognitive and social.

With the onset of puberty, children were said to enter the genital stage when their libidinal energies became focused on their genitals and the primary psychosexual task became one of finding a partner of the opposite sex with whom to begin a family.

In summary, according to psychoanalytic theory, the child moves through a series of developmental stages based on the evolution of the focus of his libidinal energies. So long as the child's basic needs are met and no significant traumas are experienced, development proceeds in an orderly fashion, culminating in the formation of a stable relationship with a partner of the opposite sex by the time the child reaches late adolescence or early adulthood.

Pathology

Within psychoanalytic theory, pathology is framed as resulting from one or more of the personality structures failing to develop or from a conflict between the basic structures. Failure to acquire either ego or superego functions is postulated to be the cause of serious disturbances such as autism or schizophrenia. The development of ego functions without the development of adequate superego functions is postulated to be the cause of such characterological disturbances as psychopathy. The development of all three structures is postulated to protect the individual from the more serious pathologies but to leave him vulnerable to the anxiety-related disorders that arise when there is an imbalance between the psychic structures that the ego cannot resolve using either conscious processes or defense mechanisms.

An id/superego conflict produces anxiety that activates the ego to search for ways to gratify the id in reality without violating superego constraints. A child experiences an id-based impulse to eat something but is blocked by superego constraints that remind him that he is not allowed to eat between meals—anxiety results. The ego immediately moves to mediate the conflict by attempting to satisfy both needs in reality. The ego might motivate the child to ask for permission to eat something. If this works, the conflict ends and the child moves on. But if this and any other reality-based solutions fail, then the ego attempts to use defense mechanisms to resolve the conflict. The child's ego convinces him that there is no good food in the house, signals the superego that candy is not really food so that the child can eat it without guilt, or develops any one of a number of solutions that reduce the anxiety. When the ego's conflict-reducing strategies become too fixed and too automatic, preventing the child from engaging in regular transactions with reality, symptoms that are usually within the neurotic range develop.

Cure/Treatment Goal

The ultimate goal of analytic work, and interpretation in particular, is the development or revision of psychic structures and functions in order to foster optimum development (O'Connor, Lee, & Schaefer, 1983). This revision is accomplished via the gradual working through of various intrapsychic issues. Working through is, in turn, accomplished by making the child conscious of conflicts through the use of interpretations that he can elaborate and expand across contexts, allowing him to move to, and remain at, the next level of development (Sandler, Kennedy, & Tyson, 1980). Working through, as facilitated by interpretation, also promotes the child's move from insight to behavioral change.

Basic Assumptions

Developmental Level and Pathology of Suitable Psychoanalytic Play Therapy Clients

Traditional psychoanalysis limits its clients to those who have clearly developed a complete tripartite personality and whose symptoms arise from anxiety produced by internal conflict. Thus, traditional psychoanalytic play therapy is not viewed as appropriate for children who have not, at least partially, resolved their Oedipal conflict. In terms of age, appropriate clients are therefore at least 5 years or older. Clients also have to be limited to those who have developed sufficient verbal skills to allow them to work within, and benefit from, this verbally based and insight-oriented approach. The best candidates for analysis are children with anxiety-based disorders such as phobias, compulsions, social withdrawal, and the like.

More recent developments in the conceptualization and practice of psychoanalytic psychotherapy—usually referred to as dynamic therapies—have, however, allowed for the treatment of much younger children and those who, in spite of their age, have not developed a tripartite personality structure (O'Connor & Lee, 1991). The dynamic therapies have also made it possible to treat children with developmental problems that are the result of an ongoing conflict and that are consequently more acute as well as those with problems resulting from environmental interference such as deprivation rather than internalized conflict (Johnson et al., 1986).

Training of Psychoanalytic Play Therapists

Because of the complexity of the personality theory underlying the provision of psychoanalysis and the complexity of the traditional treatment model itself, its use is restricted to those therapists who have completed advanced, usually postdoctoral, training at an analytic institute. The more modern variations that make up the range of psychodynamic treatment are frequently used by play therapists without such advanced training, although specific training in the underlying theory is of course essential.

Role of the Psychoanalytic Play Therapist within Therapy Sessions

In this model, the therapist serves as an interpreter. The therapist is there to make sense of the material that the child brings to sessions and to convey back to the child the meanings he discovers so as to create insight. The therapist is not there to play with the child or to become a real part of the child's experience. That is, the child does not know the person of the analyst; rather, he comes to know the way in which the analyst thinks about his verbalizations, behaviors, and experiences.

Role of Play in the Conduct of Psychoanalytic Play Therapy

The child's play serves three primary functions in psychoanalytic play therapy. First, it allows the analyst to establish contact with the child. That is, it lets the child and the analyst establish a relationship within which the work of the analysis can proceed. This is viewed as particularly important as children are seen as incapable of forming a true therapeutic alliance and therefore must have an alternate relationship to carry them through the painful periods of the analysis.

Second, the play allows the analyst to observe the child and gather information on which hypotheses regarding the child's intrapsychic functioning can be based. There is considerable variability in the degree to which these observational data are considered sufficient for the development of interpretations because the specific analysis of a child's play behavior continues to be subject to theoretical and technical dispute. The two most extreme views are characterized in the work of Klein and Bornstein. Klein (1932) emphasized the importance of analyzing the content of the child's play directly. For Klein, the child's play was the equivalent of verbalizations and therefore equally amenable to interpretation. Klein advocated extensive interpretation of the unconscious meaning of the play. Bornstein (1945), on the other hand, felt that the child's play should not be directly interpreted because the material would manifest itself in other more obvious ways, the power of the interpretation might disrupt the child's play, and one risks oversexualizing the child's material. Further complicating the discussion is the fact that, in the treatment of children, material may be available from other sources, such as the caretakers or the child's teacher. Some traditional analysts consider such material a source of potential contamination of the transference that the child can barely maintain under the best of circumstances, whereas others consider information from a wide variety of sources essential to the analyst's development of interpretations that connect the child's behavior in sessions to the reality of the child's world out of session.

Last, play is also a medium for communication between the child and the analyst. Not only can the child present to the analyst information that he might otherwise be unable to convey, but the analyst may use the play and descriptions of the play to present information to the child. The primary example of this technique is referred to as "interpreting within" the play; that is, the analyst delivers an interpretation framed to apply to the characters or objects in the child's play rather than directly to the child, facilitating the child's tolerance of complex interpretations from both a cognitive and an emotional standpoint.

The role of play in psychoanalytic play therapy can be understood in the context of what it is not. Play is not used as a form of recreation. The therapist is not a playmate but rather a participant observer. Play is not viewed as having primary abreactive value except in those cases of acute traumatic neuroses. "In the kind of cases brought to . . . analysis today, the structure of the disorder is generally so complex and the determinants of unconscious conflict so varied and manifold that no abreactive process that fails to explore unconscious defenses and ego restrictions is likely to be of more than transitory value" (Esman, 1983, p. 13). And play is not used to educate the child. The child's learning in this context is secondary to the analytic process itself, not a function of the play.

Curative Elements of Psychoanalytic Play Therapy

The primary curative aspect of psychoanalytic play therapy is in the interpretations the play therapist offers. Secondarily, the relationship and the child's play are seen as having limited therapeutic potential. Psychoanalytic theory recognizes the value of the therapist/client relationship in helping the client change but maintains that it is a transference and not a "real" relationship. That is, the therapist is there to represent significant individuals in the client's life, not himself. In the case of children's treatment, the degree to which a transference relationship is really possible seems debatable because the child must maintain his primary dependence on his caretakers; however, the potential impact of intense interactions with the person of the analyst cannot be underestimated. The potential abreactive value of the child's play is also acknowledged to be curative, although only in the very limited circumstances described eariier.

Course of Treatment

Assessment

To plan a psychodynamic intervention with a child, an analyst needs to have a fairly complete sense of the child's present level of personality organization and function. The therapist needs to know the level to which each personality structure has developed and the way in which the structures interact within the particular child. The play therapist also wants to gather as much information as possible about the potential sources of internal conflict that are producing the child's present symptoms. This information might be gathered through interviews and substantive projective testing. Also note that assessment is an ongoing part of all the analytically based treatments as the therapist seeks, over time, to understand the client at different levels and as development proceeds.

Treatment

The treatment in psychoanalytic play therapy consists primarily of the formulation and delivery of interpretations that make the child's conflicts conscious and allow for behavior change. To foster the play therapist's understanding of the child, the child must bring to the sessions material that can be interpreted. This material takes the form of play behavior or verbalizations.

To foster the production of such material, the play therapist wants to make certain play materials available to the child. These materials are selected for their symbolic content and the degree to which they pull for the types of conflicts the child is believed to be experiencing. Because the therapist does not want the child's material to be contaminated with extraneous content, the playroom supplies are limited, and many aspects of the child's interaction with the therapist need to be controlled and contained. The sessions should be very predictable, as should the therapist's behavior. The child should not have to confront much evidence that other children use the playroom or have contact with the therapist. And the therapist should reveal as little personal information to the child as possible. Having created an atmosphere in which the child is free to make his conflicts known, the therapist proceeds to assume the role of observer and interpreter.

Erikson (1940) described three steps that lead to the formulation of an interpretation. First, the analyst observes and thinks about the child's play, leading to various "interpretive hints." The child's play may, for example, metaphorically reflect an avoided person, object, or idea, or it may represent the child's effort to psychologically rearrange an experienced or expected danger. Second, the analyst continues to observe the actions of the child, that may lead to a reflection of the child's dynamic configuration of his inner/outer history. Finally, the analyst offers a therapeutic interpretation that conveys these reconstructions to the child at the appropriate time.

In traditional analysis, interpretations, the primary instrument of therapeutic change, are generally made in an orderly and systematic way (Harley & Sabot, 1980). Typically, defenses are interpreted before drives, and surface material before deeper, unconscious material. To enhance the likelihood that the child will understand and effectively receive an interpretation, the analyst should prepare the child by making comments that show the child that more than one meaning exists for his material. The analyst should also relate the defense to the unconscious material being defended against. By sharing this knowledge with the patient, the analyst helps the child participate in the analytic process and renders the pathological configuration of psychic structures less ego syntonic (Kramer & Byerly, 1978).

The terms *ego syntonic* and *ego dystonic* refer to the degree to which the ego accepts the thought, feeling, or behavior in question. When the ego accepts a thought or impulse and does not experience anxiety, that thought or impulse is said to be ego syntonic. When the ego negatively evaluates a thought or impulse and experiences anxiety against which it tries to defend the thought or impulse is ego dystonic (Sutherland, 1989).

Debate continues as to what, exactly, the child analyst should interpret. Because of the traditional foundations of child analysis, there is a tendency to focus on verbal material. Anna Freud (1928) suggested that the analyst use the child's play as a way of developing a therapeutic alliance with the child; however, once the alliance is formed, the analyst should go on to focus on verbal interactions. Undoubtedly, the child's verbalizations of real or fantasied events, thoughts, and feelings lend themselves to interpretation most readily. Similarly, the child's behavior both in and out of the analytic session might be considered interpretable.

Termination

The psychoanalytic play therapist works with the child for an extended period of time in frequent sessions. Termination is considered when the child had gained sufficient understanding of his conflicts so as to be able to better mediate them in reality. This occurs when his ego functioning has returned to a developmentally appropriate level and has been maintained there long enough to allow for some behavior change. Termination consists of reviewing the changes the child had made over time while emphasizing his ability to maintain these changes without the therapist's help.

For additional information on psychoanalytic child psychotherapy the reader is referred to:

Lee, A. (1997). Psychoanalytic play therapy. In K. O'Connor & L. Braverman (Eds.) *Play therapy theory and practice: A comparative presentation.* New York: Wiley, pp. 46–78.

O'Connor, K., Ewart, K., & Wollheim, I. (in press). Psychodynamic psychotherapy with children. In V. VanHasselt and M. Hersen (Eds.), *Advanced abnormal psychology.* New York: Plenum.

O'Connor, K., Lee, A., & Schaefer, C. (1983). Psychoanalytic psychotherapy with children. In M. Hersen, A. Kazdin, & A. Bellack (Eds.), *The clinical psychology handbook.* Elmsford, NY: Pergamon Press, pp. 543–564.

O'Connor, K. & Lee, A. (1991). Advances in psychoanalytic psychotherapy with children. In M. Hersen, A. Kazdin, & A. Bellack (Eds.), *The clinical psychology handbook.* Elmsford, NY: Pergamon Press, pp. 580–595.

O'Connor, K., & Wolheim, I. (1994). Psychodynamic psychotherapy with children. In V. VanHasselt & M. Hersen (Eds.), *Advanced abnormal psychology.* New York: Plenum, pp. 403–417.

HUMANISTIC

Theory

The interventions loosely grouped under the heading of humanistic play therapy are not based on a theory of personality as extensive as that of psychoanalytic theory. Rogers (1951, 1959, 1961) developed the humanistic model in reaction against some of the negativistic aspects of psychoanalytic theory. In particular, Rogers introduced the concept of Thanatos, or the death instinct, which was difficult because it suggested that humans had within them a drive toward the dangerous and chaotic that must be constantly held in check lest it destroy the individual or even society at large. Rogers developed an alternative model based on his belief that our primary motivation as human beings is self-actualization or the drive to maintain and enhance growth.

Rogers postulated—similar to psychoanalytic theory—the existence of different aspects of the individual's internal functioning, although these aspects are not the equivalent of Freud's psychic structures. "The *organism* is the focus of all of the individual's experience, both somatic and psychological. *Experience* is defined as everything the organism responds to or reacts to at any given moment in time" (Johnson et al., 1986, p. 124). More recently, the (1) *organism* has come to be referred to as the person or that which is made up of the child's physical being as well as his behavior, thoughts, and feelings (Landreth, 1991). The emphasis on (2) *experience* has also been linked to the notion of the child's "phenomenal field," that which is both conscious and unconscious and either internal or external. Out of experience grows a sense of (3) *self* that is composed of the combination of the person and his phenomenal field (Landreth, 1991; Rogers, 1951). "Optimal personality development is achieved when the organism's inherent tendency towards self-actualization is not markedly interfered with by experiences that force the individual to deny his thoughts, feelings and emotions" (Johnson et al., 1986, p. 126).

Pathology

The humanistic model posits environmental toxicity as the cause of the child's psychopathology. If the environment is meeting the child's needs in an appropriate way, then the child is able to strive for self-actualization and does not engage in symptomatic behavior. Contrarily, the toxic environment causes the child to deny something about himself because his experience has told him it was wrong, so he adopts the values of others, and internal conflict ensues. Pathology is the result of poor self-esteem and self-acceptance both of which are socially derived (Axline, 1947). The source of the problem is within the child only to the extent that the environment has caused the child to respond in a negative manner. Fortunately, this idea is not taken to the extreme of suggesting that there is only one good environment. A child may be born with characteristics that necessitate exposure to an environment different from that of his peers for the child to develop optimally. A retarded child, for example, may eventually perform much better if initially presented with an environment structured to an extent that would make a cognitively average child feel constrained. The model places the responsibility for creating the appropriate environment entirely on the adults in the child's life. The model Rogers proposed was adapted by Axline (1947) to work with children and elaborated by Moustakas (1959).

Cure/Treatment Goal

Since the child's pathology is seen as the result of a toxic environment, the goal is to allow the child to become more self-actualized and consequently to behave better by creating, in the play therapy sessions, an optimal environment. The therapist must provide a positively reinforcing environment, thereby reducing the conflict the child is experiencing between his self and his environment, which in turn facilitates self-actualization. This feat is accomplished through the therapist's (1) empathic responding, as evidenced in the therapist's verbally reflecting the child's behavior and emotions throughout the course of their contacts; (2) structuring the environment for the child by presenting limits where necessary, especially in the first session; (3) presenting the child with personal information about one's self when it will allow the child to grow in the relationship; and (4) maintaining one's interaction with the child either verbally or through the play.

Basic Assumptions

Developmental Level and Pathology of Suitable Humanistic Play Therapy Clients

Because the humanistic play therapies emphasize the health-producing benefits of the child's mere presence in the play therapy environment, the range of clients who can be treated is much broader than when traditional psychoanalytic techniques are used. The approach can be used with children at virtually any developmental level because the therapy environment could be adjusted to suit the needs of the children. The approach can also be used with children exhibiting a wide variety of psychopathologies because, again, the environment could be suitably modified. Further, because the treatment is viewed as very benign, there is less concern with iatrogenic effects, so there is less concern about treating large numbers of children. That is, even normal children are seen as having much to gain and nothing to lose from a course of humanistic play therapy. However, the humanistic therapies generally are not considered very useful with very aggressive children or children who engage in considerable acting out. The intense structure and the quantity of limit setting these children require runs counter to the philosophy of these approaches.

Training of Humanistic Play Therapists

Because humanistic play therapy is less technically complex than psychoanalytic play therapy, therapists who wish to practice this modality generally do not require as much advanced training as child analysts. Several institutes offer training in one of the humanistic play therapies; in fact, this model of intervention permeates the academic and clinical training of many play therapists currently practicing within the United States. Unfortunately, the research documenting the effectiveness of humanistic play therapy is rather sporadic and much of it shows the effectiveness of training nonprofessionals, especially parents, in conducting child-centered sessions (Landreth & Sweeney, 1997).

Role of the Humanistic Play Therapist within Therapy Sessions

The primary role of the humanistic play therapist is to maintain an environment that encourages the child to trust and allows for the child's growth and development. This is accomplished by implementing the basic rules of Axline's play technique, reproduced here because they have become well-known as the credo of the approach:

1. The therapist must develop a warm, friendly relationship with the child. Good rapport should be established as soon as possible.
2. The therapist accepts the child exactly as he or she is.
3. The therapist establishes a feeling of permissiveness in the relationship so that the child feels free to express his feelings completely.
4. The therapist is alert to recognize the feelings the child is expressing and reflects those feelings back in such a manner that the child gains insight into his behavior.
5. The therapist maintains a deep respect for the child's ability to solve his own problems if given an opportunity to do so. The responsibility to make choices and to institute change is the child's.
6. The therapist does not attempt to direct the child's actions or conversation in any manner. The child leads the way, the therapist follows.
7. The therapist does not attempt to hurry the therapy along. It is a gradual process and must be recognized as such by the therapist.
8. The therapist only establishes those limitations necessary to anchor the therapy in the world of reality and to make the child aware of his responsibility in the relationship (Axline, 1947, pp. 73–74).

In his book, *Play Therapy: The Art of the Relationship,* Landreth emphasizes the importance of three therapist behaviors all of which foster the development of the child-therapist relationship. The first is being "real" which is the result of the therapist's self-understanding, self-acceptance, and ability to engage in a genuine relationship with the child. Second, the therapist must be able to convey warmth, caring, and acceptance. Last, the therapist must also convey sensitive understanding, or the ability to connect to the child's phenomenal world. Landreth (1991) sees the goals of the child-therapist relationship as being to:

1. Establish an atmosphere of safety.
2. Understand and accept the child's phenomenal world.
3. Encourage the child's emotional expression.
4. Establish a feeling of permissiveness.
5. Facilitate the child's decision making.
6. Provide the child with an opportunity to assume responsibility and to feel in control.

Role of Play in the Conduct of Humanistic Play Therapy

In humanistic play therapy, the child's play is seen as the medium in which the relationship with the therapist is created. The play is also a source of information in that it gives the therapist cues about the child's internal state that can be reflected. The play may also be a means of communication because the therapist may engage in the play with the child. Last, there is an emphasis on the various functions of play in the development of the normal child, as delineated in Chapter One.

Curative Elements of Humanistic Play Therapy

The curative elements of humanistic play therapy are hypothesized to be the relationship that the child develops with the therapist, the insight the child gains from the therapist's reflections, and the freeing up of the child's drive to self-actualization through exposure to the healthy environment within the play sessions. Change in the humanistic therapies is based on emotional rather than cognitive processes (Shirk & Russell, 1996) Since pathology is the result of blocked emotions the therapist's unconditional acceptance creates an environment where emotions can be experienced and expressed and thus become an accepted part of the self (Rogers, 1942). The therapist creates an environment in which the child can play and is allowed to meet various biological, intrapersonal, and interpersonal needs in ways that do not require that he deny his self.

Course of Treatment

Assessment

Because humanistic play therapy is not based on a structured theory of personality, the therapist needs to know less than the child analyst about the child's personality structure and conflicts before initiating treatment. The humanistic play therapist wants to know as much as the psychoanalytic play therapist about the child's present developmental level because this information is essential in helping the therapist design an optimal play therapy environment. The humanistic play therapist probably wants to know much more than the psychoanalytic play therapist about the child's interpersonal life to date and his history. For example, it is of value to know with whom the child currently has positive interactions and under what circumstances as well as knowing the same information about past interactions.

Treatment

Humanistic play therapy consists of regularly and consistently exposing the child to the health-promoting atmosphere of the playroom and to the acceptance and warmth the therapist provides. The therapist's use of reflection rather than interpretation is emphasized. In delivering reflections, the therapist makes explicit his attention to the child's play, verbalizations, thoughts, and feelings. Reflections are not usually as complex as interpretations because the aim is not to create insight as to the origins of his problems but to focus the child's attention on his own processes and on the interaction with the therapist.

Termination

As with analytic play therapy, the humanistic play therapist sees termination of treatment with a child as appropriate once the child is functioning optimally given his developmental capacities. Insight is not a criterion, but the ability to maintain a positive behavior change outside the playroom is considered a necessary condition for termination.

BEHAVIORAL

Prior to the publication of the first edition of this primer, there were few examples of behavioral theory directly applied to the practice of play therapy (Leland, 1983). More recently, Susan Knell (1993, 1994, 1997, 1998) has done some excellent work on the development of a Cognitive Behavioral Play Therapy (CBPT). Her model not only includes the most recent thinking on the cognitive mediation of behavior but places a much needed emphasis on child development as well.

Theory

The concept of personality runs counter to the very nature of the models the early and the more radical behavioral theories created. These models proposed that individuals did not have stable internal characteristics; they merely responded to the stimuli presented to them in various situations. Gradually, some behaviorists moved to a model that included personality to the extent of acknowledging that there were internal processes that were unknown, that is, the black box. Mainstream behaviorism has become integrated with cognitive theory, allowing for the recognition of thought as an integral part of human behavior and, consequently, the recognition of more complex and individual behavior patterns. The cognitive behavioral model looks at the interaction of the individual's cognition, emotion, behavior, physiology, and environment (Beck, 1967, 1972, 1976; Beck & Emery, 1985). Further, in cognitive behavioral theory, language is seen as an important mediator of a child's behavior (Knell, 1997). However, traditional behavioral theorists still do not include within their models something equivalent to the concepts of personality developed elsewhere.

The primary behavioral theories of how a child learns both functional and dysfunctional behaviors include classical conditioning, operant conditioning, and social learning.

> [In] classical conditioning a previously neutral stimulus eventually comes to elicit autonomic or reflex responses . . . Watson and Raynor (1920) presented one of the earliest demonstrations of respondent (classical) conditioning in humans by developing a conditioned emotional response (i.e., fear) in Albert, an 11-month-old child. They first demonstrated that Albert was totally unafraid of furry animals, such as a white rat. When presented with a loud noise (unconditioned stimulus), however, Albert reacted with a startle and began to cry and shake (unconditioned response). When the loud noise was presented at the same time the child reached for the white rat, he began to react to the animal with the same fearful response. Thus, the previously neutral stimulus (white rat) became a conditioned stimulus capable of eliciting a fearful (conditioned) response in the child. (Johnson et al., 1986, p. 147)

Operant conditioning (Patterson, 1971; Skinner, 1972, 1974) refers to the process by which behaviors are acquired due to the presence of contingent positive reinforcers or negative consequences. If a behavior is followed by positive reinforcers, it will increase even if the reinforcers are unrelated to the cause of the original behavior. If a caretaker who picks up his child from day care at exactly the same time every day happens to arrive, several days in a row, just after the child has begun a major temper tantrum and if the caretaker is very soothing and nurturant, then he may find that the child's tantrums increase in frequency both across days at about the time the caretaker is due to arrive and over the course of each day. Similarly, negative consequences will decrease a behavior whether or not they are related to the original cause of the behavior.

Social learning theory (Bandura, 1977; Rotter, 1954) recognizes the impact of classical and operant conditioning but adds cognitive processes to the list of factors affecting the acquisition of behavior. The major contribution of social learning theory is the recognition of the fact that an individual need not actually engage in a behavior to add or delete it from his repertoire. In fact, much of a child's day-to-day behavior is learned through the observation of others instead of through direct experience. The increased emphasis on cognitive process that social learning theorists advocated led in turn to the development of cognitive behavioral interventions in which the behaviors the child is to learn are not even modeled but rather presented to the child in a more educational or instructional format.

Pathology

Given that behavioral theory does not include a specific concept of internalized personality, pathology is not defined as a disruption of internal processes as it is in psychoanalysis. Further, pathology is not conceptualized as a disruption in the individual's environment as it is within humanistic theory. Pathology is conceptualized as resulting from aberrant patterns of reinforcement. The reinforcers available and the pattern of their presentation are entirely controlled by others for the duration of the child's dependent years. Therefore, it is the interaction between the child and those who reinforce and punish him or who model aberrant behavior that creates the pathology. As with each of the other theories presented thus far, the responsibility for dysfunctional behavior is not seen as resting with the child; rather, to facilitate the child's behavioral improvement, those around the child must learn how to modify the stimuli they present, and the responses they make, to the child.

Several cognitive behavioral theorists have focused on the importance of the cognitive or language mediation of behavior and problems associated with mediational deficits (Knell, 1997). In this model irrational thoughts produce disturbances in the individual's emotions and behavior (Beck, 1976; Knell, 1997). Further, this model has taken on a phenomenological tone in that external reality (the actual reinforcement system) is no longer seen as primary (Knell, 1997). Rather, it is the individual's perception of those events that is critical (Beck, 1967, 1972, 1976). Thus, the basic premises of CBPT are: "(1) thoughts influence the individual's emotions and behaviors in response to events, (2) perceptions and interpretations of events are shaped by individual's beliefs and assumptions, and (3) errors in logic or cognitive distortions are prevalent in individuals who experience psychological difficulties (Beck, 1976)" (Knell, 1997, p. 79). Specific subtypes of the cognitive mediation of behavior are addressed by a number of authors. Verbal mediation (Meichenbaum, 1977) is the ability to talk oneself through an event. This typically reduces impulsive behavior and allows one to apply language based knowledge to behavioral situations (e.g., I learned Rule X in school and I know this is a situation in which I should apply it). Social problem solving (Shure & Spivak, 1978; Spivak, Platt, & Shure, 1976; Spivak & Shure, 1982) is self-explanatory and is important in regulating all interpersonal interactions. Last, social perspective taking skills (Chandler, 1973; Chandler, Greenspan, & Barenboim, 1974) include one's ability to understand the thoughts, feelings, and behavior of others and to use that information to enhance interactions.

More recent cognitive behavioral formulations draw a connection between individuals' interpersonal schema and their social and emotional difficulties. Simply put, interpersonal schema are a sort of cognitive template individuals develop in order to understand interpersonal interactions. The schema is made up of past experiences and the person's understanding of those experiences. The most important and powerful schema develop as a result of the child's interactions with his primary caretaker. In this way, cognitive behavioral theory draws a link to the attachment concepts so central to psychodynamic thinking about children's development and psychopathology. Shirk (1998) presents three models for understanding how interpersonal schema can cause problems:

1. The preemptive processing model, in which activated schema undermine effective information processing.
2. The schema triggered model, in which activated schema evokes associated emotions that are transferred from prior interactions.
3. The behavioral priming model, in which interpersonal schemata increase the likelihood that specific interpersonal or affective regulation strategies will be displayed (p. 9).

Cure/Treatment Goal

The goal of behavioral play therapy is to discover those patterns of reinforcements, consequences, and cognitions that shape and maintain the child's developmentally inappropriate behavior and then alter them. In cognitive behavior therapy, the goal is to discover and correct the child's problematic interpersonal schema as well as to facilitate the child's use of more cognitive/verbal mediation strategies.

Basic Assumptions

Developmental Level and Pathology of Suitable Behavioral Play Therapy Clients

As with humanistic play therapy, behavioral play therapy can be used with clients at a variety of developmental levels and with those displaying a wide variety of dysfunctional behaviors. Knell (1998) notes that CBPT is developmentally sensitive and seems best suited to children between the ages of $2\frac{1}{2}$ and 6. She further suggests that it is particularly effective for children with control issues, those who have been maltreated, and those who are anxious or depressed.

Training of Behavioral Play Therapists

Unlike the other models mentioned thus far, behavioral play therapy can be divided into a design and an implementation phase. The design of good behavioral interventions requires considerable training, especially in the area of operant conditioning. A solid foundation for this type of work can be obtained in a very focused undergraduate college program; however, training to at least the master's level is advisable. The implementation of behavioral play therapy is a different issue because the procedures, once designed, are very straightforward, requiring that the therapist observe the child for the presence or absence of specific behaviors and then apply specific rewards or consequences. Complex verbal interactions and interpretations are not seen as an essential part of the process, which is why paraprofessionals, including high school students, have been trained to implement behavioral methods successfully in relatively brief training sessions. The more complex the technique, the more training that will be required.

Role of the Behavioral Play Therapist within Therapy Sessions

The behavioral play therapist's role is to observe the child for the presence or absence of specified behaviors and then dispense rewards or consequences. It may, or may not, be necessary for the therapist to be verbally defining the process as it proceeds. Usually the pairing of verbal statements that label the target behavior and connect it to the reward or consequence that follows speeds the change process and enhances generalization of the behavior.

Role of Play in the Conduct of Behavioral Play Therapy

Play is simply the medium in which reinforcement schedules can be introduced and manipulated. Most modern-day behavior therapists recognize the fact that the existence of a positive relationship between the child and the therapist will enhance the therapist's reinforcement potential, and play is seen as a way of creating this relationship. The play itself is not seen as having particular health-producing properties; it is merely a way of engaging the child in behavior that can then be reinforced. On the other hand, CBPT emphasizes that "play provides an ideal situation for breaking the association between a stimulus and its maladaptive response" (Knell, 1998, p. 31).

Curative Elements of Behavioral Play Therapy

It is the manipulation of the child's exposure to positive and negative consequences that is primarily responsible for producing change in the child's behavior. In the more cognitively oriented behavior therapies, emphasis is on the role that altering the child's thoughts and beliefs can have in producing behavior change. In addition, it is likely that behavioral treatment involves more work outside the playroom than either humanistic or psychoanalytic treatment. The child's caretakers or teacher might be asked to become involved in collecting data, dispensing reinforcements, and extinguishing behaviors. Behavioral play therapy also can be described as essentially creating a relationship for the child in that positive reinforcement is provided for virtually all nondestructive interactions with the therapist and the environment.

Course of Treatment

Assessment

Assessments prior to beginning behavioral play therapy do not focus on the child's internal workings or the dynamics of his interpersonal interactions; the focus is on the specific problem behaviors (generally as defined by those other than the child) and/or particularly successful behaviors and those factors that facilitate or inhibit the production of those behaviors. A detailed record of those things that the child finds reinforcing and punishing is obtained. The behavioral play therapist might also want to obtain some behavioral records indicating the frequency and intensity of the problem behaviors as they are presently occurring.

Treatment

If individual treatment were to be instituted, it would consist of bringing the child to the playroom so that the play therapist could manipulate reinforcement schedules so as to produce behavior change in the child. Insight is not a goal, but the child's cognitive understanding of the process by which he behaves and is differentially reinforced greatly enhances the acquisition, maintenance, and generalization of the desired behavior change.

Various behavioral techniques have been developed based on each learning theory previously discussed. The concept of classical conditioning led to the development of systematic desensitization procedures in which the child is gradually exposed to an anxiety-provoking stimulus while his conditioned anxiety is blocked through the use of relaxation procedures. The concept of operant conditioning led to the widespread use of all types of contingent reinforcement strategies as well as to the systematic use of extinction, punishment, and negative reinforcement.

An extinction program removes the positive reinforcement that was maintaining a behavior, thereby causing the behavior to fade over time. Punishment is the application of an aversive consequence each time the undesired behavior occurs, causing the behavior to decrease in frequency. It is recommended that neither extinction nor punishment procedures be instituted in isolation; they should be paired with programs designed to provide positive reinforcement for behaviors that compete with the behavior to be eliminated. Negative reinforcement is probably one of the most commonly misused of all behavioral terms. Often the term is used to refer to punishment or unpleasant consequences the child experiences as the result of a given behavior. The assumption being that the child somehow finds this negative reaction to be positively reinforcing. In reality, negative reinforcement refers to situations where one stops an aversive stimulus as soon as the child engages in the target behavior. For example, a parent might begin yelling at a child who is sitting watching TV, telling the child to go take a bath. If the parent continues yelling until the child heads toward the bathroom and stops yelling as soon as the child gets in the shower, then one has an example of negative reinforcement.

Social learning theory led to the development of a variety of modeling procedures using either adults or the child's peers as models. In practice, CBPT almost always includes a modeling component. "As the therapy progresses, the model develops more adaptive behaviors and thought processes, and presents these to the child on a level of understanding that enables the child to begin to incorporated them into his or her own behavioral repertoire" (Knell, 1998, p. 31). The gradual emphasis on cognition in the field of behaviorism spawned a number of cognitive behavioral interventions. These include the self-instructional programs (Meichenbaum & Goodman, 1971) and interpersonal problem-solving training programs (Spivak & Shure, 1982).

Termination

Termination is indicated when the targeted negative behaviors have disappeared or been greatly reduced and desired behaviors have increased and generalized beyond the playroom.

DEVELOPMENTAL

A number of different types of play therapy can presently be clustered under the heading of developmental play therapy.

Theory

Brody (1978) developed a technique she called Developmental Play Therapy (Brody, 1992, 1997), that emphasizes the use of physical contact and somewhat structured sessions. Deriving from her work and the earlier work of Des Lauriers (1962), Jernberg (1979) developed one of the most succinct theoretical and technical models of developmentally oriented play therapy, Theraplay®. The technique is based on the notion that normal caretaker/child interactions in the first few years of life are essential to establishing the basis for the child's future mental health and that these types of interaction may be instituted later in the child's life with the same health-producing effects.

Jernberg noted that healthy caretaker/child interactions serve two functions. Primarily the interactions maintain the child at an optimal level of arousal; then, as a consequence, these activities promote the child's development. The degree to which the caretaker maintains responsibility for the child's arousal level decreases as the child develops, dropping off dramatically after the child achieves individuation at about 3 years of age. Over the course of the child's life, his need to have someone else exercise control over his level of arousal will vary considerably, depending on the situations in which he becomes involved. For example, in the case of severe trauma, both children and adults tend to become over-stimulated to a point where they become unable to care for themselves. They may wander aimlessly about or sit motionless. Whether or not they are able to express their specific needs at this point, they are in very real danger if someone does not intervene and care for them. When the crisis is over, the victim will likely return to his previous level of functioning and others will subsequently reduce their caretaking efforts. It is a delicate dance in which the needs of the caretaker and the child must be constantly re-evaluated and their interactions renegotiated.

Caretaker/Child Interactions

Jernberg (1979) identified four categories of early caretaker/child interactions: structuring, challenging, engaging, and nurturing.

Structuring activities. These are those behaviors in which the caretaker engages that somehow create boundaries for the child that reduce arousal. Structuring teaches the child that parents are trustworthy and predictable as they help define and clarify the child's experience (Jernberg & Booth, 1999). During the child's infancy, the caretaker must constantly structure the child's world, often just to make it safe. For example, a caretaker has an infant sleep in a crib; ride in a protective car seat; bathe in a small, shallow tub; and so forth. All these actions represent necessary structuring of the infant's environment to prevent accidental injury.

As the child gets older, the number and intensity of structuring activities in which the caretaker engages decrease. For the toddler, the caretaker childproofs the home by placing latches on cabinets that contain dangerous materials and putting plastic stops in all electrical outlets. The caretaker also remains quite vigilant to ensure that the toddler or preschool child does not wander off. With a preschool child, the caretaker makes sure that the child gets to bed at a reasonable hour and eats healthy meals and tries to establish self-care routines like bathing and toothbrushing. School-age children do not need as many concrete protections as younger children, but they do need to be trained to structure their own lives to a certain extent. By the time a child enters early adolescence, the caretakers limit most of their structuring to the imposition of household rules. The expectation for an adolescent is that he will now regulate much of his own behavior and that the caretakers need provide structure only to keep the adolescent's behavior within the bounds of a relatively wide range of acceptability. No longer will the caretakers decide what the child should wear so long as the clothing is situationally appropriate. No longer will caretakers monitor the child's personal hygiene so long as it too is within reasonable boundaries. Peers will take over imposing much of the structuring to which the child is exposed. The caretaker now has to learn to trust the child's judgment.

Since the publication of the first edition of the Primer, Jernberg (Jernberg & Booth, 1999) changed the name of Intruding Activities to Engaging Activities. The change primarily reflects her discomfort with the negative connotation the word intruding tends to carry rather than a reclassification of the behaviors. Jernberg did, however, express concern that the activities listed in the first edition of this text were not what she was thinking of when she referred to Intruding Activities. Rather, she saw most of the examples used as examples of Structuring Activities. Irrespective of this debate, it seems important to consider at least a subcategory of structuring behavior that include those times when caretaker intrudes on the child's physical or psychological space. While the infant is very young, the caretaker intrudes constantly to orient the infant toward relevant stimuli. A baby will cry when it is hungry, signaling the mother that it is time to nurse. However, if the baby is very agitated, he will not stop crying when the breast is presented; he may not even stop crying when a few drops of milk are placed in his mouth. At this point, the mother may blow on the infant's face or make a sudden noise to distract the infant to allow her to reintroduce the breast. In this example, the mother's intrusion into the baby's agitation lets her direct him toward the food he desired. Healthy intrusions occur when the *child* needs them, not when the caretaker's needs dominate. The caretaker is intruding to keep the child's level of arousal at an optimal level.

A caretaker might intrude on a toddler's play to direct him to the bathroom, knowing that it has been some time since the child has voided and that he has been distracted by play. A caretaker might intrude on a preschool child to slow him down when he becomes overly excited. For example, a child who is at a preschool party where there is a lot of noise and activity may gradually increase his motor behavior until he is running around wildly, bumping into both people and objects. He is still having a good time, but the caretaker realizes that he will soon hurt himself or someone else. At this point, she intrudes and takes the child, in spite of his brief protests, into another room where it is quiet. While there she holds the child and talks to him quietly until he has slowed down some, at which time they return to the party. Caretakers might intrude to settle an argument between two school-age children or two adolescents. Each of these activities involves not just the caretaker structuring an ongoing interaction with the child but initiating an interaction to provide structure.

Challenging activities.   These are activities in which the caretaker encourages the child to perform at the upper end of his present capacities so as to increase the child's level of arousal. Challenging activities push the child to move ahead, to strive, and become more independent (Jernberg & Booth, 1999). Good caretakers constantly challenge their child in gentle and stimulating ways. Picture the caretaker who places his index fingers into his infant's hand while the infant is lying supine in bed. Early in the infant's development, reflex grasping makes it impossible for him to let go of the caretaker's fingers as long as the palms of his hands are being stimulated.

Slowly, the caretaker lifts the infant's upper body off of the bed. Early on, the infant's head does not follow because he does not have the strength to lift it, so the caretaker only lifts the infant's shoulders a few inches. Gradually, the infant attempts to lift his head, and with practice he can be pulled to a sitting position while he grasps the caretaker's fingers. The caretaker has challenged the child often enough and gently enough to allow him to develop the strength and control needed to lift his head with the rest of his body. Similarly, a caretaker may hold a toy a few inches from an infant's grasp while encouraging the child to reach for the object.

As the child gets older, he will be challenged in many different ways. The older infant and toddler will be encouraged to feed himself, walk on his own, speak, use the toilet, dress himself, tie his own shoes, attempt recall of letter and color names, and develop preschool skills. The school-age child will be encouraged to learn a wide variety of factual information and increasingly will be challenged to subjugate his own needs to the needs of the group. The young adolescent will be challenged to engage in complex cognitive operations and, often, in equally complex social interactions.

Engaging activities.   This category of behavior was originally labeled Intruding Activities. Since Jernberg indicated that some of the examples of Intruding listed in the first edition of this Primer were actually Structuring Activities those have been moved to that section. This category refers to those things the caretaker does to initiate or maintain an interaction with the child. For example, a parent might initiate a game of peek-a-boo with a child who is refusing to look at the parent because the child is angry. Rather than demanding eye contact in a structuring way, the parent playfully engages the child so that the problem that triggered the anger can be addressed. A parent might find playful ways to engage a child who has withdrawn out of boredom or sadness. Through Engaging Activities, the caretaker "provides excitement, surprise, and stimulation in order to maintain a maximal level of alertness and engagement" (Jernberg & Booth, 1999, p. 17).

Nurturing activities.   These activities provide for the child's physical and emotional needs, including feeding, bathing, and changing the infant as well as soothing, kissing, and hugging him to maintain the child's current level of arousal. They are those activities that make the child feel warm, soothed, comforted, and loved (Jernberg & Booth, 1999). Initially, the caretaker provides for all the child's needs because the infant is totally dependent. As the child grows older, the caretaker spends more time providing for his emotional needs and encouraging the child to gradually provide for more and more of his own physical needs. The caretaker dresses an infant based on his perception of the child's needs given the outdoor temperature. With the preschool child, the caretaker makes the child wear a jacket outside when it is cold but accepts input from the child in deciding whether or not he needs to keep the jacket on when he is running around and playing hard. With school-age children and adolescents, the caretaker accepts considerable input from the child before overriding the child's wishes and insisting on specific types of clothing.

Pathology

If these fundamental caretaking interactions are disturbed early in children's lives, the consequences, in terms of the children's ability to engage in functional interpersonal interactions, are often dire. Virtually every model of psychopathology attributes considerable importance to these early interactions, identifying everything from autism, schizophrenia, and psychopathy to borderline and narcissistic personality functioning to their disruption. Theraplay focuses on problems of attachment including the following related behaviors: (1) problems relating to people, (2) problems accepting care, (3) problems with transitions, (4) lack of a conscience, (5) emotional immaturity, and (6) problems with trust and self-esteem (Jernberg & Booth, 1999). Further, the transactional models of psychopathology, those that emphasize the role of a person's interpersonal relationships in the development and maintenance of pathologic behavior, suggest that disruptions in the regulatory and caretaking aspects of an individual's relationship at any point in his life could result in symptomatic behavior.

A caretaker may structure the child's world either too much or too little and, depending on the child and his life situation, could either create overdependency on others for structure or an excessive drive to rebel against structure. Take, for example, the caretakers who run their home as if it were a military training facility. They have numerous strict rules and harsh consequences and accept virtually no input from the children about the running of the family. Children from such a home may grow up to need a high level of structure to function in their daily lives, or they may grow up to be laissez-faire caretakers who choose jobs that give them total mastery over their own work.

Intrusions can become destructive when they are instigated to satisfy the caretaker's needs. This is often the case when a caretaker is very needy. For example, some teenage mothers depend on their infants to feel good about themselves. They will report going in and waking up their infant during his nap because they were feeling lonesome. In this case, the child may develop an interpersonal wariness that affects his later interactions.

Note that there is often a fine line between challenging and frustrating a child. A caretaker who encourages his 3-year-old to try to pour his own glass of milk from a carton that is virtually empty is challenging the child. But the caretaker who pushes his 3-year-old into trying to pour a glass of milk from a full carton is frustrating the child and pushing him into failure experiences. If a child is not adequately challenged by the caretaker, he is likely to lag behind in developing basic skills and maintain a rather dependent posture relative to others with whom he interacts. If a child is challenged to the point of frustration, he is likely to become angry and resist becoming involved in those situations that tax his abilities in the slightest.

The earlier in the child's life in which challenging interactions become problematic, the greater the dysfunction the child will exhibit later in life. But older children and even adults may face challenges in the course of their lives for which they are ill prepared; in those cases, they benefit from having another person regulate both the challenge and the response expected. A classic example of this type of situation occurs when caretakers have very unrealistic expectations of their child, say expecting the child to be day and night toilet trained at 10 months of age. These unrealistic expectations often lead to child abuse. In this case, the child would benefit greatly from having someone intervene and adjust the caretakers' expectations to reduce the possibility of abuse. Both the caretakers and the child are facing frustrating challenges. The child in this case cannot develop bowel and bladder control that he does not yet have, and the caretakers feel frustrated because they are failing at the task of getting the child to behave in what they believe to be an age-appropriate way.

The impact of not receiving enough nurturance is generally recognized as causing children to become preoccupied with getting their needs met or making them withdraw from human interaction out of frustration and feelings of hopelessness. Too much nurturance is not generally thought of as a problem in the lives of children or adults. It is possible, however, to recognize that some children could find themselves overwhelmed by a caretaker whose nurturing is intrusive to the point that it interferes with the child getting his other needs met. This would be the case if the aforementioned teenage mother who woke her infant because she wanted to play with him did so often enough to prevent him from getting needed sleep.

Cure/Treatment Goal

The goal of Theraplay is to overcome those behaviors that prevent the child from having the kind of interpersonal relationships he needs to function optimally in the world. This is accomplished by the therapist establishing a caretaker-like relationship with the child and implementing those activities that promote the experience of positive interpersonal interactions. The therapist then works with the child to help him generalize the experience he has acquired in session to the interactions in which he engages in the world outside the playroom.

Basic Assumptions

Developmental Level and Pathology of Suitable Theraplay Clients

As with the humanistic play therapies, Theraplay is thought to be suitable for use with a wide range of clients. All the child clients share the inability to engage in satisfying interpersonal relationships but their actual and chronological developmental levels might vary considerably. Early in the development of the Theraplay method, all clients were conceptualized as having been deficient in early caretaker/child attachment-fostering and autonomy-inducing experiences. More recently, the focus has expanded to include those who lack or have deficient relationships in the present irrespective of their past history. Also, as with the humanistic therapies, Theraplay is viewed as having minimal risk of iatrogenic effects, and, therefore, client exclusion is not viewed as a priority.

Initially, Jernberg considered Theraplay to be contraindicated in cases where the child appeared to be sociopathic, traumatized, emotionally fragile, or abused. Since that time, however, she has recommended that children with such problems who also have disturbed interpersonal relationships should go through a two-phase treatment. Initially, these children should be made to feel safe and involved in a treatment that processes the trauma they have experienced. Once that is complete, the children can then be treated using the Theraplay method to focus on the damage done to their ability to trust and form attachments (Jernberg & Booth, 1999).

Training of Theraplay Therapists

Theraplay is a registered trademark of the type of therapy taught at the Theraplay Institute in Chicago. The training consists of intensive group work in which trainees learn how to engage in structuring, challenging, engaging, and nurturing interactions with peers, both as a leader and a follower. The trainees then go on to work with normal children under supervision and finally to work with clinical cases. The training is not restricted to persons with advanced degrees in the helping professions (Jernberg, 1973). In fact, Jernberg viewed one of the advantages of the technique the fact that paraprofessionals can be taught to implement it effectively.

Role of the Theraplay Therapist within Therapy Sessions

Theraplay draws a strong parallel between the functions of a healthy caretaker and those of the therapist. That is, the therapist regulates the child's level of arousal in session and promotes development. The primary difference between the caretaker and the therapist is in the degree of reciprocity involved in their respective relationships with the child. The healthy caretaker is always involved in a reciprocal relationship. That is, the caretaker must not only regulate the child's level of arousal but do so in the context of the caretaker's own needs. For example, if the caretaker is feeling ill, he will need the child to amuse himself and to stay relatively quiet. This compromise between the child's and the caretaker's needs is an essential aspect of their relationship. The therapist's relationship with the child is not reciprocal. During the session, the therapist sets most of his needs aside (other than the need to be safe). The child is the sole focus of the session resulting in a reparative level of caretaking which it is assumed the child needs in order to resume normal development.

The Theraplay therapist is there to lead the child in constructive and health-producing interpersonal interactions. The following guidelines are set forth as do's and don'ts. The Theraplay therapist:

1. Is confident and has leadership qualities.
2. Is appealing and delightful.
3. Is responsive and empathic.
4. Is in charge of the sessions at all times (Robertiello, 1975, p. 12).
5. Uses every opportunity for making physical contact with the child.
6. Insists unwaveringly on eye contact.
7. Places intensive and exclusive focus on the child.
8. Initiates, rather than reacts to, the child's behaviors, anticipating the child's resistant maneuvers and acting before, not after, they are set in motion.
9. Is responsive to cues given him by the child.
10. Uses every opportunity to differentiate himself from the child.
11. Uses every opportunity to help the child see himself as unique, special, separate, and outstanding.
12. Uses the child's moods and feelings to help the child differentiate himself and label his feelings.
13. Keeps the sessions spontaneous, flexible, and full of happy surprises.
14. Uses himself as the primary playroom object.
15. Structures the session so that the times, places, and persons are clearly defined.
16. Attempts to keep the session cheerful, optimistic, positive, and health-oriented.
17. Focuses on the present, the future, and the here and now.
18. Focuses on the child as he is.
19. Sees to it that within each session there are many different segments, each one having a beginning, a middle, and an end.
20. Offers some minimal frustration, challenge, and discomfort.
21. Uses paradoxical methods when appropriate.
22. Makes his insistent presence felt throughout the duration of a child's temper tantrum.
23. Conducts his sessions without regard to whether the child "likes" him.
24. Curtails and prevents excessive anxiety or motoric hyperactivity.
25. Attends to physical hurts.
26. When at a loss for ideas, incorporates the child's body movements into his repertoire (Jernberg, 1979, pp. 48–49).

Curative Elements and Role of Play in the Conduct of Theraplay

Play is an essential element in the conduct of Theraplay because of the technique's emphasis on the inclusion of elements of fun in the treatment. All the interactions between the child and therapist are considered to have little therapeutic value if both persons are not finding the interaction pleasurable. That does not mean that there will never be conflict between the child and therapist—there will be. The occurrence of conflict is predictable as the child's usual methods of keeping others at a distance are challenged. What is different here is that when there is a conflict, the therapist does not experience it as a rejection of himself but as a rejection of the unfamiliar aspects of the interaction. Therefore, the therapist is not put off by the child's behavior but rather drawn further into the interaction.

Course of Treatment

Assessment

Theraplay advocates the use of a rather extensive pretreatment assessment process that includes obtaining a good developmental history and general information and focusing on observing the child's pattern of interaction with significant others in his environment. The method used to collect these observations is called the Marschak Interaction Method (MIM) (Jernberg, Booth, Koller, & Allert, 1980). The MIM consists of having the significant adult and the child engage in predetermined interactions while the therapist videotapes or observes them. The interactions are coded for the presence or absence of structuring, challenging, engaging, and nurturing elements that are positive in nature. Based on the analysis of these observations, the type of interactive elements that should be included in the child's sessions are determined.

Treatment

The following innovations distinguish Theraplay from most other treatment methods:

- The therapist takes charge, carefully planning and structuring the sessions to meet the child's needs rather than waiting for the child to lead the way.
- The therapist does all in her power to entice the child into a relationship, including, if necessary, intruding on the child to begin engagement. Treatment emphasizes the interactional relationship between the therapist and the child rather than focusing on conflicts within the child's psyche.
- Nurturing touch is an integral part of the interaction.

- The therapist remains firm in the face of resistance, whether passive or active. If the child responds with anger, the therapist stays with the child throughout the duration of the angry outburst.
- Treatment involves active, physical, interactive play. There is no symbolic play with toys and very little talk about problems.
- Treatment is geared to the child's emotional level and therefore often includes "babyish" activities that many people would consider appropriate for a younger child.
- Parents are actively involved in the treatment to enable them to take home the new ways of interacting with their child.
- The therapist initially steps into the parental role in order to model, for the watching parents, a new way of relating to their child (Jernberg & Booth, 1999, p. xxviii).

The treatment proceeds in six phases. During the introduction phase, the therapist sets the ground rules and creates the child's expectations of what will take place in future sessions. During the exploration phase, the therapist and child get to know one another by focusing on mutual explorations such as checking the color of each other's eyes and hair, their relative number of teeth, their favorite foods, and so forth. The therapy then moves into the third phase, where the child tentatively accepts the process of interaction and seems to enjoy himself. During this phase, the therapist is often aware of the very subtle ways in which the child is trying to lead and control the sessions. This is followed by the negative reaction phase, in which the child resists the therapist's attempts at pursuing further intimacy. This stage often includes some very intense, aggressive acting out, during which the child tries to re-establish control over the therapist and re-create his modal level of interpersonal distance. The therapist must take particular care to not back off from the interactions in the face of the child's rage but to continue to structure the child's acting out while providing as much nurturance as possible. When this phase of treatment has been successfully negotiated, the growing and trusting phase begins. Initially, this phase consists of very positive interactions between the child and therapist, but gradually the therapist introduces others into the child's sessions so that the child's newly developed interactive style will generalize as much as possible. This may be the point at which the caretakers, siblings, or even the child's peers are included in the playroom activities.

Not only does the course of Theraplay follow a predictable path but the individual sessions are structured into three parts as well. All sessions include an opening phase during which the therapist greets the child and checks up on changes in the child since the last session. As an example, the therapist might measure the child at the beginning of each session to see how the child has grown over time. During the middle portion of each session, the therapist engages the child in planned activities that emphasize structuring, challenging, engaging, and nurturing. Each session then has a closing activity that includes transitioning the child from the session back to the outside world (Jernberg & Booth, 1999).

Termination

The last phase of Theraplay treatment is termination, it proceeds in three steps. First, the child is prepared for termination by noting the degree to which he has changed and his increasing ability to interact positively with others in his environment. Second, the termination date is announced, giving the child several sessions' advance notice. Third, there is the actual parting, this is celebrated as an acknowledgment of the child's growth and happiness with a party that often includes several of the other people who have been involved in the treatment process.

FILIAL THERAPY

Filial Therapy is a variant of Child-Centered Play Therapy in which the child's parents or caretakers are trained to conduct child-centered play sessions with the child. The primary advantage of the method is the greater impact the parents are assumed to have on the child due to their importance and availability in the child's life relative to that of the therapist. As early as 1949, Baruch was advocating planned play sessions to enhance parent-child relationships. In 1959, Moustakas talked about play therapy sessions conducted in the child's home by the parents. The term, *Filial Therapy,* was applied to the technique by Bernard Guerney in 1964. While the method has been around for some time, its use has become a growing trend over the past 10 years (Landreth, 1991). Because the basic elements of Filial Therapy are so similar to the humanistic or child-centered approaches, the review that follows will address only those areas where there is a significant difference between the models.

Theory

The reader is referred to the references that appear at the end of this section for further reading on the theoretical basis of Filial Therapy which is very comparable to other humanistic models.

Pathology and Cure/Treatment Goal

While humanistic theory in general emphasizes the importance of self-actualization in therapy, Filial Therapy focuses on remediating deficits in the parent-child relationship. Bernard Guerney (1964) indicates that the goals of the play sessions are:

. . . first, to break the child's perception or misperception of the parent's feelings, attitudes, or behavior toward him. Second, they are intended to allow the child to communicated thoughts, needs, and feelings to his parents which he has previously kept from them, and often from his own awareness. (This communication is mainly through the medium of play.) The children's sessions with their parents are thus meant to lift repressions and resolve anxiety-producing internalized conflicts. Third, they are intended to bring the child—via incorporation of newly perceived attitudes on the part of his parents—a greater feeling of self-respect, self-worth and confidence. (p. 452)

Basic Assumptions

Developmental Level and Pathology of Suitable Filial Therapy Clients

The use of Filial Therapy does not depend on the diagnosis of a particular pathology in either the child or the parents. Rather, the focus is on enhancing the relationship between the parent and child. Filial Therapy is seen as being potentially useful for virtually any parent-child dyad irrespective of the child's developmental level or diagnosis (Bratton & Landreth, 1995; Landreth, 1991).

Training of Filial Therapists

Filial Therapists must be trained in basic humanistic or child-centered approaches. They should also be trained in one or more of the specific models of teaching child-centered therapy skills to parents. Guerney (1991), Landreth (1991), and VanFleet (1994) among others have outlined such training programs. Finally, it is useful if the Filial Therapist also has training in basic parenting skills education and child development so that any related problems the parents are experiencing in their interactions with their children as the sessions progress can be addressed.

Role of the Filial Therapist within Therapy Sessions

In Filial Therapy, the therapist does not usually work directly with the child. Instead, the therapist trains the parents to conduct child-centered play sessions with their child. Besides acting in a teaching role, the therapist also supervises the parent by reviewing their reports or videotapes of their early sessions with the child.

Course of Treatment

Assessment, Treatment, and Termination

The full course of Filial Therapy is usually completed over a set number of sessions ranging from 6 to 12. Landreth (1991) presents a 6- to 8-session training format. During the first part of the treatment, the parent is trained and is closely supervised by the therapist. During the middle phase, the parent practices in sessions at home with the child and the therapist reviews the parent's report of the sessions and advises the parent as to how to proceed in subsequent sessions. As the therapy draws to a close, the parent continues the play sessions with the child and is slowly weaned from supervision.

Selected References

Guerney, B. (1964). Filial therapy: Description and rationale. *Journal of Consulting Psychology, 28* (4), 303–310.

Guerney, L. (1983). Introduction to filial therapy. In P. Keller & L. Ritt (Eds.), *Innovations in clinical practice: A sourcebook* (Vol. II). Sarasota, FL: Professional Resource Exchange, pp. 26–39.

Guerney, L. (1991). Parents as partners in treating behavior problem children in early childhood settings. *Topics in Early Childhood Special Education, 11* (2), 74–90.

Guerney, L. (1997). Filial therapy. In K. O'Connor & L. Braverman (Eds.), *Play Therapy Theory and Practice: A comparative presentation.* New York: Wiley, pp. 131–159.

VanFleet, R. (1994). *Filial therapy: Strengthening parent-child relationships through play.* Sarasota, FL: Professional Resource Press.

ADLERIAN PLAY THERAPY

Theory

There are several key elements to the Adlerian conceptualization of personality. First, like child-centered therapy, Adlerian therapy is rooted in phenomenologic philosophy. That is, children are seen as experiencing life from a subjective perspective. The therapist accepts that the world is what the child perceives it to be. Consistent with this view, each child is viewed as unique and creative. Somewhat akin to the behavioral view people's behavior is seen as goal-oriented. "One of the primary tenets of Individual Psychology, that all behavior is purposive and goal-directed applies equally to both healthy and pathological behavior. In an effort to understand what the child is trying to achieve with the symptomatic behavior, the therapist would examine its effects or results" (Kelly, 1999, p. 119). Children engage in behavior to move toward a goal. The primary drive in Adlerian theory is the need to belong. Children are seen as social beings with an inherent drive to affiliate. Specifically, children are seen as motivated by the need to belong (Kottman, 1997).

Pathology

Children are seen less as pathologic and more as engaging in misbehavior. Children who misbehave have developed self-defeating convictions that thwart their ability to get their needs met in socially appropriate ways. In Adlerian terms, the goals of misbehavior are to gain attention, to obtain revenge, to gain power, or to overcome feelings of inadequacy (Kottman, 1995).

Cure/Treatment Goal

The goals of intervention in Individual Psychology are to help the client (1) gain an awareness of and insight into lifestyle; (2) alter faulty self-defeating apperceptions and move from private logic to common sense; (3) move toward positive goals of behavior; (4) replace negative strategies for belonging and gaining significance with positive strategies; (5) increase his or her social interest; (6) learn new ways of coping with feelings of inferiority; and (7) optimize creativity and begin to use his or her assets to develop self-enhancing decisions about attitudes, feelings, and behaviors (Kottman, 1997).

Basic Assumptions

Role of the Adlerian Therapist within Therapy Sessions

As with other humanistically based play therapy models, one of the therapist's primary responsibilities is to develop and maintain a positive relationship with the child. Having done this, the therapist engages in three, stepwise behaviors. The first is to thoroughly assess the child's present functioning and life situation. This is not done through formal assessment procedures but rather is an ongoing aspect of the treatment process. The therapist's goal is to come to an understanding of why the child engages in misbehavior. What does the child believe he will get or accomplish via engaging in problematic and even self-defeating behavior? As the therapist develops this understanding, he conveys what he has learned back to the child through interpretation. As the child gains insight, the therapist becomes more active in teaching the child alternative behaviors and in helping the child to rehearse those behaviors in session. The therapist will also take an active role in encouraging the child to practice these new behaviors out of session and may work with various adults in the child's life to ensure that such generalization occurs.

Role of Play in the Conduct of Adlerian Sessions

Play serves to enhance all stages of the Adlerian Play Therapy process. Initially, the child's play behavior is a major source of the data the therapist gathers as he attempts to understand the child's view of the world and the goals of his misbehavior. As the treatment progresses, some interpretive work may be done in the context of the play before it is directly applied to the child's own behavior. And, last, play activities such as role playing provide a fun and safe medium through which the child can learn and practice alternative behaviors.

Curative Elements of Adlerian Therapy

The main curative element is the reframing of the child's self-defeating convictions by the therapist. This enables the child to engage in new, positive behaviors (Kottman, 1995).

Besides the direct work done in session, one of the most powerful tools for change, logical consequences, can be implemented by the therapist, the child's parents, and any other significant adults in the child's environment such as teachers (Dreikurs & Cassel, 1972). Logical consequences help redirect the children's misbehavior and enable them to draw more appropriate connections between the behaviors in which they engage and the outcomes they experience. Simply put, logical consequences are, just as the term implies, the consistent imposition of consequences for the child's misbehavior that follow logically from what the child has done. Punishments inflict pain or distress while logical consequences present the child with an outcome separated from the adult's anger or negative judgments about the child.

Logical consequences are realistic. They express the reality of the social order, not just that of the person applying them. Because of this, they imply a consensual judgment of right or wrong rather than an arbitrary moral judgment. A lie is bad because it hurt someone's feelings or puts the child in danger not simply because all lying and all liars are inherently bad.

Logical consequences are related to the misbehavior and are applied in a manner that respects the child. Logical consequences are concerned only with the present, not what happened in the past or what may happen in the future. Where possible, logical consequences are agreed upon by both the adult and the child in advance of the transgression and the application of the consequences. The child is given a choice and understands, in advance, the consequences of each choice. Categories of logical consequences include: (1) loss or delay of privilege (a desired activity, interaction with a desired person, use of desired objects, or access to desired places), (2) loss or delay of cooperation (I will do what you want after you have done what I want.), (3) making restitution (adapted from Kottman's notes on Gilbert, 1986).

Course of Treatment

Assessment, Treatment, and Termination

Adlerian treatment proceeds in four stages with the assessment process as an integral part of the early stages. First, the child and therapist must establish a partnership. This begins to address the child's need for affilia-tion and sets up the notion that the two of them will be working together; their behavior is goal directed. Second, the therapist explores the child's life, formulates hypotheses about the child's self-defeating convictions and methods of gaining significance. Third, the therapist shares these hypothe-ses with the child in the form of interpretations. Last, the therapist guides the child to generate alternative behavior, teaches the child more socially appropriate behavior and then practices these new behaviors with the child (Kottman, 1995). Having accomplished this, the child is ready to leave the play therapy.

Selected References

Adler, A. (1963). *The problem child.* New York: Putnam Capricorn. (Original work published 1930)

Kottman, T., & Johnson, V. (1993). Adlerian play therapy: A tool for school counselors. *Elementary School Guidance and Counseling, 28,* 42–51.

Kottman, T. (1994). Adlerian play therapy. In K. O'Connor and C. Schaefer (Eds.), *Handbook of play therapy* (Vol. 2). New York: Wiley, pp. 3–26.

Kottman, T. (1995). *Partners in play: An Adlerian approach to play therapy.* Alexandria, VA: American Counseling Association.

Kottman, T. (1997). Adlerian play therapy. In K. O'Connor & L. Braverman (Eds.), *Play therapy theory and practice: A comparative presentation.* New York: Wiley, pp. 310–340

REALITY THERAPY

Theory

In presenting Reality Therapy, Glasser (1969, 1972, 1975, 1986) did not make any reference to personality constructs. In fact, his model suggested that theories of personality are generally used to explain and subsequently justify why an individual behaves in a manner that is unacceptable to him-self, society, or both. Glasser emphasized a primary motivational force sim-ilar to the notion of libido in psychoanalytic theory and self-actualization in humanistic theory. He stated that all humans are motivated to meet basic physiologic and psychologic needs. The latter is of particular interest to the mental health professional and consists of (1) the need to love and be loved and (2) the need to feel worthwhile to one's self and others. As a result, Glasser's model emphasizes the interactional aspects of human behavior and therapy in particular.

Glasser believes that an individual's "mental health" should be de-fined by his ability to act responsibly, that is, by his ability to fulfill his own needs in a way that does not deprive others of the ability to fulfill their needs. People are not viewed as having an innate drive toward responsible behavior as per humanistic theory; instead, it is the caretakers', and later society's, duty to teach children responsibility by exposing them to love and discipline from the earliest possible moment. It is recognized that this type of learning can take place only in the context of a relationship in which the "teacher" and "student" are intensely and emotionally involved with one another.

Pathology

Glasser proposes that psychopathology results when individuals deny reality and act irresponsibly in order to fulfill their basic needs. In this context, denying reality and acting irresponsibly mean that the individual acts in a way that prevents others from meeting their basic needs. The central premise of Reality Therapy is the notion that mental health professionals actually promote pathology by focusing on the forces in the environment that caused the individual to act in a certain manner rather than unfailingly requiring the individual to act responsibly. Once individuals have acquired the skill to act responsibly, they must be expected to act in accordance with those skills and must suffer appropriate consequences if they violate the rights of others.

Cure/Treatment Goal

The goal of treatment is to teach individuals strategies for meeting their own needs responsibly. Therapy is terminated when the individual has demonstrated a capacity to meet his basic needs in socially appropriate and responsible ways.

Basic Assumptions

Developmental Level and Pathology of Suitable Reality Therapy Clients

Because Reality Therapy is based on the assumption that all clients are capable of acting in responsible ways and that treatment must be geared to the level at which the client is currently functioning, virtually any client might be considered appropriate for this type of treatment. It is a particularly viable approach for working with acting-out clients who might not respond to a less directive therapeutic approach.

Training of Reality Therapists

Glasser considers extensive experience in working with client's who display a wide range of irresponsible behavior essential to the conduct of Reality Therapy. He maintains a training institute in Canoga Park, California.

In addition to having certain basic experiences and training, the Reality therapist is (1) responsible, and willing to convey his own values to the client when needed; (2) strong, and able never to condone the client's irresponsible behavior; (3) able to understand the client's experience of being unable to get his basic needs met; and (4) able to become emotionally involved with his clients.

Role of the Reality Therapist within Therapy Sessions

Reality Therapy posits six ways in which the Reality therapist is different from the conventional therapist:

1. Because we (Reality therapists) do not accept the concept of mental illness, the patient cannot become involved with us as a mentally ill person who has no responsibility for his behavior.
2. Working in the present and towards the future, we do not get involved with the patient's history because we can neither change what happened to him nor accept the fact that he is limited by his past.
3. We relate to patients as ourselves, not as transference figures.
4. We do not look for unconscious conflicts or the reasons for them. A patient cannot become involved with us by excusing his behavior on the basis of unconscious motivations.
5. We emphasize the morality of behavior. We face the issue of right and wrong which we believe solidifies the involvement, in contrast to conventional psychiatrists who do not make the distinction between right and wrong, feeling it would be detrimental to attaining the transference relationship they seek.
6. We teach patients better ways to fulfill their needs. The proper involvement will not be maintained unless the patient is helped to find more satisfactory patterns of behavior. Conventional therapists do not feel that teaching better behavior is a part of therapy. (Glasser, 1975, p. 54)

In addition to behaving in accordance with the guidelines delineated above the Reality therapist engages the client in certain tasks over the course of the treatment. The therapist (Fuller & Fuller, 1999):

1. Focuses on being involved with the child by being warm, supportive, and interested in the child.
2. Focuses on present behavior and the emotions related to those behaviors.
3. Assists the child in determining whether or not his or her behavior is harmful to self or others.
4. Helps the child plan responsible behavior. The plan must be: small and manageable, specific, reasonable (make sense and have value), positive (what the client will do as opposed to what he will not do), begin as soon as possible, and must be repetitive.

5. Contrasts a commitment to the plan from the child.
6. Accepts no excuses for the child's failure to implement the plan.
7. Does not punish the child for failure to behave according to the plan but ensures that natural or logical consequences follow.
8. Never gives up.

Course of Treatment

Assessment

Glasser mentions very little about the type of assessment procedure that would be most useful. One assumes that the therapist would want to know a great deal about the client's past and present attempts to get his needs met and his relative success or failure. The focus once treatment begins, however, is on the present and future rather than the past; thus taking an extensive developmental history, for example, is probably viewed as unnecessary.

Treatment

Reality Therapy proceeds in three steps. First, the therapist must become involved with the client quickly and deeply. One part of this involvement is an acceptance of who the client is at that point in time. Essentially, this is the creation of the type of unconditional positive regard for the person, if not their behavior, that humanistic therapists advocate. Second, the therapist must reject irresponsible behavior while working to maintain involvement. That is, the therapist must, in a way, re-parent the individual by conveying the consistent message that he cares for the client at all times even if he does not approve of the client's behavior. Finally, the therapist must teach the client alternative, responsible ways of getting his needs met.

In the course of implementing Reality Therapy, the therapist may use any or all of the following techniques:

1. Humor.
2. Confrontation.
3. Contracts, written agreements to follow a plan developed in session.
4. Instruction, particularly when helping the client learn new skills.
5. Teaching.
6. Role playing.
7. Support.
8. Homework assignments.
9. Bibliotherapy.
10. Self-disclosure (when it is relevant to the treatment goals).
11. Summarizing and reviewing (have child restate a plan or the goals of a plan).

12. Restitution, requires that the client make amends for the negative impact of his behavior.
13. Questioning.
14. Paradox is used to help the client break set in the face of particularly strong resistance (Wubbolding, 1988).

Termination

As stated, therapy is terminated when the client has demonstrated a capacity to consistently get his needs met in responsible ways.

TRANSACTIONAL, FAMILY, SYSTEMIC, COMMUNITY, AND ECOLOGICAL THERAPIES

The one concept that these therapies have in common is their focus on the individual as part of a system. The systemic unit thought to change as a result of treatment varies from the dyad, to the family, to the social network, to the community, to some broader network of interlocking systems. Yet, regardless of the unit of treatment considered, the increasing recognition of the fact that clients do not exist in isolation, either in their day-to-day lives or in the course of their psychotherapy, is probably the single greatest advance made in the mental health field over the last few decades.

Increasingly, the psychological treatment of clients is guided by the fact that both the client and therapist are embedded within multiple systems, some of which may be overlapping while others are orthogonal. Each brings to the treatment session individual, family, peer, community, cultural, national, religious, racial, and other experiences. If the potential impact of these experiences on the treatment process is not recognized, the outcomes are likely to be less than optimal for all concerned. This is not to say that the therapist has, or would even want, control or influence within each system, only that he must recognize that the systems exist, that they are a part of the client's reality. As Glasser (1975) noted, neither the client nor the therapist can function optimally if they deny reality.

The contributions of each theoretical model of psychotherapy reviewed in the preceding pages to the formulation of Ecosystemic Play Therapy presented herein is delineated in Part II. Before proceeding with that presentation, however, we will briefly examine the impact of some of the therapist's individual experiences and beliefs on the practice of play therapy.

CHAPTER THREE

Diversity Issues

Two key areas will be discussed as we address diversity issues in play therapy. One is the therapist herself and the other is the role of culture in modern society and the mental health field in particular. The persona of the therapist plays an incredibly important but often neglected role in the way she practices psychotherapy. The therapist's philosophy, values, experiences, cultural background, family background, and so forth influence every nuance of the therapy. These variables in turn affect the style and pattern of the therapist's speech and the way the therapist dresses and moves in the session, the way she reacts to different clients, and the way clients react to her. Even the theoretical orientation that the therapist adopts and the techniques she chooses to implement are not without their determinants in the persona of the therapist. It is critical that therapists recognize themselves in their work and not hide behind rationalizations that hold that what they do in a given case is the one best intervention. Otherwise, the therapist risks becoming blind to the client's needs, and therapy may not only cease to be effective, it may even become iatrogenic.

Given the relative clinical success of child psychotherapy techniques based on widely divergent theoretical models, it is necessary to consider the possibility that it is not the theory that determines whether or not a particular intervention will be successful. Weisz (1986) found that children's improvement in therapy was unrelated to the therapist's theoretical orientation. Psychotherapy process research with adult clients suggests that clients find the therapist's ability to help them come to a new understanding of their problems most helpful regardless of the therapist's theoretical orientation (Elliott, 1984). Shirk and Russell (1996) suggest six primary change processes:

1. Insight gained through interpretation.
2. The therapist's provision of supportive scaffolding. That is, the therapist's ability to support the client as she tries to make the difficult life changes associated with therapeutic progress.

59

3. The client's development of additional skills.
4. The correction of the child's cognitive distortions through the transformation of her interpersonal schemata.
5. An increase in the client's self-esteem as the therapist validates and supports the client.
6. A reduction in the emotional interference that prevents the child from behaving appropriately as the therapy works toward enhancing the child's emotional regulation.

While our clinical understanding of these processes may derive from different theoretical models (e.g., insight is usually seen as a psychoanalytic method and correcting cognitive distortions are usually seen as a cognitive-behavioral method), Shirk and Russell (1996) propose that these occur in all effective therapy regardless of the theoretical orientation of the therapist.

Whatever the therapist's theoretical orientation, well-conducted therapy reorganizes the client's experience in a new, yet systematic, way. What the theory provides is the system by which this reorganization is accomplished. The client comes to therapy displaying pathologic and constricted behavior, unaware of how to act so as to get more of her needs met. The therapist helps the client come to a different way of understanding the problem, thereby reorganizing her experience. This new understanding creates for the client the possibility of flexible thinking and behaving, and when properly presented, it also creates the motivation to experiment with behavior change. If the system, or theory, on which the therapist bases the information she conveys to her client is clear, then the client gradually learns the system and develops an independent capacity for flexible thinking and behavior change. Although this process is more easily accomplished if the client and therapist can interact verbally, it is feasible to complete this work with children through a combination of therapeutic and verbal experiences.

In other words, it seems as if many of the people who seek therapy do so because they are experiencing difficulties to which they can find no solution. They are unable to find responsible ways to get their basic needs met (Glasser, 1975). What these individuals find helpful in therapy is the process by which the therapist helps them identify solutions to their problems. Essentially, it seems that all therapy may be reduced to a form of social problem solving. The therapist helps the client identify the problem (often the longest part of the process) to generate potential solutions to the problem, evaluate and implement the potential solutions that seem most likely to provide the desired results, and then evaluate the outcome of the efforts. The theoretical language used to complete these steps is less important than the steps themselves.

Clients who undergo psychoanalysis come away understanding their lives in terms of the impact of their past experiences and the internal conflicts that fuel their anxieties and trigger their defenses. Clients who complete a course of humanistically oriented therapy reconceptualize their experience in terms of their capacity and right to have their needs met and to create a health-producing environment for themselves. And clients who undergo behavior therapy find that they can engage in new behaviors and either garner new reinforcers or, at the very least, not lose any of the old ones.

If the therapist's theoretical orientation is not a critical variable in the outcome for the client, should the therapist concern herself with adopting a particular orientation? The answer is a resounding "Yes." The therapist's theoretical orientation, whatever it may be, is the framework against which she organizes all her thinking about the client's difficulties, the interventions to be used, and the assessment of the outcome. Without a defined theoretical framework, the therapist's thinking about a given case will be unclear and the progress through the social problem-solving steps will be chaotic. The client will be unable to gain new understanding of her problem because the therapy process is random, not logical. The therapist may, for example, identify the problems that the client had in her infantile relationship with her mother while prescribing a program designed to systematically desensitize the client to being out in public places. Both components may be important, both may even be related, but unless the therapist can systematically present the rationale for each component, the client will be left with no understanding of the process. If the client remains in the dark for too long, she may terminate therapy or, conversely, become dependent on it because it makes her feel better in a way she perceives as magical. Further, if the client cannot come to understand the process, then she cannot learn to solve her own problems, and the generalization of the changes made in therapy will be quite limited.

If the theoretical model used is not of primary importance in determining treatment outcome, then it seems that it is the therapist's adoption of a theory that is internally consistent will better enable her to conduct her work in a consistent manner and to convey clearly to her client the necessary elements of understanding and empathy. To adopt a theoretical orientation that is internally consistent, the therapist must understand both the philosophical underpinnings of the theory and her personal philosophy.

PERSONAL PHILOSOPHY AND THEORETICAL ORIENTATION

Nature of People

One important component of self-awareness requires the examination of personal beliefs about the fundamental nature of people. Do you as an individual believe that people are innately good? Such a belief is the basis for the Rogerian perspective Axline (1947) proposed in delineating her method of play therapy. But Rogers and Axline added a secondary belief:

There is within each person a drive to become the best possible, the drive to self-actualize. Axlinian play therapy is based on the notion that it is the environment which subverts this drive and produces maladaptive behavior. This premise logically leads to the development of a treatment modality that provides the child with an optimal, nonsubverting environment in which the child's own self-actualizing drive can reassert itself.

The psychoanalytic position regarding people derives from a significantly different philosophical stance. Freud struggled with the notion of Thanatos, a destructive drive or death instinct we all possess, until his own death. Whereas the humanists blamed the environment for human pathology, Freud could not resolve his observation that many of a person's self-destructive behaviors continue in the absence of apparently toxic environments. Over time, Freud's belief in the death instinct became more and more necessary in order for him to keep his overall theory of personality intact. After all, it would have been difficult for Freud to justify the concept of destructive neurotic conflicts in the absence of significant precipitants if he did not believe that within a person there is some potential for pathology, or at least some drive toward the chaotic. The humanistic and psychoanalytic theories differ on more than just a view of people's drives, including some fundamental differences in philosophic stance.

Both philosophies limit an individual's responsibility for personal behavior. The humanistic model does so by noting that individuals possess the drive to be good and that maladaptive behavior is the result of the impact of society or the environment, thereby shifting the responsibility for the problem outside the individual. Freud, on the other hand, emphasized individual responsibility over social responsibility but proposed that individuals were essentially at the mercy of their drives and histories. In the psychoanalytic model, individuals are not free to behave in ways contrary to past experience until they have developed insight.

Behavior therapy takes a virtually neutral stance regarding the nature of humans. Humans are neither good or bad; they are simply organisms who respond to the patterns of reinforcement to which they are exposed. Less radical behavioral theorists accept the possibility that human behavior is the result of an interaction between individuals and their environment, but they place little or no inherent value on one side or the other of the interaction.

Reality Therapy (Glasser, 1975), on the contrary, focuses entirely on the individual's responsibility once she has developed certain capacities for reason. Glasser's underlying belief was that individuals act in order to get certain basic needs met. Individuals have the capacity to act in any manner they choose, and they must be pressured by society to get their needs met in ways that do not violate the basic rights of others to get their needs met. In this model, behavior is valued according to the degree it meets the needs of the individual without depriving others. In cases of conflict between the needs of the individual and the needs of the majority, the good of the majority takes precedence.

These differences in the conceptualization of the underlying nature of man in some ways parallel the differences in emphasis on individual versus social responsibility in certain societies. Western, industrial societies tend to emphasize the rights of the individual although they tend to vacillate on the issue of individual responsibility. The right of the individual to get his own needs met is seen as primary unless it interferes in some very significant way with the rights of others. On the other hand, individuals are seen as victims of larger social forces. Americans strongly argue that individuals have the right to smoke cigarettes if they so choose. The only legal restrictions they are willing to place on this behavior is to limit smoking to places where the second-hand smoke will not make others ill. Juries have been awarding astronomical sums to people who have suffered the consequences of exercising their right to smoke. Who is responsible for the death of a smoker from cancer—the tobacco company who sold the product or the smoker himself who made the choice to smoke? Communal societies like those in Asia often see the need to limit the rights of the individual to benefit society as a whole. Many marriages in Japan are still arranged for children by their families. The notion is that the parents and grandparents are in a better position to see what is good for the children and for the two families that will be joined. As Japan becomes more industrialized, its similarity to the West increases but differences remain. None of this discussion should be interpreted as implying that one worldview is better than the other. Rather the goal here is to emphasize the importance of staying alert to the need to continually strive to optimally balance the needs of individuals against the needs of the many systems in which they are embedded.

Although the beliefs about the nature of people as presented in these four theories are not necessarily mutually exclusive, they are sufficiently different that they have different effects on the way the therapist conceptualizes psychopathology and therapeutic interventions. Therefore, it is important that the therapist take the first step in developing a theoretical position that is internally consistent. The therapist accomplishes this by examining personal beliefs regarding the nature of people.

Value of the Individual versus Value of the System

As reflected in the theoretical models presented in Chapter Two, the relative emphasis on the value of the individual versus the value of the systems in which that individual is embedded is a constant source of potential conflict for the therapist. On the broadest level, the therapist must question her own role in the conduct of psychotherapy.

Is the therapist there to help the child achieve insight, thus allowing for the possibility of behavior change as per psychoanalytic theory? If so, then contact with the family, school, or any representative of society seems as pointless as it does when we assume that the child has within her the capacity to self-actualize. Even a naive or idealistic therapist must realize that insight is not likely to change the child's behavior in the absence of a change in the response the child obtains from the environment. The analytic stance, however, is that the child's internal, self-responses are more important than the responses of the world to that child.

Is the therapist there to help the child self-actualize as the humanists suggest? If so, then contact with the family, school, or any representative of society seems somewhat irrelevant. The therapist is there to help the child be the best person she can be by creating an optimal environment within sessions. The needs of the child take precedence over the structures of the environment. But even the most naive therapist must accept the fact that her child client must leave the office and live in the world. Thus, the therapist is put in the position of helping the child find some middle ground between her own needs and the demands of the real world or helping the environment become less toxic if the child's growth is to generalize beyond sessions.

Is the therapist there as a behavior analyst who will discover those aspects of the child's reinforcement system that are problematic and work to reorganize those systems? If this is the case, then the therapist will want a great deal of contact with the people and systems who dispense rewards and punishments to the child and potentially very little contact with the child. The child must learn to behave in a manner consistent with the expectations of the systems in which she is embedded.

Finally, is the therapist there as an agent of society, someone to teach the child socially acceptable strategies for getting needs met, as Glasser stated? If this is the case, the therapist might again want a great deal of contact with those in the child's world so as to help the child develop the most realistic strategies possible.

Regardless of the therapist's theoretical stance, the reality is that the child is an individual embedded within multiple interrelated systems: family, school, judicial, medical, cultural, and general societal ones; an ecosystem. If the changes achieved during therapy are to benefit clients in their day-to-day lives, then these systems must be taken into consideration at every step in the process.

Family System

The first "system versus individual" conflicts that must be addressed are those involving the needs of the child versus the needs of her family. On the most pragmatic level, the therapist must face the fact that it is the child's family who brings the child to therapy and pays for the sessions. Certainly this fact should not be the basis for making many therapy decisions, but few therapists could claim that it has not entered their thinking at some point.

Second, the therapist must recognize that a child client must go home from the session and live in a family setting, which means that the child must develop some way of getting her needs met in her family. Third, the family must support, or at least tolerate, changes in the child's behavior or they can undermine the child's progress either overtly or covertly. Finally, if the child becomes very dysfunctional, the therapist may be faced with the decision of whether or not to remove the child from the family. Does the therapist consider the best interests of the family or the child? How is the decision framed? In some cases, it may be best to say that this is a decision the therapist and family reach in concert, with the best interests of the child at heart. At other times, it might be better to frame the decision as one that the child made by continuing to engage in destructive behavior which the family can no longer tolerate.

Cultural System

Second, the play therapist has to consider how to resolve potential conflicts between the child and the child's cultural subgroup.

> Franklin was a light-skinned African-American child who behaved in a manner which clearly indicated that he did not view himself as being the least bit African American. Franklin would play only with Anglo children, he referred to himself as White, and he disdained any of the ethnic foods his family prepared. His Anglo peers encouraged such self-identification and readily included him in their group. He did very well in his, primarily, Anglo school. However, his behavior greatly distressed his African-American parents despite the fact that they reported being emotionally close to their son when they were together as a family. Franklin's behavior was a particular problem when the family visited African-American relatives.

Should Franklin have been considered a candidate for play therapy? Certainly his denial of the reality of his racial background was dramatic and probably not healthy, but he was not displaying much else in the way of symptomatic behavior. Numerous value judgments would have to be made before deciding whether or not to treat this child and in determining treatment goals if the process were initiated. Many of these value judgments would tie directly into the therapist's own feelings about valuing and preserving all aspects of one's ethnicity versus the individual's need to fit in socially. One could also easily imagine that these decisions might vary considerably, based not on the child but on whether the play therapist was Anglo or African American.

Now let us look at a situation in which the conflict between the child and the culture does not involve any gross distortions of reality but merely reflects different rates of acculturation. Consider the second- and third-generation children of immigrant parents. California has been subject to a large influx of Southeast Asian refugees over the past 10 years. Some of these groups have had great difficulty adjusting to life in the United States because of the radical differences between their culture of origin and modern, U.S., Anglo culture. Many of these people were rural peasants who lived a semitribal life and now find themselves in an urban setting. While the first-generation individuals have difficulty making this transition, their children, exposed to the public school system, often adjust quickly. Extreme parent/child conflict may arise when the child's new value system and the parent's traditional values clash.

Is the Southeast Asian girl who wants to play after school with her peers rather than help with childcare, who wants to wear modern clothes, and who wants to socialize with boys in need of treatment? Certainly these behaviors may cause problems at home, but are they problems in the abstract? Does the therapist work to acculturate the family, preserve the culture of origin, or develop some compromise position? Each tactic carries with it implicit value judgments.

Society as a Whole

Besides situations in which the child's problems can be framed as conflicts between the child and the family or the child and her cultural or ethnic group, the therapist also sees many cases in which the child's difficulties are best characterized as conflicts between the child and any one of a number of other systems in which she is embedded. Primary among these difficulties are problems resulting from conflicts between the child's needs and the needs of the school setting. The behavior problems teachers report are numerous and range from children who talk too much to those who refuse to do particular assignments to those who brutally attack their peers. Many of these children need treatment, yet some are simply reacting to a toxic environment, as the following example illustrates:

> Joseph was brought to therapy suffering from numerous symptoms consistent with a severe anxiety disorder. He had nightmares, difficulty sleeping, and episodes of guilt in which he would talk his mother for hours, telling her about transgressions he had committed days, months, and even years earlier. His school performance had also begun to deteriorate. His mother had become quite concerned but had decided to talk to other mothers of children in her son's class before seeking outside help. In her discussions, she soon noted that the parents of the girls in the class reported no problems while the parents of the boys reported all types of regressive symptoms, from anxiety to bedwetting.
>
> It was then discovered that this teacher was creating classic double-bind situations for the boys in the room. One day she would criticize the boys for talking too much during class time and keep them in from recess and terrorize them, including hitting one child hard enough to break his glasses. The next day not a single boy spoke all morning, and when it came time for recess, the teacher kept the boys in again, saying that they had not participated in class as much as she wanted.

After considerable lobbying, the school district agreed to move the teacher to another school (not terminate her employment), and the symptoms the boys in the class displayed abated within weeks.

Had Joseph been referred for treatment, it is, unfortunately, very likely that play therapy would have been initiated without a sufficient investigation into the toxicity of the child's environment, based on the assumption that most teachers are really quite good. It is also likely that Joseph's symptoms would not have responded to treatment as long as he continued to be exposed to such a harsh school environment day after day.

Another example of the potential for conflict between the needs of children and the needs of the system is from a long-term pediatric hospital, where many of the children were hospitalized in casts, and many were cognitively quite impaired. These children would be brought down to the orthopedics department to have their casts removed. Once there they would scream in terror during the entire procedure, due mostly to the sight and sound of the saw that was being used. They could not grasp how a saw that cut plaster did not risk cutting their skin. The orthopedic surgeons resisted numerous approaches by the psychology staff to create a desensitization program in which the children could be enrolled several days ahead of their scheduled cast removal. The argument against such a program was that it would take too long and that the surgeons did not want to be bothered with planning that far ahead because they were usually only at the hospital 1, or at most, 2 days a week.

In the play therapist's constant efforts to balance the needs of the child against the needs of those in the multiple systems in which the child is embedded, she must constantly be aware that to some extent her role is indeed that of communicator of the social order. At her best, the therapist helps children learn to get as many of their needs met as possible while violating as few of society's rules as possible. One danger in taking this stance is that the therapist teaches conformity and not the kind of high-level functioning valued by society and exemplified by Kohlberg's definition of optimal moral development. Will a child who has been in therapy be able to go against society when the time is right? Even that question reflects a very Western/Anglo point of view in which nonconformity is valued. Many Southeast Asian and Oriental parents would be aghast at the idea of a therapist promoting anything but conformity with the social order. Again we run up against a problem created by the variability of cultural and philosophical values.

Within Ecosystemic Play Therapy, the assumption is that the play therapist's role is to work with the child to develop strategies for meeting as many of the child's needs as possible within the sociocultural context in which the child is embedded. This places the therapist in much more of an advocacy role than is typical of some theoretical models, but again, this is seen as necessary, given children's dependent position in society. The play therapist is the child's ally, but she is also the caretaker's ally and the family's ally and ultimately society's ally. This mix of roles carries with it an implicit difficulty in defining professional boundaries. It is not surprising that many play therapists choose to avoid the conflict by confining themselves to their offices and rarely venturing out into the real world of their clients. To accept the fundamental assumption made herein regarding the role of the therapist, play therapists will have to learn to recognize themselves as having an impact not just on their individual client but indirectly on a rather large array of systems, each of which may react in ways that directly affect the course of the treatment.

VALUES AND BACKGROUND OF THE THERAPIST

Ethnic and Cultural Background

As we saw in the example of Franklin, who was referred for failure to develop an identity consistent with his ethnicity, the therapist's response may very well be influenced by her ethnic and cultural background as much as, if not more than, her philosophy and theoretical orientation. Ethnicity is such a fundamental part of a person's identity and life experience that it must pervade one's approach to the world. A Caucasian living in a Caucasian-dominated culture is unlikely to truly know what it is like to be Black in that same context. What would it be like for this person to wake up one day and be Black? How would people react to her on a day-to-day basis? And how would their reactions change her behavior?

Language

A significant assumption made in the course of designing and delivering most psychological interventions is that verbal communication is extremely important and therefore to be emphasized in the interactions between the therapist and the client. This is by no means a universally accepted assumption; in fact, some cultural groups such as Native Americans might find the quantity of conversation in which the therapist seeks to engage both difficult and socially inappropriate.

Most therapists also tend to assume that universal meanings exist for certain nonverbal behaviors. Anglos view eye contact as a sign of a person's general adjustment, an ability to be trusted, and a sign of respect. Other cultures, such as those of Native Americans and Asians, tend to view eye contact as intrusive and disrespectful. Such differences exist for virtually all forms of body language.

The existence of a language difference between the therapist and the child client may lead to significant problems in the conduct of the play therapy. The primary problem is direct translation difficulties when the therapist and child attempt to translate the meaning of the verbal and body language being used. Much more complicated, however, is the translation of idiomatic language; even a skilled translator may be unable to convey the actual meaning of a culturally idiomatic term or phrase.

Play therapy is not necessarily free from problems should there be language differences between the therapist and child. Both persons may have problems translating verbal and nonverbal behavior. Play therapy's potential advantage is its pairing of an activity with language, which can be used by both the therapist and the child to create show-and-tell interactions, thereby reducing the potential for misunderstandings.

Class

The majority of play therapists come from middle- and upper middle-class backgrounds or have entered these socioeconomic levels as adults. Most clients, however, are from lower socioeconomic groups. This difference sets up a potential clash of class values. Problems may arise, for example, in the area of goal orientation. Therapists tend to be oriented to finding the underlying cause of a behavior and seeking to develop long-term solutions to the problem. They are willing to tolerate a lot of ambiguity in moving toward that goal. Clients from lower socioeconomic groups, however, tend to focus more on immediate problem solving. They want advice and concrete plans for addressing concrete problems. Both the therapist and the client may find that they are frustrated because of the mismatch of long-term goals.

Religion

The impact of the therapist's religious beliefs on her practice of play therapy may be more or less subtle. It may affect the judgments the therapist makes about the morality of the child's and the family's behavior. She might view a family's existential depression as a result of the loss of faith in either a specific religion or a specific deity. Alternatively, the therapist's rejection of her own religion may make her negate the role of religion in the lives of her clients. She might feel frustrated in the face of a family's refusal to become active participants in their child's treatment due to their belief that their life situation is "God's will" and therefore out of their control.

The therapist's religious beliefs may also interact with, and affect, other aspects of the treatment process. For example, the fact that most therapists maintain some fairly strong fantasies or hopes of rescuing their clients is widely accepted. Some religious beliefs enhance or limit this fantasy. A supervisor once told a student that the intensity of his rescue fantasies was to be expected given his Catholic upbringing. "After all," she said, somewhat tongue in cheek, "Jews can limit their sense of guilt and responsibility to situations where they fail to meet their mother's expectations. Protestants can limit their guilt and responsibility to situations where they have failed to meet work expectations. But Catholic guilt is universal. They believe they should bear some responsibility for, and experience guilt in response to, everything that goes wrong in the world." In this particular case, the student's religious background seemed to amplify his personality and his therapeutic style, resulting in intense rescue fantasies.

Family Experience

A study of child psychotherapists' childhood experiences revealed that a commonly believed folk myth may not only be true but may in fact operate to the benefit of child clients (Poal & Weisz, 1989). Namely, the belief that people who become child therapists must have had problem childhoods themselves. The study asked child psychotherapists to recall, using the Child Behavior Checklist, the types of problems they had in childhood and found that the therapists indeed reported more childhood problems than would have been expected in a random sample of the population. Next, the results of the therapist's recall were correlated with the behavioral outcomes reported for their child clients. The findings suggested that the more problematic a child therapist reported her childhood to be, the greater the improvement reported in her client's behavior. For several reasons noted in the study, this finding does not appear to be simply the result of increased empathy on the part of the therapist but potentially the result of increased personal experience with problem solving.

Aside from this direct study, there are many theories about why people become helping professionals in general and child therapists in particular. Virtually all these theories postulate problematic family experiences as underlying the choice of careers. Miller's (1981) model proposed that growing up in a household with narcissistically flawed caretakers causes the child to become excessively oriented toward meeting the needs of others as a way of eventually getting her own needs met. It seems plausible that the younger the child was when she became aware of the need to be attuned to the caretaker's needs, the more likely she is to decide to work with children later in life. This reasoning is consistent with the idea that play therapists must first heal the "child within" before they can become effective in their work.

Also, consistent with these research findings, observational experience suggests that many graduate students in child psychotherapy training programs have had less than optimal childhoods and that one of the most consistent problems is the actual absence of a clear childhood. Most of these individuals became caretakers in their families at a very young age, often before 5, and thus experienced role reversals vis-à-vis their caretakers, which resulted in a loss of appropriate childhood experiences. They were adults who rarely played; instead, they were interpersonally and intrapsychically sensitive caretakers who put the needs of others ahead of their own. Many of them report delayed childhoods, usually a period of acting out during adolescence or young adulthood, and many report no childlike period in their lives at all. Unless these people have received treatment that fosters their learning to take care of the child within, the one who has been neglected all this time, they run a very high risk of trying to take care of that child in their client's therapy. Often this action is observable when the play therapist does things in the child's session that are clearly intended to be nurturant but that ignore the child's needs at the time.

The early part of this chapter focused on how the therapist's values, beliefs, and experiences affect her practice of play therapy and her relationship with a given child. Let us now turn our attention to the issues of culture and diversity as they affect the therapy process. Several issues must be addressed here: the degree to which the concepts of culture are undergoing change, the definition of culture, the impact of culture on the mental health field, and the importance of practicing culture or diversity-competent play therapy.

GLOBALIZATION

Rather unfortunately it appears that the world is becoming gradually Westernized. This seems unfortunate not because of any specific flaws inherent in Western culture (though some might argue that there are some serious flaws), but because humanity risks losing the diversity that has contributed so essentially to the complexity and creativity of human thought. One example of such Westernization is the near universal adoption of the Internet as a mode of communication and with it the adoption of English as the language of the Internet. If we lose languages, we lose ideas that have no equivalent in another language. A favorite example of such differences is that fact that the Eskimo language has more than 20 words for what, in English, is simply snow. Language both reflects and communicates that which is important to a culture. Language is but one example of the rich heritage that is threatened by the process of globalization.

The formation of the European Union provides an excellent example of the direction in which the world seems to be headed. In the past, the differences between European countries and each one's sense of nationalism would have made such a union impossible. Globalization has overcome many of these differences and pushed the countries to join together for their mutual gain. It is clear that some of the poorer countries stand to benefit greatly from the union, but there will also be losses. One of the problems within the newly formed union is the inability of the countries to agree on a uniform set of standards for mental health professionals (Lunt & Poortinga, 1996). Even though all of these countries can be viewed as reflecting a generally Western view of psychology and mental health, their own internal differences make for significant differences in their conceptualizations of the essential training and qualifications of mental health professionals.

Globalization makes conceptualizing culture more complex. On the one hand, it appears to reduce the differences between cultural groups. On the other hand, as cultural isolation decreases the importance of understanding regional, local, familial, and individual differences increases. It becomes more important to be aware of the continuum of human differences. While each human is a unique individual, many times these individual differences become the focus of discussion among those that wish to minimize the importance of culture and other group memberships. It has become critically important to understand the relative impact of various groups and cultures on individuals both in and out of the context of psychotherapy. Essentially, culture as an object of study has become a moving target as people move freely between countries and continents. Because of this, the following should be kept in mind when considering the concept of culture: (1) cultural contacts and connections are leading to hybridization creating new cultures; (2) a heterogeneous global system is emerging; and (3) cultural complexity is increasing rather than decreasing (Hermans & Kenipen, 1998).

DEFINING CULTURE

In the context of this text, the term *culture* is used very broadly to refer to any identifiable group that shares a common language, beliefs, values, or customs that are communicated from one generation to the next. Commonly, conceptualized cultural groups include those based on race, ethnicity, religion, and national origin. Less commonly thought of as cultural groups in spite of the fact that they meet the broad definition are men, women, and the aged. Even less commonly thought about are cultural groups based on physical ability or disability and sexual orientation. It is important to recognize that membership in any one of these groups may play a very central role in the life of an individual and his identity. And, therefore, could become a central issue in the therapy process.

Triandis (1996) talks about cultural syndromes identifying these as: "a pattern of shared attitudes, beliefs, categorizations, self-definitions, norms, role definitions, and values that is organized around a theme" (p. 408). The following list of variables are important in characterizing and understanding a given cultural group:

1. Tightness: degree to which is enforced within the group.
2. Cultural complexity: the number of elements that characterize the culture.
3. Active-passive: the number of each type of element.
4. Honor: personal elements that might include the concept of shame or guilt.
5. Collectivism: the relative value placed on the group as a whole.
6. Individualism: the relative value placed on any one person in the group.

7. Vertical and hierarchical relationships: the degree to which a hierarchy exists within the group. (Triandis, 1996)

While it is important to understand the nature and of a culture as a whole, the importance of assessing the degree of meaning cultural membership has for a specific client cannot be overemphasized.

Last, it seems important to address the issue of what a group calls itself. In the past few decades many groups have chosen to move away from names that were assigned them by the dominant culture to names that more accurately reflect the nature and values of the culture. The transition from the use of the term Negroes to Blacks to African Americans is but one example of this trend. Often, members of the dominant culture become frustrated with the shift in terminology, most likely because it reflects the degree to which the group has chosen to define its own identity and to take over its own destiny. By referring to the concept of political correctness, the dominant culture trivializes the experience of various minority groups. As with addressing other aspects of diversity, the therapist should use and understand the importance of the self-label preferred by the client.

ANGLO- AND EURO-AMERICAN INFLUENCES IN MENTAL HEALTH

Because of its enormous economic, political, and military power, world thought is gradually becoming Westernized especially when it comes to the field of psychology (Marsella, 1998):

> The current Western thinking of the science of psychology in its prototypical form, despite being local and indigenous, assumes a global relevance and is treated as a universal mode of generating knowledge. Its dominant voice subscribes to a decontextualized vision with an extraordinary emphasis on individualism, mechanism and objectivity. This peculiarly Western mode of thinking is fabricated, projected, and institutionalized through representation technologies and scientific rituals and transported on a large scale to the non-Western societies under political-economic domination. As a result, Western psychology tends to maintain an independent stance at the cost of ignoring other substantive possibilities from disparate cultural traditions. Mapping reality through Western constructs has offered a psuedounderstanding of the people of alien cultures and has had debilitating effects in terms of misconstruing the special realities of people and exoticizing or disregarding psychologies that are non-Western. Consequently, when people from other cultures are exposed to Western psychology, they find their identities placed in question and their conceptual repertoires rendered obsolete. (Gergen, Gulerce, Lock, & Misra, 1996)

The trend has been to approach the cross-cultural application of Western/American psychology as a matter of finding points within existing theories that need to be modified to account for cultural differences. Consistent with Western scientific tradition, the assumption has been that single, universally applicable theoretical models can be developed. The possibility that culture creates fundamental differences requiring disparate models does not even appear to be entertained (Gergen et al., 1996). It seems time to consider the possibility that developing a single, universal psychology may not be possible or even desirable. Psychology can play a significant role in the emerging global community if "it is willing to reconsider some of its fundamental premises, methods, and practices that are rooted in Western (and specifically American) cultural traditions and to expand its appreciation and use of other psychologies" (Marsella, 1998, p. 1282). As an alternative to a more unidimensional model, "global-community psychology can be distinguished as a superordinate or meta-psychology by its concern for (a) recognizing the global dimensions and scale of our lives; (b) limiting the ethnocentric bias in many existing theories, methods, and interventions; (c) encouraging the development of indigenous psychologies; (d) emphasizing the cultural determinants of human behavior; (e) using systems, contextual, and nonlinear conceptualizations of human behavior; and (f) increasing the use of qualitative, naturalistic, and contextual research methods" (Marsella, 1998, p. 1286).

Phenomenology versus Applied Sciences

One way in which Western thought seems to be benefitting from globalization is the increasing relevance placed on phenomenology. Most Western science is based on the applied science model. In this model, the existence of a single, universal truth is endorsed and the goal of science is to uncover such universal truths. While phenomenology has a long history in Western philosophical thinking, it tends to take a more central role in Eastern thinking. From a phenomenologic point of view, all truth and knowledge are specific to the perspective of the observer. For example, there is no way to prove that what two different people see when they look at a green object is actually the same color; we can only prove that both label what they perceive using the term green. One person might, in fact, be color blind and simply have learned that identifying any leaf shape as green is most likely to be consensually validated. Phenomenology encourages us to recognize the idiosyncrasy of our own worldviews and to attend to the relative importance that the worldviews of our clients may have on the process of conducting therapy.

Impact on Psychology

The dominant Anglo culture has affected mental health practice in most of Western Europe, the United States, and Canada in the areas of diagnosis and treatment. With respect to diagnosis, it has been found that culture is more likely to have a negative effect on the accuracy of diagnosing adults than it does with children. For example, African Americans and Hispanics are more likely than Anglo Americans to be diagnosed as Schizophrenic as opposed to having Psychotic Affective Disorder (Garb, 1997). Such race bias is not as evident in studies that examine referrals for treatment, behavioral predictors, or diagnosis with children (Garb, 1997). It seems the diagnosis of children may be made less subjectively than the diagnosis of adults. This may also be the result of the fact that there are fewer diagnostic categories available for application to children thereby reducing the variability. It also seems that therapists are more sensitized to the effect of cultural and socioeconomic variables on children. Therapists sometimes seem to give children who are both of low socioeconomic status and members of a minority group a "break" when it comes to diagnosis or their estimates of the accuracy of test data (Garb, 1997). This is a relatively common practice in schools using intelligence testing. When non-Anglo children achieve low test scores, it is sometimes assumed to be the result of cultural or social deprivation instead of either genuine differences in cognitive styles or actual cognitive deficits. This attempt at being sensitive to cultural differences may end up hurting the child in the long run if it interferes with accurate and timely diagnosis of cognitive or educational problems.

When it comes to the practice of psychotherapy itself one must recognize that "counseling is a Euro(Anglo) American middle class activity based on Western cultural values" (Coleman & Barker, 1991; Coleman, Parmer, & Barker, 1993, p. 64; Sue & Sue, 1977, 1990). This leads to some specific areas of potential conflict between the values and goals of psychotherapy and the values of a given cultural group.

First, most play therapists consider the enhancement of the child's expressive capacities a primary goal of play therapy. This goal is the opposite of socially normative behavior in some cultures. Most Far Eastern cultures do not value emotional expressiveness and may have great difficulty when the child in treatment becomes more vocal at home.

Second, play therapists tend to favor the use of relatively unstructured play sessions. While many Anglo parents become annoyed and question the value of having their child "just play" in the sessions, members of cultural groups that emphasize structure and formality in interpersonal relationships may find the lack of structure virtually unacceptable. One African-American parent became quite disturbed by the fact that the therapist was allowing her daughter to address him by his first name. She felt that the child already had enough behavior problems and that the therapist was encouraging the child to act out by allowing such disrespect.

Third, play therapists rely on both the caretakers and the child to voluntarily communicate with them during the sessions, which may pose a problem if the family is from a culture that teaches that it is impolite to speak to authority figures unless they address you first. Even though the play therapist may not be too surprised to see such behavior in a child client, she may still interpret it as shyness or even excessive self-control. However, when the caretakers seem reluctant to talk and do not volunteer critical information out of respect for the therapist's authority, the play therapist is more likely to interpret the behavior as hostile resistance.

Fourth, both play therapy and parent counseling tend to stress linear logic in organizing and discussing behavior and interactions. Some other cultures, such as those of American Indians, value intuitive and holistic approaches, often placing much more emphasis on the spiritual components of human existence. The play therapist may become frustrated with the caretakers' and child's apparent inability to focus on the particulars of an event, while the caretakers and the child are confused by the therapist's seemingly endless preoccupation with insignificant details.

Overall, it is important to note that not only do cultural and philosophic issues affect the persona of the therapist and the way the therapist reacts to a given client, certain fundamental aspects of the therapy process are more or less culturally determined.

Importance of Developing a Global View

As stated in the opening of this chapter, globalization is upon us. It affects all aspects of our everyday lives from education to commerce to psychotherapy. If the practice of psychotherapy and play therapy is to remain relevant for children of the global village, then theories must be developed that give culture its rightful context. "The importance of the identification of theories appropriate for non-Western cultures becomes clearer when we realize that all humans are ethnocentric (Triandis, 1996) and suffer from naïve realism that limits the full appreciation of the "subjective status of their own construals, and, as such, they do not make sufficient allowances for the uncertainties of construal when called upon to make behavioral attributions and predictions of others" (Robinson, Kaltner, Ward, & Ross, 1995, p. 404 as quoted in Triandis, 1996, p. 407).

BECOMING CULTURALLY COMPETENT

To be optimally effective with the broadest range of clients, the therapist must develop cultural or diversity competence. This does not mean that the therapist develops culture or race blindness—the therapist who denies the differences between clients of different cultural or religious backgrounds is as likely to treat her clients inappropriately as the one who exaggerates the differences. Cultural competence means being able to recognize the differences between groups and to work with these groups without bias or prejudice. It further implies the ability to value and preserve group differences as opposed to striving for uniformity among clients. The process by which individual therapists and mental health practitioners in general become culturally competent has been described as requiring one to develop awareness, specific skills, and specific cultural knowledge.

Awareness

First, cross-cultural work requires awareness of one's own cultural attitudes, traditions, ideal and actual norms, and family and social organization. This is not an easy task because these psychosocial elements of culture operate largely outside of our awareness. They are rarely made explicit (much less questioned) because this process can threaten self-identity, can shake self-esteem, and can induce anxiety. Thus, this task is best undertaken at the postgraduate level when trainees have acquired basic clinical skills and some clinical experience. A three- to six-month seminar conducted with trainees who belong to the same cultural group and socioeconomic class has proven to be a successful format. Along with self-analysis and group disclosure regarding their own ethnic affiliations, activities, and biases, trainees can be guided in selected readings, can participate in seminar discussions, and can present their first cross-cultural cases.

There are some questions therapists can ask themselves to enhance their awareness of their own culture:

- What is my cultural heritage? What was the culture of my parents and my grandparents? With what cultural group(s) do I identify? (Locke, 1992)
- What are some of the traditions and customs practiced in my family? Where did they originate? (Locke, 1992)
- Am I a member of any minority group? What has this experience been like for me?
- What values, beliefs, opinions and attitudes do I hold that are consistent with the (Anglo) European American culture? Which are inconsistent? How did I learn these? (Thomas & Cobb, 1999, p. 51)

Second, clinicians must develop awareness of their attitudes toward other cultures. The following questions can help elicit that information:

- What are my perceptions and beliefs about members of other ethnic groups?
- What is the origin or source of most of my views toward members of other ethnic groups? What have I ever done to validate my beliefs?
- How do my beliefs affect my behavior toward persons from other cultural backgrounds?
- How do my attitudes help and/or hinder me in my interactions/relationships with children and adults who are culturally different from me? (Thomas & Cobb, 1999, p. 51)

Besides striving for general awareness, it can be very valuable for therapists to obtain close supervision for their initial assessments (treatment) of cross-cultural cases. A supervisor experienced in cross-cultural work can address special issues of transference and countertransference as they manifest themselves across cultural boundaries. Selected reference materials can be helpful to both supervisor and trainee (Adebimpe, 1981; Kadushin, 1972; Portela, 1971; Shuval, Antonovsky, & Davies, 1967; Spiegel, 1976; Westermeyer, 1979).

Experience in cross-cultural clinical settings will further facilitate the learning process, and research on a cross-cultural topic will provide information on the nuances of the field. For those wishing to devote themselves to this field, living and working in another culture for at least one year (and preferably two years) can be enormously useful. The experience should involve learning the indigenous language; participating in community activities; and acquiring a local social network of friends, coworkers, and families (Westermeyer, 1987, p. 476). Such experience will provide awareness and knowledge not attainable through seminars, supervisory sessions, or clinical settings.

Skills

Sue (1998) indicates that to practice in a culturally competent manner therapists must develop two basic skills: scientific mindedness and the ability to use dynamic sizing.

Scientific Mindedness

Scientific mindedness refers to the ability to develop, test, and evaluate hypotheses. Relative to cultural or diversity competence, this means that the therapist is first able to generate hypotheses about factors and dynamics that may be relevant to a given client based on the cultural groups of which the client is a member. The therapist does not accept these generalizations as fact. Rather, she develops creative ways of assessing the degree to which this particular client shares the commonalties of her culture. Having assessed the degree to which cultural variables apply to the client, the therapist is further able to evaluate the relevance of these variables to the diagnostic and treatment processes.

Dynamic Sizing

Dynamic sizing refers to the therapist's ability to balance the need to make generalizations and be inclusive versus individualize and be exclusive when applying her knowledge about a culture to a given client. For example, the therapist will need to know whether cultural factors that have a significant effect on an African American raised in New York City apply to an African

American raised in a small Southern town or to one raised in Liberia who has just immigrated to the United States. Related to this is the notion of balancing group versus individual differences. The individual differences within a cultural group exceed the differences between groups. Some therapists use this scientific reality as a rationale for minimizing the importance of cultural information. While it is important to remember not to stereotype individuals in the process of applying cultural knowledge, the reality of the differences in people's experiences as a result of their membership in a given culture should never be ignored.

A critical element in accurate dynamic sizing is an understanding of the impact of oppression or discrimination on the relevance of an individual's cultural identification. Discrimination tends to make one more acutely aware of their own group membership. Many Whites criticize Blacks for the emphasis the latter places on the importance of race in their day-to-day lives. "Why do you have to make such a big deal out of race? After all, a person's worth should be based on individual abilities rather than race." Such statements reflect the experience of Whites who have never been turned away from a job or rejected from a social club simply because of their race. When such rejections are a part of one's day-to-day experience, the group membership that causes such rejections takes center stage in one's self-concept. One can react by embracing one's group membership and seeking to make it a valued aspect of the self, "I am proud to be Black." Or, one can attempt to deny the difference even to the point of avoiding the group entirely. Therapy must strive to help children by recognizing and valuing all aspects of diversity.

Obtaining Culture-Specific Knowledge

In addition to developing the requisite awareness and skills, it is also important for therapists to acquire culture-specific knowledge (Sue, 1998). While acquiring awareness and skill can be an arduous process of self-development, acquiring culture-specific knowledge can be frustrating for even the most sensitive therapist. This is because so little good culturally descriptive information exists and what information there is, is often scattered across many different sources. Those familiar with the clinical psychology research will find some culture-specific information but much more of it tends to be found in the social psychology and anthropological literature. The therapist is then left with the task of trying to determine which variables are actually relevant to the therapy process.

COMMON CULTURALLY DERIVED MISTAKES

Failure to become diversity competent leads to therapist to make some common mistakes as noted by Kerl (1998):

1. Using children as translators for their parents. Bilingual children should not serve as translators because it inappropriately interferes with the adult/child hierarchy.
2. Underestimating the importance of ethnicity.
3. Overestimating the importance of ethnicity.
4. Grouping a variety of subcultures into one population.
5. Not having experience with a culture outside of play therapy so that the child cannot be understood in the context of his world and life experience.

The central theme here is that "(a) child is embedded in an interpersonal matrix that may not always change with the child, regardless of the strides the client is making in treatment. Teaching the child values or standards that are not a part of her or his family values and standards will inevitably lead to conflicts between the child and her or his parents. It is important for the therapist to proceed cautiously and to be very aware of the family's values and standards" (Brems, 1994, p. 31). The same can be said for being aware of the values and standards of the various cultural groups in which the family and, therefore the child, are embedded.

GUIDELINES FOR CULTURALLY COMPETENT PRACTICE

A number of authors have developed specific guidelines for practicing therapy in general and play therapy in particular in a culturally competent manner. These guidelines operationalize the previously presented concepts of awareness, scientific mindedness, dynamic sizing, and culture-specific knowledge. The guidelines presented in the following list were synthesized from several sources including the Association for Advanced Training in the Behavioral Sciences (1988, pp. 5–6); Coleman, Parmer, and Barker (1993, pp. 67–71); as well as Paniagua (1994) and Vraniak and Pickett (1993) as summarized in Thomas and Cobb (1999).

Awareness/Sensitivity/Empathy

When it comes to practicing culturally competent play therapy, the point of developing awareness of one's own and other's cultures is to facilitate the ability of the therapist to empathize with the client. To this end the therapist should:

- Respect historical, psychological, sociological, and political dimensions of a particular culture and/or ethnic group and be certain that the child and family feel the therapist accepts their belief system.
- Display an appreciation for strengths of different cultures.

- When working with a client of a different racial or cultural group from the therapist's own, acknowledge to the client your awareness of the difference and ask the client in a supportive way if he or she has any concerns regarding this issue.

Dynamic Sizing

As stated earlier, two issues are key when it comes to dynamic sizing. One is the ability to understand and evaluate the meaning of culture for a specific client and the other is the ability to assess the impact that a history of discrimination may have on the therapy process.

Do not generalize about all clients that belong to a particular racial or cultural group. Draw on your knowledge of cultural patterns to develop hypotheses regarding values, behaviors, and attitudes toward therapy; but always focus on understanding the particular individual with whom you are working. Be aware that many factors contribute to a person's orientation and values (e.g., socioeconomic class, dominant language, and, in the case of immigrants, the degree of embeddedness in the culture of origin versus the degree of assimilation into the dominant culture).

Recognize that social, economic, and political discrimination and prejudice are real problems for racial and cultural minority groups in the United States. Validate these realities for the client while helping him focus on ways to maximize his own personal effectiveness. Recognize that suspiciousness and mistrust on the part of minority clients may reflect a realistic response to past experience rather than paranoia or pathological defensiveness. Note that because of a history of deleterious relationships with those in power:

- Clients may display a deeper level of mistrust when forming new relationships.
- Clients may display behaviors that test the limits of the therapist's practical knowledge of the client's culture. Adolescent skepticism may be especially acute.
- Clients may want to explore the clinician as a person, including his or her authority role as well as the clinician's ability to connect with the client.
- Clients may question how much the clinician actually cares about them, and how much the clinician can be of help.

Knowledge

Two types of knowledge make it more likely the therapist will be successful with clients from diverse backgrounds. One is knowledge about how to modify the therapeutic process to suit a given cultural group. The other is knowledge of the culture itself and the way it is manifested in the system(s) in which the client is embedded.

Therapy Specific Knowledge

Eurocentric counseling techniques may or may not be appropriate; however, the counselor must determine the efficacy of a given approach based on consultation with other mental health professionals and the support system of the children from multicultural backgrounds.

To facilitate the optimum counseling process, a blend of pluralcentric (approaches that accept diverse cultural perspectives yet acknowledge the impact of the society of the mainstream culture in which the individual lives) methods and techniques may be the best solution for children from multicultural backgrounds.

Understand that interpretation is an important aspect of play therapy and can only be done accurately when the context of the client's life is taken into consideration (Atkinson, Jennings, & Liongson, 1990).

Clients may need to be taught the protocol of therapy; understanding of the purpose, nature of the process, potential content of the sessions and expected outcomes. In addition, a greater therapeutic alliance may be formed from the outset if the therapy includes therapy that is direct, active, and structured and that provide a potential solution to the primary problem within the first session or within a relatively short time frame.

For some cultures, such as Asian, discussing the potential role of medication is expected; for others, such as African Americans, immediately recommending and evaluation for medication would be perceived negatively. With Southeast Asian clients, in particular, do not insist on the child or family discussing traumatic experiences immediately; the stress that ensues could lead to attrition.

Culture Specific Knowledge

The role of play for multicultural populations should be critically examined in order that the mental health professional have an understanding of its influence on children from different ethnic groups and cultures.

Counselors working with multicultural populations must actively seek opportunities for interaction with these groups *outside the counseling situation* (Coleman, Parmer, & Barker, 1993, p. 71). They must be aware of social and community supports to which the client can be referred (e.g., social service agencies and religious organizations).

CONCLUSION

From the preceding discussion it is apparent that cultural competence on the part of the play therapist involves much more than simple awareness of cultural differences. True cultural or diversity competence requires that the therapist has good understanding of her complete ecosystem and her place within it as well as the ability and desire to become fully aware of her child client's ecosystem and the child's place within it.

Selected References

The following books are excellent starting points for those who wish to develop diversity competence:

Atkinson, D., Morton, G., & Sue, D. (1983). *Counseling American minorities: A cross-cultural approach* (2nd ed.). Dubuque, IA: Brown.

Comas-Diaz, L., & Griffith, E. (Eds.). (1988). *Clinical guidelines in cross-cultural mental health.* New York: Wiley.

Marsella, A., & Pederson, P. (Eds.). (1981). *Cross-cultural counseling and psychotherapy.* New York: Pergamon Press.

Sue, D., & Sue, D. (1990). *Counseling the culturally different: Theory and practice* (2nd ed.). New York: Wiley.

A Conceptual Framework
for the Practice of
Individual Play Therapy

Part I provided a history of the evolution of play therapy and a review of the major theories and techniques of play therapy in use today.

Part II delineates an integrated description of play therapy that was derived from elements of these theories using a cognitive developmental framework and an ecosystemic perspective. As was mentioned in Chapter One, this integrated model has come to be known as Ecosystemic Play Therapy since the publication of the first edition of this Primer. While representing a distinctive approach to the practice of play therapy, the model is still thought to be inclusive enough to serve as foundation for training new therapists or retraining experienced therapists. Ideally, readers should not indiscriminately accept any theoretical model but rather should seek to integrate what they learn into a personalized and internally consistent theory and practice of their own.

Because a developmental model underlies the material presented in the remainder of this book, Chapter Four includes an extensive review of child development based largely on the work of Piaget, Freud, as well as Wood and her associates. An understanding of developmental concepts is critical to the play therapist's ability to conceptualize everything from the nature of the child client's psychopathology to the type of activities that would be most therapeutic for a given child in a given play therapy session.

Chapter Five includes discussions about the types of child clients best suited to play therapy, the training and role of the play therapist, and the nature of the play therapy process.

CHAPTER FOUR

Theoretical Underpinnings of Play Therapy

Having reviewed the existing theories of play therapy, we now proceed to define the model presented in the remainder of this book, Ecosystemic Play Therapy, and the theory behind it. In Chapter One, play therapy was defined as

> a cluster of treatment modalities that include a variety of highly developed theoretical orientations and technical strategies. Regardless of these variations, however, all play therapy shares a common goal: the reestablishment of the child's ability to engage in play behavior as it is classically defined. Specifically, this means that the play therapist seeks to maximize the child's ability to engage in behavior that is fun, intrinsically complete, person-oriented, variable/flexible, noninstrumental, and characterized by a natural flow. High-quality play therapy as practiced by a given play therapist represents therefore an integration of the therapist's specific theoretical orientation, personality, and background with the child client's need in working toward this goal. That both the child and the play therapist may engage in behavior that might be called anything but play along their way to this ultimate goal is irrelevant. Play therapists universally recognize that treatment has been successfully completed when the child demonstrates an ability to play with joyous abandon.

Ecosystemic Play Therapy meets this general definition because it integrates aspects of existing theories and techniques with developmental theories to create a single model that addresses the total child within the context of the child's ecosystem.

The integration of theoretical models within psychology began in the 1930s but has become a growing trend as psychologists and other mental health professionals seek to combine the best of many different approaches to create optimal treatments for clients (Goldfried, 1998). A special section of the *Journal of Clinical Child Psychology* was dedicated to new models of child psychotherapy "that are anchored in developmental theory, are empirically based, and integrate features of different theoretical perspectives" (Russ, 1998, p. 2). Existing models may be combined for several reasons. First, integration is one way of addressing the acknowledged limitations of single-model approaches. Second, both eclectisism and integration are demanded by the realities of clinical work. For example, behavioral techniques work well with children manifesting toileting problems or developmental delays but are not as effective with very bright children who generally respond better to more cognitive approaches. If your client list includes both types of children, you must either switch between models or find a way to conceptually integrate what you do from one session to the next. In addition, the influx of managed care required therapists to be more accountable, creating pressure to use whatever techniques work rather than adhering to any one model (Kazdin, 1996).

The integration and development of new models has also been related to increasing recognition of the role of culture in the effective conceptualization of all aspects of mental health. Marsella (1998) proposed the development of a Global Community Psychology that is distinguished by:

1. Recognizing the global dimensions and scale of our lives;
2. Limiting the ethnocentric bias in many existing theories, methods, and interventions;
3. Encouraging the development of indigenous psychologies;
4. Emphasizing the cultural determinants of human behavior; and
5. Increasing the use of qualitative, naturalistic and contextual research methods (p. 1286).

The characteristics and goals of Global Community Psychology are entirely consistent with those of Ecosystemic Play Therapy.

The integration of models and the use of a variety of techniques has the potential to benefit psychotherapy clients. However, it is important to differentiate first between theoretical eclecticism and theoretical integration and then between theoretical eclecticism and technical eclecticism. Put very bluntly, theoretical eclecticism is detrimental to good mental health practices while theoretical integration enhances practice.

Theoretical eclecticism means therapists change the way in which they conceptualize clients' problems and treatment from one client to the next or worse yet from one problem to the next with the same client. This presents two types of problems. One is that the therapist is unable to form a coherent treatment plan because there is not stable problem conceptualization on which to build. The other is that clients are presented with inconsistencies they cannot resolve so that they don't come to understand their own treatment and consequently are unable to integrate it into their day-to-day lives.

For example, a therapist with a psychoanalytic orientation might initially hypothesize that a child's encopresis is the result of an internalized neurotic conflict. He would then proceed with treatment aimed at uncovering the conflict through the use of symbolic play. In the child's mind, the sessions would appear to have very little to do with the encopresis per se. But what if after several months of treatment, the encopresis does not resolve and the parents begin complaining to the therapist. At this point, the therapist, having discovered no underlying conflict, shifts gears and hypothesizes that the problem is both biologic and behavioral. He advises the parents to make some changes in their child's diet and toileting pattern and begins to work with the child on keeping a behavioral journal relative to encopretic episodes while showing very little interest in the child's symbolic play. It is very likely that the child will have no idea what happened to trigger the shift in the therapist's behavior. In fact, the child may now come to see the therapist as being just like other adults who initially feign interest in the child's thoughts and feelings only to become obsessed with the child's toileting if things don't go the way the adult wants them to.

While theoretical eclecticism is problematic, technical eclecticism is often very appropriate. Using a combination of medical, biofeedback, and insight-oriented strategies to address a child's asthma is likely to bring about much more rapid change than any of the techniques used in isolation. The more different techniques you want to use with a specific case, the stronger and more solid should be the theoretical orientation from which you are operating. Even the youngest clients should have the sense that everything you are doing in session fits together and that all is geared toward providing them with symptom relief and enabling them to better get their needs met. In the previous example, the therapist switched theoretical models in forming hypotheses about the child's encopresis resulting in discontinuities in the therapy process. If the therapist had worked from an ecosystemic orientation, an overarching hypothesis that the child's encopresis was the result of biologic and behavioral factors that had become complicated by unconscious conflicts over time as the problem became more of an issue between the child and those in his environment. The therapist could have then chosen to have the parents make changes in the child's diet and implement some behavioral techniques at home. Simultaneously, the therapist could have focused on the conflicts the encopretic behavior created for the child in the play sessions through various symbolic and pretend strategies.

As noted in the Preface to this volume, there comes a point when an integrated model violates enough of the basic premises of the originals from which it was drawn to require that it be considered a new model. This is especially true when one is integrating theories as opposed to techniques. Ecosystemic Play Therapy is the result of just such a process. It began by integrating "elements of several existing theories and techniques using cognitive developmental theory as an organizing framework . . . (and) a broadly systemic perspective called ecological or ecosystemic as the filter for determining which elements of the theories or techniques of play therapy that were reviewed should be retained or discarded" (O'Connor, 1991, p. vi). Since 1991, this model has been refined and expanded and taken on an identity of its own. Ecosystemic Play Therapy theory and practice has been presented in great detail in *Play Therapy Theory and Practice: A Comparative Presentation* (O'Connor & Braverman, 1997) and the *Play Therapy Treatment Planning and Interventions: The Ecosystemic Model and Workbook* (O'Connor & Ammen, 1997). Those interested in reading a comprehensive yet condensed description of the theory are referred especially to the latter text. In the following discussion and chapters, the theory and practice of Ecosystemic Play Therapy will be presented in a somewhat more diluted form suited to those looking for a solid grounding in play therapy theory and practice suitable for use with a broad array of clients.

First and foremost, Ecosystemic Play Therapy is systemic. The model accepts that the child has been affected by every system he has come into contact with over the course of his life. The model also recognizes that by conducting individual therapy with a child, the play therapist has an impact on every system with which the child currently has contact. The ecologically minded play therapist is aware that every change that the child undergoes will meet with a corresponding change in the child's environment. He understands that the child's ecosystem will not always rejoice as the child changes. In fact, the ecosystem may work very hard to prevent the child from changing and altering the system. Recognition of these ecological variables allows the play therapist to plan treatment that will maintain some degree of harmony between the child and his environment and promote generalization of those changes the child makes in sessions to the world outside the playroom.

As indicated in the reviews of various play therapy theories in Chapter Two, all theories of psychotherapy seem to contain certain basic elements, namely, a theory of personality, definitions of psychopathology, and specific ways of characterizing the goals of treatment or the way the notion of cure is conceptualized. Ecosystemic Play Therapy is no different in this regard. Let us start the discussion of these basic elements with the theory of personality—a term that is somewhat difficult to define. Basically, personality is the sum of intra- and interpersonal characteristics, attributes, cognitions, beliefs, values, and so forth that make a person unique. Within Ecosystemic Play Therapy, three main elements are considered: (1) basic motives or drives, (2) intrapsychic organization and, (3) the role of development.

Ecosystemic Play Therapy retains the concept of a motivational system, that is an integration of that proposed by the psychoanalytic, humanistic, and Reality Therapy theories. This motivational system has two levels. On a biological level, there exists the organism's motivation to act to preserve itself. This level of motivation is thought to be innate or instinctual and geared toward the survival of the species. Out of this biologic drive develop two different secondary motivations, both of which are interpersonal in nature and develop out of the child's initial transactions with the world, namely those with the primary caretaker. The first motivation causes the child to act in order to maintain positive interpersonal contacts to get his basic needs met. This level of motivation is not innate but must be learned, preferably within the child's first 2 years of life. The other interpersonal motivation develops out of the child's experience with separation/individuation and causes the child to act in ways that give him control over sources of supplies. That is, the child first learns that he must depend on others for supplies and so behaves in ways that keep the caretaker close at hand; later, as the child learns that others are not always reliable, he seeks to gain some control over supply sources so as to ensure his survival in spite of the availability of others. If all goes well, the motive to maintain positive dependent ties remains stronger than the motive for control, and the child works to get his needs met in the most socially acceptable ways. In summary, humans are motivated by a desire to maximize rewards and minimize negative consequences and, if properly socialized, to do so in ways that do not interfere with the ability of others to get their needs met. The model does not posit the existence of a drive to self-actualization per se; rather, the drive to behave in growth-promoting ways is seen as a derivative of the child's interpersonal motivation.

While hypothesizing the existence of a primary motivational system, this model also recognizes that human cognition and experience can work to override even very basic instincts, thus acknowledging the importance of examining the environment in which an individual's behavior occurs for significant positive and negative consequences that are redirecting his behavior. This integrated theoretical model also incorporates the concept of personality made up of elements consistent with the tripartite structure Freud proposed. These structures are particularly useful in helping to group various dimensions of the individual's functioning. The id simply represents the constellation of the child's drives and the primary motivational system. The ego represents the child's cognitive capacities and skills, his ability to act within his ecosystem. The superego represents the child's understanding of the rules that must be followed to get his needs met and not suffer unpleasant consequences. That these elements are acquired or refined over the course of the child's development seems self-evident because each represents a gradual increase in the child's socialization. The child's personality is not seen as an excuse for deviant behavior or as a concrete "thing" that cannot be changed. Instead, the concept of personality helps the therapist recognize the uniqueness of the child while allowing for comparisons between children or comparisons of a given child's behavior across situations.

Also important in Ecosystemic Play Therapy is the recognition of the interaction between the individual's mind and body. The relative importance of these two elements has been a source of considerable debate in psychology and is also reflected in many nature versus nurture arguments. Without getting into serious debate about the dominance of one or the other, it is simply important to note that the two constantly interact and that this interplay affects all aspects of human behavior. Considerable evidence exists to demonstrate the dramatic effects the mind can have on one's physical well being in such fields as psychoneuroimmunology and similarly the impact of various body processes and such things as drugs on the brain and behavior. As neuroscience and genetics become more scientifically sophisticated, our ability to demonstrate physiological correlates of human thought, feeling, and behavior steadily increases. One aspect of mind-body interactions that is often not specifically addressed in many models of play therapy is the significance of development. Fortunately, this is changing and most new models are anchored in developmental theory (Russ, 1998).

Before proceeding with the discussion, let us first consider what development is or means. "Individual human development involves incremental and transformational processes that, through a flow of interactions among current characteristics of the person and his or her current contexts, produces a succession of relatively enduring changes that elaborate or increase the diversity of the person's structural and functional characteristics and the patterns of their environmental interactions while maintaining the coherent organization and structural-functional unity of the person as a whole" (Ford & Lerner, 1992, p. 49). Most noteworthy in this discussion is the mention of incremental and transformational change. Children undergo incremental changes on almost a daily basis. The infant who can barely stand one day is able to take steps the next and to traverse a room the next. But, it is the transformational changes that are most significant and the hardest for adults to grasp. The way in which the child's thinking changes with the acquisition of language is virtually incomprehensible and outside of adult recall. Development also happens on many levels. There is microgenetic development; the changes that happen in the here and now. There is ontogenetic development: Change that occurs over the course of a person's lifetime. And, important to the ecosystemic model, there is cultural/historical development that occurs over recognizable periods of time. The marked change over the past 100 years in the way children are viewed and valued is an excellent example that shows up quite dramatically in the history of the assessment and treatment of child abuse in the United States. It is difficult to keep in mind that in just three generations we have gone from a "spare the rod, spoil the child" mentality to one where many think that all forms of corporal punishment are completely inappropriate. That means, in a single extended family there might be grandparents who beat their child with a belt, parents who were beaten themselves who are advised by their parents to beat the child for misbehavior while threatened by Child Protective Services with losing their children if they do, and children who are taught in special school programs how to recognize abuse such as excessive spanking and report it to the appropriate authorities. And last there is phylogenetic change or those developmental differences that occur in a species over the course of its existence. Take, for example, the fact that the mean age for the onset of puberty in girls has dropped markedly in the past several decades (Valsiner, 1997). We as a species tend to forget how extremely brief a period of time is covered in our recorded history so that the reality of phylogenetic change is usually lost. From an ecosystemic view, the first three levels of developmental change may be very important in conceptualizing both the presenting problem and the intervention.

The extreme emphasis on developmental theories within this text is evident from the fact that both elements of the individual's motivational system and his personality are hypothesized to derive from the child's interactions with the world and to change over time. The integration of a treatment model with developmental concepts is somewhat difficult because there are numerous developmental models, each emphasizing a different aspect of the child's internal or life experience. Consistent with the present trend in psychology toward the integration of theoretical models rather than just the creation of new ones, the first part of this chapter presents an integrated view of child development from birth to adolescence. This developmental conceptualization is the cornerstone on which the model rests; it is the template against which the child's history will be compared. Deviations or disruptions in the child's progress through it are the basis for formulating the major therapeutic goals and for designing the interventions that will be implemented within the play sessions. Finally, it is the yardstick against which the child's progress is measured:

a. Human psychological development continues throughout the life cycle. This means that an understanding of the phase-specific normative developmental issues, conflicts and anxieties is a key element in helping or furthering the development of an individual or group of individuals in a given age period.

b. Since the developmental view emphasizes the continuity of individual human development, the attainments of each successive phase are seen as being built upon and influenced by the outcome of the preceding phases. Underscoring the commonality of child and adult psychology, this longitudinal emphasis includes both the child and the adult as participants in the same, continuous process of development. The status of each can thus be assessed in identical terms: the degree of attainment of age-appropriate individuation and the extent of freedom from developmental-arresting forces in the individual and the environment.

c. Thus, the developmental view underlines the role of environmental influences not only in the past, as it has contributed to pathologic formations, but in the present, as an ongoing factor in adaptation.

d. Similarly, the developmental view stresses the progressive, impetus-providing role of normative growth forces in the treatment of emotional disorders, as well as in the development of personality.

e. In keeping with its emphasis on the continuity of development throughout the life cycle, the developmental view also stresses the recapitulation of earlier developmental issues—however well resolved or unresolved—in later developmental phases. This idea is particularly well illustrated by separation-individuation theory. Complementing the theory of the psychosexual stages, this additional developmental theory focuses on the development of the capacity for human relationship and for adaptation, as these arise from progressive ego development and self-object differentiation.

The separation-individuation process is most crucial during the first three years of life. Nevertheless, this process continues throughout development, ending with the process of dying and death. Again, the individual confronts the issue of incremental separation and loss of important figures in his life and the correlated internalization of the development of self.

The understanding of this process of recapitulation is important to mental health work for two reasons: It provides an opportunity for a further solution of unresolved problems as a part of normal development, and it provides the professional with both access to and leverage for facilitating such solution through early preventive intervention or treatment. One can capitalize on the inherent tendency of the human organism to repeat and gain mastery over the unresolved conflicts and the unfulfilled wants of his past.

f. The developmental view emphasizes the contiguity of normal and pathologic outcomes of development, recognizing that at each stress point and phase-specific juncture, the human being strives for adaptation and mastery. In this sense, psychopathology is seen as a failure in adaptation. From this perspective, the route, the reversibility of psychopathology, while not assured, is highlighted.

g. Finally, the developmental orientation views mental illness not in the medical model of disease entities affecting developed organ systems, but in the model of functional disturbances which impair current functioning and also impede further development in one or more of its lines or aspects. The aim of treatment or other remedial interventions is thus to enhance and facilitate those developmental processes that have been arrested. From this viewpoint, then, one treats not a syndrome but a developmentally arrested individual who has participated psychologically in the formation of his psychopathology and must similarly participate in its undoing. The patient is not a passive recipient but an active partner in a mutual endeavor (Cooper & Wanerman, 1977, pp. 4–6).

Unfortunately, when most people learn about human development they learn about specific theorists and their views on single developmental lines as if each line were unrelated rather than interdependent. That is, most students are taught about Kohlberg's (1976, 1984) stages of moral development, Erikson's (1950) stages of social development, Freud's (1917) stages of intrapsychic development, and Piaget's (Singer & Revenson, 1996) stages of cognitive development sequentially rather than simultaneously. Because of this, many students of child development never get much of a sense of what a child of a given age is like across areas of function. In Ecosystemic Play Therapy, cognitive development is viewed as the driving force behind development in other areas. Children are seen as unable to function at Kohlberg's highest level of moral functioning unless they also function at Piaget's highest level of cognitive functioning. These seems to follow logically: It seems unreasonable to expect people to apply sophisticated abstract concepts to moral situations if they have not yet developed to the point where they are capable of abstract reasoning.

The information in the following pages represents an integration of data and hypotheses from a number of different theoretical viewpoints regarding the development of children from birth to about the age of 12 using cognitive theory as an organizational framework. The material is descriptive rather than a detailed review of all the existing stage models of child development. The reader should gain a sense of what children are like at various ages regarding their cognitive, language, physical, emotional, social, and play development as well as their response to common life experiences. Although occasional reference is made to the relevance of the developmental material to the therapist's conceptualization of either child psychopathology or the play therapy process, this is not the focus. It is more important that the reader gain an understanding of normal children and their life experience prior to attempting to understand troubled children and their treatment. For convenience, the material has been organized into four levels that coincide with Piaget's four stages of cognitive development.

There are several limitations to Piaget's theory that make it less than ideal for use as an organizing framework for a discussion of development. First, it was conceptualized as a stage model, that is, children were seen as making rather sudden shifts from one stage to the next with no regressions. Current thinking postulates a more gradual shift between stages and notes that regressions are common especially when children are under stress. Second, the model does not take into account the mixed results of research on cognitive differences between the sexes. Third, it does not take social or cultural factors into account. The current sociocultural view is that individual, social and cultural factors do not interact but, rather, they have a combined and inseparable effect on a person's development and functioning (Rogoff & Chavajay, 1995). That is, "the intellectual development of children is inherently involved with their participation in sociocultural activities" (p. 871). Last, although it is not of much concern to us in the context of this discussion, the model does very little with respect to describing cognitive development after adolescence. In spite of these limitations, it is still one of the better organized and widely known models and is used here for these reasons. For other excellent references on cognitive development the reader is referred to the following:

- Greenspan and Greenspan (1991) provide excellent developmental tables showing the behavior one should expect from children at different ages. These tables cover six observational categories: (1) physical functioning, (2) pattern of relationships, (3) overall mood, (4) affects, (5) anxieties and fears, and (6) thematic expression.

- Wood, Davis, Swindle, and Quirk (1996) also provide excellent tables and descriptions of children's functioning at different ages in four categories: (1) behavior, (2) communication, (3) social functioning, and (4) academic performance.
- Johnson-Powell and Yamamoto (1997) offer in-depth insight into the diverse cultural and institutional influences on children from 12 different racial, ethnic, and cultural groups living in the United States.

The relevance of child development to psychopathology is described in some detail toward the end of this chapter. Developmental references are made throughout the treatment material in Chapters Six through Fifteen.

A DEVELOPMENTAL CONTEXT FOR THE PRACTICE OF PLAY THERAPY

Level I Children

From birth to the age of about 2, children's primary task is to learn to respond to the environment with pleasure and, in counterpoint, they fear abandonment and deprivation by others (Wood, Davis, Swindle, & Quirk, 1996).

Cognitive Development

Level I children are in what Piaget (1952, 1959, 1967) identified as the sensorimotor phase, that begins when the child is born and continues until approximately the age of 2 years. The end of the phase is marked roughly by the child's acquisition of language. At no other level does development proceed as rapidly as during the sensorimotor stage. This is an exciting level for the infant because every experience is new; nothing is similar to anything that has occurred previously. The infant takes in sensory information of all types. At this stage, all of the child's learning derives from his experience. Experience and memory are visual, gustatory, olfactory, tactile, kinesthetic, and auditory. The infant attends to and stores in memory the quality and intensity of the experience.

Experimental psychology has demonstrated the power of memory stored via these modalities, yet these are not sources of information on which most adults rely. Instead, an adult tends to rely on language to facilitate recall of events and experiences. The infant has no language to use in mediating his experience. Experiential memory is just that: experiential. He can recall something he has seen, smelled, tasted, touched, or heard before, but he cannot categorize or label it. Initially, experience is simply absorbed—there is very little interaction between the child and his world. As development progresses, the child seeks to interact with the environment, to repeat pleasant experiences and avoid unpleasant ones. A movement that makes the mobile above the cradle jiggle will be repeated, often for long periods of time. On the other hand, the sight and smell of a pediatrician's office may cause the child to scream in anticipation of pain.

Although experiential memory is quite strong, it is not readily available to recall and even less amenable to processing. It is difficult to hold an experience and look at it without putting words to the event. Freud posited that infantile amnesia, an individual's tendency not to remember anything that happened before about his third birthday, was due to the repression of the intense affects and conflicts that precede the onset of the oedipal period. It seems much more plausible that these memories are not available to later recall because there are no words by which they can be retrieved. Many an adult, however, has had the experience, often in the context of his own psychotherapy, of suddenly "remembering" a preverbal event. The intensity of the related affect may be overwhelming, and the adult will often report feeling as if he had gone back in time and were reexperiencing the event.

Early in Level I, objects exist for the child for only as long they can be experienced through one of his senses. When the child drops his spoon, he does not look for it; why should he? It has ceased to exist because it has ceased to be experienced. Similarly, when his mother leaves the room, he cries only briefly because his attention is subsumed by his experience of things he knows to exist. As this phase of development progresses, he grows able to hold a mental image of objects in his memory for ever-increasing periods of time and shows fear of loss when things are removed from his experience. He still fears that if the object is gone for long it will cease to exist, but now it can be experienced for as long as his memory can hold on to it. When a young toddler who is now standing in his living room looks for a missing toy, he looks around the living room. If one were to ask him where he had the toy last, he might be able to say that it was in the bedroom, but it is likely that he will continue to look for the object in the living room. The actual location of the object is irrelevant as the child attends, instead, to the strength of the memory. The stronger the memory, the closer the object is assumed to be.

Toward the end of this Level I, object constancy becomes firmly established and affect may be attached to an external object (Piaget, 1962). This piece of cognitive development is a key element in the child's separation/individuation from the parent (as discussed later in this chapter).

As previously noted, during Level I the child has no language by which to label, process, store, or retrieve experience and memory. During most of this level, communication is accomplished through motor movement and simple vocalizations. The infant wiggles and cries when he is wet. Unfortunately for the first-time parent, the child also wiggles and cries when he is hungry, cold, hot, sick, or experiencing any of a number of discomforts. Later, the child is able to produce more meaningful motor responses: He pulls at his diaper when wet, touches his mouth or stomach when hungry, or, clearer yet, stands in front of the refrigerator and cries. Gradually, word-like sounds come to be associated with these motor cues, and still later words will replace many of the motor behaviors.

In developing a play therapy treatment plan, the therapist has to keep in mind that children with Level I cognitive functioning require sessions that are almost entirely experiential rather than verbal. This is true whether or not the child's cognitive functioning is uniformly Level I or if the child exhibits only Level I thinking in certain, say, emotionally loaded, situations.

Physical Development

While Level I is a time of rapid cognitive development in the child's internal thought process, it is also a time of rapid changes in motor development and skill. Infants are initially able to move very little beyond waving their extremities and wriggling. Slowly they learn to orient toward objects and make attempts to move toward those objects. They learn to roll over, drag themselves on their stomachs toward an object, sit up, crawl, and walk. Each advance in motor movement allows the child to become more independent and meet some of his own needs. As with the acquisition of object constancy, increases in mobility play a part in the child's separation/individuation from the primary caretaker. A child whose motor development is significantly delayed or advanced might, for example, manifest attachment difficulties even if his relationship with his caretaker is otherwise good.

Emotional Development

During Level I, the child also develops his basic understanding of affect. It seems likely that significant shifts in physiologic state are the precursors of the child's experience of affect. Infants are capable of differentially reacting to at least three physiologic states. They know that they are comfortable when all their body systems are experiencing no more than a moderate level of arousal. This state of moderate arousal seems to be the biologic equivalent of what will later be labeled happiness.

The infant can also recognize pain when one or more body systems are significantly overaroused. The infant's physiologic response to pain is easily distinguished from contentment using even simple instrumental measures of physiologic state. This arousal pattern seems to be the biologic precursor of anxiety and anger. The infant is initially aware of the discomfort as a hyperaroused or anxious state sets in. The infant then moves to protest the discomfort. For the infant, an anger or protest response is life-preserving because it signals the caretaker when a problem exists.

Aside from recognizing optimal arousal as pleasant and hyperarousal as unpleasant and worthy of protest, the infant is also capable of a conservation/withdrawal response when discomfort persists past a reasonably long protest period. For example, the infant who is hungry will first whimper and wiggle but very shortly begin to scream in protest. He will continue screaming for a very long time if food is not forthcoming. But if food does not come, he will gradually shift into a conservation/withdrawal response and stop his protests. Again, this state is easily distinguished from both contentment and the protest response using even simple measures of the infant's physiologic state. It is characterized by a pattern of significant underarousal. This pattern, as with protest, seems to have a life-preserving function. If the infant simply persisted in raging in the face of deprivation, he would eventually exhaust himself and potentially die. The onset of a conservation/withdrawal response slows the infant's internal functioning to a level where he could continue for a considerable period without receiving necessary supplies. This conservation/withdrawal reaction seems to be the biologic precursor of depression.

No matter how hypervigilant the caretaker, the infant experiences all three of these physiologic states at some point in his early development. Every infant experiences pain at some point and therefore experiences the ensuing physiologic arousal, anxiety, and rage. And every child, at some point, finds that no matter how he protests, there may be pains from which the caretaker cannot rescue him. Ear infections are a good example of a naturally occurring event that triggers the full range of physiologic responses. Children tend to ignore the first signs of an ear infection and continue to look contented until the problem becomes quite severe. Because children tend to have a difficult time localizing pain, the parent is often unable to tell what is wrong with the child once he does begin to protest. Consequently, the ear infection builds until the child is screaming and the parent is frantic over his or her inability to provide comfort. A trip to the pediatrician locates the source of the problem, but it usually does not provide immediate relief. Many children cry themselves to sleep, a classic conservation/withdrawal response.

It appears that these experiences gradually acquire language labels over time, and by the time the child enters Level II, he is beginning to refer to these experiences as happy, mad, and sad. A considerable amount of experience and a significant increase in language skill are necessary before the child is able to differentially label these states according to the situations in which they occur. By adulthood, however, most individuals are able to describe and use most of the 400 plus affect terms that occur in the English language.

Aside from this biologic model of the infant's affective experience, Freud (1905) was one of the few theorists who described the infant's personal internal experience. Unfortunately, modern readers often have considerable difficulty with Freud's model because of his sexualization of the major aspects of each developmental phase. For example, Freud postulated that it is libidinal energy as it becomes focused on a given area of the body, such as the mouth, anus, or genitalia, that drives the child's development. He then defined libidinal energy as primarily sexual in nature, although he did recognize the life-preserving effects of this biologic drive force. The discontent with and consequent dismissal of much of Freud's work is unfortunate because the developmental aspects of the model do not suffer particularly when framed in cognitive, behavioral, or social terms.

Although he predated Piaget by more than 50 years, Freud recognized the infant's total focus on the incorporation of environmental stimuli. The infant is like a sponge, taking in every experience without attempting to filter anything out. Freud labeled this time the oral stage and talked about the focus of the child's libidinal energies being the mouth. All his energies are used to "take in," and all his pleasures are derived from such activities. From a cognitive perspective, this is entirely consistent with Piaget's description of the infant during this period. The primary difference is that Piaget talked about sensory/motor stimuli and their incorporation as relatively affectively neutral while Freud focused on the pleasure the infant derives from the incorporation process. From a biologic perspective, this is a life-saving drive in that the infant is oriented toward food intake. Given the helplessness of human infants, this dependent orientation is essential. Gradually the infant uses its accumulated experience to focus its search for food and nurturance on its primary caretaker, and the beginnings of an interpersonal relationship are formed. All this means that the emotions Level I children experience are both primary and intense. The manifestations of such emotions within the play therapy sessions will certainly follow suit. The therapist must be both emotionally and physically prepared for powerful emotional outbursts when working with a child who is still functioning at Level I or whose primary difficulties were experienced while he was in Level I.

Social Development

For all the cognitive and motor development that the child undergoes during Level I, the most critical psychological aspect of this level is the establishment of the child's initial sense of self through the processes of separation and individuation (Sroufe, 1979). Mahler (1967) described the early part of Level I as the phase of normal autism, during which the infant "seems to be in a state of primitive hallucinatory disorientation, in which need satisfaction belongs to its own omnipotent, autistic orbit" (p. 740). For the first few months, the child seems to do no more than take in its environment; responses are reflexive, and behavior is without intent. The infant is fascinated with his sensory experience and does not recognize the boundaries of his own body. What he is and what he experiences via any of his senses are one and the same.

Next the child goes through what Mahler (1972) called differentiation and what A. Freud (1965) labeled normal symbiosis. Differentiation is triggered by the infant's gradual recognition of body boundaries. The infant begins making associations between certain sensations and certain objects and notices that those objects are not always present. The infant can differentiate its primary caretaker from other people very early on. As the process of differentiation progresses, the child goes through the practicing phase (Mahler, 1972), during which he makes contact with the outside world while using the primary caretaker as a secure and stable base. This is commonly seen in children's exploratory behavior. Picture the toddler brought to a new location by his mother. Initially, he hides behind her and refuses to look at any of the new people or the environment. If he is not pushed, he will gradually begin to visually explore the environment while remaining safely behind his mother. Still later he will begin to physically explore the environment while staying very close to his mother. As the child's anxiety and concomitant arousal settle, he will move farther and farther from the mother to explore the environment, always returning to the mother periodically to verify that everything is all right and that the mother continues to exist. Erikson (1950) focused on the social component of this behavior and talked about the child's learning trust or mistrust based on the consistency and stability of the caretaker and the environment.

During this phase, a child's relationship with its primary caretaker is heavily dependent on the child's drive state (A. Freud, 1965); that is, children will seek out their caretakers when in pain and remain more distant when they are content and satisfied. This points to the biologic underpinnings of Level I development. Although the caretaker's behavior and the absence of environmental toxicity are critical to the child's healthy negotiation of Level I, neither factor will override the child's biologic endowment. The child whose neurologic structure is such, for example, that he is unable to detect environmental consistency will fare poorly at this level no matter how healthy the environment.

Play Development

At any age, play development directly parallels the child's development in other areas. For this reason it is somewhat difficult to isolate it for purposes of discussion. In spite of this let us attempt to take a brief look at play behavior as it evolves over the first two years of life. During the first 4 months, most play will involve repetitions of pleasurable physical activities that are geared toward the infant's body, primary circular reactions (Hughes, 1995). A contented baby seems surprised to find its own foot, pulls it to its mouth and releases it suddenly appearing shocked at the simultaneous stimulation of its mouth and foot. Gleefully it repeats the action over and over, seeming surprised anew each time. Between 4 and 8 months the child is more likely to repeat actions that have an effect on the environment rather than simply on its own body or secondary circular reactions. The baby will bang on the plate with the spoon only to be startled by the sudden loud sound. As soon as he realizes there is no danger he repeats the action and is soon banging out a regular torrent of noise. From 8 to 12 months, the child becomes fascinated with processes or tertiary circular reactions. The child anxiously searches for his mother who appears suddenly saying a familiar, "peek-a-boo." The child seems to instantly forget his anxiety and to focus on getting the mother to repeat the hide-and-seek process. From 12 to 18 months, the child still engages in repetitive play behavior but will seek to vary the experience from one repetition to the next. Where before the infant might have banged a spoon on the same plate endlessly he is now more likely to move around the room banging on a variety of objects seeking out novel sounds. Past 18 months, sensorimotor play begins to fade and is gradually replaced with symbolic and pretend play (Hughes, 1995).

As the child's pretend play emerges it changes with respect to three variables. First, there is gradual *decentration*. That is, the focus of the pretending moves from the self to objects or others outside the self (Fenson, 1986; Fenson & Ramsey, 1980; Hughes, 1995). The child pretends to feed a toy or another child rather than pretending to feed himself. Second, the play becomes gradually more *decontextualized*. Initially, the child needs objects that closely resemble the focus of the pretend, a toy car to represent a real car. Gradually, however, substitutions are tolerated and the child may be perfectly content to use a toy block to represent a car. Last, the child's play becomes more *integrated*. The duration of any one activity and the connections between one activity and the next gradually increase. Although the lines of development have been presented as sequential for purposes of discussion, the evolution of the child's play along all three is simultaneous.

Processing of Life Experience

While focusing on the child's internal experience and growth during Level I, it is also important to note the life experiences the child is exposed to and the possible interaction these may have with the developmental process. Doing so allows the therapist to take individual, ethnic, and cultural variations in experience into consideration.

Some important factors to consider when evaluating the child's relationship with his primary caretaker include the length of time the two spend together, both daily and over the course of Level I development. Among mothers who work, the length of their maternity leave and the options they exercise after returning to work vary considerably. Was the mother home 6 weeks or a year or more? When the mother returned to work, did the child go to another individual caretaker or to some sort of group care setting? To what extent was the father involved as a primary caretaker? Many men are now offered paternity leave and may spend some time as their child's primary caretaker. The child's understanding of changes in caretaking arrangements made during Level I will be very limited and may be experienced as extremely discontinuous if done suddenly. The infant or toddler has difficulty retaining an image of the caretaker when that individual is not present and may have a hard time learning the routine of moving between caretakers over the course of the day or week. The child is likely to react to each separation as unique and very disturbing for some time. The separations and reunions are not necessarily harmful, but the caretaker must try to help the child understand and adjust based on the child's level of understanding at the time.

Aside from noting the caretaking arrangements, the therapist should also note the likelihood that children may experience the birth of a sibling sometime during their first 2 years of life. In spite of many psychologists' recommendations that a new sibling not be added to the family while the youngest child is between the ages of 18 and 30 months, this continues to be a popular interval selected by parents. The birth of a sibling when the child is at the peak of his own separation/individuation from the parent(s) has the potential of producing some serious concerns about his own relationship with the primary caretaker.

The therapist must carefully consider each of these life events when diagnosing a child and developing a treatment plan. Strategies for obtaining this information through the taking of a developmental history are discussed in Chapter Six.

Level II Children

From the age of 2 until about the age of 6, children's primary task is to learn to respond to the environment with success and, in counterpoint, they fear personal inadequacy and punishment by other powerful forces (Wood, Davis, Swindle, & Quirk, 1996).

Cognitive Development

As noted previously, the child's transition from Level I to Level II is marked by the acquisition of language. The primary cognitive task of the Level II child, ages 2 to 6 years old, is the development of the ability to use language to categorize experience based on similar linguistic labels as well as experiential similarities and differences. Piaget (1952) called this level the preoperational phase, noting children's ability to label information and experience and their inability to cognitively organize and manipulate what they are learning. During this phase, learning becomes more language based and less dependent on experience.

Experience still tends to dominate the Level II child's information processing, which often makes for some interesting ways of looking at the world. For example, a child may learn the word "dog" and begin applying it to a few dogs in the immediate environment; often, on first encountering a cat, the child will also label it a dog. An involved adult will point out the differences between a dog and a cat, potentially saying one is smaller than the other. Upon later encountering a Pekinese, the child is likely to label it a cat. And it is not at all uncommon for a child to label the first cow he sees as a dog. This reflects the way in which preoperational children's minds acquire and store information. The "file" drawers in their head have only the most general labels, and information is loosely, and often unrealistically, grouped.

Because of this somewhat haphazard storage of information, the child is unable to perform most mental operations. Level II children have difficulty comparing and contrasting much less manipulating their knowledge. The child cannot solve simple conservation problems, nor can he cognitively reverse an action so as to determine its cause (Piaget, 1963).

Although he cannot conserve, the child is perfecting a key subskill of conservation, namely, object constancy. As language becomes a more stable component of the child's thought processes, object constancy gradually becomes a central part of the child's cognition. Thus, cognitively, this phase is really divided into two segments: one, between the ages of about 18 and 36 months, during which language acquisition is the dominant task, and the other, between the ages of about 3 and 6, during which the incorporation of object constancy into the child's thinking is dominant. It is this aspect of object constancy that seems essential to the child's successful negotiation of the last stages of the separation/individuation process as well as the process Freud labeled the oedipal conflict. Both issues are discussed at greater length within the context of the Level II child's social development.

Inextricably bound to the child's cognitive development is the fact of his entry into the formal educational process during Level II. Many children now enter preschool as early as the age of 3, and many of these preschools are no longer simple day care centers but actually include some explicit academic components. This does not take into account some of the intense infant-education programs that well-educated and upwardly mobile parents currently favor. Whether or not the child attends a preschool and, if he does, the focus of that program has definite implications for other aspects of the child's development. Further, whether or not the child attends preschool, it is certain that he will attend kindergarten and possibly first grade before he has moved out of Level II.

The expectations of academic programs for Level II children are quite varied. Some programs expect children to have acquired a relatively large store of information, including the alphabet, numbers, and colors, before they enter kindergarten. Others maintain a more social focus through at least the middle of kindergarten. Most expect a child to have acquired virtually all the prereading and premath skills prior to completing first grade. The details of a child's early academic experience may be very important in conceptualizing the child's presenting symptomatology and in developing a treatment plan, as is seen in Chapters Six and Seven.

Physical Development

The motor development of the Level II child is much less dramatic than the progress of the Level I child. During Level I, the child progresses from being virtually immobile to being able to walk quite well. During Level II, that is, from the age of 2 to 6 years, the child is working primarily to refine the motor skills he has acquired thus far. The child learns to run faster, jump higher, and throw farther and more accurately. These skills may be very important in the child's gaining peer acceptance, but they are not as important in the course of his emotional development as are other aspects of his functioning.

Emotional Development

With regard to the child's emotional development during Level II, note that a process of refinement is also involved. Emotions are now more readily recognized and may be experienced in the absence of strong physiologic cues. The child's affective vocabulary, however, tends to remain quite limited, often consisting only of happy, mad, and sad as well as a few variations on these basic categories. What expands rapidly during Level II is not so much the child's internal experience of affective states as the interpersonal aspects of their emotional experience. With a Level II child, it is very difficult to talk about his emotional experience outside the context of his social development.

Two social/emotional tasks are central to the Level II child's development: (1) the development of sense of mastery relative to both internal and external experience, and (2) the development of a stable sex-role identification. The centrality of mastery to the development of the Level II child has been recognized by authors from rather divergent theoretical orientations (Erikson, 1963; Freud, 1917; A. Freud, 1965; Mahler, 1972; Sroufe, 1979). As Mahler (1972) stated, the child's drive to mastery during this level provides him with numerous positively reinforcing experiences, resulting in a sort of general euphoria peculiar to toddlers. But remember that mastery is not a unitary concept: One aspect of mastery is the development of internal controls; another aspect involves mastery over external experience.

Both Freud (1917) and Erikson (1963) focused on the child's drive to achieve internal mastery, as exemplified by attempts at bowel and bladder control in toilet training. Consequently, Freud labeled the period from about 18 to 36 months as the anal stage, while Erikson stressed the child's struggle for autonomy versus shame and doubt. Even in Erikson's label for this struggle it is evident that the process of obtaining a sense of internal mastery is linked to obtaining a sense of environmental mastery. After all, toilet training is rarely accomplished without some involvement of people other than the child, even if these outsiders do no more than provide contingent verbal feedback. In this sense, mastery involves the child's development of self-regulation while protected by external controls (Erikson, 1950). There are, however, differences between the two components of mastery, and it is their balance that is particularly important in the child's development.

Before examining this concept of a balanced sense of mastery, let us first look at the child's development of interpersonal mastery. After all, toddlers are probably better known for their temper tantrums than for their ability to be toilet trained. In fact, if you were to ask any adult, with or without children, to identify something they know about children between the ages of 18 months and 6 years, they would probably indicate that they know about the "terrible twos." Virtually all parents can recall a time when their 2-year-old had a rage episode equivalent to a small nuclear explosion. Even children considered average in many ways can have temper outbursts that are long (20 to 30 minutes) and dramatic (screaming, head banging, breath holding, aggression, and so on). These tantrums reflect the child's final step in becoming a person independent of his caretakers and demonstrating the power of his "self" to get his needs met.

What these tantrums accomplish for the child is largely dependent on how the parent reacts to their occurrences. The good parent is able to act as a container for the child's rage, recognizing and accepting it and protecting herself or himself and the child from its potentially damaging effects. The "good" parent is also capable of helping the child identify ways he can get his needs met in spite of, not because of, the temper outburst. The following examples illustrate the delicate balance that is the desired outcome of this period of development.

Imagine the 2½-year-old child who has had a very busy day, say a holiday at the home of relatives. Due to the celebration, the child misses his nap and is never quiet all day. As evening rolls around, the child becomes quite frantic, running and laughing in a driven sort of way. The good parent recognizes that the child has become exhausted and that, in response, his inhibitory mechanisms are failing. The parent informs the child that it is time to go to bed—a dramatic temper outburst ensues, during which the child insists that he is not at all tired. The good parent is able to acknowledge that the child does not feel tired and is very angry at having his good time interrupted while proceeding to get the child ready for bed. Sometimes this type of tantrum escalates into hysteria on the child's part; again, the good parent recognizes the child's need for sleep and does not give in by letting him stay up longer or by getting angry at him. The good parent holds and soothes the child and puts him in bed, often while he is still screaming, confident that he will be asleep within seconds. In this interaction, the child learns that there are times when the parent can be counted on to override his wishes in order to act in the child's best interest. In other words, he learns that there is a limit to those things over which he will be allowed to become master.

Let us now look at the Level II child's development of mastery in another interaction with a good parent. Imagine a 2½-year-old playing in the yard with his father. They are having fun when the father says that it is time to go indoors. The toddler protests and, when it appears he will not get his own way, starts to run away from the house toward the street. The father rushes after the child, picks him up, and physically transports him inside, acknowledging the child's anger while indicating his need to protect the child from the cars in the street.

Imagine this same scenario a year or so later. The parent again says that it is time to go in the house; the child becomes angry enough to try to get away and in so doing heads for the street. This time the good father is likely to stand his ground while verbally warning the child about the danger ahead and the need to return and enter the house. If the child's development is proceeding appropriately, a child of about 3 or 4 will stop at this point and look to see if his father is following. When the child notes that his father is not, he stops and waits. If the father were to turn toward the house at this point while repeating that it was time for the child to come in, very likely the child would follow, albeit at some distance. Both parent and child watch each other carefully to see what the other is doing, but both pretend to ignore the other. It is an elaborate dance during which the roles of leader and follower are constantly renegotiated. Once in the house, the father might acknowledge the difficult choice the child faced and his pleasure at the child's decision to come into the house.

Now imagine this scene again as the child reaches the end of Level II and is about 5½ years old. Parent says that it is time to go in—if the child is going to protest, he does so immediately. He may say no and again head away from the house toward the street. The father reiterates his desire for the child to enter the house and turns and walks away, confident in the knowledge that the child will follow shortly. This time there is virtually no double check by either the child or the parent. Both now know who is leading in this situation. The child is allowed room to be the master of his own behavior because he has demonstrated an ability to keep himself safe in the process.

One other example illustrates how control is completely given over to the child as development proceeds. When the child is young and the parent is in a hurry to get the child dressed to leave the house, the parent completes the job without encouraging or even wanting the child to assist. If the child does not want to wear what the parent has selected or wants to help in the process, the parent often overrides his wishes in order to get the task completed. When the child is a little older and better able to assist with dressing, a skill presumably achieved when no one was in a hurry, then the parent is likely to compromise by, say, having the child put on one sock and shoe while the parent puts the other one on him. By the time the child reaches the end of Level II, the parent is likely to expect the child to select his own clothes and dress himself.

In each situation, notice that the child gradually gains a sense of control or mastery in the world through the successful negotiation of interactions with a good parent. In the first example, the parent overrode the child's wishes in order to act in the child's best interest; in the second example, the parent negotiated, over time, an arrangement whereby the child could exercise some personal freedom and control within a situation over which the parent had ultimate control. In the last example, the child eventually gained almost complete autonomy and control.

In conceptualizing the child's development of a sense of control, the therapist must understand that the child must learn to control both the external environment and his internal processes. The development of these two types of control may proceed very differently. Some children will compensate for feelings of inadequate control in one sphere by developing excessive control in another sphere. The child of an alcoholic parent may become very overcontrolled and pseudomature in the face of the unpredictability of, and his lack of control over, the parent's behavior. Erikson (1950) referred to this developmental level by its primary conflict, namely, initiative versus guilt. Will the child develop a sense of his ability to operate on his environment, or will he become immobilized by an internal sense of guilt and failure?

Two very useful psychoanalytic terms help label the connection of the sense of mastery to the individual's approach to problem solving (Sutherland, 1989). Individuals may be *autoplastic* in that they attempt to change themselves or their behavior in response to problems in the environment. That is, they do not expect others to change but rather tend to see their own responsibility for problems. Alternatively, children may be *alloplastic* in that they attempt to change the behavior or others or the environment. When faced with a sibling who will not share a toy, does the child find another toy—an autoplastic adaptation—or does he scream for a parent to come and mediate the situation—an alloplastic strategy? Most people use both strategies at various points in time or when faced with specific types of problems but most people also tend to have a dominant strategy that they use first when faced with virtually any sort of problem. The concepts of autoplasticity or alloplasticity should not be confused with locus of control. The first refers only to the child's perception of who or what has to change in order to resolve a given problem. The latter refers to where the child sees the power to change the problem residing. Ideally, a child who is autoplastic will also have an internal locus of control. He believes he should be the one to change when faced with a problem and believes he has the power to effect the necessary changes. A child who is autoplastic but tends to externalizing the locus of control is very prone to depression. He believes he is the only one who should or can change in a problem situation but believes he has no power to effect the outcome. Similarly, a child who tends to be alloplastic and but tends to internalize the locus of control can become very frustrated because he believes other should or can change but that they have no power to effect the outcome even if they do. These children tend to resort to using force to make others change. Children who are alloplastic and maintain an external locus of control see others as very responsible and powerful and may see themselves as perpetual victims.

Understanding the degree to which the child has been able to develop a sense of mastery and control is critical to the effective treatment of most children because it appears that many children who enter treatment have either achieved entirely too much control over their life situations or not nearly enough control. Problems with impulse control, temper outbursts, overcontrol, pseudomaturity, aggression, and the like constitute most of the presenting problems for children referred to treatment.

As the child enters the second half of the preoperational stage, when the incorporation of object constancy becomes the dominant process, he becomes more concerned with his gender-role identification. The onset of this intrapsychic process is apparently triggered by the development of the child's object constancy to the point that he is able to compare himself to others in a realistic fashion. He is now fully able to appreciate the differences between men and women and recognize that his own gender places him in one of these categories. Given the social preference many cultures award males, it is no surprise that many female children become jealous of the male gender and the male role.

Unfortunately, partly because of their limited understanding of child development, many parents and, in turn, many child therapists manifest some rather inaccurate beliefs regarding children's gender-related development. First, it is important to be aware that three minimally related tasks are involved. The first task is the development of children's *gender identity,* that is, their conceptualization of themselves as either biologic males or females. This task is usually accomplished during Level I and is virtually irreversible by the time a child is 2 years old. The second task is the development of a *gender role,* children's propensity to behave in ways consistent with the social stereotypes of masculinity and femininity. This task is accomplished during Level II and is a component of the child's negotiation of the oedipal conflict. Cross-gender-role behavior is often of significant concern to parents, especially when seen in a male child. Both parents and therapists often assume, incorrectly, that such behavior is indicative of same-sex object preference. *Sex object preference* or choice refers to an individual's choice of sex partners and is the third and final task within the realm of the child's gender-related development; it may not be completed until the child is an adolescent. Each task is viewed as essentially independent. In other words, a child may develop a sense of self as male or female somewhat independent of his biologic gender. Then a child may develop gender-role behavior that may not be stereotypically consistent with either his biologic gender or gender identity. Finally, a child's sex object choice may not be stereotypically consistent with the child's gender, gender identity, or gender-role behavior. Consider, for example, the biologic male who develops a female gender identity (transsexual), pursues a sex change, and behaves in ways only somewhat stereotypically feminine and then enters into a sexual relationship with another female. Whether or not one views such behavior as "healthy," it points to the fact that gender-related development is extremely complex and not a unitary phenomenon. This is also an area where the nature versus nurture arguments run rampant. Many place an inordinate emphasis on the probability that all gender-related and sexual behavior is biologically determined. Certainly, there is growing medical evidence that this may be more true than we ever imagined. On the other hand, there is no question that there are enormous cultural and social influences at play. What is accepted as normal behavior for boys and girls varies greatly from one culture to another and typically from one socioeconomic group to another within a given culture.

Because sterotypic gender-related development is so valued in Western society, several related psychoanalytic concepts, namely, penis envy and the oedipal conflict, are discussed. Freud (1917) labeled this stage the phallic period, focusing on the relative social value of the male role by focusing on the perceived value of the male's sex organ. This is another point at which Freud lost followers because of the degree to which he sexualized a childhood phenomenon. One particularly troublesome aspect of Freud's conceptualization of this period of the child's development was his focus on the concept of penis envy. Freud saw the female child's desire for a penis as a necessary condition for the onset of the oedipal conflict in girls. Particularly noteworthy is that Freud so valued stereotypic gender-role behavior that he postulated that the successful resolution of the oedipal conflict was essential to both the male and female child's attainment of at least a neurotic level of personality functioning. Persons who did not develop stereotypic gender-role identification were thought to be quite severely disturbed.

The following discussion is an extremely distilled presentation of Freud's (1917) conceptualization of the Level II or phallic child's development, that was presented in more detail in Chapter Two. At some point early in this level, both boys and girls realize that boys and men have a penis and that girls and women do not. Given the presumed value of this organ, girls become preoccupied with obtaining one while boys become preoccupied with keeping theirs. The little girl looks to her father to provide her with a penis, and when, over time, it becomes apparent that he will not do so, she longs to become impregnated by him so that she could have a child, that is theoretically postulated to serve as a penis substitute. When it becomes apparent that this solution also will not come about in reality, the girl returns to her mother for solace and identifies with her in the hopes of eventually attracting a man.

The male child, on the other hand, has no reason to turn to the father because he already has a penis. Instead he seeks to possess the mother who has, from the very beginning, provided him with most of his nurturance.

Unfortunately, he has a rival for possession of the mother in the father. The little boy also notes that neither his mother nor sister now have the penis that he, in his egocentric state, believes they once had. He looks around and notices that his father still has one, and so he assumes that this powerful male must be responsible for this state of affairs. As with the girl, it soon becomes apparent to the boy that the mother will not help him get rid of the father, and he becomes even more fearful of the father's retribution and the possibility of castration. In defense, he becomes the father's ally so that he will be valued and not attacked. In other words, both boys and girls are seen as not having resolved this conflict until they finally identify with the same-gender parent in order to obtain the approval of the parent of the opposite gender (A. Freud, 1965).

The general concept of oedipal conflicts and the concept of penis envy in particular are very difficult for non-analytic psychotherapists to accept and incorporate into their schema for conceptualizing child psychopathology and potential treatment issues. In responding to this personal difficulty, they often disregard certain facts about the Level II child's conceptualization of the world and his knowledge of the relative social value of the male and female gender roles.

This discomfort can be minimized if the oedipal conflict and penis envy are reframed in cognitive developmental terms. This integration of theories represents the trend in psychology toward attending to the similarities rather than differences among models. Penis envy is actually a very real possibility among 3-year-olds who have yet to develop any sense of the concept of equivalence because their ability to conserve has yet to develop. The 3-year-old cannot value what he cannot see. It is all well and good to tell a 3-year-old girl that she also has important sex organs that are internal, but that will not compensate for the natural valuing of visible, concrete objects in which 3-year-olds engage. If they see another child with a toy similar to one they have at home, they assume the new toy to be theirs and want it now. Assurance that they have one of their own at home does little to calm them. Add to this the relative social value most cultures place on being male, and it is fairly easy to accept concepts such as a boy's oedipal desire to usurp the role of the most powerful male he knows and to possess the most significant female he knows. It also becomes clear why girls do not go through an oedipal conflict similar to that of boys: They do not have either a desirable object or the relative social status to lose. Within this framework, even a concept such as penis envy becomes more logical and acceptable. No, not every girl wants a penis, but very few girls could say that they never wanted social power and status at least equal to that of their male peers.

Social Development

As can be seen from the previous discussion, the social development of the Level II child is bound to the child's emotional development. Mastery is a self-perception that occurs, in part, relative to other people in the environment. Gender-role identification is by definition a comparison of the child to a reference group. It is the child's growing ability to categorize and to compare and contrast that make these aspects of development possible.

Socially, the preoperational child gradually becomes quite focused on comparing himself to his peers. If one places a young Level II child in a peer group setting, the child's tendency to ignore his peers unless they have something he wants is obvious. The child is too preoccupied with his own needs and strategies for getting those needs met to bother with anyone who cannot address his needs, much less anyone who might prove to be in competition for resources. By the time the child is 5 or 6, however, he will have developed a very strong pattern of attending to peers and even of viewing them as potential sources of both material and emotional supplies. At either age, children are likely to cluster around a child they perceive to be obtaining a steady supply of reinforcers from the environment. The child with the only cookie is suddenly everyone's friend.

As children interact with their peer group, they begin to establish relationships based on perceived similarity. This action follows from the basic behavioral principle of modeling. Children are more likely to imitate a model they perceive as similar to themselves than a model they perceive as different. Little boys emulate their fathers and other little boys while little girls emulate their mothers and other little girls. As they engage in this process, they will also identify themselves not only as boys or girls—something most can do as they enter Level II—they will work to match the stereotype associated with their gender. Boys will learn not to cry, and girls will learn not to be aggressive. Identification with the stereotype is quite powerfully entrenched by the time children leave Level II. And as they engage in this comparative process, the children will come to realize that they have more in common with other children than they have with adults, and the relative value placed on peer relationships will rise accordingly.

Play Development

Pretend play dominates the activity of children between the ages of 2 and 6 although its complexity increases significantly over the course of Level II. Early on, the child's pretending is quite active and he is very much a part of it. He enjoys pretending to ride a carousel horse or push toy. He runs, jumps and is generally fully engaged in his activities. Toward the age of 3 and 4 the child's imagination grows. Interest in miniature pretend toys that allow the child to control and externalize the pretending are of progressively more interest. Similarly, the child becomes interested in toys and materials that allow him to accomplish something, to demonstrate his increasing prowess. Art materials and drawing become a significant interest. Unfortunately, drawing on "forbidden" surfaces like furniture or books also becomes more likely as the child literally seeks to make his mark upon his ever expanding world. By the age of 5, the child is able to engage in elaborate fantasy play and will enjoy the use of a wide array of props. At this time the child also shows a beginning interest in very simple card or board games. It is toward the end of Level II that the child becomes very interested in peers as play partners and is more able to be social and to share (Hughes, 1995).

Processing of Life Experience

As with Level I children, the therapist must always be alert to potential positive and negative interactions between Level II children's ongoing development and their actual life experience. As mentioned in the discussion of the Level II child's academic training, in the United States, children enter the public school system at the age of 5 or 6. The play therapist should also be aware of the significant differences between the demands placed on the kindergarten child and the first grader. For children who have been in day care on a part-time basis, kindergarten may not be significant change in their experience. For those who are in full-time day care, it may mean that they go to school half the day and day care the other half, significantly disrupting their daily routine. Regardless of the ease with which they make the transition into kindergarten, most children experience some difficulty upon entering first grade, finding the length of the day and the degree of structure confining and demanding. They usually adjust quickly, but some transition period is to be expected. School additionally complicates matters because the system has difficulty accepting the variability in the rate of individual children's development and so expects more similarity between children than may be realistic. This response, in turn, is experienced as excessively demanding by some children and as infantilizing by others.

Many other events may occur in the lives of children between the ages of 2 and 6 years. Some have become so common in recent years as to warrant specific consideration.

The birth of another sibling during this time is common and always has been—very few children are older than their next sibling by more than 2 or 3 years. When there is a 6-year or more difference, then the therapist must consider that each of the children may have had experiences similar to those of a youngest or only child. Parental divorce has become very common and often occurs when the child is in the lower elementary grades or even preschool. Parents no longer tend to stay together "for the good of the children," so they feel able to divorce earlier. Change in residence either separate from, or related to, a parental divorce is also very common. Many children move to new residences on a fairly regular basis, often staying in one place no more than a year or two. This degree of transience affects the child's development of stable and meaningful interpersonal relationships. Another event common in the lives of preschool and early school-age children is the death of a loved one or a pet. Children at this age are first really aware of the fact that death means you do not get to be with that person or animal anymore, and some may find the concept quite frightening, partially because of their limited understanding. Each event has its own impact on the child's way of thinking and reacting to the world, especially as the events interact with children's unfolding sense of mastery and their conceptualization of themselves as masculine or feminine.

Let us look at the potential impact of a divorce on a Level II child as an example. How it will effect the child will depend on the gender of the child, the gender of the primary caretaker and which parent it is who moves out of the home upon the divorce. For the sake of this example, let us assume the child is a 3-year-old boy whose primary caretaker was his mother and whose father moves out of the house. First, if the child has not already generalized his attachment to his mother to include his father he may become more possessive and clingy with his mother and rejecting of his father. Second, he is likely, due to the egocentricity of children in this phase, to either believe he caused the divorce or to believe he can bring his parents back together. Last, he may choose, even if only temporarily, to behave in a more feminine manner so as to align more closely with his mother and reduce his perceived risk of her getting rid of him the way she got rid of daddy.

Level III Children

From the age of 6 until about the age of 9, children's primary task is to learn skills for successful participation in groups and, in counterpoint, they may experience guilt for failing others. From the age of 9 until about the age of 12, children learn to invest in group process and struggle with conflict their desire for independence and their need for others' approval (Wood, Davis, Swindle & Quirk, 1996).

Cognitive Development

Level III children, ages 6 to 11 years old, are in the phase of concrete operations, which is marked by the acquisition of the ability to conserve, classify, and serialize (Piaget, 1952, 1967). These skills are not acquired all at once but are usually in place by the time a child is about 6 years old. Conservation simply means that children are able to use cognitive processes to override experiential input to make their perceptions more consistent with reality. No longer is the sandwich cut in half more than the sandwich is left whole. No longer is the can of soda poured into a short, fat glass less than the can of soda poured into a tall, thin glass. Now children can compare and contrast information based not just on their experience of it but on what they "know" to be true. During this period, children become obsessed with organizing all the information they have acquired to date and all the information they are acquiring into the absolutely correct category. It is a time when they prefer things to be black or white and resent those facts or experiences that are gray. For example, many children are somewhat annoyed when they learn that the category mammals includes not only dogs, cats, and cows they learned to discriminate during the preoperational phase but also whales and dolphins. Some children react with exasperation over the seemingly pointless rules adults invent.

During this phase, even more of the child's learning is based on language as opposed to experience. However, experience is still important because the child has only a limited ability to engage in hypothetical thinking and may have trouble grasping new information that he has never experienced. Because of the shift to language-dominated information storage, processing, and memory retrieval, the child gradually loses direct access to many of the memories and experiences acquired during the sensorimotor and even early preoperational stages. When memories are retrieved, it is often in, what appears to an adult, a rather haphazard manner. Children during Level III still tend to retrieve information according to emotional priority or similarity of the experience. That is, if you ask two Level III children who are fighting which one started the fight, both will answer that the other one did. And, more importantly, both will believe what they are saying. If John wanted Matt's truck and took it from him, that caused Matt to hit John, then John would say that the fight started when Matt hit him. John would say this because, to him, it is the point at which he became aware of his pain and subsequent anger at Matt; before that he simply wanted the truck. True and consistent serialization of memory by temporal sequence does not occur until the child enters Level IV at about the age of 11.

Between the ages of 6 and 11, school becomes a dominant part of the Level III child's life experience. At age 6, most children enter the first grade and must contend with a full day of school for the first time, a pattern that will continue, without a break, for at least the next 12 years. In determining the impact of school on the child's development, the therapist must be aware that each grade is not the same in terms of the child's experience. As previously stated, kindergarten and first grade each present the child with particular adjustment difficulties. Many children also face specific problems in adjusting to the third and sixth grades as well.

Third grade is often experienced as difficult partly because children who have not yet made the transition into formal operations thinking are introduced to various concepts that are difficult to conceptualize concretely. The best example of this phenomenon is the introduction of multiplication to third graders. Although multiplication can be explained as nothing more than consecutive addition, it is more easily conceptualized as a process of grouping sets. The latter conceptualization is quite difficult for children who think concretely; therefore, they often approach learning the multiplication tables as a rote memory task that they do not really understand. Thus, they are faced with learning at least 100 isolated bits of information, an overwhelming task even for a relatively bright child. If multiplication seems abstract to a child of 8 or 9, imagine how he experiences the introduction of division, which usually occurs in fourth grade.

Many children also experience sixth grade as difficult for reasons similar to those that made third grade difficult. At the age of 11, the normative age for sixth graders, many children are indeed making the transition into formal operations thinking, but many are not. Most academic programs proceed as if all the children are functioning at the same level. Based on school districts' assumption that most sixth graders will acquire formal operational thinking during the course of the year, the academic programs shift to curricula heavily loaded with reading and writing assignments. This shift is most difficult for children whose cognitive development is lagging somewhat. If these children also differ from their peers in the areas of motor or physical development, they are at risk for serious negative self-evaluations and criticism from their peers.

Physical Development

As with the preoperational child, the concrete operations child does not undergo dramatic shifts in motor functioning when compared to the transitions the sensorimotor child makes. Between the ages of 6 and 11, the child gains considerable motor coordination, acquiring those skills needed to participate in the sports his peers play. The child learns to throw, catch, and kick a ball; to jump rope; to climb trees; to run; and to skip. These skills may not be essential to the child's having a successful adult life, but they can be very influential in determining the course of his relationships with peers. And advances or delays in boys' and girls' motor development are likely to have differential effects. Boys with quite advanced motor development are often very successful in team sports and therefore able to garner many friends. Boys with delayed motor development are often made scapegoats by their male peers. Girls are less likely to experience such marked social consequences as a result of either advanced or delayed motor development.

While the motor development most Level III children undergo is a matter of quantitative change, toward the end of this level many are experiencing the profound qualitative physical changes associated with the onset of puberty. This is more likely to be the case for girls than boys, but it is possible for either gender. Unfortunately, this physiologic variability further enhances the possibility that some of the children will feel ostracized because they are different. As noted in the section on Level III children's social development, such children have great difficulty accepting personal differences without seeing themselves as at least less than their peers if not bad.

Emotional Development

As children enter Level III, they have, if all has proceeded as it should, resolved their oedipal conflicts. Freud (1905) labeled this the latency period and posited that it was a time during which the child confronts no major psychosexual conflicts. While it may be true that the child is not experiencing any major change in the sexualized aspects of his nature, Level III is hardly the period of quiescence that Freud suggested. Once children are able to conserve, they develop a capacity for internally generated emotions that were not previously possible.

Freud believed that it was the process of resolving the oedipal conflict that caused the child to develop a superego. Again, a cognitive explanation of the child's development of a conscience seems more parsimonious. It is clear that by the age of 5, children have begun internalizing some of their parent's prohibitions. That is, the child conserves rules and expectations even when the parent is not physically present (Piaget, 1962). The conservation of parental rules even in the parent's absence allows the child to begin to judge his own behavior and experience the affect appropriate to that evaluation. Thus, the child is able to experience an internally based, negative self-evaluation or guilt.

Whether one calls this process of internal evaluation a superego or a conscience or merely includes it among other developing cognitive operations, it is an essential element for the growth of the child's repertoire of affective experience. While it is still true that even most Level III children will use only happy, sad, or mad to label their affects, they are beginning to be able to categorize affects not only by the internal sensations that are generated but by the situations in which they occur. The Level III child knows that anger in response to being hit is not exactly the same as anger experienced in reaction to having his teacher pay more attention to someone else's work than his own. He knows that sadness in reaction to the death of a pet is not the same as the sadness he experiences in reaction to the divorce of his parents. The physiologic variations on which the child bases his affect are as limited as they were when he was born, but he is building the experience base that gradually allows him to access the myriad of affect words available in the English language. These words do not reflect variations in affect as much as they reflect the specifics of the situation in which the affects occur. Consequently, the child eventually learns that the sadness experienced at the death of a pet is called mourning or grief while the sadness experienced months after the divorce of his parents might best be labeled depression. He also learns that jealous means coveting the attention someone else is getting, while envious means coveting someone else's possessions or accomplishments.

Social Development

Not only does the ability to conserve have profound effects on children's affective experience, it dramatically alters their social exchanges as well. As they develop a stable internalized set of social rules, children rely less on having their behavior governed by external authority and are now able to exhibit a morality of reciprocity (Piaget, 1932, 1962). In other words, children now perform certain behaviors not just because they are instructed to do so but because they can now put themselves in the other person's place in order to evaluate their actions. Thus, children may now behave simply because they can anticipate the effect their actions will have on others by putting themselves in the recipients' place.

As the ability to conserve allows the child to develop an internalized set of rules that govern his behavior, so too it allows him to develop a stable internal representation of self (Piaget, 1963). Further, as noted in the section on Level III cognitive development, children become preoccupied with categorizing every object and experience with which they come in contact. This combination of a stable self-representation and a cognitive predilection for categorization and comparison causes Level III children to begin evaluating themselves socially. During this level, the child's narcissism abates sufficiently to allow him to see himself as different from others; thus, the process of peer comparison and socialization becomes a dominant task. This process is accomplished through interactions with others in the environment, most particularly peers. Level III children move to compare every aspect of themselves to those around them. Who is the tallest, thinnest, smartest, fastest, prettiest, nicest? Who can jump the highest, eat the most, burp the loudest, and giggle the longest? The child is bombarded with new information about himself, both good and bad. The information must be compared to the child's fledgling self-representation and either discarded or incorporated. Once information has been incorporated, it becomes part of the basis on which future self-evaluations are made.

Erikson (1950), who noted the importance of the child's entry into school, saw the major developmental task of this period as the child's resolution of the conflict between industry and inferiority. The child begins comparing his own capabilities to those of peers and subsequently either is able to approach and address new tasks with confidence or experiences various feelings of inferiority that inhibit creative productivity. In addition, on entering school, children begin to transfer some of their positive feelings and expectations outside the home to peers (A. Freud, 1965). This is the final part of the individuation process, as the child invests in peers much of the libidinal energy previously attached to the mother.

Play Development

While the child may still engage in a great deal of pretend play at the beginning of Level III, organized games of various types dominate by the end. Hughes (1996) discusses several aspects of play development over the course of Level III. First, much of the child's play during this stage focuses on the acquisition and display of various skills. "Whether by skateboarding, shooting baskets, roller skating, wrestling, jumping rope, performing stunts on a bicycle, throwing a Frisbee, or climbing a tree, each generation of children inherits or invents a wide assortment of motor activities that allow them to show off in front of peers and adults and establish their positions within the peer group" (p. 109). Second, children often become avid collectors of any of a number of objects. The acquisition, sharing, and exchanging of collectibles becomes a way of demonstrating status and knowledge as well as a focus for social activity. Third, children develop play rituals during this stage such as using "paper, rock, scissors" or "one potato, two potato" to select who should go first at a game. These rituals are an enactment of concrete operations thinking as they lend order to the child's world and are taken very seriously by the participants. Children during this stage become progressively more interested in games with rules. Everything from card games to board games to semi-pretend games like "Capture the Flag" appeal to children this age. Often, the more rules the better the children like the game. Many an adult has watched in amazement as a group of pre-adolescent children use up all of their play time enthusiastically engaged in laying out and negotiating the rules to a game they will not have time to play. This is the age where children begin to play organized sports. Whether or not one favors the competitiveness inspired by such games they are a significant part of most children's lives as contemporary society becomes more industrialized and technological. Organized sports seem to provide a bridge from the carefree games of childhood to the intensity, competition and team nature of the work lives of most contemporary adults.

Processing of Life Experience

The life experiences of Level III children can be extremely variable, and their life histories should certainly play a part in the formulation of a viable treatment plan. Events common to the lives of many an American child in this day and age might include any of the following: illness or death of a parent, parental divorce, family moves, illness or death of a sibling, birth of a sibling, significant change in family status, and so on. Regardless of the experiences to which the child is exposed, he will certainly process them from a concrete perspective that means the child is somewhat preoccupied with the facts of the event and may want to discuss them at length while comparing them to other events he perceives as similar. What adults often find difficult is the degree to which the Level III child shows an intellectual curiosity about events and his tendency to associate them to other events in what appears a rather haphazard way.

Upon the death of a grandparent, the Level III child, while certainly experiencing grief, may also ask numerous questions about the situation. How did grandfather die? What did they do with grandfather's body once he died? Is it dark in the coffin when it is closed? What happens if rain seeps into the coffin underground? These questions may appear callous to adults who are in the midst of their own grief, but they merely reflect the child's attempt to integrate the experience into his present store of knowledge. Further, the child might very well launch into a virtually identical series of questions on seeing a dead animal by the side of the road and might, in fact, become very upset. The adult must be able to recognize that to the Level III child a death is a death and that discrimination of events becomes possible only toward the end of this level. The specific interaction of trauma with the developmental functioning of the Level III child is discussed in the "Pathology" section that follows.

Level IV Children

Early in this stage children's primary task is to learn to apply their individual and group skills to new situations and they tend to struggle in their search for their identity as an independent person (Wood et al., 1996). However, relatively few clients over the age of 12 or 13 are treated primarily with play therapy. Of those who are, even fewer are actually functioning at Level IV. Therefore, this discussion of the development of Level IV children, ages 12 to 18, is fairly limited.

Cognitive Development

Level IV children engage in formal operations thinking, that is marked by the child's increasing ability to process information in the abstract. No longer are children bound to experience; they can think in the "as if" mode, understand things they have never seen or experienced, and both formulate and test hypotheses. Language becomes the dominant mode for learning about the world, both internal and external. For the first time, their conception of time is consistent with reality, although they may still have difficulty with concepts such as "forever." With the acquisition of a more consistent perception of time, children store and retrieve memories in temporal order as opposed to the emotional sequencing typical of the Levels II and III children. As with other cognitive processes, formal operations thinking was once thought to be acquired in an all-or-none manner but is now viewed more as a set of skills that are gradually acquired between the child's eleventh birthday and young adulthood. In fact, although Piaget did not distinguish different stages of cognitive development after the child reaches the age of 11, many authors contend that children continue to undergo both quantitative and qualitative cognitive changes for many years and, potentially, throughout their lives.

Language development is not a primary task for the Level IV child; the focus is on expanding and fine-tuning one's vocabulary. Of particular importance to the play therapist is the fact that the child can now engage in abstract thinking and is much more likely to use a variety of emotional terms that reflect subtle variations in their internal experience. No longer is a child simply happy, mad, or sad; now he can be ecstatic, morose, blue, furious, homicidal, and so forth.

The academic experience of Level IV children is more programmatically variable than that of children at previous stages. Some school districts break their educational programs into elementary, middle, and high school programs, while others divide them into elementary, junior high, and high school or other variations. Often these programs are housed in different buildings with different catchment areas; that means that a child makes transitions from one school to another and from one peer group to another between any two of a number of grades. Depending on the program, a sixth grader might be at the top of the elementary school social ladder or the bottom of the middle school ladder. Some children are even so lucky as to move from one school system to another and spend two consecutive years at the bottom of the social status hierarchy. Teachers who work in school systems that have junior high schools often indicate that eighth graders are a miserable group to work with because these students are both in the early throes of puberty at age 13 and are caught between the newly arrived seventh graders and the top of the hierarchy ninth graders. They thus act moody and competitive, in the manner of many an unhappy middle child. It is important that the therapist understands the school system so as to understand the child's position within, and reaction to, that system.

Physical Development

As the child enters into Level IV, he also enters into puberty, with all its associated physical changes. It is a time of the physiologic turmoil that has been established in both clinical and popular literature. It is not that puberty must be a difficult period for children but that it creates the possibility of internal as well as external stressors. Not only does the onset of puberty have its own inherent problems, but the differences in the ages at which children enter puberty adds to the likelihood of differential and potentially negative self-evaluation beginning during Level III. As their cognitive development proceeds, however, children are better able to evaluate information they receive about themselves in light of the situation they are involved in and the character of the messenger as opposed to just deciding whether or not it matches their internal self-representation. Thus, the Level IV child who is called dumb when he fails a test is able to judge whether or not the teacher and the test seem fair, whether or not his test performance reflects his actual ability or the influence of some other variable such as time spent studying, and the reliability of the person delivering the epithet before deciding whether or not to incorporate "dumbness" into his self-concept.

Emotional Development

Freud (1917) labeled adolescence the genital period because it is during this phase that he saw the individual's libido becoming focused on his now developing sex organs. It is recognized as a period during which the child develops the capacity for the full range of human emotion and the cognitive capacity to more effectively defend against those affects when necessary.

Social Development

Erikson (1950) spoke of the individual's struggle for identity versus role confusion as adolescents attempt to integrate themselves into adult society. In many ways, adolescence may be viewed as a second toddlerhood. During the first toddlerhood, the child negotiated with the parent for an individual yet primarily dependent role. During the second toddlerhood, the Level IV child is negotiating for both increasing individuality and a transition to self-reliance. These negotiations may be quite stormy as the Level IV child strives to maximize his individuality and control in the face of the reality and benefits of his dependent position. One way this conflict is manifested is in the young Level IV child's ambivalence about physical contact. Often the child feels that it is inappropriate for him to receive physical affection from his parents long before he loses his desire for it. It is not uncommon for the average 10- or 11-year-old to be very embarrassed about being hugged or kissed by a parent when other people, most especially peers, are present. But when he is alone and in a good mood, he may become extremely cuddly and affectionate.

Play Development

During Level III, the child's play behavior becomes more sporadic and disguised. As they struggle to become adults, adolescents rarely play with identifiable toys or games usually out of fear of looking "childish." But it is often easy for them to let everyday activities degenerate into play. A group of teenagers may get together to hold a car wash to raise money for their school or a charity. Initially, they will be very serious and task oriented. They will try to stay dry and maintain some sense of decorum. Gradually, as they get wet and tired, they begin to "accidentally" spray one another with the hose or to throw soapsuds or sponges. As the day progresses, the focus may shift from fund-raising to simple fun-raising. Such activities are also a way to channel growing sexual interests as one targets a specific person as the target of the play, often using the play as a reason for sporadic physical contact (Hughes, 1996). More serious games often become avocations at this age with a growing interest in being really good as something like chess, cards, or tennis. Pretend play at this age is usually context specific. You are allowed to dress in costume for a Halloween party and to act out the role of your character. You are also allowed to pretend in the high school play. But pretending in general and certainly pretending with toys is seen as juvenile and to be avoided. Somewhat sadly, adolescents slowly give up the pleasures of spontaneous childhood play and accept the more serious, focused and usually goal oriented play of the adult world.

Processing of Life Experience

Children who have entered Level IV will process events in a manner very similar to that of adults. Note, however, that most children do not enter this phase in one sudden leap—they move into it gradually over a period of several years. The young adolescent is as likely to process events that are emotionally loaded at the level of concrete operations as at the formal operations level.

Some events that predictably occur for the child at the beginning of Level IV include transitions from one school to another, with the concomitant stress, and entry into puberty. This tends to be a very difficult time because Western society does not have any clear way of signaling the child's entry into adulthood. A girl may enter puberty as young as the age of 8 or 9 and she will be able to drive at age 16, but she will not be legally considered an adult until 18 and will not enjoy the full legal privileges of adulthood until 21. How does she define her social role for the 10 to 13 years in between? Is she a child, an adolescent, an adult? If an adolescent chooses to go to college, the period of transition from childhood to adulthood may be even more protracted and less clear.

The play therapist working with young Level IV adolescents must also be aware of the many social pressures to which children of this age may be exposed. Adults generally recognize the pressure to be sexually active and to experiment with drugs or alcohol that Level IV children are exposed to, but these children are also pressured to dress in a particular manner, listen to certain music, enjoy activities with their peers, and generally disdain anything adults like.

It is evident by now that children's development does indeed interact with every component of their functioning and is reflected in every aspect of their day-to-day lives. An understanding of the child client's developmental level is critical to the therapist's awareness of the very "nature of the beast" with whom he is working. In addition, a thorough understanding of child development is essential to the therapist's understanding of the children's psychopathology, as is evident in the following material.

PATHOLOGY

The topic of psychopathology is complex and tends to be made more problematic by the tendency to rely on a natural sciences conceptualization and a generalized failure to keep in mind the degree to which culture and social-historical factors come into play. Because a natural science model dominates psychology there is a tendency to see various diagnostic categories as something real and immutable. Most mental health practitioners see schizophrenia as a real, measurable, documentable illness. This, in spite of the fact that a person demonstrating a schizophrenic cluster of symptoms would be more likely to be diagnosed as manic depressive if hospitalized in the United Kingdom rather than the United States. In some other cultures hallucinations are not seen as particularly pathologic and may even be considered an indicator of the hallucinator's spirituality. Even more disconcerting is the fact that diagnostic categories supposedly grounded in science change regularly by vote of those practitioners responsible for creating the *Diagnostic and Statistical Manual of Mental Disorders IV (DSM-IV)* (1994). In spite of these conceptual problems, it is clear that many children suffer and that many are capable of causing considerable suffering in others.

Another significant factor with respect to the diagnosis of psychopathology in children is the failure of most diagnostic systems to take either the underlying pathogenic process or child development into account. Most diagnostic systems consist of symptom checklists that do not take into account how the child came to display the observed symptoms. Depression, for example, might be biochemical, reactive, or the result of a history of causative factors. Since treatment needs to be aimed at changing the internal process. Symptom-based diagnostic systems are of relatively little utility when it comes to treatment planning. Shirk & Russell (1996) propose a model based on six etiologic categories derived from three theoretical models. From dynamic psychology come disorders based on internal conflict or ego deficits. From cognitive psychology come disorders based on skill deficits or cognitive distortions. And, from client-centered psychology come disorders based on low self-esteem and emotional interference. Later, in the same text, the authors match each etiologic category to the specific psychotherapy process most suited to address it. *The Diagnostic and Statistical Manual of Mental Disorders IV* only incorporates development in terms of separating a handful of childhood disorders from those experienced by adults. Failure to take child development into account presupposes that all mental illness is experienced and manifested in the same way at different ages. Again, relative to depression we know this not to be the case. It seems imperative that a diagnostic system that integrates a broadly based (ecosystemic) model of etiology with a comprehensive model of child development be created (Greenspan & Greenspan, 1991; Tolan, Guerra, & Kendall, 1995).

Within Ecosystemic Play Therapy, the definition of psychopathology is limited to *the inability to get one's needs met adequately and/or the inability to get one's needs met in ways that do not interfere with the ability of others to get their needs met.* A symptom or behavior that does not meet either or both of these basic conditions is not considered pathological and, therefore, is not viewed as an appropriate target for treatment. As children initially find that their needs are not being adequately met they may engage in a variety of behaviors in an attempt to resolve the problem. Hopefully, this experimentation results in nonpathologic behavior but, along the way other problems may arise. A pathologic behavior may inadvertently be reinforced and thus become a part of the child's behavioral repertoire. For example, some 2-year-olds find out that their temper tantrums are very effective and thus engage in more and more of them as they seek to get their needs met. Alternatively, the child may find a behavior that gets one need met but actually interferes with other needs being met. The pseudomature child who acts very grown up in order to avoid abuse at the hands of an alcoholic parent often misses out on the important tasks and joys of childhood. These behaviors are adaptive. No matter how dysfunctional they appear to an outsider they represent the child's best attempt at coping. Often these behaviors are referred to as *pathogenic adaptations* (Rappoport, 1996).

Besides developing less than effective behaviors as they seek to get their needs met children may also develop problematic interpersonal schemata (Shirk, 1998). An interpersonal schemata is a sort of cognitive template with which the child approaches social interactions. A child who has a strong, positive relationship with his caretaker will bring his expectations that others will be warm and nurturing to his interactions with other adults. Conversely, a child who is abused will come into other relationships expecting abuse. On some level such beliefs may protect the child but taken to the extreme they may interfere with the child's further development and overall mental health. Problematic interpersonal schemata are the cognitive equivalent of the behavior evidenced in the child's pathogenic adaptations. Both are the result of the child's inability to get his needs met effectively. And, in both cases children become stuck in a cycle of thought and behavior that prevents them from seeing the original need any more much less able to see how to modify what they are thinking and doing.

Ecosystemic Play Therapy proposes several broad categories of pathology, based on the degree to which present scientific study has been able to identify an interaction between the child's manifest behavioral or emotional pathology and his underlying biologic or physiologic functioning. The categories are admittedly overly simplistic and do not represent discrete groupings but rather clusters along a continuum. These categories are presented here based on the assumption that they should have an impact on the play therapist's development of a reasonable treatment plan.

Biologic Factors

First, the therapist must consider those types of pathology that, given the present state of science, have been determined to have considerable biologic underpinnings. These types include autism, schizophrenia, and an assortment of neurologic, endocrinologic, and physiologic disorders. Generally, these disorders require interventions above and beyond play therapy. Pharmacologic and educational interventions are, for example, often a priority. This is not to say that children with these disorders cannot benefit from play therapy but that the play therapist should be sure to not develop a treatment plan that ignores the child's underlying biologic endowment. After all, one would not attempt to make a mentally retarded child gifted; one would hope to maximize the mentally retarded child's functioning at any given point in his development.

Second, the play therapist must recognize that some pathologies are not specifically biologic but may represent the sequelae of underlying biologic deficits or disorders. This category includes Fetal Alcohol Syndrome children as well as those often labeled "learning disabled," or children with any of a range of mild to moderate central nervous system disorders, including epilepsy. For those children who fall into the first category, play therapy may be of great value but often will need to be accompanied by other forms of intervention. In these cases, the play therapist must recognize the often complex interaction between children's biology, behavior, and transactions with the world. It seems reasonable to include, in this group, those children with chronic physical or medical conditions that do not necessarily have a specific neurological component, such as diabetes, asthma, kidney problems, and the like. It is unclear how these disorders, and the medications those afflicted with them must take, interact with the child's personality, but it does often appear that many of these children develop dysfunctional and yet avoidable emotional and behavioral symptoms in response to their illnesses.

Finally, the therapist must consider those children whose biologic endowment appears entirely intact if not superior. These children possess the capacity not only to function very well in the world but to have transactions with their world that benefit both themselves and those around them.

The range of disturbance a child exhibits may vary both across and within categories. Those children who fall into the category with significant biologic impairment tend to demonstrate the most severe psychopathology, while those with superior biologic endowment sometimes appear more impervious or adaptable. However, the therapist must also recognize that the variability within these categories often exceeds the variability between them. It is possible to identify rather high functioning autistic children as well as extremely psychotic and disorganized, intellectually gifted children.

Learning Problems

Focal problems with learning that do not involve obvious biologic deficits or mental retardation have received progressively more attention in the field of education over the past 20 years or so. Although the cause of learning disabilities is not very clear the fact that these can and do interact with a child's overall psychological development is clear. Educators now recognize the myriad types of highly specific learning disabilities children may manifest, including Reading Disorders, Mathematics Disorder, and Disorder of Written Expression all of which are listed in the *DSM-IV*. Mental health practitioners are beginning to hypothesize the existence of specific emotional learning disabilities. "Children's problems with emotion, then, can take many forms. These include, but are not limited to, problems with affect modulation, emotional constriction, limitations in the capacity to understand contextual cues for emotion expression or control, and emotional lability" (Shirk & Russell, 1996, p. 188). The existence of even more specific disorders have also been hypothesized. "Alexithymia is a disturbance in which one is aware only of the physiological aspects of affect, such as increased heart rate, perspiration, and dry mouth, and is unable to name or give symbolic representation to an emotional experience" (James, 1994, p. 14) Dyssemia is the inability to read, interpret or use non-verbal affective cues in the self or others (Nowicki & Duke, 1992).

Developmental Deviations

Regardless of the ceiling a child's biologic endowment imposes, many of his psychological symptoms may be conceptualized from a developmental perspective. The child's development may be considered to be delayed, uneven, or both. This model does not consider the possibility of advanced development in the way some individuals label a child an "overachiever," that is, a child performing above his capacities. In this model, such a child would be viewed as having uneven development in that some areas of his functioning lagged behind others. Developmental deviance is assessed, for the most part, relative to the child's chronological age.

First, the therapist must consider the child's overall developmental level; that is, one must look at the gestalt of the child's development. How does the world perceive the child? Does the child strike others as being younger or older than his chronological age? This general view of the child is critical to understanding that child's experience in the world both outside and inside the playroom. Those readers who grew up looking, physically, much older or younger than their chronological age must certainly recall how it affected their transactions with the world.

> Caroline, who entered college at age of 16, was always able to appear very sophisticated and at least several years older. She was generally able to interact well with her new, mostly older, peer group. She was often asked out on dates by male peers. She lamented, however, that these were often first and last dates because the men seemed to become quite overwhelmed when they discovered her to be "underage."

While these experiences are often directly recalled by adolescents, who generally hate to look young, they affect the lives of younger children in often overlooked ways. A child who, because of physical, cognitive, or emotional developmental delays, is viewed by the world as much younger than his chronological age is often subject to differential expectations. Parents and teachers may not expect age-appropriate behavior, and, human nature being what it is, children tend to rise or fall to meet others' expectations. Delayed children are often subtly or directly encouraged to remain dependent and to limit their peer interactions. At school they are sometimes shielded from their peers by well-intentioned adults who want to protect them from the harsh feedback for which school-age children are often known. This does not mean that parents, teachers, peers, and others should never adjust the demands placed on children displaying developmental deficits; it is critical, however, that others consistently evaluate whether or not their treatment of the children is based on realistic limitations or on projections that do not match the children's true underlying capacity.

It is worth noting that such projected and inappropriate expectations are often foisted on children who are capable of acting in some ways older than their chronological age, as often happens to certain children who may be labeled "depressed." The literature on the behavior of children of alcoholics contains some of the best descriptions of these pseudomature children. Their depression slows them down so that their behavior appears more controlled, and often they manifest considerable verbal skills through which they tend to interact with adults rather than peers. Gradually, their families, and others with whom they interact, come to expect them to be adultlike at all times. In class they are quiet and withdrawn, and teachers often react with shock and considerable criticism if, and when, these children engage in even the most age-appropriate forms of acting out. The families of these children similarly come to count on these children to help meet their needs and may be unable to see or tolerate the fact that the children have needs of their own. This overestimation of the children's functional level gradually results in the children having even fewer of their needs met and an exacerbation of their symptoms.

It is relatively easy for the play therapist to become caught up in the same set of misperceptions the child encounters in the real world. Consider the child who comes to therapy appearing so regressed and hostile that the therapist feels compelled to structure and contain the child in a way that prevents his ever really being able to interact in a nurturing and supportive manner. Over time his therapy may come to reproduce the child's transactions with the world in a repetitive and less than growth-promoting way. The therapist is merely another authority figure demonstrating a limited capacity to meet his needs. The same unproductive pattern may also be established with the pseudomature child, who may come to the session and demonstrate an exceptional desire and ability to talk. The play therapist, particularly one who is more analytically inclined, may become enthralled by the child's apparent capacity for cognitive processing and, again, repeat the type of transactions the child has with the world. Therapy comes to be a matter of thinking and not doing, and again the child's needs go unmet. The therapist's evaluation of the child's overall developmental level is therefore a key element in determining the course of the treatment, particularly early on.

Prior to beginning the child's treatment, the therapist must also consider the unevenness of the child's developmental progress across the areas assessed. While global developmental lags or apparent pseudomaturity are often signs of significant psychopathology, uneven development is often an underlying cause of even greater disturbance. Consider the mentally retarded child who at the age of 10 has an overall IQ of 60. This child also has the language skills of a 6-year-old and motor skills that are not significantly below his chronological age. It is likely that this child will be experiencing some developmentally related distress but that, given a relatively normal environment, he will not manifest many emotional or behavioral problems. Consider, on the other hand, the 10-year-old child who has an overall IQ of 140. This child also has the language skills of a 6-year-old and slightly slower than expected motor development. Even within a normal environment it is likely that this child will be so frustrated with his inability to communicate his thoughts and feelings in a manner consistent with the complexity of his inner world that he will manifest significant emotional and behavioral sequelae.

Interaction of Trauma with Developmental Level

In developing hypotheses regarding the nature and origins of the child's developmental deviations, it is very important that the therapist understand the interaction of the child's developmental level with his experience of trauma. That is "the interplay of processes of growth and development and interaction of the individual with the environment (should be) the basis for conceptualizing adjustment and intervention" (Kazdin, 1995, p. 259). This understanding will help the therapist understand both children's symptoms in reaction to recent or ongoing trauma and the likely residuals children who experienced trauma at earlier levels of development carry. Obviously the pattern of interaction will be very complex and vary considerably from child to child, but certain trends are noted in the literature and observed in clinical practice.

Level I

If an infant experiences trauma during Level I, he will protest, usually by crying. This protest is instinctual and informs the caretaker that something is physiologically wrong with the infant. If the caretaker is unable or unwilling to provide for the infant's needs after he has begun active protest, the infant's system will eventually shut down as exhaustion sets in, resulting in symptoms such as sleep disturbance, loss of appetite, reduced energy level, and withdrawal. This physiological shutdown appears to be one of the earliest manifestations of reactive depression and protects the infant from death due to exhaustion. Piaget (1952) stressed the fact that these reflexive behaviors are the infant's only mechanism for coping with stress. Otherwise the infant depends on the caretaker for physiological regulation and tension management (Sroufe, 1979).

When psychopathology results from trauma in the very young child, it stems from the child's experience of basic reactions, not cognitively based internal conflicts (Arieti & Bemporad, 1978). Further, because the infant has no ego to protect himself, his reaction to trauma is often severe (Spitz, 1946). Last, since the infant cannot direct affects outward until he achieves object constancy (Graham, 1974), this affect cannot be readily diffused and so its intensity is maintained over time.

The long-term impact of trauma experienced during Level I is entirely dependent on the capacity of the child's caretakers to regulate and repair the damage done. It is quite possible for a young child to experience a single traumatic event sometime before his second birthday and demonstrate no behavioral or emotional sequelae or cognitive recall of that event later in life. If the trauma or its consequences persist for some time, then the long-term effects may pervade the child's functioning because they have become an integral part of the child's basic approach to the world. The disturbances are likely to be profound, with significant manifestations in the child's inability to form close interpersonal relationships, to manage dependency needs appropriately, and, sometimes, to use language effectively in interpersonal communication.

The therapist should also be aware that Level I children store information in memory without any particular organization. It simply is stored as it is experienced; that means that a Level I child is likely to associate emotions experienced in response to a trauma with any other stimuli that were perceived and stored proximally. That is, the child who must endure a painful medical procedure may store the negative emotions associated with that procedure in a group with the sights, sounds, smells, and so forth that he was experiencing at the time. This is why Level I children become so sensitive to, and fearful of, many stimuli associated with their pediatrician's office. It is also the rationale for providing the child with a treat immediately after the trauma in the hopes of overcoming the negative memory with a positive one. What is important here is the fact that so many of the child's reactions at this age may be based on temporal or proximal associations, not on any real connection between the stimuli. Thus when the older child attempts to recall trauma experienced during this level, he may also pull up seemingly unrelated memories because of the way they were stored.

Level II

Because the Level II child is still not capable of forming stable internal representations of objects (Piaget, 1963), the child evaluates things relative to himself and his own rather unstable perceptual schema. Generally, this seems to imply that a preschool child, even when able to attach emotion to objects, is still only happy, sad, angry, and so on when the objects that initially elicited those feelings are present. Thus the therapist would expect the child's emotional world to be highly variable and normally filled with euphoria and despair but not generally dominated by one pervasive affect, either positive or negative. Toddlers and preschoolers are, in fact, noted for their frequent and intense mood swings.

Trauma experienced at this level may therefore appear to have a rather fleeting impact on the child, who seems to quickly revert to his more usual way of functioning once the trauma is over. Mahler (1972) noted the preschool child's seeming imperviousness to long-term negative reactions to events. If, however, the trauma is repeated or prolonged, the aspect of development most likely to be affected is the child's development of autonomy. If something prevents the child from developing autonomy, the child may try to control himself rather than the environment and will develop a depressivelike symptom pattern (Erikson, 1950). Without sufficient individuation, the child cannot give up infantile ideals and is therefore prone to disappointment and depression (Sandler & Joffe, 1965). Alternatively, if the child develops excessive autonomy in reaction to failing to get his needs met during this level, then the aggressive pursuit of control may pervade his interactions with the world.

Because of the strength of children's early cognitive/affective schemata, the overall feeling states children experienced during this phase will have great permanence (Wadsworth, 1971). Further, as noted, Level II children's affect tends to swing back and forth from very positive to very negative. When traumas are experienced during this time period, the child may tend to continue to display highly variable affects as he gets older, continuing to react to objects and events as either very positive or very negative. This is the pattern hypothesized to exist in the histories of individuals diagnosed with Borderline Personality disorders.

Level II children's processing and storage of traumatic experiences are only somewhat more sophisticated than that of Level I children. At this level memories are stored both in the order in which they were experienced and in clusters. The Level II child is beginning to sort his experience and can now store happy experiences with other happy experiences and sad experiences with other sad experiences. Level II children actually seem more likely to store together memories that evoked similar affects than to store together experiences with similar content. That is, they might be better able to recall and talk about events that have made them happy than to recall and talk about all the times they got presents. This means that children are likely to dredge up a number of other unpleasant memories when they experience a new trauma. When they are unhappy, they will usually say that they are always unhappy and that things never go their way. Similarly, when they are older, they may recall several traumatic events that occurred during this time period as all having occurred at virtually the same time.

Level III

As children enter Level III, their ability to experience a variety of stable affects and to differentiate those affects one from another and from one event to another expands rapidly. Traumas experienced during Level III are much more likely to be accompanied by several different affects, with the child somewhat able to hold these simultaneously in experience. No longer is something necessarily all bad or all good—now the child can recognize positive and negative aspects and the beginnings of ambivalence.

Additionally, the child is increasingly able to respond to events experienced cognitively rather than just responding to those that occur in reality. The Level II child may have scary or sad fantasies, but these are often pure fantasy and not related to any real but as yet unexperienced event. The Level III child can be sad, or angry, or scared by real things he has not experienced but that have been described to him or which he has constructed in his mind. The death of a friend's father is likely to be very anxiety-producing for the Level III child, not because of its direct impact on his life but because he suddenly finds himself worrying about the possibility of his own father's death. Further, the morality of reciprocity now allows the child to feel guilty for actions he has never taken but only thought of taking. This change in processing means that Level III children do not have to directly experience an event in order to find it traumatizing; thus the therapist's consideration of the impact of the child's environment has to be much more extensive.

Level III children are also capable of sorting and storing their memories of traumatic experiences much more realistically than either Level I or Level II children. There is still some likelihood, however, that they will store and retrieve memories of traumatic events in ways that seem somewhat odd to adults. For example, what the child thought or felt about the event and the event itself are likely to be recalled by the child as equally solid facts. If a child who was abused experienced his attacker as very old and very tall, he may later have trouble recognizing the attacker on sight if, in fact, the person is an older adolescent who is relatively short.

Level IV

According to Piaget and Inhelder (1969), the child holds onto a view that reality may match his ideals well into adolescence. That is, to the adolescent, there seems to be little reason that the world cannot be made into a perfect, ideal place within his lifetime. This expansive egocentric idealism tends to shield the young adolescent from some of the unpleasant realities of life during a particularly difficult developmental period. However, as reality invades and breaks down the adolescent's idealism, he or she often becomes very moody and disillusioned and may, by the late teens, become quite depressed or angry.

Having assessed the child's development across areas as is described in Chapters Six and Seven, the therapist is in a position to evaluate both the child's global developmental level and any unevenness that may be present. Therapy then begins by focusing on the child's lowest functional area. For both the uncontrolled and the pseudomature children described previously, an underlying problem may be dependency needs that were never adequately met earlier in the child's life. If this is the case, their initial therapy sessions might look quite similar. If, on the other hand, it becomes clear that one child is attempting to cope with a relatively recent trauma and that his symptomatic behavior is laid over relatively normal and even development, then his initial sessions will look quite different.

Pathology Unrelated to Developmental Level

While much of the problem behavior that brings children to therapy can be conceptualized as manifestations of either developmental lags or developmental unevenness, some behaviors or responses do not fit this frame. These are behaviors that are considered pathologic when appearing in children of any age, such as motor or vocal tics; preoccupation with objects; peculiar speech or ideation; eating disturbances; sleep disturbances; extreme or constricted emotions; physical aggression; running away; inappropriate sexual behavior; intentional destruction of property; and suicidal ideation, threats, or attempts.

These behaviors are best conceptualized from a behavioral perspective by analyzing their antecedents and consequences. What situations trigger the onset of these behaviors? What factors escalate or decrease the frequency of these behaviors? In which contexts do these behaviors occur? How does the child's environment respond when the child engages in these behaviors? What does the child gain or lose when he engages in these behaviors? The concept of negative attention is particularly without merit in the context of conducting this type of analysis. It is very unlikely that a child will engage in a behavior simply to elicit negative interactions with another person. What seems to be a much more parsimonious explanation is that he will engage in behaviors that bring him a sense of control over a situation in spite of the fact that these also elicit negative interactions. The child who can engage in behavior that makes an adult scream and yell has a unique power that can be used to distract the adult from other issues or to control the beginning and endings of interactions.

When any pathologic behaviors occur that do not seem developmentally related, the therapist should examine the child's ecosystem very carefully. The presence of these behaviors tends to reflect relatively severe, dyadic, or systemically based problems with which the child is unable to cope.

Pathology Related to Dyadic Interactions

Dyadically based pathology is seen when two seemingly functional individual's are unable to effectively get their needs met in the context of their interactions with one another. It is not uncommon, for example, for a competent mother to find that she simply has a great deal more difficulty getting along with one of her children than she does with the rest. Perhaps they are temperamentally mismatched. Perhaps the child physically resembles the abusive exhusband. Whatever the cause the source of the pathology does not necessarily lie within either individual but somewhere in the interactions between them. Therapy in such cases may be both effective and, sometimes brief, particularly when both persons are basically quite functional and, therefore, have considerable resources on which to draw.

Pathology Related to Systemic Factors

Systemically based pathology is seen when there is a mismatch between the needs of the child and the needs of the system in which he is embedded. This may be as simple as behavior problems seen in a child who attends an afternoon kindergarten so that he is no longer able to take the nap he needs as he did in preschool. Often problems arise in families when the developmental level of the family and the development of a first or last child do not coincide. A couple with one child who is much younger than the rest may find they have more difficulty raising this last child once the rest of their children have moved out of the house. The couple is ready to begin adjusting to an "empty nest" while the remaining child is still very much in need of the comforts provided by the nest. Systemically based problems can also arise when the system itself is pathologic. One should never rule out the possibility that the child's behavior problems are actually his best attempt at coping with a seriously disturbed system. This should be a prime consideration if the therapist discovers that other children in the same system are also manifesting difficulties.

CURE/TREATMENT GOALS

Given the broad definition of pathology laid out in the previous section the primary goals of Ecosystemic Play Therapy are to:

1. Maximize the child's ability to get his needs met effectively and in ways that do not interfere with the ability of others to get their needs met;
2. Maximize the child's attachment to others as a primary way of ensuring that the child gets his needs met in a socialized manner so as to avoid egocentrism and sociopathy; and
3. Return the child to a level of functional development consistent with his biologic endowment. As stated by Vernberg, Routh, and Koocher (1992) the aim of therapy is to "help children regain footing on a developmental pathway more likely to lead to adequate adaptation in subsequent periods of life" (p. 73).

This means that, ideally, the child's personality structures, emotions, cognitions, and social interactions will all function optimally given his developmental capacities at the time of termination. Further, the changes in the child's overall functioning will have at least begun to generalize to the world outside the playroom as evidenced by the child's being able to get his needs met in ways the environment can accept. These overall goals remain the same whether one is doing long- or short-term therapy. The length of the treatment is determined by the complexity of the problems the child is experiencing and the ability of the environment to support the therapy process for the child outside of the therapy sessions. Complex social problems such as long-term abuse cannot be treated by short-term therapy. Similarly, when children are embedded in pathogenic environments, such as living in an alcoholic home, short-term therapy may have no more effect than tossing a glass of water on a forest fire. Therapists must not give in to external economic and sociopolitical forces when faced with the needs of such children. On the other hand, therapists should be very active in examining the possibility that resolving a key problem and enlisting the supports naturally available in the child's ecosystem may make short-term therapy effective in the majority of cases.

Play therapists who maintain a developmental emphasis also recognize that treatment may have to resume when the child enters a new level of development. The changes that the child and the child's ecosystem make may not be appropriate at a later point in the child's development and may therefore need to be revised so as to be consistent with subsequent developmental expectations.

As with any of the other theories of play therapy, Ecosystemic Play Therapy makes some basic assumptions about various elements of the treatment process and the participants that derive from the model presented so far. These assumptions are detailed in Chapter Five.

Basic Assumptions of Ecosystemic Play Therapy

Aside from the various theoretical concepts that underlie Ecosystemic Play Therapy, a number of ideas are critical to understanding this treatment modality although these do not derive, as clearly, from a particular theoretical base. These ideas include the type of clients thought to be best suited to this form of treatment, the type of training the therapist requires, and the assumptions made about what it is that is curative or health-promoting in the conduct of the play sessions.

PLAY THERAPY CLIENTS

Developmental Level

Because the techniques the play therapist uses covary with the child's developmental level, Ecosystemic Play Therapy can be adapted for use with all children, from the lowest functioning to the highest. At the lower levels of functioning, the treatment is geared toward the creation of corrective experiences that cause the child to reorganize the assumptions she has made about the world and her place within it. At the higher levels of functioning, the treatment is less experiential and more cognitive. The aim is to have the child understand her world and her place within it on a verbal level so that any changes she makes in her behavior may generalize more rapidly. At these higher levels, the child is not seen as needing to try out every new behavior in reality but to be capable of a certain amount of cognitive problem solving. The therapist need only understand the child's developmental level within various areas of functioning in order to make the necessary adjustments to the treatment method.

Pathology

As with other developmentally oriented play therapies, Ecosystemic Play Therapy places considerable emphasis on how deficits in the child's early and current interactions with the caretaker affect the creation and maintenance of many types of pathologic behavior. Therapy is viewed as an attempt to remediate those deficits in the context of a very human interaction between the child and therapist. In addition to this emphasis, Ecosystemic Play Therapy also take into account those ecological variables that created and now maintain the child's difficulties. The play therapist considers working with the child, the parents, the school, the child's peers, and so forth. This flexibility means that play therapy can be adapted for use with children across the full range of psychopathologies. One advantage of a developmentally organized model is that it allows for treatment of even the most severely acting-out child so long as her safety can be maintained because the play therapist accepts the responsibility for structuring the sessions to a degree consistent with the child's developmental level and psychopathology.

The techniques described in this text assume, for the most part, that the child is being seen as an outpatient. But even if the child is so disturbed that she requires inpatient or residential treatment, the structure of the individual play sessions does not have to change substantially. In general, the primary shift made, when doing inpatient work, is to intensify the treatment by making the sessions more frequent and potentially longer. Some children who are in acute crisis may even benefit from as many as two sessions per day, especially when suicide is a concern.

ECOSYSTEMIC PLAY THERAPISTS' TRAINING

To adequately conduct play therapy, the therapist should be trained to at least the master's level in psychology or a related discipline. She needs to have had course work in child development, child psychopathology, child assessment, family systems theory, and therapy as well as play therapy. Also essential is that she have a supervised play therapy practicum of at least 6 months' duration. Listed below is a summary of the current International Association for Play Therapy (IAPT) requirements for becoming a Registered Play Therapist (RPT):

Academic Training

A. A master's degree in an appropriate medical or mental health profession from a regionally accredited educational institution. Content areas of graduate study, from an accredited university, must include: (1) Child development, (2) Theories of personality, (3) Principles of psychotherapy, (4) Child and adolescent psychopathology, and (5) Legal, professional, and ethical issues.

B. A minimum of 150 clock hours of instruction in Play Therapy (all 150 hours may not be taken from the same instructor). Content areas must include: (1) History, (2) Theory, (3) Techniques/Methods, and (4) Applications to special settings or populations.

Clinical Experience

A. Two years of supervised experience including 2,000 direct contact hours related to the area in which the applicant received a master's. One year of this experience (1,000 hours of direct clinical work) must be at the post-master's level.
B. The applicant must have provided a minimum of 500 direct contact hours of play therapy under supervision.

Continuing Education

Once registered, Play Therapists will need to complete 36 hours of continuing education every 3 years to maintain their registration. Eighteen of these hours must be specifically in play therapy, and granted by an IAPT approved provider.

Although formal course work and practicum are essential components of the play therapist's training, it is also critical that she have developed certain personality characteristics mentioned in many elementary texts on psychotherapy and counseling. Five specific valuable traits are:

1. The ability to display empathy or "an accurate understanding of the client's world as seen from the inside. To sense the client's private world as if it were your own, but without losing the 'as if' quality . . ." (Rogers, 1961, p. 284).
2. The ability to show the client respect. The therapist's "attitude is nonevaluative, nonjudgmental, without criticism, ridicule, depreciation, or reservations. This does not mean that the counselor accepts as right, desirable, or likeable, all aspects of the client's behavior or that he agrees with or condones all his behavior . . . Yet the client is accepted for what he is, as he is" (Patterson, 1974, p. 58).
3. The ability to display genuineness in that "within the relationship he is freely and deeply himself, with his actual experiences accurately represented by his awareness of himself" (Rogers, 1957, p. 97).
4. The ability to be concrete, to engage in "the fluent, direct and complete expression of specific feelings and experiences, regardless of their emotional content" (Truax & Carkhuff, 1967, p. 32).
5. The ability to tolerate ambiguity and tentativeness (Brems, 1994).

The play therapist must also have resolved any residual issues she has relative to her own childhood experience; otherwise there is the danger of her trying to resolve those experiences through the client's therapy. This resolution is best accomplished if the therapist completes at least 6 months, and preferably more, personal therapy. During this treatment, particular attention should be paid to those childhood themes that manifest themselves in the therapist's present thoughts and behaviors. Through therapy, the play therapist should also develop self-respect and self-esteem, self-awareness, and a willingness to self-explore as well as an awareness of her personal style (Brems, 1994). In addition to receiving personal therapy, the play therapist should be supervised by a senior play therapist for at least one year. During this time, the therapist should work on discovering the way her history and personality effect and direct how she conducts play sessions, thus allowing her to make maximum use of her personal experience without her needs overriding those of her child clients.

In addition to having resolved her own childhood issues, the play therapist must be able to play. Play may be the natural medium of childhood, but adults often experience it as very foreign and awkward. Adults are not used to pretending, to physical interaction, or to acting on impulse, so it is often easy for them to distance themselves from the child's play and take an intellectual, analytic stance. While this is a useful skill when it is under the therapist's control, it can interfere by preventing the therapist from creating good corrective experiences for the child when it happens reflexively. A creative play therapist must be able to not only follow the child's play but occasionally enhance or lead the activity in the playroom.

A female therapist was just beginning to work with an 11-year-old boy, Thomas, who was very resistant to becoming involved in psychotherapy. At first they tried talking, but he soon became silent and just sat in the corner. The therapist attempted to shift to play sessions to reduce the situational pull for conversation. Although Thomas initially attended to her attempts, he soon withdrew again. After several sessions of almost complete inactivity, the therapist came up with an idea that was both interpretive in nature and very playful.

She built a wall across the playroom, using furniture to separate herself from the client. She verbalized his concerns about not wanting to interact with a "girl" and said that she could empathize with his position and she would make sure that it did not happen. Then she set a wastebasket on her side of the wall but close to where Thomas was sitting. She sat a few feet away and started wadding up sheets of paper and tossing them toward the basket. All the while she was verbalizing her desire to be good at this game and her confidence in the fact that Thomas was probably sure that she could not do it. The therapist reported during supervision that, for the first time in days, Thomas watched everything she was doing, although she said "He did sort of look like he thought I was crazy."

At first, the play therapist made every shot she attempted, but when she observed that Thomas was moving a little closer, she began occasionally shooting wide until one of the paper wads landed on his side of the divider. He jumped a little but made no move to retrieve it. Soon a large number of paper wads were on his side, and she asked him to toss them over the wall to her so that she could continue her game. Thomas casually tossed one of the papers back and then another, and because the therapist had moved very close to the wastebasket, she managed to deflect one of his throws toward it, commenting "Oh, that one almost made it in." Of course, Thomas' next throw was much closer to the basket—his involvement had begun. Initially, he threw only those wads of paper that landed on his side of the barrier and did not talk much at all. Soon, however, he was reaching over the wall to grab for papers and bragging to the therapist about his throwing skill.

The therapist continued to build the wall over several sessions, commenting on how it no longer had to be as high or as solid but that it still seemed necessary to make Thomas feel safe. The basketball game continued, with a gradually decreasing number of paper wads available so that more sharing had to occur. After about three sessions, play therapy was fully under way. This therapist had been able to use her inherent childishness to devise a strategy that allowed Thomas to keep his initial safe distance while he began exploring the possibility of entering into a working relationship with her.

ROLE OF THE ECOSYSTEMIC PLAY THERAPIST IN SESSION

As can be seen in the preceding example, the therapist's initial task is to establish a helping relationship with the child. Once the relationship has been established, the therapist provides alternative, corrective experiences for the child and promotes cognitive reorganization through the use of interpretation and problem solving. Sometimes this means leading the sessions, sometimes this means following the child. Sometimes this means being fully engaged with the child, sometimes this means taking a much more distant, observing role. Always this means working to understand the child's experience and attempting to convey that understanding back to the child either in language or action. Further, it is the play therapist's role to be constantly aware of the child's present developmental level and needs and to work within the context of those factors. The general role of the play therapist in conducting Ecosystemic Play Therapy is to work toward maximizing the child's functioning first within sessions and then in day-to-day life.

Finally, the play therapist also views herself as an advocate for the child, recognizing that by choosing to work with an individual child, she has entered into a number of systems from the child's viewpoint. In practice, the therapist sees occasional interventions in any one of the systems the child is involved in as an integral part of the child's treatment. This means that working with the child's parents, family, school, peer group, the legal system, or the health care system is all well within the play therapist's potential role. This book focuses on the implementation of individual play therapy from an ecological perspective; it does not detail the advocacy perspective that is also an essential aspect of effective work with children and their families. The delineation of the advocacy role will have to wait for future writings because it is beyond the scope of the material to be covered here.

NATURE OF THE PROCESS

Role of Play

Within the therapy, play serves many purposes. It is a medium within which various psychological and educational techniques may be employed. Children in play therapy may be learning things such as social skills, they may be receiving differential reinforcement for behavior change, or they may be provided with concrete, factual information that corrects the myths that drive their anxieties.

Play is also a vehicle for communication between the child and therapist. It allows the child to enact those things for which she does not have words. This is seen as a conscious process, the equivalent of the "show me if you cannot tell me" tactic used in interviewing sexually abused children. Similarly, the therapist can show the child things that would otherwise require language more complex than the child is capable of understanding. This type of play is based on primary symbols where pretending to drink is substituted for actually drinking (Scarlett, 1994). But the communication function of play also works on the unconscious level: The child often reveals, through her actions, thoughts and feelings of which she is totally unaware. This type of play is based on secondary symbols where pretending to drink represents the child's need for nurturance (Scarlett, 1994). This is really no different from the nonverbal communication adults engage in during essentially verbal therapies. What is different is the degree to which this may be the therapist's primary source of information about the child's intrapsychic functioning.

Play is also the vehicle for the creation of the child's corrective experience. Either the therapist or child may set up play interactions that allow the child to reexperience an event or relationship in a different way and with a more positive outcome than that of the original event. It is this aspect of play therapy that often seems underemployed in some other models of child therapy. When the child is able to re-create in play those situations over which she needs to gain mastery so as to proceed with her development, it is a marvelous process. Many children, however, have confronted such an array of destructive experiences that it seems less likely they will hit on a series of optimally corrective experiences on their own. Terr (1983) noted that the victims of the Chowchilla bus kidnapping often engaged in secret repetitive play centered on their experience of the incident for years without managing to obtain a sense of either mastery or catharsis. In these cases, the therapist can create play experiences that help the child resolve critical issues and proceed with normal development.

It is important to remember that, not withstanding the therapeutic context, play is beneficial in and of itself. From the ages of 3 to 5 play encourages children to develop their verbal and representational skills. It provides a vehicle for conflict resolution with peers and to develop empathy and moral values. From the ages of 6 to 9, role-playing becomes a forum for self-expression but this is also the time when children become aware of rules and rule making. They learn to manage competition in a controlled way. From the ages of 10 to 12 children engage in more group play and learn social skills while just enjoying themselves and relaxing (Barasch, 1999). "The process of playing itself is consolidating and integrative; it provides children with the resources to make sense of emotional experiences on their own. It is only after such consolidations take place that verbal interpretations of repressed ideas or conflicts [such as those used in therapy] can be meaningful to the child" (Slade, 1994, p. 82).

Curative Elements

Corrective Experience

Since the publication of the first edition of the Primer, there has been a continual increase in the emphasis placed on the critical and central role of corrective experiences in the therapy process. "In a survey of 12 leading therapists representing different schools of thought, the corrective experience was uniformly described as 'essential,' 'crucial,' 'basic,' and 'critical' to the change process" (Goldfried, 1982). But what, exactly, are corrective experiences? In this context, they are defined as one of two types of events that trigger essential shifts in the child's thinking. On the one hand, the therapist may *behave* in ways that disconfirm the child's underlying pathogenic beliefs (Shirk, 1998). That is something the therapist does causes the child to think differently about her interactions and, therefore, to begin to behave differently. On the other hand, the therapist may *provide* the child with new information or an alternate understanding of past events that causes the same shift in the child's thinking and subsequent behavior. Corrective experiences involve a certain amount of both retrospective and prospective problem solving. The child learns what went wrong in the past and how to use this information to prevent the same problems in the future. Without corrective experiences, the activities in the play therapy session become therapeutic play at best and repetitions of the child's dysfunctional past at worst. The therapist must be able to conceptualize the type of experiences that will foster the correction of those of the child's:

past experience, present assumptions about the workings of the world, patterns of behavior and social interaction, and, finally, the child's developmental lags.

This notion of corrective experience is not unique to play therapy; it has been framed variously by different authors. Certainly, Theraplay (Jernberg, 1979; Jernberg & Booth, 1999) is a primarily experiential mode of treatment. But perhaps the best description of the importance of the experiential component of child psychotherapy was presented by Levin (1985):

> The corrective developmental experience is an interactional rather than intrapsychic model of treatment and is, therefore, applied most rationally at that point in the life cycle where important psychical processes are negotiated through actual exchange within a dynamic, mutually regulated interactional system. What is "corrective," however, is not limited to the emotional or affective aspects of interaction, which, after all, constitute only one developmental line. . . . Corrective experience as a meaningful concept applied to the treatment of early childhood psychopathology implies the facilitation of simultaneous changes across multiple developmental lines (affective, cognitive, physical-motor, social, linguistic, and so on) within a context of gradually shifting, forward moving interactional tasks (Sander, 1983). Thus, I have chosen corrective developmental experience to designate a model of treatment in which the confirmation and disconfirmation of experience and expectation applies to the current and ongoing organization, disorganization, and reorganization of experience as it unfolds within a complex interactional system of which the therapist is but one formative element. While recognizing the influence of the child's past on the child's present, the corrective developmental experience is continuous and coterminous with the child's current developmental experience and its respective tasks and issues. (p. 301)

In spite of the central role of corrective experiences these are only of value to the child client if they happen in a certain context. As noted in the discussion of the therapist's role in conducting play therapy, three elements are essential to the production of therapeutic change. First, the therapist creates the relationship or setting in which the work of the therapy is to take place. The therapist must engage the child. "We should point out that even . . . novice therapists' patterns of participation, taken at a very abstract level include . . . 3 factors: information seeking, technical work (interpretation, confrontation) and the provision of affirming encouragement—perhaps the triadic heart of therapeutic engagement (Mook, 1982 as discussed in Shirk & Russell, 1996, p. 120). Only then can the therapist engage in the work of providing the child with a new understanding of her problem, through the creation of corrective experiences in the playroom, through verbal processing, or, preferably, by pairing the two methods. However, even the establishment of this new understanding of the problem and the knowledge that choices exist may not, in and of itself, provide the impetus for behavior change. The therapy must also provide experiences, either in reality or in fantasy, that allow the client to sense the value of making choices and instituting change. If at all possible, the therapy should also provide those experiences that allow the child to experiment with new behaviors in her relationship with the therapist.

The Relationship

The importance of the existence of a relationship between the child and the therapist is emphasized in every form of play therapy. Even the most clinically behavioral therapist will acknowledge behavioral procedures work best when the child is positively engaged with the therapist. In spite of this much of the play therapy literature tends to portray a false dichotomy between the child-centered therapists and virtually everyone else. The sense conveyed is that only child-centered therapists really value the child and their relationship with that child. This view comes about largely because child-centered therapy posits the relationship as the central curative element of the therapy. This should not minimize the value placed on the relationship within other play therapy modalities and certainly not within Ecosystemic Play Therapy.

A positive relationship between the therapist and child is a key factor in the corrective experience. "In essence, the therapeutic relationship provides an opportunity for constructing new expectations about how significant others will respond to the self. Therapist's responses to the child that are discrepant from well-developed expectations provide enacted evidence that could potentially disconfirm problematic interpersonal schemata" (Shirk, 1998, p. 12). The very nature of the therapist-child relationship becomes one aspect of the corrective experience. Conceptualized as part of the change process the therapist-child relationship serves three functions.

First, the relationship provides a form of support for the child. The support allows the child to reappraise stressful situations outside the therapy differently while developing and maintaining self-esteem. In this context, it is very important for the therapist to balance warmth and control. This is entirely consistent with the Theraplay approach where the degree of control exerted by the therapist within the context of a warm and fun relationship depends on the developmental level and psychopathology of the child. Child-centered approaches that focus on warmth may be more suitable for young children who are more dependent on adult attention while older children may need to focus on developing increased competence in order to build self-esteem (Shirk, 1998).

Support also serves as scaffolding on which the child makes developmental advances. The therapist moderates the stress the child is experiencing so as to allow a match between the external stimulus and the child's capacity to cope. Further, the support provides a social context for learning higher order social perspective taking and problem solving. The therapist provides the child with support and feedback the child uses to make therapeutic gains.

Second, the relationship serves as the basis for a working alliance. A positive relationship between therapist and child is associated with the child becoming more involved in the work of therapy, specifically in disclosing problems and discussing feelings (Shirk & Saiz, 1992). In the context of the relationship it is easier for the child to acknowledge problems. It is important to remember, however, that the focus should be on building a helping relationship not just a positive relationship (Shirk, 1998). The therapist and child will have a relationship unlike any others in the child's life and the central purpose of their interaction should always be to help the child.

Last, the development, maintenance and successful use of the relationship is a therapeutic technique in and of itself. That is the therapist conceptualizes all aspects of the relationship as potential corrective experiences. Because people tend to interpret new experiences in ways consistent with their faulty schema (Baldwin, 1992; Safran, 1990a, 1990b) and those schema are quite stable (Main, Kaplan, & Cassidy, 1985; Safran, 1990a, 1990b) simple corrective experiences may not be sufficient. There is some indication in the research that change can only occur when the individual is aware of the problematic schema (Kiesler, 1988; Weiss, Sampson, & The Mt. Zion Psychotherapy Research Group, 1986) meaning that the cognitive work of interpretation and problem solving are still necessary parts of the treatment no matter how positive the therapist-child relationship.

Interventions Matched to Underlying Dynamics of the Problem

Typically, the literature suggests matching "therapeutic orientation (e.g., psychoanalytic or cognitive-behavioral) to diagnostic category (e.g., dysthymia or conduct disorder). Alternatively, matching change process and case formulation of pathogenic process" (Shirk & Russell, 1996) seems a more promising and more effective therapeutic strategy. This is true because the behaviors in which therapists engage in session is typically not as different as differences in theoretical orientation would lead one to believe. For this reason, strong correlations between positive outcomes and any one particular theoretical model of therapy or play therapy. Instead, it seems more logical to conceptualize the underlying cause of the child's difficulties and then to implement interventions specifically focused on those causes.

Shirk and Russell (1996) proposed six basic case formulations, that is, ways of conceptualizing the nature of the problems the child is experiencing. They proceed to match these to 12 psychotherapy change processes:

Linkages between Case Formulations and Change Processes

Basic Case Formulation	Associated Change Process
Internal conflict	*Insight/interpretation* Emotional experiencing
Ego deficit	*Supportive scaffolding* Symbolic Exchange
Cognitive skill deficit	*Skill development* Affective education
Cognitive distortion	*Schema transformation* Corrective relationship
Low self-esteem	*Interpersonal validation/support* Skill development
Emotional interference	*Emotional regulation* Emotional experiencing or abreaction

Note: Italic change processes represent the primary methods of intervention (Shirk & Russell, 1996, p. 327). Used with permission.

Curative Elements of the Therapist's Behavior

As mentioned previously, the role of the ecosystemic play therapist is to develop a helping relationship with the child, to create the corrective experiences the child needs, to engage the child in the cognitive work of understanding the present problems, to engage in problem solving so as to lessen the impact of future problems, and to reinforce change as it occurs.

To create the relationship, the ecosystemic play therapist must be able to create for the child those therapist-offered conditions discussed previously: empathy, genuineness, and warmth (Rogers, 1942, 1951). The creation of the relationship or setting in which the therapeutic work is to take place must begin with the intake session and continue through termination. The following list of therapist behaviors that create and maintain the therapeutic setting is culled from the lists proposed by Axline, Jernberg, and Glasser and detailed in Chapter Two. The therapist:

1. Develops a warm, friendly relationship with the child. Good rapport should be established as soon as possible.
2. Accepts the child exactly as he or she is.
3. Establishes a feeling of permissiveness in the relationship so that the child feels free to express his or her feelings completely (Points 1 to 3, Axline, 1947, p. 73).
4. Is responsive and empathic.
5. Places intensive and exclusive focus on the child.
6. Is responsive to cues given him by the child.

7. Keeps the sessions spontaneous, flexible, and full of happy surprises.
8. Structures the session so that the times, places, and persons are clearly defined.
9. Attempts to keep the session cheerful, optimistic, positive, and health-oriented.
10. Conducts his sessions without regard to whether the child "likes" him.
11. Curtails and prevents excessive anxiety or motoric hyperactivity.
12. Attends to physical hurts (Points 4 to 12, Jernberg, 1979, pp. 48–49).
13. Relates to (the child as himself), not as a transference figure (Glasser, 1975, p. 54).

The creation and maintenance of the therapy setting are necessary but not sufficient conditions for therapeutic change. That is, the setting is not curative in and of itself but provides the situation in which the work of the therapy can take place (Tuma & Sobotka, 1983). The effective therapist must therefore be able to work while maintaining the setting, the work in this case being the creation of corrective experiences and the offering of verbalizations that help the child better understand her thoughts and feelings and their relationship to her behavior. Essentially, the therapist must behave in such a way that the patient feels safe enough to give up pathogenic adaptations (Rappoport, 1996). Following is a list of therapist behaviors culled from the work of Axline, Jernberg, and Glasser that describe what the therapist must do to create corrective experiences for the child. The therapist:

1. Establishes those limitations necessary to anchor the therapy in the world of reality and to make the child aware of his responsibility in the relationship (Axline, 1947, p. 74).
2. Is in charge of the sessions at all times (Robertiello, 1975, p. 12).
3. Uses every opportunity for making physical contact with the child.
4. Insists unwaveringly on eye contact.
5. Initiates, rather than reacts to, the child's behaviors, anticipating the child's resistant maneuvers and acting before, not after, they are set in motion.
6. Uses every opportunity to differentiate himself from the child.
7. Uses every opportunity to help the child see himself as unique, special, separate, and outstanding.
8. Uses himself as the primary playroom object.
9. Sees to it that within each session there are many different segments, each one having a beginning, middle, and an end.
10. Offers some minimal frustration, challenge, and discomfort.

11. Uses paradoxical methods when appropriate.
12. Makes his insistent presence felt throughout the duration of a child's temper tantrum.
13. When at a loss for ideas, incorporates the child's body movements into his repertoire (Points 2 to 13, Jernberg, 1979, pp. 48–49).
14. Requires that the child becomes involved in the therapy as a person who is responsible for his behavior.
15. Emphasizes the morality of behavior by facing the issue of right and wrong which, in turn, solidifies the therapeutic relationship.
16. Teaches children better ways to fulfill their needs. The therapy will not be maintained unless the patient is helped to find more satisfactory patterns of behavior (Points 13 to 16, adapted from Glasser, 1975, p. 54).

The range of experiences a child may encounter in her life is virtually unlimited, and the impact of each experience may be positive or negative, depending on assorted contiguous variables. For example, not every child experiences the death of a parent in the same way. For some children, the death is a devastating event that becomes the point around which many of their assumptions about the world are organized. Yet other children may feel relieved, in spite of their grief and guilt, that a tyrannical parent is gone, never to return. A child's reaction is also mediated by her developmental level to the degree it affects the way she understands the event, the available support system, the reaction of that system to the event, and so on. Unfortunately, most of the contiguous variables are out of the control of any one individual, much less the child, and thus the impact of a given life situation may be devastating in spite of what the child or those around her do at the time. If a child is born with a neurological impairment that affects her ability to respond to her caretakers in a consistent manner, it is likely that she will display deficient interpersonal attachments at some point later in life no matter how heroic the efforts of the mother during the child's infancy. Certainly, it may be possible to remediate some of her early experience when the child's development has proceeded to a point that allows for more consistent responses, but until then, the people in the environment may need to learn rather specialized patterns of stimulating and responding to this child.

In the same way that the child's range of life experiences is virtually unlimited, so too the range of experiences to which a child may be exposed in the context of her treatment is vast, and again, the impact of each depends on a number of contiguous variables. The therapist has two advantages in regulating the impact of the child's in-session experiences when compared to the ability of other people in the child's life to regulate the impact of out-of-session experiences. One advantage is the therapist's training in models that allow her to predict the way a given event will interact with the child's developmental level and produce a specific set of outcomes.

A therapist should know that the impact of a parental divorce on a child will be very different if it happens when the child is 2 years old rather than 5 or 15 years old. The therapist's other advantage is the ability to control in-session events much better than most out-of-session events can be controlled. Most notably, the therapist holds her needs and feelings in abeyance in order to make the child's needs and feelings primary in a way that would be unrealistic and unhealthy on a round-the-clock basis in the real world.

To take advantage of these two factors, the therapist must have ready access to a knowledge base that allows for the developmental conceptualization of the impact of the child's experience, a recognition of her ability to control the child's sessions, and a willingness to exert such control when it is in the child's best interest. Chapter Four presented the theoretical basis for understanding the interaction of the child's experience and her developmental level. In Part III a model is presented that the play therapist can use to conceptualize the impact of various client/therapist interactions so she can plan their use in sessions.

David was a 6-year-old child who had already been in therapy for a year in an attempt to resolve his rather pronounced depression. Whenever David became frustrated, he became appropriately angry but never directed the anger outward. Instead, he became quite self-destructive. A series of unfortunate accidents in David's life had led him to believe that he had no choice but to withhold his anger or risk being abandoned.

After a full year, David still rarely showed any signs of being angry when he became frustrated with limits that were set; instead, he became very quiet and sad. Reflections of his anger and fear of abandonment coupled with reassurance that the therapist could withstand anger did little to change David's style. He understood the therapist's statements, he was just too afraid to try anything different. Finally, in one session, during which many limits had been set, the therapist said "I'm sure you must be sick and tired of hearing me say no and that it makes you very angry. You know you cannot hit me, but you can hit the Bobo doll." At that point David glanced at the doll and smiled but made no move to approach it. The therapist then took David by his hands, led him over to the doll, and proceeded to hit the doll with David's hands while saying, in a childish voice, "I'm so tired of never getting to do what I want. You are such a mean and rotten person. Sometimes I just want to beat you up even though I know that isn't OK." David then began laughing and enthusiastically hit the doll.

What followed were numerous sessions in which David allowed himself to express his rage at both the therapist and others in his life by attacking various figures in the playroom. Often, however, he was still so self-conscious about his anger that he would have the therapist look the other way or close his eyes before expressing himself. Much later in his treatment, David was able to choose to express anger directly at the therapist, albeit in a rather indirect way: He would get a toy gun that shot rubber darts and shoot them at the ceiling over the therapist so that the darts would drop onto the therapist's head. He repeated this behavior several times with the therapist, who openly reflected how much better David seemed to feel now that he had found a way to be angry at the therapist. Additionally, the therapist repeated a reassurance that David had heard many times, namely, that no matter how intense, David's anger would never drive the therapist away.

The turning point in David's therapy seems to have been the point at which the therapist pushed David into breaking the pattern of his response to anger. David was not only encouraged to be angry but initially to have fun doing so. Up until that point David had not been able to use his awareness of his choices to make changes in his behavior. The activity the therapist created helped him experience a tiny bit of acting out that was not followed by abandonment, and this experience decreased David's anxiety to a point where he could allow himself to express negative emotions more directly.

As noted in the previous example, the therapist must be willing and able to be directive and controlling as needed to promote the child's progress and development in the context of creating corrective experiences. The degree of structure should be related to the type of pathology, skills deficit problems and developmental lags require more structure (Shirk, 1998). Very few practitioners of play therapy would argue against this valuing of the child's experience in therapy. But many would argue against the degree of control over these experiences that the play therapist assumed. Ecosystemic Play Therapy requires that the therapist maintain control of the direction and content of the therapy. This does not mean that the therapist continually forces the child to engage in specific activities or talk about certain content material. And it certainly does not mean that the therapist acts in a manner that overrides the child's needs at any given point. It does mean that the therapist is willing to override the child's behavior when she understands that the behavior actually interferes with the child's needs being met. A play therapist would be able to restrain a child in spite of the child's screams of protest if the therapist understood that the child needed to be contained at that time. This understanding arises out of a solid clinical formulation based on the theoretical concepts presented in Chapters Two and Four.

This stance runs counter to the view of many humanistic play therapists. The following analogy to describe the play therapy process has been used by a therapist who considers himself humanistic. The child who comes to play therapy is like a seed. The therapist creates an environment that serves as the soil in which the seed can grow, and he provides interactions which act as the water and fertilizer to promote growth; but he cannot force the seed to grow any faster than it is able. In fact, he cannot force it to begin to grow at all. Having created the nurturing environment, the humanistic play therapist can only wait for the child's internal, growth-promoting forces to become active. He noted that if the therapist attempted to force the child-seedling to grow faster or in a particular direction, he would irreparably harm it. The analogy emphasizes the importance of the role of the child's internal processes in promoting her own health within play therapy and structures the role of the play therapist as the facilitator of that growth.

The same type of analogy could be used to conceptualize the roles of the child and therapist in Ecosystemic Play Therapy. The child is viewed not as a seed upon entry into therapy but as a plant that has been growing for a number of years. The child-plant comes to the therapist having lived in an environment that has affected its health and pattern of growth. The child-plant has been stunted, misshapen, traumatized, or neglected. The therapist will seek to provide new soil for this plant and to water and fertilize it each week. But she will also shape its growth. She may prune back portions of the plant which have grown wild and which use so much energy that they threaten the health of the main portion of the plant. She may even trim back new growth in some areas to foster the more even and healthier growth of the entire plant. And, most importantly, she will work with others in the child-plant's environment in the hopes of ensuring that the growth which occurs in session is appropriately maintained between sessions.

This analogy notes that the energy for growth and certain basic characteristics belong to, and originate within, the child. Those are things the play therapist tries to work with, not against. But the analogy also notes that the direction of the child's growth and to some extent the rate of growth are responsibilities that the therapist must accept. The more dysfunctional the child and the lower the child's developmental level, the more prominent the therapist's responsibilities.

While creating corrective experiences for the child in session it is also important for the therapist to work with the child's caretakers to ensure that these experiences are also carried out in the child's natural environment.

In the psychotherapy of children, particularly in the early years of life, the important experiential moments are not long gone and the original "cast" is, in most cases, still available. By working psychotherapeutically with the caregiving parents at the same time as the child, we are, in effect, correcting certain aspects of the child's developmental experience at their sources, in the original and ongoing caregiver-child interaction. This is the level at which the reorganization of recognition-expectation-response patterns is most essential if the child's reappraisal of possibilities for interactional relatedness in the therapeutic situation is to be generalized to the family system as well. Thus, if there are therapeutic manipulations in the corrective developmental experience, they are undertaken through the caregiver and caregiving family in helping family members to observe, understand, and modify patterns of interaction that are counterproductive to the child's ongoing development. Even here, however, I do not believe that the process of intervention is tantamount to manipulation. In many instances, the most effective and enduring changes in caregiving attunement and responsiveness come from insight into the sources of faulty family interaction in the caregiver's own developmental experience a generation earlier, rather than from teaching, advice or suggestion (though these may be needed in situations where the parents simply do not know how to do some things). Optimally, through the consolidation of new interactional (and, in some cases, intrapsychic) structures and the development of insight into current patterns of interaction, the caregiver's adaptive and parenting resources will expand to the point where both the therapeutic and the actual caregiving environments provide comparable and compatible growth-promoting developmental experiences for the child. (Levin, 1985, p. 305)

Although much of what a child acquires in therapy will come out of the corrective experiences she has in session, changes will also be produced by the verbal and cognitive work completed during the session. In fact, what most effective therapy has in common is that it gives clients an opportunity to come to a new understanding of their situation and to therefore experience themselves as having response choices. Research with adult clients suggests that they find shifts in their understanding of their problems to be uniquely therapeutic, apparently irrespective of the theoretical framework the therapist uses (Elliott, 1984).

Within Ecosystemic Play Therapy, arriving at a new understanding of their situation or problem is merely the first step in a problem solving process that will result in behavior change and improved functioning, that is the improved ability to get one's needs met effectively and appropriately. In this text the term cognitive processing or processing an event in therapy are synonymous with the concept of problem solving. That is the child first comes to define his internal schemata (beliefs about the problem) differently. Then the child develops an understanding of the impact of the problem and a range of potential solutions. The child then selects one or more of these solutions and implements it. Having followed through on the new behavior the child then evaluates the outcome and determines whether to use that behavior again in the future or to try another alternative.

It is relatively easy to see how problem solving can be applied to present tense problems the child is experiencing but how does it apply to the therapeutic processing of events in the child's past? Let's say a child's parents divorced when he was 5 and the child felt terribly responsible at the time and tried to manage these feelings by becoming overcontrolled and adultlike. At this point, the child defines his problem not as having anything to do with the divorce as related to the fact that other children do not like him. In response to feeling hurt and rejected he engages in even more controlling behavior with his peers driving them further away. The goal of therapeutic processing is to help the child identify the problem as unresolved feelings of helplessness relative to the divorce that are not being effectively addressed by his controlling behavior with his peers. He must then brainstorm ways to address ongoing feelings of responsibility for the divorce preferably within his interactions with his parents rather than his peers. He must also develop strategies for interacting with peers in a noncontrolling way so that his needs for peer affiliation can be met. He might even go so far as to seek out peers for support in managing his negative feelings about the divorce. Having done this, the event has been very effectively processed.

The critical role of problem solving strategies in play therapy are briefly addressed in Chapter Seven and then again in Chapter Nine.

Usually, children who come to therapy have lived within the bounds of a world created by their thoughts, feelings, and past experiences which is so confining that they no longer perceive themselves as having any power to change their circumstance. Their lives have come to control them, and they are without options. The therapist strives to produce insight in the child which, in this case, means an understanding of the cause and nature of the child's pathogenic adaptations (Rappoport, 1996). The importance of pairing cognitive processing with experience in the child's sessions cannot be overemphasized. Most of the cognitive work will be accomplished through the therapist's use of interpretation. (Chapter Nine presents a conceptual framework for the development and delivery of interpretations.) The child's cognitive processing of in-session experience is also fostered when the therapist:

1. Is alert to recognize the feelings the child is expressing and reflects those feelings back in such a manner that the child gains insight into his behavior (Axline, 1947, p. 73).
2. Uses the child's moods and feelings to help the child differentiate himself and label his feelings (Jernberg, 1979, p. 49).
3. Teaches children better ways to fulfill their needs. The therapy will not be maintained unless the patient is helped to find more satisfactory patterns of behavior (Adapted from Glasser, 1975, p. 54).

The therapist reinforces changes the child makes. This may be done through direct reinforcement techniques such as providing the child with points, stars or special privileges in session. The therapist should consistently use verbal reinforcement which, might be offered directly to the child or delivered in comments made to the child's caregivers while the child is present. The therapist may also point out for the child positive outcomes made possible by the child's change in behavior. This is especially important when the child is trying a new behavior and the changes in the environment are small. Say a child who has been using tantrums to get her way suddenly asks her mother for something quite politely. In spite of the change in strategy the mother still denies the request. The child is likely to use this to demonstrate to the therapist the usefulness of tantrums over politeness. The therapist must be quick to point out that while she didn't get what she was requesting she also didn't get punished for the tantrum so that some degree of improvement was achieved. In this type of situation it will also be important for the therapist to work with the parent to ensure that the child's attempts at behavior change are indeed rewarded at some point.

COURSE OF TREATMENT

The treatment phases are the focus of the next few chapters. Chapter Six and Seven cover the intake and pretreatment assessment process used in Ecosystemic Play Therapy. Chapters Eight through Twelve cover the ecosystemic treatment process itself and Chapter Thirteen discusses termination.

PART III

The Course of Individual Play Therapy

The remainder of the book is written in the second person so as to make it read more like a manual for the conduct of play therapy rather than a theoretical text, consistent with the author's goal of writing a work that teaches the reader how to do play therapy. Many books that provide a theoretical rationale for a given approach to child therapy are available, but very few integrate theory and practice, and still fewer focus on practice. The goal of the remainder of this volume is to provide a practical introduction to the implementation and conduct of play therapy.

The next six chapters take the reader through the process of individual play therapy from beginning to end. The discussion is organized in line with the six treatment phases reported in the Theraplay literature: introduction, exploration, tentative acceptance, negative reaction, growing and trusting, and termination. The introduction phase includes the intake and assessment processes discussed in Chapters Six and Seven, respectively. This is the time when the child is introduced to the problems to be addressed, is familiarized with the nature of the work to follow, and is initially exposed to the therapist's personal style. The phases of exploration, tentative acceptance, and negative reaction are grouped under the general heading of the beginning of treatment in Chapter Eight. The growing and trusting phase is the longest one and the one in which the bulk of the therapeutic work takes place. This phase and the therapeutic strategies needed to conduct the work of play therapy are presented in Chapters Nine, Ten, and Eleven. Collateral work is the term used to refer to any work in which the therapist engages with people in the child's ecosystem other than the child herself. Strategies for conducting collateral work over the entire course of the child's treatment are presented in Chapter Twelve. Termination, the last phase of the treatment process, is discussed in Chapter Thirteen.

The didactic information in Part III is heavily illustrated with case examples. Most of these examples are self-contained; however, two cases are presented in segments across Chapters Six through Thirteen. That is, the intake material is presented in Chapter Six, the assessment material in Chapter Seven, the information on the beginning of treatment in Chapter Eight, the process of the therapy in Chapters Nine, Ten, and Eleven, the collateral work in Chapter Twelve, and the termination information in Chapter Thirteen. Because it may be difficult for some readers to get a real flavor for these cases due to their fragmentation across chapters, two additional cases are presented in their entirety in Chapter Fourteen. Of the four full cases presented either across chapters or within Chapter Fourteen, two present very specific examples of short-term treatment including individual session plans while the other two present a more general picture of two long-term cases.

CHAPTER SIX

The Intake Process

Play therapy begins the first time the client or, in the case of a child, his caretaker, makes contact with you or your representative. Usually this first contact is by telephone and consists of an inquiry regarding some aspect of treatment or a request for an appointment. The caretaker has no doubt gone through a great deal to get to the point of making this call, and the response received may be critical in determining whether or not treatment for the child is pursued. Many clients are lost following the first contact, and still more following the first visit. Those who make it past those points often last only a few sessions before they drop out. Yet many become successfully involved in treatment and continue whether treatment takes weeks, months, or years until all are satisfied with the outcome. What differentiates those clients who continue past the first few contacts? There are client-related variables over which you have no control. Finances may be a problem or the family system may simply not be able to muster the emotional resources necessary to begin an endeavor such as therapy at this time. However, many other variables are under your control. In describing the stages of the intake process, the potential impact of your behavior on the client's likelihood of following through with treatment is discussed.

REFERRAL CONTACT

The initial interaction in the intake process is usually a telephone contact between the child's caretaker and yourself. For the purpose of this discussion, we assume that the caretaker is, in most cases, one of the child's parents. Policies regarding the extent of the information to be gathered during the initial phone contact vary from practitioner to practitioner and from agency to agency. Some practitioners suggest obtaining virtually all the demographic information and history, extending this first contact to considerable length.

The format presented here describes a shorter and less comprehensive initial contact that focuses on obtaining the following information: basic demographic information; (names of family members, home and work addresses and phone numbers) and a description only of the presenting problem, not the history. The latter information is a difficult portion of the contact to control because it tends to be very lengthy. Throughout the telephone contact, you should remember to consistently label and reflect the parent's affect as the parent talks about the child's problem so as to establish rapport while setting the pattern for subsequent interactions. Additionally, at this time you should convey to the client certain basic information regarding policies, practices, and fees. This might include available appointment times, the format of the first few sessions, and payment policies.

Even something as mundane as obtaining demographic information may affect the likelihood that the parent will follow through with keeping the first appointment. Although a computer can take the parent's name and address and set up an appointment time, it is unlikely that very many people will take their child to a therapist who has a computer answering the phone. It is critical that the basis for a therapeutic alliance or working relationship be developed from the outset. One way of doing this is to connect with the parent's affect. The idea here is not to sympathize with the client, to join in the client's pain, but to convey a genuine understanding of the difficulty of the situation so as to enhance the client's belief that you will be able to help the parent find a solution. To do this, you must be able, at some point, to restate the affects and motives that have driven the parent to seek treatment for the child.

Initially, parents tend to claim altruism as their primary motivation—after all, their child is having problems and they want his suffering to stop. Underlying this child-based motive the parents are often experiencing powerful negative emotions of their own. For some parents, it is fear that they are failing as parents, that their child is displaying behavior, thoughts, or emotions that are "bad" and against which they feel helpless. Often this helplessness generates sadness, that jeopardizes the parents' ability to follow through with treatment because it saps their energy. For other parents, their child is causing them problems they want stopped immediately. They are angry, embarrassed, or both. Their child is misbehaving in school or at home, and they have tried everything to no avail. Feelings of helplessness are in place, but in this case the parents are angry, not sad. These parents are often on the verge of wanting to have their children live elsewhere, if only temporarily.

> Mrs. Arnold called a therapist requesting information about residential treatment centers that would admit her daughter, Jennifer, 9 years old. The girl, Mrs. Arnold stated, was completely out of control. The therapist reflected the anger in Mrs. Arnold's voice, noting her apparent exasperation. She responded immediately by saying that she had indeed had enough. Jennifer was making her miserable and threatening to destroy her marriage and

her family. As she and the therapist discussed the difficulty of placing a child in that particular geographical area, Mrs. Arnold began to ask what type of treatment they would implement for her daughter in such a place. The therapist presented some basic behavioral strategies and asked if Mrs. Arnold had tried any of them at home. Mrs. Arnold stated that she had but that she had such difficulty with basic behavior management that she soon gave up. The therapist suggested that while exploring possible placements they might work on developing some behavior management strategies that Mrs. Arnold could use at home. Mrs. Arnold began to protest, saying that nothing worked. At this point, the therapist empathized and reflected Mrs. Arnold's feelings of helplessness and discouragement. Mrs. Arnold readily admitted these feelings and began to talk about all the things she had tried with her daughter and failed to implement successfully. This gave the therapist an opening to reflect her feelings about failing as a parent and her desire to find someone who could make it right even if it meant parenting her daughter for her. At this point, Mrs. Arnold began to cry and for the first time requested more immediate help, saying that maybe it would be possible to avoid placing her daughter.

Based on this mother's initial request, a list of referrals would have sufficed. However, empathizing with and reflecting her anger, frustration, and pain led her to pursue less drastic means of altering her situation. She successfully initiated and completed treatment for her daughter with collateral sessions of her own.

Having identified the emotion or motivation that has pushed the parent into making the initial contact, you must then go on to provide the parent with some sense that the problem, and in turn her feelings, can be addressed. This does not mean that you should promise a cure—nothing in this world comes with an absolute guarantee, least of all play therapy—but the parent must feel that you believe the situation can be improved or, again, the parent will have little motivation to follow through with treatment.

Often the parent's pain during this first contact can seem almost overwhelming. The parent, the child, and the family have probably been experiencing discomfort for some time, and their desire for immediate relief may be expressed through some fairly demanding behavior. Therapists tend to get drawn into taking care of the parent at this point, frequently to no one's advantage.

One factor motivating these attempts to help the parent is the rescue fantasy most of those who enter the helping professions hold dear. Certainly, most therapists go into this business to help people, and not doing as much as possible at any given point tends to threaten their benevolent and altruistic self-image.

A second factor motivating some therapists' attempts to help the parent is a belief that a demonstration of skill will motivate the parent to pursue further treatment. Often the pull to take care of the parent and the parent's pain results in the therapist providing rather extensive advice, especially if the presenting problem is a fairly straightforward, behavioral one. Unfortunately, this approach may actually solve the immediate problem and keep the parents from following through with necessary treatment.

Say, for example, that a mother calls and, among other things, mentions that her child is encopretic. By the end of the phone call, the parent has agreed to come for an intake session but asks, quite insistently, what can be done in the meantime. As this mother seems particularly competent, you mention a book on encopresis and very briefly outline a few simple steps to implement over the next few days. The parent never comes to the intake session. During a follow-up phone call, the mother says that the encopresis has indeed cleared and that although her child is still painfully shy and quiet, she is sure he will grow out of this and does not feel that treatment is indicated at this time. In response, there is little you can do other than to let the mother know that you will be available should she need you in the future.

This is not meant to disparage either telephone hotlines or consultation services that provide parents with information regarding childcare, behavior management, or other parenting advice. These services certainly have a place and can be very helpful in addressing some of the questions facing new parents. In addition, some of these hotlines focus on child abuse prevention and serve an excellent crisis intervention function. You should be wary, however, of the parent who demands a quick fix. There is a fine line to be walked with such a parent. You will want to provide the parent with enough supplies to encourage a return visit but not so many that the parent feels satiated and sees no need to complete treatment. Such a parent is often characterized by a tendency to put personal needs ahead of those of the child. Usually, the parent is really seeking treatment to address her problems and is less interested in the child's distress.

Finally, reality forces us to address those times when the problem the parent is calling about is so immediate that something must be done. In these cases, the principles of crisis intervention should form the basis of your response. These cases may involve a suicidal or dangerously psychotic child, or they may involve cases where the family is so stressed by a child that there is a real risk of imminent child abuse.

A complete discussion of crisis intervention is not within the scope of this book, however, we briefly review the basic principles used to stem the crisis and establish the basis for a subsequent working relationship using a case to illustrate.

CRISIS INTERVENTION

Mrs. Jones called her nephew's therapist late one Friday afternoon and stated that the therapist must do something about her 4-year-old niece immediately or she was sure she would abuse the child. The niece was one of four of Mrs. Jones' brother's children whom she had taken in when her brother abandoned them. The therapist worked at a residential treatment center at the time and was the caseworker for Mrs. Jones' oldest nephew. The therapist knew from the family history that the 4-year-old had severe pica and was possibly psychotic. The therapist also knew that the woman had two children of her own and that abuse had occurred in the home in the past.

Step 1: Identify the Immediate Stressor

The therapist asked Mrs. Jones to tell him what was happening at the moment. She said that she could not cope with the child's pica anymore, that it was disgusting. In fact, the child had just eaten several bugs and had attempted to eat her feces.

Step 2: Join with the Client

The therapist accomplished this step relatively easily by empathizing with the level of hypervigilance that living with this child required. When Mrs. Jones agreed, the therapist added that it must be especially difficult with four other children in the apartment. Mrs. Jones again agreed. The therapist then identified the additional stress it must cause her to have a husband who was unable to assist with the child care. (Several caseworkers in the past had noted that the husband appeared to be a paranoid schizophrenic with delusions of grandeur centered on his being a physicist whose time was spent studying discarded computer printouts while not holding a job.) In spite of the fact that she had never talked about her husband before, the stress of the crisis eased Mrs. Jones' admission that he was just like having another child who required her care.

Step 3: Establish Your Authority as Someone Able to Address the Problem

Having identified that Mrs. Jones was feeling completely overwhelmed and needed respite from her situation, the therapist asked if she had contacted Child Protective Services (CPS). Mrs. Jones said she had called them but had been told that if she was sufficiently under control to call CPS for help, she was certainly under sufficient control to not abuse her child. One should not necessarily blame CPS for their response—it was late, it was Friday, and Mrs. Jones sounded very rational, even in a crisis. This particular caseworker was also unaware that Mrs. Jones had abused the children in the past.

At this point, the therapist took a rather authoritarian stance. He asked if Mrs. Jones knew where the CPS office was located. She said that she did. He then instructed her to pack a bag for her niece and take her to the CPS office and leave her there. She was aghast; surely they would arrest her. She could not abandon this child and not suffer consequences. The therapist assured her that he would call ahead and inform CPS of the level of the crisis and that Mrs. Jones would be able to leave the child there without trouble. She remained unconvinced. The therapist talked about the legal mandate of CPS to protect children and assist families. He assured her that if all else failed, she could leave the child there without letting anyone see her do it. He further assured her that if there were problems, he would speak on her behalf. In other words, the therapist established himself as having the authority to give her permission to abandon this child, having recognized the impossibility of the situation.

Step 4: Gather Additional Information

Now that Mrs. Jones had a way out of the crisis, she was somewhat calmer, and she and the therapist began discussing strategies for protecting the child from consuming anything else. She talked about having the older children rotate through an observation schedule. She talked about keeping the child in her room if necessary. And she talked about ways she might get out of the apartment for a little while. The therapist also suggested that they plan to have the child evaluated by a psychiatrist as soon as possible to determine an appropriate treatment strategy. The therapist assured her that he would call CPS immediately and hung up.

Although CPS was not thrilled to hear from the therapist, they did assure him that they could place the child on an emergency basis if Mrs. Jones contacted them at any point during the weekend. When the therapist called Mrs. Jones back, she had calmed down considerably and felt she could make it through the weekend if a psychiatric evaluation could be arranged for early the following week. The therapist said that he would work on it and call her on Monday.

Step 5: Develop a Long-Term Treatment Plan

When the therapist called back on Monday, he had arranged for the niece to visit a child psychiatrist. Following the visit, it was determined that the child required residential care. Mrs. Jones admitted that she could no longer care for this child and that she wanted to release her for adoption. The outcome is not a happy one, but it saved the child from potentially serious abuse and allowed her to receive the treatment she so desperately needed.

An Alternative Intervention

Another type of crisis intervention interview meant to be used with children is called a *Life Space Intervention* (Wood & Long, 1991). The steps in conducting such an intervention are as follows:

1. *Focus on the incident* so as to convey support and understanding of the child's stress* and to start the child talking about the incident.

---

* The word child was substituted for the word student throughout the quote.

2. *Children in crisis need to talk* in sufficient detail to clarify and expand understanding about the reality of the incident and to decrease the child's emotional intensity while increasing reliance on rational words and ideas.
3. *Find the central issue and select a therapeutic goal.*
4. *Choose a solution based on what the child values.*
5. *Plan for success* by rehearsing what will happen and anticipating the reactions and feelings (of self and others) when the solution is actually put into action.
6. *Close down the interview and prepare the child to assume responsibility* for subsequent behavior.

The Life Space Intervention is an excellent way to engage a child in cognitively processing a distressing event and applying problem-solving strategies that allow the child to manage the event and return to or develop more functional behavioral strategies.

The therapist's fear that the family will not follow through with treatment for a child who seems very disturbed may lead a therapist to tell the parent that the child has a serious emotional disturbance. The problem here is that parents often are not the best reporters of their children's behavior.

> A mother called and reported that her daughter showed no empathy and no remorse after negative interactions with other children and that she would like the child to be in treatment. The therapist initially thought that this sounded like the beginnings of some serious characterological problems and readily agreed to see the child. Well into the second intake session the therapist discovered that what the parents meant by lack of empathy was that the girl, 5-years-old, always wanted to have her own needs met before the parents' needs and that she never seemed to have her fill of attention from the parents, not exactly unusual behaviors in preschoolers.

Even if the problem is very serious, it is questionable whether or not the parents' increased anxiety will induce them to obtain treatment or whether it will cause them to increase their defenses, inadvertently allowing them to continue as they have. Suppose a parent describes a family situation that sounds very pathologic, say one child is seriously threatening or even hurting another child. The therapist becomes concerned and labels the family situation as pathologic during the initial phone contact. Rather than pushing the parent to seek treatment, the label pushes the parent into hiding for fear of further condemnation. This fear of condemnation may occur even when the parent, who is calling to obtain treatment for the child, is also a victim, as may be the case when a woman is unhappy with an alcoholic husband who is making her children miserable. She finally rallies and calls to obtain services for one child who is regressing in the face of the familial stress, only to be confronted by a therapist who labels this a seriously disturbed family and empathizes with the mother's feelings of victimization. Instead of feeling empowered to help her child, she feels helpless to change the larger picture and does nothing, telling herself it is not that bad.

At the opposite end of the continuum from the therapist who overwhelms the client during the initial phone contact are some therapists who fail to do enough to encourage a parent to follow through with treatment. Failing to get beyond the parent's labeling of the child's problem to the identification of the parent's experience at the point of seeking help will often prevent the parents from following through with play therapy. Again, as children rarely self-refer, the parents must be the ones who are experiencing sufficient distress to make them call for treatment.

> In the earlier case of Mrs. Arnold, the child absolutely did not want to become involved in treatment. Jennifer felt that there was nothing wrong with her and that everything would be just fine if her mother would stop doing things that made her angry. But Mrs. Arnold was in extreme distress and already felt abandoned, stating that her daughter's school staff did not see how big the problem was and that her husband's only response to the problem was to tell her that she was not a strong enough disciplinarian. It was the therapist's reflection of Mrs. Arnold's pain, anger, and feelings of isolation from support systems that calmed her to the point that she was able to initiate treatment. If the therapist had failed to address Mrs. Arnold's needs, it is very unlikely that she would have pursued that initial session.

One final task that needs to be taken care of before the child is brought to a session is helping the parent identify how the child will be told about the referral. This may occur over the telephone or during the intake interview with the parents if the child is not going to come to that first session. Many, if not most, parents will not tell their child about their intent to call a play therapist, and many will not ever label the problem for the child. Many parents have no intention of telling their child any more than that they are going to visit a friend. It is unwise to attempt to start a therapeutic relationship with a lie; it is best to use this as the point at which to begin to expect the parents to communicate with the child in a clear and direct manner. They should be encouraged to label, for the child, some of the specific behaviors or interactions they find problematic and the fact that they have decided to seek outside help to resolve these problems.

ESTABLISHING THE STRUCTURE OF THE INTAKE INTERVIEW

Having established the specifics of the referral problem and having decided that there is the possibility that play therapy will be an appropriate treatment, you must now set the appointment for, and determine the structure of, the intake sessions. A key element in structuring these sessions is determining who should attend. This is not a simple decision. Will you want to see the entire family, the parents alone, the identified problem child alone, or some combination of the above?

The primary problem with conducting a family intake as the first step in the intake process is that it may create faulty expectations for both the parents and the child about the nature of the work to follow. The family may, quite reasonably, expect that there will continue to be a lot of information shared once treatment is under way. Or they may believe that they will be intimately involved in the treatment process. These expectations are not problematic in and of themselves but rather in the degree of discrepancy between the treatment plan you actually intend to implement and what the family thinks will occur. The presence of several children may also make it difficult to gather the quantity of historical information needed in treatment planning. During initial family interviews, parents tend to focus virtually all their discussion on the difficulties the identified patient is experiencing and to spend the full time scapegoating the child, that can humiliate the child and lead him to believe that you are on the parent's "side." Neither condition sets the best groundwork for a working relationship.

In spite of these problems, it is often very useful to conduct a family interview at some point during the intake process even if you fully intend to work with an individual child for the bulk of the treatment process. The following case example illustrates some of the additional information such an interview can provide.

> Sue was seeking therapy for her 5-year-old son. She and her husband had adopted Teddy and his 3-year-old brother about 9 months earlier. Sue reported that while the 3-year-old seemed to be adjusting very well, Teddy was having problems, as manifested by bedwetting and rather pervasive, though low-level, defiance. He did not have temper tantrums; he just refused to do things such as getting ready for school in the morning. Sue's primary complaint, however, was that Teddy just did not seem to be developing an attachment to either her or her husband. He seemed distant and controlling. Her reaction was probably best summarized by her statement "We adopted these boys because we wanted children, and Teddy is not a child. He is like another adult sharing our living space. It is not at all what I had in mind." Although this statement reflects Sue's needs in this situation, it is also a powerful statement about Teddy and the nature of their interactions.
>
> During his interview, Teddy was entirely charming. He was verbal and polite. He sat very still, talked constantly, and denied any negative feelings at all. He eventually admitted to missing his biological mother a little, but said that he very much enjoyed his new family. Other than the fact that he seemed a little too controlled for a 5-year-old, he appeared to be very functional.
>
> A family interview was scheduled, and the observed change in Teddy was remarkable. He still sat very still and talked constantly, but now he was overwhelmingly controlling. The family session was used primarily to gather basic demographic information that had not been collected to date. When

the therapist asked where the parents worked and their work schedules, Teddy answered, and correctly. When the father started to say that he was about to change jobs, Teddy broke in and finished the explanation. When the mother was asked to describe the family's daily routine, Teddy took over and did a remarkable job. Teddy was, in fact, so good at what he did that the therapist did not initially recognize that he was gathering most of the information from a child. As the play therapist became aware of the process, he began to be more explicit about whom he expected to answer his questions, but still Teddy jumped in. Even when the therapist thanked Teddy for the information and said ". . . but I would like to hear what your mother has to say," Teddy would find some way to deliver the essential information. Not only was Teddy intrusive, but, amazingly, he was often accurate. His lack of manifest attachment became more clear as he never really moved to interact with his adoptive parents during the interview but worked very hard at remaining engaged with the play therapist. On the other hand, his attempt at attaching to the parents by controlling them and finding out everything he could about their lives and feelings was also apparent.

Teddy was a very intelligent child who was trying to keep his world safe by knowing all about it and controlling it. He had difficulty discussing negative effects because his primary negative emotion appeared to be anxiety, which is rather difficult for a 5-year-old to conceptualize, much less describe. In this case, the family interview added significantly to the play therapist's understanding of how Teddy and his symptoms fit into the overall functioning of this newly formed family.

If you are not going to begin by seeing the entire family initially, then you must decide who should come to the first few sessions. One option is to see the parents alone. When the referral is for a younger child, say, 8 and younger, this seems to be the arrangement of choice. If you are going to obtain a good sense of the problem and take a complete developmental history, you will need approximately 1½ hours, which is too long for most children to sit in the waiting room without having an understandably negative reaction. Even if you continued and saw the child for ½ hour, he would likely feel he did not get his fair share of your attention.

Older children—those over 8—may feel left out and "talked about" if not included in the first intake session. It is prudent to treat these children as competent to make decisions regarding their needs and treatment and to talk to them on the phone about the initial intake session. With these children, you can explain the process of the initial intake and ask them if they would like to be present or if they would prefer to wait until the next session, which will be primarily devoted to talking to them. Explain to the child that you will be taking a developmental history, that is, asking the parents to describe what things in their family have been like since before he was born. Specify that regardless of whether or not the child chooses to attend the first session, he will not be allowed to be in the office while you talk to his parent(s). This reinforces the existence of an appropriate parent/child role boundary and establishes you as having a certain amount of authority in the therapy situation. Given this information, most children choose not to come to the first session and feel empowered by their choice.

Regardless of what you or the child decide, you should be aware that some parents will resist coming to an initial session without the identified child client because they do not see themselves as the client, either now or at any point in the future. In such cases, you will need to make an effort to convey the fact that the parents will be vital information providers throughout the process and that their help will always be needed in keeping the treatment on the right track. You should emphasize the degree to which they can facilitate their child's treatment and provide some assurance that there is no hidden plan to treat them unless, at some point, all were to agree that it seemed warranted.

There is very little advantage to seeing the potential child client alone for the first intake session because most likely a certain amount of the working relationship will be created virtually at the outset, and there is always the possibility that the child will turn out not to be a good candidate for treatment at this time or with you. Additionally, the session will often have to remain very unfocused because you have little or no idea as to the context of the problem, or even much sense of the problem itself. If you would like to see the potential child client very early on in the intake process, then split sessions are probably most advantageous.

In a split session, you see the child for part of the session and the parents for another part. As mentioned, if the child is to come to the first session, it is inappropriate for him to be present in the room while the parents relate the history. However, you do not want to ignore the child either. To resolve this problem, it is generally a good idea to spend a small amount of time with the child before meeting with the parent; you can then meet again with the child at the end of the session.

You should be aware of potential problems in the conduct of split sessions. If you see the child first and then the parent, the child may fear that you will reveal the content of his session to the parent. If you see the parent first, then the child may fear that the parent is telling you bad things about him and may be reluctant to come to his portion of the session. One strategy for minimizing these problems is to ask the child how he would like to structure the session, listing his two choices.

A third alternative for split sessions is to see the parent and child together and then the parent alone and then the child alone. This format tends to address everyone's concerns about having a say without creating the appearance that you are taking sides. We talk more about the use of this format when we discuss structuring the ongoing treatment sessions.

Since each initial intake strategy has its benefits and risks, it may be best for you simply to select a strategy and then stick with it so that you become knowledgeable regarding the impact of your technique and can recognize and address problems where they arise. When the child does accompany the parents to a session, be it the first one or subsequent sessions, it is beneficial to address the child first when meeting the family in the waiting room. You may want to warn the parents that you will do this by explaining the importance, for the child, of establishing an immediate sense of the uniqueness of the therapy relationship. This explanation should prevent parents from feeling slighted. Also, you will need to establish a way of identifying the child client, especially if they will be bringing more than one child to the office.

When you enter the waiting room, identify yourself to the child and offer your hand for a handshake. This is best done once you have positioned yourself in a relatively natural position at or below the child's eye level, which is usually easily accomplished by kneeling or sitting on the floor. You do not want to look so silly that the child discounts you, but some accommodation to the child's size is usually appreciated.

> When Danny, a 4-year-old, came to his first session, he laid on the floor of the waiting room, running a toy car along the carpet. When the therapist came out to get Danny, his mother signaled that Danny was not happy and did not want to come to the session. Danny ignored the therapist as he said "Hi, you must be Danny." When Danny did not move, the therapist laid down on the floor next to him and commented on the car Danny had. As the therapist laid down, Danny looked out of the corner of his eye as if to check to see if the therapist would really stay. The therapist tried to lie flat enough so that Danny could look into his face without really moving his head. At one point Danny glanced at him and the therapist smiled; Danny smiled back, and they were off to a good start. Danny came to the office quite readily a few minutes later.

INTERVIEWING THE PARENTS

Before beginning the information-gathering portion of the intake interview with the parents, spend some time discussing with the parents the nature of the therapeutic contract they are entering into. Specifically, you must be clear about who is to be considered the client. Is treatment being rendered to the child alone, making him the primary client, or is the treatment plan to include others? Will the parents and the child be considered the primary treatment unit and therefore the clients? Or will the child be viewed as embedded in a family system with a resulting need to define the family as the client? This is not just a pragmatic issue but a philosophic/theoretical question as well. Do you render treatment to the child in relative isolation, in cooperation with the parent, or to the child as an integral part of the family system? Or do you go even further and see the child as an individual embedded in multiple systems, each of which will be affected by the therapy? Taking the last stance does not necessarily imply the treatment of the entire family; it does, however, imply the conceptualization of the child and his treatment as having a relationship with, and an impact on, many systems and individuals and is the approach taken in

Ecosystemic Play Therapy. Within this approach, it seems to be most accurate to define the family as the client or unit that will change as the result of the child's treatment.

Once the client has been identified, you should discuss other pragmatic aspects of the therapy contract before actually conducting the intake interview: review fee schedules, payment policies, insurance and scheduling issues, confidentiality, and other considerations. Confidentiality is one of the first issues to be affected by the decision to consider the family as the client. If the child were to be the client, the expectation that the child's confidentiality was quite far reaching would be created. If the parents and the child were to be considered the clients, the boundaries of confidentiality between them would be less pronounced. Since you will view the child as one member of a family system and you will see yourself working with the child to affect that system, then the entire family is considered the client and the boundaries of confidentiality become even less clear. Family therapists have noted all along that confidentiality is quite problematic within their approach.

In any case, it is imperative that you go on to advise the parents of the limits of their and their child's confidentiality, even if some of these limits are relatively artificial. Parents must clearly understand that if they reveal any information that suggests that they, or any member of their immediate family, is a clear and present danger to a known individual or to themselves, then confidentiality must be violated and the problem referred to the appropriate authorities. In this relatively simple statement, it is clear that you have assumed some professional responsibility for more than just the parents or the child as a result of your having defined the family as the client. Given this stance, you would feel as compelled to address the suicidal threats of your client's sibling as you would any threats your client makes. Obviously, this is not an easy stance to take but it is necessary and even desirable if the treatment is to be optimally effective.

Next the question arises as to how specifically you inform the parents of the child abuse reporting laws. Some therapists consider the general endangerment statement mentioned previously to be sufficient. Others note that child abuse reporting involves not only present danger but past occurrences as well and feel therefore that information regarding endangerment is not sufficient. These therapists, who are rapidly becoming the majority, favor explicit divulgence of the reporting laws, namely, that the parent be told that if you suspect that any child in the family is now, or has ever been, the victim of abuse, then confidentiality must be violated. Some therapists go so far as to define abuse, but this seems excessive, especially given the many definitions of abuse used by law enforcement, school, and mental health personnel.

You must also inform the parents as to your policy of revealing to the child information the parent provides. This issue becomes problematic when significant family secrets exist. Suppose the family has never told the child that the man he believes to be his biologic father is not, and it becomes apparent that the child's subconscious awareness of this fact is a major issue in the current conflict. Ideally, you would first work with the parents, encouraging them to talk to the child. But what if they refuse? Do you want to have established the position that you will be the one to decide whether or not to reveal the information to the child? Do you want to be placed in the position of feeling compelled to continue to work with the child in spite of the destructive family secret? Or do you terminate work with the family if they refuse to comply? This is a very complicated situation that is best resolved on a case-by-case basis. It is wise, however, to come to an explicit a priori agreement with the parents about the process by which decisions regarding what information should be made available to the child will be made so that there will be an established format for discussion should a problem arise.

Finally, it is important to discuss with the parents the limits of their child's confidentiality. The imperatives that compel you to report when the child is a danger to self or others or when the child is a victim of abuse are the same as those that govern the limits of the parents' confidentiality. Differences arise relative to the child's right not to have information conveyed to the parents. Most play therapists do not reveal specific session content to parents on a regular basis; instead, they share the process with the parents using more general descriptors. Others describe session contents much more freely. Virtually all play therapists agree that in most cases it is useful for the parent to have a good understanding of the problems the child is currently working on and to understand the general nature of the treatment approach being used at any given point. For this reason, it is often useful to make an initial contract with the parents as to the type of information that you will give them under routine circumstances. Whichever stance you take, the parents should be informed ahead of time so that they will not feel deceived or shut out at some later point.

The decision to consider the family the unit of change also complicates the intake in that the boundaries of the information to be collected are less clear to both you and the parents. Everyone involved in a child's play therapy must remember that the child is the focal point and that the determination of the relevance of any particular piece of information is based on whether or not that fact had, has, or will have an impact on the child's life and treatment. This means that you should gather some information about each of the parents as individuals and information about them as a couple but that you want only that information relevant to your understanding of the child and his ecosystem. Unfortunately, it is often impossible to determine which types of information will be relevant a priori, and therefore you have to go ahead and gather the data and sort them out later. It is easiest to stay on track during the initial interview and keep the parents comfortable if you ask them to describe their family at different points in the child's life (we discuss obtaining this type of developmental history later in this chapter). Beyond the direct questions you ask the parents, you will also be gathering information through your observation of their interactions with you.

Having reviewed the basic therapy contract and the limitations of confidentiality, you then proceed to conduct the intake interview. For a detailed presentation of how to complete a comprehensive systems review with the parents please consult *Play Therapy Treatment Planning and Interventions: The Ecosystemic Model and Workbook* (O'Connor & Ammen, 1997). Before discussing the actual information to be obtained, let us review the goals of the initial interview with either the parent or the child:

1. To establish rapport with the patient:
   a. By supplying the proper emotional climate for the interview.
   b. By structuring the purpose of the interview.
   c. By clarifying misconceptions about (play therapy).
   d. By dealing with inadequate motivation.
   e. By handling other resistances and preparing the (parent and child for play therapy).
2. To get pertinent information from the (parents and child):
   a. By listening to his spontaneous account.
   b. By focusing on selective data.
3. To establish a tentative clinical diagnosis.
4. To estimate the tentative dynamics, in terms of inner conflicts, characterologic distortions, mechanisms of defense and their genetic origins.
5. To determine the tentative etiology.
6. To essay tentatively the assets, strengths, and weaknesses of the (parents and child) actually and latently:
   a. By estimating the areas of living in which the patient is succeeding and failing.
   b. By determining the motivations for therapy.
   c. By exploring the level of insight.
   d. By estimating the tentative prognosis.
7. To make practical arrangements for therapy:
   a. By tentatively approximating optimal goals.
   b. By tentatively selecting the therapeutic method.
   c. By accepting the patient for treatment or arranging for another therapist.
   d. By making appropriate time arrangements.
   e. By making financial arrangements.
8. To arrange for essential consultations and psychologic testing. [(Wolberg, 1954, p. 198) Words in parentheses were substituted to make the guidelines consistent with the conduct of play therapy.]

The first item to be covered is a discussion of the presenting problem. You will have obtained this information during the initial phone contact, so at this point you are attempting to get more detail. It is particularly useful if the parents can operationally define the types of problems they are seeing. This not only encourages specificity, it usually reduces the number of value judgments that the parents include with their descriptions.

> Mrs. Arnold, who had called wanting to place her daughter in residential treatment immediately, could say over the telephone only that Jennifer was completely out of control, that she was terrible all the time, and that something must change immediately. During the intake interview, when Mrs. Arnold had calmed down somewhat, the therapist asked her to operationally define Jennifer's problems. At first Mrs. Arnold resisted, and then she began to focus on Jennifer's incredibly intense temper outbursts. These explosions often lasted for more than a half an hour and usually did not end until someone had been hurt, property was destroyed, and/or the girl had run away from home for several hours. As the intake continued, it became apparent that the problem was limited to these outbursts and other low-level defiance. Jennifer was not doing too badly in her Special Education class, although she had few friends.

Once you have clarified the referring problem and its concomitants, you will be able to discriminate the amount of information you need to gather about the systems in which the child is embedded. No matter what the problem is, you must gather extensive information about the past and present structure and functioning of the child's family. You may also need to gather more or less detailed information about the child's school history if the problem has generalized to that setting. Or you may want to gather a detailed medical history if you discover that the child has had a major illness or traumatic injury or an ongoing medical condition because these often become intertwined with emotional and behavioral difficulties. Other areas that may need to be explored include the child's involvement with peers, juvenile justice, extended family, childcare providers, and so forth.

The bulk of the intake interview focuses on obtaining a thorough developmental history. The format for taking this history is somewhat different from the more traditional, medically oriented developmental history because the emphasis is on organizing the child's psychological history against the framework of his development rather than on the timing of various developmental milestones per se.

In this type of interview, the reporter is repeatedly asked to describe the family and the child within the family at various points in the child's development. The occurrence of the developmental milestones are used as markers along the course of this descriptive history to help gauge whether or not the child's overall development was age-appropriate at various points in time.

The parents are first asked to describe their family at about the time the child being referred was conceived. The parents are then asked to describe the child and the family when the child:

1. Was born.
2. Was an infant.
3. First began to be mobile.
4. Began to talk and moved into toddlerhood.
5. Was a preschooler.
6. Entered kindergarten.
7. Was in the early school years, with special attention to the third and sixth grades.

What is critical here is that you are not simply gathering information about the child but about the systems in which the child has been embedded over the course of his life. You want to know what the parent's lives were like at each of these points. You also want to know their mental status at these points. How did each parent react to finding out that the mother was pregnant with this child? If the child was unwanted, what made them decide to keep the child? During the course of the pregnancy, was the mother happy, sad, anxious? How did the parents react to the child's birth, and so forth? This information is critical to understanding the subsequent interactions of the family members and the child's response to those interactions.

> Mrs. Williams reported that her marriage had been stormy for the first 10 months and that things became much worse when she became pregnant. Her husband, who had always been very jealous, became enraged and physically attacked her when he found out she was pregnant. At one point, she cried out that she could not breathe because he was choking her. He responded by saying that he hoped the baby would die. His anger did not abate during the course of the pregnancy, and it came as no surprise that he abused the infant once it was born.

The final portion of the intake interview with the parents is having the parents discuss the child's functioning in the areas covered by a traditional mental status exam: appearance, speech patterns, affect and mood, thought content and process, short- and long-term memory, intelligence, general fund of information, social judgment, and apparent insight. The exact information to be gathered in each area is detailed in the description of the child's intake interview that follows. You will probably find that many of these areas will have already been covered in various portions of the interview and so need not be repeated. Such information is a reference point for confirming or questioning the material the child provides during his intake interview.

Before concluding the intake session, you should give the parents the opportunity to discuss any specific goals they have for their child's treatment. Having just reviewed all the intake information, the parents may be able to generate some fairly reasonable desired outcomes. Usually, however, parents tend to generate rather general goals that include the overall welfare of their child. These goals can be modified and specified prior to initiating treatment through cooperative discussions among the parents, the child, and yourself.

The following cases are discussed from intake through termination over the next five chapters. In the first case, the problems, although severe, are quite focused making the case suitable for time-limited treatment. The second case is very complex where the only viable treatment option is long-term play therapy. In differentiating a long- and short-term case, two variables are generally considered. The first is the complexity of the problem as well as its duration. The more systems involved with the problem, the more likely it is that short-term treatment will not be feasible. The other variable to consider is the relative health of the systems in which the child is embedded. Again, the less healthy and supportive the child's environment, the less likely the case will be amenable to short-term treatment. Determining the complexities of the case and maintaining a fairly narrow focus during the intake are the initial differences between a long- and a short-term case.

CASE EXAMPLE: AARON

Aaron was brought to treatment by his mother, who was very concerned that he had no peer friendships and seemed overly mature and rigid.

Aaron was an only child. The parents had been married for 5 years when they planned to have Aaron. The mother's pregnancy and delivery of Aaron were without complication. Aaron was reported to be an easy infant and toddler whose developmental milestones were achieved within or well ahead of normal limits.

When Aaron was 2 years old, the family went on a trip. While Aaron and his mother were away from their hotel on a walk, the father had his first, intense bout of multiple sclerosis. When Aaron and his mother returned, they found the father fully paralyzed. The family reacted with terror, and over the next few weeks the father only partially recovered. Over the next 4 years, the father continued to deteriorate rapidly, and at the time of the intake he was completely bedridden and unable to feed himself.

Aaron was reported to have been constantly involved with his father's care from the first and was considered to be a big help because he was so well behaved.

CASE EXAMPLE: FRANK

Frank was referred for continued treatment when he was 10 years old upon entry into a residential program for his extreme school problems. As neither parent was available to be interviewed, the history was gathered primarily from records.

Virtually nothing is known about Frank's family life from the time of his birth until he was 2 years old. There is some suspicion that one or both of his parents were substance abusers.

When Frank was about 2 years old, his mother had a second child who died within a relatively short time from what was believed to be Sudden Infant Death Syndrome. It is known that at that time Frank's mother became severely depressed, possibly to the point of becoming bedridden for about 6 months. Frank's previous therapist also suspected that the mother was abusive during this period. The quality of Frank's relationship with his father during this period is unknown.

When Frank was about 3½ years old, he set a fire in the home in which his family lived. Frank supposedly went to warn his mother, but she ignored him. He then went and got his cat and took it out to a front room but was unable to get the cat away from the house. His mother died in the fire, as did the cat he had attempted to rescue.

Frank continued to live with his father for the next 4 years. When Frank was about 4½ years old, the family dog bit him on the bottom half of his face. (The scar from the incident extends from one side of Frank's mouth to below his chin.) Frank was treated at the local emergency room and then taken home. The next day Frank's father took the dog out, telling Frank they were going hunting. Once out in the open, the father shot the dog in front of Frank, claiming it was an accident but saying, at the time, that at least the dog would not bite Frank again.

Little is known about Frank's life over the next 3 years. What is known is that when Child Protective Services intervened, they found that Frank and his father had been living in a car for some time. Frank was removed from the father's care; gross neglect and suspected physical abuse were cited as the reasons.

Over the next year, from roughly 7 to 8, Frank was moved to several different foster homes, each of which found his behavior virtually unmanageable. He was finally placed in a therapeutic group home, where he began to receive treatment. Shortly after that, it was discovered that Frank's father had severely sexually abused him. The abuse consisted primarily of subjecting Frank to anal intercourse as a form of punishment. Each time, the father initially made Frank stand in the corner or spanked him, and then, when Frank displayed little or no reaction, the father became enraged and sodomized Frank. When this information was uncovered, Frank was referred to a treatment program for sex abuse victims. He was treated in that program for almost 2 years, at which point it was determined that more intensive remediation of his school problems and more intensive psychotherapy would be beneficial. At that time, Frank was transferred to a residential program, which allowed him to return to the group home on weekends. It should be noted that by this time Frank referred to the woman who ran the group home as his mother.

Frank's academic history was abysmal. At the age of 10 he could barely read and lacked even basic academic skills. Similarly, his history of peer relationships, either good or bad, was nonexistent. He was known to have become physically aggressive on several occasions, targeting the woman who ran the group home. He had also killed a kitten during his stay in the therapeutic group home.

INTERVIEWING THE CHILD

Having interviewed the child's caretakers and obtained as much of the relevant background information as possible, it is now time for you to proceed to interview the child.

Before beginning the child's interview it is important to consider whether this is to be a clinical or a forensic interview especially if it is a known or suspected abuse case. The primary purpose of a clinical interview is to get the information needed to commence treatment while the primary purpose of a forensic interview is to gather the information needed to proceed with a legal action. Unfortunately, referral agencies such as Child Protective Services do not always keep the differences distinct in their own minds and refer children for therapy when what they really want is more information to confirm or disconfirm abuse. Other differences between clinical and forensic interviews include:

1. Clinical interviews assume the child is telling the truth the child's subjective reality is accepted. The goal of a forensic interview is to uncover the truth and alternative explanations for what the child perceives to be reality are sought out.
2. In a clinical interview, the therapist is an advocate for the child while the interviewer should maintain a neutral stance in a forensic interview.
3. In a clinical interview, general information about the abuse is sufficient to proceed while details are imperative in a forensic interview.
4. Last, in a clinical interview, how the information is obtained is not relevant. The therapist may ask leading questions and have the child demonstrate those things he cannot describe in words. In a forensic interview, the way in which information is gathered is strictly governed. Leading questions are explicitly forbidden and the child needs to make every effort to put all of the information into words (Adapted from Raskin & Esplin, 1991 as presented in Steinmetz, 1995).

For a list of do's and don'ts with respect to conducting a forensic interview with children see "Interviewing Children: Balancing Forensic and Therapeutic Techniques" by Melissa Steinmetz in the May/June, 1995 issue of the *National Resource Center on Child Sexual Abuse News*.

Irrespective of the type of interview, the interview format will need to be structured to the child's developmental level. With Level I children, the interview will be extremely limited, focusing primarily on you and the client becoming familiar with one another. Interviews with Level IV children may appear very similar to the standard intake you would complete with an adult.

A more detailed description of the strategies used for interviewing children than that presented here can be found in *The Clinical Interview of the Child* (Greenspan & Greenspan, 1991). They propose the following guidelines. The therapist should:

1. Attend to all levels of communication, including body language and metaphorical or symbolic communication.
2. Consider the responses he gets in the context of the child level of functioning along multiple lines of development (e.g., behavior, socialization, communication, language).
3. Be aware of the concept of multiply determined behavior. That is that the same behavior may have multiple reasons for being.
4. Understand the concept of developing a causal formulation rather than just a diagnosis. For example, instead of diagnosing a child as Attention Deficit Disorder the therapist would develop a case formulation indicating whether the attention problems were neurologic in their origins, the result of severe anxiety or the result of a combination of the two.
5. Learn to balance personal perceptions with concrete data. That is the interviewer should never disregard his own sense of the child's functioning but rather should anchor these observations to know reference points. Is the child's language really very advanced or does it just appear so because the interviewer has been meeting with a series of developmentally delayed children for the past few days?

With these guidelines in mind the therapist should first note that in all fairness to the child, one of the first things that should be discussed are the limits of the child's confidentiality. This can be a little awkward since the child may not even understand why he is there or what your role is, but it may also prevent the therapy from beginning on a very bad note.

> Cindy was brought to therapy by her mother as a result of her gradually increasing withdrawal and bedwetting. The therapist was a trainee who was eager to become involved with this little girl, who appeared very fragile and needy. She immediately began to explore the presenting problem with Cindy. Much to the therapist's surprise, Cindy almost immediately revealed that she was being sexually abused by her father. The therapist found herself in the position of having to break confidentiality without ever having warned the child of the circumstances under which this might happen so that the child could make an informed decision regarding the content of the session.

This particular example was chosen because many would argue that the child's welfare was actually benefited by circumventing her rights. While this may be true in the short-term, one would certainly have to question the underlying assumption that children's rights have no inherent value as well as questioning the impact such an initial interaction would likely have on the future course of therapy. In addition, the feelings of loss of control and helplessness that the child experiences may be perceived as parallel to the abuse rather than as protection from it.

The limits of the child's confidentiality should be presented in a simple and straightforward manner. It is easy to let the child know that when he tells you anything that suggests that he is a danger to himself or to others, or that someone has ever hurt him, or is currently hurting him, then you will have to tell others so that he remains safe. If needed, you can give the child specific examples, but generally children seem to understand the issues at hand with very little difficulty.

A problem that arises immediately, however, is that in most cases the child's right to confidentiality is very limited. It is the parents who are, from a legal perspective, generally considered the clients and therefore the holders of the privilege with regards to treatment information. Certainly, if the parents wanted information from the child's record they would be able to get it. Further, as previously noted, you will have defined the family as the client from the outset, creating certain problems regarding boundary definition and maintenance.

Given that the confidentiality extended to the child by law is so limited and that you may want to provide the parents with information in order to facilitate the child's treatment, you should prepare and reassure the child by telling him that no information will be shared with the parents unless he is forewarned. This does not imply that the child will be asked to consent to the provision of information, only that he will be informed before it happens. Most children accept these limits with little reservation because they tend to respect the fact that more attention is being paid to their rights and feelings than is true in most of their transactions with adults.

Having covered the limits of confidentiality, it is prudent to then explain your role to the child. Children's misconception about therapists can be quite extreme, and often they have been told no more than that they are going to see a doctor, so they enter the interview expecting a physical exam or worse. A relatively simple explanation, using the following steps, goes a long way with children up to about 10 or 11 years of age. First, ask if the child has ever had to go to the doctor when he was sick. It is quite unlikely that you will encounter a child who has never been sick, but if you do, then proceed to ask if he has ever known someone who had visited a doctor.

Second, engage the child in a discussion of the fact that he had some symptom—a headache or sore throat—which signaled the parents that something was wrong so they took him to the doctor. The doctor then examined him to see if he could figure out what was wrong, and when he did, he gave the child medicine and maybe told him some things to do that would make him feel better.

Proceed to draw an analogy to therapy. Tell the child that his parents have observed certain behaviors that have signaled to them that he is not well, but that this time it is not his body that is in discomfort but his feelings. You present yourself to the child as a feelings doctor, someone who works with children when their bodies are basically fine but their feelings are bothering them. You let the child know that because you do not work with kid's bodies there is no physical exam and no physical treatment, especially no shots. You let the child know that instead of a physical exam there is a feelings exam, during which you will try to find out all about the child's feelings and the nature of the problem by talking. The child should be made aware that this may take quite some time but that once both you and he have an idea of how and why he is feeling bad, then you both can go on to figure out ways to try to help him have more pleasant feelings. Most Level II and Level III children find this a very acceptable explanation that focuses on their needs and does not criticize them for their present state.

Referral Problem

The information-gathering portion of the child's intake interview begins in much the same way as that of the parent's interview: Ask the child to talk about the referral problem. The explanation of the therapist's role (previously described) creates an immediate opening for interviewing the child in the form of conducting an emotional checkup. Start by asking the child what he knows about the parent's motives for bringing him to a "feelings doctor." Many children will not know why they have been brought or will initially deny knowing. Given the way in which your role has been described to the child, you could engage him in discussing those behaviors that the parents have observed that made them think that he was having some unpleasant feelings.

"You know how we said that your mom or dad knows that it is time for you to go to the doctor when you have a fever or a bad stomachache because those are signs that something is wrong with your body? Well, let's talk about the signs they have seen that told them you are having some bad feelings." In this manner, you can lead into a discussion of the presenting problem. If the child resists or seems lost, you might present some of the specific concerns that the parents mentioned.

A few children will say that they have no bad feelings and, at this point, you may have to say "None, ever?" If the child persists in saying no, then you might pursue one of two strategies. You might say "Well, you are pretty lucky and maybe we will not be working together for very long at all." This allows the child to relax and to see that you are not going to force him into discussions he does not want to pursue. It is generally a good strategy to use with children who are relatively passive and fearful during the intake. With the other strategy you say "Well, I know of at least one bad feeling you have. You must be pretty angry that your parents have brought you to a feelings doctor when you don't need one." Many children who are actively resisting the intake process and indeed are angry will immediately verbally agree with this statement. You can then proceed to note that one of the treatment goals he might want to pursue is trying to discover how he can convince his parents that he really does not need to come to therapy. At this point you can reengage in a discussion of those things the child thinks motivated the parents to seek treatment and proceed as before.

Having gained a sense of the child's conception of the referral problem, you can move on to asking the child to describe situations in which he experiences different affects such as happiness, sadness, or anger. The intensity of these affects can be discussed as well as their frequency. If you are careful to stick with the role initially presented, then usually it is not too difficult to talk about the child's negative affects without making him feel that you will judge him negatively if he is not always happy. Even the most oppositional child can admit that he gets angry at his parents a lot and that being yelled at or punished is not very much fun and makes him angrier and maybe even sad.

Focusing on the child's experience of negative affects facilitates the development of a treatment contract between you and the child. The two of you can agree to focus on trying to find out more about when he feels sad or angry and then see if the two of you can figure out ways to decrease the frequency and intensity of those feelings. Using this format, you will be able to get children as young as 4 years to develop initial treatment goals and to make a relatively educated commitment to the treatment process. This format also allows you to provide the child with the sense of having an active role rather than a passive one of responding to questions. This in turn makes for a smoother transition to the first treatment session, where you will want to ask fewer questions and have the child display more initiative.

In completing an ecosystemic intake interview, it is important to cover not only the child's present functioning but to get a sense of the child's view and functioning of the other systems in which he is embedded.

Mental Status

Play therapists rarely conduct formal mental status examinations with new child clients; however, many cover more areas of the exam than they realize. The exam, whether completed in full or in part, can be a useful tool for gathering comprehensive information about the child. For a detailed presentation of the Mental Status Exam and strategies for completing a comprehensive systems review with the child please consult *Play Therapy Treatment Planning and Interventions: The Ecosystemic Model and Workbook* (O'Connor & Ammen, 1997).

Appearance

You should attend to the child's appearance and develop hypotheses about how it affects his transactions with the world. Is the child's appearance consistent with his chronological age, or does he appear much younger or older? Is the child so attractive that he draws attention from others? Or does he have some oddity in appearance that might invite scapegoating? If the latter condition exists, is the oddity permanent or changeable?

Speech Patterns

Unusual speech patterns may reflect more serious underlying disorders of emotion or cognition, specific language disorders, or normal developmental variations, such as stuttering in 3- to 4-year-olds. In some cases they may also affect other's perceptions of the child's age and/or cause the child to become a target for scapegoating.

Orientation

In this part of the exam, you assess whether or not the child is oriented to person, place, and time. Does he know who he is and who you are? Does he know where he is? Does he know the time of day, the day of the week, the month, and the year to a degree appropriate for his age level?

Affect and Mood

Information about the child's affect and mood is usually gathered by observation during the course of the rest of the interview, although it may be assessed more directly. You will want to know if the child is capable of experiencing and displaying a full range of affects and if those affects are consistent with the situation in which they are displayed.

This portion of the interview may be one of the better points at which to inquire about the child's self-destructive ideation and behaviors. Assessing the suicide potential of children is not something with which many professionals feel terribly comfortable; however, it is essential that you do ask because the problem is quite widespread and does not go away when ignored. You should be aware that suicidal ideation and attempts have been documented in very young children; they are particularly at risk because their impulse control and their ability to judge the lethality of their chosen method is so limited.

Leading into the subject of suicide is usually relatively easy. While you have the child talking about his bad feelings, you might reflect on the fact that it sounds like his negative feelings, such as anger, sadness, loneliness, or the like, sometimes become very intense and you wonder if, at those times, he has ever thought about hurting himself. The use of the word "hurting" rather than "killing" is done not to be discreet but to assess for lower level self-destructive behavior, such as getting hurt "by accident" or cutting, burning, or hitting oneself. If the child answers "Yes" to this initial question, proceed to ask about the types of self-destructive behavior in which he has engaged. Once you have gathered this information, or if the child has answered "No" to the initial question, proceed to ask if he has ever wished he was dead. This is an important question because many children who may not have thought of actively pursuing suicide have wished they were dead, reflecting very intense negative affects.

The final step in assessing the child's suicidal ideation is to ask him whether he has admitted to ever wishing he was dead or not, if he has ever thought about killing himself. If the child answers "No," then this portion of the interview is over; if he answers "Yes," then you must proceed to inquire as to the:

1. Intensity and frequency of the suicidal thoughts.
2. Child's plan for killing himself:
   a. Circumstances under which he would follow through with his plan
   b. Method he would use
   c. Feasibility of the chosen method
3. Child's perception of the resources to which he might turn if he ever felt like following through with a suicide attempt.

The more concrete the child's responses to any of these questions, the more concern you would have about his safety. The primary decision you will have to make is "Can this child be safely maintained in his home with outpatient services, or is a more intensive intervention required?" Unfortunately, a complete discussion of the therapeutic management of suicidal children is outside the scope of this volume; for additional information, see *The Suicidal Child* (Pfeffer, 1986).

It is also a good idea to assess the child's homicidal ideation and behavior. Although rarely do children follow through on such thoughts, they should be explored, for as we have seen in the case of Frank, even very young children may kill another person. This topic should be explored using the exact same format as that used for assessing suicide potential. You might lead into the discussion by asking the child if he has ever wished that someone he knows would just disappear, and proceed from there.

Thought Content and Process

You need to assess the clarity of the child's thinking, not only to rule out the possibility of psychosis but to determine the impact of the child's cognitions on his day-to-day behavior. It is important to inquire about hallucinatory experiences, although these are somewhat difficult to assess in younger children. One strategy for conducting this part of the assessment is to ask the following series of questions:

1. Have you ever been playing alone, walking down the street, or just concentrating on something and thought you heard someone call your name, and then when you went to see who it was there was no

one there? (Virtually every child will acknowledge some variation on this experience.)
2. Why, or how, do you think this happens? (At this point, you should assess whether or not the response is commensurate with the child's cognitive developmental level.)
3. Do you ever hear more than your name, like any other words or talking when you know that no one else is there or which no one else can hear?
4. Have you ever seen anything that no one else can see?

Each of these last two questions, if answered positively, should be followed by an inquiry regarding the nature of the child's experience. When do the phenomena occur? What is happening to the child at the time? What is the content of the phenomena? For a more complete discussion of the assessment and interpretation of hallucinatory phenomena in children, see *Hallucinations in Children* (Pilowsky & Chambers, 1986).

Short- and Long-Term Memory

The child's memory is usually assessed informally as the interview proceeds. It can also be assessed more formally by asking the child to complete a task similar to the Digit Span subtest of the Wechsler Intelligence Test for Children—Revised. Long-term memory can be assessed through the child's recall of events.

Intelligence

You need to estimate the child's intelligence, given your observations during the intake interview. Often mental health professionals are terrible at making such estimates, so it is important to remember that this estimate will actually be a reflection of the way the child comes across on first meeting a new adult, not necessarily indicative of his actual cognitive potential.

Fund of Information

The child's general fund of knowledge is simply assessed as the interview proceeds, although you might want to add a random sample of general questions to the interview to both assess general knowledge and relax the child by lightening the content of the interview periodically. Suitable questions could be culled from any of the children's intelligence tests.

Social Judgment

Your two sources of information regarding the child's social judgment in the context of your interview with him are the kind of behavior he exhibits during the interview and the degree to which such behavior is appropriate for a child, at a given developmental level, in this situation. One would expect most Level I children to exhibit considerable reluctance to approach a stranger, while Level II children would approach but have some difficulty warming up to a stranger. Level III children should be able to exhibit much more socially appropriate behavior. Therapists tend to be delighted when a young child comes readily to the first session and engages very quickly and warmly; however, this is often a symptom of the child's level of interpersonal neediness or affect hunger more than a sign of mental health.

Apparent Insight

Assess the child's level of insight into the presenting problem and the thoughts and feelings associated with it. Is the child aware of the problem? Does he have any idea what motivates him to behave in the ways that triggered the referral? While judging whether or not the child's level of insight is appropriate, you must again keep in mind the child's developmental level and recognize that the capacity for self-observation and true insight tends not to develop in children until at least Level III.

Other areas frequently assessed in intake interviews include the following (adapted from La Greca, 1983):

1. Interests:
   a. What does the child like to do (in spare time)?
   b. What does the child like to do alone?
   c. What does the child like to do with friends?
   d. What does the child like to do with family members?
2. Fears/worries:
   a. What kinds of things is the child afraid of?
   b. What kinds of things make the child nervous and jumpy?
   c. What kinds of things does the child worry about?
3. Self-image:
   a. What does the child like or dislike about himself or herself?
   b. What can the child do well, relative to peers?
   c. How would the child describe himself or herself?
4. Somatic concerns:
   a. Does the child have any headaches or stomachaches?
   b. Does the child have any other kinds of body pains?
   c. How often does this happen?
   d. What does the child usually do?
5. Aspirations:
   a. What would the child like to do for a living when he or she gets older?
   b. What are other things the child would like to do when older?

6. Fantasy:
   a. What kinds of things does the child daydream about?
   b. What kinds of things does the child dream about?
   c. If the child could have any three wishes, what would they be?

Current Social Situation

Having completed the Mental Status Exam, the interviewer now proceeds to get the child's perception of his environment and his functioning within it. With children, it is somewhat easier to obtain a developmental history if you work from the present to the past. This is consistent with children's tendency to recall recent and emotionally charged events most easily.

Family

The child should be asked to describe his present living situation and his feelings about the situation and each of the people who compose his nuclear family. This portion of the interview may be accomplished by having the child complete a Kinetic Family Drawing (Burns & Kaufman, 1972).

School

What are the child's favorite subjects? Which are his least favorite? How does he get along with his teachers? How does he do on his schoolwork? How does he behave in school?

Peers

You should also gather information about the child's relationships with peers, both at home and at school. How does he describe his peers? Does he identify himself as having particular friends; if so, how does he describe those friends? What does he like to do with his friends?

Social History

During this segment of the interview, be alert to the probability that the child will not be able to provide a temporally organized accounting of his history. Children at Level I or II may not even be able to temporally organize the elements of a single event. Level III children will probably be able to organize the elements of a single event but may be unable to locate that event very accurately within their histories. Regardless of the child's organizational capacities, you should allow him to convey information in whatever manner he chooses rather than attempting to guide him through a temporal presentation that may frustrate him and convince him that you are more interested in the way he tells the story than the content. You can always go back at the end and ask some questions to help you place the information you have gathered in sequence.

Family

For this portion of the interview, you will be asking the child about ways the family has changed over time. Has there been a divorce, a remarriage? Have additional siblings been added to the family since this child? Have any of the older children moved out of the home? More important than the child's ability to recall such events is his description of his reaction to those events. What did he think about them? How did he feel at the time they happened, and how has he adjusted since?

School and Peers

Similarly, you will want to know how the child's school and peer relationships have changed over time. Has the child changed schools; if so, how often? Has the child's status relative to his peers changed? Has the child's academic performance changed? Has the child's behavior toward adults and/or peers in school changed over time?

Having completed the intake interview it is a good time to give the child the opportunity to engage in some discussion of his goals for his treatment. Children as young as 9 years old have been found to be capable of reaching reasonable treatment decisions (Weithorn, 1980). It is important to include at least older children and adolescents in making decisions regarding their treatment whenever possible and to actively involve them in discussing the goals of treatment. Not only is their participation appropriate from an ethical standpoint, but it may have other positive effects in terms of decreasing the resistance to treatment that sometimes comes with being excluded, and of enhancing motivation. (Adelman, Kaser-Boyd, & Taylor, 1984)

Not only can young children be viably involved in making treatment decisions, they are more capable of responding to all the aspects the intake process described so far than most adults, professionals included, tend to believe. With children of all ages, it is best to engage in less direct questioning than one might use with an adult. Children tend to feel interrogated and to resist the response demand of questions if too many questions are strung too close together. It is often best to substitute simple commands for questions where possible. For example, the therapist might say "I'm interested in knowing more about your friends. Tell me about the kids you like to play with at school." With this format, the child is clear as to the information you are pursuing and is not concerned about the possibility of double meanings, as he might be if you ask instead "Do you have a best friend?"

A Level I child is going to have difficulty following most of the intake process, especially if it is conducted in a question and answer format. For children functioning at this level, many of the content areas have to be kept very brief or dropped entirely. It is important, however, not to let the child's limited expressive language and ability to provide you with information deter you from providing him with as much information as possible in a very simple format. You should always attempt to describe the nature of the relationship and the reason for initiating treatment. Reflections of some of the child's possible concerns can also be useful in helping orient the child to the treatment process.

Once the child enters Level II, it is generally possible to complete inquiries in all the content areas described herein. With children functioning at this level, it is not the content of the intake that needs to be adjusted but the format in which the information is gathered. Level II children may need you to provide much more information and examples of what you expect from them before they become involved in the process. They may also need you to be very concrete in specifying the information you want. This is the developmental group that is most likely to say "Well I had a tummy ache yesterday but I'm OK now" when asked how they are feeling or if they have had any bad feelings lately. With Level II children, you may have to spend time, at intervals, clarifying vocabulary. You want to begin to become familiar with the kinds of words the child uses to describe things, and you want to begin to familiarize him with your vocabulary. Only if the child's behavior is very disorganized or impulsive will the establishment of limits and the session structure have to take precedence over information gathering. However, in most cases, the child will engage quite readily once he understands the context of the interview.

Level III and IV children can be expected to provide relatively complete intake information and be actively engaged in the therapy process from the beginning. The Level III child will be able to provide relatively limited information about his internal state and feelings unless these are related to specific events and interactions. The Level IV child will be able to provide progressively more information about his internal processes and feelings in hypothetical situations and even in the absence of a specific event or interaction.

Before concluding the intake interview, you should tell the child what will happen next. If there will be a decision-making process that includes the possibility that the child will not return, then he should know this, and the intake interview should end as cleanly as possible. If you are quite certain that there will be a next session, then you should tell the child a little about what the first therapy session will be like. The explanation might be as simple as informing the child that work will begin by you getting to know more about him by spending time together, during which things can be more relaxed and fun. This means that during the next session you will not be asking nearly so many questions and the child will have the opportunity to do some things as well as talk. You might also want to mention to the child, and the child's caretaker, the type of clothing the child should wear to sessions. Suggest that the child wear play clothes so that neither you nor he need worry excessively about protecting his clothes from things like clay or paint.

CASE EXAMPLE: AARON

Aaron was very adultlike during his intake interview. He was unsure as to why his mother had brought him to therapy, although he thought it might have something to do with the fact that he sometimes got in trouble at school for being bossy. He quickly added that he had to be bossy because the other kids were constantly doing things they were not supposed to do and the teachers seemed unable to get them to behave better so they needed his help.

Aaron described his family and home in detail. He described events in good temporal order and tended to include information such as how long the drive on a particular trip had taken or where and when they had stopped to have lunch. None of his stories contained any but the most superficial descriptions of affect. He talked about his father's illness in a very matter-of-fact way and denied any strong emotional reactions to the changes that had taken place over the years other than noting that the adjustments were sometimes difficult though necessary.

Aaron reported no peer relationships. Instead, he noted how other children's behavior made it difficult to like them. He admitted to getting angry if someone bothered him or touched his things.

Aaron's mental status was remarkable for the lack of affect he displayed, although he could use words to report having had various feelings in the past. He was obviously very intelligent and surprisingly controlled and controlling. He wore a button-down shirt, that still showed evidence of having been ironed, dress pants, and a belt—clothes he had selected himself. He got out of his chair only with permission. He often tried to redirect the interview or to cut it off by discussing objects in the room and asking if he could use them.

Aaron could not think of any reason he should be in treatment, although he admitted that he was sometimes a little nervous and that it would be nice to have someone to play with. At this point he was referring to the therapist, not to a desire to play with peers.

CASE EXAMPLE: FRANK

Frank was generally able to recall information consistent with that gathered from his history during his intake interview. However, because of his expressive language difficulties and extreme lack of trust, he tended to limit his statements to extremely concrete reports. He especially limited his discussion of any emotions.

Frank acknowledged that he set the fire that killed his mother and that he meant to do it. He said that he lit some papers in the kitchen and then, when the fire started to spread, he became frightened. At that point, he tried to get his mother to get out of her bed, but she refused to comply and told him to go away. He went and got his cat and went out to the front room but could not open the door to go outside. He was rescued by firefighters, but the cat died.

Frank also recounted the incident when he was bitten by the dog and said that his father became very angry that he had taunted the dog and provoked the attack. Frank noted that although his father claimed to have shot the dog by accident, he believed he did it on purpose. Further, he believed the father did it, not to protect Frank but to punish him for taunting the dog. The logic Frank believed his father followed was "If you can't treat a dog the way you are supposed to, then you can't have a dog."

Frank described his current group home parent as his family. He described no interactions with any of the other children placed at the home or with any of the children at school.

Frank's mental status exam revealed a child who was basically intact except for very limited speech with concomitantly limited ability to recall events and organize his verbalizations. His affect was extremely flat, and he lacked any apparent insight into the reason for his placement in a series of treatment programs or into the reason he engaged in the behaviors that had triggered those referrals. He was minimally engaged in the intake process and did not seem to care one way or the other if he returned to future sessions.

The complete histories of both the child and the family form the first block for building a developmental conceptualization of the case. With this information you will formulate some general hypotheses that can be further tested during your assessment of the child. The hypotheses you develop from the history are framed as "because this happened during this developmental phase, this is the expected outcome, and this is the logical intervention." Only the hypothesis development is addressed herein; the treatment planning component is addressed in the next chapter.

Case Example: Aaron

Aaron's first 2 years of life had progressed optimally until he was exposed to a single, yet ongoing, traumatic event: the onset of his father's multiple sclerosis. The trauma specifically involved the father's loss of body control. The therapist hypothesized that Aaron would manifest significant control issues in his life because he was making the transition from Level I to Level II when children develop their style of control, relying on an autoplastic, alloplastic, or mixed style.

Case Example: Frank

Frank experienced multiple traumas over the course of his early development. It appears that his relationship with his parents may have been adequate during the first year or two of his life. Beginning with the death of his brother, however, he was exposed to almost continuous trauma.

Given that his brother died when Frank was transitioning from Level I to Level II, the therapist hypothesized that Frank would have some difficulty developing attachments and considerable difficulty managing his aggression. Specifically, he expected Frank to vacillate between hostile and dependent relationships and to display explosive, aggressive behavior consistent with that seen in a 2-year-old.

During the time when Frank should have been embroiled in Oedipal issues he caused his mother's death by fire and then was immediately involved in a sexually abusive relationship with his father. The therapist hypothesized that Frank would have significant problems with gender-role identification and separating sex from aggression. The therapist also hypothesized that Frank might express anger through setting fires.

Frank was kept in an abusive relationship with his father throughout his transition from Level II to Level III, therefore, the therapist hypothesized that Frank would have been so preoccupied with trying to protect himself that he would not have had the energy available to go on to form peer relationships and that these would continue to be problematic.

Once you have formulated these general developmental hypotheses regarding your client, you are ready to proceed with the assessment phase of the treatment process.

CHAPTER SEVEN

Assessment, Case Formulation, and Treatment Planning

The course of Ecosystemic Play Therapy delineated in the next few chapters differs from most other play therapy models because the degree of your involvement in determining that course is quite extensive. You begin by thoroughly assessing the child and family to determine the child's present level of developmental functioning and the issues and conflicts to be addressed. This is a critical phase whether the intended treatment is to be long- or short-term. In fact, shorter term treatment often requires a more intensive assessment process so that the goals can be very specifically defined and the treatment carefully planned. You then use this information to develop a treatment plan with specific goals. Therapy proceeds through an introductory phase, a working phase, and on to termination. All the while you are attempting to maximize the child's functioning relative to her developmental capacities and to convert actions into language wherever possible and appropriate.

ASSESSMENT AND DIAGNOSIS

Treatment planning depends on an accurate assessment of the child's development across areas of functioning and an accurate psychological diagnosis. In this context, the assignment of the child to one of the diagnostic categories of the 1994 *American Psychiatric Association's Diagnostic and Statistical Manual on Mental Disorders (DSM-IV)* or any other system is not a critical aspect of the diagnostic process. Diagnosis rather is used to refer to the clinician's formulation of a psychological explanation for the client's current pattern of symptoms and level of functioning. These developmental case conceptualizations are much more descriptive of the underlying pathologic process and therefore are more useful than a diagnosis in the development of a treatment plan (Shirk & Russell, 1996). Most of the information the play therapist needs to develop—a diagnostic formulation and an appropriate treatment plan—is obtained from the intake interviews with the parents and child. In certain circumstances, however, you will need additional information, to be obtained through a more direct assessment process.

The following discussion of the assessment process intentionally precedes the discussion of setting up the playroom because it is generally advisable that the assessment process be completed in a location other than the playroom. This stance reflects the different and often conflicting processes associated with assessment as opposed to play therapy. Many evaluations resemble school tasks that may be unpleasant for the child, so it is less than desirable to have the child associate therapy with school in this manner. Thus, the use of a room other than the playroom may alleviate some of the child's associations. Further, because assessment tasks often involve testing the child to failure, you do not want her to come to therapy assuming that her behavior is going to be judged as either a success or failure. The less the assessment process resembles traditional testing and the more it consists of observational play sessions, the more likely that you will want to conduct the sessions in the playroom. If so, before proceeding you should consult Chapter Eight for a discussion of how to set up the playroom.

Diagnostic Play Sessions

One option for obtaining information beyond the initial interview is to use diagnostic play sessions. The most comprehensive text on the conduct of play-based assessment is *Play Diagnosis and Assessment* (Schaefer, Gitlin, & Sandgrund, 1999). Although several structured techniques exist, most play therapists rely on rather unstructured play sessions. The reliability of this approach is quite variable, largely dependent on the individual therapist's skills. In most cases, it is advisable that the sessions be somewhat structured, at least to the extent that they present the child with specific materials. One such use of these semistructured diagnostic play sessions is to explore the impact of specific trauma on the child victim.

The Erica Method is a derivative of the Lowenfeld World Technique (1939, 1950), which consisted of miniature toys—trees, houses, cars, people, and so forth—and a sandbox in which Dr. Lowenfeld let the child build a "world." The child's constructions then were a source of material for interpretation.

Lowenfeld's technique was modified at the Erica Institute in Sweden until it became a comprehensive projective technique used to assess children's psychological functioning. Allis Danielson published a manual for the Erica Method in 1965; this manual contributed to making the Erica

Method the most widely used technique for diagnostic observations of children in Sweden and other Scandinavian countries.

The materials consist of 360 miniature toys that are kept in a 12-compartment cabinet. The toys are divided into 12 categories based partly on whether they are peaceful, aggressive, moving, active, or static. A small piece of clay is also included so that the child may create whatever she desires should she miss something among the toys. On the floor are two metal boxes, one filled with dry sand and the other filled with wet sand. These boxes are placed in a wooden frame on which the child and examiner sit.

The child is seen for three sessions that are scheduled as close together in time as possible. The use of three sessions improves the validity and reliability of the method by allowing for comparison of the child's constructions over time. You would be particularly interested in whether the child's constructions improve or deteriorate over time. At the end of the session, the child's construction is photographed and a record form completed.

The record form organizes the therapist's observations into four categories: sequence, form, composition, and content. Sequence includes such factors as response latency, the pace of the child's work, and the length of time required to complete the work. Form includes the materials the child uses, the manner in which she uses the sand, and the type of play in which she engages. Composition refers to the way the child organizes the materials used. The seven types of composition that reflect progressively increasing intellectual and developmental functioning are: (1) indifferent—the toys are randomly placed; (2) sorting—like toys are grouped together; (3) configuration—the toys are arranged in geometric patterns; (4) simple category—the toys are grouped based on conceptual similarities; (5) juxtaposing—a few related toys are placed near one another but in no relation to the whole; (6) conventional groupings—small, realistic arrangements of toys are created; and (7) meaningful wholes—the toys are arranged to create larger, more complex scenes. Three additional types of compositions are thought to reflect pathology: (1) chaotic—the toys are dumped about the sandbox; (2) bizarre—the child juxtaposes unusual elements; and (3) closed—the scenes the child creates are surrounded by walls and fences. The content category includes themes developed within or across the child's sessions.

The information gathered from the three sessions is used to develop four types of diagnostic formulations. The developmental diagnosis is a description of the child's functioning across areas. The milieu diagnosis describes the relationship between the child's constructions and her real world. Somatic/psychosomatic diagnoses include descriptions of the interactions between the child's medical/biologic functioning and behavior. The psychopathological diagnoses are the more traditional descriptions of the intrapsychic variables that contribute to the child's problem behavior. These diagnoses can be used in planning the child's treatment, which can be conducted either traditionally or with additional Erica Method sessions. (Erica Method discussion adapted from an article by Sjolund, 1983.)

The interviews some law enforcement officials and mental health practitioners use in the diagnosis of the sexual abuse of young children are an example of the moderately structured diagnostic play techniques. Viewpoints regarding the legal and psychological usefulness of such interviews widely vary even among those who profess a child advocacy orientation. On the one hand are those who see such interviews as a way of reliably substantiating the child's experience and limiting the child's exposure to investigators, attorneys, and the court system, especially if the interviews are taped. On the other hand are those who point out that the reliability of the material obtained during these sessions may not be particularly good and that tapes of such sessions have been used to discredit child witnesses in court.

Strategies for conducting unstructured diagnostic play interviews are as unlimited as the number of practitioners who use them. The range extends from variations of the World Technique to purely observational methods in which you provide the child with a variety of play materials and some very limited instructions that give the child permission to use the materials as she sees fit. You then observe the child's choice of materials; the type of play in which she engages—its structure, organization, completeness; the symbols used; and so forth. This information is interpreted in a manner consistent with your theoretical orientation. A psychoanalytically oriented therapist would interpret the content of the child's play at various levels of symbolism; a humanistically oriented therapist might observe for the child's capacity to engage in health-promoting behaviors either in reality or fantasy; a behavioral therapist might consider the session a sample of the child's behavior, noting her attention span, ability to use materials, orientation to the therapist, and so forth.

Note that observations of a child's play behavior can be used to assess her developmental level. Play, like other child behaviors, follows a predictable developmental sequence. An excellent discussion of play and development can be found in "Cognitive-Developmental Considerations in the Conduct of Play Therapy" (Harter, 1983). Observations of the child's play development can be used to develop hypotheses about other aspects of her development and both treatment strategies and goals.

You might use any of these techniques, depending on the aspect of the child's internal functioning or ecosystem that requires clarification.

Formal Testing

Formal psychological testing is not a routine part of most play therapists pretreatment evaluations. However, it can be invaluable in clarifying the child's overall developmental level and pinpointing areas where development is proceeding unevenly. As we previously noted, developmental lags are very common in children presenting for treatment, but it is uneven development that can prove particularly problematic.

Cognitive Testing

This portion of the evaluation can help identify the child's current cognitive developmental level. This information may be useful to you in three different ways. First, knowledge of the child's present cognitive functioning allows you to understand how she has processed her experience to date. Second, it allows you to gauge the play therapy process and content to the child's level in such a manner as to maximize the learning she will do in sessions and the speed with which improvements generalize. Finally, knowledge of the child's cognitive level can help you develop appropriate expectations for her behavior both in and out of sessions. That is, it may be used to help identify the range of the child's functional potential.

In any of these contexts, IQ scores are not particularly valuable because they simply compare the child to a normative group, yielding some sense of deviation rather than a sense of the pattern of her cognitive functioning or developmental level. The child whose Full Scale IQ on the *Wechsler Intelligence Scale for Children-III* (WISC-III) (Wechsler, 1991) is about 100 based on a Verbal IQ score of 130 and a Performance IQ of 70 is very different from the child who achieves 100 on all three measures. Further, two children with identical Verbal and Performance IQ scores could have obtained them based on very dissimilar performances. One child might have made good use of verbal skills, preferring to learn new material via auditory channels, while the other child might have processed visual information more readily. On the other hand, an analysis of the WISC-III subtests and the child's responses to specific items will tell you much more about her style of thinking and help you identify those strengths or weaknesses that might inhibit or potentiate treatment progress.

The normative information intelligence tests like the WISC-III can help you compare the child's cognitive functioning to other children her age, but it is not always very useful in treatment planning. For example, a child's low scores in Arithmetic, Object Assembly, Block Design, and so forth do not necessarily tell very much about the child's day-to-day cognitive style. Additionally, one must always keep in mind the potential inappropriateness of using many standardized intelligence tests to assess children who are not Anglo or Euro-American. Further, the results of most intelligence tests do not readily translate into a developmental conceptualization of the child's functioning. As described in Part II, the child's cognitive developmental level will determine the way both general life experiences and in-session experiences are processed. Therefore, a good understanding of the child's cognitive developmental level is essential to the conduct of effective therapy sessions.

Projective Testing

Various projective instruments can be used to identify the child's level of psychosexual development in a manner consistent with psychoanalytic theory and the range of her emotional experience and coping styles. Projective testing can identify not only the child's current functioning but residue of unresolved trauma and conflicts from earlier developmental stages.

Projective testing may also be useful in helping identify the way the child thinks about the world. Typical questions that can be addressed through projective testing include: How does this child expect interactions between adults, or between children, or between adults and children to proceed? How does she conceptualize the roles of significant others in her environment? To whom would she turn for help in case of a problem? What kinds of outcomes does she expect in various situations? How does she conceptualize herself in the world? Is she powerful or helpless? Is she good or bad? All these beliefs about the world will affect or directly manifest themselves in the child's treatment at some point. If you are at least minimally aware of your client's most significant organizing thoughts and beliefs, then you can anticipate their appearance and successfully address them in treatment.

Developmental Assessment

Cognitive testing can identify children's present level of functioning and give some sense of the probable range of their potential, and projective testing can measure children's personality functioning, but the formulation of an adequate play therapy treatment plan requires that you also have a sense of the child's overall developmental level across her full range of functioning. Several instruments are excellent tools for assessing children's development across areas of functioning; the two instruments discussed here are the Vineland Adaptive Behavior Scales (VABS) and the Developmental Therapy Objective Rating Form.

The VABS (Sparrow, Balla, & Cicchetti, 1984) are designed as a structured interview to be conducted with someone who knows the child well, usually the primary caretaker. The instrument is so well known and widely used that here we only briefly discuss it.

The VABS are used to gather information about the child's functioning in five domains: communication (receptive, expressive, and written), daily living skills (personal, domestic, community), socialization (interpersonal relationships, play and leisure, coping skills), motor skills (gross and fine), and maladaptive behavior. The items in each subdomain consist of operationally defined behaviors. The target behaviors are hierarchically arranged by the age at which they are normatively achieved.

The interviewer checks off each behavior that the respondent reports the child as engaging in on a regular basis. The instrument measures habitual, rather than optimal, functioning. To maintain rapport and help prevent the respondent from skewing their responses to the high end, the items are not presented directly; the information is gathered through a very open-ended interview, with specific probe questions used only when the information needed to complete a given scale is not provided spontaneously.

Once all the data have been gathered, the raw scores are converted into standard scores, national percentile ranks, adaptive levels, and age equivalents. As with other tests with items hierarchically arranged based on developmental norms, the initial items that the child does not pass on each scale become the intervention goals.

Regarding treatment planning, the VABS provide a considerable amount of very useful information. Unfortunately, because of the test's atheoretical, norm-referenced nature, many of the items do not translate readily into concepts consistent with any particular developmental model, which can make the information obtained somewhat difficult to integrate with your general conceptualization of the child's functioning. The exceptions to this are the socialization and maladaptive behavior scales both of which can be quite useful.

The Developmental Therapy Objective Rating Form (DTORF)* is "a developmental rating instrument employing an ordinal scale for assessment of a student's social-emotional development . . . which emphasizes the sequential process of item mastery and direct application for program implementation" (Wood, Combs, Gunn, & Weller, 1986, p. 46; Wood, Davis, Swindle, & Quirk, 1996). The DTORF is particularly useful in treatment planning for two reasons. First, the ratings allow the therapist to conceptualize the child's overall development while noting any unevenness between domains. In addition, the DTORF was designed as part of an overall Special Education intervention program for emotionally and behaviorally disturbed children so that the goals identified for each student rated can be directly translated into interventions.

The DTORF is divided into four domains: Behavior, Communication, Socialization, and Academics. Within each domain, the items range from very basic and low level behaviors at the awareness level to very complex behaviors reflecting high levels of integrated, coordinated social and cognitive activity. For example, the first objective in the Socialization area is "To be aware of others." The last objective in the sequence, on

---

* At this time a DTORF-R (1999) is available. Current research and refinements of the DTORF-R and a test kit can be obtained by writing Developmental Therapy-Teaching Programs, Box 5153, Athens, GA, 30604-5153 or by e-mail at mmwood@arches.uga.edu. There is also a website: www.uga.edu/dttp.

the other hand, is "To demonstrate the ability to generally sustain mature group and individual relationships in which there is mutual reward." The objectives are sequenced into five separate stages of development, Stage One being the lowest level and Stage Five the highest (Wood et al., 1986, p. 46).

The primary tasks and the normative ages for each stage are as follows: Stage 1—ages 0–2, learning to respond to and trust the environment; Stage 2—ages 2–6, learning individual skills; Stage 3—ages 6–9, learning to apply individual skills to group procedures; Stage 4—ages 9–12, learning to value one's group; and Stage 5—ages 12–16, learning to apply individual and group skills to new situations (Wood et al., 1986). Unfortunately, in terms of parsimony, the stages of the DTORF and the levels proposed in Part II of this book do not exactly overlap because the DTORF proposes four rather than three stages prior to the child's turning 11 years of age. For reasons somewhat less than clear, the DTORF divides Level III, which corresponds to the concrete operations stage of cognitive development, into two stages. But if this aspect of the DTORF is overlooked, the models are virtually identical.

The DTORF contains sequences of 171 hierarchically arranged, operationally defined objectives that encompass a developmental age span from birth to the age of 16. The rater simply begins at the earliest developmental level in the area to be rated. Each criterion behavior that is judged evident in the child's repertoire at least 80 percent of the time is checked in sequence. The rater proceeds down the list until she reaches a behavior in which the child does not engage regularly; this behavior becomes a treatment goal. The rating form can also be used to assess progress as treatment proceeds.

"Construct validity for the DTORF was established in the initial Developmental Therapy model which draws on the research findings and theory reviewed in Chapter Two (of the Developmental Therapy text by Wood et al., 1986). Each DTORF item is referenced to this knowledge base. Content validity for use with severely emotionally disturbed students initially was established by field testing over a five year period with more than 400 severely emotionally disturbed students served in four different locations. Since the first field testing, the DTORF has been used with several thousand students, ages two to sixteen, with a range of handicapping conditions including the autistic, mentally retarded, severely multiply handicapped, deaf, severely emotionally disturbed, schizophrenic, and socially and behaviorally handicapped as well as nonhandicapped and gifted students" (p. 72).

For use in planning a child's play therapy program, only the Behavioral, Communication, and Socialization domains are rated. Typically, you identify three to six goals for a child, one or two in each of the three areas. Although not every item can be directly translated in the work you will be doing in the playroom with the child, most will. Additionally, many of the goals could be communicated directly to the child's parents or teachers so that others in the child's environment could be working to enhance the generalization of the improvements made over the course of the treatment. In the following box, Developmental Therapy Objectives, is a list of the Behavior, Communication, and Socialization items on the DTORF.

DEVELOPMENTAL THERAPY OBJECTIVES*

Behavior Objectives

Stage 1

0. To indicate awareness of a sensory stimulus with any responses away from or toward source of stimulus.
1. To react to sensory stimulus by attending toward source of stimulus by body response or looking.
2. To respond to stimulus by sustained attending to source of stimulus.
3. To respond spontaneously to simple environmental stimulus with a motor behavior.
4. To respond with motor and body responses to complex environmental and verbal stimuli.
5. To actively assist in learning self-help.
6. To respond independently to several play materials.
7. To indicate recall of routine by moving spontaneously to next activity area without physical stimulus.

Stage 2

8. To use play materials appropriately, simulating normal play experience.
9. To wait without physical intervention by adult.
10. To participate verbally and physically in sitting activities such as work time and juice and cookie time without physical intervention by adult.
11. To participate verbally and physically in movement activities such as playtime, mat time, games, and music activities without physical intervention by adult.
12. To spontaneously participate verbally and physically in activities without physical intervention.

---

* This list of objectives is from The Developmental Therapy Objectives: A Self-Instructional Workbook (Wood, 1979, pp. 99–132). The case examples following each item in the original text were deleted for the sake of brevity.

Stage 3

13. To complete short, individual tasks with familiar material independent of any teacher intervention.
14. To accept praise or success without inappropriate behavior or loss of control.
15. To convey awareness of basic home, school and community expectations for conduct.
16. To give simple reasons for home, school and community expectations.
17. To tell other, more appropriate ways to behave in a given situation.
18. To refrain from inappropriate behavior when others in the group are losing control.
19. To maintain physical and verbal control while participating in group activities including transitions and group play.

Stage 4

20. To respond appropriately to choices for leadership in the group.
21. To indicate beginning awareness of one's own behavioral progress.
22. To implement appropriate alternative behaviors.
23. To indicate flexibility in modifying procedures to satisfy changing needs of the group.
24. To participate in new experiences with verbal and physical control.
25. To respond to provocation with verbal and physical control.
26. To respond to critical interpersonal and group problems with constructive suggestions for solutions.

Stage 5

27. To seek to develop new personal habits or skills related to the world of work.
28. To identify and develop a desired positive role within a group.
29. To openly accept responsibility for the results of one's own actions and attitudes.
30. To demonstrate understanding and acceptance of concepts of law and order in the school and community through deliberate behavioral choices or through verbal means.
31. To endorse and participate in group self-governance.
32. To independently apply the rational processes of information gathering, analysis, conclusion, and generalization in solving personal problems.

Communication Objectives

Stage 1

0. To produce sounds.
1. To attend to person speaking.
2. To respond to verbal stimulus with a motor behavior.
3. To answer question by naming single object with a recognizable approximation of the appropriate verbal response.
4. To spontaneously use recognizable single word approximation in several activities to describe or label a situation, object, or event.
5. To produce recognizable single words in several activities to obtain a desired response from adult or to label object for adult.
6. To produce recognizable single words in several activities to obtain a desired response from child or to label object for child.
7. To produce meaningful, recognizable sequence of words without a model to obtain a desired response from others or to label object.

Stage 2

8. To answer a child's or adult's questions or requests with recognizable, meaningful, relevant word(s).
9. To exhibit a receptive vocabulary no more than two years behind chronological age expectations.
10. To use simple word sequences to command, question, or request of another child or adult in ways acceptable to classroom procedures.
11. To use words to share minimal information with an adult.
12. To describe simple, tangible characteristics of both self and others.
13. To use words spontaneously to share minimal information with another child.

Stage 3

14. To use words spontaneously to describe personal experiences, ideas, or work.
15. To use words or gestures to show appropriate positive and negative feeling responses to environment, materials, and people or animals.
16. To participate in group discussions in ways not disruptive to the group.
17. To describe characteristic attributes, strengths, and problems in self.
18. To use words or nonverbal gestures to show pride in own work and activity or to make positive statements about self.

19. To describe characteristic attributes of others.
20. To verbally recognize feelings of others.
21. To use words to show pride in group achievements.

Stage 4

22. To channel feelings or experiences through creative, nonverbal media such as art, music, dance or drama.
23. To indicate behavioral awareness of one's own behavioral progress.
24. To explain how the behavior of others results from one's own behavior.
25. To use words to praise or personally support another individual.
26. To use words to express own feelings spontaneously and appropriately in the group.
27. To use words to initiate positive relationships with both peers and adults.
28. To spontaneously express cause and effect relationships between feelings and behavior in self and other members of the group.

Stage 5

29. To make verbal statements which are generally complex in structure and figurative or abstract in content.
30. To demonstrate spontaneously the ability to choose verbal responses in provocative group situations which suggest conciliatory aims.
31. To verbally support others by recognizing their contributions and including their comments or ideas in own responses.
32. To describe multiple motives and values in social situations.
33. To express own values, ideals, loyalties and beliefs spontaneously and without adult assistance.
34. To use communication skills to sustain positive interpersonal and group relationships.

Socialization Objectives

Stage 1

1. To be aware of others.
2. To attend to other's behavior.
3. To respond to adult when child's name is called.
4. To interact with adult nonverbally to meet own needs.
5. To engage in organized solitary play.
6. To respond to adult's verbal and nonverbal requests to come to him.

7. To demonstrate understanding of single verbal requests or direction given directly to child.
8. To produce recognizable single words in several activities or obtain desired response from an adult or to label object for adult.
9. To produce recognizable single words in several activities to obtain a desired response from child or to label object for child.
10. To produce meaningful, recognizable sequence of words without a model to obtain a desired response from others or to label object.
11. To exhibit a beginning emergence of self.
12. To seek contact with adult spontaneously.

Stage 2

13. To participate spontaneously in specific parallel play activities with another child using similar materials but not interacting.
14. To wait without physical intervention by adult.
15. To initiate appropriate minimal movement toward another child.
16. To participate in a verbally directed sharing activity.
17. To participate in interactive play with another child.
18. To participate in cooperative activities or projects with another child during organized activities.

Stage 3

19. To model appropriate behavior of another child.
20. To share materials and take turns without verbal reminders.
21. To lead or demonstrate activities for a group activity.
22. To label simple social situations with value statements such as right/wrong, good/bad, fair/unfair.
23. To participate without inappropriate response in activity suggested by another child.
24. To describe won experiences in the sequence of occurrence.
25. To indicate developing friendship preferences for a particular child or children.
26. To seek assistance or praise for another child.
27. To assist others in conforming to group rules.

Stage 4

28. To identify with adult leaders, heroes or other real people.
29. To describe group social experience in the sequence of occurrence.
30. To spontaneously suggest appropriate group activity directly to the peer group.

31. To express awareness of social actions of others which are different from one's own in the same situation.
32. To show respect for the opinions of others.
33. To openly express interest in the opinions peers hold about oneself.
34. To respond to critical interpersonal and group problems with constructive suggestions for solutions.
35. To recognize and discriminate among opposite values in social situations.
36. To draw inferences from social situations.

Stage 5

37. To show understanding of and respect for situations, feelings and perspectives of others (empathy).
38. To participate in reciprocal relationships in a variety of roles.
39. To make personal choices in social situations based upon one's own values and principles.
40. To indicate self understanding by describing goals, adequacies, inadequacies and inconsistencies between what one is and what one would like to be.
41. To demonstrate the ability to generally sustain mature group and individual relationships in which there is mutual reward.

Having identified the target behaviors or developmental issues and the relevant psychological conflicts, where they exist, you are ready to proceed with the development of a treatment plan.

CASE FORMULATION AND GOAL DEVELOPMENT

As stressed throughout this volume, the play therapist has a primary role in developing and implementing a treatment plan that will maximize the client's developmental functioning while minimizing her symptomatology. To be effective regarding both the outcome of the treatment and the time and money invested by the child's caretakers, you should be operating from a clear treatment plan at all times. This plan may change over time, but it should be maintained so as to provide the knowledge base from which you are working.

Some of the goals you will be working toward will have been developed by the child and/or parents during the intake interview and need to be incorporated into your treatment plan. The remainder of your goals will be developed out of your review and interpretation of the data you have collected through the intake and the assessment processes and your observations.

The development of good, comprehensive treatment goals is a complex portion of any form of treatment. It becomes more complicated when you are attempting to take so many different aspects of the child's life and ecosystem into consideration as you proceed. The process is somewhat simplified by dividing the plan into three phases.

In Phase 1, describe the child's present pattern of functioning across as many areas as possible. To create this description, use information from the child, her family, other reporters, and any assessments that are available. Be careful to develop an overall description of the child's functioning into which her problem behaviors have been incorporated. The goals developed out of this phase of the analysis involve specification of the developmental steps through which the child will need to proceed to achieve an optimal level of functioning. These goals lie primarily in the areas of the child's emotional and social functioning.

In Phase 2 of the analysis, develop hypotheses about the origins of the child's present pattern of functioning. What are the source(s) of the lags in the child's development as well as those problems that are not developmentally related? Originating factors that must be addressed are not based in the child's past experience; they are those factors that are a part of the child herself, her endowment, as it were. You may be unable to address these factors in the course of the child's treatment, but they are crucial in determining both the strategies to be used and what can reasonably be expected to be the child's optimal level of functioning. In a manner consistent with psychoanalytic treatment, you must also recognize that residue of the child's past may be a significant roadblock to altering her present pattern of behavior. This is not to imply that therapy can undo or alter the past but to ensure that you consider the context out of which the child's behavior has grown. The goals resulting from this portion of the analysis consist primarily of listing those experiences from the child's past that will have to be addressed. The treatment plan may consist of either making sure that the child is exposed to experiences which counter the impact of the original experiences or working to help the child integrate her past experience into her present life on a cognitive and emotional level.

In Phase 3, develop hypotheses as to what factors maintain the child's present pattern of functioning. These factors may derive from any portion of the child's present life situation—her ecosystem—including factors the child contributes as well as those the child's family, school, peers, and so forth contribute. Some of your goals will target factors which need to be weakened or eliminated so that they do not interfere with the child's progress; other goals will target factors which need to be strengthened so that they maximize her progress. Again, it may not be possible or even desirable to address all these points in the child's treatment, but they may have significance, indirectly, in the overall management of her case.

The Child's Present Pattern of Functioning

Development Level

What is the child's overall level of developmental functioning, and what are her needs? In which domains is the child functioning well, and in which is her performance deficient? To what extent can the child's current difficulties be framed as developmental deviations as opposed to behavior that would be considered atypical regardless of her level of functioning? Independent of the way the child's developmental level is assessed, whether by interview, rating scale, or formal testing, each question must be addressed before treatment can proceed. It is the therapist's conceptualization of the child's developmental functioning against which all the other information about the child will be viewed and upon which all subsequent treatment planning will be based. Treatment first needs to be geared toward the child's lowest level of functioning in any one domain while attempting to take advantage of her strengths in other domains. In the middle phase of treatment, the therapist plans sessions to enhance the child's movement along the developmental continuum, gradually approaching age appropriateness in as many domains as possible. Termination is considered when the child's functioning appears as close to being developmentally and age-appropriate as possible given her particular endowment. Following each goal listed below is a code indicating the domain (B for Behavioral, C for Communication, and S for Socialization) and the item number from the DTORF.

CASE EXAMPLE: AARON

Using the DTORF, it was determined that at the age of 6, Aaron was functioning at Stage 4 in the Behavioral domain, Stage 3 in the Communications domain, and Stage 2 in the Socialization domain. Given his age, Aaron should have been functioning at the early Stage 3 across all domains.

Goals: Aaron will be able to: (1) respond appropriately to either being selected or not being selected to be the leader in a group activity (B-20); (2) indicate a beginning awareness of his own behavioral progress (B-21); (3) use words or gestures to show appropriate positive and negative feeling responses to the environment and people or animals (C-15); (4) participate in group discussions in ways that are not disruptive to the group (C-16); (5) initiate appropriate minimal social interaction with another child (S-15); and (6) participate in interactive play with another child (S-17).

CASE EXAMPLE: FRANK

Using the DTORF, it was determined that at the age of 10 Frank was functioning at Stage 2 in the Behavioral domain, Stage 2 in the Communication domain, and Stage 2 in the Socialization domain. Given his age, Frank should have been well into Stage 4 in all domains.

Goals (Wood, 1979, pp. 93–132): Frank will be able to: (1) use play materials appropriately (B-8); (2) spontaneously participate, verbally and physically, in activities without physical intervention (B-12); (3) exhibit a receptive vocabulary no more than 2 years behind his chronological age (C-9); (4) use words to initiate minimal conversations with an adult beyond making requests (C-11); (5) participate spontaneously in specific parallel play activities with another child using similar materials but not interacting (S-13); and (6) initiate appropriate minimal social interaction with another child (S-15).

Cognitions

In conceptualizing the child's cognitive functioning, two different issues must be addressed. First, you must determine the child's present level of intellectual functioning and develop hypotheses as to her intellectual potential, and, on the other hand, you must determine which of her thoughts and beliefs organize her thinking and approach to the world. That is, you must identify core beliefs which are based in the child's experience and which may or may not have any basis in her present reality.

It is not necessary to have a specific measure of the child's intelligence, especially if her overall functioning is approximately in the average range. After all, it is not the child's IQ that directly affects the nature of her treatment but the way she processes information and stores it in memory. Therefore, it can be very useful for you to know if the child has any overall cognitive deficits or any specific learning disabilities. With regards to learning disabilities, you should recognize that some learning difficulties will have a greater impact on the child's overall functioning and the nature of the treatment than others. For example, the child who has a specific disability in mathematics may be frustrated in school, but it is unlikely that it significantly affects her ability to relate to family and peers or that the techniques you use will need to be modified in any significant way. On the other hand, a child whose overall intelligence is near normal but has a specific disability affecting receptive and expressive language is much more likely to be experiencing difficulties in her social interactions and will require a treatment plan consistent with her overall intelligence but not heavily language-based.

The consistency between this integrated model and cognitive behavior therapy is reflected in the fact that both recognize that children's thoughts and beliefs can play a significant role in maintaining their dysfunctional behavior. These cognitions must be identified so they can be changed if any behavior change over the course of therapy is to be expected. Often the child's core misbelief(s) about the world is not discernable at the beginning of treatment, although portions of it may be hypothesized. These hypotheses can be used in treatment planning virtually from the outset.

CASE EXAMPLE: AARON

Aaron's cognitive functioning was assessed using the WISC-III. He obtained a Full Scale IQ of 130 with little deviation among his subtest scores. This suggests that his intellectual abilities are well ahead of his expected developmental level and will greatly facilitate his use of cognitive strategies in the play therapy.

Virtually all of Aaron's cognitions were age-appropriate. He did, however, demonstrate unusual cognitions regarding his father's illness. In spite of the fact that he was exposed to most of the aspects of his father's care, he had virtually no understanding of the illness. His parents believed that he was too young to understand any of the details. In his desire to understand the continual changes in his life, Aaron had made many assumptions which meant that, given his preoperational level of thinking at the time, many of the facts he strung together had very little to do with each other in reality. One of his particularly disturbing beliefs was that if he were very, very good, what was happening to his father would not happen to him.

Goal: Aaron will demonstrate age-appropriate knowledge of his father's illness.

CASE EXAMPLE: FRANK

Frank was assessed just prior to his admission to a residential special education program where he was placed because of persistent school failure. On the WISC-III, which was administered to Frank when he was 10, he obtained a Full Scale IQ of 82, with a Verbal IQ of 72 and a Performance IQ of 96. Although Frank's overall intellectual functioning was below average, he impressed his teachers as being somewhat brighter. What was most pronounced was his extreme language disability. Receptively, he could not follow any statements longer than simple sentences delivered at a relatively slow rate. The introduction of any abstract terms into the conversation caused him to completely lose the content. Expressively, Frank limited himself to very brief statements, generally avoiding verbal interactions whenever possible.

Frank's relatively low cognitive functioning, his serious language deficits, and his traumatic life experiences combined to delay his cognitive development considerably. In spite of his age, Frank was still functioning at the early concrete operations level of thinking, as demonstrated by his inability to serialize even a simple sequence of events.

Due to Frank's history of catastrophic abuse, he held numerous beliefs about the world that interfered with his day-to-day functioning. First and foremost, he believed that although he was dependent on adults for both emotional and physical supplies, all his interactions with them would lead first to their abusing him and then to their abandoning him. Frank's feelings of dependency therefore alternated with his belief that the adults in his world were either unable or unwilling to meet his needs on a consistent basis. He also believed that his peers were incapable of gratifying any of his needs and in fact that they were in competition for the limited supplies which were available; thus his peers were to be avoided or attacked. A very significant belief not uncovered until later in his treatment was Frank's view of himself as possessing incredible destructive power. He believed that he had killed his mother to protect himself and that no one else could be as effective as he was in caring for himself. After all, the courts had merely sent his abusive father away, so Frank lived with the fear that he might return, while he knew his mother would never disappoint him again.

Goals: Frank will: (1) be able to describe his feelings in simple sentences and to report a brief series of events in sequence; (2) seek to get some of his needs met by others, first adults and then peers; (3) report less fear that he will be abandoned by adults; and (4) report decreased intent to hurt others.

Emotions

What is particularly important here is the child's repertoire of affective experience, the degree to which she is aware of those feelings, and her ability to express those feelings either verbally or in action. Also, the therapist needs to have some sense of the motivation underlying the child's behavior and, as with affects, the degree to which she is aware of those motivations and able to express them.

Generally, anxiety is the dominant affect children entering treatment experience. It may be hidden under layers of defense or secondary emotions, but it is usually present. You will have to work to address both the affects that the child manifests in her verbalizations and behavior and the underlying affects and anxieties.

CASE EXAMPLE: AARON

Aaron appeared quite pseudomature upon interview, and his mother confirmed that this was his style across settings. His affects were well modulated and never intense. When he experienced something he did not like, he expressed his discomfort in a very direct manner. If his statements did not stop the interaction, he seemed very confused and became very anxious. Aaron desperately wanted to be in control at all times and resisted becoming involved in activities anyone else suggested. At school he insisted on doing his work his way. If he had to follow directions, he found some way to make it sound as if they had been his idea in the first place.

Goals: Aaron will: (1) manifest less anxiety across situations; (2) be able to accept input from others in both academic and social situations; (3) manifest a greater variety of affects; (4) instigate more requests that others meet his needs; and (5) not become anxious when exposed to small amounts of disorder or mess.

CASE EXAMPLE: FRANK

Frank entered therapy with an extremely constricted affective repertoire. He rarely smiled, cried, or became overtly angry. In fact, he rarely interacted with anyone else, especially his peers. When Frank talked, it was generally in a monotone, although he occasionally slipped in some slight variations. Frank was unable to report any variation in his own affect other than being able to say he was angry if directly asked. If frustrated to the point of becoming angry, he usually acted out in some destructive way. Many of Frank's behaviors seemed motivated by his desire to get all that he could from someone before they abandoned him.

Goals: Frank will: (1) be able to verbalize his affects; (2) be able to recognize variations in his affect; (3) be able to label his affects in a variety of situations; and (4) use language to delay his tendency to act out.

Psychopathology

As discussed in Chapter Four in Ecosystemic Play Therapy psychopathology is framed as the inability to get one's needs met effectively and/or appropriately. The latter always meaning the ability to get one's needs met without interfering with others getting their needs met.

CASE EXAMPLE: AARON

Aaron's need for nurturance and affection had been consistently met since birth although the increasing seriousness of his father's illness meant his mother had less and less time for him. Unfortunately, because he was so focused on his parents and their problems he was unable to appropriately seek out and receive nurturance from his peers. There was some sense that Aaron's need for safety may not have been adequately met in that he may have believed his father's illness was contagious. The bulk of Aaron's difficulties stemmed, however, from his intense need for control which interfered with his ability to gain simple pleasure from everyday experiences and tended to make him controlling and somewhat hostile toward peers.

Goals: Aaron will: (1) experience an increased sense of safety as he gains a better understanding of the nature of his father's illness; (2) recognize and express a desire for nurturance from other adults in his environment and from his peers; and (3) learn to get more of his needs for nurturance met by relinquishing some of his need for control.

CASE EXAMPLE: FRANK

Frank had been unable to get his needs met either effectively or appropriately since a very young age. His need for nurturance and attachment had not been adequately met since before the age of two due to his experience of abuse by his mother. This need was only partially being addressed in his current life situation as he felt moderately attached to his foster mother but did not see himself as deserving or receiving nurturance from other adults much less peers. His need for safety was met inappropriately in that it was achieved at the cost of his mother's life. Even then his safety was only temporary as his father became abusive. Later, he was not even safe with animals once bitten by the family dog. His need for a sense of control and mastery over his environment was never met effectively or appropriately. He was inappropriately controlling from the time he set the fire that killed his mother right up through the temper outbursts he continued to display.

Goals: Frank will be able to: (1) express the desire for and receive nurturant input from other adults in his life; (2) express his desire for and receive nurturant input from his peers; (3) express his ongoing need to feel safe and to be protected by the adults around him; (4) develop a more accurate sense of what he can and cannot control; and (5) develop strategies for feeling in control that do not involve interpersonal aggression.

Response Repertoire

How does the child respond to stress, to situational demands, to feeling needy? Does the child tend to try to modify the environment (alloplastic change) or herself (autoplastic change), or does her response vary across situations? Maybe this is a child who will engage in significant autoplastic change if she perceives that any of the adults around her are feeling distressed. Some children will do this to keep the adults at a distance, fearing that if they do not keep an adult's distress to a minimum, they risk retribution or excessive demands from that adult. This is often the case with children of alcoholics, who become very quiet and well behaved if they notice that the parent has been drinking in hopes of avoiding a conflict. Other children will do this to build up credit with the adult, ensuring that they will be able to get their own needs met at some point in the future. This may occur when the child's parents are so narcissistic that they are unable to care for her unless their own needs are taken care of first.

Other children may tend to alloplastic change. They whine when frustrated, strike out when angry, and insist that the world take care of them. Most children, however, exhibit both autoplastic and alloplastic behavior in different situations. They may handle their anger alloplastically when at school by beating up peers but handle it autoplastically at home by hiding in the closet and biting on a blanket.

CASE EXAMPLE: AARON

Aaron also tended to solve virtually all problems autoplastically, but rather than focusing internally, he tended to focus on his immediate environment. Aaron kept his playroom at home absolutely immaculate. His mother reported that Aaron still had every piece of every game he had ever been given and that he knew exactly where everything was on each shelf. He maintained his clothing the same way and was always dressed immaculately. He rarely played with other children because they would not play by his rules and they made a mess. He never let any other children touch any of his toys.

Aaron was able to verbally request attention from both of his parents on a regular basis.

Goals: Aaron will: (1) not manifest undue anxiety in situations in which others have control; (2) not manifest undue anxiety in unstructured situations; and (3) instigate requests to play with peers.

CASE EXAMPLE: FRANK

Frank tended toward autoplastic responses to stress and frustration as his initial reactions. He simply refused to comply with anything that disturbed him; he walked away or sat like a lump. He did not fight, either verbally or physically, unless pushed. If his refusal to respond was not respected, Frank would become enraged and physically violent. In the recent past he had killed a kitten and severely injured his group home parent, and he required prolonged physical restraint at school to prevent him from hurting peers and staff. It later became clear that he was also prone toward violence if he felt that he were about to be rejected or abandoned. Thus he tended to act out if another child got his or her needs met first, fearing that the adult would not have sufficient resources left for him and would therefore neglect or reject him.

Frank's anxiety was virtually invisible at the outset of treatment. If anything, he appeared impervious to interpersonal stress so long as basic supplies were not at stake. Later it was noted that Frank acted out aggressively whenever memories of his abuse, or the various traumatic events in his life, were triggered. Any word or action in any way related to fire was particularly effective in setting off inappropriate behavior.

Goals: Frank will: (1) not use either withdrawal or violence as ways of managing frustration; (2) substitute words for actions whenever possible; and (3) manifest less anxiety in response to the recall of events from his history.

Origins of the Child's Present Pattern of Functioning

Most of the information contained in this part of the treatment plan is hypothetical unless discrete, identifiable trauma can be identified in the child's history. Part of what you try to address in conceptualizing the origins of the child's difficulties is why this child has reacted this way to this particular set of circumstances. This task is similar to that of the behavior therapist who is trying to assess why a stimulus or set of stimuli cause her client to make a certain response under certain circumstances. The hope is that by understanding how the child's past has created the dynamics of her present interactions with the world, you will find ways of intervening and creating an alternative dynamic style.

Child-Specific Factors: Endowment and Developmental Response

In developing cause-and-effect hypotheses regarding the interaction of the child's past with her present functioning, it is usually easiest to begin by examining those things that the child brought to her interactions with the world, that is, *her endowment*. This line of thinking is not meant to blame the child for her present state; it is an attempt to recognize that each child is unique and brings certain conscious and unconscious variables into her world. This concept is easiest to recognize in those cases in which a child has been born with recognizable congenital defects, such as blindness or deafness, or a physical handicap. If you view the child's contribution as existing along a spectrum, then next along the continuum are those children whose behavior is attributable, at least partly, to less visible defects, as is the case with autistic or hyperactive children. These children's parents often recognize that they are different from birth, although it may be some time before the condition is actually diagnosed. Learning-disabled children lie somewhere toward the less impaired end of the continuum, although they too may have been viewed as different by others from very early on in their lives. Last, even completely normal children bring to any situation the limitations their development to that point has placed on them. No matter how bright the 3-year-old, she is still a Level II child and can only process information in a very simplistic way and react accordingly. She cannot understand complex explanations of traumatic life events no matter how good the explanation or how hard she tries. It is these developmental limitations that you must understand to effectively conceptualize the child's understanding and response to events at any point in time. This interaction of events with the child's developmental level is referred to as the child's developmental response and is a key part of establishing the focus of the corrective experiences that will be built into the play therapy sessions.

The complete histories of the two children now discussed were presented in Chapter Four. Certain facts have been repeated here to help you understand how the child processed the events when they occurred.

CASE EXAMPLE: AARON

Aaron appears to be a very normal child with better than average intellectual capacities. As with Dennis, these skills have allowed him to resort to autoplastic attempts at modifying his environment more readily and successfully than most children.

Goal: Aaron will demonstrate the use of alternative stress management strategies across a variety of settings.

CASE EXAMPLE: FRANK

Frank's limited cognitive functioning and his severe language deficit significantly determined his present functioning in two ways. First, most likely his limited language contributed to his not being removed from his father's care earlier. Frank was never able to tell anyone about the abuse he was suffering, and there is little doubt that he would have had difficulty formulating the reports even if he had wanted to tell anyone. Second, Frank's limited cognitive capacity was responsible for his being able to process his experience only in a very primitive manner. He was unable to cognitively sort out the differences between the various traumas he experienced, and therefore they were all stored together in his memory. He could not recall one without recalling the others, which in turn made his response to stimuli that triggered recall of any one of the traumatic events very intense. Last, the young age at which Frank's trauma began adds to the likelihood that he never fully understood what was happening to him or why it was happening. He most likely processed these events in a very concrete and egocentric manner. Evidence of this is found in the fact that he firmly believes he intentionally killed his mother even though he was only three at the time of the fire.

Goals: Frank will be able to: (1) differentiate the situations, serialize the events, report antecedents and consequences, and label the affects associated with each traumatic event in his history; and (2) be more realistic in his appraisals of the control and power he had at the time the abuse was occurring and his subsequent responsibility for either the way he was treated or the outcome of events such as the fire.

Ecological Factors

Having considered the child's contribution, if any, to the origin or structure of her present difficulties, now turn to the examination of her ecosystem for variables that contributed to her current pathology. The variables include family, peers, and broader systems.

Family. The child's family is the primary system in which she is embedded and has therefore powerful potential to either create pathology or mediate against the negative effects of a pathonomic event. Many a therapist is quick to blame the parents for the child's distress, an attitude fostered by the disease models of psychopathology, which frame the parents as the pathogenic agents, and the humanistic model, which postulates the environment as the trigger of all dysfunction. But no matter how effective and well functioning the family, they cannot protect the child from everything. Some children experience trauma at the hands of peers or teachers or others; sometimes children simply cannot function at the level they, or others, would like. The impact of the family on the child's functioning and their ability to support the child in treatment need to be carefully considered when formulating a treatment plan.

CASE EXAMPLE: AARON

Aaron's difficulties stem almost entirely from his and his family's response to his father's physical deterioration due to multiple sclerosis. Up until the time of his father's first attack, Aaron had been developing normally, if not precociously. Since that time, Aaron continued to develop and be precocious in most areas while his father steadily lost functional capacities. A gradual reversal of roles occurred, with Aaron becoming the adult male in the family as the father became the dependent child.

Goal: Aaron will engage in a greater proportion of age-appropriate behaviors over the course of a given day.

CASE EXAMPLE: FRANK

Frank's pathology was entirely the result of the trauma to which his mother and father subjected him. However, in this case there is the additional complicating factor of a severe language disability, whose impact on Frank's processing and storage of the trauma he experienced we covered in the previous discussion of cognition.

Goals: Frank will be able to: (1) verbalize his awareness that his parents were extremely pathologic and that their treatment of him was not his fault; (2) express his sadness at the fact that he has lost both his parents; (3) express sadness that his biological parents were not good parents; and (4) express his anger at his biological father for the way he treated him.

Peers.   The impact of relationships with peers on the creation of a child's pathology is often overlooked when planning for a child's individual treatment. Peers can have a pronounced impact on a child, especially if she is stigmatized in some way that invites ridicule.

Peers did not play a significant role in the origins of the pathology of any of the cases presented here. Frank and Aaron tended to remain aloof from peers and rarely encountered any resistance to such a stance. Diane and Dennis were both very good at maintaining appropriate peer interactions. None of these children were able to get a significant portion of their basic needs met through their peer interactions, so they were minimally motivated toward such interactions.

Broader systems: School, hospital, juvenile justice.   The impact of the other systems in which the child is embedded on the creation and maintenance of her difficulties is also an often neglected area in developing the individual treatment plan. Children are unique in their position of relative dependence and helplessness vis-à-vis many of the adults in their lives. They must do what teachers, doctors, legal representatives, and others tell them. Often in situations where the child's parent is incompetent, the child has no one to protect her interests against the interests of the systems in which she is trapped.

CASE EXAMPLE: AARON

Aaron had little or no contact with any systems outside his family and school. The school system had responded to his needs fairly well, although they tended to reinforce his overcompliance and complain about the degree to which he wanted to control every aspect of his schoolday.

Goal: Aaron will initiate requests that others meet some of his basic needs.

CASE EXAMPLE: FRANK

Frank's failure to develop a substantive bond with any adult as precipitated by the abuse and neglect his parents inflicted was complicated by his being moved from one foster home to another over the first year and a half after he was removed from his father's care. The social service system taught Frank not to attach even if people were nice to you because they would abandon you relatively soon.

Not until his placement at the therapeutic group home where he remained for 3 years did Frank began to develop an attachment to the woman who ran the home. The stability of this placement was the result of the time and energy of the therapist who treated Frank for the duration of his placement.

Goal: Frank will demonstrate the development of a unique attachment to an adult in his life.

Additionally, events may occur during the course of the therapy that are, or could be, extremely detrimental to the process of the treatment. Some of these events will be well outside your control, but you may be able to mediate the impact of others.

CASE EXAMPLE: FRANK

As Frank began to show real improvement in his treatment, the woman who ran the group home where Frank resided and whom Frank referred to as his mother decided that she could no longer manage Frank in her home and asked that he be placed elsewhere. This was a legitimate decision on her part but one that had devastating implications for the long-term outcome of Frank's treatment. The therapist worked hard with Frank's caseworker to try to develop a plan to keep Frank in the group home, all to no avail.

While the therapist had been unable to intervene effectively in preventing Frank's move to yet another home, he was able to intervene in another situation that could have had serious negative consequences for Frank. Over the course of Frank's life, he had been repeatedly separated from people with very little warning and with no time to mourn and say his goodbyes. Even when he was moved from the group home where he had lived for years, it was accomplished without giving Frank any notice. These sudden separations reinforced Frank's tendency not to attach to any of the people in his environment because they might suddenly be gone.

When a new group home was located, it was at some distance from the residential program, and the decision was made to move Frank to a school placement closer to his new home. This decision was made and Frank was moved in the space of less than 1 week. The expectation was that in a single session Frank would terminate with the therapist he had been seeing for over a year.

The therapist worked to educate the caseworker on the negative impact this move would have. He pointed out that this action would in effect nullify most of what Frank had accomplished by convincing Frank that the therapist really did not care about him after all. After much convincing and a little threatening, arrangements were made to transport Frank to three additional termination sessions over a 2-month period, allowing Frank to mourn the loss of his group home and the residential program and to make the transition into his new program, all with the same therapist. With this support, Frank was able to make a smooth transition to the new placement.

Factors Maintaining the Child's Present Pattern of Functioning

In this final stage of the data analysis, you develop hypotheses as to the factors that maintain the difficulties that the child is presenting. As with the previous stage of the analysis, you must integrate the information you gathered from the child, her family, the assessment, your observations, and any other sources with your theoretical model of child development and pathology. This part of the data analysis may generate goals not directly addressed in the course of the child's treatment but that will be in the overall management of her case.

Child-Specific Difficulties

At this point, you will have examined the child's present pattern of functioning and those child-specific factors which originated that pattern. Now it is time to examine those aspects of the child's functioning that maintain her difficulties or specifically interfere with her growth.

Endowment. Some children have little chance of ever functioning at an age-appropriate level simply because their biologic endowment precludes it. In most cases this is determined by deficits in either the child's cognitive or neurological functioning that cannot be remediated. Occasionally, a child has a physical disorder that substantially interferes with her functioning optimally in other areas for some period of time, such as the severely asthmatic child whose peer relations suffer because of the restrictions her illness imposes on her diet and exercise. Depending on the severity of the problem, complete or even partial remediation may be more or less possible.

CASE EXAMPLE: AARON

Aaron's endowment seemed to be well within normal limits. Unfortunately, his intellectual capacities allowed him to be overly dependent on an autoplastic approach to problem solving.

Goal: Aaron will initiate requests for information and assistance in problem solving from adults in his environment.

CASE EXAMPLE: FRANK

Frank's limited cognitive functioning and his severe language deficits made it difficult for him to progress developmentally. He had difficulty processing events or carrying out simple social interactions. He was virtually unable to interact with age mates even if he wanted to because of his limited communication skills. Verbal expression of affect was similarly difficult.

Goal: Frank will initiate interactions with peers using nonverbal strategies where possible.

Developmental level and response.   The child's developmental level, especially when it is discrepant from that expected given her age and biologic endowment, can play a significant role in maintaining her present difficulties or even cause new ones. For example, if the child behaves very immaturely she may invite censure or ridicule from peers or even adults. Further, the therapist must assess whether the child is still conceptualizing and responding to events at the developmental level at which they occurred. That is, is the 10-year-old child who was abused as a toddler still thinking about her abuse like a two year old (the abuse was my fault and I hate my abusive mother) or is she able to think about it like a 10-year-old (I shouldn't have been abused no matter what I did and I realize I both love and hate my abusive mother)?

CASES EXAMPLE: AARON

Aaron displayed behavior that appeared to be in advance of his chronological age which brought him substantial reinforcement from adults. Aaron's pseudo-maturity prevented his establishing stable friendships with his peers.

Goal: Aaron will demonstrate more variability in his affective expression consistent with his developmental level.

CASE EXAMPLE: FRANK

The extreme discrepancy between Frank's developmental level and his chronological age interfered with his interacting positively with peers. When he was 10 and acting like he was 5, this was not too much of a problem because Frank was rather small. However, when Frank was 11 he began to grow, which highlighted for both peers and adults the discrepancy in his functioning. Adults changed their expectations for Frank's behavior even though he had made virtually no other changes. Similarly, Frank's peers began to reject him for being too infantile.

Goal: Frank will initiate social interactions at his developmental level.

Cognitions.   Both the child's cognitive functioning and her thoughts and beliefs about her world can significantly interfere with her ability to move toward emotional health.

CASE EXAMPLE: AARON

Aaron's cognitive abilities were also a strength and allowed him to implement many autoplastic attempts at problem solving. As with Dennis, Aaron's skill in this area made it difficult for him to risk attempting other problem-solving strategies. In addition, his belief that he might contract the disease that afflicted his father if he did not behave well dramatically interfered with his willingness to take any risks.

Goals: Aaron will: (1) demonstrate a more realistic understanding of his father's illness; and (2) engage in some play activities for the first time without experiencing unmanageable anxiety.

CASE EXAMPLE: FRANK

Frank's limited cognitive functioning made it difficult for him to process new information or to rework old information and experience. He tended to be locked into his particular approach to the world. In addition, those beliefs about the people with whom he interacted (described in the section on Frank's present pattern of functioning) significantly interfered with his ability to interact in an age-appropriate manner.

Goal: Frank will demonstrate increased flexibility in his thinking by engaging in simple problem solving.

Emotions.   To what extent does the child's present emotional repertoire maintain the difficulties she is experiencing? For most children entering treatment, the degree of anxiety they experience interferes with one or more aspects of their development. For some children, their emotions are so powerful that they have virtually no energy to invest in anything beyond attempts at affect management. In either case they must find new ways to manage their emotions if further development is to take place.

CASE EXAMPLE: FRANK

As previously mentioned, Frank's affective repertoire was extremely limited because, except for occasional violent outbursts, he tended to remain emotionally neutral. The problem appeared to be that the unpleasant events in Frank's life had become cognitively connected to one another. It was as if Frank had a file drawer in his head, where all traumatic memories were stored along with their associated affects. The memories could not be retrieved separately, and they, along with their negative affects, tended to be reactivated whenever something triggered similar unpleasant affects in the present.

Goals: Frank will be able to: (1) differentiate past affects from present affects; and (2) recall past trauma without experiencing affective flooding.

Response repertoire.   Which of the child's response styles facilitate developmental progress? To what extent do each of the response styles interfere with such progress?

CASE EXAMPLE: AARON

Aaron's overcontrolling behaviors brought him considerable positive regard from adults but prevented him from engaging in positive interactions with his peers. Aaron's emotional repertoire was fairly constricted, and he was constantly experiencing such high levels of anxiety that he did not have the energy to invest in interacting with others. Further, his attempts at autoplastic adaptation did very little to address the concerns that created his anxiety.

Goals: Aaron will: (1) demonstrate an increased understanding of his father's illness; (2) verbalize his understanding that he cannot catch his father's illness; (3) be able to approach adults with questions about the progress of his father's illness and especially about his concerns that his father might die imminently; and (4) be able to engage others in conversations about his fear of dying.

CASE EXAMPLE: FRANK

Frank's primary responses to stress were either withdrawal or rage, neither of which facilitated his getting his needs met in his interactions with peers or adults.

Goal: Frank must develop alternative ways of responding to stress in order to get his needs met more effectively.

Ecological Difficulties

In this portion of the analysis, you develop hypotheses about those environmental factors that interfere with the child's functioning optimally. Here you should also look for those factors that can be anticipated to interfere with the progress of the child's treatment.

Family.   The first system to be examined is that of the family.

CASE EXAMPLE: AARON

Aaron's father was dying from his rapidly advancing multiple sclerosis; he was not expected to live more than another year. In the meantime, it was becoming very hard for him to engage in any activities with Aaron due to his loss of muscle control. His continued rapid deterioration triggered repeated episodes of mourning in all family members.

At one point, Aaron's mother said that although she recognized that Aaron's behavior was not normal for a 6-year-old and this made her sad, she was not sure she really wanted him to act like a 6-year-old. After all, she said, then her situation would make her feel like she was a single parent with an in-fant (the husband) and a 6-year-old. This way, she admitted, Aaron was no trouble and was, in fact, a great deal of help. This was anticipated to be the major interference in Aaron's progress in treatment.

Goals: Aaron will: (1) see that both his parents are involved in the treat-ment process; (2) see that his mother acts as his primary caretaker but that both parents make all treatment decisions jointly; and (3) be able to verbally mourn the gradual loss of his father.

CASE EXAMPLE: FRANK

Early in Frank's placement at the residential educational program in which he was treated, one of his foster siblings developed a life-threatening illness re-quiring numerous hospitalizations and round-the-clock care. As a result, the group home parents were constantly involved with the sibling, spending most of their time at the hospital, which meant that they were unable to visit Frank and were not there when he went home on weekends. This greatly enhanced Frank's sense of abandonment and his belief in the unreliability of adults as caretakers.

It was anticipated that the fact that Frank had no permanent family who could serve to buffer the emotions he would experience in therapy might prove a major factor in his failing to progress in therapy.

Goal: Frank will be able to seek support from others as his therapy progresses.

Peers.   Once the child begins to exhibit abnormal behavior, ridicule from peers becomes even more likely. One of the most difficult types of problems to treat is the severe victimization of children who are scape-goated. Even if such children can manage to change the behavior that draws the negative attention of their peers, the image or reputation they have created for themselves can be virtually impossible to reverse.

CASE EXAMPLE: AARON

Aaron did not interact with any peers. Given his age, the other children did not seem to care much whether or not he was involved. He had not been negatively characterized by either the children in his school or those in his neighborhood.

Goal: Aaron will initiate interactions with peers both at home and at school.

CASE EXAMPLE: FRANK

Frank's peers had already identified him as odd, a characterization that was not helped when he offhandedly told them that he had killed his mother and was not sad about it. They preferred not to play with him, although they did not usually antagonize him. Frank was best accepted by several younger children.

Goals: Frank will: (1) demonstrate an ability to approach age mates in an appropriate manner; and (2) be able to elaborate on the circumstances of his mother's death in conversations with his peers.

Broader systems: School, hospital, juvenile justice.   A limited advocacy approach is a logical extension of your taking an ecological perspective with respect to the child's difficulties. Such an approach requires that you consider the impact non-family systems may have on the health and development of the child in treatment.

CASE EXAMPLE: AARON

Aaron was not involved with any systems other than his family and school. No special school programming had been instituted.

CASE EXAMPLE: FRANK

Frank lived in constant anxiety that his father would someday return to claim him because the legal system failed to either place the father in jail or terminate his parental rights. The latter had never been effected only because Frank was considered unadoptable. However, it would have occurred immediately if his father had ever tried to reenter his life.

Frank's placement in a residential Special Education program furthered his belief that no family or facility could manage his behavior. At the time of his admission, there was already a plan, for political reasons having nothing to do with Frank or his well being, to move him to another residence at some point in the future.

Goals: Frank will: (1) verbalize his understanding of the fact that the legal system would work to prevent his father from ever reentering his life; and (2) demonstrate his ability to be involved in planning his future placements.

GOAL SYNTHESIS

At this point, you will have developed an extensive list of goals for the child who is entering treatment. Many of the goals developed will be interrelated, so you can facilitate treatment planning by grouping the goals into categories. Following are the integrated goals for each case being presented.

CASE EXAMPLE: AARON

The formation of a close therapeutic relationship in which Aaron could practice giving up some of his overwhelming need for control is the primary goal of therapy. As soon as Aaron is able to trust the therapist with a certain amount of control over their interactions, the goal is to transfer that trust from the therapist to Aaron's mother.

Once therapy effectively reduces Aaron's intense need for control, the focus is on helping him recognize and express his intense anxiety and his unmet needs, especially in his relationship with his mother. At this point two issues need to be addressed. One issue is the competition between Aaron and his father for the mother's attention, along with the father's gradually decreasing ability to meet any of Aaron's needs. The other issue is Aaron's need for concrete information about his father's illness. It is hoped that if Aaron can be assured that his needs will be met no matter how little his father is able to provide and, in fact, no matter how much his father needs, he will become substantially less anxious. It is also hoped that information about his father's illness and prognosis will help Aaron worry less about his own, and his mother's, health and begin to prepare for his father's death.

To help prepare Aaron for his father's death, therapy will aim at helping him maintain a relationship with his father that recognizes the father's extremely limited ability to be active in meeting Aaron's needs. Therapy will also work to help Aaron separate his experience of his father's deterioration from his father's experience of the process, that is, to help Aaron to empathize with his father's condition rather than identify with it. While working to maintain this relationship to whatever extent possible, it will also be important for Aaron to be able to talk about the changes that have taken place in his family thus far and those that will take place in the future.

Once Aaron's anxiety at home begins to decrease, the goal of treatment will be to encourage him to focus some energy on using his peers to get some of his emotional needs met, which will require that he become less controlling in his interactions with his peers and that his affective and behavioral repertoire be expanded and freed up.

During the termination process, Aaron will be encouraged to use his family and peers to get his needs met in age-appropriate ways.

Because Aaron's case is being used as a specific example of short-term play therapy the exact goals as stated in the treatment plan are listed here. The many goals derived from Aaron's intake and pretreatment assessment were synthesized into the following general goals:

1. Aaron will demonstrate a marked decrease in anxiety and his accompanying obsessions and compulsive behavior. Related to this, he will be better able to handle unpredictable or messy situations.
2. Aaron will recognize, express, and make use of a broader range of affects.
3. Aaron will also demonstrate a better understanding of his father's illness and be able to discuss his thoughts and fears about dying and death. He will begin to grieve the loss of his father.
4. Aaron will reduce the amount of time he needs to be in control and will allow others opportunities to control interactions.

5. Aaron will maintain a strong sense of attachment to his mother and will be better able to ask to have his needs for nurturance met.

CASE EXAMPLE: FRANK

The primary goal for Frank's treatment is the establishment of a close and trusting primary relationship Frank could learn to rely on because it appears that the trauma in his history has caused him to engage in excessive interpersonal separation and autonomy. He has yet to demonstrate attachments to any of the staff at the educational center he is residing in. It also seems that he is losing some of his attachment to his foster mother as she becomes involved in coping with the illness of his foster brother. Within the context of the therapeutic relationship, his anxiety about being abandoned needs to be addressed.

As the therapeutic relationship becomes established, it will be important to help Frank label his affects more consistently and to use words to delay his impulses where necessary. First, Frank needs to learn to recognize his affects in the present. Second, he needs to learn to verbally label these emotions. Third, he needs to differentiate past from present affects. As this process proceeds, it will be important for Frank to learn how to use the relationship to help him manage his anxiety so that he will feel less of a need to withdraw from interactions.

The third phase of the treatment is to help Frank learn to use his cognitions and language to delay acting on his impulses, especially aggression. To accomplish this objective, he has to learn how to serialize events so that he can better recognize the antecedents and consequences of various actions.

The fourth phase involves Frank's using his newly acquired skills to process the events in his history. He needs to learn how to manage the anxiety that is triggered when he recalls past trauma. He then has to learn how to label the affects that are a part of his memories. Finally, he has to develop an understanding of the antecedents and consequences of those events.

The fifth phase of Frank's treatment requires that he learn how to interact with his peers. First, he has to learn how to use play materials appropriately on his own. Second, he has to learn how to engage in parallel play. Third, he has to learn how to engage in minimal social interactions.

The termination phase of Frank's therapy will be particularly important in the overall treatment planning because the separation is likely to reactivate some thoughts and feelings about the separation first from his mother and later from his father. As therapy comes to a close, Frank should be able to be involved in planning for his future.

TREATMENT PLANNING

Treatment planning is an extremely important part of the overall play therapy process, yet it is one of the most difficult aspects to delineate. The pretreatment process occurs in three phases. During the intake and assessment phases of treatment, you gather data about your client and her ecosystem. During the goal formulation and synthesis phase, you integrate the material you have gathered with a theoretical model and develop many hypotheses about your client's functioning and develop treatment goals. Treatment planning is the last phase of the process; you determine the strategies you will use to help your client achieve the goals developed in the second phase. You will decide which aspects of the child's ecosystem should be targeted for intervention, the general types of interventions you will want to use, and specific techniques to be used in your sessions with the child to produce the fastest, most stable, and most cost-effective progress.

Determining the Context(s) in Which Intervention(s) Will Occur

Depending on the treatment goals identified for the child, interventions may be initiated within one or more components of her ecosystem. You will have to decide where your interventions will be best directed.

Individual

As a play therapist, your first interest is in determining whether or not the child is a good candidate for individual treatment. It seems unlikely that there are very many children who could not benefit from a course of play therapy and certainly none who could be harmed by it so long as the child is not made to feel stigmatized by the process. But the decision to initiate therapy should not be made on the basis of the fact that the child will not be harmed but on substantial evidence that she will benefit. In addition, it is important to consider whether or not the child is candidate for long or short term individual treatment and which will be the most cost-effective intervention in the long run. Short-term therapy is not cost effective if it means that the child will continue to be symptomatic and will eventually require intensive intervention. For example, suicidal children are usually not good candidates for short-term therapy even though the immediate danger may be alleviated with such treatment. In these cases, if the underlying issues are not resolved it is very likely the child will become suicidal again at some later point and might even require hospitalization. Even relatively long-term therapy is substantially less expensive than a short-term hospitalization. Most managed care companies can be made to see the value of dollars spent on long-term therapy in the present if it means preventing high cost hospitalization in the future.

Family

A related decision a play therapist often faces is whether the child's needs will be best served by individual or family intervention. Family therapists inevitably argue that family therapy is preferable, while play therapists inevitably favor individual child work. An ecological perspective allows you to remain somewhere in the middle, recognizing the value of interventions directed at the individual, the family, or both. There is no easy way to determine which approach is preferable overall, even when the theoretical and philosophical differences are set aside. Individual child work seems particularly useful when the child's difficulties are not a direct result of systemic family difficulties and the family is generally functioning well. This may be the case when children are traumatized outside the home, experience behavior problems related to a chronic illness, or have specific problems with their peers. Individual therapy may also be the treatment of choice when the family system and its members are so dysfunctional that work must be done to stabilize the individual members before the problems of the system can be addressed.

The continuum between individual and family therapy seems to have five intervals. At one end is absolute individual treatment, in which the child's parents are excluded from the process as much as possible. Second is parallel treatment, in which the therapist treats the child individually and works with the parent(s), but there is very little cross communication or even overlap in the goals being pursued. Third is joint parent/child treatment; both the parent and child attend the same session, and treatment is aimed at reducing problems in the dyadic relationship. Fourth is filial treatment (B. Guerney, 1964a, 1964b; L. Guerney, 1983, 1991, 1997; VanFleet, 1994) in which the child only occasionally attends the sessions. In this case the parent becomes the therapeutic agent, and the therapist's role is to train the parent to be a good change agent. Fifth is family treatment, in which all family members attend sessions and interventions are directed at resolving systemic difficulties. The decision about which type of treatment to implement is entirely case-dependent, based on your assessment of the child's and the family's particular strengths and weaknesses and your training and experience. This means that you may occasionally, to be professionally and ethically responsible, have to refer cases with needs which are not consistent with your training and approach.

Peer

Certain interventions may be best directed at the child's peer group. Some of these interventions may be carried out directly, others through the child's parents, and still others through the child herself. Unfortunately, the child's problems in her peer interactions may be very resistant to change within the context of a one-to-one therapeutic relationship with an adult therapist. One of the more effective interventions that can be directed at the child's peer problems is group play therapy, one form of which is to be described in Part IV.

Other Systems

Successful remediation of the child's difficulties may be best attained by working with other systems in which the child is involved. The variety of interventions that can be aimed at these systems is as extensive as the number of systems. Some of the appropriate interventions might be carried out by you, in your role as a play therapist, while others might be better implemented by individuals within those systems. School interventions, for example, might be implemented by you, but it probably makes more sense for the child's teacher, counselor, or school psychologist to carry out the intervention.

Regardless of the point(s) in the child's ecosystem at which you determine interventions should be made, you will still have to decide which type of intervention will be most effective and whether or not you will be the one to implement it.

CASE EXAMPLE: AARON

Aaron was not thought to need an intensive individual play therapy program because reality-based family problems seemed the primary source of the anxiety he was experiencing.

Family work would have been ideal in Aaron's case but was not possible because of his father's extremely poor health. For this reason, collateral work with Aaron and his mother was seen as the next best alternative. The goal was the creation of a relationship in which Aaron could return to being a child without taxing the system beyond its capacities. An additional goal was establishing the mother as Aaron's primary source of information and support as he tried to adjust to the continual deterioration in his father's health.

Since Aaron's anxiety created interpersonal problems that significantly interfered with his having successful peers interactions, it was decided that peer group work would be useful once Aaron's anxiety about his home situation abated somewhat.

No interventions were planned with systems other than Aaron's family and peers.

CASE EXAMPLE: FRANK

In reviewing Frank's treatment goals, many goals could best be addressed in the context of individual play therapy. The primary goals in this aspect of the treatment were Frank's inability to establish a relationship with another person, his pervasive fear of retraumatization, and his general difficulty identifying and managing his own emotions.

Family-of-origin interventions were not possible in Frank's situation; however, collateral work with the group home parent Frank considered his mother was implemented. The goals here were to help her develop plans to manage Frank's behavior when he was home on weekends, develop strategies for maintaining the relationship between her and Frank while he was in residence, and engage her assistance in helping Frank generalize to his home environment the changes he made in session.

Because Frank was in residence, it was possible to consider implementing some direct interventions with his peer group. Initially, however, Frank's interaction with them was so limited that this was not considered a priority.

Interventions in the residential setting were also indicated because Frank's acting out was endangering others. The goal was to actively involve the staff in enhancing Frank's interpersonal skills and in working toward generalization of the gains he might make in therapy. Finally, the need to communicate as much of the treatment process as possible to Frank's caseworker was considered vital to the development of a good long-term plan for Frank's treatment and placement.

Determining the Type of Intervention to Be Used in Each Context

Having identified those components of the child's ecosystem that are to be targeted for intervention, you next have to make two decisions. One is whether or not this will be a short or long term case. As previously mentioned this decision is usually based on the complexity of the problem and the degree to which the child's ecosystem is healthy enough to promote and support change. Children with complex problems who live in unhealthy ecosystems cannot be made suddenly healthy through short term work irrespective of the demands of a third part payor. This is not to say some benefit can not be derived from a brief intervention in such cases but the goals will have to be both very clear and very circumspect. The other decision you will make at this time has to do with the types of interventions you will implement. You have many choices in terms of specific interventions, some of which are discussed in Chapters Nine and Ten. For the sake of discussion, the specific intervention techniques are grouped into three general categories: problem solving, educational, and therapeutic.

The problem-solving approach is the least intrusive general style of intervention for the play therapist. This category includes any interventions in which the client or members of her ecosystem are involved in developing and implementing strategies that address some aspect of the problems she is experiencing. Although there are many different problem-solving techniques, they all include at least four steps. Step 1 is to identify the problem. If possible, the problem should be operationally defined. Step 2 is to brainstorm for solutions. At this point, any solution is acceptable, no matter how outlandish it may be in reality. The goal is simply to be creative and flexible in generating alternatives. Step 3 is to select one of the solutions, generated by brainstorming, for implementation, based on the ability of the individuals and the systems involved to actually implement the suggested plan in reality. Step 4 is to implement and evaluate the proposed solution. If there are problems with implementation or outcome, the process begins again. The value of this approach to the verbal-cognitive aspects of Ecosystemic Play Therapy are discussed at some length in Chapter Nine.

Educational approaches are somewhat more intrusive than problem-solving approaches because they tend to not involve the client as actively in the process. The individual who is the target of the intervention tends to fall into a passive student role, with the therapist taking an active teacher role. This need not happen because it is possible for the client and therapist to engage in a mutual search for information that will be useful in addressing the client's problems, but it tends to occur more often than not. As with problem-solving approaches, a wide variety of educational intervention techniques are available that might be appropriate for use in the treatment of children. All the techniques are similar in that they involve the transmission of factual information from one person to another. Further, the techniques do not generally encourage the processing of the information transferred on an emotional level.

Emotional processing is the goal of the therapeutic interventions, which are more intrusive than either of the other techniques in the breadth and depth of the work to be accomplished. Therapeutic techniques also presume the greatest disparity between the knowledge base of the therapist and client. Not only is the therapist expected to know certain factual information, as in the educational approaches, but she is expected to bring a unique understanding of the client's emotional life to the situation. Partly because of the complexity of therapeutic interventions, a very large number of techniques are available.

Problem-solving and educational interventions are also discussed briefly in Chapter Twelve because they might be used in collateral work with the parents.

CASE EXAMPLE: AARON

Aaron seemed to need only very brief individual therapeutic intervention, with more significant therapeutic interventions aimed at the family system. Aaron's goals also called for an extensive educational approach to be implemented by the mother, the therapist, or both. Further, once some of Aaron's anxiety was alleviated by the individual and familial interventions, a therapeutic intervention would be aimed at remediating Aaron's peer problems.

CASE EXAMPLE: FRANK

In Frank's case, there did not seem to be any indication for using anything but a therapeutic approach in his individual sessions. A problem-solving approach and an educational approach seemed best suited to interventions with his group home parent. Finally, a problem-solving approach seemed to be the most likely intervention for residential staff to use.

Determining the Therapeutic Strategies to Be Used in the Child's Play Therapy

The final step in the treatment planning process is determining the specific therapeutic strategies to be used in the sessions with the child. This, as with every step of the process, is a relatively abstract task and therefore rather difficult to delineate.

Individual

In determining the content of the child's individual sessions, you must first decide how structured you want the sessions. Will the sessions be relatively unstructured, with the child having free rein to select materials and generate the degree of interaction she chooses? Will the sessions be semistructured, with only a few toys and materials available and the therapist having considerable say in the degree of interaction? Or will the session be very structured, with specific materials set out and the therapist entirely determining the degree of interaction? The degree of structure will depend largely on the child's developmental level: The lower her developmental functioning, the more structured the therapy. This fact runs parallel to the reality of children's interactions with adults in that the younger the child, the more adults will take responsibility for providing the appropriate structure. Some children, especially those with particularly traumatic histories, may need time to become familiar with the therapist before the sessions become too structured and interactive, but most can move right into more intense interactions.

Second, you have to decide how much experiential work the child will be doing in session. Again, the lower the child's level of developmental functioning, the more one would expect to do experiential work in the play sessions. You would not expect a 2-year-old to engage in verbally oriented psychotherapy, so there is little reason to expect an older child whose personality organization is like that of a 2-year-old to do so. If you decide to do experiential work with the child, you have to decide whether the child's experiences in therapy will be aimed at challenging her present style of interactions, at reviving and redoing events from her history, or perhaps both.

Independent of the decision as to whether or not to use experiential tasks in the child's sessions, you have to decide how much of the work will be done verbally, on a cognitive level. You have essentially three choices. You can use experiential techniques alone with very little verbal overlay. This approach might be most effective with children functioning at a very low developmental level. Second, you can use experiential techniques with a substantial verbal overlay. This approach is most effective with children who are at a developmental level in which they are trying to convert actions into words, that is, trying to learn to talk rather than acting out. Or you can use verbal interventions alone with a very small experiential component to the therapy. This approach seems most valid with children who are functioning at the higher developmental levels.

The conceptual models used in designing the specific experiential tasks to be used and verbalizations to be made in a given session with a given child are presented in Chapters Nine and Ten.

CASE EXAMPLE: AARON

Aaron had experienced a significant trauma at the age of 2, and his symptomatology was hypothesized to be the result of the residual of that trauma as it interacted with the course of his development. For this reason, highly structured and experiential sessions were to be implemented. One goal was to circumvent Aaron's tendency to talk about problems rather than attempting to do anything about them. Because the trauma was quite old and had not been abusive in nature, the therapist did not feel the need for a substantial introductory period but felt that the structured sessions could begin with the second session. As Aaron became used to the experiential approach, the use of verbally presented interpretations would increase to foster age-appropriate cognitive processing of Aaron's internal experience. A more verbal approach would have to be taken in implementing the educational portion of Aaron's treatment, in which he was to learn more about his father's illness.

CASE EXAMPLE: FRANK

Because Frank's history of trauma began when he was about 2½ years old, it was hypothesized that his limited ability to initiate interpersonal interactions stemmed from developmental residual of very early Level II issues. Since this was Frank's lowest level of functioning, it was decided that treatment initially should be focused to that developmental level by being very structured and experiential. The need to use an experiential approach was also determined by Frank's very low language-processing skills. It was also decided that the initial experiences in the sessions would be designed to challenge Frank's style of interaction, while later experiences would be designed to facilitate Frank's working through the traumatic events in his history. Last, it was determined that because so much of Frank's life experience had been traumatic, there would have to be a substantial warming up period at the beginning of treatment to allow him to become familiar and, at least, somewhat relaxed with the therapist.

Collateral

If collateral work is to be conducted weekly either with, or without, the child present, then the specific strategies to be used and the content of those sessions also need to be determined. Those interventions are covered in Chapter Twelve.

THE FEEDBACK SESSION AND TREATMENT CONTRACTING

The Parents' Session

The feedback sessions are the final contacts between you and the family before the child's treatment is initiated. In the session with the parents, you should review the data that have been collected, present the synthesized list of goals, and present the treatment plan you developed to address those goals. It is important for the parents to feel that none of what is presented is carved in stone and that they have the capacity to negotiate for changes in the goals or the treatment plan. The aim of the feedback session is not to convince the parents that you have developed the one correct formulation of their child's case or the one correct treatment plan but to maintain and further their involvement in the treatment of their child.

The actual contract developed is usually verbal but may be written. A written contract signed by all tends to imply more of a commitment on everyone's part. The contract may specify either the number of sessions to be completed or the operationally defined goals to be attained. Even if the treatment is anticipated as a long-term proposition, intervals at which an evaluation of the child's progress will be made should be set. One option is to create a contract that is renewable at regular intervals. For example, the child will be seen for 8 weeks, at the end of which time treatment will be reevaluated and a decision made as to whether to continue for another 8-week block or to plan for termination. The family should understand, from the beginning, that the termination process takes a minimum of two sessions once it is initiated.

A well-conducted feedback session will fully engage the parents and facilitate both their continuation of the therapy over time and increase the likelihood of their, and their child's, regular attendance at sessions.

The Child's Session

Many play therapists neglect to conduct a feedback and contracting session with the child as well as the parents, especially when the child is relatively young. As with the parents' feedback session, a session conducted with the child can significantly increase the child's understanding of, and commitment to, the therapy process. Ethically, it facilitates the child's provision of informed consent. This does not mean that the child is placed in the position of deciding whether or not treatment is to be implemented because that is the parents' responsibility as the child's primary caretakers. The child should be encouraged, however, to negotiate with regards to the goals and, to some extent, the treatment process, which may mean that the child's therapy contract is somewhat different from the parents' treatment contract. A clear example of this situation often arises out of the play therapist's attempts to develop a treatment contract with a very resistant child:

> Bill was 9 years old and adamant that he was not going to participate in the therapy process even if his parents were going to bring him every week; he would just sit there in silence. Bill had been referred for oppositional, aggressive behavior both at home and school. He admitted that he hated getting in trouble all the time and that it made him sad and angry. He said that he did not know why his parents had brought him to therapy because there was nothing wrong with him; it was everyone else who caused problems. After multiple attempts to engage Bill, the therapist finally said that she believed that Bill did not want to be there but that somehow he had managed to convince everyone else that he needed to be. She asked him what he had done to convince everyone that something was not all right. With only a little prodding, Bill began listing the behaviors that got him in trouble and that, he believed, had triggered his referral. He still blamed everyone else for causing the negative interactions he was listing, but at least he was admitting that the referral had not just developed out of thin air. At this point the therapist suggested that their contract for treatment focus on helping Bill figure out ways he could convince everyone that he did not need to be in therapy. She cautioned that this might take some time as it had taken him a long time to convince them that he needed to come but that she was willing to help all she could. Bill agreed to this contract and treatment was underway.

Whenever possible, children should also be aware, from the outset, that the therapy relationship will not go on forever, especially when the therapist knows she will be available only for a set length of time, as is the case with graduate students in field placements or interns. Children do have a limited sense of time, but they can grasp the notion that this relationship will have an end, especially if it is tied to another big event in their future, such as the end of the school year. Alternatively, you might simply inform the child that this is a working relationship which will come to an end when the goals delineated have been achieved, with special note made of the fact that the child will have plenty of warning before that happens. Many therapists do not want to do this, fearing that it will prevent the child from forming a stable therapeutic relationship. Ethically, however, this is essential information if the child is to form a therapeutic relationship based on informed consent.

In many ways, the feedback session with the child is a transition phase between the intake and assessment processes and the therapy proper. It is the beginning of the introduction phase, as it is labeled in Theraplay (Jernberg, 1979). You establish the structure of the sessions and begin to create certain short- and long-term expectations for the child.

CASE EXAMPLE: AARON

Aaron's feedback was somewhat unusual for the degree of specificity the therapist attained in defining the treatment goals. The therapist identified Aaron's fears about his father's illness and the degree to which those fears paralyzed Aaron in his day-to-day life. The therapist also identified Aaron's lonesomeness relative to his peers and the need to increase Aaron's ability to make friends. Aaron agreed that he was not very happy and that he would like to be more comfortable, especially with other children. He agreed to work with the therapist twice a week for 5 weeks.

CASE EXAMPLE: FRANK

Frank's did not have a feedback session per se; rather, the intake, assessment, and feedback were all accomplished in one session. Because Frank had been in treatment for 3 years at that point, he was quite willing to continue. He was informed that the new therapist worked in a style quite different from that of his former therapist but that they would take a few sessions to get used to each other before getting down to more serious work. The initial focus of the sessions was to facilitate Frank's adjustment to his new placement.

CHAPTER EIGHT

Beginning Treatment

SETTING UP THE PLAYROOM

The Physical Plant

Although a play therapist is rarely able to set up a playroom from scratch, this chapter is organized as if that were the case. Note that the playroom described might not be considered ideal for conducting play therapies other than the one presented herein. However, the elements can all be easily modified to suit various other settings, techniques, clients, and situations.

The ideal playroom is large enough for some gross motor activity without the child being in danger of bumping into furniture and yet not so large he feels lost and isolated from you. Unfortunately, this is a bit like saying you should use enough but not too much in a recipe. The minimum playroom size is about 10 by 10 feet and no larger than 16 by 16 feet. If the room is sometimes to be used for seeing groups of children, then it must certainly be larger—a room about 15 by 25 feet is excellent for group work.

No matter how large the room, it is useful to have one half of the floor covered with linoleum tile and the other half carpeted, to allow messy activities on one side without constantly worrying about the carpet being damaged. The carpeted side allows for quiet activities or rough and tumble activities that are more comfortably carried out on a padded surface. A small sink on the tiled side of the room is very useful as a source of water for the sandbox, for water play, or for painting and cleanup.

It is also very advantageous to have a bathroom adjoining the playroom, to prevent the child from using an urgent call from nature as a way of avoiding the therapeutic work. Many a therapist has given in to the child's urgent plea to use the bathroom, only to find his client gone for 15 or more minutes. Wherever it is, the bathroom child clients will use should not have a lock on the door. It certainly will not add to your sense of control over the therapeutic relationship or enhance the child's sense of safety if you have to cajole him to come out.

If there are windows in the playroom, replace the regular window glass with either safety glass or plastic. No one wants shards of glass flying when a momentary lapse in the child's management of his anger makes him fire a block at the nearest breakable target. The windows should also have latches that only an adult can manipulate.

> Several years back, a play therapy intern, Kyle, was working in a turn-of-the-century Victorian building. At one point a fellow intern, Susan, whose office was across the hall, cried out in a tone that conveyed sheer panic. Kyle flew across the hall, only to find Susan's 8-year-old client halfway out a third-story window in spite of her efforts to restrain him. The two managed to drag the child back in, but both have been very wary of windows in either their offices or playrooms ever since.

Equipment

You must first consider what major pieces of furniture you want. At a minimum, a table and a few chairs are necessary. The table should be high enough to feel comfortable to a child of latency age. Smaller children will kneel on a chair without too much discomfort, but older children will feel insulted by "baby-sized" furniture. Aside from that equipment, only two other items are particularly useful. One is a large storage cabinet that locks. A playroom with a walk-in closet that locks is excellent, but a tall metal cabinet or cupboard also serves the purpose. Second is a sand tray or table. The best one is the type meant for nursery or kindergarten use; it has a deep plastic tray built into a frame that is up on legs like a table. The better kind comes with a wooden cover that lifts off. This apparatus looks like a standard kindergarten table when the cover is on and thus serves a dual purpose.

Play Materials

You now want to select the play materials to be included. Therapists' views of toys and play materials vary widely. Psychodynamic play therapists tend to present the child with a very limited number of toys that have been selected for their particular symbolic significance in the treatment of that child. Most also have individual toys and materials for each child and a way to store them separately so that they remain undisturbed between the child's visits. In a traditional psychoanalytic practice, where the analyst is seeing only 5 to 10 clients four to five times a week, this is feasible. However, in a clinic setting, where the playroom may be used by several different therapists with a total caseload of 20 plus children each, this approach becomes a logistical nightmare. Therapists who consider themselves humanistic tend to envision the ideal playroom as one that vaguely resembles Santa's workshop. Since the goal of this therapeutic modality is to provide the child with an environment that fosters optimal growth, development, and self-actualization, the plethora of toys and material does make sense. The therapist hopes to have the "right" object(s) available for each child, the right object being one that appeals to the child enough to encourage its use, carries some symbolic meaning, and can be used in resolving the particular issue the child is facing at the time. To have such perfect objects on hand for every child at any given point, you need a rather extensive inventory.

Ecosystemic Play Therapy places much more emphasis on the interaction of the child and therapist than on the interaction of the child and the play materials—thus, the ideal playroom is virtually bare. Often the room is devoid of even furniture. This strategy is entirely consistent with the Theraplay method (Jernberg & Booth, 1999). Any toys present have been preselected for use by the child to be seen; usually there are no more than two or three toys available at one time. This is actually consistent with Landreth's recommendation to parents regarding toys used in their Filial Therapy sessions (Landreth, 1991). He indicates that using certain toys only during the play session make these more special to the child. This practice does limit the chance that the child will stumble on a toy that facilitates the spontaneous and unexpected expression of a problem, but it allows for a level of focus often lost when he finds the toys more interesting than the therapeutic relationship or process.

Setting aside the issue of the availability of toys, there is still the issue of what needs to be included in a playroom inventory. Toys should be selected to reflect the needs and interests of children at each developmental level discussed in Part II. The list of possibly useful toys is virtually endless, so the following discussion focuses on those toys that are considered most useful.

Level I Play Materials

Remembering that Level I children are at the 0- to 2-year age level, the toys most appropriate are those which are either particularly nurturant or those which stimulate sensorimotor functioning. Nurturant toys let the child address issues surrounding caretaking and bonding and also tend to incorporate a strong sensorimotor element. Nurturant toys that are useful in therapy with Level I children include the following:

- *Baby bottle:* Each child with whom a baby bottle will be used should have his own, for sanitary reasons. The very inexpensive translucent plastic bottles sold at supermarkets are best because they are virtually indestructible.
- *Baby blanket:* A flannel blanket takes up little space and can be used with either the child or a doll. Older children tend to use such a blanket for dress up or to create a tent or "fort."

- *Baby powder and/or lotion:* These items can be used with either the child or a doll and they let the child experience or imitate typical caretaking. They can also be used to foster minimally threatening physical contact between the child and therapist when and where appropriate.
- *Stuffed animals:* These are often children's primary transitional objects outside of therapy, and they have considerable potential for use in session. The problem is how to select the toys and make them available. Too many stuffed animals are distracting and tend to prevent the child from developing a primary attachment to any one. Having only one or two may not sufficiently entice the child to interaction. However, in spite of the latter possibility, it is best to err on the side of having too few rather than too many stuffed animals. One excellent stuffed animal is actually a hand puppet turtle about 10 inches in diameter and quite overstuffed so that it is very squeezable and makes a nice pillow. The person using it can also pull in the turtle's head and front legs, which fascinates young children. More about the inclusion of puppets in the playroom is discussed later in this section.
- *Attention getters:* This open-ended category includes all those things that infants and toddlers find totally fascinating, ranging from very colorful and expensive European wooden toys to empty cartons and other discards. The purpose of having some of these high-interest toys on hand is that they can be used to help focus the child's attention and to enhance interaction with the therapist. Toys that are solely intended for solitary use, like a noisy pull toy, are therefore not very useful. Other simple but useful toys are balls, blocks, noisemakers, and musical instruments. Balls should be colorful, and one should be big enough to lay the child over and use as a way of rocking him. Toddlers can use blocks to build and then knock down towers, an activity most will repeat for long periods of time. Noisemakers and musical instruments attract a child's attention and can be used to express affects nonverbally.

Art materials are not particularly useful with Level I children if either the therapist or the child structures the use of the materials toward the creation of any end product. Children at this level can only minimally control their fine motor coordination and certainly cannot reproduce elements of their inner or outer world in their art. Level I children do, however, greatly enjoy the sensorimotor qualities of art materials. They are fascinated by the properties of the different materials, the colors, textures, and smells, and the degree to which the materials respond to their actions by smearing, dripping, or molding; Level I children can become involved with art materials for very long periods of time if the materials are used these ways. Children usually find finger paints, tempera paints (paired with large brushes and large sheets of paper), and Play-Doh® or clay most attractive.

Level II Play Materials

As a child enters Level II, he becomes much more interested in using toys to engage in pretend play. Initially, he tends to include himself in the midst of the pretend activity, but as development proceeds, the pretend activity tends to be projected onto the toys to a greater extent. That is, initially, the child tends to create a pretend airport scene by pretending that he is the pilot or even the airplane, but as he gets older he tends to use a toy airplane and small figures to create the pretend scene while he serves as the omniscient narrator. To cover this developmental range, you should have an array of pretend toys available from each of the following categories: interactive toys, costumes, and miniatures.

Interactive pretend toys are those the child uses to pretend to engage in some real or fantasy activity. They may be either child- or full-sized objects. Interactive pretend toys tend to appeal to the younger Level II child. A well-outfitted playroom would include toy telephones; dishes and pretend food; appliances (stove, refrigerator, iron and ironing board, and others); and equipment from various settings the child is familiar with (office, preschool, school, hospital, and so on).

A pair of toy telephones is an excellent stimulus for enacting difficult communications. The phones can be used to call people who do not usually come to the play sessions or to role play discussions with unpleasant content:

> Six-year-old Michael had great difficulty expressing anger. In one session, he became very angry with limits the therapist was setting. He went to the toy shelf and took out the toy telephones, brought one phone to the therapist, and took the other to the opposite side of the room. He instructed the therapist, "When I say `Ring,' pick up your phone." Michael then pretended to dial and said "Ring." The therapist picked up the phone and said "Hello." Michael slammed down his receiver as if to hang up on the therapist. This interaction was repeated a number of times until Michael's anger began to dissipate. At this point, his communication was still nonverbal, but the phones had given him some way to structure these initial expressions.

Toy dishes and pretend food allow the child to explore issues of nurturance and caretaking at a postinfancy level. The child can feed or be fed, can frustrate or gratify. Children often use toy dishes in conjunction with Play-Doh as the pretend food. These toys can be particularly useful with children who are experiencing eating difficulties or those who have experienced abuse or neglect and are still anxious regarding the satisfaction of their basic needs.

Child-sized household appliances can enhance the child's ability to engage in the same kind of play that toy dishes and pretend food foster. In addition, the appliances often encourage the child to enact scenes from home. In these enactments, children may display the roles that characterize the various members of their family, or they may present important content material.

Just as child-sized household appliances let the child enact scenes from home, so do pieces of child-sized equipment that represent other environments the child is exposed to help him enact scenes from those settings. The equipment with the most universal value for child clients are things that represent the school environment. Often even simple art materials such as a ruler or an easel have a high stimulus pull for "school" play, which can be either positive or negative, depending on the emotional valence school carries for the child. For some children, school is so aversive that any objects which create a link between school and the playroom have the potential to disrupt the working relationship, especially early in the treatment.

Costumes or materials for dressing up appeal to children but get mixed reviews from therapists. Those favoring this type of play material cite children's natural tendency to model the behavior of those around them and to use play to rehearse for the roles they will have later in life. To foster this type of play, you should include items such as adult clothing, hats, or other items that characterize various professions, such as a briefcase, stethoscope, jewelry, and necktie. Unless you have considerable storage space, you will have to limit these items to those few that could be used in a variety of ways.

Others who favor costumes in the playroom lean more to the use of drama as a therapeutic medium; they include in their materials those that allow the child to enact fantasy as well as real roles. Materials that enable the child to become a prince or princess, a monster or an angel, an animal, an astronaut, or a super hero all have potential uses in treatment.

Those against the inclusion of costumes in the playroom speak primarily of management problems. Costumes let the child become someone else. This is not a problem for the average child with few significant behavior problems who recognizes the boundaries between himself and his costume-created characters because such a child does not use the character as an excuse to act out in a destructive manner. However, younger children and more disturbed children tend to have much more difficulty maintaining some psychological distance between themselves and their costume-created character. Such a child becomes his character. If such a child were to dress up like a soldier, he would find it very easy to justify acting like a soldier and dismiss the usual playroom rules as not applying. In this situation, would you set limits on the "soldier" or the child? If the choice is the soldier, the child may become very argumentative because he is a soldier and under no particular obligation to listen to your directions. If the choice is to set limits on the child, you may find that the child is not available so long as the costume is intact, again setting the stage for negative acting out. Following is an excellent nonclinical example:

> Matthew, a 2½-year-old, became totally infatuated with cowboys and took the opportunity to become one whenever possible. At the beginning, these transformations did not even require a costume, so his shifts back and forth were less than obvious. Later on, the costume he preferred became quite elaborate and took time and adult assistance to be put on or taken off. But the real problem came when adults tried to interact with Matthew. When he was a cowboy, his name was no longer Matt, so he did not respond when spoken to or simply informed the speaker that his name was not Matt. The transformations were also under his control: He became a cowboy when it was convenient for him, not for the adults. When Matt was a cowboy, none of the usual household rules applied, particularly in terms of limits. If the cowboy wanted to eat cookies just before dinner, that was okay because cowboys could do that. If Matt still was not allowed to eat the cookies, he burst into tears and became very argumentative, presenting the rights of cowboys in some detail. If the cowboy did something that Matt was not supposed to do and was reprimanded by an adult, he would look the adult squarely in the eye and say "You can't yell at me because I am not Matt, I am a cowboy." A response indicating that the cowboy had better listen up was usually met with feigned indifference as he walked away.

Now you may be saying "So where is the problem? This is an interesting variation on normal toddler oppositionality and individuation but it's not particularly difficult." If this is your reaction, you are right: Matt rarely actually did anything that required significant intervention, and he eventually came to depend on a costume to initiate the transformations between boy and cowboy so that adults could recognize him more readily. But what if he were your client and decided he did not like the way a session was going and became a cowboy and refused to interact unless you pretended to be a horse, and a relatively nonverbal one at that? Or what if he became aggressive as a cowboy and then became enraged at your attempts to set limits because you were not respecting his role? What if, as is common with Level I and II children, he did not want to remove the costume when it was time for the session to end? The presence or absence of costumes is not going to completely eliminate this problem—after all, Matt initially required no costume. Further, resistance comes in all forms and must be addressed accordingly. But costumes that are anything but very simple and do not pull excessively for aggressive acting out may be more problematic than valuable, especially with children functioning at the lower developmental levels.

Toward the end of Level II, pretend toys that maintain some distance between the child and his fantasy material become more popular. Because children throughout Level III continue to enjoy these toys, a discussion of their use is presented in the section on play materials for those children.

Level II children tend to greatly enjoy art materials. From the ages of 2 until about 4, they still tend to focus on the sensorimotor aspects of the materials, as do Level I children. Gradually, however, they come to give their creations content labels, although these labels may be inconsistent. A 3- or 4-year-old may start out painting a picture of a deer, watch his creation develop and decide it looks more like a bear, and then when the black paint he is using to add hooves to the deer smears too much, he may decide that the whole thing looks more like a car and to proceed accordingly. These shifts do not bother the child; they represent the fluidity of the pre-operational child's thinking. Toward the end of this level, when the child is 4 to 6 years old, he will become much more invested in creating two- and three-dimensional representations of his inner and outer world.

Level II children's desire to create representational art greatly exceeds their cognitive and fine motor skill. They are equally likely to focus on the process of creation as the content. For this reason, materials which allow the child to do his best possible work with minimum frustration should be available, so that content can take priority. Felt pens are probably the single most favorite drawing medium of Level II children, with crayons a close second. With felt pens, children tend to produce bold drawings that convey a lot through the intense colors. Unless fine tip pens are used drawings done with felt pens tend to be fairly simplistic and to look fairly flat because shading is difficult to accomplish with this medium. In spite of the fact that many children see crayons as "babyish" these do lend themselves to a rather broad range of artistic expression. Drawings can be made quite elaborate and shading and texture are easily accomplished. Tempera paints used with medium-sized brushes also appeal to this age group and are great for promoting simple, relaxed yet bold pictures. Whatever drawing or painting medium is used, the paper available to Level II children should be rather large. It need not be the big sheets of newsprint you would provide for the Level I child, but it should be bigger than an 8½ by 11-inch standard sheet. Watercolors are generally inappropriate for inclusion in the playroom because they are a very difficult medium for children to use successfully.

During Level II, children also develop the capacity to use art symbolically. That is, they can convey feelings through the quality of the work, not just its content. A family fight might be depicted as a whirl of color on a sheet of paper that is eventually torn up rather than as a picture of people fighting. These symbolic skills can be enhanced through the use of specific techniques, such as the Color-Your-Life Technique (O'Connor, 1983), which make them available to the child as a form of communication within the sessions.

Level II children also enjoy producing three-dimensional works of art. As with the two-dimensional media provided to children at this developmental level, any three-dimensional materials should be relatively easy to use. Level II children still tend to enjoy Play-Doh but may also enjoy clay or plasticine. If you use plasticine, make sure it is one of the softer varieties because nothing is more frustrating than trying to make something out of an extremely hard ball of plasticine that will not yield to the pressure of a 5-year-old's fingers.

More structured art materials such as coloring books or craft kits rarely have their place in the playroom because they tend to limit both the content and creative process that the child might otherwise bring to the task. However, some of the available therapeutic coloring books might be suitable as ways of introducing sensitive material into the sessions of a particularly resistant or defended child. For example, certain coloring books are designed to introduce information about sexual or physical abuse or alcoholism into the child's session.

Level III Play Materials

On average, Level III children have reached a point at which they are better able to differentiate fantasy from reality. Unfortunately, their extremely concrete approach to the world and their fascination with the factual may prevent them from playing out those fantasies. Many want to engage in "big" kid play, such as traditional board games, or in sports, neither of which lend themselves easily to interpretive, insight-oriented work. Fortunately, the safety and permissiveness of the playroom often allow Level III children to become actively engaged in pretend play with a variety of toys.

Children whose development is consistent with that of children 6 to 11 years old are more likely to engage in pretend play with materials which allow them to maintain some distance from their fantasies. Miniature pretend toys do just that because they include all those items which allow the child to portray his thoughts and his world in miniature. Small people, animals, houses, cars, dolls and dollhouses, and so forth are all essential for promoting this type of play. These miniatures can be readily accumulated from a wide variety of sources; Playmobil® manufactures some very useful ones. Playmobil produces sets that include anywhere from 1 to 12 people and the equipment needed to create a particular scene. The adult figures are 2¾ inches tall; the child figures are about 1¾ inches tall. All the figures are virtually indestructible and movable. The sets include an incredible number of pieces, many of which are too small for a very young child to use.

One small set includes a father, mother, baby, and baby carriage. There are hats for the father and mother and a blanket for the baby. One of the medium-sized sets consists of everything needed to create a rather traditional classroom: a teacher, pupils, desks and chairs for all, usable blackboard, map with stand, hats and backpacks for all the pupils, and a hat and briefcase for the teacher. Two medium-sized sets re-create a hospital operating room and a patient room. Some large sets include fire engines, a western town, ambulances, pirate ships, and on and on. There are several problems with these sets. First, the sets cannot be ordered directly from the manufacturer at this time, so you must buy/order from local toy stores. Second, the sets tend to be very traditional. The classroom teacher is a woman with glasses; the firefighters are all male; and so on. If you have several sets, you can keep the people together in a box separate from the rest of the pieces in each set, allowing the child to choose whatever characters suit his play. The final problem is the limited number of ethnic/minority figures included in the sets. Again, if you buy several sets, you can combine the figures and eliminate this problem.

Dolls and dollhouses have always been considered an essential element in playrooms. There are many to choose from; most of the better ones are available through school supply companies. They may be quite expensive, but they have been designed for use by many children and are therefore sturdy and simple. One problem you may have encountered over the years is trying to find a dollhouse that reflects the variety of living arrangements your child clients experience. Children may live in single-family houses, duplexes, apartments, and high-rises, and of course the possible layout of these residences is virtually endless. One recommended solution is to eliminate the dollhouse from the playroom but keep the dollhouse figures and a wide variety of miniature furniture, appliances, and other household items. In the absence of a dollhouse, children tend to create more free-flowing households spread across the floor. Those children who need more structure may use the blocks to create constructions that the play figures can inhabit.

Aside from materials or equipment that let the child enact general scenes from real life or fantasy, you can select other pretend toys to met the needs of a particular client, as the following nonclinical example illustrates:

> Ryan was hospitalized at age 4 for complications of flu. Because he was quite dehydrated, the insertion of the intravenous needle was very difficult and required repeated attempts at three different sites on his body. Ryan tried to be cooperative but eventually became extremely distressed, screaming and protesting actively. The next day, when the intravenous fluids had helped him feel a little better, he asked to go to the playroom in the hospital. Once there, he discovered a box of real-life hospital supplies, including an intravenous set. He took one of the baby dolls and the set and proceeded to restart the baby's IV over and over. Each time he had his father hold the baby doll's hand, saying "The baby is scared and is going to cry so he needs a hand to hold." For the next 2 days this play dominated Ryan's time in the playroom. The third day he was discharged and asked to go to the playroom one last time. He set about giving the doll an IV again. However, he said to his father "You don't have to hold the baby's hand this time, he isn't going to cry." Immediately after finishing this enactment, Ryan proceeded to play something else, having apparently resolved his anxiety.

The types of art materials that Level III children enjoy using are quite varied, although the older Level III child is interested in materials that can be used to create more realistic representations of his world or fantasy. Level III children usually like to produce both two- and three-dimensional artwork. For their two-dimensional work, they like standard sized sheets of paper (8½ by 11) rather than the larger sheets younger children prefer. They also tend to prefer white paper rather than colored paper. Level III children show decreasing interest in tempera paints as they get older and an increasing interest in felt pens and crayons. Interest in crayons fluctuates over time; most children tend to prefer the control and intense color they can obtain with felt pens. Toward the end of Level III, children may decide that the colors produced by felt pens are unrealistic and prefer colored pencils that allow them to shade their drawings. Even with children at this developmental level, watercolors are a very difficult medium to work with and do not seem well suited to the playroom, where content and process are of greater value than technical skill.

For their three-dimensional work, Level III children again tend to prefer media that allow them to create realistic products. At this level they prefer regular clay to Play-Doh. A large container of water-base clay (of the type potters use) works well and can be kept soft simply by adding water. Unfortunately, objects made of such clays are very fragile if left to air-dry and not fired in a kiln. One solution is to purchase the self-hardening clays, which work well but are relatively expensive.

Another solution is to treat objects made of clay the same way you would treat constructions made of blocks. That is, inform children that once a session ends, the child's clay construction will be rolled back into a ball and returned to the container for use next week. If this is the plan you decide to follow, then stick to it no matter how symbolic or beautiful a child's creation turns out to be. The child who produced something particularly symbolic may have been able to do so because you said that you would not keep the object around where others might see it. If you save beautiful objects, the child comes to feel that you preserve his creations only when they please you. In the first case, the child might feel he was tricked, in the latter case that he is valued only when he is able to produce a fine product. Neither are good contexts for the conduct of the therapeutic work. If you find the policy of routinely destroying the child's creations cruel, you can mediate it by using a camera with instant-developing film to take a picture of each of the child's productions before destroying them.

Level III children also tend to show an increasing interest in construction toys such as Legos®, Lincoln Logs®, Tinker Toys®, and Erector® sets, but these are generally less than satisfactory items to include in the playroom for a variety of reasons. Lincoln Logs and Tinker Toys are poor choices because they are fairly difficult to use but, more importantly, they make dangerous weapons. Erector sets require considerable skill and tend to distract the child from the work of the session. Lego toys are probably the most useful of the group. They are easy enough to use that a younger Level III child could successfully complete a simple construction, yet they can be used to make more complex constructions which appeal to older Level III and even Level IV children. One strategy for preventing the child from becoming preoccupied with the technical details of creating something with Legos is to make sure you get rid of any of the boxes or papers that show completed objects. Level III children are sufficiently concrete that they will immediately try to reproduce what they see and will easily become distracted from the work of the session.

Some older Level III children also enjoy putting together models, which are generally a mixed blessing, somewhat akin to traditional board games. The primary drawbacks are the degree of structure most models impose and the complexity of the directions. That is, the content is entirely predetermined and allows the child to express very little creativity, and the directions may require so much of the child's attention that he is really not available to do the work of therapy. Models are discussed further in terms of their use with Level IV children.

Another group of play materials that appeal to Level III children are board games. Here you might decide to use either traditional games or some of the many therapeutic board games currently available. Complex, traditional board games like chess or Monopoly® have no place in the playroom because they tend to focus the child on the mechanics of playing the game rather than the work of the session. Simpler games like Candyland®, Chutes and Ladders®, or checkers can be quite useful, especially when the goal is to help the child learn to follow rules and take turns. The board game format can also be used to introduce a wide variety of content material to the sessions through such games as The Talking, Feeling and Doing Game (Gardner, 1973), Imagine (Burks, 1978), The Ungame (Zakich, 1975), or Reunion (Zakich & Monroe, 1979).

Regardless of the game(s) you choose to use in sessions with a particular client, it is important that you do not attempt to throw the game to the child (Cooper & Wanerman, 1977). Most children catch on when an adult plays a game at significantly less than capacity. This does not mean you set out to win regardless of the child's needs, only that you focus on the process of playing the game rather than on either winning or losing. One way to do this is to have two games available, one based on luck and one based on skill. You can show the child that you both have an equal chance of winning at games of luck but that you have a better chance at winning a game of skill. A good game of luck is Candyland because it can be played several times in a single session, increasing the odds that you and the child will each win at least once. Checkers is a good game of skill, again because it can be played several times in one session. It is also one whereby you can teach the child a simple strategy that increases the chances that he will win. (Simply instruct the child to move his pieces forward and toward the center of the board whenever possible.)

It is also important that you do not let the child cheat at the games you play in sessions (Cooper & Wanerman, 1977). When the cheating first occurs, you should interpret the child's behavior in a manner consistent with the guidelines presented in Chapter Nine. If the cheating persists over time, it may be appropriate for you to set limits on the child's behavior. For example, you might offer the hypothesis that the child's cheating may be one of the reasons he has trouble getting along with his peers. If the child acknowledges the interpretation but continues to cheat, you might want to begin blatantly cheating yourself while saying that the game does seem to be a lot more fun when you ignore the rules. This usually triggers a lively discussion of the relative fairness of the child's cheating versus your cheating. Alternatively, you may decide to set limits by saying that the child does not seem ready to play games yet because he is unable to follow the rules and then follow through by not making the game available the next time he comes to the session.

Level IV Play Materials

Children over the ages of 11 or 12 are in a difficult position both socially and when it comes to the type of play materials they feel comfortable using. As the child enters preadolescence, his cognitive ability to compare himself to others is greatly enhanced. Suddenly he is very self-conscious and generally very motivated to conform to peer standards and expectations. Preadolescents are also under substantial social pressure to appear adultlike and to prefer adult toys. This change often causes them to disdain play materials they may have greatly enjoyed only a short time earlier. The child may or may not experience this disdain as internally consistent. That is, some preadolescents may see themselves as very grown up and find that they do not miss their childhood playthings. Other preadolescents may want to look grown up but may still feel like children and feel grief at the loss of their toys. In either case, it is a rare preadolescent or even adolescent who is willing and able to sit through a 50-minute therapy session and do nothing but talk. For this reason, you need to have a range of toys available if you will be working with Level IV clients.

Younger Level IV children may still show considerable interest in pretend toys, especially miniatures, once they feel safe in the playroom. A 12-year-old who gives in to his wish to use blocks and toy soldiers will create a scene that is dramatically more complex than one a 10-year-old would create. Similarly, the 12-year-old may show renewed interest in a mechanical toy he has not used in years because he is now fascinated by its internal works. Level IV children's interest in younger children's toys may come not only from the fact that they are hardly out of childhood themselves but that their cognitions have become so much more complex that they can look at their old toys in new ways.

For the Level IV child who is in transition from preferring to use toys in therapy to preferring to sit and talk, it may be very useful to have some simple toys available with which he can occupy his hands while he talks.

Level IV children often use Lego toys this way, not really building anything but sitting and snapping the pieces together and taking them apart over and over. Sometimes a model kit can serve the same purpose, in which case the model should be simpler than one the child would select for himself so that he does not need to spend much time looking at the directions but can work and talk at the same time.

As children enter Level IV, their interest in art materials tends to drop off dramatically. Their increased ability to compare their work to that of others or to compare the appearance of the object drawn to the appearance of the object in the real world makes them very critical of their productions. They often refuse to draw, saying that they are not any good at it. Of course there will be those children who have some real talent, of which they are aware, and for them the creation of artworks in sessions can be very productive for both artistic and therapeutic purposes. At this level children may show an interest in some quality art materials with which they can create realistic products. Unfortunately, art materials can be very expensive, and therefore most play therapists are able to maintain only a very limited inventory. One inexpensive medium that allows for the creation of rather sophisticated and expressive works is charcoal used on newsprint.

Finally, a word of caution. If you are planning to work with Level IV children, you may want to consider a playroom setup in which the toys are kept out of sight even more than you would otherwise. Children at this level may rigidly adhere to their first impressions. If they walk into a treatment room that strikes them as "babyish," they may develop a resistant posture which is hard to overcome in future sessions.

Having set up the playroom in a manner that will suit the needs of your client and having obtained the appropriate play materials, you are ready to begin the play therapy proper. To make the transition from the format of the intake sessions to the format of the initial play sessions, the child may need some reorientation. It is best to make the expectations for these sessions explicit. Remind the child of the treatment contract as it was presented in the intake feedback session. Then present verbally the focus and structure of the initial sessions. This transition might be as simple as saying to the child:

> The last time we met we talked about how sad and angry you sometimes feel and you said you would like it if you could have those feelings less often. Well, we are going to get together each week for a while and see if we can figure out how to do that. The first time we got together I asked you a lot of questions and I found out a lot about you. Now I would like to get to know you a little better. But this time I do not want to ask you more questions. Instead I would like to spend some time with you and just get to see the kinds of things you like to do and the kinds of things you do not like. As I get to know you, we will talk more about your feelings, but for now let's just do something. You can do whatever you would like, play with the toys, talk, whatever. . . .

This introduction assumes that you will have some initial unstructured sessions; if this is not the case, the transition may be even easier. This transition might be as simple as saying to the child, "The last time we met we talked about how sad and angry you sometimes feel and you said you would like it if you could have those feelings less often. Well, I would like to try an experiment to see how hard it is for you to be happy and have fun. [You may need to explain the word experiment.] This is an easy experiment because I am just going to see if I can make you laugh. First, I am going to try to make you laugh by telling a joke or two, but if that does not work I may have to check to see if you are ticklish." In either case, you have made it clear to the child that the format has changed from that of the intake sessions and have made both your, and the child's, roles fairly clear.

The Initial Session(s)

Anna Freud compared the introduction, exploration, and tentative acceptance phases of the child's treatment to a seduction. The analogy may be oversexualized, but it is accurate in many ways. You are initially working to make the child feel safe in an unfamiliar environment with an unfamiliar person so that you can join together and engage in a process totally foreign to the child—a difficult situation at best. Freud recommended that very little work (interpretation) take place during this phase of the treatment so that the child's defenses are not overwhelmed before he has a chance to develop a safe and protective relationship with the therapist. In these initial sessions you are creating a "holding" relationship—one in which the child is sure of your ability to contain his most frightening and destructive thoughts and feelings in such a way that neither of you are harmed.

Even before you can create the appropriate holding environment, the child must accept you as a part of his ecosystem. Throughout the intake and assessment process you were an intruder in the child's ecosystem, but with the onset of the treatment you become a integral part of that system, hopefully as an ally of the child. But the child cannot allow a stranger to become part of his ecosystem. He must first be convinced that you have something to offer. You have already offered undivided attention, and that impresses most children, but others hold out and want to see more of what they can expect. Freud did magic tricks for her clients and simply became someone familiar, fun, and safe in the child's world. You might be more intrusive and demonstrate your desire to interact with the child on his level. However it is accomplished, this tentative acceptance phase or seduction, if you will, is a necessary early step in the implementation of play therapy with any child.

Jim was a 6-year-old client referred to play therapy because his mother worried that he seemed overcontrolled and somewhat depressed. The parents had divorced some years back and Jim never really seemed to recover. During the intake and pretreatment assessment Jim was exceedingly well behaved. He answered all questions directly, sat quite still and never did anything even vaguely impulsive. In order to create an initial alliance and to transition between the intake and the treatment itself the therapist suggested he and Jim conduct an experiment. This immediately appealed to Jim's intellectualized style. The therapist noted that Jim seemed very serious all of the time and questioned whether or not Jim had any happy feelings left inside of him at all. He pointed out that sometimes, happy feelings hid themselves in ticklish places just waiting to come out. He suggested that he try tickling various part of Jim's body to see if they could make happiness come out. Jim hesitantly agreed and initially sat very still while the therapist gently tried to tickle places like the side of Jim's neck and the area around his elbows. Both noted that no happiness seemed hidden in these locations. Then the therapist moved on and squeezed just above Jim's knees. Jim immediately started laughing and even slid off the chair onto the floor saying, "I just love being tickled." At this point, he readily agreed to work with the therapist to see if there were other ways they could make happy feelings come out and sad feelings fade away.

This real alliance with the child may be considered the equivalent of the therapeutic alliance that is a prerequisite to the successful psychoanalytic treatment of adults. This real alliance also represents, in large part, the childhood equivalent of the transference neurosis. Transference neurosis is the term used to refer to those thoughts, emotions, and behaviors that are brought to the session as reflections of the person's history or life experience but not as reactions to the reality of the therapy process. The transference neurosis is essential to the conduct of traditional psychoanalytic work because it is the context in which the client brings material to the sessions.

Child analysts have long debated the child's capacity for developing classical transferences, inasmuch as the child's parents, the original objects with whom his infantile relationships were formed, around whom his infantile relationships were woven, are still an integral part of the child's life. Anna Freud's initial analytic stance held that children were unable to develop transference neuroses, but she later modified her position (A. Freud, 1965) to observe that a transference neurosis can develop in children but not to the same extent as the transference neurosis of adults. From an analytic perspective, then, the issue is one of the degree to which a child can project his images of the significant people in his life, namely his parents, onto the person of the therapist when the parents are not only still alive but are still very powerful figures in the child's day-to-day world. Since true analysis is thought to be dependent on the development of this stable transference neurosis, the question of its development is crucial.

Today, child analysts continue to discuss the too-infrequent appearance of transference neuroses in children with varying degrees of agreement (Chused, 1988; Harley, 1986; Sandler, Kennedy, & Tyson, 1980; Tyson & Tyson, 1986). Chused, for one, very clearly suggested the possibility of transferences occurring in children, although they do differ in some respects from adult transferences. He pointed out that:

> in children, as in adults, Oedipal conflicts are a significant feature of the transference neurosis, with these conflicts reflecting not only pathogenic experiences during the Oedipal period but also organizing pathology derived from earlier preoedipal phases. When the developmental level of the child's ego functions, including cognitive development, affect tolerance, narcissistic vulnerability, and maturity of defenses are taken into account, as well as the nature of the child's attachment to his current objects (Tyson & Tyson, 1986), a thoughtful analytic procedure, with strict attention to the analysis of resistance and to countertransference interferences, can lead to a full-blown transference neurosis in the child patient. (pp. 55–56)

Furthermore, the transference can and does develop even in the throes of any developmental phase the child happens to be negotiating, regardless of the libidinal zone shifts. What is more crucial than the child's independence from primary objects in the development of transference neurosis, however, is the degree of internalization he has developed. Developing greater stability with advancing age, internalization allows for greater flexibility in the analyst's ability to interpret libidinal and aggressive strivings with their concomitant fantasies. Chused (1988) argued that it is not the need or wish for gratifying objects that brings children to analysis; rather, it is the unconscious conflicts over gratification, conflicts rooted not in current relationships but derived from past experiences and their incorporation into psychic structure, which pose more substantive difficulty. "Potentially gratifying objects are frequently available in our patients' lives; the problem is a patient's inability to be gratified" (p. 75).*

Whether or not one agrees that children are capable of developing a transference neurosis, there is no doubt that children can and do develop powerful working relationships with their therapists which may or may not include certain projections. Most therapists need only recall the number of times that their child clients have slipped and called them mommy or daddy, regardless of the therapist's gender, to realize that some amount of projection occurs over the course of the child's treatment. What is true, however, is that children cannot use their intellect to maintain the belief that their therapists are not a part of their everyday world in the same way that adults can. That is, children not only project a certain amount of their experience with people in their "real" world onto the therapist, they also project their experiences with the therapist and therapy onto people and

---

* The discussion of children's transference potential was adapted from "Advances in Psychoanalytic Psychotherapy with Children" (O'Connor & Lee, 1991), in M. Hersen, A. Kazdin, and A. Bellack (Eds.), *The Clinical Psychology Handbook,* pp. 580–595. New York: Pergamon Press. Adapted by permission.

situations outside the playroom. It is this tendency of the child to mix the world in the playroom with the world outside the playroom that typically contributes to the existence of a real relationship between the child and the therapist regardless of the therapist's wishes or efforts.

While child analysts would prefer that the child client develop a transference neurosis strong enough to exclude the development of a real relationship, there are those who argue in favor of the reverse, the most vocal advocate of this position being Glasser (1975). He insisted that therapists must interact with the client as themselves and not as transference objects. Glasser would have the therapist maintain certain values and work to convey these to the client. The therapist is not a neutral screen on which fantasies can be projected but a strong and stable individual who is the child's reference point for taking responsibility for his behavior. Theraplay (Jernberg, 1979; Jernberg & Booth, 1999) therapists take a very similar stance. Both views argue that the child must be aware of the person of the therapist and pushed to interact with that person in a warm and supportive relationship. Both also argue that such a relationship is critical if the child is going to have the courage and stamina needed to change his behavior.

Traditional child analysts work to maintain a transferential relationship with the child. Reality and Theraplay therapists work to maintain a real relationship with the child. The most productive relationship you could develop with a child client would have elements of both approaches. The child will certainly project onto you his feelings, beliefs, and fantasies about other people in his world. The relationship must involve some elements of transference or at least of projection because the child will never really know who you are. He will not know what you do after work, where you live, your life history, so he will fill in the gaps in his knowledge with fantasy. On the other hand, it is impossible to prevent the development of a real relationship between you and your clients. If the child goes home and talks about you and the play session, then you have entered that child's ecosystem in a way you cannot entirely control. Certainly, thoughtful and well-timed communication with the child's parents will dull the impact of whatever the child might say, but the fact is that you, as the child perceives you, are now a member of the family. You must recognize the uniqueness of your position and move between your role in the child's real world and your role in his fantasy world, attempting to effect the necessary changes in both. It is this hybrid relationship, one part reality and one part projection, that becomes the container for the child's negative feelings as they are played out. It is this relationship that gives the child the supplies needed to initiate change. And it is the desire to maintain this relationship that motivates the child to continue to develop over time.

The following paragraphs present the therapist's preparations for the initial sessions with Frank and Aaron.

CASE EXAMPLE: AARON

Aaron's presentation throughout the intake process made planning the intake sessions somewhat difficult. Clearly, Aaron had some cognitive awareness of the problems he was experiencing and a willingness to come to therapy based on his understanding that it might help ameliorate those difficulties. On the other hand, his anxiety was so intense that he did not appear to have developed any emotional connection with the therapist, as manifested by his desire to control absolutely every moment of their interaction. Based on the latter observation, the therapist decided to divide Aaron's initial sessions into three phases. The first two sessions would be ones in which Aaron had total control of the session content and format. In the next two sessions, he and the therapist would take turns controlling one half of the session. In the last two sessions of the initial phase, the therapist would control the session format, letting the content flow where it might. The transition from the intake to the initial sessions was made by telling Aaron that the therapist had learned a lot by controlling their first contact and that, since they had agreed to work together to help Aaron feel less nervous, he thought Aaron should have a turn at controlling the sessions. This, it was suggested, would tell the therapist a lot more about Aaron and would help the work get off to a good start.

CASE EXAMPLE: FRANK

Because of Frank's traumatic history and his tendency to remain very withdrawn, the therapist decided to keep the initial sessions very neutral and to allow Frank to take control of the session contents. The transition from the intake was done very simply by acknowledging that Frank was not very happy in residence and by suggesting that therapy might start by trying to facilitate his adjustment. The playroom was set up to offer three choices of activities: (1) an open sand tray table with a large number of small animals, people, and vehicles strewn about in the sand; (2) a dollhouse with a set of family figures; and (3) a board game designed to teach children basic safety rules.

Depending on the child and the nature of his difficulties, it may take anywhere form a single session to several months for you and he to form a good working relationship. The signs that this relationship is established include the passage of the child's negative reaction phase (discussed in Chapter Nine), the child's increasingly active involvement in the in-session activities, and the child's increasing responsiveness to the interpretations you offer. As the child settles into the relationship, you are ready to move into the working phase of play therapy.

Making Play Therapy
Sessions Therapeutic

As stated in Chapter Four, the belief that *corrective events* are the essential curative element of play therapy is a cornerstone of Ecosystemic Play Therapy. As you will recall a corrective event is one that violates either or both the child's past experiences and core beliefs (internal schemata) and causes the child to come to a new understanding of the problem. Armed with this new understanding, the child is then able to engage in problem solving that generates new, more effective and more appropriate ways of getting her needs met eliminating pathogenic adaptations. Further, Ecosystemic Play Therapy posits it is the therapist's *primary role and duty to work actively to ensure the child's play therapy sessions contain corrective events.* These events may be either experiential or cognitive in nature. Once an event occurs the therapist then works to assist the child in developing a language based understanding of the problem that will guide the child in future attempts to problem solve and get her needs met.

The Ecosystemic Play Therapist remains equally goal oriented whether the treatment plan calls for long- or short-term play therapy. However, the shorter term the therapy, the more limited and focused the therapist's goals must be. As stated by Sloves and Peterlin (1993) short-term play therapy "goes against the grain of several models of Axlinian/Rogerian play therapy. The therapist is sympathetic, friendly and empathic, but rarely permissive in the relationship. While the therapist respects children's ability to solve problems, it seems unfair to let them do it in their own time, especially when the therapist possesses the collective knowledge of other children who, in similar circumstances, have confronted similar problems. The therapist, as ally, does everything to hurry the therapy along without frightening the child into passivity, active resistance or flight. The therapist guides the child while maintaining the positive transference in the face of a constantly threatening negative transference" (p. 304).

Some writers suggest a dichotomy in which child-centered play therapists are focused on the relationship between themselves and the child while other types of play therapists are not. To the same extent that this seems an entirely false dichotomy so too does the dichotomy that depicts all child-centered therapists following the child's agenda while all other play therapists follow their own agenda. As stated repeatedly in this text, no therapist can be optimally effective in the absence of a positive relationship with her child clients. Similarly, a therapist cannot be optimally effective unless she has created a working alliance with the child that merges the child's agenda with that of the therapy. It is within the context of this positive relationship and working alliance that the therapist is goal-oriented and works to ensure that corrective events occur within session.

PLANNING THE EXPERIENTIAL COMPONENT OF THE CHILD'S PLAY THERAPY

One way for you to organize your conceptualization those therapy experiences that may serve as corrective events for your clients is to examine the Theraplay concepts of structuring, challenging, engaging, and nurturing (Jernberg & Booth, 1999) as these occur in each session. That is, certain naturally occurring aspects of play therapy fit each category as discussed in Chapter Two and can have the same positive impact on the child that the interactions have when they occur between the child and her caretaker.

Structuring

Structuring activities are those that organize the child's world in such a way as to keep her safe. Many aspects of each play therapy session provide a structure for the child that facilitates her feeling safe and enhances her using the health-promoting aspects of the session. A play therapy session has, by definition, a structure of its own that is designed to help the child get her needs met. The session starts and ends at a set time, on a given day, and in a specific location. The child is given some instruction as to the overall purpose of the play therapy and the format each session will follow. Each structure allows the child to anticipate the session, plan its content, and leave a given session secure in the knowledge that another will follow at some interval. Given the importance of structuring activities to the child's development, it is advantageous for the play therapist to communicate as much as possible about the nature and structure of the treatment process to the child directly rather than simply letting the child discover the rules and consistencies for herself.

Transitions In and Out of the Playroom

Among the naturally occurring structuring aspects of the play session are the transitions the child makes in and out of the playroom. The therapeutic value of the rituals used to mark the beginning and ending of each session are often overlooked in favor of the content of the session proper.

Many children seen in play therapy have difficulty controlling their impulses; most children with impulse control problems have difficulty making transitions between activities. Teachers often report that these children cannot stop an activity without significant intervention by an adult. For these children, the creation of rituals that delineate the session can be a critical part of their beginning to develop impulse control. Other children may come to therapy with separation anxiety; for them, the transition away from the person who brought them to the session to the playroom and then the reverse process at the end of the session may be extremely anxiety-provoking. Still other children engage in play behavior in session that would be difficult for the outside world to tolerate. These children may need transition rituals to help them contain their play to the playroom.

Impulsive children may have difficulty with something as simple as getting to the playroom from the waiting room if any sort of distance must be traversed. They may have difficulty staying in the playroom during the session. Or they may have difficulty terminating the play at the end of the session. Sometimes simple focusing, transitional activities will provide enough structure to overcome these problems, for example:

> Susan, a play therapist, worked at a clinic where the playroom was located at the end of a long hallway lined with offices. It was a constant struggle to get children to the playroom without either disrupting work in the offices or creating anxiety in the children about how far away from their parents they were going. For three different clients, Susan devised three different solutions. For Joey, an impulsive, hyperactive 6-year-old, she developed a plan to race Joey to the playroom. To slow Joey down, they raced walking backward while looking down at their feet. For Tim, another impulsive 4-year-old boy, she developed a plan to give him a piggyback ride down the last half of the hallway if he could walk down the first half of the hallway without stopping or making a sound. And with Jill, a rather lethargic 7-year-old, she simply hid a small food treat in the playroom before each session and then let Jill know what was waiting for her when she got to the playroom. At the end of a session, each strategy was reversed to help the children get back from the playroom to the waiting room.

Impulsive children may also need a warning or series of warnings that the play session is drawing to a close. Some will do well if you verbally remind them that there are 10 minutes, then 5 minutes, and then 1 minute left to the session; others do better when guided to watch the clock. Still others do best if you set a kitchen timer at the beginning of the session and place it in a prominent location.

Children with separation anxiety often benefit from these same rituals, but they tend to like transitions that make more of a game of the separation. In this case, structure the transitions so that they occur in smaller units, to desensitize the child to the process. The children may enjoy trying to find the therapist who is hiding a few steps away as they move to the playroom. Or they may prefer to make a game of going back to the waiting room to check on their caretaker at various intervals during the session. This last technique needs careful structuring so that it does not become a management problem through which the child is actively avoiding the work of the therapy:

Tommy, 5-years-old, created a game in which he would surreptitiously come back to check on his mother twice during the session. His mother was to try to spot him before he saw her. The therapist maintained control over the times when Tommy could leave the playroom but guaranteed that it would happen twice each session. During the play sessions, the therapist taught Tommy some basic problem-solving skills using the game as a vehicle. They developed strategies for varying the time of the sneaking-up attempts, the direction of the approach to the waiting room, and ways to open the door very slowly. As time progressed, Tommy got better at sneaking up to the waiting area and did not need to have his mother see him before he returned to the playroom. Once the interaction had become less important, the need to go and check up on his mother also faded.

Lucy, a 7-year-old, had trouble leaving the session. She and her therapist developed a hiding game they played before the end of every session. The playroom in which Lucy was seen had no windows and so became very dark if the lights were turned off. Toward the end of the session, Lucy would turn off the lights and count to 5 before turning them back on. During that time, the therapist would move about the room so as to surprise Lucy with her location when the lights came back on. When the session was over, Lucy was careful to turn off the lights and close the door, as if to preserve the room until she could be surprised again at the next session.

Finally, some children's in-session behavior is markedly inappropriate relative to the expectations of their day-to-day environment. They may be very aggressive, ritualistic, bizarre, or regressed. You must provide these children with clear transitions to help them contain their behavior to the playroom so that they do not experience excessive negative reactions on the outside. Parents and teachers rarely appreciate your returning to them a child displaying behavior more deteriorated than that which preceded the session:

Tina, a 5-year-old, engaged in some very regressive play during her sessions: She wanted to be a baby and held and rocked. When the therapist tried to end any given session, Tina would engage in lots of acting out, both in the playroom and the waiting area. She would run, yell, be aggressive toward the therapist, and refuse to leave the playroom, talking baby talk all the while.

After several fairly unpleasant endings in which the therapist had to set very strong limits, he developed what turned out to be a very effective transition ritual. He would meet Tina in the waiting room and they would head to the playroom. With every three steps, they would pretend that Tina was one year younger, and she would behave accordingly. Upon reaching the playroom door, Tina would become an infant and the therapist would pick her up and carry her into the room. At the end of each session, the process was reversed.

In each of these situations, the focus on the transition ritual proved to have both pragmatic and therapeutic value. The rituals made the transitions more efficient so that the children spent more time in the session proper. The rituals also helped the children experience success in moving between activities and reduced their anxiety in effecting separations. The rituals remind you that therapy takes place not just when the child is engaged in some symbolic activity which you actively interpret but from the time she is first aware of your presence until she loses that awareness. Finally, the type of transition rituals the child chooses to engage in may give you additional information about her developmental level. The higher the child's developmental level, the less she should need concrete rituals such as games of peek-a-boo, and, in fact, the less she should need to engage in any type of transition ritual at all.

Limit Setting

Another natural form of structuring every therapist engages in is limit setting. It is generally accepted that limit setting has considerable therapeutic value because it teaches the child about the boundaries of acceptable behavior, demonstrates your interest in keeping her safe, and helps her develop interpersonal responsibility. Even the most fervently child-centered therapists acknowledge that "children do not feel safe, valued or accepted in a completely permissive relationship" (Landreth & Sweeney, 1997, p. 23). Limit setting is also entirely consistent with the Reality Therapy (Glasser, 1975) model, in which the parents' early efforts at organizing their child's world so as to help the child get her needs met in acceptable ways are viewed as the primary force pushing the child toward emotional health and optimal socialization.

Much of the limit setting you engage in during play sessions is somewhat less than intentional. The child is constantly exposed to differential reinforcement as a result of your verbalizations and behaviors. Each time you make a vocalization, whether positive or negative, you are differentially valuing the child's behavior. You cannot reflect on everything the child does, nor can you be fully and actively involved every minute of the session. As your responses vary, so does the child's behavior over time. If you respond more actively when the child talks as opposed to when she acts, then she will begin to talk more. The reverse will occur if you attend to the child's behavior and minimize the content of her verbalizations. The fact is that the child is likely to experience all your positive behaviors as powerful reinforcements, so you must try to use this fact to the child's advantage. You should not be talking just to talk. You should conceptualize your responses, actions, and verbalizations as structuring the child's play session as a result of either the content you convey or by the mere fact of their existence.

According to Landreth and Wright (1997), the limit setting practices of therapists have not changed significantly over the past 30 years. Therapists most often set limits on aggressive behavior toward the therapist, aggressive behavior toward the equipment or toys and those behaviors that threaten the child's health and safety. Most allow socially unacceptable behavior such as swearing. While there seems to be broad agreement on those behaviors on which the therapist should set limits there is much less agreement about the form those limits should take.

Landreth (1991) suggested the following steps to the limit setting process: (1) acknowledge the child's feelings, wishes, and wants; (2) communicate the limit; and (3) specify acceptable alternative behavior. If the situation permits, it seems beneficial to add two other details to these steps. One is to specify the reason for the limit as you communicate the fact of its existence. This helps children understand and internalize the rationale for behavior rather than to simply follow the rules. The other is to provide the child with several alternative behaviors in step three so as to allow the child to make a choice. It is even better if the child can be engaged in generating at least one of the alternatives. This makes the child an active participant in the problem solving and decreases her dependence on the therapist. If these rather indirect steps do not succeed in limiting the child's behavior he goes on to suggest removing the problem toy or material from the playroom and, ultimately, ending the session. Although he gives many examples of problems in the playroom he never mentions the most problematic situation of aggression toward the therapist. This specific problem is addressed in the following section on the use of restraint.

Although this is the tactic many analytically oriented and humanistically oriented play therapists use ending the session as a form of limit setting is a notion that runs counter to Ecosystemic Play Therapy in which structuring activities including limit setting are viewed as essential to the child's progress in therapy. What does the child learn if you end the session? One message would be that you do not want to be around when the child acts out in a negative way, which is certain to have a powerful structuring effect but is also likely to reproduce the dysfunctional transactions the child has within her ecosystem outside the playroom. The child simply learns to equate loss of control with abandonment and comes to fear her own impulses for the potential they have to cause her to be isolated. A second message might be that you are unable to control the child and must resort to exiling her rather than addressing her behavior. If you are truly unable to control the child, then it is unlikely that the therapy has any chance of being successful. After all, what chance do parents have of successfully raising a child if they are unwilling or unable to intervene with control when necessary? You must be able to either provide the structure necessary to control a given client yourself or be able to draw on resources that will allow for that type of control. If you truly lose control of a session, with the result that either you or the child is injured, you create a problem from which the therapy process is unlikely to recover. The child learns that no one is safe, and so trust is virtually impossible to re-establish.

The termination of a given session makes it appear that therapy is contingent on the child behaving appropriately, which seems like a contradiction in structures. If the child could behave appropriately all the time, she would not need the therapy, yet she cannot come to therapy if she does not behave appropriately. Further, you would have to consider the possibility that ending the session might reinforce the child's using negative acting out to escape unpleasant sessions.

Physical Guidance

The use of physical contact as a way of directing the child's behavior and setting limits in play therapy is a fairly controversial topic. Unfortunately, as society has become sensitized to the issues of physical and sexual abuse virtually all physical contact between adults and children has become suspect. A fundamental rule governing all physical contact between therapist and child is that it should always happen solely based on the needs of the child not the needs of the therapist. Obviously, this eliminates any sexualized contact as such is the purview of adults not children but the rule is not as simple a notion as it appears to be. If a therapist takes hold of a child's hand to prevent her from throwing a block at a window whose needs are being addressed? Interestingly, this depends, in part, on what is going on in the therapist's mind at the time. If the therapist has become frustrated and angry at the child's ongoing noncompliance and impulsively grabs the child's hand it is likely the therapist is responding to her own needs not those of the child. In this case, the child learns that adults impulsively react with physical aggression just the way children do. If, on the other hand, the therapist is aware this child is feeling out of control and, from a therapeutic standpoint, needs to know that adults are capable of helping her manage her anger and acting out then physically preventing the child from throwing the block is probably a good therapeutic choice.

If the child has her behavior under control and the therapist uses physical guidance to gently structure her activities then there is little risk the contact will escalate the child's behavior:

> Bill became interested in a gun that shot rubber tipped darts. He began to play with it by shooting the darts around the room. The therapist was aware that Bill had difficulty managing his own behavior and that problems often

got quickly out of hand. Rather than waiting for the dart shooting to become a problem, she immediately suggested Bill shoot at a target and immediately drew a crude bull's eye and hung it on the wall. As she walked back past Bill (who was still shooting at the ceiling) she put her hands on his shoulders and turned him toward the target while reflecting how much Bill was enjoying the gun and restating her suggestion that he shoot at a target. She then positioned herself just behind Bill facing the target creating a frame as it were to direct his behavior. Bill proceeded to shoot the target and the therapist immediately provided verbal reinforcement. As it became clear that she had successfully redirected Bill's behavior she moved away from him decreasing her physical control while increasing her use of verbal guidance.

In this example, the therapist used verbal cues first and then immediately moved toward physical action. She did not wait for the behavior to escalate to the point where limit setting became necessary. This is an ideal circumstance. The therapist has clearly understood the child's needs and provided only as much assistance as was needed to help the child meet those needs in an appropriate way. In this case, the physical contact was incidental to the overall structuring the therapist was doing and probably went almost unnoticed by the child. However, when physical contact is not a part of the therapeutic routine or if the child is already beginning to lose control, touching the child can easily escalate the acting out behavior. The child perceives the therapist to have become controlling and potentially a threat to her well being and so responds aggressively. This is where clinical acumen becomes a critical variable in the outcome of the situation. A therapist must know when to rely on language and when to use physical contact as well as being able to differentiate between a child who is angry but manageable and one who has genuinely lost control. Prevention and early intervention are always preferred modes of therapeutic response to children's aggressive and dangerous behaviors in session. Physical management of the child's acting out should always be a last resort.

Ideally, the amount of physical guidance the therapist uses with the child should be directly related to the child's developmental level. With Level I children, physical guidance can be a routine part of the interaction. One expects healthy parents of healthy children who function at the 0 to 2 age level to routinely structure the child's world with touch. The parent holds the child's hand to make sure they get safely from point A to point B. Similarly, the therapist may take an impulsive child's hand when walking from the waiting room to the playroom. It is important to pair this type of touch with language because "by associating physical intervention with positive, supportive words, the student will begin building associations between words and behavior" (Wood et al., 1996, p. 13). Physical guidance should be used only in a relatively limited way with Level II children and rarely used with Level III children. The goal in all cases is to gradually substitute verbal guidance for physical guidance. Eventually, the hope is that even the external, verbal guidance provided by adults will be replaced by the child's own internal controls.

Restraining

If you are effective in setting limits, are not willing to end disruptive sessions, and are working with any but the most mildly disturbed children, there is the distinct possibility that you may encounter a situation in which you will have to restrain a child client. When the child's behavior reaches a point where it is out of control and is a clear danger to self or others, very few mental health professionals would disagree that either physical restraint or containment of the child is in order. Certainly anyone who has worked with children in a psychiatric inpatient setting has seen situations where children needed to be, and were, restrained. There is less agreement as to the appropriateness of restraining children in the context of outpatient play therapy. Many play therapists would rather end the session or involve the child's parent than restrain a child themselves.

It is possible, however, that the act of restraining the child may fit quite appropriately within the overall treatment plan. Restraint is certainly consistent with the philosophy of Reality Therapy (Glasser, 1975) and with the Developmental Therapy–Developmental Teaching model (Wood et al., 1996). In Reality Therapy, clients are held responsible for their behavior and allowed to experience natural and logical consequences. Further, clients are thought to make better and faster progress when such consequences are regularly and routinely imposed. In the Developmental Therapy–Developmental Teaching model, there is recognition that sometimes children lose the ability to control themselves and need an adult to help them regain it. Even the Theraplay model that is based heavily on positive interaction and contact notes that it is important for the therapist to restrain the child who is acting out (Jernberg & Booth, 1999).

Natural consequences are those that would occur if the behavior were to happen in the real world without artificial interventions. A cavity is the natural consequence of not brushing teeth. A burn is the natural consequence of touching a hot stove. Usually these potentially dangerous consequences happen to children only by accident, but when they do happen, one trial learning is usually the result. Less destructive natural consequences include social ridicule when a person fails to bathe regularly or hunger if one forgets to take lunch to school.

Logical consequences are those that may not happen naturally but make sense. A parent is probably not willing to let her child get a cavity to teach her the value of toothbrushing. Most parents turn to nagging or behavior modification, which takes the responsibility away from the child and places all the control in the hands of the parents. A logical-consequences approach would have the parents inform the child that since they are unable to force her to brush her teeth in order to prevent cavities, they will have to take control over other things that also affect tooth decay, until she is willing to brush her teeth regularly. The parents would then cut all sugar out of the child's diet and potentially serve all vegetables and fruits raw until such time as the child brushes her teeth. The parents do not nag and do not argue; they just take control over those aspects of the environment that are theirs to control rather than trying to control the child.

If restraint procedures are presented correctly, the child may experience them as a logical consequence, thereby fostering rather than diminishing the child's sense of responsibility. The message to the child must be "If you are unable to control yourself and persons and property are endangered, then I will have to provide protection until you demonstrate renewed control." The message is not that you will arbitrarily or capriciously control the child; in fact, the message is not that you are controlling the child at all. The message is that you are being protective and supportive while the child works to regain control.

In the context of play therapy, this approach means that you must be able to remain positive and supportive while the restraint takes place. This in turn means that you must implement restraint before you become either angered or frightened by the child's behavior and that you are confident enough with the procedure that you do not become anxious. Once begun, restraint procedures should not end until the child has been able to clearly demonstrate regained control.

Aside from the importance of imposing realistic consequences on a child's dangerous acting out, the use of restraint is in many cases developmentally appropriate. When an infant rages, her caretaker does not simply allow the behavior to continue—the caretaker moves to contain the child, to calm and even nurture her. When the toddler rages and throws herself on the ground and begins to bang her head, the caretaker again moves in to contain and soothe. The caretaker serves a regulating function until the child develops sufficient self-regulating capacities. These episodes teach the child that the caretaker is willing and able to withstand her rage while keeping them both safe. Restraint is then a normal child/caretaker interaction and is consistent with the Theraplay philosophy.

As with any other situation in which you make physical contact with the child, you must be alert to the possibility of legal problems arising. Such problems generally are easily avoided if those bringing the child to therapy are informed of the nature of the treatment and the possible types of therapist/child interactions that may take place before treatment is initiated. Very few parents have difficulty with the idea of restraining the child in the abstract, but many become much more concerned when it actually happens. If it ever becomes necessary to restrain a child in session, then it behooves you to allow for time to debrief both the parents and the child when the incident comes to a close. Both the parent and child should understand exactly what happened to precipitate the restraint. Both should review exactly the steps that were taken before and during the restraint procedure to ensure the child's safety. And both should understand that you are not angry with the child or the parent and that no one needs to apologize for what happened.

One distinct advantage of a highly interactive form of play therapy relative to the possibility of having to restrain a child is the fact that the method allows you to predict, with a fair degree of accuracy, when the child will act out, as the result of two independent variables. First, the degree of control you exert allows you to judge the pace of the child's movement through the phases of treatment. Second, as noted in the description of Theraplay in Chapter Two, this type of therapy goes through predictable phases, the first three of which are exploration, tentative acceptance, and negative reaction. The transition between tentative acceptance and negative reaction is usually predicated by a slight but gradual increase in the child's resistance to your interventions. In a short-term course of treatment, the negative reaction often occurs in the third or fourth sessions.

Your ability to predict the peak of the child's negative reaction phase does, in this case, give you some control over when it will occur. If the child has a history of severe acting out, then you should expect the negative reaction phase to be severe and plan accordingly. As you begin to see the child's resistance increase, take careful note of those things that seem to act as triggers. As you become aware of the pattern, try not to engage in these potentially provocative behaviors toward the end of the session. Then set up several sessions in which you have extra time available should the child need it and proceed to interact normally with the child even if it means she will act out. Since you will feel prepared for the situation, you will be able to react calmly and see through to the end of any negative interactions that might arise.

You can also prepare the parents for the outburst and help them process it when it occurs. You might have the parent observe a number of sessions in either the room or through a one-way mirror. If you are the only professional or staff person available in case restraint needs to be implemented, it is preferable to have the parent in the room so that you can comment to the parent on what is taking place and involve her if needed. If two therapists and an observation setup are available, it can be useful to have the parent and one therapist behind the mirror observing you and the child, to allow the parent and observing therapist to do as much processing as possible without disturbing the flow of the child's session. Finally, videotaping sessions in which you suspect that acting out may occur can be very useful:

> Mrs. Hernandez was brought in to review videotapes of each of her foster son, Jacob's, first three sessions. After the first session, she commented on the intensity of Jacob's initial attachment to the therapist. She was surprised that he seemed to be having so much fun and noted that he seemed more relaxed than he did at home. While Mrs. Hernandez viewed the tape of the second session, the therapist pointed out how Jacob was beginning to resist the therapist by engaging in a lot of "play" hitting and pretending to bite the therapist. He hypothesized that Jacob would engage in a major temper

outburst, of the type he had at home on an almost daily basis, during one of the next two sessions. Jacob did indeed have a major outburst during the next session and had to be restrained for nearly 45 minutes before he could calm himself. When she viewed the tape, Mrs. Hernandez cried and said she was incredibly relieved to have a professional finally see and experience the kind of behavior she had to cope with on a daily basis. She reported that Jacob had never displayed this behavior with his previous therapist or during the brief time he was hospitalized in an intensely behavioral psychiatric facility. She also reported that this episode had ended differently than the ones at home because Jacob usually would not allow anyone to nurture him in order to bring the episode to a close.

However, even with the best planning, at times the child may act out suddenly and with minimum warning. In these cases it is best to follow through with limit setting and attempt to involve the parents in calming the child so that the session can be brought to a reasonable end. Whether the child's acting out is foreseen or a surprise, most play therapists agree that there are times when she needs to be protected. However, even among those who agree on the above philosophical/theoretical stance with regards to restraint, there is disagreement as to the best way to contain the child. Whatever method you choose to implement in case of emergencies in your office, the child's caretakers and potentially even the child should know exactly what you will do if she loses control. The primary types of restraint techniques available are a time-out room, mechanical restraints, and physical restraint.

A time-out room suggests that no adult is willing or capable of serving a restraining function; in fact, the child may be symbolically or actually abandoned in their rage while isolated in a "safe" space. There are occasions when placing a child, alone, in a time-out room is necessary for everyone's welfare; however, you must seriously consider the appropriateness of the powerful message this sends the child about her capacity for being with people.

Mechanical restraints include all the devices used to "anchor" the child, such as posies, hand or foot restraints, tethers, seat belts on chairs, and harnesses. Mechanical restraints are rarely used outside institutional settings and are rarely used even there. The advantage of such restraints is that they provide a child with a high level of safety when used properly. Additionally, they allow you to stay close, even when the child is wildly out of control. On the other hand, mechanical restraints tend to send the child the same message as time-out rooms, namely, that you are somewhat incapable of controlling her. Mechanical restraints also tend to carry with them a somewhat sadistic aura. They smack of the Middle Ages, though it is unlikely that they raise that sort of imagery in the child.

Physical restraint is when an adult(s) holds the child until she regains control. The many different techniques for physically restraining children each have their own benefits and detractions. Regardless of the method of restraint to be used, the individuals who are to implement it should be thoroughly trained. It is advantageous for all mental health professionals who work with children to learn basic restraint techniques, much like medical professionals are required to learn cardiopulmonary resuscitation (CPR). Several organizations provide such training, and they are easy to contact through local school district or law enforcement offices.

The many techniques for physically restraining a child each carry both certain logistical and interactional implications. To help you make decisions about the use of any restraint in the treatment of a given child, let us examine three of the most common restraint positions.

In the baskethold position, you seat the child in your lap, with her back to your abdomen while you cross the child's arms around her and contain her. The pragmatic advantage to this hold is that it is quite easy to maneuver the child into this position even while you are seated. The pragmatic disadvantage is that the child can swing her head back against your face or chest quite forcefully. The emotional advantage to this hold is that the child remains upright and has some mobility while being more or less hugged by you. One risk of this position is that it prevents you and the child from making eye contact, so communication may be less than effective, which may prevent you from calming her as quickly as you might otherwise.

Several organizations that teach safe restraint techniques recommend the prone hold. In this restraint, you place the child facedown on the floor and then kneel and straddle the child's buttocks or lower back. Use your hands to hold down the child's arms. From a pragmatic point of view this is a very safe hold in which neither you nor the child are likely to get hurt. However, it can be very difficult to maneuver a child into this position, especially if you are attempting to do it on your own. From an emotional standpoint, this hold has all the limitations of the baskethold and then some. The child cannot see your face, so communication is thus limited. Further, the combination of lack of eye contact and the prone position may activate a sense of victimization, especially in children who have a history of sexual abuse.

The last restraint is the supine hold, which is executed in exactly the same manner as the prone hold except that the child is lying on the floor faceup instead of facedown. Pragmatically, this position is slightly easier to achieve than the prone hold. Unfortunately, this hold is not as safe as the prone hold because the child can raise her head and bang it against the floor and she can easily spit at you. On the plus side, the supine hold allows for that all-important eye contact, which increases the chances that the child may be calmed somewhat faster than in either of the other two holds. There is still a tendency for children to feel as victimized when held in this position as they may in the prone hold. Again, the advantage is that, so long as they can see your face, they can see that you are not angry and gain some assurance that you are not planning to hurt them.

In the case of outpatient play therapy, physical restraint initiated by the therapist alone or with the assistance of another therapist or the child's caretaker is the best choice of interventions when the child has lost control.

Before initiating the restraint, you should make a clear statement that labels the problem behavior, the reason the behavior cannot continue, and the consequences which will follow if the child does not stop. If there is time, you might also suggest an alternate behavior in which the child could engage to vent her feelings. Say the child starts to hit you. You would say, "You cannot continue to hit me because I do not want to be hurt. If you are angry, you could hit the pillow or yell at me. (You may attempt to physically redirect the child at this point.) If you do not stop hitting, then I will have to hold you until I am sure you are ready to stop."

If the child does not stop the behavior within seconds of your verbal warning, then you should move to restrain her. Sometimes this action will be sufficient to signal the child that boundaries do exist and allow her to regain control; however, this is rarely the case the first time you attempt to set a significant limit. Once the child is positioned in a restraint hold, you should begin to help her regain control. First and foremost, you should attempt to maintain eye contact with the child at all times. When speaking, you should use a very low-key voice which clearly conveys that you are in control no matter how difficult a time the child is having. You should reflect the child's distress simply and directly, not overstating the obvious because doing so will only agitate her. Suggest things the child might try to do to regain control. You might suggest that she take a deep breath, relax one limb, or close her eyes and picture herself at a place she likes.

If another person is helping you with the physical restraint, he should have been previously instructed to not say anything at all so long as the child is being restrained. All the child's interactions should be with you alone, to ensure that she will associate the trigger behavior, the consequences, the eventual safe outcome, and you in one unit.

Once you have initiated restraint, do not release the child until she has regained control, no matter how long this process takes. The best way to make sure you do not release the child too soon is to require that she follow some simple direction before you will let her go. Have her take three deep breaths along with you. Or have her lie very still while you count to 10. If you do not follow the restraint through until the episode is over, the results will be worse than if you had never initiated the limit setting. The child simply learns that you are no more trustworthy than anyone else in her life, that you will not remain available for the duration on her intense neediness even when she is out of control. The therapeutic relationship is likely to be seriously damaged.

In Chapter Eight, we described how Kyle, an intern, prevented a fellow intern's child client, Peter, from jumping out of the playroom window. The situation did not end there, however, for as Kyle pulled Peter back into the room, Peter became enraged and tried to physically attack Kyle:

At first Kyle tried to turn Peter over to his intern therapist, Susan, but every time Kyle let go, Peter headed for the window or began to destroy the office/playroom. Kyle held Peter in a baskethold for about 10 minutes, during which time Peter's behavior continued to escalate. When Peter was very nearly successful in biting Kyle's arm, Kyle instituted a supine hold and maintained it for about 20 minutes before Peter discovered that he could twist hard enough to bring his head close to Kyle's hands and he again tried to bite. After numerous warnings, Kyle moved Peter into a prone hold, maintaining this hold for a full hour, during which Kyle tried to engage in every calming and supportive behavior he could imagine. Throughout the episode, Peter screamed that he would kill Kyle as soon as Kyle released him and that he would break everything he could find.

Unfortunately, Susan's supervisor intervened at that point and insisted that Kyle release Peter because the restraint was obviously not helping. Kyle repeated Peter's threats and asked for support in finishing the interaction because Peter was obviously still terribly out of control. This statement was supported by Peter continuing to scream as loud as he could throughout the entire interaction between Kyle and the supervisor and repeating each of his threats. When the supervisor, whose theoretical orientation was not the same as that of Kyle's supervisor, insisted that Peter be released, Kyle gave in. Peter immediately proceeded to smash every object in Susan's office, to pull bookshelves off of the walls, to smash a fire extinguisher through the railing of the stairs in the hall, and to throw most of Susan's possessions down the stairs, all while the supervisor interpreted the behavior. When Peter finally wore himself out, the supervisor took Peter for a walk outside while they talked about what had happened.

While Susan's supervisor saw his intervention as successful, Susan, Kyle, and Kyle's supervisor did not agree. Susan was put in the position of having to work with a client who had been allowed to destroy her office. She substantially withdrew her energies and felt safe only when the window to her office had been nailed shut. Peter went on to use climbing out of windows as his primary method of acting out. Over the next few months he had to be pulled off the roof of his group home several times. He was finally placed on substantial doses of sedative medications and maintained until treatment could be initiated with another therapist.

When the acting-out episode ends, you should spend some time nurturing the child to demonstrate that you are not angry that the child lost control, only pleased that she was eventually able to regain control. You should also spend a few minutes reviewing what happened. Repeat what the child did that triggered the need for restraint. Repeat the alternative behaviors in which the child could have engaged to express her feelings in an appropriate way. Briefly review the steps taken to help the child regain control and any significant material that she revealed during the course of the episode. Finally, note how pleased you are that the child was able to regain control. It is best that you do not say anything about the child's future behavior. That is, it is best not to say that you hope that it does not happen again or that if it does happen again the outcome will be the same because either statement seems to be asking the child to repeat her behavior.

Given all this, it is not the least bit surprising that many, if not most, play therapists opt for other strategies for managing a child's in-session acting out. However, be aware that there is very little else which can transpire between you and your child client that will have the same therapeutic impact as the successful management of a full-blown rage episode. The child learns that even her most extreme feelings cannot hurt you or cause you to act out against her. She learns that you mean what you say and intend to follow through on requiring that she demonstrate responsible behavior in sessions. And she learns that play sessions are indeed very safe. The bond that will form between you and the child once you survive such an episode is so intense that it is difficult to describe to someone who has never experienced it.

> The third session with Jacob, mentioned earlier, began the same way the others had. Jacob greeted the therapist very warmly and came readily into the playroom. The therapist spent about 10 minutes drawing a picture of Jacob, a task that helped orient Jacob to the interaction in a fairly structured way. Then the therapist moved to engage Jacob in some rough-and-tumble play, as he had done in the first two sessions. Jacob tried to direct the interaction from the beginning. He grabbed the felt pens away from the therapist and refused to open his mouth when the therapist wanted to check and see if his new tooth had come in yet. When the play started, he tried to push the therapist over and then pretended to bite his hand. When the therapist moved to redirect the aggressive behavior, Jacob began to hit the therapist. At no time did Jacob appear angry; it was as if his behavior was several steps ahead of his feelings. He wanted to be in control but did not seem to be particularly upset by the interaction. When the therapist moved to redirect the hitting, Jacob became enraged and attacked full force. The therapist then moved to restrain Jacob. Jacob was unable to regain control for a full 45 minutes. During this time, the therapist instructed Jacob, in very soothing tones, as to how he might regain control. The therapist was calming and reflected Jacob's anger but also insisted that Jacob must relax and take three deep breaths in time with him before he would release him. After about 30 minutes, Jacob began to cry but was still attempting to hurt the therapist. The therapist became even more soothing, pointing out that he thought they were near the end. Slowly, Jacob relaxed and began to cry quietly. He relaxed to the point that the therapist agreed to release him.
>
> Immediately on releasing Jacob, the therapist reflected how difficult the time had been for Jacob and admired the amount of work he had done to regain control. Then the therapist began to be very nurturant: He held Jacob and wiped his forehead with a cloth. As soon as he could, the therapist had Jacob's foster mother enter the playroom and take over the nurturing. While she held Jacob, she stated her pleasure in being able to nurture Jacob because he rarely allowed her to do this after he had become enraged at home. And she acknowledged that usually she was so angry when Jacob acted out that she could not interact with him for hours after any one episode. To finish the session, Jacob and the therapist reviewed what had happened with

the foster mother present, to allow for comparisons to what happened during similar episodes at home.

While structuring activities are very important in helping maintain the child in an optimal state of arousal while keeping her safe, challenging activities help push the child toward higher developmental levels.

Challenging

Play therapists do not often think of themselves as challenging their child clients in play sessions. Generally, in fact, therapists consciously try to avoid activities that require much skill on the child's part. There are, however, a great variety of ways in which the child is and can be challenged by you, the play session, and the session contents.

One way you should challenge the child is by developing session structures and contents that are geared to a point just slightly above the child's present developmental level. During the intake and assessment, you determined the child's level of functioning in a number of areas: cognitive, emotional, behavioral, and social. You then developed treatment goals that included improving the child's functioning across areas. However, in the discussion of child psychopathology it was noted that unevenness in a child's functioning across areas is generally more problematic than overall delays in function. Therefore it is important that treatment begin by focusing interventions on the area in which the child is functioning the lowest. It is important to develop in-session activities that will regularly challenge the child to function at a slightly higher level.

For example, you would not expect a child who has difficulty interacting with others on any level to come to play therapy and suddenly and spontaneously develop a working relationship. Instead, you would work to create experiences that provoke minimal interaction upon which you could build:

Collin was an extremely disturbed, 10-year-old child who could not maintain appropriate interactions with others for even a few minutes. He would either withdraw and focus on objects in his immediate environment or become so intrusive that the other person would withdraw. In his early play therapy sessions, he worked hard to avoid the therapist by hiding or engaging in bizarre ritualistic behavior. The therapist decided to use a Level I social interaction to begin building a relationship. She first gave Collin a few small, chewy candies to get his attention focused. Then when she had his interest she hid one or two candies somewhere on her person and encouraged Collin to hunt for them. Initially, the candies were easy to find because they were set on the top of a shirt cuff or on the top of her outstretched leg. Gradually, however, she moved the locations to ones closer to her face so that Collin had to look at her to find the candies. Still later the game was changed so that Collin had to make appropriate eye contact for 30 seconds before she would give him a hint as to where the candy was hidden. By gradually increasing the challenge required to complete a simple therapeutic task, Collin's behavior was shaped.

Another way you will routinely challenge your clients is through the use of paradoxical directives or statements. Paradoxical statements are ones in which you say the opposite of what you mean in order to challenge the child to comply. For example, you might tell an angry child who had just struck you that you are sure she cannot hit the doll you are holding as hard as she just hit you. Very few children will resist the challenge to hit the doll—you have successfully redirected the attack on you. Paradoxical directives and statements are most often used in the context of behavior management both in and out of sessions.

You must be cautious not to sound sarcastic when using paradox because sarcasm cues the child to the double meaning of your statements. In addition, sarcasm is generally taken as an affront and as such may push the child to become very angry. If you were to say, in a sarcastic tone, "I'll bet you can't calm down" to a child who is in the middle of a tantrum, you are likely to find her escalating rather than calming. If, instead, you were to say "I have never seen a child who is so good at looking angry. I'll bet everyone knows for sure when you are mad. You look so angry right now I'll bet you can't make your face look any angrier," the child is likely to take up the challenge—you have begun to manage the behavior by getting her to follow a direction.

Intruding/Engaging

As mentioned in Chapter Two, Jernberg changed the name of this category of therapist behavior from Intruding to Engaging. In spite of the change, it seems clear that therapists will want to do both in sessions.

Few play therapists think of themselves as wanting or needing to intrude upon their clients. The very word "intrude" runs counter to the supportive and somewhat distant stance the humanistic therapists take. And yet the primary activity in which every play therapist engages, namely, the production of verbalizations, of whatever type, is intrusive. After all, how often do most children have to put up with hearing an adult comment on their activities and the meanings of those activities while they are playing? It is a process that most children find somewhat disruptive, especially early in the treatment. Certainly, the child experiences poorly timed or worded reflections and interpretations as so intrusive and disruptive that she rejects them. In these cases you have used intrusion to meet your own needs, not those of the child, and have met with the expected outcome of such an action. But there are many times when you intrude in ways that are in the child's best interest and that therefore serve a therapeutic purpose.

The well-timed and well-worded interpretation is probably the most common and effective of all your intrusive behaviors. A good interpretation will have all the hallmarks of an intrusion in that it causes a shift in the child's thoughts and actions. The various aspects of delivering interpretations and their impact on the child are discussed at length later in this chapter.

Therapists also intrude in many other situations regardless of their theoretical orientation. Most therapists will, for example, intrude on a very withdrawn child. Suppose the child had pulled into the fetal position and remained there for more than a few minutes. In this case you would attempt to intrude on her space either physically or verbally. You might coax the child, show her toys, or stroke her face or arms. All these actions intrude on the child's space but in a way designed to maximize her interaction with you. If you think in terms of optimal parent/child interactions, then you realize that no parents would allow their child to withdraw for any length of time without attempting to reinvolve her in social interchange. Similarly, parents intrude when their child becomes overstimulated and they attempt to slow her down. You might first verbally intrude on a child who seems to be losing control of her behavior and remind her of the limits that apply in the playroom. If that does not slow her, remove any objects she is using or treating inappropriately. If the child continues to escalate, then you may need to restrain her as previously described. All these actions are certainly as intrusive as they are structuring.

Engaging behavior may also run counter to some therapist's view of their role in session. Through engaging behaviors the therapist insists that the child recognize the therapist's presence and that the two remain, literally, engaged throughout the session. The therapist is not a passive observer in the session nor is she an object the child can ignore. If therapeutic work is to take place the child and therapist must be allies in the work of therapy. The child must view the therapist as someone capable of and committed to helping improve the quality of the child's life. At the same time the therapist wants to prevent the sessions from becoming so serious and overwhelming that child's strengths and skills are overwhelmed. A skillful therapist know when to work and when to say to the child, "Boy you just did some really hard work. I think we should both take a break and just play for a few minutes." While proceeding to play catch or tickling game with the child.

Nurturing

Nurturing is generally something that comes easily, often too easily, to play therapists. Most people who enter the mental health field—and child work in particular—have a great desire to help and take care of others. This is an area in which it may be more difficult for you to manage your behavior in such a way that you consistently act in the child's interest rather than your own. It is very easy to nurture a crying child by hugging and consoling her. But have you helped her understand her pain or simply helped her put it away so that it will not bother her at that moment? Later in this chapter, there are several examples of intrusions and challenges being used to help a child keep her pain active in order to explore it and nurturance being held off until the elements of pain that needed to be addressed became clearer are presented.

For clarity, let us consider the plight of a child with a physical problem rather than an emotional one. The child awakens in the middle of the night crying and complaining of abdominal pain. The pain is so intense that the mother cannot console the child and calls the pediatrician. Should the pediatrician, anxious to help both the mother and child calm down, suggest giving the child aspirin and a hot water bottle, or should she suggest that the mother probe the child's abdomen to see if she can localize the source of the child's pain? The one action will give both mother and child almost immediate relief, the other may detect acute appendicitis, which would be exacerbated by the hot water bottle and a delay in obtaining surgical intervention. The mother must be able to delay optimally nurturing her child so as to check the source of the pain. Then, if appendicitis were detected, she may have to delay some forms of nurturance, such as giving the child something to drink, even longer while the child is readied for surgery.

While there are situations when certain types of nurturance may need to be withheld to care for the child optimally, there are also situations in which nurturance may have to be forced on the child. A child who has been acutely ill may require the life-saving intravenous administration of fluids and nutrients, although very few children would plead to have a needle stuck in their hand for hours. The treatment of autistic children often requires that they be held and stimulated in ways that force them to recognize their caregiver's presence. These activities are intrusive, structuring, challenging, and nurturing all at the same time, such as when a mother leans in and turns the child's face to hers as she gives the child a kiss.

One form of nurturing play therapists use to varying degrees is feeding. There are many pros and cons to introducing food into the play session, and you should consider them before making a decision in any given case.

The primary argument against therapists bringing food to a child's session derives from the psychoanalytic model. Providing food for the child is seen as contaminating the transference by creating a real, dependent relationship, a concern when the child already tends to take a very dependent stance vis-à-vis others in her environment. But this concern must be examined in a developmental context. For a level I child, being fed is one of the main motives for interpersonal interaction. When a breast-fed baby is hungry, it will not accept consolation from anyone except its mother—after all, she is capable of meeting the infant's needs. As the child enters Level II, food is still an important part of many of her interactions. Snack time at nursery or preschool generally carries very positive emotional valence. By the time a child enters Level III, food will have lost much of its interpersonal nurturing value. The Level III and Level IV children who have developed normally eat because they are hungry, not because they need interpersonal supplies. If you introduce food in such a way that the child interprets it as a substitute for interpersonal supplies, you run the risk of creating eating problems where there were none.

The other main argument against bringing food to the child's sessions is that it tends to be a ritual which is very hard to eliminate later and which can interfere with the conduct of the session. With regards to the first issue, it is true that if you bring food to any one of the child's sessions, you had best be prepared to bring it to every session after that through termination. If this is not something you are willing to do, then do not start. With regards to the second issue, it is true that eating and drinking can become rituals by which the child avoids the work of the therapy. The first 15 or 20 minutes of the session may be taken up by eating, drinking, going to the bathroom, and cleaning up. If you are going to introduce food into the session, make sure that it is a very simple finger food and that whatever you bring is the same from week to week. Do not encourage the child to bring food from home. If you do so you lose all control of the impact of food on the session. Children can end up bring food that is difficult to eat or very messy and the whole session can be taken up with preparation, eating and clean up activities.

The advantages to the use of food in the sessions are pragmatic and developmental. The main pragmatic issue is that children often come to play sessions directly after school and do not have time for a snack, so they are legitimately hungry. A hungry child is not very likely to attend to the work of the session. In these cases, if you can direct the parent to provide a routine, simple snack for the child prior to the session, or if you can provide such at the beginning of the session, it may do a lot to improve the child's overall cooperation. As noted, it is perfectly appropriate for a child who is functioning at Level I or II to have food as a primary motivator for interpersonal interactions. In these cases, the quantity of the food is relatively unimportant to the child. She does not need to get it all at once but is quite happy to receive small, even tiny, quantities of food over the course of the session. Drinks served in baby bottles are more interesting than drinks served in cups, even though the latter method is an easier way to consume a large quantity of liquid.

If food is introduced into the therapy of a child in a developmentally specific way, then it is much less likely that the child will want to continue to have food in the sessions once that developmental phase is mastered. In two of the four cases presented in this text, food was introduced to help the children focus on identifying their dependency needs and their fears about allowing themselves to be dependent. In both cases, the child's desire for continuing the food lasted only a few sessions and was soon replaced by more age-appropriate ways of obtaining interpersonal supplies.

The more common form of nurturance provided to child clients is positive physical contact. Touch is generally important to the child's well being (Barnard & Brazelton, 1990) and to the child's physiologic, social and body image development as well as to her management of stress (Jernberg & Booth, 1999). Yet positive physical contact may be even more controversial than the use of restraint and carries with it its own potential ethical and legal problems. As noted previously, in this day and age, when the problems of the physical and sexual abuse of children are in the forefront of adults' thinking, the idea of physical contact between an adult and a child tends to make everyone a little nervous. Some daycare centers have gone so far as to refuse to change children's diapers for fear of increasing the potential for sexual abuse claims. These centers inform parents that they must come to the center to change the child's diaper if it is to be done at all. Clearly, such a situation is regrettable because it is not in anyone's best interest.

But what of physical contact between a child and her therapist? In particular, what about physical contact between a child and a therapist of the opposite gender, or even one of the same gender? The philosophy behind Theraplay (Jernberg, 1979, Jernberg & Booth, 1999), Developmental Play Therapy (Brody, 1992, 1997), and Ecosystemic Play Therapy is that physical contact between a child and an adult is not only appropriate but therapeutically mandated if the child is functioning at or below Level III:

> Touching, then, is a communication between the one touching and the one touched. Through her hands—body parts almost miraculously capable of an infinite variety of pressures, delicate to strong—the toucher communicates thew quality of her presence. Her touches tell the one touched how the toucher feels about him. In response, the one touched—all without words, and moment by moment—expresses his experience of being touched. Expressive touch is the first mode of communication, the first give and take in the life of the human individual. It is the foundation on which all later verbal and nonverbal communication must build. (Brody, 1997, p. 161)

The value of nurturant contact is coming to be emphasized even in therapies where touch is not necessarily viewed as a central component. Take for instance the following case example from *Multi-Systemic Structural Strategic Interventions for Child and Adolescent Behavior Problems* (Tolan, 1990) where the therapist addresses failure to attend to limits on what he may and may not touch in the therapist's office while the therapist is talking to the boy's mother:

> Moving just as swiftly, the therapist grabbed the little boy and threw him over her shoulder, hanging him upside down by his feet. His response was a mixture of giggles and protests. When he began to swear, she immobilized hands and feet, and tickled him. Jeff's family gasped. "Jeff, don't hurt the doctor," they warned. Jeff tried to spit, so she tickled him some more, then

deposited him in a folded ball on his mother's lap. Taking her cue, his mother caressed and restrained him, and finally released him to continue him own activity while they continued to talk. Throughout the rest of the session, Jeff tested, and either his mother or the therapist would playfully remind him that they were bigger and stronger and fully intending that he should be accountable to the limits we had set. At the end of the session Jeff recognized the therapist with a big hug and a kiss. (Comrinck-Graham, 1990, p. 23)

The need for touch exists regardless of the gender of either the child or the therapist and is true regardless of the child's history. In fact, it seems that the more pathologic the child's contacts with adults in the past, the more appropriate physical contacts in the course of her therapy are indicated. This is even true in the case of sexually abused children (Jernberg & Booth, 1999).

Michelle, a developmentally delayed 4-year-old, was referred to treatment because she constantly approached adult males and attempted to sit in their laps. She would do this whether or not she knew the man. Once seated, she would wriggle around and grind her bottom into the man's pelvis. This behavior was viewed as a direct result of the sexual abuse she had suffered at the hands of her father. Her mother was afraid that if this behavior continued, Michelle was at risk for further abuse.

As soon as she began her therapy with a male therapist, Michelle repeatedly attempted to sit in his lap. Several times she caught him off guard, and, as he later reported to his supervisor, he was surprised at how sexualized her behavior was. Initially, the therapist attempted to redirect Michelle's behavior. He would let her sit next to him and hold his hand, but he would not let her sit on his lap. This intervention and other attempts at distracting her had no effect. If anything, the behavior escalated. Finally, the therapist's supervisor suggested that instead of keeping Michelle at a distance, the therapist might try to treat her for what she was, a fragile, early level II child. The therapist agreed and went to the next session armed with a baby blanket and baby bottle. Before Michelle could approach him, he introduced a new game, the "baby game." He told Michelle that several times during each session they would pretend that she was a baby and he would take care of her. At this point he picked her up and laid her across his lap, with her bottom well off to the side. He put the blanket over her, put the bottle in her mouth, and began to rock her. She accepted every bit of his nurturance without protest.

The clearly infantile nature of the interaction allowed Michelle to accept it without feeling threatened by the possibility of sexually inappropriate consequences. The game allowed her to get her needs met in a developmentally appropriate way. The introduction of the game dropped the frequency of Michelle's attempts to sit in the therapist's lap to zero. The change was generalized by having an uncle who lived nearby spend time taking care of, and babying, Michelle on a regular basis.

Although the intervention just described was very successful, it was not easily implemented. Initially, the therapist felt very uncomfortable having any contact with Michelle for fear of exacerbating the problem. He was also reluctant to explain it to the mother, who wanted Michelle to stop approaching males. However, when he did spend time with Michelle's mother, she immediately understood the intervention and understood why the nurturing she had been providing was not the same as that which a male could provide. She even understood the need for Michelle to develop a healthy pattern of interacting with men so as to remediate the problems triggered by the abuse she had suffered.

This example points to the need to prepare parents for every aspect of the therapy process, no matter how benevolent the intervention might seem. The parent needs to be aware of the child's developmental level and the types of caretaker/child interactions that would be appropriate for a child at that level. The parent also needs to be made aware of how the interaction can be kept from having any sexual connotations by making it appear very infantile and nurturant. The point here is not to force contact with the child who does not need it nor to cause regression in children who have developed to at least the end of Level III. The goal is to create those health-promoting, nurturant contacts that the child who is functioning at Level I or II needs to progress normally.

As with physical guidance the therapist's behavior must always be guided by the needs of the child. In a study of adult client's experiences of being touched by their therapist 5 elements were found to affect whether clients perceived the interaction as positive (Horton, Clance, Sterk-Elifson, & Emshoff, 1995). The first four factors were hypothesized as important based on an earlier study by Gelb (1982) who found that clarity regarding boundaries, the congruence of the touch, the patient's perception of control over the contact and the patient's belief that the contact was for their good not that of the therapist were all associated with positive experiences on the patient's part. The 1995 study found empirical support for the first three factors and added a fifth, the patient's perception that a positive therapeutic alliance had been established. It seems that, for adults, the benefits of touch are related to their perception of the contact as appropriate in the context of both the situation and the therapeutic relationship.

It becomes clear then that the child may initially experience nurturance, like structuring, challenging, and intruding, as either positive or negative. All four categories of interaction can be withheld from, imposed on, or provided to the child in therapeutic ways. It is the needs of the individual child that determine the appropriateness of a given activity in the course of a particular session and over the course of the child's treatment. The nature of these therapeutic interactions is planned based on knowledge of optimal parent/child interactions and their effect on children's development and mental health. And the positive or negative outcome of implementing such interactions is determined by assessing the child's progress along appropriate developmental lines and by progress toward the resolution of her faulty assumptions and beliefs about the world.

Additional ideas for in-session activities are in *Activities for Children in Therapy: A Guide for Planning and Facilitating Therapy with Troubled Children* (Dennison & Glassman, 1987). The book contains more than 200 activities for use with children between the ages of 5 and 12. These ideas cover relationship building and self-disclosure, affective awareness and communication, social skills, school, termination, and follow-up. Other sources for activities include *101 Favorite Play Therapy Techniques* (Kaderson & Schaefer, 1997) and *Play Therapy Treatment Planning and Interventions* (O'Connor & Ammen, 1997).

Many effective techniques for use with children exhibiting specific psychological disorders are in The Practice of Child Therapy (Morris & Kratochwill, 1983) and Therapies for Children (Schaefer & Millman, 1977). The corrective experiences you create for the child in the session will be therapeutically effective regardless of the cognitive or verbal work that accompanies them. For children functioning at Level I, you will have to rely on the experiences to effect most of the therapeutic change. As the child's developmental level increases, so does the potential impact of cognitive and verbal therapeutic interventions.

PLANNING THE VERBAL COMPONENT OF THE CHILD'S PLAY THERAPY

Language plays a critical role in the healthy emotional functioning of children and, therefore, it must play a critical role in their play therapy. Put quite simply, "language processes . . . importantly constitute child psychotherapy, promote normal development, and are responsible for or correlated with childhood dysfunction" (Shirk & Russell, 1996, p. 228). There is a strong correlation between language problems and psychiatric problems in general (Cantwell & Baker, 1984). Specifically, language problems have been found to be correlated with externalizing behavior problems (Burke, Crenshaw, Green, Schlosser, & Strocchia-Rivera, 1989; Davis, Singer, & Morris-Friehe, 1991; Hindshaw, 1992; Piel, 1990) as well as internalizing problems (Evans, 1987; Stevenson, Rickman, & Graham, 1985). The function of language in health versus pathology seems related to the child's ability to use language as a bridge from action, to symbol to thought as well as its integral role in emotional experience and regulation.

The term *emotional experiencing* is used to define the process by which one both experiences (on an almost physiologic level) and recognizes (on a cognitive level) an emotion. The process by which children come to use incorporate emotional experiencing into their day to day lives in the course of normal development is fairly similar to the way the process occurs treatment.

In play therapy, the therapist can facilitate a child's emotional experience by breaking it into steps (Shirk & Russell, 1996). The first step is the elicitation of the emotion. This is consistent with the process of creating corrective experiences for the child in session as previously described. Second, the therapist helps the child to register the emotion by providing a verbal label for the feeling. It is not at all uncommon for a child to describe a physical sensation instead of an affect, such as describing a stomachache rather than anxiety. The child recognizes the physiology of affect but has not registered it as an emotion per se. The verbal label provided the therapist converts a physical sensation into a cognitive experience thereby drastically improving the chances the child can manage it effectively. Last, the therapist reflects the identified feelings back to the child drawing attention to the pattern of the child's emotional episodes across sessions. This allows the child to become more facile at recognizing and using emotion in everyday interpersonal exchanges.

In order to facilitate the child's emotional experiencing in session there are several things a therapist can do (Shirk & Russell, 1996). First, put emotional experiences in context. Children may have difficulty responding to an open question as to how they felt in a given situation. If, however, the therapist first asks the child about details of the experience that may relate to the emotion the child may have an easier time. Thus the child who is unable to say he was scared when his father told him to turn of the TV and go to bed may be able to do so once he has described the fact that, at the time, his father was screaming, shaking his fist and turning red in the face. Second, the therapist may need to find a way to scaffold the child's emotional experience. Having the child draw pictures of an affect or use something like the Color-Your-Life Technique (O'Connor, 1983) to create concrete representations of feelings the child can hold onto while attempting engage in processing. Third, the therapist may need to use indirect methods to illicit a child's feelings. Talking about a situation in which a child was abused may overwhelm the child and prevent accurate recognition of feelings. Talking about a mother bear who talks harshly to her cub may be much less threatening. Last, the therapist needs to remain in the present as much as possible. Children have a hard time remembering how they felt in past situations. Sometimes something as simple as role playing a past event can help the child access the emotional experiences she cannot remember out of context.

Once the child has begun to experience and recognize her own affects she must then learn to regulate them if they are to serve their function in ensuring that her needs get met effectively and appropriately. Using a information processing model, Garber, Braafladt, and Zeman (1991) describe the steps by which emotional regulation occurs. First, there is the perception of the emotion, the emotional experiencing, and the recognition of the need to regulate that affect. Second, the individual interprets that emotion coming to a cognitive understanding of the cause of the emotion and a determination of who or what is or should be responsible for altering it. Third, comes goal setting during which the individual decides what needs to be done to alter the affect. Fourth, is response generation, which involves brainstorming concrete actions to be taken. Fifth, comes evaluation, where the pros and cons of the ideas brainstormed in the fourth step are critically evaluated and one idea is selected above the others. Last, the individual enacts the selected idea. While it is assumed that this process occurs within the individual and that it is not necessarily entirely conscious it is entirely consistent with the steps involved in therapeutic problem solving as described later in this chapter.

Specific strategies for organizing the therapist's verbalizations have been developed over the past decade. These strategies take into consideration both technical variations that allow for the treatment of a broader population and advances in the understanding of child development. This portion of this chapter addresses three types of verbalizations the therapist often makes: questions, informational statements, structuring statements, responses to questions from children, running comments and finally interpretations.

The Therapeutic Impact of Common Therapist Verbalizations

Questions

There is some debate as to the value of questions within the context of ongoing therapy. One issue in the discussion of the use of questions involves the therapist's intent or purpose in asking the question. Questions are usually asked for one of three reasons: to clarify the child's behavior or verbalizations, to gather information, or to express the tentativeness of a statement the therapist makes rather than to attempt to gain a response from the child. In all cases, questions are somewhat unique among your array of verbalizations in that they are generally asked to satisfy your needs as opposed to addressing the child's needs. The problem with questions is that the respondent tends to interpret them as containing possible hidden messages, even if that is not your intent (Gordon, 1970). If you were to ask the child "Don't you like school?," for example, she is likely to pick up the message that you think she is supposed to like it. Because of their inherent demand quality, questions also have the tendency to make the child stop talking, become defensive and argumentative, and to feel pressured and infantilized (Gordon, 1970). For these reasons, it is often best if you can keep the number of questions to a minimum and instead provide many more interpretive statements of the type described later in this chapter.

There is general agreement that you may ask clarifying questions in order to better understand how the child experienced an event (O'Connor, Lee, & Schaefer, 1983). These questions would be limited to attempts to have the child elaborate on material presented within the session. For example, a child is telling a fairly long and elaborate story, and while she is doing so, you lose track of the people to whom the pronouns the child is using actually refer:

> The other day when I was at school my teacher got real angry at Tommy and me for fighting on the playground. He wouldn't let me take a turn at kickball cause he said some of the other kids hadn't had a turn yet. Then I got mad and yelled at him. Then we started hitting each other. Then he came over and was all red in the face and grabbed the ball and then he said to sit down. He hit me and knocked me down.

Even if you listened carefully to this story, it is difficult to tell who "he" is at various points. In this case, it would behoove you to admit that you had become a little lost and ask some questions clarifying the attribution of the various behaviors in the story. In this case, it turned out that the final blow was actually delivered by the teacher, who had great difficulty controlling the responses this particular child triggered.

In those situations where you have missed a considerable amount of the detail included in the child's statements or actions, it might be better to use some strategy other than direct questioning. Suppose the story just given had been considerably longer and replete with unclear pronouns. Reasonably, you might not want to disrupt the flow of such an emotionally laden story; however, if you wait until the end to begin attempts at clarification, then the child may not feel like doing the necessary backtracking.

As an alternative, you might comment on how long and interesting the story had been and express your interest in making sure you understood the whole thing by having the child act out the story in some way. The enactment might include having the child use small figures to represent characters in the story. You would be sure that each figure was clearly labeled and proceed with the retelling of the story by having the child attribute dialogue and actions to each figure. Alternatively, you might encourage the child to illustrate the story or to act out the story dramatically. Each alternative lets you clarify your understanding of the child's material without disrupting the flow of the content or making her feel discouraged regarding her ability to communicate effectively.

Clarifying questions are not usually planned, and the need to use them may vary considerably from session to session. The timing of these questions is rather straightforward because they are generated in response to the child's verbalizations or actions. In spite of the apparent innocuousness of clarifying questions, they can be quite disruptive to the course of the therapy if overused. A few focused, clarifying questions let the child know that you are interested in what she is conveying but are unclear with regards to some of the details. Too many questions may seriously disrupt the flow of the child's story and discourage her from proceeding. Likewise, a question which reveals that you have missed some key element of a very long story a child has just told may cause her to withdraw the story completely and move on to something else. This behavior is often accompanied by a "what's the use?" attitude and silence on the child's part. This type of situation often arises when treating children with language or speech disorders:

> When Jose, a developmentally delayed 5-year-old, entered therapy, his speech was virtually incomprehensible. The therapist was tempted to ask him to repeat much of what was said, but each time she did so Jose either stopped talking altogether or turned away from her in obvious anger and frustration. The therapist began, instead, to comment on Jose's actions and play rather than the content of his speech. They labeled objects and actions together and drew pictures that included what little content the therapist was able to glean from Jose's verbalizations. After a few months of these sessions, the therapist was better able to understand Jose's unusual speech patterns and Jose, in turn, was more likely to accompany what he said with explanatory behaviors and gestures, so communication was greatly enhanced.

You may also need to ask information-gathering questions at various points in the session or in the course of the treatment. A child whose parents are divorced may spend time with each parent, moving between two houses as often as several times a week or as infrequently as a few times a year. Whether the transitions are regular and planned or erratic and spontaneous, you may need to inquire as to where the child spent a given block of time so you have a context in which to interpret further discussions or play behavior. Similarly, when she comes to the next session, you may wish to ask a child who missed a session due to illness if she is feeling better. One problem with these types of questions is that there is not always a natural point at which to interject them. Should the therapist ask about the child's visit to her father's house for the weekend at the beginning of the session, when the topic spontaneously arises during the course of the session, or near the end of the session? Clearly the impact of the question will partly depend on timing.

Any question asked early in the session has the potential of structuring the content of the session from that point on. The child who missed a session due to illness may have been sick only for a day or even a few hours and may have therefore felt well for the entire week between the sessions. In this case it is very possible that the child might not even mention the illness spontaneously during the following session. Once you, however innocently, inquire about the child's health, she becomes aware that you are interested in this "old" news and may spend some time discussing it at the expense of more immediate concerns. The significance of this issue is even greater if the child is sick often, say with asthmatic children. In such a case, the child's willingness to discuss the illness spontaneously might be considered important in judging therapeutic progress. Obviously, you should carefully consider the value of the information needed versus the way the child is likely to interpret the question before proceeding.

Finally, there are times when you may choose to make a statement in which you are not entirely confident. Often this hesitancy is conveyed by an interrogative tone of voice or inflection. This is a trap many novice therapists fall into. The term trap is used here intentionally because this category of questions seems almost entirely counterproductive. If you are so unsure of the content of what you are about to say, then it is best not to say it at all, or at least not until the situation seems more clear. If you go on to make such qualified statement/questions, the child is likely to react to the material in several ways. First, she may be aware that you are not sure of what is being offered and therefore choose to ignore the content. Second, she may feel compelled to respond and again choose to avoid the content simply as an oppositional response to the perceived demand. Third, she may fear that the reason you are being so tentative is that the content is somehow difficult even for you.

> Jennifer, a 7-year-old client who had been sexually abused, came to her first session appearing very anxious. She had insisted that her mother remain in the room during her intake interview, so this was the first time that she was alone with her male therapist. Noticing Jennifer's anxiety, the therapist said, "You seem nervous; do you think it's because it is scary being alone in the playroom with me after what happened to you?" This statement was so vague that Jennifer not only failed to respond, she seemed to become even more anxious. The therapist recognized his error and chose to proceed with a very simple task that involved drawing and coloring.
>
> He and Jennifer were sharing crayons that lay in the middle of the table. At one point, the therapist's hand brushed Jennifer's hand as they reached for crayons. Jennifer pulled back so hard and fast that she hit her elbow on the arm of the chair and began to cry. The therapist immediately moved to check Jennifer's elbow to make sure that she was all right. This time he said, "Oh, that must have hurt a lot, let me check to see that you aren't bleeding." He gently took Jennifer's arm and checked it. While still holding her hand, he said, "Nope, no blood but I'll bet it hurts a lot anyway. You sure did jump when our hands first touched. I'm sure it scared you because you are a little frightened being in this room alone with me. You are a little afraid that I might do 'bad touches' (Jennifer's term) like your Uncle John did. Well, that is not going to happen. In fact, we are going to work together to see if we can't make the scary feelings that started when Uncle John did the bad touches go away." Jennifer visibly relaxed, and the two spent a full 15 seconds just looking at each other.

In this case, the therapist was able to recover from his error very quickly and the client was also amenable to proceeding. In other cases, the tentativeness of the therapist's initial comment might have convinced the child that if the therapist was so uncomfortable with the topic it must indeed be too awful to be discussed and therefore motivated her to avoid the topic in the future.

Informational Statements

Many statements you will make during the course of a child's play session are designed not to elicit information from the client but to convey information. These include structuring statements, responses to client questions, and running comments.

Structuring Statements

Structuring statements include those comments you make to create the frame of the work or session for the child. Often the first session will consist of providing the child with considerable information regarding the nature of therapy, the therapist, and the therapeutic relationship. The structure and content of this introductory session were discussed at some length in Chapter Six. Many times, however, you will have to convey additional information to the child as the work proceeds.

Some such statements will frame the time constraints of the sessions, such as when they will begin and end or how much time is left to a given session. You will also want to make the child aware of upcoming breaks in therapy due to vacations or work schedules.

Other structuring statements may restate the limits that will be enforced during the session, including the basic rules: no hurting others, no hurting one's self, and no damaging property. Also included will be statements about trips to the bathroom, snacks, and so forth. If you do a reasonable job of anticipating the child's needs, you will be able to avoid the problem of her asking a lot of direct, pragmatic questions that you have to address. However, no matter how well you are able to anticipate the child's needs and behaviors, she is likely to ask at least a few questions sooner or later, and you must be prepared to respond.

Responses to Client Questions

Some readers may be wondering why one might consider questions the child asks problematic or deserving of anything more than a direct response. The problems arise for exactly the same reasons that make questions the therapist asks problematic for the child. The primary issue here is the fact that questions may convey hidden agendas or double meanings. Because of the potential for double meaning, when a child asks a question, it is generally considered strategically wisest for you to interpret any question you are asked before responding. When interpreting at this level, you are usually just reflecting, that is, reframing the content of the question to include the child's affect or motive. For a more complete discussion of interpretive strategies, see the material presented later in this chapter.

The interpretation serves two purposes. First, it helps clarify the context of the question. It also gives you time to develop an appropriate response if needed. For example, suppose the child asks if you see any other children in the playroom. Potentially, she could be asking about the uniqueness of her relationship with you, but the underlying issue might be sibling rivalry, a fantasy of you as a parent surrogate, or even concern about the depth of her own pathology in that she is attempting to discover how many other children need treatment. Other excellent examples of the multiple potential meanings of a child's questions can be found in *Play Therapy: The Art of the Relationship* (Landreth, 1991). Interpretation allows you to attempt to verify the specific motives underlying the question, reducing the chances of addressing the wrong issues.

Other questions children ask often fall into one of three categories: practical, personal, and relationship. Practical questions, assuming no underlying motives, are readily addressed. They may include such things as requests to go to the bathroom, the amount of time left to a given session, and the number of sessions left before a vacation or before termination. These seemingly innocent questions, which novice therapists often answer without a moment's hesitation, are very likely to mask alternate agendas, particularly resistance.

Personal questions rarely reflect mere social interest on the part of the child. Clients may ask you whether or not you are married, if you have any children of your own, where you live, how old you are, and more.

One young girl used to continuously ask her student therapist strings of personal questions. He interpreted some of these as the desire to have him as a parent, others as reflecting her desire to contact him outside of sessions. He tried multiple other interpretations, yet the string of questions continued interfering with any other session content. In supervision, he talked about his discomfort with the supervisor's direction not to respond to the content of her questions. He felt that if he just answered her they could move on to other material. Yet he agreed that on the few occasions he did answer, it did not reduce the driven quality of her interactions. He said he would hold off a little longer.

Finally, the supervision team hit on the notion of interpreting not the content of the questions but the fact that she asked them so repetitively by suggesting that it was very important for her to feel she was in control of the sessions. This interpretation tended to make her very angry because it disrupted her control, but the rate of her questioning slowed dramatically. Over time it became apparent that this girl exhibited many controlling behaviors in sessions at times when her mother had decompensated to the point of moderate thought disorder. This led to more focused discussions of the correlation between her in-session behavior and her mother's condition.

Still later, they were able to discuss ways this girl could get her needs met even when her mother was not functioning well.

Relationship questions are also rarely asked without an underlying motive or agenda. These questions might include asking if you see any other children, if you like any of the other children more, if you would like to adopt the child, and so forth. Clearly, these questions beg for more than a simple and direct response. The child is usually asking about the depth of the relationship, often at a point when she is considering investing in it further herself:

> Jacob, the little boy discussed in the limit-setting portion of this chapter, had been in a foster home for a very long time without ever being adopted. The foster parents would tell him that they wanted to adopt him but could not while his behavior was so difficult. The following dialogue between Jacob and his therapist, Steve, occurred about 30 minutes into the physical restraint procedure that was initiated when Jacob lost control during the third session.
>
> Jacob asked if Steve had children. Before he could answer, Jacob asked why Steve didn't go home and restrain his own children. Then Jacob asked if Steve was married, and again, before Steve could answer, Jacob asked why Steve didn't go home and restrain his wife. At that point Steve was able to reflect Jacob's question, saying "You want to know if I would do this to anyone I love?" Jacob started to scream "I know you wouldn't do this to someone you love. You don't love me?" This last was intoned as a question, and Steve reflected it, saying simply "You don't believe I could love you." At this point Jacob collapsed into hysterical crying, saying "No, you don't love me, no one loves me and no one ever has." Jacob cried solidly for about 15 minutes while Steve talked about how sad Jacob felt when he thought about having been left by his biological mother and continuing to live in limbo with his foster mother. This depth of interaction would never have been possible so early in his treatment if Jacob's questions had not been actively interpreted.

Running Comments

Running comments sum up what the child has said, thereby familiarizing both you and the child with her productions and laying the groundwork for later confrontations and interpretations. Some authors in play therapy often call running comments reflections. Regardless of what they are called, these statements do not add any information to the interaction, they merely restate it. Beginning play therapists often make the mistake of repeating things the child has said virtually verbatim. The child says, "Look, the car is going to crash into the wall. Then the therapist says, "Oh, the car is going to crash into the wall." Usually the child looks at the therapist like she is a halfwit and proceeds to play. For this reason, it is usually best not to make running comments regarding verbalizations the child makes to avoid sounding like an endless-loop tape recorder. Rather, liberally direct running comments at the child's behavior and the content of her play. For example, you should say, "Oh, the car crashed into the wall" when the car has crashed and the child has said nothing.

When delivered in this manner, running comments model verbalizations for the child, demonstrating their importance and easing her toward the eventual goal of talking rather than "showing." Running comments also demonstrate the therapist's interest in the child's activity, thereby fostering her continued output (Kramer & Byerly, 1978).

Critical Therapeutic Processes: Interpretation and Problem Solving

Interpretations are the primary therapeutic verbalizations the therapist makes in the course of a child's treatment with play therapy. In most traditional, psychoanalytic literature, the use of the term interpretation is limited to labeling statements more specifically referred to as genetic interpretations, or those that provide the child with the opportunity to connect current behavior with past experience or recall (Lewis, 1974). For the purposes of this discussion, the term interpretation is used to refer to any statement the therapist makes that adds to the child's awareness of her internal processes or behavior.

What is the point of interpretation? Essentially, as derived from the psychoanalytic theory, interpretation is needed to insure that unconscious material becomes conscious so it can be used by the client. Within Ecosystemic Play Therapy interpretation has two highly related uses. One is that it can help create a common language the therapist and child can use to access events in the child's life that may not have previously put words to but rather simply experienced. Such experiences or memories are relatively unavailable for therapeutic exploration and resolution. In this initial work you will not necessarily be attempting to change the child's cognitions regarding an event or experience but potentially trying to *create* some cognitions regarding the same. The other, primary reason to use interpretation is that it helps define the problems the child is experiencing in new ways so that these become available to be addressed with subsequent problem solving.

Yet one must be cautious and not overwhelm the child and his play. It is important that one facilitate the play first. Scarlett (1994) emphasizes the importance of playing with the child and helping to develop it so that it takes on curative properties. One example of this is therapist intervention in children's post-traumatic play. Post-traumatic play has been defined as play that is repeated endlessly, without variation by children who have been traumatized in some way (Gil, 1991). This type of play seems to have the effect of prolonging the trauma rather than facilitating mastery as would be the effect of healthy play. The child who endlessly reenacts the exact circumstances of her sexual abuse with puppets would be an example of such play. In these cases it is recommended that therapists gently disrupt the play, say by introducing a superhero who rescues the child at the last minute so that the child can begin to master the trauma rather than simply repeating it. Once the child's play begins to serve a health promoting function that functioning can be enhanced through the effective use of interpretation and cognitive problem solving.

In play therapy it is the process of interpretation that lends meaning to the child's play. Interpretation helps the child become aware of secondary symbols in his play providing an avenue for communication and therapeutic work or problem solving (Scarlett, 1994). "As words become means of referencing internal experiences, what is inside and outside, what is wish and what is reality, what is conscious and unconscious become more distinct" (Slade, 1994, p. 93). The process of play therapy can be understood as taking events or emotions and making meaning out of them so that the conflicts or problems they engendered can be addressed and resolved (Slade, 1994). Play is the way children make meaning. Disorganized, nonrepresentational play does not represent a jumble of symbols gut rather the child's inability to make meaning at a fundamental level. The therapist guides the child in becoming organized. In doing so the therapist: (1) labels characters, objects, activities and states in the play; (2) links characters, objects and actions together; and (3) links events together as they emerge (Slade, 1994). The child learns to tell the story of his experience because she believes the therapist will listen, engage and play with her. As the story or narrative emerges the child can take an observing stance, can look at the play and can make the relevant connections to her own life.

Delivering Interpretations Effectively*

To help therapists present interpretations in an "orderly and systematic way," Lowenstein (1957) described different levels of interpretation: preparation (Lowenstein, 1951), confrontation (Devereaux, 1951), clarification (Bibring, 1954), and interpretation proper. During the preparation stage, the therapist points out the common elements among events the child has related as well as her tendency to behave the same way in each situation. Confrontations draw on both immediate and past material to make the child aware that a defense is being used. Clarifications lay further groundwork for the delivery of the interpretation proper. Lowenstein also noted that interpretations may have different structures and functions. He

---

* The discussion of the therapist's use of interpretation was adapted from O'Connor, K. & Lee, A. (1991). Advances in psychoanalytic psychotherapy with children. In M. Hersen, A. Kazdin, and A. Bellack (Eds.). *The Clinical Psychology Handbook,* New York: Pergamon, pp. 580–595. (Adapted by permission)

classified interpretation as follows: interpretation of the unconscious intent, functional interpretation—disclosing the function of a given psychological phenomenon within the framework of the personality—symbolic interpretation, and genetic interpretation, by which the genesis of a phenomenon is reconstructed.

Lewis (1974) proposed another model with levels labeled as follows: setting statements, attention statements, reductive statements, situational statements, transference interpretations, and etiological statements. Setting statements create the therapeutic setting; that is, they structure the therapeutic interaction in some way. Setting statements might include telling the child the rules of the playroom, the purpose of the sessions, and the duration of the contacts. Attention statements are the therapist's attempts to translate the child's actions, feelings, and thoughts into words. These statements involve secondary thought process and aim to consolidate existing gains while eliciting new material. Reductive statements organize emotions or behaviors the child previously perceived as dissimilar or discontinuous into a common form or pattern. Situational statements provide for the child a context in which the emotional or behavioral patterns elucidated by the reductive statements have occurred. Transference interpretations are important in helping the child recognize the uniqueness of the relationship with the therapist. They also help the child differentiate the therapist from the other people currently active in her life. Further, these interpretations help maintain and make use of the child's imperfect and unstable development of the transference neurosis. Etiological statements link the child's current behavior and affect with earlier developmental events and reactions. "Glenn (1978) classified interpretations thus: (1) defense interpretations, (2) descriptions of conflict, (3) interpretation of drive derivatives and the content of fantasy, (4) reconstructions, (5) transference interpretations, and (6) interpretation of displacements" (O'Connor, Lee, & Schaefer, 1983, p. 549).

The model of interpretive levels presented here integrates the models just described with a model the author developed to train and supervise doctoral students in clinical psychology. The model has five levels, discussed in the order in which they would be presented to the child.

Reflection.   The first level of interpretation can best be described as reflection. These reflections are not exactly the same as the reflections child centered therapists refer to; these are statements you make that add an affirmative or motivational component or label to the child's material. Shirk and Russell (1996) refers to this as the "subjective elaboration" of the child's play in that the therapist adds psychological or motivational content to concretely described events presented by children. They further state that although this process has been minimally studied it may be a powerful element in the play therapy process. In offering a reflection to a child who is throwing blocks across the playroom at a doll you might say "You sure look angry as you throw those blocks." Or, alternatively, "That doll must be scared that those blocks might hit her." If the block throwing erupted just as the child was about to discuss a painful event, you might reflect "I think that throwing blocks is your way of almost breaking our rule about damaging the playroom so that I will pay attention to what you are doing and forget what you were about to say." When the child builds a tower out of blocks, you might note the child's apparent pride with the product or her fears that, by making the tower taller, she risks knocking the whole thing down. If the child then goes on to knock down the tower on purpose, you might observe the child's displeasure with the product or her relief at having controlled its destruction.

Reflections serve multiple purposes. First, they help children label their internal experience while expanding their vocabulary of affective terminology. This is important in that experience is more readily processed both at the time and in the future if it is paired with language. Also, children often have very limited affective vocabularies, consisting of no more than happy, mad, and sad. Without a somewhat expanded vocabulary, it may be difficult for the child to appreciate some of the subtleties of the interpretive process. Third, reflections alert the child to the importance of her affect in the therapeutic process. In other words, they reinforce the child's attention to, and revelation of, affect. Last, reflections create an opportunity for you to validate your perceptions of the child's affect.

Present pattern.   The second level of interpretation, present pattern interpretation, requires that you identify and label patterns observed in the child's material within sessions. Initially, only patterns observed in the child's material within a single session are interpreted in order to ensure that the child has the information required to evaluate the pattern interpretation available in immediate memory. You might point out that the child came into a session, drew a picture and then tore it up, built a tower out of blocks and then knocked it down, and then made a snowman out of clay only to squash it. Along with repeating the sequence of behavior for the child, you might note that in each case destruction preceded the completion of the work. Later, you would offer pattern interpretations for behavior occurring across sessions. Identification of these patterns helps the child see that behavior does not occur at random but that it is somewhat consistent over time. Again, these statements let the child become a participant in the therapy process by sensitizing her to relatively concrete examples of the meaning and repetition of behavior.

If you are not used to thinking in terms of the repetition of behaviors or themes within the child's play session, they can be somewhat difficult to identify. One strategy for developing an awareness of the repetitive nature of a child's session is to audiotape or videotape a session and then proceed to transcribe your and the child's behaviors onto a sheet of paper. The transcription should be simple, allowing one line for each new behavior in which either of you engaged. Often this procedure reveals the pattern and allows you to develop some hypotheses about the dynamics of the child's behavior:

> John came to the supervision team very frustrated about the way the last few sessions with his client Tina were going. He said that all she wanted to do was play in what appeared to be a very random manner. The group agreed to help John code a videotape of Tina's last session to see if they could discover a pattern. The following coded transcript was developed using the first 25 minutes of the tape:
>
> > Tina asked John if she could engage in a behavior he had previously forbidden.
> > John denied her request.
> > Tina built a fort with the furniture and shut John out and then pretended to dial the emergency number, 911, saying that bad guys were coming.
> > When Tina heard the bad guys coming closer, she invited John into the fort and then proceeded to dial the emergency number, 911, to get them help.
> > Tina engaged in several brief behaviors and then asked John if she could do something else he had forbidden.
> > John denied her request.
> > Tina went into her fort and dialed 911.
> > Tina pretended the bad guys were coming, invited John into her fort, and then dialed 911.
> > Tina then engaged in several new behaviors before asking John if she could engage in yet another inappropriate behavior.
> > At this point the pattern was clear. Tina used dialing 911 as a way of (1) symbolically getting her needs met and (2) protecting her from the bad guys. This fit with Tina's history. She had entered therapy when it was discovered that her father, who was her primary caretaker, had been sexually molesting her over the past 2 years. In a recovery group for sexually abused children, they had taught Tina to dial 911 if she ever needed help. Tina now used 911 as a magical symbol, pretending that whoever answered would deny her nothing and would protect her from harm. Tina was able to involve the therapist in this fantasy only when she felt very threatened by external forces. John went to the next session armed with a host of potential interpretations.

Simple dynamic. At the third level—simple dynamic interpretation—you go on to point out for the child connections between her affect or motivation (as it was labeled in previous reflections) and patterns of behavior (as labeled in previous pattern interpretations). Again, as with early pattern interpretations, you should limit your first simple dynamic interpretations to behaviors within a single session. For example, you would observe, for the child mentioned previously, "I've noticed that every time you make something, like the painting, tower, or snowman, you start out very proud of what you are doing but then you begin to worry that maybe it isn't good enough. And then, before you finish whatever it is you are making, you destroy it so you never have to find out if it is going to turn out good or bad." You have simply translated your formulation that for this child, planned failure is experienced as much less anxiety-producing than inadvertent failure into a form she can understand. Once the child has become accustomed to your making simple dynamic interpretations for in-session behavior, you proceed to making simple dynamic interpretations of behavior observed across sessions. At this point, you are moving toward more traditional types of interpretation by helping the child understand the dynamics of her behavior in the recent past. Through simple dynamic interpretation, the child is encouraged to see the continuity of affects and meanings across behaviors. Children are sensitized to the internal feelings, processes, and motivations that guide their behavior. Because simple dynamic interpretations are built off of the two previous levels of interpretation, each of which the child has come to accept independently, acceptance of the interaction of the two is less likely to be resisted.

Generalized dynamic.   Level IV, or generalized dynamic interpretations, identify for children the operation of their personal dynamics across both in- and out-session behaviors. Again, as with pattern and simple dynamic interpretations, generalized dynamic interpretations build on statements you have previously made. To illustrate the process by which you might arrive at a generalized dynamic interpretation, let us look at an example involving a 7-year-old boy, Clark:

> Clark has begun the last six sessions by asking the therapist for a privilege he knows is against the office rules. Each time after the therapist has refused his request, Clark is silent for 10 to 15 minutes. The content of the material Clark has brought to these sessions has been particularly painful. The therapist has consistently made reflections regarding Clark's desire to obtain special favors from the therapist, his anger at not receiving such attention, and his apparent desire to avoid the painful material by staying silent. By the third session, the therapist felt comfortable making a pattern interpretation by noting that the last three sessions had begun in a very similar manner. With these pieces in place, the therapist went on to make a simple dynamic interpretation that connected Clark's anxiety regarding the material they had been discussing with his tendency to try to set up an argument with the therapist so as to avoid the discussions.
>
> A little while later, Clark began to describe a big argument with his mother just prior to going to the dentist. This argument started when Clark asked to be allowed to ride his bicycle on the highway to the dentist's office. The generalized dynamic interpretation that the therapist then made pointed out the similarity between Clark's behavior in and out of sessions. "You know, we have noticed that when something you don't like is about to happen in the session, you ask for something you know you can't have. When I say no, it gives you an excuse to get angry and then not talk to me about

what it is you really don't like. From what you've just told me, it sounds like that is what happened with your mom. You didn't want to go to the dentist, but instead of telling her so, you asked if you could ride your bike. She said no and you got so angry that you and your mom had a fight which made you late for your appointment at the dentist."

This type of generalized dynamic interpretation encourages the child to begin applying the therapy process outside the sessions. Further, these interpretations make the child aware that not only is the material she directly enacts during the session open to interpretation, but so is the material from any aspect of her life. Last, although it is not something with which therapists usually like to concern themselves, generalized dynamic interpretations facilitate generalizations of insights and behavior changes the child achieves in session to life outside the playroom.

Genetic interpretation. Finally, both you and the child are ready for what many therapeutic writers consider the only type of interpretation: the genetic interpretation. At this level you draw a connection between the child's current behavior and her history. For the child Clark in the previous example, the therapist went on to offer a genetic interpretation that identified Clark's history of maternal deprivation as the source of his fear of directly approaching requests to get out of unpleasant situations. Clark's mother was so narcissistically preoccupied that she was unable to respond to his fears or anxieties in a supportive manner. However, she could be engaged if Clark misbehaved. Over time, Clark chose to engage her in a conflict in an attempt to avoid fear-provoking situations rather than appealing to her to help him face the situations directly.

Modulating the Impact of the Interpretation

Aside from attending to the sequence and level of the interpretation, you must also consider the potential impact of a particular interpretation on the child. Direct and specific association of the child's play to the interpretation is cautioned since it often leads to constriction of the child's play behavior (O'Connor, Lee, & Schaefer, 1983). Further, the impact of interpretation must be adjusted whenever the child is perceived to have limited ego strength. The limitations may be due to pathology or age. Adolescents are generally viewed to be in need of modified interpretation due to the ego fragility their attempts at separation/individuation from the parents create. If you want to make a given interpretation but perceive the child as being unable to hear it if it were presented directly, you might temper its impact by offering the interpretation, within the context of the play, in an "as if" format, or within the context of the relationship, before interpreting it to the child directly.

Interpreting within the play.   Interpretations offered within the context of the child's play may often contain relatively powerful material without disrupting the activity. To do this, you simply frame the interpretation according to a character in the child's pretend play and then offer the interpretation to that character rather than directly to the child. Suppose that a child who is referred for separation anxiety is playing with a doll and enacting a scene in which a child is leaving for school. You could take the opportunity to reflect the doll's anxiety at leaving, her fear that something bad might happen to her mother while she was gone, or her wish that some adult would take pity on her and let her stay home from school. There may be opportunities for offering this type of interpretation in ways that are even less obvious. Suppose that the child is enacting a scene in which an adult is leaving to go somewhere. You could use this situation to reflect on the fact that the adult doll does not seem nervous or worried about what will happen to the rest of the family. You might even use the opportunity to introduce some problem-solving strategies that the child might use. "You know, that grownup probably isn't nervous because she knows that she can call home and check on her family as soon as she gets to her friend's house."

"As If" interpretations.   These are interpretations offered to the child as representative of children's common experience. You might say, "You know, other boys your age might feel very angry if their teacher scolded them in front of the whole class." These allow the child some distance from the content while also conveying to her a sense that her experience is probably not unique and therefore not so anxiety-provoking.

Interpreting in the context of the relationship.   Another strategy for limiting the impact of interpretations is to interpret only within the context of the relationship. This technique can be especially useful when you are trying to establish a working relationship with a child or when working with more resistant children:

> Lisa was an adolescent girl who was being seen in modified play therapy by a young therapist, Pam. Every week, Lisa, who rode public transportation to the clinic, was late for her session. Each time she would go into a long discussion of why she was late: Her employer made her work overtime, the bus was late, or she had trouble getting the right change for bus fare. These discussions would serve as a takeoff point for involving Pam in social conversation. Lisa wanted to know where Pam got her hair cut or bought the clothes she was wearing. Lisa wanted to know where Pam had lived before coming to California and what Pam thought about the area. Through this social interchange she was able to use up more than half the remaining time.
>
>   After several sessions like this, Pam began to interpret not the content of Lisa's questions but Lisa's motivation for asking them. Lisa would begin to apologize for being late and Pam would say "Now I'm supposed to act like a mother and say that you must do better. Then we can begin to argue about

whether or not being late is your fault and that will kill a little time." Lisa would say how much she liked an article of clothing that Pam was wearing and Pam would say "Now I'm supposed to act like one of your school friends and get into a fashion discussion and that will also kill some time." This went on for about 15 minutes before Lisa said "Oh fine, we might as well talk about what went on at home this week." Although her resistance continued to surface occasionally, this type of interpretation always worked to reveal her motives and to reengage her in the therapy process.

Interpreting to the child directly.   When the child is fully prepared for an interpretation, then you may proceed to deliver it directly in the standard manner. The child is considered ready when she has heard all the components of the interpretation separately and is relaxed and focused enough to hear what you are about to say. Do not offer direct interpretations in an off-hand way; they should reflect the seriousness of the work at hand. Yet all interpretations need not be ponderous either. Some may simply identify the emotion or motivation that drives the child's behavior and, once they have been repeated several times across different situations, may come to be like a private joke between the child and the therapist. The child has truly internalized the work when she begins to do or say something and then smiles, turns to you, and says, "I know, I know this is just like. . . ."

Aside from the type of interpretive statements you make being very important, the timing of those statements can make or break their therapeutic effectiveness. If you suddenly think of a terrific generalized dynamic or genetic interpretation and offer it to the child without the proper preparation, there is a chance that she will not only reject the interpretation but resist further involvement in the therapy process for some time to come. Just because you thought it was a wonderful insight does not mean the child will agree or is ready to hear it.

For this reason it is important that you offer reflections and present pattern interpretations at a high rate over the course of the therapy. Offer simple and generalized dynamic interpretations less frequently, genetic interpretations even less frequently. Never offer simple dynamic, generalized dynamic, and genetic interpretations if less than 10 minutes remain in the session. This time buffer ensures that you will have time to work through the child's reaction to the interpretation before she leaves the session.

Simple dynamic interpretations may be offered early in the child's treatment, but generalized dynamic and, especially, genetic interpretations should wait until the child has entered into a working relationship with you and is comfortable with the therapy process. Usually this does not occur until after the negative reaction phase of treatment is, at least partially, resolved. The one exception to this rule occurs when treating children who have some significant trauma in their history. Often it is best if you make some statement that gently acknowledges this trauma early in the treatment process:

Jim brought Mark, a 6-year-old client, into the playroom for their first session. Jim had not conducted the intake with Mark, but he knew that Mark had been subjected to some particularly sadistic sexual abuse by an uncle and that there was an ongoing court case. He also noticed how anxious Mark was upon entering the playroom. As they sat down at the table, Mark asked if he could draw and Jim readily agreed. Mark proceeded to draw an extremely graphic picture of some of the abuse he had suffered and to label the abuser as his uncle who would soon be going to jail. Before Jim could respond, Mark laid the picture to one side and asked if he and Jim could play checkers. In spite of the fact that Jim was overwhelmed by Mark's sudden disclosure, he managed to say "We can play checkers, but before we do I want to say that I know you figured I would ask you questions about the abuse and that you hoped drawing the picture would get that part over with. I know it is hard to talk about, and you've already done more than I expected you to for today. I already know a lot about the abuse, so before we talk about it anymore, let's spend a few sessions just helping you feel safe in the playroom with me."

Now that you have a sense of the types of corrective experiences you will be trying to create for the child and the types of cognitive and verbal work in which you will engage, we can proceed to examine the ways both elements can be adjusted to meet the needs of children at different developmental levels over the course of their treatment.

Reappraisal

Shirk (1998) has defined a process he calls *reappraisal* that lies somewhere between the process of interpretation and problem solving as they are defined in Ecosystemic Play Therapy. He states: "The critical therapeutic task, it seems, involves the identification and reappraisal of maladaptive interpersonal schemata in the context of a supportive therapeutic relationship. Reappraisal could take a variety of forms including:

1. Helping the child identify situations that rapidly elicit specific expectations.
2. Relinking expectations with the relational context in which they were formed.
3. Differentiating the original context that shaped expectations from new situations.
4. Identifying emotions that are triggered by expectations.
5. Promoting tests of expectations in new situations with careful consideration of both confirming and disconfirming evidence" (p. 13).

In the words of Ecosystemic Play Therapy, maladaptive interpersonal schemata are fixed ways of thinking about interpersonal interactions that are not effective in getting the child's needs met effectively or appropriately.

That is the child has become stuck responding to certain situation in maladaptive ways because past experiences have led him to think about such situations in very fixed and rigid ways. The child who expects all adults to be abusive because his own mother was abusive is a simple example. This maladaptive schemata has the positive effect of preparing the child for the worst in any interaction but on the negative side it may also provoke the child into being so anxious around adults that he acts out and engenders their anger thus making his schemata a self-fulfilling prophecy.

In following the reappraisal steps with such an abused child, the therapist would first need to help the child see that any interactions with new adults rapidly elicit the expectation of abuse. The therapist then needs to facilitate the child's seeing that this expectation was formed not in current experience but in the context of a long relationship with an abusive caretaker. The child can then be encouraged to look for ways in which adults in his current interactions are dissimilar from his abusive caretaker. Next the therapist can attune the child to the anxiety that is triggered by the expectation of abuse. Last, the therapist can lead the child through various interactions that help him get better at realistically differentiating potentially abusive adults from nonabusive ones and noting how successfully doing so, rather than applying the general schemata, reduces the child's anxiety. As you will see in the following discussion, this process of reappraisal is very similar to the more general problem solving process seen as essential to the effective practice of Ecosystemic Play Therapy.

Problem Solving

Everything discussed so far in this chapter has been leading up to the implementation of problem solving in the play therapy process. Within Ecosystemic Play Therapy, it is the effective use of problem solving that crystallizes the corrective events that the play therapist has been able to create for the child either experientially or through language. It is also the problem solving process that enables the child to generalize what he learns in therapy for application to life outside the playroom. This is not to say that all play therapy must be accompanied by mechanically implemented cognitive problem solving. A good deal of the problem-solving process may never even be apparent to the child and yet the play therapy can still be highly effective. What is important is that problem solving concepts organize what the therapist does in session.

Over the course of Ecosystemic Play Therapy, the therapist takes the child through a stepwise process. First, the therapist develops a relationship with the child that is helping in nature and thereby establishes a working alliance. Both the therapist and the child are aware of the problems that are to be addressed in the therapy. Second, the therapist facilitates the child's play as a way of cementing the relationship and providing an initial and important mode of symbolic communication. Gradually, the therapist goes on to the third step in which he attaches meaning to the child's play through the use of interpretation. This step must be implemented slowly so that the child is not overwhelmed and the play interrupted. The focus of the third step is to develop a detailed description of the nature and dynamics of the child's problems upon which the therapist and child agree. As the child comes to this understanding, the stage is set for engaging in the fifth step; problem solving. It is the problem-solving process that enables the child to conceptualize new and different ways of potentially getting his needs met effectively and appropriately. As a part of the problem-solving process the therapist goes on to encourage the child to critically evaluate these new solutions and behaviors and to practice these both in and out of session. As the child practices his successes and failures are fed back into the problem-solving process and his behavior is refined. As the child generalizes his ability to get his needs met effectively and appropriately in the real world therapy draws to a close. This entire therapeutic process can be focused on very circumscribed problems and be completed effectively in only a few sessions or it can be used to address more complex and chronic issues requiring months of treatment. In any case, the problem-solving process remains relatively unchanged.

As was described in Chapter Seven, the problem-solving part of the therapy can be thought of as occurring in four steps. The first step is to define and operationally describe the problem. The second is to brainstorm solutions to the problem. The third is to evaluate those solutions and select one or more for the child to implement. The fourth and final step is to evaluate the effect of the child's plan to see if the proposed solution worked or if additional problem solving is needed to ensure that the child's needs are being met optimally and in the most appropriate manner. As will be discussed further in Chapter Fifteen, children can be cued to follow these steps with four key words: Problem, Plan, Action, Answer.

Problem

When defining the problem to be addressed, it is critical that it be framed in a way that makes it a problem the child experiences directly. Therefore, "I hit my sister" is not usually a problem for most children while "I got punished for hitting my sister" is. If the problem is not one that is directly distressing to the child then, given his naturally egocentric nature, he will have minimal motivation to solve it. It is difficult for many children to get comfortable with this part of the process. They are so used to being told that one of their behaviors is problematic for others that they have lost touch with what it is that distresses them. Because the goal of Ecosystemic Play Therapy is to enable children to get their needs met effectively and appropriately it is useful if some, if not most, of the problems be phrased in terms of an unmet need. To go back to the hitting one's sister example, if the problem can be traced to the fact that the younger sister touches and breaks his toys then the problem could be stated as, "I need a way to keep my toys safe" or "I need my parents to show their respect for me by protecting my toys from my little sister." These last two are much more sophisticated problems and will not come without some coaching and practice.

Plan

This is the part of the process that is probably the most important in helping the child to break the set created by previous pathogenic adaptations and develop new ideas and behaviors. Creativity is a must so censoring should be kept to a minimum. All ideas for solving the problem are acceptable at this stage no matter how unrealistic or inappropriate. Many children immediately begin to generate ideas adults love to hear like, "I should just ignore her." These should be actively discouraged as they are rarely realistic (How many adults can just ignore someone who is bothering them?) and rarely solve the child's actual problem (meet his needs). If need be the therapist can take the lead in generating some silly solutions.

Action

During this part of the process the child selects the plan to be implemented from the list just generated. As a part of doing this the plans are evaluated using three criteria: (1) Is the plan possible in reality? Having Martians abduct your sister may sound like a good plan but it is not likely to happen; (2) Will the plan meet the underlying need? This may be somewhat hard to judge but it is the central reason for engaging in the process; and (3) Is the plan appropriate? Will it cause someone else not to get his needs met? The Martian abduction plan is not only unrealistic it will cause the sister and the parents pain and is, therefore, not appropriate. Having selected a plan that meets all three criteria the child must then agree to implement it when the next problem occasion arises. This is a good time to role play so that the child experiences the use of the new plan in the safety of the playroom.

Answer

Once the child has had the opportunity to implement the plan, the therapist and child answer this question, "How did the plan work?" Again, the same three criteria used in the Action phase of the process are used. Having evaluated the outcome the decision may be that the plan worked well and should be used again in the future. Evaluation may reveal that the plan worked but the outcome was not as good as desired so a decision is made to modify the existing plan. Alternatively, the plan may have been failure necessitating a return to the previous list of brainstormed plans or starting the problem solving process over again.

With all that is entailed, it is obvious that engaging in the problem solving process could be painful and very time consuming taking all of one or more sessions. This creates some questions to be considered. How does one get a child initially interested in problem solving? What sort of problems are suited to the process? Does the process need to be taught to children directly? How much responsibility should the therapist take for ensuring that the process is completed? How long should the process take?

To get a child interested the problems identified must be important to him. However, it is generally best not to start with the unmet needs that are central to the reason the child is in therapy. To start this way would probably overwhelm the child because she does not yet have the skills needed for the task and may not even be able or willing to identify the problem as yet. Instead, the therapist should start by using the process to solve small problems that arise in session. Virtually any action requiring a decision can be framed as a problem to give the child multiple, easy opportunities to develop problem solving skills. Simple dilemmas such as trying to decide what to do first or who should have the first turn at a game are excellent choices. Anytime the child enacts or describes an event that had a poor outcome it is the potential opportunity for problem solving.

The process can either be taught to children directly or simply modeled or both. Whether or not it is taught directly it is usually the modeling which is most significant in training a child to use problem solving. It seems best to begin by modeling the process by addressing small in-session problems. Once the child begins to apply the process spontaneously, the steps can be taught quickly, usually in just a few sentences. Then the process can be applied to progressively larger and more central problems.

The degree of responsibility the therapist needs to take for ensuring the completion of the problem solving process depends on several factors. The first, is the stage of the treatment. Early in the course of the therapy the therapist should make sure the process moves very quickly and is relatively painless. Similarly, the younger the child the more responsibility the therapist will need to take. Lastly, the more emotionally loaded the material the more the therapist may have to guide the process so that the child does not become overwhelmed.

The duration of the problem solving should be proportional to the importance of the problem while keeping the child's attention span in mind. Early in the therapy process or when working with young children the entire process might be modeled by the therapist in just a few sentences:

> Karen was a child who felt the overwhelming need to please adults. She was so careful that she seemed never to want anything for herself. Given free choice of what to do in her first play therapy session she virtually froze looking for some sign as to how the therapist wanted her to proceed. After numerous reflections the therapist interpreted Karen's fear of displeasing the therapist and immediately proceeded to identify the problem by saying, "You're so worried about what I want you to do that you can't even decide what you want to do. If you pick something you worry you might make me unhappy but if I pick something I worry I might make you unhappy. We have

a problem. We are both stuck." Proceeding immediately to brainstorm the therapist said, "One way out of this would be to have someone or something else make the decision for us. We could let the puppet choose. We could put several ideas in a hat and then pick one. We could make a numbered list and throw dice to see what number comes up. Which do you think might work?"

Karen responded by shrugging her shoulders. The therapist said, "Oh no I just asked you to make another decision and you got stuck again. Let's see. You didn't seem to like the idea of a puppet choosing so lets roll the dice to see which of the other two plans we should use. If it's an even number we'll put ideas in a hat and pick one. If it is an odd number we'll make a numbered list and roll the dice again. You roll one die and I'll roll the other." In these couple of sentences the therapist let Karen know it was alright not to like an idea he had generated, selected a plan for making an initial decision and involved Karen in implementing the plan.

They rolled the dice, then proceeded to list several play ideas on paper and put them in a cup so as to draw one out. The therapist held the cup but had Karen draw out the idea, indirectly making the choice of activity her decision. As Karen began to play, the therapist said, "That plan worked well you didn't have to worry about whether or not I would like the activity so you got unstuck and were able to start playing."

The therapist reflected Karen's initial paralysis for less than 10 minutes before implementing the problem solving as he was concerned about her experiencing an overwhelming amount of anxiety during just their first session. Once he began the problem solving, a total of 5 minutes elapsed before Karen had begun to play.

An older child or one who is dealing with a key therapeutic issue may be able to tolerate spending several sessions problem solving especially if the process is made fairly concrete:

Robert had come to therapy following several episodes of fighting at school. In just a few play sessions, he was able to recognize that the fights were a reflection of his anger at his father who had failed to show up for scheduled visitations (the parents were divorced) over the past 6 weeks. Robert was able to identify the fact that his need to have contact with his father was not being met as a problem he wanted to address. During some brainstorming he decided he wanted to talk to his father directly but felt safer doing it over the phone. He immediately noted that one problem with the plan would be his father's ability to twist things around so that he, Robert, felt he was expecting too much. Over the remainder of the session and for a second full session Robert and the therapist wrote a script for Robert's phone call to his father. They wrote out everything Robert would say and possible responses his father might make. For each of the father's potential responses they wrote out additional things for Robert to say. Then they wrote a closing statement for the phone call during which Robert would tell his father that he loved him and that it made him sad and angry to miss visits. This was to be read no matter what else the father said.

Between the next two sessions, Robert made the phone call. During the following session, he related that he and the therapist had planned for every contingency in their script and that he felt the phone call had gone well although his father had become very angry about being put on the spot. Over the next several weeks, Robert's father did not call and it seemed as if the plan had failed. Then with no notice the father showed up for one of Robert's soccer games and took him out for ice cream afterwards. Though the problem of missed visits was not entirely solved with this one intervention it so bolstered Robert's ability to express his anger at his father directly that there were no more fights at school.

Irrespective of what goes on in the session the central focus of Ecosystemic Play Therapy is problem solving ways for the child to get his needs met more effectively and appropriately. This should remain first and foremost in the therapist's mind at all times. So long as the therapist is thinking that way she might as well think out loud and model the process for the child. If the modeling is effective it should be relatively easy to begin to engage the child in the process. Once engaged, the child is acquiring the skills she will need to solve his own problems first, in-session and then in the real world. Having acquired the skills the child's mental health becomes self-sustaining and the play therapy may come to an end.

CHAPTER TEN

Developmental and Phase-Specific Modifications of Ecosystemic Play Therapy

CORRECTIVE EVENTS AND INTERPRETATIONS AT DIFFERENT DEVELOPMENTAL LEVELS

As the child's development proceeds, the relative mix of corrective event and interpretation will shift in the play sessions. The lower the child's developmental level, the more the therapy will have to rely on corrective events for its impact. The higher the child's developmental level, the more interpretation and problem solving become the primary therapeutic tools.

Level I

For Level I children, virtually all the work of therapy will have to be done via corrective events. The 2-year-old is not capable of verbally processing either the internal or transactional difficulties he is experiencing. He is, however, quite capable of learning from experience. In working with children at this developmental level, you become, in large part, an extension of the caretaker. While the child is in your office, there is no question but that you are in a parenting role. The therapeutic strategy with children at this level is to create experiences that undo what they have experienced to date, thereby producing changes that can generalize to the world outside the playroom. It is very important that the child's caretaker be involved in this process as much as possible so that the child does not become confused about the nature of your role versus the caretaker's role.

With Level I children, very little interpretation will be used. This does not mean that language and verbal work are not important in the treatment of younger children, only that they are not prominent components. At this level, you should label objects, actions, and emotions as often and as clearly as possible, to provide the child with a language base that can be used in later problem solving. It is also a way for the child to compare situations and his reactions to situations, which is the beginning of true interpretive work.

Level II

With Level II children, corrective events are still the dominant therapeutic tool, but these are overlaid with interpretive work. At this level, you can think of your role as the narrator of the events that occur in session or as the child's observing ego. The child is not yet able to step out of himself to observe and comment on his behavior, so you must do it for him. You become the "little voice" that comments on the child's feelings and motives. You also become the child's empathic voice, the one that gives him input about the reactions of others in the environment.

Level III

The Level III child moves more readily between language and experience. Therapy becomes a true blend of corrective event and interpretive work. Unlike children at the other levels of functioning, Level III children tend to vacillate more in their functioning. At this level, the child still thinks very concretely but is capable of processing his experience using language. Sometimes the child thinks things through before he acts, while other times he thinks after he acts. Early in Level III, the child still acts and feels like a child and feels most comfortable when playing, especially with his peers. Toward the end of Level III, the child will sometimes try to act like an adult, while at other times he will act very much like a child. It is a difficult series of transitions for the child to make, and not surprisingly, more children are referred to therapy at this age than at any other.

Level IV

Play therapy with young Level IV children means coping with the vacillations in functioning seen in Level III children, only in an even more exaggerated way. Preadolescent children not only experience the mixed pull between childhood and adulthood, they tend to move between concrete thinking and more abstract thinking. Most of the time they prefer to conduct the work of therapy verbally and are able to maintain themselves for most of a therapeutic hour. However, most of the time they at least want to do something with their hands while they talk. In-session activities tend to be less geared toward the therapeutic and more toward reducing the child's anxiety so that he can focus on the verbal therapeutic process.

CORRECTIVE EVENTS AND INTERPRETATIONS IN THE DIFFERENT PHASES OF PLAY THERAPY

Virtually none of the components that make up each play session remain constant over the course of the child's treatment. Both your role and the child's behavior vary, in a fairly predictable manner, over time. Both the number and intensity of the corrective events that you create for the child are quite high at the beginning of treatment and do not usually taper off until the end of the growing and trusting phase. Similarly, the degree of control you exert will be highest at the beginning of treatment and lowest at the end.

The flow of interpretations does not follow as simple a linear pattern as does the degree to which you control the sessions. Remember that there are five hierarchically arranged levels of interpretation: reflection, pattern, simple dynamic, generalized dynamic, and genetic. These levels are offered to the child in order of decreasing frequency over the course of his treatment. That is, you will offer the most reflections and the fewest genetic interpretations. The number of reflections you offer will be very high at the beginning of the treatment but gradually decrease over time. Each of the other types of interpretation will gradually increase over the course of the child's treatment until their frequency and intensity reach a peak about two-thirds of the way through his treatment, after which they gradually decline through termination.

Play therapy follows the same six phases as those reported in Theraplay (Jernberg, 1979) literature: introduction, exploration, tentative acceptance, negative reaction, growing and trusting, and termination. In play therapy, the introduction phase actually occurs over the course of the intake and assessment process. This is the time when the child becomes familiar with the problems to be addressed, is familiarized with the nature of the work to follow, and is initially exposed to your personal style. The phases of exploration, tentative acceptance, and negative reaction are grouped together under the general heading of the beginning of treatment and were discussed at some length in Chapter Eight. The growing and trusting phase is the longest and the one in which the bulk of the therapeutic work takes place. Termination is the last phase of the treatment; it is completely discussed in Chapter Thirteen.

Beginning

Since the details of the beginning phase of therapy were discussed in Chapter Eight, the focus here is on the use of corrective events and interpretation within those first few sessions. The therapeutic experience you create for the child during the first few sessions sets the stage for the rest of the treatment, which is often the problem with doing an intake interview and assessment session with the child before beginning the therapy sessions. During the intake, the child becomes familiar with the task of responding to your questions. He learns to be relatively passive because your agenda seems to have little room for his input. Not surprisingly, many children sit rather passively when, during the first therapy session, you suddenly turn the responsibility for creating the agenda over to them, as is the case in psychoanalytic and humanistic play therapy. It is generally wiser if you do not make such a dramatic shift but maintain some control over the course of the child's treatment.

The beginning of a course of play therapy consists of three phases: exploration, tentative acceptance, and negative reaction. During all these phases very little emphasis is placed on working through specific events or issues from the child's history. Instead, the emphasis is on the development of a real relationship between you and the child in the here and now. You begin by creating experiences that help you and the child get to know one another. You must know the child as he is now, and he must know you as you are in your role as a play therapist.

Once you and the child are familiar with one another, you proceed to involve the child in experiences you have planned to help remediate hypothesized deficits in his early interactions with his primary caretaker. These activities are fun, but they interfere with the child's ability to maintain his usual degree of interpersonal distance. During this phase, the child seems to accept your intrusions, although you may be aware of an almost constant undercurrent of resistance as he attempts to maintain his equilibrium. In the last phase of the beginning of the treatment process, the negative reaction phase, the child openly rebels against your intrusions into his usual pattern of interactions. He may become very angry and aggressive, and you must be careful not to withdraw in the face of these rejections or you risk replicating the experiences he has had in every other interpersonal interaction in which he has engaged. The child must discover that you are like no other person in his world. You are responsible, in that you will care for him whether or not he likes it at the time. By the time the beginning portion of the treatment is over, you and the child will have developed a powerful bond that holds the two of you together as allies through the anxiety of the growing and trusting phase.

In conceptualizing the types of behavior you will be engaging in during the beginning phase of play therapy, the following guidelines are useful. You will be actively reflecting to the child as many of the affects and motivations present in the playroom as is humanly possible, thus allowing both of you to become familiar with the relative importance of affect in his life experience. As a general rule, you will be doing very little deep interpretation early in the therapy, except for the possible use of interpretation to let a child know that you are aware of certain trauma in his history.

You may know that a child has been severely abused, but he does not mention it in the course of the intake process. In this case, you might look for the opportunity to make a genetic interpretation relative to something the child does in one of the early sessions which makes it clear that you have this information. For example, a child flinches slightly when you make a sudden move in the first session. Rather than simply modifying your behavior, you might apologize to the child and say that you understand how sudden movements might scare him given the number and the severity of the beatings he has received in the past. This allows you to communicate your knowledge to the child in a way that does not require him to either confirm or disconfirm it.

The degree to which you will be structuring the initial sessions depends on the child's developmental level, his past experience in therapy—if any—and whether or not he has experienced recent trauma. The lower the child's developmental level, the more you will need to structure the initial sessions by pushing him to interact with you and follow the limits of the playroom. If the child has been in therapy previously, you may want to match the amount of structure he experienced during those sessions for at least your first few sessions together. However, if the child's previous therapy experience was negative, you may want to structure the first few sessions to be very different in order to disrupt the child's comparison of the two. Finally, if the child has suffered a recent trauma, you may want to leave the first few sessions relatively unstructured and be minimally intrusive so that he can begin to feel safe in the playroom with you before having to interact with you directly.

Regardless of the structure you impose in the very early phases of treatment, you should make sure that you have a very substantial structure in place before the child enters the negative reaction phase of the treatment. A solid structure will allow you to manage the child's negative reaction in a firm and therapeutic way without requiring you to suddenly shift your style in a way that might confuse and produce additional anxiety for him. If you have left the first sessions totally unstructured, telling the child that he may do what he likes, he may be quite surprised when you actively set limits on his throwing blocks at the wall during the fourth session. Not only must he process whatever actual behavior you engage in while setting limits, he must attempt to understand the shift in your behavior and whether or not that means there is a shift in your feelings toward him. On the other hand, if you have structured the sessions all along, there will be no shift in your behavior. Once the negative reaction phase has passed, gradually decrease the amount of structure you impose on the sessions to a level consistent with the child's developmental level.

Case Example: Aaron

STAGE: INTRODUCTION AND EXPLORATION

Stage Goals: Aaron will:

1. Demonstrate a marked decrease in anxiety and his accompanying obsessions and compulsive behavior. Related to this, he will be better able to handle unpredictable or messy situations.
2. Recognize, express, and make use of a broader range of affects.

Sessions 1 and 2

Participants: Aaron and the therapist.

Materials: Stratego® (complex board game), small human figures and vehicles, crayons, tempera paints, large and small paint brushes, large and small paper.

Experiential Components: Because of the extreme nature of Aaron's anxiety and the rigidity of his self-control, the therapist decided to use the first six sessions to make the transition from Aaron having total control to the therapist having total control of the sessions. The transition from the intake to the initial sessions was made by telling Aaron that the therapist had learned a lot by controlling their first contact and that, since they had agreed to work together to help Aaron feel less nervous, he thought Aaron should have a turn at controlling the sessions. This, it was suggested, would tell the therapist more about Aaron and would help the work get off to a good start.

During the first two sessions, Aaron chose an activity that was considerably above his developmental level and very clean, namely, he wanted to play a complex board game. It was apparent that he had to force himself to sit still for an entire hour of playing the game and that he found the rules and the prospect of losing very anxiety-provoking. The therapist constantly reflected these feelings, but Aaron continued to insist on playing the game.

Verbal Components: During the course of the session, the therapist made the following interpretive statements.

Reflections: "You like this game because it's meant for kids older than you so you feel very grown up." "It sure is hard to sit still for so long." "You look very worried." "You seem to be very frustrated with all the rules of the game." "You sure look happy when you capture one of my pieces."

Pattern Interpretations: "That's about the fifth time you have stopped the game to read the rules and make sure we are playing the right way." "Every time I capture one of your men you check the rules again." "Every time I capture one of your men you look panicky." "Every time you capture one of my men you look very proud."

Simple Dynamic Interpretations: "It seems like you get very worried any time things aren't going just right for you and you hope that following rules will make them better." "Checking the rules helps you feel like you aren't doing anything wrong that is causing you to lose your game pieces to me." "You

seem pretty sure that if you follow all the rules you just have to win the game."
"Winning is very important to you; it is one way you feel good about yourself."

Generalized Dynamic Interpretations: The only interpretation delivered at this level was to note that the therapist bet that Aaron played games just the same way at home. The therapist also noted that Aaron's mother had reported that Aaron got so caught up in reading the rules of a game when they played at home that they could never finish a game and hardly played any more.

Genetic Interpretations: None were delivered at this time.

The therapist also engaged Aaron in problem solving related to game strategy. The goal of the game is to use playing pieces that represent soldiers and bombs to protect one's flag. Once play begins pieces can only be recon-figured one move at a time (bombs can't be moved) because of this a lot of ad-vanced planning is required. At one point, it became apparent that Aaron had not planned well and that many of his stronger pieces were not near his flag. The therapist noted the problem and suggested several alternatives. Aaron could concede a loss and start another game. Aaron could keep going with his pieces as they were. Aaron could ask the therapist for a 15-second exception to the rules so that he could rearrange some of his pieces. Without much hesi-tation, Aaron chose the latter and continued to play although he still insisted the therapist rigidly follow the rules. The therapist interpreted this to mean that while rules helped insure that things went well, sometimes breaking the rules just a little bit helped one feel better and more in control.

Collaborative Components: During this stage, the therapist met with the mother after each session to give her a little feedback about how the sessions went. The therapist also began problem solving with the mother as to how she might provide Aaron with a better understanding of his father's illness. Aaron's mother began to work through various groups to locate children's books on both Multiple Sclerosis and death and dying.

STAGE: TENTATIVE ACCEPTANCE

Stage Goals: Aaron will:

1. Demonstrate a marked decrease in anxiety and his accompanying obses-sions and compulsive behavior. Related to this, he will be better able to handle unpredictable or messy situations.
2. Recognize, express, and make use of a broader range of affects.
3. Reduce the amount of time he needs to be in control and will allow others opportunities to control interactions.

Session 3

Participants: Aaron and the therapist.

Materials: Tempera paint, large and small paint brushes, large paper.

Experiential Components: Control over the content was divided between Aaron and the therapist. The therapist took control of the first half while Aaron took control of the second half. The therapist began the third session by having

Aaron paint. Aaron agreed only reluctantly and wanted to wear an apron to protect his clothes. He held the paint brush by the tip farthest from the bristles and complained when the therapist, purposely, let some of the colors mix together. During his half of the session, Aaron continued painting, a reflection of his tentative acceptance, but insisted on using smaller brushes and being much neater than the therapist had been.

At the end of the session, the therapist asked Aaron's mother, with Aaron standing right there, to make sure that Aaron wore old clothes to the next session so that it would not matter if he got dirty.

Verbal Components: During the course of the third session the therapist made the following interpretive statements.

Reflections: "You sure hate a mess." "You look like the 'Rule Fairy' is going to come in here and get very mad at us for breaking the rules of painting and making a mess." "It seems like you believe painting is supposed to be serious not fun." "I think you're putting up with this just because I'm an adult and not because you're having any fun." "You don't seem too happy at all." "Now that its your turn to be the boss you look much happier." "You look more relaxed using little brushes and being neater."

Pattern Interpretations: "Every time I try to make our painting just a design you try to turn it into a picture of something." "You keep switching between looking almost scared and almost angry." "You keep trying to make up rules for painting just like we had rules for Stratego." "You keep telling me how to behave. You sound like you are the grownup."

Simple Dynamic Interpretations: "Life gets a lot scarier when there aren't rules to tell you what to do." "Making a mess is very scary." "You look happy when we are painting a picture of something and angry when we're just making a silly design. I think you believe that there should be reason for everything you do and that having fun is not a good enough reason." "You really seem to think that bad things will happen if you are not in control all the time." "Now that you are the boss you seem much happier but I noticed we aren't making any silly pictures, only serious ones."

Generalized Dynamic Interpretations: "I think this business about rules and being the boss is the reason you can't play at home. You worry so much about the rules and doing things just right that it sometimes seems easier just not to do anything at all." "When you follow all the rules, adults really like it and give you lots of compliments but I'll bet other kids don't always like your telling them the right way to do things." "I'll bet you really don't like to play with other kids because they don't always do things the way you think they are supposed to and that makes you nervous." "Even though other kids sometime seem sort of out of control, it must get sort of lonely not having friends your own age."

Genetic Interpretations: "I think you started all this following the rules business once your dad got sick and your mom needed you to behave because she was busy taking care of your dad."

The therapist also engaged Aaron in problem solving related to balancing goal orientation and fun. He noted that Aaron seemed to get very anxious when they weren't painting a picture of something specific. They brainstormed ways Aaron might try to overcome his anxiety without necessarily having to draw specific pictures. The therapist suggested that Aaron try deep breathing to relax. He also suggest that they try to draw things you couldn't see, like happiness or cold, so Aaron wouldn't have a sense of there being a right way to paint these. In the end, Aaron tolerated the therapist putting his hands over Aaron's eyes for brief periods of time so that Aaron could try drawing without having to attend so much to the details.

Collaborative Components: This continued as before.

STAGE: NEGATIVE REACTION

Stage Goals: Aaron will:

1. Demonstrate a marked decrease in anxiety and his accompanying obsessions and compulsive behavior. Related to this, he will be better able to handle unpredictable or messy situations.
2. Recognize, express, and make use of a broader range of affects.
3. Reduce the amount of time he needs to be in control and will allow others opportunities to control interactions.

Session 4

Participants: Aaron and the therapist.

Materials: Tempera paint, large brushes, and large sheets of paper.

Experiential Components: When Aaron came to the fourth session, the therapist again decided that they would paint, only this time the therapist was much messier. He got paint all over Aaron's hands and refused to allow Aaron to wash them until the time was up. Aaron tolerated this with the look of someone who is being kind of a crazy person. His tentative acceptance was being pushed to the limit. When the second half of the session began, Aaron asked to go to the bathroom to wash his hands. The therapist agreed and went with him. Because the sink was quite high, Aaron needed help, and the therapist took the opportunity to begin to play at a level appropriate to Aaron's age. He made soap bubbles on Aaron's hands and then shook them over Aaron's head so that they fell like snow. He got water everywhere as he "found" stray bubbles that had to be rinsed away.

Aaron was furious but channeled it into verbalizations. He said that his mother would be angry at the therapist. He admonished the therapist to stop acting like a child. And then, finally, he started to cry and throw water back. Although he was crying, he remained engaged, using up the rest of the session. When the time was up, the therapist began to dry Aaron off and straighten out his clothes. Then, in a very gentle voice, delivered the genetic interpretation described in the following section. Aaron did not respond much, but his crying slowly subsided. His negative reaction phase was not completely over—it would manifest itself in short bursts over the next few sessions—but he had begun the growing and trusting phase.

Verbal Components: During the course of the session the therapist's interpretive statements were virtually the same as in the previous session except to focus on the fact that while Aaron first got very anxious when the therapist behaved in silly, unpredictable ways, he soon got very angry. The therapist also noted that Aaron seemed very surprised when he wasn't able to control the therapist just by getting angry. The primary addition to this session was the intense genetic interpretation.

Genetic Interpretations: Because this was to be short-term work and because the cause of Aaron's difficulties was so obvious, the therapist delivered a genetic interpretation relatively early in the treatment process. When Aaron began to cry the therapist said, "I know that sometimes it is a little scary when you cannot be the boss of everything. Sometimes you think that if you stop being the boss for even a minute you will stop growing up and start to move backward like your dad." Aaron continued to cry, but did not move away from the therapist. The therapist continued, "I know that you and your mom have talked, and that she told you that your dad has a sickness you cannot catch. It is very scary to watch your dad get worse and not be able to help him, but nothing you do will make him better. Nothing anyone does will make him better. Losing control or having fun will not make your dad get worse and it won't make anything bad happen to you."

The therapist also engaged Aaron in problem solving related to his problem with the way the therapist was being silly about the clean up. He suggested Aaron try to ignore the therapist (while he did not give up being intrusive and keeping Aaron engaged). He also suggested Aaron could just have a tantrum and yell and scream at the therapist. He suggested Aaron could try to "out-silly" the therapist and fight back with bubbles. Although Aaron heard the therapist's suggestions he was clearly too anxious to really follow through although he did briefly attempt each of the therapist's suggestions. When Aaron began to cry, the therapist noted how none of the solutions had really worked but that crying seemed to focus Aaron less on being anxious and angry and more about being sad that he couldn't control everything.

Collaborative Components: This session was followed by a short meeting with Aaron's mother in which she was instructed as to how she might help Aaron over the next few days. (This session is discussed further in Chapter Twelve.)

The fact that the trauma which had triggered the onset of the problems in Aaron's relationship with his parents was, in a sense, ongoing, the growing and trusting phase of his treatment was somewhat complicated. As Aaron tried to give up his incredible controls, there were some negative reactions from his parents, who needed him to be very adultlike so as not to add any more stresses to their lives. Most of these reactions were addressed in collateral therapy with the mother and father. Family sessions were not possible due to the father's difficulty in breathing if he sat upright for any length of time.

CASE EXAMPLE: FRANK

The introduction phase of Frank's treatment was essentially completed during the intake. Frank was told that he would be resuming therapy, this time with the interviewer, and that they would meet every Monday morning for 1 hour. Based on the goals set for Frank's treatment and his extremely traumatic history, it was decided that the exploration phase of his treatment should be fairly long so that he would not become overwhelmed by anxiety at the outset. The structure of these sessions was kept to a minimum in order to appear consistent with the type of treatment Frank had received in the past.

Upon entering the room for his first session, Frank chose to play in the sandbox with the human figures and animals. He set about building a very elaborate scene with a zoo, hills, and roads. Throughout the session, he completely ignored the therapist. At no time did he make eye contact, nor did he verbally acknowledge anything the therapist said. The therapist was fairly persistent in reflecting the feelings of the various characters in the play and even went on to connect some of the animals' feelings to the way Frank might be feeling about being in a new residential program. At the end of the session, Frank left without comment, although he nodded in agreement when the therapist said, "See you next week."

During the second session, Frank chose to play a board game that was designed to teach children facts about personal safety. This was seen as a considerable movement from the previous week since Frank was now choosing to interact with the therapist. After only several moves, Frank chose a card that required him to discuss why it was important for children not to play with matches. Frank became very uncomfortable, gave a simple response, and moved on. The therapist felt that, even in this early session, he should not let Frank's discomfort and its source go unrecognized. He said, "I'll bet that question was particularly difficult for you since your mom died in a fire you set." This time Frank not only acknowledged the statement but added that it was always uncomfortable for him until he knew whether or not new people with whom he had to interact already knew about his history.

Given Frank's openness during the second session, the therapist decided to become more directive during the third session so as to complete the exploration process. When Frank came to the third session, he again chose to play the safety rules board game but seemed vaguely disinterested in the process. The therapist said very little, which decreased Frank's interest in the game even more. Frank began to change the rules to get things moving, and the therapist took this opportunity to take control. He said, in a joking voice, "OK, so you're bored. Nobody said you could just change the rules. I'm bored, too. I would rather play. I know how to change this game." At that point, he lightly tossed one of the playing pieces at Frank, who immediately returned fire. The tentative acceptance phase of the work had begun. At this the therapist said "OK, now we play." He got up and reached for Frank, who was already running around the table laughing. The rest of the session was full of attempts at catching and running away, with the therapist reflecting the change in Frank's mood and noting how quick and strong Frank was.

The fourth session began with a run-and-chase game immediately upon Frank's entering the room, only this time the therapist caught Frank and gently tickled him. Frank laughed, and Frank and the therapist proceeded to discover which parts of Frank's body were ticklish and which were not. Frank was also encouraged to see if he could find a way to tickle the therapist. During this session, Frank made several moves to, playfully, run out of the door. Each time the therapist caught him and said that Frank must stay in the room until the session was over. Frank's affect remained positive, but his physical resistance gradually increased. The therapist anticipated that the negative reaction phase of therapy would begin in the next session.

Frank's next eight sessions were all very similar, consisting of a gradual process of negative reaction. Frank would try to run out of the room, and the therapist had to constantly guard the door. Frank became much more intrusive with the therapist and would grab or hit him. At no point, however, did Frank lose control; he just became steadily more aggressive. The therapist reflected how strong Frank was and challenged him to try to get out of various holds that the therapist would initiate. These tug of wars usually resulted in a sort of modified rocking as the therapist held Frank close and Frank tried to push away. Gradually, Frank moved to more passive resistance by refusing to make eye contact with the therapist or pretending to be asleep. The therapist then initiated a game of peek-a-boo in which he lifted Frank's eyelids to see if he was still there. After about 8 weeks, Frank began to relax, and it was clear that the negative reaction phase was coming to an end. Frank began to become more dependent during the sessions and wanted to be held and rocked. The growing and trusting phase of the treatment began.

Growing, Trusting, and Working Through

As the child comes out of the negative reaction phase, he enters the longest phase of the therapy, that of growing and trusting or working through. During this phase, the child must accomplish two related pieces of work. First, he must accumulate experiences that compensate for deficits in his relationship with his caretaker to date. These are the corrective events of therapy, the reparenting, if you will. You must begin this work by addressing the child's earliest unmet needs and proceed to work forward from that point. All the while you attempt to move the child to a point where he is functioning at a level consistent with his capacities in all of the areas that were assessed at intake. As the child moves through this developmentally appropriate sequence of experiences, he must also integrate, or work through, any traumatic experiences that have occurred in his past.

This is the main way Ecosystemic Play Therapy differs from both Theraplay and Reality Therapy, neither of which place any emphasis on the exploration and integration of the child's past during the course of treatment. It is necessary to view the child's past as no different from any other component of the child's ecosystem. That is, the child's past is real, and it contributes to the structure of the child's ecosystem as it exists in the present. To function fully in the present, the child must not deny the reality of his past. Instead, he must integrate it into his present so that he can benefit from that which was positive in his history and overcome that which was negative. The working through of past experience is accomplished primarily through the use of interpretation and problem solving.

The growing and trusting phase generally begins with an emphasis on the present. The child must be able to function optimally in the here and now, starting with the interactions with the therapist. Working through the child's history does not usually begin until the child has made some progress in his overall functioning. However, these processes tend to overlap in time more than they exist as discrete and consecutive aspects of the treatment. For the sake of convenience and clarity, the two processes are separated here, to allow you to get a sense of the types of corrective events that are used to promote the child's growth in each area.

The Developmental Work

The corrective events that enhance the child's developmental functioning are those which most closely mirror the interactions between a healthy caretaker and child. These consist mainly of the type of structuring, challenging, engaging, and nurturing activities delineated in Chapters Two, Nine, and Ten.

CASE EXAMPLE: AARON

STAGE: GROWING, TRUSTING, AND WORKING THROUGH

Stage Goals: Aaron will:

1. Demonstrate a marked decrease in anxiety and his accompanying obsessions and compulsive behavior. Related to this, he will be better able to handle unpredictable or messy situations.
2. Recognize, express, and make use of a broader range of affects.
3. Demonstrate a better understanding of his father's illness and be able to discuss his thoughts and fears about dying and death. He will begin to grieve the loss of his father.
4. Reduce the amount of time he needs to be in control and will allow others opportunities to control interactions.
5. Maintain a strong sense of attachment to his mother and will be better able to ask to have his needs for nurturance met.

Session 5

Participants: Aaron and the therapist.

Materials: An assortment of messy and finger foods.

Experiential Components: During the fifth session, Aaron and the therapist tried to eat small portions of different foods without using any utensils. First, they tried to eat very runny fruit gelatin with their hands, then they tried to eat dry cereal with no hands, and then they tried to pick up single, small pieces of candy from a plate by trying to get them to stick to the tip of their tongues. These activities were used because they combined the type of nurturance a typical 2-year-old would enjoy with a sense of noncompetitive mastery. Aaron tried to stay neat, but with a little challenge from the therapist he soon gave up and dove into the activities.

Verbal Components: During the course of the session, the therapist made many fewer interpretive statements. He focused on identifying the connection between Aaron's anxiety and his controlling behavior and those brief moments when Aaron could have fun once he relinquished control. He also noted how Aaron's needs were better met when Aaron was less focused on the right way of doing things.

The therapist also engaged Aaron in problem solving related to finding new ways they could eat foods. The goal was to get Aaron to brainstorm ways of getting his needs met without being so locked into the rules. For example, Aaron wanted to eat the cereal with a spoon (which was not available). Aaron showed some creativity when he pulled a piece of paper from his pocket and folded it to use as a utensil. The therapist then suggested they try different methods to see which got the most pieces of cereal in your mouth at once (got your needs met the most effectively). They tried fingertips (too few pieces), fistfuls of cereal (you picked up a lot but a lot fell on the floor instead of into your mouth), touching your tongue to the cereal (not a lot of pieces but very neat), and finally tipping the bowl toward your mouth and using your tongue (the most effective). This time Aaron was able to modify his behavior in ways that met his needs even if these didn't seem to fit the rules exactly.

Collaborative Components: Part of the time with Aaron's mother was spent educating her as to how a preoperational child like Aaron processed information. This was done to facilitate her talking to him about his father's illness. She had, for example, never considered the possibility that Aaron might fear that his father's illness was contagious.

Session 6

Participants: Aaron and the therapist.

Materials: Chocolate pudding and large sheets of heavy paper.

Experiential Components: During the sixth session, Aaron and the therapist used chocolate pudding as finger paint on a very large sheet of paper. By the time they were finished, they had chocolate pudding up to their elbows and proceeded to a washing-up experience similar to that which followed the fourth session. This time Aaron fought back when he got splashed. Although he was a little aggressive, he behaved in a manner perfectly consistent with his chronological age of 6.

Verbal Components: The interpretive work and problem solving done during this session was virtually identical to that done in the previous session.

Collaborative Components: At this point, Aaron's mother was reporting a marked change in Aaron's interactions with peers. She said that he was playing outside most of the time and that he had actually taken one of his toys outside to let another child play with it.

Session 7

Participants: Aaron, the therapist, and Aaron's mother.

Materials: Chocolate pudding and large sheets of heavy paper.

Experiential Components: During the seventh session, Aaron and his mother duplicated the chocolate pudding/finger painting the therapist had done with Aaron in the sixth session. The therapist engaged Aaron in teaching his mother how to do the activity. This gave Aaron some controls but also put him in the position of being able to verbalize what he needed in the activity. It also served to transition the focus of the session from the interactions between Aaron and the therapist to those between Aaron and his mother. It was observed that Aaron regressed somewhat during this session in that he tried to be neater and got angry when his mother didn't do things just right. This was expected to the extent that Aaron's mother represented the original conflict between Aaron's needs as a child and his mother's need to have a very mature and well-behaved child.

Verbal Components: During the session, the therapist made the following new interpretive statements:

Simple Dynamic Interpretations: "Every time your mom tries to be the boss you seem to get mad but you seem to put up with me being the boss." "It's harder to figure out the right thing to do with your mom. You know she usually likes you to be neat but the fun part of this activity is the chance to be messy."

Generalized Dynamic Interpretations: "I'll bet the same sort of thing happens at home and in school. At home you know your mom wants you to behave because she is so busy taking care of your dad but now sometimes you just want to be a kid and have fun. You and your mom will have to figure out how to balance the two. At school the teacher likes how well behaved you are but your friends think you're too bossy. Maybe at school you could try to be very well behaved in the classroom and more silly out on the playground."

Genetic Interpretations: No new material was added.

The therapist also engaged Aaron and his mother in problem solving related to where and when silly or messy behavior was not only tolerable but to be encouraged. They decided to set aside some "Silly Play" time each day and to use the playroom Aaron had at home. His mother readily agreed that it was all right for him to make messes in his playroom so long as they didn't spill over into the rest of the house. Verbalizing the differences in their needs and problem solving creative ways to achieve balance became the focus of the remaining sessions.

Collaborative Components: Not surprisingly, Aaron developed a powerful father transference toward his male therapist. He tended to see therapy as his chance to have a healthy father who could supply the controls that made him feel safe. The reality of Aaron's desire to have the opportunity to interact with a healthy male role model was addressed in collateral work with his mother, who increased her efforts at having Aaron spend time with his grandfather and an uncle.

Session 8

Participants: Aaron, the therapist, and Aaron's mother.

Materials: An assortment of finger foods including cut up fruit, cereal, and chewable candies.

Experiential Components: During the eighth session, Aaron and his mother played some noncompetitive games that involved them feeding one another. Each would close their eyes and try to guess what the other was feeding him or her. Each would see if they could tell the foods apart by touch or smell. During this session, they engaged in a lot of rough-and-tumble play as well. Throughout, the therapist tried to remain as peripheral to the play as possible. He commented verbally but did not become involved in the activities. The goal was to promote as much generalization of the therapy gains as possible to Aaron's interactions with his mother.

Verbal Components: The only new interpretive material that was delivered was the therapist's observation that Aaron's mother was an even better play partner than the therapist, especially since she was around so much more. All problem solving that was done focused on balancing Aaron's and his mother's needs both in session and at home.

Collaborative Components: At the end of each of these sessions, the therapist had begun to hold meetings with the mother and the father by phone. These sessions were initiated when it became apparent that the father was somewhat threatened by Aaron's growing attachment to both the therapist and a male nurse who had been hired to come in each day to help with the father's care. During these phone sessions, the therapist and parents brainstormed ways the father could remain actively engaged with Aaron as his physical health continued to deteriorate. In the weeks since treatment had begun, the father had stopped reading a nightly story to Aaron because he no longer had the energy to talk for more than a few minutes at a time. The result of these telephone contacts was that the father decided to come for the final session and be a part of celebrating the gains that Aaron had made. This was a heroic and expensive undertaking because transportation had to be arranged through a paramedic unit.

Session 9

Participants: Aaron, the therapist, and Aaron's mother.

Materials: Headache® (a simple board game) brought to the session by Aaron and his mother.

Experiential Components: In preparation for termination, the therapist asked Aaron and his mother to bring from home a game they enjoyed so that they could play it in the office for the ninth session. They brought, Headache, a developmentally appropriate board game that Aaron played without his usual rigidity and without becoming upset when he lost. Both mother and son were instructed to verbalize their feelings about the game as they played.

Verbal Components: No new interpretive information was delivered. The therapist focused on verbally reinforcing the gains Aaron had made as well as the positive interactions between Aaron and his mother. Problem solving continued to focus on balancing their needs and making sure that they had fun.

Collaborative Components: Aaron's termination had been planned when he began his ten-session course of treatment. By the time the eighth session was completed, many of Aaron's referral behaviors had disappeared. Both his parents and school personnel reported significant changes in his behavior, particularly with regards to increased spontaneity and playfulness. Although they noted a slight decrease in his level of compliance, they considered this to be both manageable and age-appropriate.

As a result of the increasing communication between the therapist and Aaron's father over the last few weeks of the treatment, it was decided that the father would attend the last session. The decision was also made that the session should be in the office and not at Aaron's home—although this would have been easier—to facilitate the generalization of the feelings Aaron had experienced in connection with the playroom, not just the therapist, to his father. Aaron and his mother planned the contents of the last session and arranged to have the father transported to the office.

CASE EXAMPLE: FRANK

Frank came to therapy having experienced severe trauma beginning when he was 2 years old. As noted at the time of intake, it was hypothesized that these traumas had prevented him from receiving the protection and nurturance a toddler usually receives. For this reason, the therapist decided to devote a major portion of the growing and trusting phase of Frank's treatment to experiences that would begin to make up for this deficit.

As soon as Frank's initial negative reaction was over, the therapist introduced food into the sessions. The goal was to reverse Frank's experience of having to feed his mother by creating a situation in which he could be fed. The foods used were bite-sized candies, peanuts, and raisins, fed to Frank while he lay relaxed in the therapist's arms. Frank was also given drinks from a baby bottle filled with apple juice or soda. These sessions continued for several months.

During this time, the therapist constantly reflected Frank's affect and the patterns that appeared in Frank's behavior. Slowly, these began to crystallize into more dynamic interpretations. Frank's intense neediness in session was linked, through generalized dynamic interpretations, to his missing his foster mother while he was in residential placement and later to the fact that his foster mother was becoming less available due to the illness of Frank's foster sibling. These feelings were in turn compared, through the use of genetic interpretations, to Frank's feelings about the neglect he had suffered due to his mother's death and his father's abuse.

As the number of genetic interpretations increased, Frank began to deny missing his mother until one day he said that he had killed her intentionally, that she had sexually abused him, and that he was glad she was dead. Up until that time, Frank had always maintained that his mother had been a very good person. This information had been unknown previously and changed the nature of the therapist's interpretations significantly. Now he focused on the grief Frank must have experienced because his biologic parents had never provided him with the type of care he deserved. These interpretations triggered Frank's first discussions of the sexual abuse his father perpetrated. He stated that the abuse had been violent and that he was still afraid that his father might come one day and try to hurt him. During this period of the work, Frank was still spending most of every session being held, tickled gently, and hugged.

As the therapist focused more and more on the abuse that Frank had suffered and its impact on his need for nurturance in the present, Frank began to need physical contact with the therapist less. They stopped the feedings in session, and Frank would come to the office and play with Play-Doh. This huge leap in his developmental functioning was used as a cue that the working through of the historical material could proceed in earnest.

Working through Traumatic Historical Experiences

You begin the child's treatment by creating experiences that will foster the development of a strong bond between you and the child. You then move to alleviate some of the early developmental deficits that the child experienced. Eventually, the child begins to feel somewhat satisfied; he begins to give up his old ways of getting his needs met and to explore new, more functional patterns of interacting. At this point the child's self is sufficiently stabilized and his relationship to you anchored in enough positive experience to allow you to begin to work through any traumatic, historical material that may have contributed to his present style and functional deficits. The point here is not to dredge up all previous trauma just for the sake of reviewing them. Before doing any historical work the therapist must first determine that residual of the trauma, usually problematic interpersonal schema, are still interfering with the child's ability to get his needs met effectively and appropriately. If this is the case, the therapist begins by creating new experiences for the child that activate elements of his history interpretation is then used to identify the interference and problem solving is focused on ways to reduce this interference in the present.

These corrective events should be planned to re-create some aspect of the past experience. The experiences might re-create either in reality or symbolically the type of interaction, the setting, the actual event, or the feelings the event triggered. Often these experiences can be created through the introduction of certain materials. A toy gun might be introduced into the playroom for a child who saw someone shot, medical equipment might be brought in for a child who had experienced a serious accident or injury, or a baby doll and infant supplies might be provided for a child having difficulty adjusting to the birth of a sibling. Sometimes the work can be initiated not so much through the introduction of a specific toy or material as through the use of that material in a specific way. Paints can be used to paint pictures, but they can also be used to reflect emotions or to be messy. Play-Doh can be used to make food for a neglected child, or to make bad guys who can be squashed in the case of victimized children. The issue here is not so much the material but the way in which you facilitate the use of that material to help the child work through his past experience.

CASE EXAMPLE: AARON

Because Aaron's family was able to allocate only a brief period of time to a course of treatment, the therapist decided to focus on the developmental issues in the play therapy sessions and to address the historical issues through collateral work with Aaron's parents. This is a simple and effective way of containing the amount of information to be addressed in session when doing short-term work. The details of this collateral work are in Chapter Twelve.

CASE EXAMPLE: FRANK

As Frank was able to be moved toward less dependent types of play in his sessions and into more expressive ones, the therapist decided it was time to begin processing Frank's history. The process was initiated by gradually increasing the number of genetic interpretations so as to connect more and more of Frank's present emotions, thoughts, and behaviors to the things he had experienced in the past. Each time such interpretations were made, Frank became very anxious and attempted to move on to some other subject.

Eventually, Frank and his therapist began to make people out of the Play-Doh; the people were almost immediately identified as Frank's parents. During one session, the therapist sat and held Frank as he had early in the treatment and said that although he knew it would be very difficult, he wanted Frank to try to recall the events of the day when his mother died. Frank began to become quite agitated, but the therapist held tight, and Frank began to recount his history. Consistent with Frank's rather concrete thinking and his limited ability to judge time, the recounting made it sound as if every trauma in his history had occurred on the same day. He had, indeed, stored all the trauma together, so it was no wonder it easily overwhelmed him. At the sessions end, the therapist was as nurturing and supportive as he could be, acknowledging how difficult the session had been for Frank and pointing out that, for the first time, Frank had been able to think about all the events in his past at one time and not erupt into aggressive acting out, except for squashing the Play-Doh figures.

In this context, the therapist began to identify for Frank the degree to which the rage at his parents still interfered with his being able to get his needs met on a day to day basis. Because of his anger and fear he never felt safe. Because of the constant background of rage he experienced day to day things that might only be annoying instead produced outbursts of seriously dangerous behavior. And, because he still felt some guilt about setting the fire that killed his mother he maintained an intensely ambivalent preoccupation with fire. In sessions, they began to work on ways of ventilating Frank's rage so that it did not erupt in day to day interactions. They also began to look at why and how Frank had set the fire and the terrible consequences it had had. They began to problem solve other ways Frank could express fear and anger without setting fires. All of this cognitive and reality based work was interspersed with considerable ongoing pretend play.

Over the next few sessions, Frank and his therapist continued to make models of Frank and his parents. They enacted some of the traumatic events, and the ritual of squashing the Play-Doh figures to return them to their containers expanded into rituals of mutilating the parent figures while recounting the rage Frank had experienced. He began to stick any long pointed object he could find in the playroom into the figures, symbolically avenging the rape he had endured. One day he chopped the mother figure into tiny pieces and piled them into a frying pan that he placed on a toy stove. The therapist, somewhat taken aback, managed to offer the following genetic interpretation: "This reminds me of how your mother died after she hurt you." Frank looked genuinely surprised and asked what had made the therapist think of this. The therapist pointed out the similarity between cooking the mother on the stove and burning her up in a fire. At this Frank overturned the pan, spilling the pieces of the mother onto the burner. It was done with little emotion, and Frank went on to clean up the Play-Doh at the end of the session.

From that point on, Frank's overall behavior seemed to stabilize. The improvements the therapist had seen in session began to generalize to the classroom and the residential program. Frank increased his attachment behavior toward his female teacher and one of the male counselors and even began to interact with some of his peers. The therapist did not feel that termination should be considered yet because of some changes that were about to occur in Frank's life, the most potentially destructive of which was that he would soon be told that he would not be returning to the group home he had lived in for the past 3 years or to the woman he referred to as his mother. Instead of working toward termination, the therapy became focused on engaging Frank in problem solving directed at his day-to-day experiences.

Once you begin to work through the child's past experience, both the quantity and quality of the emotion you and the child experience during the session are likely to intensify. When, in the previous example, Frank spontaneously "cooked his mother on the stove," the therapist was virtually overwhelmed by his emotional response. When Frank attempted to talk about his past rather than acting on it, he was virtually overwhelmed. The emotional responses of both the child and the therapist are often discussed under the headings of transference and countertransference, respectively. The effective management of such transferences is essential to a good therapy outcome and is discussed in the following chapter.

CHAPTER ELEVEN

Transference and Countertransference

In this section, the term *transference* is used somewhat unconventionally. Psychoanalytic writers generally restrict the term to refer to those emotions, thoughts, and behaviors that are brought to the session as reflections of the person's history or life experience but not as reactions to the reality of the therapy process. The client's transference is desirable because the aim of analysis is the working through of these archaic complexes. The child's ability or inability to develop a transference neurosis was discussed in Chapter Eight. The therapist's transference or countertransference (as it is usually termed) is generally considered problematic because it interferes with the therapist's ability to objectively process the client's material.

More recent writings on the therapy process tend to use the word *transference* to refer to all the emotions, thoughts, and behaviors that either the client or therapist bring to the therapy session, the logic being that no one can isolate herself from her past experience and that any experience a person has in the present is intimately tied to everything that has gone before. The hope in this case is that the therapist is more fully aware of the impact of her past on her present functioning. With this awareness comes the ability to use what one has learned from the past to work in the present. The goal of therapy is to create this same sort of awareness in the client, allowing the client to use her past experience rather than be victimized by it.

In this volume, the term transference is used in a manner consistent with this more general definition, but it is even more inclusive. Herein the term is used to refer not only to the emotions, thoughts, and behaviors that an individual manifests within the context of the therapeutic relationship but to the treatment-related interaction between the child or the therapist and the child's ecosystem. That is, transference on the part of the child also occurs when she reacts to events within her ecosystem in a manner consistent with issues occurring in the therapy. Similarly, countertransference refers to the emotions, thoughts, and behaviors that you bring to your interactions with the child's ecosystem. Transference issues of all types make it difficult for both you and the child to maintain much-needed role boundaries over the course of the treatment. The problem of blurred boundaries is further complicated when you take a broadly systemic approach to the conduct of play therapy.

When you define yourself as a play therapist in the psychoanalytic sense, you establish a set of boundaries that greatly reduces the potential for transference and countertransference problems. You are not yourself with the child; you are more distant and more "objective." You are minimally involved with the child's ecosystem and totally uninvolved with the child outside the therapy session. These boundaries, while somewhat artificial, create a sense of safety for everyone involved in the child's treatment.

Should you involve yourself in the child's ecosystem as is consistent with Ecosystemic Play Therapy, the boundaries are not nearly so clear. You might decide to work with the child's parents or even with siblings. You might be called on to attend an educational planning meeting at the child's school. You might become involved in helping plan a child's placement outside the home. You might even become involved with the legal or medical system if your client has difficulties in those areas. How then do you define your limits and boundaries within this model of play therapy?

Three factors ultimately define your role as a play therapist. First is your level of training and expertise. You must know the limits of your knowledge. If you do not know much about the school, medical, or legal system, you should not become involved in those areas on your client's behalf. You should, however, make it a point to familiarize yourself with persons you could refer your client to in the event of a problem in any one of those areas. Similarly, if you have no training in couples or family therapy, then you should not attempt to become involved with the child's family on that level. Again, you should know professionals you could refer the family to if that type of work is needed.

Second, is that you are able to recognize the limits of your time commitment. If you are in private practice and are seeing 20 or 30 clients a week, you cannot go to school meetings and do family work and be available to do crisis intervention with every child. Your work will have to be defined by the time you have available; you should be straightforward in informing your clients of the limits of your practice. Again, you should develop resources you can refer your clients to should the need arise.

Third is the matter of knowing your personal limits. No one person can be everything to even one child much less be everything to every child. What type of work makes you the most comfortable? Maybe you prefer to be heavily involved with a few very disturbed children and their families. Maybe you prefer to maintain a reduced level of involvement with less disturbed children. Or maybe you prefer a caseload that includes a mix of children. Whatever you prefer, you must know when to say no. In fact, it is preferable if you can communicate your limits to the family before beginning treatment so that they can decide whether or not the services you will offer meet their needs.

Using theory to establish a priori limitations on the nature of your role in conducting play therapy with a given child does not seem to make much sense. If you want to adopt such arbitrary rules in order to protect yourself from becoming over- or underinvolved with your clients, that is fine but accept that any limits you set are somewhat artificial. On the other hand, if you wanted to be all things to all people, you could be trained as a social worker, psychologist, school counselor, teacher, physician, lawyer, and so forth. For the sake of your sanity, you set limits somewhere and identify your preferred modes of intervening. When you apply an ecosystemic perspective to the practice of play therapy, you gain substantial freedom in planning and selecting your role because it encourages you to take all the child's ecosystem into consideration, regardless of where and how you yourself plan to intervene. The following pages review some of the more common transference and countertransference problems so that you can manage them within your work.

TRANSFERENCE

You should be alert to the three types of transference children commonly engage in because they may cause problems in the therapy process. At some point in the course of a child's treatment, she is likely to develop a parental transference toward you. She may begin to react toward you as either the bad or the good parent—if the therapy is going well, it is usually the latter. This reaction may manifest itself in a number of ways. The most obvious manifestation is the child's beginning to call you mom or dad. The assignment of titles is rarely gender-dependent because children tend to call both male and female therapists mom. Sometimes a child will attempt to directly engage you in discussions about your own children and then begin to talk about what it would be like if you were her parent. At other times, this transference will not manifest itself directly in the session but when the child is at home or in school. Children may actually say to their parents that they would rather have you for a parent.

However it is manifested, parental transferences can directly threaten the continuation of the treatment if not managed appropriately. It is important to help the child label the transference as a fantasy that will never be realized. You should actively interpret the needs and motives that underlie the child's desire to have you as a parent. Usually, such a child is experiencing an intense need state that she does not perceive the parent as capable of gratifying. The appearance of this type of transference also needs to be addressed with the parents, who may feel very threatened by the depth of their child's attachment to you. They will need to know what types of needs the child is attempting to communicate so that they can work to address them instead of being put off by feelings of rejection.

A second common transference reaction occurs when a child begins to perceive the therapist as omniscient and all-powerful. If you help her generate a solution to a problem that works when she tries it, the result may appear magical, especially to a younger child. If you intervene with the parents and the parents' behavior changes, your ability may seem even more magical. The child comes to expect you to fix everything and may be very disappointed when this does not happen. This situation is actually a common developmental phase that children go through with their parents, first occurring when they are in Level II and gradually beginning to realize that although their parents are very powerful, they cannot protect them from everything. This situation again occurs when children enter Level IV and can suddenly see their parents as fully human and capable of mistakes.

This type of transference causes fewer problems in the overall course of the therapy than does parental transference, but it should still be addressed. The child's needs and motives for wanting an all-powerful guardian should be actively interpreted and addressed in the therapy. And the parents should be aware of the feelings that are driving the child's fantasy about the therapist.

The last transference problem to be discussed here concerns the child's taking emotions, thoughts, or behaviors out of the playroom and into her ecosystem rather than into the playroom. The child who is not allowed to use guns at home but may use one in therapy suddenly begins to pretend to shoot at members of her family for a few hours after each therapy session. The child who has become very dependent in therapy becomes very clingy and dependent at home. The child whose behavior was already problematic at home begins to deteriorate soon after therapy begins. None of these situations is uncommon, but any of them can make the parents feel that therapy is making the problems worse, not better.

As with each of the other types of transferences, it is important that you actively interpret for both the child and her parents her underlying needs and motives. These problems can often be managed by instituting more ritualized transitions in and out of the session which make it clear to the child that the playroom is a unique environment with its own rules and expectations. (The use of transition rituals was discussed at length in Chapter Nine.) If possible, discuss the likelihood of carryover with the parents before it occurs. Also discuss strategies for managing the behavior. Many parents feel that because you allow a behavior in session, you expect them to allow it at home. They are often relieved to find out that you hope that they will set limits on their child at home to help the child differentiate between what is appropriate in one environment versus another.

CASE EXAMPLE: AARON

Not surprisingly, Aaron developed a powerful father transference toward his male therapist. He tended to see therapy as his chance to have a healthy father who could supply the controls that made him feel safe. The reality of Aaron's desire to have the opportunity to interact with a healthy male role model was addressed in collateral work with his mother, who increased her efforts at having Aaron spend time with his grandfather and an uncle. In sessions, this transference was managed by involving the mother in a therapeutic role toward the end of the work and by arranging for the father to be transported to the final session so as to draw for Aaron a concrete connection between the therapist and the father.

CASE EXAMPLE: FRANK

The most significant transference problem that occurred in the course of Frank's treatment was the tendency of his behavior in session to carry over into his ecosystem, particularly when he was feeling either very needy or overwhelmed by his recall of past trauma. While Frank was able to be very appropriate during sessions, the reduced structure he experienced out of session caused him to deteriorate. Because Frank was in a residential program, the therapist decided not to work on containing Frank's behavior but on strategies to make the residential environment better able to meet Frank's needs. This goal was accomplished through collateral work with Frank's teacher and residential program counselor. These interventions are discussed in Chapter Twelve.

COUNTERTRANSFERENCE

In all cases, countertransference is best managed by maintaining a level of self-awareness that allows you to get your needs met outside the child's play sessions. The solution may require that you go through treatment of your own or that you regularly seek out supervision, but it is an issue that must be actively addressed before it has a negative effect on your child clients and their families.

Most of the countertransference problems that arise in the treatment of children appear to stem from a single source, namely, the therapist's experience of being raised by parents who, for one reason or another, manifested a narcissistic flaw. In her book *The Drama of the Gifted Child,* Miller (1981) identified reactions to parental narcissism as the primary reason individuals choose to become analysts. The argument she presented generalizes quite readily to persons who enter any of the helping professions, and most definitely to those in the mental health fields.

Miller noted that most analysts have at least one parent with a significant narcissistic flaw. That is not to say that these parents display narcissistic personality disorders, rather that at various levels or intervals they are unable to accurately read and then gratify their child's needs. Instead, they tend to look to their children to met their own needs. For some parents, this is the result of drug abuse, for some it may be the result of depression, and for still others it may be the result of a primary character flaw. If the child is bright, she learns to work to meet the parents' needs in the hopes that they will eventually be capable of returning the favor. To accomplish this, the child must get to be very good at reading the needs of others and delaying her own gratification. These experiences and subsequent skills, Miller said, become the foundation of the child's later attraction to the field of analysis. The child is merely continuing the pattern of interpersonal interaction that she began very early in life. Miller went on to identify the danger this poses to the welfare of the analyst's clients if the analyst does not thoroughly understand and manage it. Emphasis is on the analyst's need to maintain, for herself, an ecosystem that consistently meets her needs so that she does not fall into the trap of expecting clients to meet her needs.

This core experience in the histories of many mental health professionals drives their desire to care for others, often to the point of having very unrealistic expectations of their ability to effect change. The therapist wants to be all things to all people and takes on an advocate role relative to the child. You come to believe that every child can be saved if only you make the right intervention at the right time. You believe that you can influence not only the child but every dimension of her ecosystem as well. The primary risk here is of professional burnout. When reality hits you full force, you feel depressed and tend to withdraw so that your failure to meet the child's needs is not so obvious.

There is research to suggest that the degree and type of countertransference a therapist manifests can be related to the child's diagnosis (Shachner & Farber, 1997). Children who were diagnosed as dysthymic tended to elicit the most positive countertransference. Children diagnosed as conduct disordered elicited more negative countertransference. Therapist tended to engage in the most countertransferential actions (actions based on the therapist's feelings rather than the facts of the case) in response to children diagnosed as borderline. Generally, this supports the notion that more disturbed clients trigger more negative countertransference in the therapist and more acting out of those negative feelings.

Related to this situation are the anger and frustration you experience when a child does not improve. You feel that you have done your best to meet the child's needs, so now she should meet yours, or at least make you feel better by improving. These feelings are most prominent in the cases of children in whom you have invested a great deal of time and energy. Regressions on the child's part can be especially frustrating. Children who display borderline features and who regress frequently often activate these feelings in virtually everyone with whom they come in contact, not just their therapists. Again, there is a tendency to withdraw from these children over time.

Brems (1994) identified four types of countertransference. *Issue specific countertransference* is used to describe those feelings elicited by the therapist's own unconscious material. This is the type most referenced in the psychoanalytic literature. *Stimulus specific countertransference* involves negative reactions on the part of the therapist to stimuli outside the therapy that are not directly related to the child such as the divorce of the child's parents. *Trait specific countertransference* is seen when the therapist manifests certain character traits in all interactions with children even if they are inappropriate for a given child. This can be seen in the therapist who feels the need to have every child enjoy the session so that she overstimulates children including her hyperactive clients. Last, *child specific countertransference* occurs when the child is able to elicit from the therapist the exact same reactions she elicits from others in her environment. This last one is particularly problematic because it makes it very difficult for the therapist to effectively create corrective experiences for the child in the sessions. No matter what type of countertransference you are experiencing it is not the feelings that matter rather how you manage those feelings so as to ensure that you continue to act in the best interests of the child that matters.

The last countertransference problem to be addressed derives from the therapist's identification with her clients or their parents. Brems identified four types of identification. First, identification with the child is a problem when the therapist begins to react to the child's parents in the same way as the child. All children enter treatment because their parents no longer feel that they are able to meet the child's needs for themselves and therefore need the assistance of a professional. This means that all child clients can rightfully see their parents as failing to provide for them in some way. Problems begin when you agree with the child's perception and do not question the impact of the child and the ecosystem on the creation of the child's current life situation. This loss of perspective is particularly easy when the child's parents are indeed negligent or even destructive, as in the case of child abuse. You come to view the parents as bad and incapable of changing even if their circumstances changed. You must be constantly vigilant for this loss of perspective because it undermines not only the treatment of the individual child but your ability to work with the parents and to maintain an ecosystemic perspective. Alternatively, the therapist may be put in the position, especially in child abuse cases of having to make a recommendation to the court as to the necessity of terminating parental rights when the parents really are incapable of changing. The details of how and when to make such a determination are beyond the scope of this book. Suffice it to say that such decisions should be made with extreme caution and only after having carefully considered whether or not the therapist's affects have clouded the picture.

Second, the therapist may come to identify with the child's parents. In this case the therapist begins to view and to treat the child the same way her parents do. This is particularly easy when pleasant, well-educated parents are attempting to cope with a very seriously disturbed child. This type of countertransference is essentially the reverse of the type described in the previous paragraph.

Third, reactive identification occurs when the therapist dislikes certain characteristics of the parent and begins to behave consistently in the opposite manner. A therapist might not like a parent's rigid attention to neatness and cleanliness so that she begins to encourage the child to be sloppy and messy in session. This sets up a conflict in which the therapist has already taken sides. Last, there is projective identification, where the therapist takes on the child's unacceptable needs or emotions as if they were her own. This differs from simple identification with the child in that the therapist is not able to recognize the fact that the feelings originate from the child. A neglected child might appear to accept her situation in therapy while managing at the same time to cause the therapist to begin feeling hurt or deprived. This is not to say the child does this consciously but rather that she has found a subconscious way of engendering feelings in others. This type of problem is described in much of the clinical literature on work with adult borderline clients. Irrespective of the nature of the identification these should be considered a form of countertransference and thus in need of careful management. Again, it is not the feelings of identification that are, in and of themselves, problematic but rather the degree to which these prevent the therapist from acting in ways that are in the best interest of the child.

CASE EXAMPLE: AARON

Aaron's life situation was such that it tended to pull for sympathy. His father was dying very slowly, and everyone, including Aaron, knew it, which tended to make others protective of Aaron, preventing them from challenging the maladaptive ways he got his needs met. It also prevented people from providing him with some of the concrete information he needed to understand what was happening to his father and the impact it would have on his life. One of the therapist's sources of support was several other therapists, all of whom said they were not sure they could work with a child in that situation. Although each therapist would have rallied to implement the needed interventions had Aaron been their client, their recognition of the effort required helped support the therapist through the course of the treatment.

CASE EXAMPLE: FRANK

Frank pulled for virtually every form of countertransference possible. The extreme abuse he had suffered at the hands of both his biologic parents tended to draw others into protective caretaking. The degree to which he rejected attempts at interaction tended to cause others to become very angry at him as they tired in their efforts to help. The abuse he suffered at the hands of a system that had been unable to find him a placement which provided a consistent primary caretaker tended to make adults have fantasies of adopting Frank. However, the fact that he was the reason, whether intentional or not, that his mother had died tended to scare people off.

The therapist's discovery that Frank was not going to be able to return to the woman he referred to as his mother upon leaving residential treatment caused him to have such a strong sense of hopelessness that it was difficult for him to continue to work with Frank. Two things made it easier for the therapist to stay fully involved in the treatment through this crisis. One was the dramatic improvement Frank had manifested in only about 10 months of therapy, because this created hope that he would survive this latest assault on his development. The other was the therapist's cognitive awareness that Frank would need treatment now, more than ever, that kept him engaged. To avoid directing his anger at Frank, he targeted several people who were responsible for Frank's placement and vented as much of his frustration as possible with them in order to facilitate the development of the best possible placement plan.

If the proper corrective experiences and the proper cognitive and verbal work are done with the child, she will soon become fully engaged in the growing and trusting phase of the therapy. Once this occurs, she will begin to make changes, and if the transference and countertransference issues are properly managed, these changes may be quite rapid. To ensure that the changes the child makes in therapy generalize to her world outside the playroom, you must conduct at least some collateral work with significant others in the child's life. Strategies for conducting this collateral work are presented in the following chapter.

CHAPTER TWELVE

Collateral Work

As has been stressed throughout this book, you must consider the child's entire ecosystem when planning and implementing a course of play therapy. The focus is on the intervention to be carried out with the individual child, but you should not ignore the potential value of intervening or at least facilitating interventions with some of the other individuals or systems that comprise the child's ecosystem. Most often these interventions will be directed at the child's parents or family, but they might also be directed at individuals or systems in schools and hospitals or at various legal systems. The term *collateral* is often used to refer to work done with the parents or to work done by the parents with the child under the direction of the therapist. In this chapter, all the interventions you might implement within the child's ecosystem are discussed under the heading collateral work.

COLLATERAL WORK WITH PARENTS

Collateral work with parents is critical if play therapy is to successfully meet the child's individual needs. Parent guidance also facilitates the generalization of the gains the child makes in treatment. Collateral work with the child's parents can take many forms. It may be designed to support the child's treatment by maintaining your alliance with the parents or to facilitate the flow of information. It may be designed as a time in which you and the parents are engaged in mutual problem solving. It may be educational in nature; that is, your time is spent giving the parents information about such things as their child's particular pathology, behavior management strategies, or even general parenting skills. Or the work with the parents may be therapeutic in nature. Therapeutic work can be carried out in three ways. First, the parents may be engaged as the therapists for their child, with you filling the role of clinical supervisor. Second, the parents may be involved in joint or family sessions with the child. Third, the parents may be involved in individual or couples treatment of their own that parallels the work being done with their child.

Play therapists tend to view the sole purpose of collateral work as the engagement of the parents in the child's treatment as an ally of the therapist. Although this is a very desirable goal, it is best if it is not your first aim. Remember that it is the parent who brought the child to treatment and, at the point of referral, it is likely that the parent's emotional needs are at least as great as those of the child. Often therapists make the mistake of assuming that by caring for the child they will please the parent and reduce the parents' needs. In fact, your caring relationship with the child may have the reverse effect: The parents may feel that they were truly incompetent and that they were responsible for their child's distress. They may feel that they were so generally bad that even an hour of contact a week with a stranger (you) makes their child feel and act considerably better. When these feelings are aroused in the parents, they tend to work, albeit unconsciously, to sabotage the sessions. For this reason, it is best to at least begin the collateral work with the child's caretakers with the goal of addressing their immediate needs and conflicts.

Addressing the parents' needs in such a way that the parents are available to continue to support the child's treatment generally means that you will have to meet with them on a regular basis. Since most parents cannot afford two therapy sessions per week and since most children find a full, 50-minute hour somewhat long, the use of split sessions is a good way to meet everyone's needs. In a split session, the parents meet with you for 20 minutes, and the child's play session is 30 minutes long. Whether to see the parents at the beginning or the end of the hour has significant implications. Parents usually prefer to meet at the beginning of the hour so that they can tell you about the events which have occurred since the child's last session. If you use this format, the parents may be able to provide you with information that is very helpful in planning the content of the child's session.

There are three drawbacks to this format. First, the child may feel that the parent is "telling on" him and therefore come into the session feeling quite anxious about your reaction to whatever the parent has told you. Second, the child may come to feel that your primary alliance is with the parent because you always see her or him first. The child may end up feeling that you will take the parent's side in the event of a disagreement. Third, you will never have the opportunity to give the parent any information about the nature of the child's sessions in case there is something the parent should watch for or do in the time before the next session.

The alternative is to see the parent for the last 20 minutes of the session, a format that also has drawbacks. This format may make the child feel that you are telling the parent about his session, even if you provide extensive reassurance as to the confidentiality of the material. This format may

also create a situation in which you do not find out about some very significant information until it is too late to use it in the child's session.

In spite of the problems associated with the first format, it gives you
the most information. It also sets up a situation in which the content of the
child's most recent session is "old" news, so the parent is less likely to want
to know exactly what transpired. In any case, you may want to give your
child clients, especially the older ones, the choice of how they would like
the sessions to proceed. Once you explain that the primary purpose of the
meetings is for you to find out about the child's week, they usually agree to
the first format.

Regardless of the format you select, the other significant goal of any
collateral work with the parents, besides addressing their needs and conflicts, is the formation and maintenance of a good working alliance that
supports the child's treatment, which is accomplished largely through the
active exchange of information. Except for parents who understand and accept the nature of true analytic work, it is virtually impossible to expect
parents to support, over time, a treatment protocol from which they are virtually excluded. The parents must be kept informed as to the treatment
goals, the general nature of the sessions, and the progress of the treatment.
Without this information, they are likely to become frustrated and anxious
and eventually terminate treatment.

The parents who are totally unaware of the fact that many children's
behavior gets worse with treatment before it gets better may terminate just
as the therapy is beginning to be most effective. Similarly, you cannot be effective in your work with the child if you are not fully informed as to the ongoing status of the child's behavior and ecosystem. If you do not know that
the parents are contemplating a divorce or that the maternal grandmother
has just died, you may misunderstand a great many of the changes you see
in the child's play session. The active and accurate exchange of information
between you and the parents is the single most effective way to maintain an
alliance that will support your work with the child.

Beyond simply exchanging information, it may be helpful for you
and the parent to engage in problem solving regarding some of the behaviors the child is exhibiting at home or in school. A substantial portion
of this type of work consists of developing appropriate behavior management strategies. This is certainly the case for the child whose primary
problem is poor conduct, but it may also be true for the child who is depressed, withdrawn, or even self-destructive.

It is useful to use with the parents the same problem-solving strategy
you plan to use with the child so that everyone has the same experience
base, thus allowing the parent and child to engage in problem solving on
their own when possible. The standard four-step model that you use in the
child's session is advised. Step 1 is to have the parents operationally define the problem they would like to resolve. Step 2 is to have parents
brainstorm for possible solutions to the problem. Remember that at this

stage creativity, not practicality, is the goal. Step 3 is to evaluate the solutions generated in Step 2 for their practicality and to choose the one that will be implemented. Step 4 is to implement and evaluate the effectiveness of the solution implemented. If there were problems in the implementation, then the process begins again.

Since most of the problem solving in which you engage will be directed at behavior problems, it is usually a good idea to present the parents with some basic information about behavior management. Behavioral concepts such as positive and negative reinforcement, consequences, extinction, and punishment are often poorly understood and misapplied by parents. A simple review of each concept may uncover some problems the parents are having instituting a consistent behavior management plan. A discussion of the use of natural and logical consequences may also do a lot to improve the parents' behavior management skills.

As mentioned in Chapter Nine, natural consequences are those that would occur following a child's behavior if there were no intervention. The examples given were: If you touch a hot stove you get burned, and if you do not brush your teeth, you get cavities. Parents often choose not to allow the natural consequences to occur because they think them too harsh, only to become even more harsh when imposing consequences of their own devising.

Logical consequences are those that do not occur by themselves but that follow logically from the child's behavior. Too many parents impose a consequence which makes the child feel bad regardless of whether or not that consequence is in any way related to the problem behavior. Often this consequence becomes standardized as the punishment for a wide variety of infractions. For example, many parents may routinely take away the child's television watching time. "If you don't finish your lunch, you won't watch any television." " If you hit your brother again, you won't watch any television." Not only does the consequence appear capricious, but it eventually loses its effectiveness. Logical consequences follow from the behavior. "If you don't eat some of your lunch, you will be hungry and you will not be able to eat anything else until dinner time."

> Sara's mother was truly upset by the daily battles that ensued when she tried to get 9-year-old Sara to bathe. Bath time usually became a physical struggle that exhausted both Sara and her mother.
> In talking with the therapist, the mother was able to identify the natural consequences of Sara's failing to bathe. She knew that Sara might become uncomfortable and that after a few days she would probably be ridiculed by her peers. But she feared that the teacher or the parents of the other children would think her an unfit mother. As she thought about the situation, she decided that the natural consequences were preferable to the ones she was currently imposing. She informed Sara that there would be no more battles over bathing and that when and how Sara took a bath were now her own responsibilities.

To enhance the intensity of the consequences, she added a few logical consequences as well. She informed Sara that since clean clothes would only get immediately dirty if placed on a dirty body, she would not be doing any of Sara's laundry until the day Sara chose to take a bath. She added that she would not bother to change Sara's bed until that time.

To take care of her own feelings, the mother called Sara's teacher and told her of the plan and asked if the teacher could say something special the next time Sara came to school clean.

For several days Sara did not take a bath, and the mother despaired that the intervention would have any effect. Then one morning Sara wanted to wear to school a particular shirt that had not been washed. She ranted, raved, and cried, but her mother simply repeated her intent not to wash clothes to be put on a dirty body and stayed calm. She reflected Sara's frustration while pointing out the degree of control Sara had over the whole situation. Sara finally went to school in a different shirt. She came home that evening and took a bath, during which time her mother started a load of laundry. The next morning the mother complimented Sara on her appearance but made no remark about the bath. From that point on Sara took a bath virtually every day without any reminder from her mother.

Mrs. Wilson came to therapy with a problem that had no real natural consequence. She complained that her son and, as a matter of fact, her entire family, were slobs who never picked up their things from the living room. She felt she deserved to be able to sit down in her living room at the end of the day and relax without having to look at everyone's personal belongings strewn about. The family agreed that this was a reasonable expectation but had habituated to Mrs. Wilson's nagging to the point that none of them responded unless she screamed.

Working with her son's therapist, Mrs. Wilson developed a very effective logical consequence for the problem. She obtained a large cardboard box, masking tape, and a felt pen. Then she announced to her family that she expected the living room to be clear of personal belongings by 6 o'clock each evening. Any item she found after that time would be marked with the date it was collected and placed in the box. Items could not be retrieved from the box for 5 days from the time they were collected. She also said that she would no longer nag and that she would not even alert people to the approach of the 6 o'clock deadline.

Only one item ever made it into the box. The sight of Mrs. Wilson armed with her box, tape, and felt pen sent family members scurrying to pick up. Mrs. Wilson got her clean living room and her family was relieved of her nagging.

Problem-solving approaches and behavior management often work best when combined with an educational approach. Parents who bring a child to treatment often need to be provided with a relatively large amount of information in order to work more effectively with you and their child. One of the initial points they will need to be educated about is the process of play therapy. Most treatment programs find that adequate preparation of the family is essential to continuation of the child's treatment beyond a very few sessions. Many a play therapist has been asked, in the course of treating a child, "How is just coming here and playing going to help my child get better?" Often one of the underlying questions is "Why am I paying so much for you to play, rather than work, with my child?" Play therapists often inadvertently perpetuate the myth that simply playing attentively and supportively with the child will effect a dramatic change. While this may be true to a certain extent, the covert message to the parents is often "You have not been, and are probably incapable of, playing well with your child." If this message needs to be heard by the parent, then it needs to be anything but covert.

Adequate education of the parents regarding the child's treatment ensures greater cooperation relative to all aspects of the process, from bringing the child to sessions, to supporting the therapist's work with the child, to paying the bill. At a minimum, parents should be informed of the play therapist's theoretical orientation and the pragmatics of the treatment process. The pragmatics include:

1. How often will the child be coming to sessions?
2. How long will each session be?
3. How much will each session cost?
4. Will the parent get to talk to the play therapist and if so, when and for how long?
5. What will go on during an actual session, and will the parent get to hear all about it?
6. How long will it take before treatment effects become manifest, and how will the parent know if the treatment is working?
7. What will be the duration of treatment from assessment to termination?

Some of these questions are easily answered and routinely discussed during the intake (see Chapter Six), while others are difficult to answer definitively at the outset of treatment. For example, in the case of questions regarding treatment duration, it is often wise to present the parents with an expected range so that they can begin to adjust their thinking accordingly. It is essential to keep parents informed regarding every aspect of the treatment plan and course as the work proceeds. One way of informing both the parent and child about the process of play therapy is to have them read Nemiroff and Annunziata's (1990) *A Child's First Book about Play Therapy*.

While much of the educational work with parents will focus on the treatment process itself, some parents will need to be educated regarding their child's current functioning and, where appropriate, the prognosis. This may involve educating the parent to both developmental norms and the degree or manner in which their child's pathology relates to his overall developmental functioning.

Many parents, even those who have had several children, may have some very unrealistic expectations about child development. Many do not know the norms for a child's attainment of the various developmental milestones. And many more will not have much understanding of the impact of changes in the child's cognitive functioning over time. For example, virtually everyone knows that 2-year-olds have frequent temper tantrums, but very few parents know why or how their management of those tantrums is likely to affect their child's behavior in the future. Education regarding child development may help reduce the parents' anxiety because it helps them develop appropriate expectations for their child's behavior.

Parents whose children manifest more serious or unusual disorders often need you to take an educational approach. This is usually the case when there is an interaction between the child's deficit cognitive, emotional, or behavioral functioning and another disorder, as with children who are learning-disabled, epileptic, autistic, chronically ill, or have Tourette's Syndrome. Often simultaneous referral to a support group is appropriate.

Parents whose children display fluctuations in functioning may also benefit from an educational approach. One such group of parents are those whose children can best be diagnosed as manifesting a Borderline Personality Disorder. Although there is considerable debate as to the origins of the disorder, its behavioral concomitants, and the feasibility of diagnosing it in children, many therapists have begun reporting an increase in number of their child clients who appear to fit the syndrome from a developmental perspective. These children often manifest extreme fluctuations in every aspect of their day-to-day functioning. Their affect, judgment, behavior, reality testing, and ability to tolerate separations may all be affected. When the child is fairly bright and generally high functioning, the fluctuations the parent observes can be confusing and frustrating.

One characteristic the higher functioning subgroup of Borderline children share is the tendency to do quite well at school so long as their days are very structured but to do terribly at home. The parent often reports behavior of near psychotic proportions and despairs at the fact that no one outside the home ever sees it. This discrepancy may be further exacerbated by the fact that the child may act very differently with one parent versus the other. Often it is the mother who is the focus of most of the child's acting out. For these parents, an explanation that the children experience their primary anxiety around issues of separation and individuation from the parent is often even more confusing. Why then don't they become worse when away from home? Why don't they act out more with the father? What the parents need to understand is that totally unemotional separations like going to school may not activate these children's fears, so their cognitive ability to remember that they will rejoin their families at the end of the day remains intact. At home, however, they are engaged in numerous emotional transactions with the parents and whenever these transactions become even vaguely negative, they become very anxious, fearing abandonment and often acting out in quite bizarre ways. Parents' whole attitude and style of interacting with their child can change when they can see that their child's behavior is driven by anxiety rather than oppositionality.

Bibliotherapy can be a very efficient way to convey a large amount of pragmatic information to a parent without using session time. Many good books on a broad range of topics ranging from coping with chronic illness, to alcoholism, to divorce are available to parents and children. Unfortunately, very few books about children's psychopathology are written with the pragmatic perspective parents find so helpful, so it is up to you or someone you designate to translate the mass of available information into something the parent can use.

Finally, many parents benefit from education in specific parenting skills. There are many parent training programs available; see Parent Effectiveness Training (Gordon, 1970), Systematic Training for Effective Parenting (Dinkmeyer & McKay, 1982), and Active Parenting (Popkin, 1983), for example. All you need do is find a program that meets the needs of the parents with whom you are working and proceed to implement it.

Some parents need more than problem solving or educational interventions if their child is to benefit from play therapy. For these parents, therapeutic interventions may be very useful. Three different ways the parents can become involved in a therapeutic approach include: (1) having the parent(s) function as the child's therapist(s) under your supervision; (2) including the parents in joint or family sessions with the child; and (3) involving the parents in individual or couples therapy of their own parallel to the child's treatment.

The Parents as the Child's Therapists

A number of techniques involve the parents directly in the child's treatment. One of the most traditional is filial therapy (Andronico, Fidler, Guerney, & Guerney, 1967; Guerney, 1964). Another technique that involves parents directly in the treatment of their children is Theraplay (Jernberg, 1979).

Parents may be involved in their child's treatment in whatever manner the therapist can devise. The parents may sit in on some sessions or may observe sessions with or without a commentator to help them process what they are observing. The parents might be included in specific structured activities with their child. Alternatively, parents might be assigned tasks to accomplish with the child between sessions.

One assignment that is useful with virtually all parents and their children is the institution of Special Time at home. The concept is quite simple: to noncontingently provide the child daily with 10 to 20 minutes of parent contact time over which he has complete control. The concept is based on the notion that many children's symptoms involve secondary gain in the form of obtaining parental attention and creating, in the child, a sense of control over the environment. Interventions that provide those reinforcers without waiting for the child to display symptoms can potentially be very effective.

The parent should set aside approximately 15 minutes a day for the child, during which time the parent is to be completely and totally focused on meeting the child's needs as he communicates them. The child is encouraged to ask the parent to engage in any activity he enjoys. The only limitations are that the activity must be safe, possible (financially, logistically, and so on), and that it be something which can be completed in 15 minutes. The time limit is strictly enforced, to prevent either the parent or child from skipping nights and then doing a 1-hour make up session. The only aspects of Special Time that the parent controls are when it begins and when it ends. The key elements are the parent's undivided attention and the fact that the child controls the activities in which they are to engage.

A parent should be encouraged to label the time and develop cues for its beginning and ending. Some parents simply call it (Child's name) Time and set a kitchen timer to mark the beginning; the ring of the timer marks the end. In other parent/child dyads, defining the time is much more of a ritual, such as unplugging the telephone and retreating to a designated space in the house, based on the child's needs. Some parents may need to practice their Special Time roles in a play session with the child in order to learn to give up their control and to be fully oriented to the child's needs.

Parents often raise many questions or complaints in response to the recommendation that they institute Special Time. One is that they simply do not have the time to do it every day. This concern can usually be addressed by having them review their daily schedule and helping identify a block of time that is open or an activity that could be replaced with Special Time. Some parents may simply extend the child's normal bedtime ritual by 15 minutes, others may decide to eliminate one television show, while still others may decide that it is easiest to get up 15 minutes earlier in the morning. If a parent seriously resists committing to even 10 minutes a day and you believe that the resistance is based solely on the time issue, then you must consider the probability that there are very serious problems in the parent/child relationship and you should begin questioning the parent's ability to adequately care for the child. In such a situation, it appears that the first order of therapy is to address this problem in some form of family therapy rather than trying to work with the child individually.

Other parents resist by saying that they already spend considerably more than 15 minutes a day devoting themselves to their child. This may be a very realistic appraisal, in which case it is important to let them know that they do not necessarily need to add time to what they are already doing but simply to label one 15-minute block Special Time. Explain the need for doing this in terms of the young child's need for concrete labels in order to recognize objects and events. Many parents can recall some event along the order of the following:

> Joe took his son, Tim, out to do some Christmas shopping. At lunch they stopped at a fast-food restaurant, and Joe, in the spirit of the season, allowed Tim to get a large ice cream sundae with his lunch. Now this was clearly not

something that Joe would allow at home, and he considered himself to have given Joe a major treat, although he did not label it as such. A little while later Tim saw a store window full of candy and began to plead for some.

Tim: "Just this time. For a special treat, please?"

Joe: "No. You already had a treat."

Tim: "What treat?"

Joe: "Remember you had a sundae?"

Tim: "That wasn't a treat, that was lunch. You didn't say I couldn't have anything else if I had a sundae. If you had I wouldn't have eaten it. I didn't really want it. I wanted to get some candy."

In this example, everyone gets stuck, largely because the father's need to feel generous is allowed to override the child's need to have some input as to how he would like to have his needs met. Joe becomes angry because he feels that Tim did not appreciate the sundae, and Tim becomes angry because he could not have candy. The problem could have been avoided if the sundae had been clearly labeled as a treat—the idea being that only one treat that day would be presented—and Tim had been given some choice in the matter.

All these factors need to be very clear when instituting Special Time if it is to have the desired effect. Once they have instituted Special Time, many parents are dismayed at the fact that they may have spent an entire day taking a child to the zoo or the circus, only to find that the child reminds them that they have not yet done Special Time later that afternoon. This reflects the child's need for the time as well as his difficulty in consistently recognizing the time spent with the parent and its value.

Some parents worry about giving their child total control over anything, much less 15 minutes of their time. What if the child wants to do something dangerous, ridiculous, or disgusting? Obviously, dangerous activities are not to be allowed, but most ridiculous or disgusting activities are not without their merits.

One mother reported that after doing Special Time with her 8-year-old son for about 2 weeks, he asked to spend the entire time burping. Since the mother had often complained that she found burping offensive, she realized that the son was testing her commitment to doing what he wanted to do. Wisely, she agreed, and her son did indeed spend 15 minutes burping, creating various sounds and tunes as he did so. During his play session that week, the son cheerfully reported that his mother had actually let him burp for one of his Special Times. He responded positively to interpretations, noting the fact that he must feel that mom really meant what she said about Special Time being his. He then spontaneously reported that he would not do it again because it had used up all his time that particular day and not really had a chance to play with his mother.

Parents also ask whether or not they should do 15 minutes on days when the child is behaving very badly. They should be reminded that this time is to be noncontingent—after all, even a bad child deserves

15 minutes of parental attention a day. A parent can be encouraged to wait until he catches the child between episodes of negative acting out but to go ahead and offer the time no matter what happens during the day. However, the idea of a noncontingency does not apply should the child begin to act out during Special Time. If the child becomes aggressive or loses control, then the parent should calmly end Special Time for that day, reminding the child that they will have time again the next day. If the acting out continues, then the parent should engage in his usual forms of limit setting.

Finally, parents ask what they should do if all the children in the family want Special Time or if the child wants Special Time with both parents. Here flexibility and creativity should be encouraged to ensure that every child who wants Special Time can have it every day. Some families have arranged it so that half the children have Special Time with the father one night while the others have it with the mother. The following night the routine is reversed. Others have arranged for the child to have Special Time with each parent each night.

Occasionally, a child will be so passive that he genuinely cannot think of anything to do during his Special Time. In this case, the parent may offer a list of possibilities but should not do anything until the child has at least indicated a preference. When listing activities, parents should be encouraged to mention those that are not particularly goal-oriented and are noncompetitive, including things like blowing and chasing bubbles, tickling, wrestling, feeding each other dry cereal, drawing a picture of each other, playing hide-and-seek, having a water pistol fight, and having a pillow fight. The idea is to be with the child, to engage in interactive rather than parallel play.

Special Time is useful with virtually all children, but it can be especially valuable as a precursor to having the parent institute more rigid behavioral controls. A parent who will be setting limits on his child's physical aggression might be asked to record a baseline of the aggressive behavior for 1 week and to begin Special Time as a way of inoculating the relationship with the child against the stress that will be produced when the parent starts to more rigidly enforce limits.

When you recommend something to the parents that the child will perceive as positive, always do so when the child is not present. The information should then be conveyed to the child by the parents rather than the play therapist, to allow the child to see the parents as good, in and of themselves, rather than seeing them as simply yielding to the control of the good therapist.

Conjoint Parent/Child Sessions

The therapeutic strategies discussed so far have involved the parents in their child's therapy in, more or less, the role of a therapist. Sometimes it is useful to have the parent directly involved in the child's treatment in more of a client role through the use of joint or family therapy sessions. This technique allows the parent and child to be in similar roles relative to the therapist and may promote more of an alliance between them. A complete discussion of family therapy, play or otherwise, is beyond the scope of this volume, so we turn our attention instead to the conduct of joint sessions with one or both parents and the child.

The format for conducting this type of work was briefly discussed in Chapter Six. The session is divided into a 15-minute session with the parent and child, a 15-minute session with the parent alone, and a 30-minute session with the child alone. With this format, the therapist uses the joint 15-minute session to help the parent and child engage in social problem solving using incidents that have occurred since the last play session. The 15-minute session with the parent alone is used to review the status of the family and the parent's perceptions of the child's functioning. The time with the child is then used to conduct a standard play session.

> Mrs. Thomas and Penny, her 9-year-old daughter, entered treatment because of Penny's extreme separation anxiety. Over time it became apparent that Penny and her mother often had significant arguments that were largely the result of misunderstanding each other's intentions. Three-part sessions were instituted so that these arguments could become the target of intervention without subsuming the content of the play sessions.
>
> The joint portion of the session started with Mrs. Thomas and Penny each describing their version of one of the arguments they had during the week. They then engaged in problem solving guided by the therapist. The incidents they chose to work on ranged from arguments about completion of homework to Penny's peer problems to conflicts between the parents as to how to respond to Penny's behavior. With the therapist's assistance, they were usually able to empathize with each other's view of the problem and to reach realistic compromise solutions.
>
> Mrs. Thomas' 15-minute sessions varied in their focus. Sometimes they were educational in nature, aimed at enhancing her parenting skills or her understanding of Penny's psychopathology. Sometimes the sessions were largely supportive, aimed at empathizing with Mrs. Thomas' experience of strain as a result of trying to parent a very difficult child. And sometimes the sessions focused on the latest conflicts between Mrs. Thomas and her husband and the impact of these events on Penny's behavior.
>
> Penny was then able to use her play sessions to focus on issues other than the arguments she might have had with her mother. In general, her sessions involved themes of separation, fear of criticism, and her need for a great deal of attention and nurturance from adults.

This format had the added advantage of providing a concrete way of reinforcing appropriate boundaries between Mrs. Thomas and her daughter. They could separate out the problems that were theirs, those that were Mrs. Thomas', and those that were Penny's.

Very often, as the play therapist interacts with a client's parents it becomes evident that the parents could benefit from treatment of their own. Further, it is easy to slip into the role of providing this treatment without overtly contracting to do so. Initially, you are seeing the parent for 15 to 20 minutes each week, and your conversations focus on the child and his treatment. Gradually, you find that the parent's time has expanded to 30 to 40 minutes and that the content primarily, if not exclusively, focuses on the parent and his difficulties unrelated to the child. At this point you may become angry at the parent for using up the child's time and attempt to set limits that only alienate the parent, often to the point of feeling abandoned. The net result may be that the parent terminates treatment for both himself and the child.

This situation can be relatively easily addressed if you follow some simple rules from the outset. First, set the parent's time and stick to it, no matter how important the content of a particular session may seem. If this decision becomes a problem, remind the parent that the treatment contract is to provide for the child, which requires maintaining the length of each of the child's treatment sessions. Second, always clearly identify when the parent has moved onto something that is an issue of his separate from his interactions with the child (Chetik, 1989). While recognizing these issues, it is important to empathize with the parent and to recognize the importance of a given issue while stressing that your primary task is to address parent/child interactions. It is easy to become enmeshed in the view that anything which affects the parent affects the child. This is to some extent true, but it is also true that all families should have appropriate boundaries which shield the child from some of the parent's experience. If it becomes apparent that you are relabeling material on a regular basis, then it is time to suggest that the parent seek treatment for himself. Here you should reflect how often parental issues arise, how important they are, and that the time limitations of a collateral session seem to prevent the parent from having these issues addressed and his needs met in the way he deserves.

Parallel Individual/Couples Treatment of the Parent(s)

Finally, you may face the possibility of a request from the parent to provide his individual treatment yourself. This is a fairly natural outcome if you have developed and maintained a good working alliance with the parent from the outset. The decision as to whether or not to do this is best based on your perception of your ability to meet the needs of both the child and parent as clients while maintaining appropriate boundaries. If you have been able to accomplish this throughout the initial collateral work, it is likely that you will be able to continue to be effective while seeing the parent and child separately. If, however, these issues have been problematic during the collateral work, there is little to suggest that separate sessions will bring about a significant improvement.

Peter, a 10-year-old boy, was being treated within the context of a residential program for children with severe behavior problems. Peter was extremely withdrawn, dependent, and engaged in some autisticlike behaviors. During the course of Peter's stay, it was discovered that his mother was terribly involved in controlling Peter's bowel movements, asserting that without such intervention he would have serious symptoms.

The mother wanted the staff to administer laxatives and enemas during the week, while she would continue them when Peter was home on weekends. The staff did not comply and did not note any problems with Peter's bowel functioning during the week. A medical workup revealed no problems, and the mother was informed that she should immediately cease her ministration during Peter's home visits. The possibility of referring this case to Child Protective Services as abusive was entertained, but a plan to attempt collateral treatment of the mother and son was determined to be a better first step.

Peter's individual play therapy sessions, which had been initiated earlier, did not change. They continued to be rather unstructured and geared toward helping him become more spontaneous and interpersonally interactive. Initially, the time with the mother was geared toward channeling her intrusive involvement in her child's bowel functioning into other, more productive interactions. The therapist assumed that she had a great desire to help her child and would readily become involved in nonbowel-related tasks. Instead the mother resisted every step of the way, constantly attempting to resume the laxatives and enemas. Gradually, it became apparent that this was a very narcissistic woman who derived most of her sense of self-esteem from her ability to parent. Unfortunately, her idea of good parenting was the establishment of total control over her child. She did not appear emotionally invested in him other than for the sense of accomplishment she could derive from her ministrations.

The therapist then took a different tack in the collateral sessions and began to powerfully empathize with the lack of reinforcement this mother received from her son and her need for such feedback. He identified that not only could she not control Peter's bowels, but that he was not appreciative when she tried. He identified that having the boy sleep in her room with her did not provide her with any of the gratification she might get from a relationship with an adult male. He identified how her fearing that this child was totally unable to care for himself kept her at home full-time and prevented her from getting any of her adult interpersonal needs met. As this focus continued, the mother shifted from talking about her son's difficulties to talking about her own frustrations and disappointments with having such an impaired child. She also identified that it was guilt which kept her so overwhelmingly involved in her son's life.

Peter's therapist continuously recognized these as important issues for the mother while noting that they were beyond the scope of a 20-minute session each week. After considerable direction and hand-holding, the mother sought her own treatment. At this point Peter's therapist began to help her clarify which issues were directly child-related and therefore appropriately discussed during the collateral sessions and which were more intrapsychic and therefore more appropriate for discussion with her own therapist.

As these boundaries became clearer and the mother was able to get some of her needs met through her therapy, her need to control her child abated considerably. She was able to stop administering laxatives and enemas. She was able to allow him to fix simple meals for himself, to have a room of his own, and to insist that he sleep in his own bed at night. She was even able to allow him to play outside with children from the neighborhood and to spend the night with a friend. As she loosened her controls, she discovered that her child was much more competent than she had assumed. She also found that she now had time to get some of her interpersonal needs met elsewhere. The relationship between mother and son began to approach normalcy, and both were very pleased.

CASE EXAMPLE: AARON

The collateral work with Aaron's parents was extensive. The weekly sessions were split. During the mother's portion of the session, the therapist worked in several different ways. Part of the time was used to share information about Aaron's progress; part of the time involved educating the mother about the normative behavior of six-year-old children so that she could judge the changes in Aaron's behavior over the course of treatment in context. Part of the time was also spent educating her as to how a preoperational child like Aaron processed information. This was done to facilitate her talking to him about his father's illness. She had, for example, never considered the possibility that Aaron might fear that his father's illness was contagious. Finally, some of the time was spent providing support for the mother as she attempted to cope with extremely stressful life circumstances.

Aaron's mother was also directly involved in Aaron's treatment for the seventh through the tenth and final session. During these sessions, the mother gradually took over the therapist's role while the therapist acted as her coach. During the seventh session, she and Aaron duplicated the chocolate pudding/finger painting the therapist had done with Aaron in the sixth session. During the eighth session, they planned some noncompetitive games that involved them feeding one another. Each would close their eyes and try to guess what the other was feeding them. Each would see if they could tell the foods apart by touch or smell. During this session, they engaged in a lot of rough-and-tumble play as well. In preparation for termination, the therapist asked Aaron and his mother to bring from home a game they enjoyed so that they could play it in the office for the ninth session. They brought a developmentally appropriate board game that Aaron played without his usual rigidity and without becoming upset when he lost. Both mother and son were instructed to verbalize their feelings about the game as they played.

During these sessions, the therapist had begun to hold sessions with the mother and the father by phone. These sessions were initiated when it became apparent that the father was somewhat threatened by Aaron's growing attachment to both the therapist and a male nurse who had been hired to come in each day to help with the father's care. During these phone sessions, the therapist and parents brainstormed ways the father could remain actively engaged with Aaron as his physical health continued to deteriorate. In the 10 weeks since treatment had begun, the father had stopped reading a nightly story to Aaron because he no longer had the energy to talk for more than a few minutes at a time. The result of these telephone contacts was that the father decided to come for the final session and be a part of celebrating the gains which Aaron had made. This was a heroic and expensive undertaking because transportation had to be arranged through a paramedic unit.

CASE EXAMPLE: FRANK

Neither of Frank's biologic parents were available to be involved in any collateral work. Limited collateral work was initiated with the woman who ran the group home Frank resided in and with the woman who ran the home he was moved to upon discharge. In both cases, the interventions consisted primarily of supportive work, during which information about Frank's functioning was shared. Some problem solving with respect to the development of appropriate behavior management strategies was also conducted.

Frank's previous therapist had conducted extensive collateral work with Frank's foster mother, including joint sessions that focused on facilitating the parent/child attachment and subsequently directly involving the foster mother in Frank's treatment. Split sessions were used to educate the foster mother as to the nature of Frank's posttraumatic reactions and potential intervention strategies she could employ. Split sessions were also used to provide support and crisis intervention services when Frank's aggression was extreme.

COLLATERAL WORK WITH SCHOOL PERSONNEL

Aside from the time children spend at home with their parents, the time they spend in school is the most significant portion of their day. School can play a role in triggering and maintaining pathologic behavior in children, or it can be a part of the solution to the child's problem. If school staff or the child's peers react negatively to the changes therapy produces in the child's behavior, then continued improvement will be very difficult to attain. If the school supports the changes the child makes, the child is likely to rapidly progress toward health. Because of school's impact on the child's mental health, interventions that positively effect the child's school experience can significantly enhance the child's overall progress in therapy.

CASE EXAMPLE: AARON

Aaron's therapist had no direct contact with Aaron's school. Instead, Aaron's mother contacted his classroom teacher and explained that Aaron was in therapy and asked her to be tolerant if Aaron's behavior deteriorated temporarily. Fortunately, the teacher was very supportive and said that she would not mind at all if Aaron acted out a little; in fact, she felt she could encourage him to be a little more playful.

CASE EXAMPLE: FRANK

Because Frank was in a residential facility, interventions in his school program were relatively easy to accomplish. The therapist consulted with the school personnel in a number of areas. First, he provided the staff with information about Frank's overall functioning and the impact of his history on his development and his present response patterns. Second, he worked with the staff to plan an educational program that would emphasize Frank's social and emotional development without stressing him to the point of excessive acting out. Last, and most importantly, he worked with Frank's teacher to develop a series of classroom interventions that would facilitate Frank's growth in therapy and the generalization of those improvements.

Frank was lucky enough to have a teacher who was very open to becoming directly involved in Frank's treatment. She had individual sessions with Frank for two ½-hour periods each day. During those sessions, she repeated many of the corrective experiences the therapist had implemented during the week, mainly highly physically interactive experiences designed to build Frank's level of trust. The teacher's interactions balanced the therapist's interactions by giving Frank a female with whom he could interact in a highly structured yet nurturant way. The teacher also pulled for the processing of additional historical material because her first name was the same as that of Frank's biologic mother. Because the therapist and teacher were able to work so closely together, it was as if Frank were receiving treatment at least five times a week.

COLLATERAL WORK WITH MEDICAL PROFESSIONALS

When treating children with concomitant medical problems, you may have to communicate with the medical professionals who are treating the child. It is critical that you understand the impact a child's illness may have on his behavior.

Many chronic illnesses have a powerful impact on children. One therapist reported that a group of severe asthmatic children, aged 6 to 12, with whom he worked had all entertained thoughts of suicide. The children said that they knew that their condition might someday kill them, and sometimes it seemed better to decide for yourself when you would die than to have your condition decide for you.

The child's illness will affect the child differently at different stages of development. Level III children who develop diabetes are likely to resent their disease and be afraid of injections should they be needed, but they tend to adapt fairly quickly. Level IV adolescent diabetics, on the other hand, tend to act as if they are impervious to the long-term effects of their illness and to ignore their symptoms on a day-to-day basis. They will eat what they want when they want and then play with their insulin dose in an attempt to counteract their sugar intake.

It may also be very important for medical professionals to understand the effect that a particular form of psychopathology may have on a child's response to illness or a given medical procedure.

COLLATERAL WORK WITH REPRESENTATIVES OF THE LEGAL SYSTEM

The legal system is one of the other subsystems of the child's ecosystem in which you may be asked, or need, to intervene. Unfortunately, the role of legal advocate is one for which very few mental health professionals are well prepared. Additionally, the legal system tends to operate from a set of basic assumptions that are very different from those of the mental health system. As one judge said, "Mental health professionals often become enraged at judges who do not act, as they see it, in the best interests of the child in a given case. What they do not understand is that the judge is there, not to protect the child or any other individual, but to ensure that the rules of the legal system are followed to the last detail." Although there are significant differences between family court proceedings, which are much more relaxed than criminal court proceedings, the fact is that even family court judges have very little background in child development, child psychopathology, family systems, or any of the other knowledge bases which would make it easier to act in the child's best interest. Even attorneys who are assigned child welfare cases usually do not have much knowledge about what makes the children they represent tick.

The overlap between psychology and the law may be an area in which a new group of professionals may be trained at some point in the future. This would be a great boon to the thousands of children who enter the legal system each year. An excellent example of such training for professionals involved in making custody decisions is presented in *The Best Interests of the Child* (Goldstein, Solnit, Goldstein, & Freud, 1996). Until specialists in child mental health and the law come into their own, therapists who work with children may occasionally find themselves pulled into an advocacy role.

Henry was 5 years old when he witnessed his mother stab and kill the woman he considered his primary caretaker. This woman had been living with Henry, his brother, and mother for at least a year and had assumed many of the childcare responsibilities in that time. The killing was apparently the result of a domestic argument. When the police arrived, Henry led them to the place where his mother had hidden the knife she had used in the killing. Henry and his brother were placed in a foster home while their mother awaited trial. After several weeks, Henry was placed in treatment because he was failing to adjust to his placement and was acting out aggressively.

When the mother's trial began, Henry's therapist inadvertently discovered that the district attorney who was prosecuting the mother intended to have Henry testify against his mother. The therapist protested that this was inhumane; one spouse cannot be forced to testify against the other, why should a child be forced to testify against his mother? What impact would this have on future interactions between Henry and his mother? When the therapist called the district attorney's office and asked who was supposed to represent the child's interest in this situation, they responded that no one was usually appointed to represent the rights of witnesses because they were not thought to be in jeopardy. However, they acknowledged that if someone were to represent the child, it would be an appointee from their office. Further, they acknowledged the fact that this might create a conflict of interest, in which case they would appoint an outside attorney.

Following the phone call, the therapist wrote letters pleading the child's case to the child's caseworker, the mother's attorney, the district attorney, the family court judge, and the criminal court judge involved with the case. Several days later, the child was dropped from the witness list, not because it was in his interest but because the therapist had revealed that the child's IQ was in the mildly retarded range, rendering him a virtually incompetent witness in terms of a criminal proceeding.

CASE EXAMPLE: FRANK

Since Frank was a ward of the state, considerable collateral work had to be done with Child Protective Services. Although Frank's CPS social worker was to serve as his primary advocate and had full legal power to make all "parenting" decisions on his behalf, the fact is that she was also a state employee who had to work within the system. The duality of her role became apparent at times when precipitous decisions were made to change Frank's placements to suit his caretakers rather than to serve Frank's interests. Only considerable collateral work by Frank's two therapists over the years prevented or delayed some of these moves.

As work with the client and his caretakers produces changes in the child's behavior and ecosystem, the work of the therapy turns to promoting the stabilization and generalization of the improvement being made. When the treatment goals have been attained and the child and his ecosystem seem stabilized, it is time to begin the termination process.

CHAPTER THIRTEEN

Termination

The last questions to be considered in conducting play therapy involve termination. The two central questions are: How does one know when it is time to terminate therapy? How should termination be effected?

Ideally, termination should occur when the goals that were developed at intake are achieved. This sounds like a very obvious point, but it is usually not as simple a decision as it seems it should be. One complicating factor may be that the treatment goals have evolved and changed since the treatment began. Therapy may uncover additional material that needs to be worked through. Children are not always able to discuss everything that has contributed to their condition at the time they enter treatment. Often, like adults, they simply do not know what is the matter. For example, children may reveal that they have been the victims of abuse once they come to sense the safety of the playroom and their relationship with the therapist.

The goals for a child's treatment may also change if the child enters a new developmental level while she is in therapy. Her capability of classifying information and experience in new ways will create a need to reprocess her experience in a manner consistent with her current level of understanding. This does not mean that a child who has experienced a traumatic event should be in treatment until she enters adulthood; it does mean that adults should be sensitive to the child's changing needs over time.

Colleen was 2 years old when she drank enough lye to severely burn her throat, esophagus, and stomach. Prior to the accident, she was described as a very active and precocious toddler who was very independent, clearly a child in the early phase of Level II development. The accident caused her to be hospitalized for 6 weeks. During this time she was fed through a tube that went directly into her stomach and forced to stay very still in her bed. Twice she was subjected to very painful procedures which stretched her esophagus so that the scar tissue which was forming did not seal it off. She was totally helpless. Her Preoperational thinking led her to understand, in spite of what adults told her, that she had been a very bad girl and now she was being punished by having very bad things done to her. She also decided that it was not good to explore the world because it was obviously full of hidden dangers from which adults could not protect you. After she healed, Colleen's behavior remained controlled, passive, and dependent.

When Colleen entered Level IV thinking at age 9, she began to understand that it was not all exploratory behavior that was bad, just toddler-like curiosity. Her increased awareness of the world led her to see an ever increasing number of hidden dangers and to even more passive behavior. She became hypervigilant with her younger sibling who was now 2½ years old.

When Colleen entered Level V and began to experience some pressure from her peers to become more independent, she instead became more clingy and stayed at home more. She compared the exploratory behavior of her preadolescent peers to the exploratory behavior in which she had engaged as a toddler and decided that it too was very dangerous.

With each developmental advance, Colleen did not gain perspective on what happened to her; instead, she generalized the initial traumatic experience and developed more intense symptoms. Unfortunately, the treatment which was initiated at the time of the accident was not maintained long enough to assure that Colleen had really worked through her experience.

In the event that the child's environment continues to be toxic, exposing her to new insults, long-term or repeated treatment may be indicated, which is often the case when the child is a victim of in-home abuse. Unfortunately, the child welfare system's ability to protect children is considerably less than optimal and the chances of a child being exposed to ongoing abuse are very high. In these situations, treatment is aimed at inoculating the child against the environmental stress so that she eventually becomes able to tolerate it or manage it on her own.

An alternative to planning the termination once the treatment goals have been attained is to preplan the termination date. This is an advantageous approach when the goals of the treatment are fairly circumscribed, when there is a limited amount of time available to either the therapist or the child, or when the caretaker's motivation to follow through with the child's treatment seems low.

In either of the first two situations, you can develop a treatment contract based on a preset termination date or a set number of sessions. The latter approach is more reasonable because children tend to miss a fair number of sessions due to illness. Short-term interventions planned around 8, 10, or 12 sessions can be very effective and produce long-term changes in the child's behavior. The typical course of Theraplay (Jernberg, 1979; Jernberg & Booth, 1999) is designed around an 8-session frame, while the play group described in Part IV is designed as a 12-session intervention.

When the therapist will be available only for a set period of time, it is critical that both the child and the child's caretakers be aware of this limitation. This situation is common in settings that train therapists, as the student's or intern's rotation may be only a year or less. It is advisable that the date of the therapist's departure be made clear even when there will be the option of transferring the child to another therapist if the treatment goals have not been achieved. Making the clients aware of the potential limits of the treatment is essential if the client is to provide truly informed consent. Further, even if the decision is to proceed with treatment, it seems that the child should have the right to limit her involvement in treatment if she feels that the overall length of treatment is too short.

Another option, which works well when the caretaker's motivation seems limited, is to develop a renewable treatment contract. The initial contract between you, the child, and the child's caretaker might specify that the need for treatment will be evaluated at six-session intervals. If, at any of the reevaluation points, the decision is to terminate treatment, then two termination sessions will be scheduled. In other words, you will see the child for a total of 8, 14, 20, and so on sessions. This type of reevaluation schedule can help maintain everyone's sense of involvement and progress even when the treatment is planned as a long-term process from the outset.

The length of long-term treatment may vary considerably, depending on your theoretical orientation, the facility in which you work, and the type of children and families who make up your caseload. Many therapists consider eight to ten sessions a long-term case; others do not see 2 years or more of treatment as excessive. Given a comprehensive approach to play therapy, the completion of eight therapy sessions following the intake and assessment sessions seems to be the minimum time required to make an effective intervention. At the other end of the continuum, it is unlikely that a child should be in therapy for more than 2 years if the interventions being conducted are optimally effective. There will be exceptions at both ends of the spectrum.

This brings us to the issue of terminating a child's treatment not because she has attained her goals or because therapy has been of long duration and it is time to see if the child can make it on her own, but because there is no evidence of progress. This is an extremely difficult and yet ethically necessary decision. How long after the child ceases to make progress should you continue to see her in treatment before recommending either termination or transfer to another therapist? The answer should only be partially dependent on the nature of the child's pathology. In most cases, if the child goes eight to ten sessions, or one of the reevaluation intervals set in the initial contract, without making any discernible progress, then termination or transfer should be considered.

There are two likely exceptions to this rule. One exception occurs in the treatment of children whose primary referral problem involves failure to develop significant interpersonal attachments. In these cases it may take some time for the child to develop enough of a relationship with you to allow the work of the therapy to begin. Further, termination or transfer of the child may exacerbate rather than alleviate the symptom of attachment failure. The other exception occurs in the treatment of children whose environment continues to be toxic. These children may not progress in therapy in the usual sense; instead, they are maintained by therapy. They may reach an acceptable level of functioning in a fairly short time but need to continue with treatment in order to maintain those gains in the face of ongoing stresses.

Whether to terminate a child's therapy or to transfer her to another therapist in the face of minimal progress is a decision that you must very carefully weigh. If the child is terminated, will she feel that she has failed at therapy and been rejected by you? If this is a likely outcome, then you must consider what can be done to ameliorate this situation. Perhaps one very small goal could be set and therapy terminated once it is achieved. Perhaps a few sessions spent reviewing and celebrating the progress the child did make will provide for a better ending. Whatever the case, the child should not leave therapy feeling that you simply do not like her anymore. In other words, no matter how badly the therapy has progressed, the child must feel that she has, in some small way, succeeded and that you and she have ended your work together amicably. Although this may not be possible, especially if the child's caretakers are angry or disappointed, it is certainly the desirable outcome.

Once the decision to terminate therapy has been reached, it is crucial that termination be thought of as an essential part of the treatment process, not just an inevitable and unpleasant event. From the child's point of view, termination makes very little sense. Children enter the therapy relationship at a point when they are experiencing particular difficulties. They learn to trust and rely on you, and then, as they begin to feel considerably better, you end the relationship. To avoid this kind of an effect, you must do considerable planning well before terminating the relationship. When it is well planned, the termination can be as much of a corrective experience for the child as any other part of the process.

The implementation of an effective termination process depends on the child's having a realistic understanding of the nature of her relationship with you. The child must understand that this is a work- or goal-oriented relationship which differs significantly from any other relationship in which she will ever enter. She must understand that you are an ally, not a friend, parent, or peer. The development of a clear contract at the outset of the treatment greatly facilitates this differentiation. In the same way that you will review that contract with the child's caretaker at various intervals, you should also review the contract with the child. She may not be able or willing to enter into a contract at the outset of treatment, but you should be constantly alert to opportunities to establish goals on which you and the child can agree.

If the child is made aware of the goals of the treatment fairly early, her awareness can be maintained through your use of interpretations. The way you and the child interact will be different from the way the child interacts with other adults in her environment, but maybe not dramatically so. It is interpretations that differentiate the therapeutic relationship from all others. No other adult in the child's life will limit their verbalizations to this peculiar form, and the child cannot help but become aware of this over time. In addition, if at least occasionally your interpretations draw connections between the problems for which the child entered treatment and both her current and past behavior, then the working nature of the relationship will be further reinforced.

If the child can be helped to understand that the therapy relationship is a working one, then she can also be involved in appraising her progress toward meeting those goals. These appraisals should occur on a regular basis, certainly at intervals of no more than 6 to 8 weeks. As the time for termination approaches, your reflections of the child's gains should become more frequent. You should also begin to verbally reinforce the child's gains, noting that the need for the two of you to continue working together will soon come to an end. This procedure desensitizes the child to the idea of the relationship ending because it warns her of the inevitable.

As the child is alerted to the impending end of therapy, it is time to either set a termination date or to announce the number of sessions remaining. The lower the child's developmental level, the more concrete the cues that signal the end of therapy should be. The date can be circled on a calendar and the passing days crossed off as the date approaches. Alternatively, you might set out one candy for each of the child's remaining sessions, allowing her to eat one at the end of each session. The longer the child has been in treatment, the more sessions should be allowed for termination.

The length of the termination process must be proportional to the length of children's treatment because you must expect children to recapitulate the main elements of their therapy. That is, children tend to replay their therapy in a condensed form as it draws to a close. This does not always happen, but it happens often enough that you should plan for it. Children who have not engaged in regressed, infantile behavior since the very beginning of their therapy may suddenly want to be held and nurtured once again. The real problem is that children also tend to repeat their negative reaction phase, if only briefly. Why recapitulation occurs is not entirely clear, but it seems that the threat of the loss of the therapeutic relationship triggers sudden and massive regression. The children engage in the behaviors which brought them to therapy in the first place in an attempt to convince you that you are still needed. Therapists who are not aware of how common this process is are frequently convinced by the sudden resurgence of the child's acting out that therapy should continue, only to find that the child is doing just fine again within a couple of weeks.

Recapitulation is managed quite easily if it is actively interpreted. The child's anxiety and feelings of loss should be reflected, as should her hope that she can find a way to prevent the termination. Following the increased intensity of interpretation that is needed to bring the child successfully through the recapitulation process, the work of the therapy should turn to working through the child's reaction to this separation as compared to separations in her past through genetic interpretations. Finally, you should spend some time reviewing the major discoveries and changes the child has made since treatment began. Initially, you should deliver these observations in a format similar to, if not identical to, previous interpretations, to allow the child to see the review as part of the work. While interpretation is essential to the management of the recapitulation process, it is also important that you begin shifting the nature of your role somewhat as the relationship draws to a close. Stop bringing in new tasks; instead, join with the child in celebrating the gains she has made over the course of the treatment.

This is not the time to relax the boundaries of the therapeutic relationship. You want to leave therapy as the child's therapist, not as the child's friend. Maintaining your role ensures that you will be able to continue work through the child's response to the termination to the very end. It also ensures that the child will be able to return to therapy with you should that become necessary at some point in the future.

As the child is able to put her feelings about termination in perspective, then the work done in the child's sessions should rapidly decrease. Just as you would not offer a significant interpretation in the last few minutes of a given therapy session because the child would not have time to process it, so too you should not be uncovering new material as therapy draws to a close.

However and whenever treatment draws to an end, part or all of the last session should be a true celebration of the child's progress over the course of the treatment, to both foster the child's sense of accomplishment and provide a clear ending ceremony. Along this order, there are questions about continuity of contact with the child after the therapy is over. Should the child be able to visit, call, or write you? Should you plan a follow-up? Should non-therapy contacts between you and the child occur? For the most part, the end of treatment should be the end. On the other hand, the child and her caretakers should be aware that a return to therapy is possible if the child needs it. To this end, it is very reasonable to give the child your business address and telephone number so that she can contact you in the future if needed. One of the easiest and most professional ways to do this is to give the child one of your business cards.

ENDING THE TREATMENT

CASE EXAMPLE: AARON

STAGE: TERMINATION

Stage Goals: Aaron will:

1. Maintain a strong sense of attachment to his mother and will be better able to ask to have his needs for nurturance met.
2. A secondary goal of maintaining Aaron's attachment to his father was added at termination, in hopes that Aaron would not prematurely grieve and separate from his father.

Session 10

Participants: Aaron, the therapist, and Aaron's mother and father.

Materials: Cupcakes and juice brought by Aaron and his parents.

Experiential Components: At the beginning of the last session, Aaron was giddy with excitement. He helped push his father's wheelchair into the playroom and set about showing him the room and explaining that this was where he and his mother and therapist had done all the activities he had told his father about. The beginning of the session focused on a review of the content of Aaron's sessions and the progress he had made. There were several very painful points in this process at which the fears everyone had about the father's health were discussed, but the family processed the discussion beautifully. The session then turned to a celebration. The activity planned essentially involved a lot of physical contact between all the family members in a playful way. Aaron delighted in climbing on his father, even though the father's physical response was very limited. The session included a lot of mixed emotions and a lot of tears but general joy that Aaron was so much happier and his play so much healthier.

Verbal Components: The therapist primarily reviewed Aaron's gains and reinforced the changes the whole family had made. Although it is not typical for the therapist to make any genetic interpretations this late in therapy the therapist felt that it was important to do so in this case. The therapist repeated an earlier interpretation that identified the father's illness as the source of great anxiety that Aaron had tried to manage through his compulsive and controlling behavior. He noted how difficult the father's deterioration was for everyone because it was scary and meant that the father was moving closer to dying. Last, he mentioned that, no matter how scary things got it was always important to remember that Aaron was a child who sometimes needed a break to relax and have fun even if things around him were very serious. This information was repeated so that the whole family could hear it together and could take the directive to maintain Aaron's childhood in spite of the adversity they were facing with them out of the playroom.

Collaborative Components: Both parents were given the option of phone contact with the therapist should they have any questions as to how to maintain Aaron's gains as the father's health deteriorated. It was also suggested to the mother that she might consider returning Aaron for additional brief therapy upon the father's death should any of Aaron's symptoms recur at that time.

CASE EXAMPLE: FRANK

Frank's individual play therapy lasted for 1 year, at which time he was transferred to a therapeutic group home where he received milieu rather than individual therapy. Because of the structure of the residential school program, the termination had to occur in two phases.

Initially, Frank had to be prepared for a 1-month separation because of the school's summer break. Because a final group home placement had not yet been arranged, plans were made to place Frank in a different group home for the month. This meant that Frank would have to leave all the people who had been responsible for his care for the last 10 months, adjust to the temporary placement, return to the school for several months, and then move to a permanent group home placement. Given Frank's difficulties with attachment, this was anticipated to be a very problematic, yet unavoidable, plan.

One week before the scheduled transfer to the temporary group home, Frank revealed that he had stolen and hidden some matches and was very afraid that he was going to set a fire. His anxiety at the separation and feelings that he was being neglected and abused were reflected and acknowledged. The similarity between his setting a fire in response to being neglected and abused by his mother and his desire to set a fire now was presented in a genetic interpretation and reflected. After much discussion, the therapist decided that Frank would not be safe in the group home at that time, and plans were made to admit him to a psychiatric hospital as soon as the school program closed for the summer break. Frank was fully involved in this process and saw the hospitalization as demonstrating the therapist's and staff's commitment to protecting him.

Frank was hospitalized for about 1 week, during which time the hospital staff was extremely nurturant and supportive. As Frank habituated to the separation from the staff at the school program, his mood stabilized and he was successfully placed at the temporary group home.

When Frank returned to the school program, work on his final termination began immediately. From the outset he was aware that therapy would be time-limited and that he would be leaving the program for good within a couple of months. This time Frank had a better sense that he would survive the separation, and instead of becoming overwhelmed by his anxiety, he began the recapitulation process in a more controlled way. This began with his becoming quite needy so that he required much more physical contact with both his teacher and his therapist. Soon, however, his rage over the separation became very active and was played out in several very violent therapy sessions.

It was clear that Frank's emotions relative to all the separations he had ever experienced were being activated simultaneously in a manner consistent with the Preoperational processing which he had used to store the old trauma as they occurred. Because of his current Level III cognitive functioning, he was able to make more conscious connections between these events as well as discriminating between them. He identified that he was experiencing an intense mix of sadness and anger similar to his reaction to the death of his mother, to being taken away from his father, to being moved through several group homes, to being moved away from the woman he currently identified as his mother, to having to leave the school program, and to leaving therapy. All these events came to be symbolically represented by the cat that had died in the fire which killed his mother. The cat had never hurt him, and he missed it terribly. It also represented his fear that somehow all these losses where his fault. Arrangements were made for Frank to have a cat at the new group home, and this became a significant transitional symbol.

The peak of the recapitulation process occurred over the course of three sessions. In the first two sessions, Frank became violent in his interactions with other students, necessitating his removal to a time-out room. Both events happened early in the morning on the only day of the week that his therapist worked at the school program. Upon his arrival, the therapist entered the time-out room with Frank and worked to calm Frank. Both times Frank became immediately assaultive, which was interpreted as a signal that he needed to be held and kept safe by the therapist. The first of these holding sessions lasted over 1 1/2 hours, during which time virtually all the material presented in the previous paragraph was identified and interpreted. By the end of the session, Frank was able to identify his grief and to tolerate it without becoming enraged. The second session lasted 45 minutes, during which most of the material from the first session was reviewed and integrated. During both sessions Frank was extremely violent, attempting to hurt both himself and the therapist, yet he remained surprisingly available to interpretive work, probably because he was so used to it by this point in the therapy.

At the end of the second of these episodes, the therapist noted the pattern of his finding Frank already in the time-out room upon his arrival at the school. He interpreted Frank's fear that his rage could destroy the therapist and noted Frank's need to discover just how much the therapist could withstand. He suggested to Frank that they plan ahead for their next battle. He observed that the floor in the time-out room was very hard tile and that he would rather restrain Frank in a room where there was carpet, but, he added, this would be possible only if Frank were sufficiently in control that he was not already in the time-out room when the session began. Frank immediately agreed and then suggested that instead of the time-out room they meet in the gym, where they could lay down mats prior to the session. Frank and the therapist shook hands to finalize their agreement, and Frank returned to school calm and happy.

The oddness of this conversation never struck Frank. He had been completely out of control first thing in the morning before two consecutive sessions, requiring long, painful periods of restraint, and yet here he was agreeing to remain in control the following week so long as the therapist promised to restrain him. The following week he was in much better control. He helped the therapist lay down the mats and then initiated some play which required that he be held. Soon, however, he wanted to be held and nurtured. He was relaxed and happy for the duration of the session. The therapist interpreted Frank's gradual acceptance of the termination and his increased sense of control and safety, which Frank acknowledged readily.

The remainder of his sessions involved a review of the content of Frank's therapy and the progress he had made. As the date of his transfer to the therapeutic group home drew near, his entire school program was geared toward celebrating the progress he had made. Because of Frank's need for concrete objects to facilitate his transition to the new program, several of these objects were made and others bought. In therapy, he and the therapist drew pictures of special sessions they remembered and put them together in a "termination book." Frank and his teacher made arrangements to go around the school program and take photos of the people with whom Frank had worked. And the therapist, teacher, and counselor all bought Frank small symbolic gifts, one of which was a stuffed toy cat.

Frank's transfer to the new program was accomplished without incident, and he seemed to adjust to the new personnel quite well. To provide some continuity over the course of his adjustment to the new program, he saw his therapist three more times at 1-month intervals. During these sessions, the content gradually shifted from missing the school program to his interest in his new placement. During the final session, Frank and his therapist had a small party.

TRANSFERRING CHILD CLIENTS

At times, either by necessity or by design, you wish to transfer your client to another therapist or to another treatment modality rather than terminating her at the end of treatment. Some of these changes may be necessary for your own reasons, but hopefully most will be initiated for the child's benefit. There may be times where you need to transfer a child to another therapist due to illness, change of employment, or pregnancy. There may also be times when a change of therapists is necessitated by the failure of the therapeutic relationship. The majority of transfers to other treatment modalities such as family or group therapy are initiated when the child's individual goals have been achieved and you want to move on to address certain ecosystemic goals.

Transferring the Child to Another Therapist

As mentioned, it may be necessary to transfer the child to another therapist for one of two reasons: Either you are no longer to treat the child for reasons of your own, or you have decided that your therapeutic relationship with the child is so poor that the child should be transferred to see if therapy can progress. The strategies for conducting the transfer are quite different in the two situations.

If you must transfer a child with whom you have a good working relationship, you want to make every effort to transfer the relationship as well as the child. In other words, you want the child to make a strong connection between you and the new therapist. Whenever possible, it is good to make the connection in as concrete a fashion as possible. The process should occur in two parts, the second of which includes three subphases.

Initially, you should alert the child to the impending transfer while providing some explanation for its occurrence. That is, make the child aware that the problem does not lie with her, which should create a lead-in to a rather standard termination. The child will perhaps engage in some recapitulation, although it may not be as intense as in the case of a true termination. As the child is ready to move on, you should review the treatment goals that have been achieved and those that have not. The goals achieved should be the focus of some celebration so that there are some good feelings associated with the termination. Both you and the child can feel that something has been accomplished and that she will not be starting over from the beginning. The goals yet to be accomplished should be the focus for explaining the need to transfer the child as opposed to terminating therapy. All this could reasonably be accomplished in one or two sessions.

Next, it is very advantageous if you can arrange for you and the new therapist to conduct several joint sessions with the child. These joint sessions will proceed through three phases. Ideally, one session would be allotted for each phase, but they could be compressed if needed. The first phase is to conduct a session in which the new therapist is very passive, directing only a few nonthreatening remarks to the child. During this session, you might make a point of telling the new therapist key things about both the child's life history and her therapy history. As you do this, you should let the child know that you are doing it to relieve her of the burden of having to tell these things all over again. With an older child, you might discuss, prior to the session, whether she wants to relay the history or wants you to do it. This part of the process makes the child aware of the fact that you and the new therapist have communicated and that the new therapist does know quite a bit about her. You and the child should also demonstrate a typical session for the new therapist. It is good to involve the child in this as much as possible, potentially by asking her which aspects of your sessions she thinks the new therapist should be most aware. This minimizes the chance that the child will resist the new therapist by saying "Well, my old therapist never (always) did. . . ."

The second phase of the joint session process should involve you and the new therapist as equals. You might select an activity in which you can take turns interacting with the child. Or you might say that the child enjoys a particular activity and suggest the new therapist try that with the child. During this phase, you and the new therapist want to say and do just about the same amount within the given time frame. You also want to interact with one another a great deal so that the child perceives a strong working relationship between you both.

The last phase of the transfer consists of your taking a very passive role while the new therapist and child do the bulk of the work of the session. An ideal way to accomplish this is for the new therapist and the child to plan and then hold a good-bye party for you. They might meet alone for a few minutes at the end of the second session to plan the party. Then during the third, and last, transfer session, they might meet alone at the beginning to get ready and then to call you in for the last half of the session. This creates an alliance between them in mourning your departure, providing a solid base for the work of their first few sessions after your departure.

If you are transferring the child to a new therapist because your working relationship is not good, then you want to transfer as little of the relationship as possible by minimizing the connections the child makes between the two of you. If the child is to be transferred, the same feelings may arise. You might decide that it would be best for the child not to be aware of any communication between you and the new therapist beyond a knowledge that you are aware of one another. Certainly, joint sessions would be inadvisable.

Instead, you should terminate with the child, ending the problematic relationship as cleanly as possible. It may be very helpful to allow some time to lapse before the child begins with a new therapist so that she can look on it as a new beginning rather than a change superimposed on feelings of failure. If you are accepting such a referral, it is usually best to make no more than a passing reference to the previous therapist, possibly by pointing out some ways in which your work is different.

Transferring to Another Treatment Modality

Sometimes a child accomplishes all her individual goals in therapy but family or peers issues remain. In these situations, it can be highly advantageous to transfer the child to a different treatment modality either with you or someone else as the therapist. This is often an excellent plan for children who have suffered severe in-home abuse, whether or not they are, or will be, living in the home. You might begin to address in individual play therapy the developmental and intrapsychic problems that the child has developed subsequent to the abuse. As the individual issues are resolved, you might decide to address through group work the social skills deficits manifested by most abused children. Moving the child from individual to group work may also help her separate from the treatment process more gradually and consequently manifest fewer and less intense recapitulation symptoms. During this time, you or another therapist might be treating other members of the family to stabilize them as individuals with the family system. As each individual moves toward improved functioning, then family sessions could be initiated to address the remaining family system's issues, an approach that is particularly useful when one or more of the family members is extremely dysfunctional.

Family Therapy

If you are the one who will be conducting the family therapy, then it is important that the child understand that this type of transition will be made from very early on in her treatment. Besides making family therapy a part of your treatment contract, you should make an extra effort, in the course of conducting the child's individual sessions, to define yourself as an ally of the family system first and the child as a member of that system second. You can accomplish this objective by skewing the type of interpretations you make to address more systemic than individual or intrapsychic issues. If you maintain this stance, it should be relatively easy to move between family and individual sessions or to make the transition from individual to family sessions. A distinct advantage of your conducting both the individual and family work is that you are in a unique position to help build and reinforce appropriate interpersonal boundaries. You can, for example, clearly label issues as belonging to the child, the parents, the siblings, or the family system and engage the appropriate individuals in addressing the problem.

One disadvantage to your conducting both the individual and family work in a given case is that those family members whose interpersonal boundaries are particularly weak may perceive you as more committed to the welfare of your individual client than to the welfare of the family. In such cases you may decide to transfer the family to another therapist as you begin to terminate your sessions with the child. The period of overlap, if any, should match the needs of the child. For some children, you will simply terminate your work and make a referral to an independent family therapist. This strategy usually works best when you want to create a clear boundary between your work with the child and the needs of the family, which helps prevent the child from expecting the family sessions to be anything like her individual sessions.

In cases where the individual play therapy with the child has gone well and the family is pleased, it may be advantageous for you to encourage the transference of the working relationship onto the new therapist. In such cases, the procedure followed should be very similar to the process previously described for transferring a child. The process might be divided up as follows:

- Schedule two or three termination sessions with the child, building to a family celebration during the last session.
- Schedule a joint session with the family, your child client, yourself, and the new therapist in which you actively facilitate the family's providing relevant information to the new therapist. During this session, the new therapist directs most of her comments about the material to the family, thereby beginning to develop a relationship with them.
- Schedule a final joint session in which you assume a very passive role and the new therapist takes control of the sessions. At the end of this session, the new therapist notes that this was the last session you are attending. The new therapist should reflect that the family will miss you, note the progress that has been made so far, and encourage the family to say their good-byes.

Group Therapy

As with transfers of child clients into family therapy, the process of transferring child to group therapy depends on whether you, or another therapist, will be conducting the group. A prime advantage to your conducting the group is that you can help the child integrate the progress she has made individually into the work she will be doing in the group. The group becomes a very obvious continuation of her therapy experience instead of seeming isolated or discontinuous. For example, you may work with a child and you both come to recognize the impact that her intrapersonal functioning is having on her interaction with her peers. If you also agree that you have resolved most of the child's individual issues, then you and she may contract to address peer issues in a peer context prior to termination.

In this case, the termination of individual sessions should still be marked by a celebration to note the progress the child has made to date. The celebration might also note that, in making such progress, the child is now ready to move on and address a new treatment context in which you are sure she will do well. There are times when you might decide to see a child in both group and individual work concurrently, which brings us to an interesting point. The primary problem in conducting both individual and group therapy with a child is the potential for disruptive levels of sibling-like rivalry to develop among the group members, a rivalry that will be heightened if you are seeing several of the children in concurrent individual therapy. To prevent this happening, it is recommended that you see either all the children in concurrent individual and group sessions or none of the children in both.

If the child is to be treated in a group conducted by another therapist, then you may or may not decide to terminate the individual work. Since children tend to do very different types of work in each modality, there may be great benefit to conducting the two simultaneously. You simply want to be sure that you and the group therapist remain in close contact regarding the child's progress. Regardless of who will conduct the group phase of the child's treatment, the group format described in Part IV is useful.

CHAPTER FOURTEEN

Case Examples:
Dennis and Diane

In the body of this text two cases were presented to illustrate the various steps of the intake, assessment, and treatment processes. Unfortunately, the use of that format meant those cases were discontinuously presented across many chapters and may, therefore have been difficult for the reader to follow. In this chapter, two cases are presented in their entirety with as little explanatory text as possible. The presentation format is exactly the same as it was in the body of this volume so the reader should be able to refer back easily to the comprehensive explanatory material as needed. Sections of each case are presented in table form showing data or hypotheses on the left and the treatment goals derived from that information on the right. It is hoped that this format will help the reader track exactly how the treatment goals were derived from the case information. As with the cases presented earlier one is a short-term and one is long-term. Dennis was seen for short-term therapy and the goals and content of his eight therapy sessions are presented in detail. Diane was seen in therapy over a much longer period and the goals and content of her therapy sessions are presented in more of an overview.

DENNIS: SHORT-TERM ECOSYSTEMIC PLAY THERAPY

Identifying Information

Dennis was a very handsome white male who was 9½ years old at the time of referral. He was brought to the school psychologist for treatment by his parents at the suggestion of Dennis' Special Education teacher, who expressed concern about Dennis' periodically striking himself in the head with his fist while he was completing written work.

Intake

The intake was completed in two sessions. Dennis' mother and father attended the first session and provided an extensive general and developmental history. Dennis attended the second session by himself where a brief history was taken and a mental status exam completed.

Dennis was the youngest of three children and the only boy born to this family. The pregnancy and delivery were without complication. All Dennis' developmental milestones were reported to have been achieved well ahead of normal limits. Dennis' early history was unremarkable except that the family moved approximately every 2 years. The father was in the Foreign Service, and the family had first moved overseas when Dennis was 5 years old. They moved to a second foreign country when Dennis was 7.

Dennis attended English-speaking schools and did well academically. When his classroom teacher noted that Dennis was having trouble completing his schoolwork, Dennis began spending 2 hours a week in a Special Education resource room. His Special Education teacher found Dennis extremely quiet and prone to hitting himself in the head with his fist while he was completing written work.

The parents reported that Dennis was very outgoing at home and had many friends. They did not see any unusual behavior when he was at home. He enjoyed spending time with his family, and they did many things together. They did note that Dennis seemed to be very sensitive and spent a lot of time processing his interpersonal interactions.

Dennis was very quiet throughout his intake interview and reported that his parents were seeking treatment because his teachers thought he was dumb. When pressed, he admitted that he did hit himself in the head while at school and seemed very embarrassed.

Dennis' behavior during the intake was divided into two very different styles. Whenever the content involved anything academically related, he was quiet, avoided eye contact, and became obviously uneasy and physically tight. When the content centered on his family or his peers, he became talkative and animated and interacted warmly with the therapist. He reported loving his family very much and noted that as the youngest he was often the center of attention. He said that he had a lot of friends and that he liked being on the school soccer team. He had long lists of likes and dislikes and engaged in lengthy discussions about any topic that came up.

Dennis' mental status exam was unremarkable except for his ability to talk about his internal process. He seemed to invest a lot of energy in self-observation and to be able to describe not only how he felt but why he felt that way. He readily admitted that school generated a lot of bad feelings and that he would be very happy if therapy could make some of those go away.

Assessment

Following the intake, Dennis was administered a fairly comprehensive evaluation. The primary goal of the evaluation was to determine the basis for Dennis' apparent self-abusive behavior as was reported by his Special Education teacher. During classroom observation as well as during the intake, it was noted that Dennis hit himself only while he was trying to complete written assignments. In fact, it had been his consistently below-average written work that had triggered his referral to the Resource Room for 2 hours of help each week. The Special Education teacher suspected that Dennis had a language disability.

Upon evaluation, it was discovered that Dennis had a Full Scale IQ of 140 with comparable Verbal and Performance IQ scores. These scores placed him in the very superior range of intellectual functioning. One of Dennis' particular strengths was his vocabulary. Further evaluation confirmed that Dennis was a gifted child who did not have a language disability but a writing disability. Handwriting was difficult for Dennis because he could not remember the steps for producing each letter with a pencil; therefore he used virtually all his energy trying to decide which way to move his pencil next when writing and lost the ideas he wanted to put down. The striking himself in the head served as a kind of "reset" button Dennis used before initiating a correction to cue himself that the pencil was moving in the wrong direction. When Dennis was interviewed, his language was extremely complex and his interactions well above age level.

Dennis was also administered several personality tests as well at the Developmental Teaching Objectives Rating Form (DTORF). The personality tests revealed poor self-esteem relative to his intelligence and academic abilities, general shyness and a tendency to withdraw in the face of academic tasks. The DTORF information follows:

Using the DTORF, it was determined that at the age of 9½, Dennis was functioning at Stage 4 in the Behavioral domain, Stage 3 in the Communications domain, and Stage 3 in the Socialization domain. Given his age, Dennis should have been functioning at the early Stage 4 in all domains.

Dennis will be able to:

(1) Indicate a beginning awareness of his own behavioral progress (B-21);

(2) Implement appropriate alternative behaviors in the context of interpersonal interactions (B-22);

(3) Describe characteristic attributes, strengths, and problems in himself (C-17);

(continued)

DTORF (Continued)

(4) Use words or nonverbal gestures to show pride in own work and activities or to make positive statements about himself (C-18);

(5) Seek assistance or praise from another child (S-26);

(6) Assist others in conforming to group rules (S-27).

GOAL DEVELOPMENT

The headings in this section parallel those used in Chapter 7. The reader is referred there for descriptive information regarding each area from which treatment goals are derived.

The Child's Present Pattern of Functioning

Developmental Description

In spite of the slight lags measured on the DTORF the general impression Dennis gave was of a somewhat older child in that he was particularly well behaved and polite. Dennis did not offer much spontaneous conversation but when he did speak he used fairly sophisticated language.

(7) Dennis will act in a manner consistent with his chronological age, as demonstrated by the use of more spontaneous verbalizations.

Dennis' developmental functioning varied depending on the amount of language the situation demanded. When in class he appeared behaviorally advanced but socially delayed. When doing something nonacademic like playing soccer he seemed quite socially skilled.

(8) Dennis will display developmentally consistent behavior across situations.

Cognitions

Dennis' interactions with the world all derived from his core belief that he was stupid. He was, he thought,

Dennis will:

(9) Manifest fewer signs of anxiety when engaged in writing projects;

DTORF (Continued)

one of the dumbest children in his class and feared that he would be retained in the fourth grade. Beyond this he seemed to have developed very normally and to be a very functional child.

(10) Verbalize his belief that he is very intelligent.

Emotions

Dennis displayed the ability to experience and report the full range of affects appropriate to his age when he was in a comfortable situation. Generally, however, he was so afraid of failing or appearing stupid that he drastically constricted the expression of his emotions. In fact, it appeared that he often had difficulty enjoying a positive social interaction, although his affect tended to remain neutral rather than becoming negative.

Dennis will:

(11) Be able to complete school projects without experiencing severe anxiety;

(12) Manifest a greater variety of affects;

(13) Verbalize his internal, affective state.

Pathology

Dennis' need to feel good about his own cognitive and academic abilities was not being met effectively. Further, his need for a sense of mastery relative to cognitive tasks was not being met effectively.

Dennis will:

(14) Demonstrate an increased valuing of his cognitive and academic abilities;

(15) Be able to demonstrate increased mastery by performing better on school tasks once his anxiety has decreased.

None of Dennis' needs were inappropriately in that nothing he did interfered with the ability of others to get their needs met.

(continued)

DTORF (Continued)

Response Repertoire

Dennis tended to manage virtually every situation autoplastically. He rarely told anyone if something bothered him, and he was seen by one and all as a very compliant, cooperative child. Both adults and peers described him as very nice. If he encountered a problem, he assumed it was his fault and attempted to change his behavior. In spite of his profound graphomotor disability, Dennis had never told anyone that writing was difficult and never complained that he could not finish his work in the time allotted. Even his striking himself in the head was an attempt to force himself to perform as others expected.

Dennis will:

(16) Manifest less anxiety during performance situations;

(17) Instigate more requests that others meet his needs;

(18) Verbalize his belief that he is not stupid;

(19) Not engage in self-abusive behavior when experiencing performance anxiety.

Origins of the Child's Present Pattern of Functioning

Child Specific Factors

Endowment

Dennis' superior intellect had allowed him to develop optimally in most areas of his functioning. His severe graphomotor disability was the basis for his belief that he was stupid and the primary trigger for virtually all the problem behaviors that brought him to therapy. It is also likely that he resorted to autoplastic changes more readily than most children his age because he had the capacity to do so.

Dennis will:

(20) Be able to include his graphomotor disability as one component in a rather lengthy description of himself and his skills;

(21) Demonstrate the use of alternative stress management strategies while at school.

Developmental Response

Because Dennis' learning disability did not manifest itself until he was

DTORF (Continued)

well into Level III functioning, it
was hypothesized that his overall
developmental picture would be
both age-appropriate and healthy.

However, because his problem directly interfered with his ability to
master individual tasks it was hypothesized that he would manifest
general feelings of being unable to
perform adequately.

(22) Dennis will be able to separate
his learning disability from his
overall perception of himself and
his abilities.

Ecological Factors

Family

Dennis' family was assessed as extremely functional and supportive.
What they may have inadvertently
contributed to his situation is their
high level of achievement motivation. Both his parents were very
successful, as were his two older
sisters. In his position as the
youngest child and the only boy,
Dennis had certainly come to understand how much his parents valued him: They perceived him as
perfect and loved him for it. Somehow he had failed to hear that they
would continue to love him no
matter what he achieved.

Dennis will:

(23) Be able to ask his family for
support in addressing his graphomotor disability;

(24) Understand that his special
place in his family is not jeopar-
dized by his academic difficulties.

Peers

Dennis' peers played no significant
role in the development of Dennis'
maladaptive thoughts or behaviors.

(continued)

DTORF (Continued)

Other Systems

Dennis' father's job required that the family move quite often to various locations around the world. Because of these moves, Dennis had never been in the same school for more than 2 years, and he was in schools that had little to offer in the way of pupil services. When it was noted that Dennis was not completing written work, he was placed in a Special Education program for 2 hours a week. Although this was a well-intentioned plan on the part of the school, it considerably reinforced Dennis' belief that he was stupid. Other than his interactions at school, Dennis had not had significant contacts with any other systems.

(25) Dennis will verbalize a desire to go to the Resource Room program without verbalizing any sense of shame.

Factors Maintaining the Child's Present Pattern of Functioning

Child Specific Factors

Endowment

Dennis' graphomotor disability was both the primary originator of his present problems and one of the most important factors maintaining his poor self-esteem.

(26) Dennis will be able to list his graphomotor disability as one aspect of an otherwise positive self-description.

Dennis' very attractive appearance tended to make people respond to him in a very positive way. Combined with his behavior it seemed to make them underestimate the severity of his difficulties and to conclude that he just needed to try harder to succeed academically.

(27) Others will manifest a more realistic appraisal of Dennis' difficulties and assist him as needed.

DTORF (Continued)

Cost/Benefit Analysis of Beliefs, Emotions, and Behaviors

Since Dennis displayed behavior that appeared to be in advance of his chronological age, it brought him substantial reinforcement from adults. Fortunately, Dennis was also able to interact with his peers in an age-appropriate way.

(28) Dennis will demonstrate more variability in his affective expression consistent with his developmental level.

Dennis' negative self-evaluation of his cognitive and academic abilities prevented him from succeeding in other academic areas as well as preventing him from behaving in a spontaneous manner when interacting with others.

Dennis will:

(29) Perform better on non-writing tasks once his overall negative self-evaluation improves;

(30) Manifest more spontaneous, happy behavior in more situations.

Ecological Factors

Family

Dennis' family was stable and intact with no job transfers anticipated for at least 2 years. No interference with the progress of treatment was anticipated.

(31) Dennis will see that his parents are actively engaged in the treatment process and interested in his welfare.

Peers

Dennis had very good peer relations who served as his support system for the nonacademic portions of his life.

(32) Dennis will initiate requests for support from peers with regards to his academic difficulties.

Other Systems

Dennis was receiving minimal Special Education support services at the time of intake. No other systems were actively involved in his life.

(32) Dennis will become as involved as possible in planning his academic program by stating his preferences and engaging in some problem solving with his parents.

Case Formulation and Goal Synthesis

For Dennis, the primary goal of therapy is the reduction of his intense performance anxiety. The formation of a therapeutic relationship is a part of this process but not a central goal in and of itself because it is not anticipated that Dennis will have any problems entering into such a relationship.

Dennis' initial goal is the recognition and labeling of his affect across a variety of settings and experiences. The underlying goal here is to help him separate his feelings about school and his school performance from his overall conceptualization of himself. This is necessary so that Dennis will not experience school problems as a threat to his overall self-esteem and, therefore, as totally overwhelming.

Once Dennis becomes able to recognize that his feelings of being bad and stupid were actually limited to certain tasks during the course of the schoolday, the goal of the therapy is to engage him in problem solving. The problem-solving component of the therapy will be geared toward identifying ways Dennis could address both his actual graphomotor problem and the feelings it generated with his verbal and physical self-abuse as the initial target behaviors. He will also be encouraged to develop strategies for obtaining more noncontingent support from his family and peers.

As Dennis generates potential solutions to his problems in therapy, the goal is to help him find ways to implement these goals outside the sessions. He will be encouraged to involve his family, peers, and school personnel in helping him attain his goals. As these solutions become effective in reducing Dennis' anxiety, therapy will focus on expanding and freeing up his affective and behavioral repertoire.

Termination will involve helping Dennis become more active in his peer relationships so that they can provide continuing support throughout his school career.

In summary the 32 treatment goals derived from the intake, assessment and case formulation were clustered into 7 individual goals and one collateral goal. Because this was conceptualized as a short term treatment the goals selected were all highly interrelated. It was also assumed that only very preliminary work would occur on the more comprehensive goals such as adjusting Dennis' self-esteem or perception of his place in his family. On an individual level Dennis will:

1. Be able to describe himself more realistically. He will manifest a generally positive self-image in which his graphomotor disability plays a very circumscribed role (gratification of his need for approval and self-esteem).
2. Show an increase in spontaneous behavior including a greater range of affects and affective expression.
3. Manifest less anxiety during academic tasks and a reduction in his self-abusive behavior.

4. Increase the frequency of his requests for assistance from peers and relevant adults especially his regular and Special Education teachers.
5. Manifest an overall improvement in his school performance particularly on non-writing tasks (gratification of his need for mastery).
6. Indicate an awareness that his special role in the family is not threatened by his academic difficulties.
7. Show beginning awareness of his own behavioral progress.

Collaterally:

1. The relevant adults in Dennis' environment will demonstrate a clearer understanding of his academic disability and will provide better and more consistent support in their attempts to ensure that his needs are being met.

Pretreatment Decisions

Determining the Context(s) in Which Intervention(s) Will Occur

Individual.   Individual play therapy was implemented with Dennis to help him develop a sense of self that was somewhat impervious to the negative feedback he was receiving regarding his academic skills and performance. The other goal was to have them provide Dennis with as much support as possible as he attempted to remediate school problems.

Family.   Collateral work with the parents was also initiated to involve them in helping generalize beyond the playroom the changes Dennis would make.

Peer.   Since Dennis was not experiencing any difficulties relative to his interactions with his peers, no interventions were planned for that group.

Other systems.   Consultation with Dennis' school was considered essential to his making reasonable progress in treatment because it was the primary context in which his symptoms were manifested. The goal was to help them develop a school plan that would allow Dennis to function at a level consistent with his cognitive capacity.

Determining the Type of Intervention to Be Used in Each Context

Dennis was a good candidate for short-term individual therapy; however, it seemed that the most effective interventions could implemented through Dennis' school. A problem-solving and an educational approach were to be used with the school personnel and Dennis' parents.

Determining the Therapeutic Strategies to Be Used in the Child's Play Therapy

Dennis' development was appropriate in virtually all areas. Given that he was functioning well within Level III, a heavily experiential approach did not seem necessary. The therapist did decide to use some very structured and experiential sessions at the very beginning, to disrupt Dennis' pattern of anxiety and rigidity in interactions with adults when academic content was even discussed. The goal here was to desensitize him to his fear of failing at academic tasks. The rest of the treatment was to be quite open-ended, with an emphasis on the use of verbalizations so that Dennis could learn to apply his cognitive skills to the development of strategies that would help him feel successful in school.

Feedback and Treatment Contracting

At Dennis' feedback session only his anxiety and bad feelings about schoolwork in general were addressed. Dennis agreed that he would like to feel much less anxious about schoolwork and that he was willing to try to learn some new ways of coping besides hitting himself in the head.

Treatment Plan

STAGE: INTRODUCTION AND EXPLORATION

Stage Goals: Dennis will:

1. Be able to describe himself more realistically. He will manifest a generally positive self-image in which his graphomotor disability plays a very circumscribed role (gratification of his need for approval and self-esteem).

3. Manifest less anxiety during academic tasks and a reduction in his self-abusive behavior.

Session 1

Participants: Dennis and the therapist.

Materials: WISC-R subtest graph, pencil and paper, bean bag, and target.

Experiential Components: Because Dennis had no previous therapy experience and no traumatic history, the therapist decided to take control of the sessions from the beginning. The therapist opened the first session by giving Dennis some very specific feedback about his performance on the intelligence test using a photocopy of the subtest graph from the cover of the record form. This allowed them to discuss Dennis' relative strengths and weaknesses as well as to illustrate that even Dennis' weaknesses were, in the vast majority of cases, well above the norm. The therapist also described in some detail the exact nature of Dennis' disability. As they discussed his skills Dennis' smile got bigger and bigger although he sometimes looked at the therapist as if to check that the therapist wasn't lying to him.

Following the test feedback portion of the session therapist said, "The first two times we met I asked lots of questions and you took a whole bunch of tests. That was a lot of work. Now we are going to do a different kind of work. I am going to teach you how to relax so that your writing will get to be a little easier. Before I teach you about relaxing though, I need to know some more about you." The therapist then proceeded to ask Dennis about some of his favorite places to go where he felt all quiet inside and his favorite colors, music, animals, and so forth. This was the extent of the exploration phase of the treatment because Dennis and the therapist had been able to spend a considerable amount of time together over the course of conducting the intake and initial assessment.

Once the interview was done, the therapist proceeded to teach Dennis a progressive deep muscle relaxation strategy. As muscle relaxation was achieved, it was enhanced through the use of visual imagery. Dennis was taught to imagine a secret hideout that he could get to only by walking across a wide meadow. Once in the hideout, Dennis was to imagine being surrounded by his favorite things. The room was painted his favorite color, and his favorite music was playing on the radio. He could look out the window to a stream where his favorite animals, deer, had stopped to drink. While he was there, he could do whatever he wanted because no one was around to make demands. The relaxation training was followed by two short activities.

The activities in this session were designed to contrast tasks on which Dennis performed poorly with one's on which he did well. The obvious choice for a poor performance task was have him write something. If needed, the intensity of this experience could be increased by timing him. Tossing bean bags at a target was conceptualized as a very low level task at which Dennis would perform very well. The distance between Dennis and the target could be used to adjust the level of difficulty of the task as needed.

Verbal Components: The goal of the initial part of the session was to begin helping Dennis to put his academic difficulties in context. As the test data some tentative problem solving was done by the therapist as to how one could see one's self as very smart in some areas and as having terrible problems in another. In spite of the fact that this was just the beginning of the treatment the therapist was able to make some significant interpretations because Dennis was already fairly well aware of the nature of his difficulties. The therapist made the following interpretive statements.

Reflections: The therapist reflected changes in Dennis' affect including his anxiety during the writing task and his pleasure at hearing that he was smart and at being able to accomplish relatively difficult bean bag tosses.

Pattern Interpretations: "This is the second time you've mentioned how much you don't like subjects like language arts and social studies." "This is the third time you've told me how much fun it is to throw the bean bag at different targets."

Simple Dynamic Interpretations: "You seem to get so worried when you have to write or do some kinds of schoolwork that you don't like doing them at all." "You seem to be really happy when you are doing something that doesn't remind you of school at all."

Generalized Dynamic Interpretations: "I'll bet that you get even more worried in class when its time to do written work than you do in here." "Seeing how much you like throwing the bean bag at targets gives me an idea of why you love to play soccer."

Genetic Interpretations: No genetic interpretations were made at this time.

The therapist also engaged Dennis in Problem Solving relative to how to make both the writing task less painful and the bean bag toss even more fun.

Collaborative Components: The therapist met with the parents for an extensive feedback session about the nature of Dennis' academic difficulties. They were so relieved to learn that there was a very focal reason for the problem that they immediately began to problem solve ways they could make learning and school easier for Dennis. The offered to get him a typewriter or word processor and special tutoring in typing if that would help bypass his disability. They also offered to buy him a tape recorder so that he could dictate his answers to schoolwork which they would then transcribe. All in all it was clear that they would help Dennis in any way they could.

A meeting was also held with Dennis' school personnel. They were somewhat surprised when they learned of his high level of intelligence. Like the parents they were somewhat relieved to find that he had such a focal disability. The teacher immediately agreed to modify her procedures for Dennis. He was given more time to take written tests. She agreed he could dictate homework. She even agreed to make up some special tests for him that were multiple choice rather than fill in the blank or short answer. All personnel agreed to meet again in 4 weeks to determine if these changes were sufficient and effective.

STAGE: TENTATIVE ACCEPTANCE

Stage Goals: Dennis will:

1. Be able to describe himself more realistically. He will manifest a generally positive self-image in which his graphomotor disability plays a very circumscribed role (gratification of his need for approval and self-esteem).

3. Manifest less anxiety during academic tasks and a reduction in his self-abusive behavior.

Session 2

Participants: Dennis and the therapist.

Materials: Large paper and markers, bean bags.

Experiential Components: Dennis' tentative acceptance was manifested in his complete cooperation with the relaxation training which was conducted during the first part of the session. The exercise was completed in much the same way as it was during the first session. Upon completion it was suggested that Dennis begin to practice the relaxation on his own at home especially just before he went to sleep at night or right after he woke up in the morning.

The next activity involved the therapist tracing an outline of Dennis' entire body on a large sheet of paper. Dennis and the therapist then began filling in the outline with both his features and clothing as well as written descriptions of Dennis' characteristics. The goal was to include things he was good at as well as things that were difficult for him so as to begin to create a more rounded self-image. Many neutral characteristics such as his eye color and hair color were included for variety. Each characteristic was labeled with a plus a minus or a zero to indicate whether Dennis viewed the characteristic as good bad or neutral. When it came time to include the graphomotor disability the item was written by the therapist in fairly small letters inside the outline of Dennis' writing hand so as to symbolize how contained the problem was. Dennis and the therapist took turns writing the characteristics so that Dennis would have experience both writing (anxiety provoking) a dictating (not anxiety provoking).

After the drawing was completed it was laid on the floor while Dennis and the therapist took turns throwing bean bags at it. When the bean bag landed on the drawing the person who threw it had to give an example of the characteristic on which it landed or name another characteristic that Dennis gave the same valence.

Verbal Components: Since the ongoing goal was to have Dennis build a better and more rounded view of himself the therapist continued with the following interpretive statements.

Reflections: Feelings of happiness, anxiety, relaxation and frustration were all reflected along with Dennis' periodic self-consciousness at being the focus of such close scrutiny and discussion.

Pattern Interpretations: "You sure do hand the pen back to me in a hurry when you decide its my turn to write again." "That's the fourth negative characteristic you've added in a row." "Most of the bad things you say about yourself have something to do with school."

Simple Dynamic Interpretations: "You seem much more relaxed when you can dictate your answers rather than having to write them." "Talking about school seems to bring up some pretty bad feelings." "Talking about things you do with your family seems to bring up a lot of happy feelings."

Generalized Dynamic Interpretations: "I'll bet you spend a lot of time in school worrying and feeling stupid, especially when you have to do written work." "I'll bet you like just about everything about time away from school except for homework."

Genetic Interpretations: No genetic interpretations were made during this session.

Problem Solving: The therapist helped Dennis brainstorm other things he could say about himself as well as how to keep a balanced view of his good and bad points. Anytime Dennis appeared to become anxious the therapist helped him problem solve how he might reduce his anxiety level (at this point they focused on using the relaxation strategy or asking for help).

Collaborative Components: No additional collaborative work was done at this time.

STAGE: NEGATIVE REACTION

Stage Goals: Dennis will:

1. Be able to describe himself more realistically. He will manifest a generally positive self-image in which his graphomotor disability plays a very circumscribed role (gratification of his need for approval and self-esteem).

2. Show an increase in spontaneous behavior including a greater range of affects and affective expression.
3. Manifest less anxiety during academic tasks and a reduction in his self-abusive behavior.

Session 3

Participants: Dennis and the therapist.

Materials: Tape recorder, crayons and paper, tempera paint with large brushes, fingerpaint and large sheets of paper, bandana folded as a blindfold.

Experiential Components: Dennis' manifestation of a negative reaction to therapy was very brief. At the beginning of the third session he complained about having to do the relaxation exercises saying they were boring. As he and the therapist brainstormed how to make them less boring they came up with some ideas that involved Dennis trying to relax while the therapist tried to distract him. They also agreed to make an audio tape of the relaxation that Dennis could take home to use in his practice sessions. Just these slight shifts got Dennis reinvested in the process and brought the Negative Reaction phase of the therapy to an end.

   The goal of the activities in this session were to get Dennis to focus less on performance and more on having fun. To start he had to think of a word. Then he had to write the word. Next he drew a picture that went with the word using markers. After that he drew another picture to go with the word using tempera paint, large brushes and large paper. Lastly, he repeated the drawing using finger paints. Whenever Dennis became too focused on the product the therapist would blindfold him and have him complete that stage of the writing or drawing process without looking. When Dennis asked, the therapist did provide verbal directions to help Dennis complete something while blindfolded. As they went along the ideas for drawings got sillier and the therapist set progressively shorter time limits for completing each step so that the focus was on the process and not the product.

Verbal Components: The therapist continued to differentiate anxiety producing activities from pleasurable ones. During this session the therapist also focused on the fun associated with spontaneity.

   Reflections: The therapist reflected the same feelings as in previous sessions with the addition of reflecting Dennis' apparent need for achievement as he focused on trying to do everything just right.

   Pattern Interpretations: "I noticed you sort of roll your eyes just before you have to write something." "You spend an awful lot of time on the marker drawings putting lots of details in your pictures." "You speed through the finger paintings without paying much attention to what you are doing at all."

   Simple Dynamic Interpretations: "You sort of decide something is going to be hard to write even before you start and then get to worrying right away." "You like to draw with markers because it gives you a chance to show me how good you are at drawing." "You seem not to like the finger paints much because it is almost impossible to make a good drawing with them." "It seems harder for you to get into an activity if it isn't something you can do well." "If you can't do something well it seems like it makes you feel bad about yourself."

Generalized Dynamic Interpretations: "I'll bet you avoid things at home and at school when you don't think you can do them well. In fact, I'll bet that is why you hardly ever do your homework."

Genetic Interpretations: "I think that all this worrying about doing well started way back when you found out you couldn't write as well as the other kids in school. Since then it has kind of grown so that anything that is even a little bit hard makes you think badly about yourself."

In this session Problem Solving focused on how to make each of the tasks more fun and less anxiety provoking.

Collaborative Components: No additional collaborative work was done at this time.

STAGE: GROWING, TRUSTING, AND WORKING THROUGH

Stage Goals: Dennis will:

1. Be able to describe himself more realistically. He will manifest a generally positive self-image in which his graphomotor disability plays a very circumscribed role (gratification of his need for approval and self-esteem).
2. Show an increase in spontaneous behavior including a greater range of affects and affective expression.
3. Manifest less anxiety during academic tasks and a reduction in his self-abusive behavior.
4. Increase the frequency of his requests for assistance from peers and relevant adults especially his regular and Special Education teachers.
5. Manifest an overall improvement in his school performance particularly on non-writing tasks (gratification of his need for mastery).

Session 4

Participants: Dennis and the therapist.

Materials: Large sheets of paper, small container of chocolate pudding, small container of vanilla pudding, towels and wet washcloth for clean up.

Experiential Components: This session again began with practicing the relaxation exercise but with the addition of two components. During the first phase the therapist demonstrated for

The goals of the experiential component of this session were to get Dennis to have fun doing a totally non-goal-oriented activity as well as to enjoy being in the position of being helped. Now that Dennis had learned the relaxation procedure quite thoroughly, the idea of his trying to stay relaxed during different activities was introduced. Thus mastery would be accomplished by maintaining relaxation, something he knew he could do in one setting, in a variety of new settings. The therapist started by teaching Dennis how to use relaxation to overcome being ticklish. He showed Dennis that a tense muscle reacted to tickling much more strongly than a relaxed one. Then they worked on having Dennis stay relaxed through progressively more intense tickles. Once Dennis was able to do this the idea of staying relaxed while thinking about schoolwork was introduced. Because this was such a big shift for Dennis it was only practiced very briefly and in sort of a lighthearted way.

The remainder of the session was spent having Dennis finger paint on giant sheets of paper with chocolate and vanilla pudding. When Dennis proved initially reluctant the therapist proceeded to roll up Dennis' sleeves and coat his hands with pudding. He then pretended he was an artist using Dennis' arms as his paint brushes. No attempt was made to draw anything in particular the focus was on having fun. Periodically, the therapist would ask Dennis to 'clean' one of the brushes (hands) by licking his fingers. At the end of the session the therapist helped Dennis clean up.

Verbal Components: In addition to the interpretive work the therapist made every effort to verbally reinforce even the slightest attempts to ask for help on Dennis' part. At one point Dennis' sleeve began to roll back down and Dennis called the therapist and then nodded toward his sleeve. The therapist said, "Oh, you need help with your sleeve. No problem. I'm glad you asked."

Reflections: These were the same as in previous sessions.

Pattern Interpretations: "You are really getting the hang of how to have fun and be silly." "You don't seem to ask for help; instead you just sort of point and grunt."

Simple Dynamic Interpretations: "You sure seem uncomfortable about having to ask for help." "I think you worry that I won't think you're good at something if you have to ask for help." "You sure do love rowdy play, like being tickled. I think that's partly because there is no way to be either good or bad at being tickled. It is just plain fun."

Generalized Dynamic Interpretations: "I'll bet asking for help in school is hard because you worry other people will think you are stupid if you can't do it on your own."

Genetic Interpretations: "Once you decided you weren't good in school you sort of learned to lots of things to try and hide rather than having to ask for help."

During this session Problem Solving was kept to a minimum so that Dennis could focus on the process of the interaction.

Collaborative Components: No additional collaborative work was done at this time.

Session 5

Participants: Dennis and the therapist.

Materials: Blocks, two sticks and a ball, pencil and paper, chair.

Experiential Components: This session was divided in two parts. During the first part Dennis used the relaxation strategy to try and stay relaxed during discussions of academic tasks and, finally, role plays of Dennis completing academic assignments. The role plays included tasks that included writing as well as verbal responses. For the writing tasks Dennis' first just pretended to write and later actually used the relaxation strategy while writing first single letters and then short words. The therapist alternated playing a very supportive teacher and one who kept pressuring Dennis to work faster. The tone was kept playful throughout.

The next set of mastery tasks involved having Dennis stay relaxed while he playing games, which required that he desensitize himself to both the competition and the prospect of losing. This was done first with cooperative games. In one Dennis and the therapist took turns adding blocks to a tower to see how high they could build it before it fell over. Each time they competed only with their previous record. Then they played a game where they had to transfer a ball from one end of the playroom to the other. Each of them had a stick and they had to work together to pick up the ball without using their hands and carry across the room. Not only did this help Dennis learn needed peer social skills it was a way of getting him to accept help with tasks in a way that was very nonthreatening.

Verbal Components: This session was less interpretive and more focused on working together.

Reflections: Same as in previous sessions.

Pattern Interpretations: "I've noticed you like to take the early turns at tower building." "It seems like you want me to give directions on how we should work to get the ball across the room." "Even though you look really frustrated when we drop the ball I've noticed you don't say anything."

Simple Dynamic Interpretations: "I think you want me to take the later turns in tower building so that it will be my fault if it falls down. I think you still want to avoid failing because even something as unimportant as tower building might make you feel bad about yourself." "This game with the ball is sort of confusing for you. When we drop the ball you get frustrated but you're not sure who to blame. That's what makes it a good game you can't blame yourself or feel bad when it doesn't go well."

Generalized Dynamic Interpretations: "In sports and in school it is always better when you work together because there is more chance for success and someone to share the blame if it doesn't work out." "I'll bet you don't worry about much at home except what your parents will think about your bad grades in school."

Genetic Interpretations: Earlier interpretations about the origins of Dennis' negative self-evaluation were repeated.

All of the problem solving done in this session was focused on how to complete the games successfully. These were true joint efforts in which the therapist tried to use Dennis'.

Collaborative Components: Now that Dennis was using his relaxation during role plays of academic tasks both his regular and Special Education teacher were invited to a session that Dennis led. During this session he demonstrated how he practiced deep muscle relaxation. He also described how the technique helped him focus. Then he led the two teachers through a sample relaxation session of their own. Following the session both teachers agreed to provide whatever assistance they could to Dennis when he needed to use his relaxation training to manage a classroom task.

Session 6

Participants: Dennis and the therapist.

Materials: pencil and paper, incomplete homework assignments, dice, Chutes and Ladders, checkers and checkerboard.

Experiential Components: This session was divided into three parts. During the first part Dennis practiced using his relaxation training while first, role playing completing academic tasks and then while actually completing some unfinished homework assignments.

The next part of the session was designed to make Dennis' appraisal of his own skills and self-esteem more realistic and less pessimistic. During this part of the session Dennis and the therapist first rolled dice keeping track of who rolled the highest number each time. The therapist used the dice to demonstrate to Dennis that no matter what strategy one used the relative number of each person's wins and losses stayed about the same. The therapist emphasized that winning or losing games of chance ought to have very little effect on one's self esteem as they were not based on personal action but rather on luck. Since the players moves in Chutes and Ladders were based on rolls of the dice Dennis was readily able to see it as a game of chance and to relax and enjoy playing it rather than focusing on the outcome. He and the therapist competed to see who could come up with the silliest way to roll the dice.

The last third of the session was designed to show Dennis how asking for help could radically change his skill level and, therefore, his self-appraisal. The therapist initiated playing checkers with Dennis and soundly beat him during their first game. When Dennis started to look dejected the therapist disclosed the fact that he knew a strategy that made it much easier to win. Dennis hesitated for several turns before asking the therapist to teach him the strategy. The therapist immediately complied teaching Dennis to always move his checkers toward the midline of the board. They were unable to complete the next game but when the session ended both had captured an equal number of the other's pieces. Dennis beamed with pride.

Verbal Components

Reflections: Same as in previous sessions.

Pattern Interpretations: "You seemed to like the games of chance like dice and Chutes and Ladders better." "You sure liked the second game of checkers better than you liked the first."

Simple Dynamic Interpretations: "You liked the games where you didn't have any control over winning or losing because then you didn't have to worry about screwing it up and feeling bad about yourself." "It was easy to feel better about checkers once you asked for and learned a strategy for winning." "Asking for help was hard but using the help was easy and fun."

Generalized Dynamic Interpretations: At the generalized level the therapist first gave an instruction rather than an interpretation. He suggested that Dennis attend to those activities during the school day that were luck versus those that depended on skill and to see how success or failure at each made him feel. The therapist also went on to interpret Dennis' fear of losing his parents' love and approval if he didn't start to do better in school. Because there was already some improvement in his school performance Dennis was able to say that he already worried about this one less and less.

Genetic Interpretations: No additional genetic interpretations were made this far into the treatment.

No specific Problem Solving was done during this session. Instead, the therapist pointed out how Dennis' request for instruction at checkers brought him immediate knowledge and success at the game. The implication was that asking for help might be a good solution to many of the times Dennis experienced difficulty.

Collaborative Components: Following this session the therapist again met with Dennis' school personnel. The report from Dennis' teacher was overwhelmingly positive. She said that he was now completing all of his work and that the accuracy and completeness of his answers was dramatically improved. She also noted that he seemed much more open and personable in class. Based on this report it was recommended that Dennis be placed in a part time program from gifted children that the school was starting while he continued to receive Special Education assistance on an as needed basis.

STAGE: TERMINATION

Although Dennis' treatment had been roughly planned for 8 sessions. Dennis actually initiated the termination at the beginning of session 7 prior to the therapist bringing up the topic. Dennis started by saying that he was feeling much better, that he had not hit himself for weeks and wondered if he needed to come to sessions any more. He said that although he liked the therapist a lot, he would like to join the soccer team at school, which had practice at the same time as his sessions. The therapist agreed that termination seemed appropriate, and they planned two final sessions.

Stage Goals: Dennis will:

1. Be able to describe himself more realistically. He will manifest a generally positive self-image in which his graphomotor disability plays a very circumscribed role (gratification of his need for approval and self-esteem).
4. Increase the frequency of his requests for assistance from peers and relevant adults especially his regular and Special Education teachers.
6. Show beginning awareness of his own behavioral progress.

Session 7

Participants: Dennis and the therapist.

Materials: Paper and pencils, large paper and markers, actual schoolwork, checkers and checkerboard, pair of squirt guns.

Experiential Components: Since Dennis had initiated a discussion of termination this session began by repeating a task from the first session. The therapist again traced Dennis' outline on a large sheet of paper and then proceeded to work with Dennis to fill it in with both features and written out personal characteristics. Now that Dennis could place his learning handicap in perspective relative to his overall cognitive functioning, his overall self-esteem was much more stable. He enjoyed his placement in the program for gifted children and was investing more time and energy in school-related peer activities, which allowed him to move more of his positive experience with peers into the academic part of the schoolday. The focus of the discussion during this session was on the differences between how Dennis had felt when he started therapy and how he felt now.

After completing the drawing the therapist had Dennis briefly practice the relaxation strategy while completing a little of his homework. Again, the focus was on the difference between Dennis' initial performance and his current skills. Emphasis was placed on the degree to which he had mastered his own anxiety and self-doubt.

With the pragmatic portion of the session out of the way Dennis was given the choice of playing checkers or playing with the squirt guns. Although he initially chose to play checkers he asked to play with the squirt guns as it became apparent there would not be time in the session OT complete the checker game. During the squirt gun play the therapist emphasized the number of different things they could do with the guns to encourage Dennis' spontaneity. They shot at targets, they shot at each other. They squirted water into their own mouths and into each other's mouths. The made small stand-up figures out of paper and attempted to knock these down. None of these activities took more than a minute or two and the emphasis was on fun.

Toward the end of this session Dennis and the therapist took time to plan the final session termination party. The therapist suggested Dennis bring two children from his class to help them celebrate. Since Dennis' sessions were held at school this was not a logistical problem. The therapist then used a problem solving format to guide Dennis in planning what to do during the final session. Dennis selected Chutes and Ladders and squirt guns as his desired activities. He also decided that a real party needed food and drink. He and the therapist negotiated with Dennis' agreeing to bring either cupcakes or cookies (depending on what his mother would agree to) and the therapist agreeing to bring fruitjuice and cups.

Verbal Components: The first part of the session involved a discussion of Dennis' progress to date. The therapist spent a lot of time praising Dennis for the excellent progress he had made and for his ability to generalize the relaxation training to various tasks during the school day. This discussion continued throughout the completion of his drawing of himself.

Reflections: The primary focus was on the increase in Dennis' positive and the decrease in his negative affects.

Pattern and Simple Dynamic Interpretations: No new interpretations were made at these levels.

Generalized Dynamic Interpretations: An effort was made to tie virtually all of the discussion to Dennis' experiences either at school or at home.

Genetic Interpretations: No genetic interpretations were made during this session.

All of the problem solving was focused on evaluating Dennis' progress and planning the final session. Specific problem solving was done relative to every detail from the pros and cons of inviting various children in his class to determining the session activities and a menu that all the children would enjoy and his mother would find acceptable.

Collaborative Components: No additional collaborative work was done at this time.

Session 8

Participants: Dennis, two peers of his choosing, and the therapist.

Materials: Cups, juice, paper plates, napkins, Chutes and Ladders, paper, markers and squirt guns.

Experiential Components: The goal of the last session activities was simply to give Dennis experience of using problem solving in interactions with his peers and to provide a basis for his further generalizing the gains he had made in therapy to life outside the playroom. Towards the end of the session Dennis' teacher and his elementary school counselor (who also led the gifted program) stopped by to congratulate Dennis and share a cup of juice.

Verbal Components: No new interpretations were made. The motives and affects of all the boys was actively reflected in support of the problem solving in which they engaged. Problem solving was initiated to manage even the slightest disagreements amongst the boys. It was used to determine the sequence of activities, who got the first turn at games, who got the first choice of cupcakes and so forth. Because it was used frequently each episode of problem solving was kept very brief and efficient with the therapist taking the lead to keep things moving.

Collaborative Components: During a final meeting with Dennis' parents the therapist reviewed Dennis' progress and made suggestions about how the parents might work with Dennis' schools in the future to ensure that Dennis did not regress.

   On follow-up it was noted that Dennis was doing very well in the part-time gifted program at his school and that he had reduced his time in the Special Education Resource Room to one hour every other day. During this time he mostly worked on longer assignments that he could not complete in class.

Transference and Countertransference Issues

Transference

Because Dennis' therapy was focused on a very specific problem and its correlates, there was very little opportunity for transference reactions to occur. The only reaction that arose involved Dennis' attempts to interact with the therapist as a peer/friend whom he idolized. This situation was managed through interpretations that labeled Dennis as the creator of the changes which had occurred and the therapist merely as the diagnostician who had figured out what the problem was in the first place.

Countertransference

Dennis and his situation did not pull for much in the way of problematic countertransference. He was the kind of case that helps insulate a therapist from any lack of progress with other children. One issue, however, is worth noting in this case. The therapist occasionally wondered to what extent Dennis' extreme physical attractiveness combined with his intellectual giftedness triggered the fast response he got from everyone in Dennis' ecosystem. The school made exceptions to their policies, and the teacher made exceptions to her classroom plan, virtually without hesitation. The therapist felt sure that the response would not have been so dramatic had Dennis been a child with average intellectual functioning. This may be a case where countertransference worked heavily in the child's favor.

DIANE: LONG-TERM ECOSYSTEMIC PLAY THERAPY

Identifying Information

Diane was brought to treatment when she was 11 years old upon her discharge from a residential treatment center. Her mother wanted Diane to receive treatment to facilitate her transition back to living at home.

Intake

The intake was completed in two sessions. Diane's mother was seen first to obtain a complete history. Diane was seen second to obtain a history and mental status as well as to get a perspective on Diane's perceptions of her problems.

Diane was the fourth of five children. The mother's pregnancy and delivery of Diane were without complication. The mother reports, however, that Diane was the most difficult of all her children during infancy. Diane was terribly clingy. She screamed uncontrollably if her mother tried to put her down. She slept in her parents' bed for most of her first 2 years. The mother reports that Diane also seemed to be extremely sensitive to environmental stimuli and to have trouble calming herself. When Diane was about 2 years old, the mother returned to working four evening shifts per week. During that time Diane's father cared for her: Diane seemed to make a sudden and dramatic adjustment, as if she did not really mind being separated from her mother if her mother was away and completely inaccessible. At this point Diane was weaned from breast-feeding without difficulty and suddenly began sleeping through the night. She was no longer clingy and seemed to tolerate being left alone, although the initial separations each day were still difficult.

When Diane was 2½ years old, her mother gave birth to her fifth and last child. Diane entered nursery school about 6 months later. Both events occurred without particular incident or reaction on Diane's part.

All Diane's developmental milestones were achieved within or ahead of normal limits.

The parents were separated when Diane was 8 years old. The mother moved out of the family home for about 1 year, leaving the children with her husband and continuing to visit the children during her separation. At the end of the year, the mother returned to the home. The parents' marriage lasted six more months. When the parents divorced, the children stayed with the mother. Within a relatively short time Diane set two fires that did substantial damage. She also showed increasing signs of a thought disorder. She was placed in a psychiatric hospital for 6 months and then in a residential treatment center for 18 months.

Diane was quite cooperative during her intake interview and readily able to state that she was there to help her make the transition from her residential placement to living at home. She admitted to some anxiety about the transition process but said she was mostly just glad to be home.

Diane was able to provide only the most minimal history. She knew when her parents had divorced and the houses the family had lived in over the years. She also knew when she had been placed in residential care and how long she had been in each of the two placements. She could state that she had been hospitalized following a fire-setting incident but denied that it had been as serious as others said or that she had ever set the second fire. She seemed unable to recall much about the last 2 years of her life, although she said she had enjoyed both facilities. She also seemed unable to recall any aspects of her last 2 years of psychotherapy. A portion of this recall failure seemed resistant or at least defensive in nature; however, it also appeared that Diane could not recall these things because they were over. She could not seem to recall much information, positive or negative, about any time period in her life.

Diane was looking forward to returning to school and meeting new friends. She had already decided that she would tell everyone that she had been away at a private boarding school for 2 years and that she had returned because her family could no longer afford to pay the tuition. She had already played with one of her old friends and said it had been a lot of fun.

Diane's mental status was remarkable for her inability to report any of her internal processes. She was happy to be home, she never wanted to go back to residential placement, and that was that. She was enjoying the intake and liked the therapist but seemed unable to discuss anything but the present and very recent past. She also seemed fearful that if she admitted to any negative feelings the therapist would judge her negatively and admitted to being afraid she might be rehospitalized if she experienced any negative affects at all.

Diane was able to say that her primary goal for treatment was to stay out of the hospital. She quickly added that she was sure that she could do that on her own as all that was in the past and that she really did not need therapy.

Assessment

Because Diane had been in residential treatment where several evaluations had been completed additional testing was not performed at the time of intake. On a previous assessment, completed when Diane was 10 years old, using the WISC-R Diane had achieved a Full Scale IQ of 145 consisting of comparable Verbal and Performance scores. Her academic performance was at least two grades above her school placement.

As a part of the intake Diane's mother completed the DTORF.

Using the DTORF, it was determined that at the age of 11, Diane was functioning at Stage 3 in the Behavioral domain, Stage 3 in the Communication domain, and Stage 3 in the Socialization domain. Given her age, Diane should have been functioning in Stage 4 across all domains.

Diane will be able to:

(1) Convey awareness of basic home, school, and community expectations for conduct (B-15);

(2) Give simple reasons for home, school, and community expectations (B-16);

(3) Use words or gestures to show appropriate positive and negative feeling responses to the environment and people or animals (C-15);

(4) Describe characteristic attributes, strengths, and problems in herself (C-17);

(5) Label simple social situations with value statements such as right/wrong, good/bad, and fair/unfair (S-22);

(6) Describe own experiences in the sequence of occurrence (S-24).

GOAL DEVELOPMENT

The Child's Present Pattern of Functioning

Developmental Description

Upon interview Diane gave a mixed developmental picture. Sometimes she appeared older than her chronologic age because of her vocabulary and general fund of knowledge. At other times she impressed

(7) Diane will manifest more consistent developmental functioning.

DTORF (Continued)

one as a child much younger than her chronologic age because of her difficulty reporting even the most basic information and her tendency to become very concrete.

Diane's developmental functioning fluctuated greatly from one situation to another and in her interactions with some people versus others. At her best she seemed like a very socially adept child capable of reading people and situations quite well. This usually occurred in emotionally neutral situations with other adults or peers. Under stress she regressed to impossibly low levels where she had trouble accessing anything but her own very egocentric view of the situation. This type of behavior was more often manifested in her interactions with her mother or other authority figures.

(8) Diane will be able to retain more developmentally appropriate functioning in the face of stressful or emotionally loaded situations.

Cognitions

In spite of her intelligence, Diane demonstrated extremely concrete thinking, especially in emotionally loaded situations in which she was involved. For example, she was quite anxious during an electrical blackout in her neighborhood. She tried to calm herself by insisting that there was no blackout, only that the lights and appliances in the house were not working. She said she knew this because the water was running and the cuckoo clock was ticking. No argument noting that

Diane will:

(9) Demonstrate increased capacity to engage in cognitive activity when anxious;

(10) Be able to match events with their antecedents;

(11) Use a larger affective vocabulary.

(continued)

DTORF (Continued)

neither the water nor the clock required electricity or that all the
other houses were dark made a
dent in her belief.

   Aside from these occasional
irregularities in her thinking,
Diane demonstrated no other unusual beliefs. Her recall of events in
her history was very poor: She
rarely demonstrated any ability to
pair events with the reason for their
occurrence.

Emotions

Diane's affect at the time she began
therapy was extremely limited. In
virtually all situations, Diane could
only report that she was happy. She
did admit that she did not like when
people became angry with her but
said she felt OK as soon as the interaction was over. Diane admitted
that she was sometimes frightened
when she was caught doing something wrong. At one point Diane
said that she rarely knew how she
felt in a situation until after it was
over and she was able to look back
and examine her behavior. In those
situations she could use her intellect to deduce how she must have
felt.

   As noted in the presentation
of Diane's cognitive functioning,
her experience of anxiety often significantly impaired her ability to
process information in a manner
consistent with her intelligence and
overall developmental level.

Diane will be able to:

(12) Recognize her own affects;

(13) Recognize the affects of
others;

(14) Become moderately anxious
without losing her cognitive processing skills or engaging in destructive behavior.

DTORF (Continued)

Pathology

Diane's needs for attachment were not being adequately met due to fluctuations in her ability to perceive the nurturance provided by others.

(15) Diane will experience more consistent feelings of attachment.

Diane's need for safety was not being consistently met as she often felt adults got angry at her rather capriciously.

(16) Diane will feel safe (not at risk of having others get angry at her) a greater proportion of the time.

Diane's need for control was not being met appropriately in that she often did things that interfered with others getting their needs met.

(17) Because Diane will safe more often her need for control will subside. This diminished need will be addressed through more socially appropriate activities.

Response Repertoire

Diane had a mix of autoplastic and alloplastic response strategies, but her ability to use either consistently was quite poor. When anxious or bored, Diane engaged in considerable self-stimulating or fantasy activity, including masturbation, reading novels with considerable aggressive content, and collecting and hiding small objects that either were, or appeared to be, dangerous, such as matches, firecrackers, and rough pieces of metal.

In interpersonal situations that were affectively neutral, Diane was quite able to get her basic needs met using language. She was good at asking for what she wanted and working with either adults or peers toward obtaining those ends. She

Diane will:
(18) Verbalize an awareness of her tendency and ability to copy the behaviors of others and will demonstrate a more consistent use of this skill;
(19) Engage in additional solitary activities that decrease her anxiety;
(20) Engage in less volatile behavior at home;
(21) Be able to discriminate reality from fantasy.

(continued)

DTORF (Continued)

was also very good at imitating the behavior of those around her so that her behavior in a group was always appropriate. This behavior tended to give adults the impression that her acting out must be purposeful since she was capable of being appropriate. It also meant that her school behavior tended to be excellent because she was very good academically and could work with peers so that rarely did anything make her uncomfortable.

At home, however, where Diane was surrounded by people about whom she had very strong feelings, she tended to act out much more often and much more destructively. If an interaction became frustrating or anxiety-producing, Diane tended to do things to bring the situation to a close. Usually this involved lying. Once Diane had told a lie, however, it contaminated her thinking to the point that it became incorporated as part of her reality, so she no longer knew what the "truth" was. If she could not end the interaction verbally, then she would escalate, first into physical threats and then into actual violence or running away.

Origins of the Child's Present Pattern of Functioning

Child Specific Factors

Endowment

Diane was noted to have significant abnormalities in her pattern of response to stimuli from birth, suggesting that in spite of her

(22) Diane will be able to differentiate her cognitions, emotions, and experiences from those of others in her environment.

DTORF (Continued)

intellectual skills she was neuro-
logically immature or impaired at
birth, although these deficits were
no longer measurable by the time
she entered the elementary school
grades. Given the intensity of the
problems during Diane's infancy,
as reported by her mother, it is
likely that there was a significant
interference with the primary
bond. That is, it appears that
Diane's neurological sensitivity
triggered intense dependency on
her mother and did not allow for
appropriate differentiation over
the course of the first 2 years.
Diane's extreme intelligence allowed her to continue to develop
in other ways but was not sufficient
to correct for the failure to
differentiate.

Developmental Response

Diane appears to have had some
type of neurologic problem during
her first year to 18 months of life,
which made it difficult for her to
tolerate her environment without
considerable protection, as provided by her mother. This created a
situation in which Diane was intensely attached to her mother for
the first 12 to 18 months of her life,
to the exclusion of interactions with
others. However, when Diane separated from her mother at about the
age of 2, the separation was accomplished suddenly and unexpectedly.
Given this inappropriate attachment and subsequent separation,

Diane will:

(23) Manifest a more stable and secure attachment with her mother;

(24) Manifest more stable and age
appropriate attachments to peers;
and

(25) Be better able to distinguish
fantasy from reality.

(continued)

DTORF (Continued)

the therapist hypothesized that Diane would manifest problems in her significant interpersonal interactions. The therapist further hypothesized that because Diane's problems manifested so early in her life, the impact on her subsequent functioning would be severe and would include distortions of reality, especially when relationships became too close or too distant.

Ecological Factors

Family

Diane's failure to achieve differentiation from her mother was probably complicated when her mother moved out of the family home for approximately 1 year when Diane was 3 years old. The move was a precursor to the parents' divorce, after which the mother gained custody of the children and became their primary caretaker once again. Although Diane showed no signs of being distressed by these events, it seems likely that they were contributing factors in the creation of her pathological attachment to her mother.

Since that time, Diane's mother and her siblings seem to have been largely responsible for the level of adjustment which Diane had achieved in spite of the degree to which her early neurologic deficits had prevented the development of a differentiated self. Her mother constantly rehearsed social interactions with Diane so that she

Diane will be able to:

(26) Differentiate her cognitions, emotions, and experiences from those of her family members;

(27) Instigate requests for assistance in preparing for social situations.

DTORF (Continued)

rarely entered a situation without knowing how to behave. When Diane was involved in negative interactions, her mother helped her cognitively process them until Diane understood at least some of the antecedents and consequences. Also, her mother engaged in substantial limit setting through the use of natural and logical consequences so that Diane's home life was inordinately well structured and predictable.

Peers

Because Diane's difficulties developed before she was old enough to develop any significant peer attachments her peers played no role in the development of her pathology.

Other Systems

Diane's placement, first in a psychiatric hospital and then in a residential treatment facility, from the time she was 8 until she was 10 years old, compounded her failure to develop a healthy bond with her mother, although it did enhance her differentiation. Given the fluctuations in her behavior, it was likely that she would require placement at some time in the future. If this were to be the case, the manner in which the separation was effected could be critical in determining whether it had a positive or negative effect on Diane's overall development.

Diane will:

(28) Be able to verbalize her thoughts and feelings regarding her past placement experience;

(29) Demonstrate a full understanding of the reasons for any future placements should they occur.

(continued)

DTORF (Continued)

Factors Maintaining the Child's Present Pattern of Functioning

Child Specific Factors

Endowment

The neurologic deficit Diane experienced in infancy was not manifest in her functioning at the time of intake. Diane's cognitive capacities allowed her to function above grade level academically and to maintain fairly positive peer interactions. However, her inability to process affectively loaded stimuli made progress past the most concrete level of interpersonal interaction virtually impossible.

(30) Diane will use her intellectual capacities to insert affect into situations based on her understanding of what is happening.

Cost/Benefit of Beliefs, Emotions and Behaviors

Diane's egocentric world view made it easier for her to feel in control of her world unfortunately it sometimes prevented her from having good interactions with others.

(31) Diane will develop better empathic skills so that her view of the world is less egocentric and she is able to develop better interpersonal relationships.

Diane's difficulty with reality testing made her see danger in more situations than was realistic and definitely interfered with her relationships with others.

(32) Diane will manifest more accurate reality testing and better interpersonal relationships.

Diane's intermittent destructive behavior often got her in trouble and had resulted in her loss of freedom upon hospitalization.

(33) Diane will engage in less destructive behavior.

Because of Diane's difficulties people often simplified her world (hospitalization being the most sever example) so that Diane experienced less anxiety and better interpersonal interactions.

(34) Diane will feel better able to cope with the world outside of the hospital so that she does not need that protected environment.

DTORF (Continued)

Ecological Factors

Family

Diane's mother was just about to divorce her second husband at the time Diane was referred for treatment. Since this man had come into the family while Diane was in residential treatment, she had very little attachment to him and, indeed, seemed glad that he would be gone. However, Diane's biological parents' divorce was thought to have been one of the events that precipitated her initial hospitalization. The possibility of Diane reacting negatively in the manner of an unconscious repetition was very high.

Since her family had lived without Diane for 2 years, it was anticipated that their tolerance for her acting out would be fairly low. The possibility of their actively rejecting her in the event of a crisis was considered a major danger in working toward other treatment goals.

Diane will:

(35) Be able to verbally differentiate the present divorce from the initial divorce on both a pragmatic and an emotional level;

(36) Verbalize her awareness that her family will hospitalize her again if it becomes necessary to protect her but that they believe this will not happen;

(37) See that her mother as actively involved in the treatment process, with the stated goal of maintaining her at home.

Peers

Diane had generally good peer relations. She even had a few friends who knew that she had been in residential treatment and did not seem bothered by it.

(38) Diane will request support from her peers in addressing some of her interpersonal anxiety.

Other Systems

Diane was not involved in any other systems outside her family at the time of intake. Shortly after the intake, at her request she was placed in a program for intellectually superior students.

(39) Diane will continue to be as involved as possible in planning her academic program.

Case Formulation and Goal Synthesis

The primary goal of Diane's treatment is the development of a close and trusting relationship she can rely on while developing an appropriate level of interpersonal differentiation. This is necessitated by the fact that Diane appears to have failed to fully differentiate from her mother, therefore demonstrating fluctuations in attachment and cognitive and emotional functioning. The goal of the therapeutic relationship is not attachment but differentiation.

A major goal of the differentiation process is to increase Diane's ability to discriminate both her own and others affects and cognitions. The emphasis here is on Diane's developing the capacity to recognize and label her own affects rather than relying on her ability to deduce her feelings from her behaviors. Initially the goal is for Diane to differentiate between her own affect and that of the therapist. Later, the goal will be for her to differentiate between her affect and that of members of her family and, finally, to differentiate between her affect and that of her peers. As a part of this process, Diane should be better able to discriminate fantasy from reality. A critical and immediate aspect of this will be Diane's ability to discriminate the present divorce from the divorce that triggered her initial decompensation and hospitalization.

As Diane becomes better able to recognize and label her affects, the goal of treatment will be to help her develop ways to manage her anxiety. This will be a critical step in the treatment because any experience of anxiety appears to significantly interfere with Diane's ability to use her cognitive skills to her benefit, often resulting in acting out. Since Diane has such a limited sense of self, the initial management of her anxiety will probably have to be accomplished by the therapist.

Once Diane is better able to reliably recognize and label affects, then the goal will be to have her use this skill in combination with her intellectual skills to delay her tendency to act on impulse. Specific target behaviors include her running away and her aggression. To facilitate generalization, the therapy needs to help Diane work toward understanding the antecedents and consequences of various interpersonal behaviors as well as the rights of others. The latter objective includes the development of some elemental empathy.

The goal of the final phase of the treatment is to have Diane's newly acquired interpersonal skills generalize to her interactions with peers and her family, including the attainment of more consistent functioning across settings and time. If, at any time, Diane's behavior deteriorates to the point that she requires an out-of-home placement, the goal of her therapy then is to attempt to involve her in the decision-making process, hopefully allowing her to see herself as having some control over the course of her life even when she is in extreme distress. Without this sense of control, most likely Diane will begin losing her sense of self in the process and, consequently, resist others attempts to intervene or passively submit without expressing her needs.

The termination process will be particularly important in Diane's therapy because it is likely to reactivate her fears regarding differentiation and autonomy. The goal is to have her use the process to establish a stronger sense of her own capacities without allowing her to simply transfer her dependency onto another person in her environment.

The 39 goals generated from the intake and assessment material were clustered as follows:

1. Diane will experience less anxiety and better reality testing allowing her to track and relate incidents more accurately. (Goals: 6, 10, 14, 16, 19, 21, 25, 28, 29, 32, 34).
2. Diane will experience, verbalize and make use of a broader range of affects resulting in a more realistic sense of self. She will better recognize affective states in herself and others. (Goals: 3, 4, 11, 12, 13, 30, 31).
3. Diane will demonstrate better interpersonal attachments (Goals: 15, 23, 24, 37, 38).
4. Diane will exhibit less variability in her behavior (Goals: 7, 8, 9, 20, 27).
5. Diane will be better able to differentiate her thoughts, feelings and behaviors from those of others in her environment (Goals: 18, 26, 35).
6. Diane will demonstrate a better understanding of social rules and the consequences of her behavior including engaging less destructive behavior. (Goals: 1, 2, 5, 33, 36).

Pretreatment Decisions

Determining the Context(s) in Which Interventions Will Occur

Individual. Diane was thought to be a good candidate for individual play therapy because of her inability to manage her emotions well in any close interpersonal relationship. The primary goal was to increase Diane's ability to develop a well-differentiated yet close relationship. The other goal was the enhancement of Diane's problem-solving and reality-testing skills.

Family. Collateral sessions with the mother were also indicated because of the differential pattern of Diane's behavior at home versus that at school. This component of the intervention was to focus on assisting Diane's mother better manage her behavior at home and to involve her in helping generalize to the home setting the gains that Diane made in therapy. Joint sessions with Diane and her mother were also planned, to allow for direct work on increasing the differentiation between them.

Peer. Since Diane's peer relationships were one of the stronger aspects of her current functioning no specific peer interventions were planned. It was decided that her peer relationships should be carefully monitored as she reestablished herself in the community. There was some fear that, outside the protected environment of the hospital, Diane's relationships might become more volatile or that she might easily be led into problem behavior due to her poor judgement.

Other systems. Since Diane was experiencing very few problems outside the home, no interventions in other systems was considered necessary. The school was made aware of the nature and severity of Diane's difficulties so that they could monitor her progress and alert the mother immediately if problems began to occur.

Determining the Type of Intervention to be Used in Each Context

Diane's long-term individual goals also seemed best served by a therapeutic approach; however, a problem-solving approach seemed best suited to addressing the issues involved in her making a smooth transition from residential placement to living at home. A problem-solving and an educational approach were to be used with Diane's mother. An educational approach was to be used with personnel at Diane's school.

Determining the Therapeutic Strategies to be Used in the Child's Play Therapy

Diane had displayed difficulty regulating her interactions with the world since birth, and although she appeared well socialized in some settings at the time of referral, it was apparent that this facade could give way to some very primitive and destructive acting out if she felt excessively stressed. Because of the potential for serious acting out, the initial sessions were to be very structured but more verbal than experiential. As Diane's adjustment became evident, more experiential sessions designed to challenge her way of interacting with the world would be used. Throughout Diane's sessions there was to be an emphasis on the use of verbal interaction as well in order to facilitate Diane's application of her intellectual skills to her interpersonal interactions.

Feedback and Treatment Contracting

Because Diane came to her first session expecting to begin therapy to help her make the transition from her residential placement to life at home, she did not have much of a feedback session. The first half of her first session was devoted to a discussion of her therapy experience to date and discussing some ways the new therapy would be different. She was a little nervous about the idea of treatment that would involve more activity and less talking, but she agreed that she was ready for a change.

Treatment Plan

STAGE: INTRODUCTION AND EXPLORATION

Diane was coming to this new phase of her treatment with a long history of both outpatient and residential therapy. She had expectations that therapy would involve substantial talking and problem solving. For this reason her therapist decided to let Diane structure part of each of the first few sessions while he structured the rest of the session, which would allow them to compare and contrast the styles of this new therapist with the styles of the previous therapists. Since Diane had stated that she was coming to therapy to facilitate her transition from residential treatment to living at home, the focus of the initial sessions was presented as being a transition from one therapist to another. A few toys were made available, including several felt pens and paper, a rubber ball, and some human figures.

Diane had also been in treatment prior to being seen by an ecological play therapist. The introduction phase of her treatment was completed during the first half of the first session, where the overall structure of this course of therapy was compared to what she had done before. The days and times of her appointments were set, and the exploration portion of her therapy was begun. The therapist planned to leave Diane's first few sessions relatively unstructured so as to be consistent with her previous treatment experience.

Diane spent her entire first session talking about nothing in particular. She responded to direct questions when the therapist asked them but otherwise seemed to be trying to fill the time without touching on anything that was emotionally loaded. She refused to talk about her previous treatment, saying that it was over and now she wanted to talk about the future. If pressed, she claimed not to remember much about the facility she had just left.

STAGE: TENTATIVE ACCEPTANCE

Diane's next three sessions were very similar to her first. However, during her fourth session she mentioned that she knew another child who had been treated by her therapist and that this child had told her that the therapist had sometimes held him and played tickling games. Diane had a definite gleam in her eye as she related this information. The therapist said "That is true. I've been waiting until we knew each other a little better before I started to really play. I thought you might need some time to make the switch from one therapist to another. You look like you are about ready now though, so . . . ." At this point he reached for Diane, who squealed in delight, and proceeded to discover all her ticklish spots. With this, Diane moved easily into the tentative acceptance phase of treatment.

STAGE: NEGATIVE REACTION

Although Diane occasionally became aggressive during any physical interaction with the therapist, she was always easily redirected. Her previous therapy had included considerable limit setting carried out in the context of a residential treatment facility, so the experience of being restrained was not at all new. For this reason Diane's negative reaction phase was quite limited. Several times the therapist made a game of restraining Diane, saying that she was getting a little too rough and needed to calm down. Diane complied within a minute or two. Gradually, Diane began to talk more about the things that were going on at home and at school-the growing and trusting phase of the work was begun.

STAGE: GROWING, TRUSTING, AND WORKING THROUGH

Diane did not come to therapy with a particularly traumatic history, although her experience included multiple significant shifts in the intensity of her relationship with her mother, the most recent being the 2-year placement out of the home. This, in combination with the hypothesized neurologic deficit that Diane manifested during the first 18 months of her life, appeared to have contributed to her failure to develop good object constancy in spite of her intellectual capacities. This lack of object constancy was manifested by Diane's inability to recall, much less process, events from her past. What little she did remember of her life prior to the age of 11 was so contaminated with fantasy material as to be virtually unrelated to the initial experience. The primary contamination occurred when Diane would overlay her present feelings on the events she was recalling. If she felt good now, then she had felt all right during the event she was recalling. If she felt bad now, she had felt bad then. Because of this extreme lag in Diane's social and emotional functioning, the therapist decided to work almost exclusively in the here and now and to create corrective experiences that could be compared to events in Diane's recent past.

Because Diane did not recall much of her past in a realistic or consistent way, she did not perceive herself as having any unmet needs. In session she did not need to have physical contact with the therapist unless a situation became extremely stressful in the present, which usually occurred when Diane's mother made it clear to the therapist that she was upset with something Diane had done in the past week. Diane would become very anxious, and her motor behavior would increase markedly to a point that the therapist would choose to intervene and calm her by holding her in a fairly tight hug.

Virtually all the corrective experiences used in Diane's treatment were based on role plays of recent negative interactions she had encountered with either her peers or various authority figures. During these enactments the therapist provided virtually all the information about Diane's feelings and the feelings of the other people involved. Diane would generally ask how the therapist knew that she had felt a certain way, and he would specify the behavioral indicators which led him to his conclusion. At one point Diane revealed that she never knew how she felt. If she looked inside it was just blank. She said that she had to wait until the interaction ended and then look back at what she had done to figure out how she felt.

At that point Diane seemed to become a more active participant in the uncovering and labeling of her own feelings. It was at this point that the therapist began to work through some of Diane's history by drawing comparisons between the events and feelings of the present and those of the past.

The growing and trusting phase of Diane's treatment consisted largely of problem-solving sessions directed at events that had occurred throughout the week. These events were generally minor infractions of school and social rules that might not be viewed as entirely inappropriate for a preadolescent. What was striking in Diane's case, however, was her extreme difficulty processing these events afterward.

Often she had difficulty identifying the problem, the first step in problem solving. She understood that someone had responded negatively to something she had done but was not always sure what exactly had happened. In one incident, school personnel first discovered that Diane had provided lunch tickets that did not belong to her to other children at her school. When they searched her locker, they discovered that Diane had in her possession a large number of school lunch tickets that belonged to several other students. Not only was there a question of how Diane had come to have all these tickets, but the school had a strict policy against students selling lunch tickets to one another.

When Diane was questioned, she claimed that an older student she did not know had given her the lunch tickets when she was playing on the school grounds one weekend. She said that she had taken the tickets home and asked her mother what she should do with them and that her mother had told her to turn them in to the school office first thing on the following Monday. Diane's mother confirmed this occurrence. Somehow Diane had simply never followed through on the plan.

Diane was unable to explain why she had kept the tickets, other than to vaguely imply that she thought she would get in trouble if she tried to return them. She was afraid that she would be questioned about how she came to have them in her possession. She was baffled by the school personnel's angry response to the fact that she had passed some of the tickets on to other students. After all, she had not sold the tickets, she had given them away. She could not accept that what she had done was the same as "passing stolen merchandise," although she understood that the latter was a crime. The more the therapist pushed Diane to label the problem in the situation, the more agitated Diane became, so finally the problem was labeled as failing to follow through on the mother's initial direction to return the lunch tickets that were not hers.

Next the therapist tried to help Diane brainstorm solutions to the problem. She could have had her mother accompany her when she returned the tickets. She could have returned the tickets anonymously. She could have simply left the tickets in a place where a teacher would find them. She could have thrown the tickets away. She could have asked other children if they had lost any lunch tickets. Diane did well with this part of the problem solving, apparently because it was a purely cognitive step.

When it came to trying to identify which of the plans would work the best, Diane was again baffled. She could not evaluate the relative appropriateness of the solutions. She could not identify her own affect in the situation, so she could not identify which of the solutions would have made her feel all right. She could not identify with the children who had lost the lunch tickets in the first place, and she certainly could not see why the school personnel might have questioned her story about the unknown boy who gave her the tickets in the first place. As Diane again became agitated, the therapist explained the emotions and reactions of the different people involved in the incident. In so doing he created an explanation of the sequence of events that Diane could follow cognitively, although she continued to say that she did not understand why people had made such a big deal about the whole thing.

In the end, Diane was complimented on her initial attempt at solving the problem by going to her mother. She was encouraged to use this plan again in the future and to follow through with the solutions that were developed.

It was difficult for all the adults involved in this situation to believe that a child as intelligent as Diane could be oblivious to the consequences of her actions. Everyone tended to feel that Diane was simply attempting to manipulate her way out of a bad situation. And yet everyone agreed that Diane had appeared totally lost when they had talked to her. They acknowledged that some elements in Diane's story had changed many times, and yet Diane was always adamant that she was telling the truth and denied that she had ever said anything inconsistent with her current story. This event dramatically emphasized the degree to which negative emotions continued to interfere with Diane's reality testing and her object constancy.

The remainder of Diane's treatment continued with the same plan, all the while trying to help Diane establish appropriate boundaries and an adequate sense of self. The treatment was complicated by several major setbacks when Diane decompensated to the point of requiring hospitalization because her very destructive impulses had begun to get out of control. Usually these were manifested as self-abuse in the form of cutting at the skin around her toe and fingernails, increases in suicidal intent, or setting small fires. When Diane was able to leave the hospital, therapy began again, with very active attempts at reestablishing the relationship and working to enhance Diane's sense of self.

STAGE: TERMINATION

Diane's therapy continued for about 3 $^1/_2$ years. Termination was planned when her behavior had remained stable for 6 months. During that time, Diane still manifested occasional lapses in judgment and reality testing, but these lapses did not interfere with her behavior. During the course of her treatment, Diane had transitioned into, and become settled at, Level IV functioning in many areas. Her cognitive development was the first to advance to Level IV, followed closely by her overall interpersonal behavior. Her emotional functioning was at early Level III when things were relatively calm. With this level of emotional functioning, Diane was no longer subject to the extreme vacillations of mood that had interfered with her adjustment prior to starting therapy. This was the single greatest improvement Diane had made.

Due to the length of her treatment, Diane's termination was planned 6 months in advance. At that time she was involved in a discussion of her progress over the past 6 months, and she agreed with the therapist that termination was in order. A termination date which coincided with the Christmas holidays was selected so that Diane would have time to get settled into the coming school year before ending therapy. The date was marked on a calendar, with the intervening sessions circled. Sessions were crossed off the calendar as the weeks proceeded.

Although Diane's treatment had involved very little playing over the last year, she wanted to play again many of the games she had enjoyed as a way of recapitulating and reviewing the therapy. In spite of this regression, most of the work of therapy was done on a verbal level without particular incident. Most of the sessions focused on Diane's anxiety about having to function on her own and on the development of strategies for coping with that anxiety as well as creating a support system which could provide for her some of the things that therapy had provided.

At this point, Diane had made a substantial investment in peer friends. The needs that therapy had met for her over the years were identified, as were ways her friends could be involved in taking over some of these needs. She role played discussions with her friends in session and then repeated the interactions at home. In the next session she processed the interaction and planned what she might do next. This problem-solving approach helped her decathect the sessions and begin to accept more and more responsibility for managing her life and her interpersonal interactions.

Over the last few weeks, Diane began to report feeling that she might decompensate. She noted some transient distortions of her reality testing but none that persisted. Her increasing anxiety was constantly reflected and related to her difficulty being independent due to her need for considerable help from others in reading interpersonal situations and deciding how to behave. The availability of people in her environment who could do this for her was acknowledged, and the fact that she could return to therapy in the future if she needed to was restated. With this reassurance to anchor her, she was able to terminate without incident. Diane returned to treatment when she was 21 years old because she was experiencing considerable anxiety over moving away from home. The course of this treatment is unknown.

Collateral Interventions

Diane's mother was extensively involved in several types of collateral work. She and Diane had both split and joint sessions with the therapist. The content of the split session time varied. Sometimes it was primarily directed toward sharing information; at other times it was directed toward educating the mother as to the nature of Diane's pathology and the long-term prognosis. At still other times it was directed toward crisis intervention and providing the mother with support in coping with such a difficult child. The joint sessions involved problem solving directed toward problems that had occurred during the previous week.

Diane's mother was also seen in individual therapy by Diane's therapist for the treatment of problems unrelated to the difficulties Diane was experiencing. This provided the therapist the opportunity to help the mother develop strategies to ensure that she got her own needs met in spite of vacillations in Diane's functioning. The mother's increased ability to take care of herself made her more available to work with Diane.

In the course of treating Diane, the therapist was involved with her school on several occasions. For the most part he attended educational planning meetings in which he provided input on Diane's classroom placement and strategies for managing Diane's behavior.

On several occasions he was called by the school to intervene in behavioral crises. One involved the lunch ticket incident related in Chapter Seven. The school was not sure whether they should call the police, which was their standard response to such incidents. The vice principal did not follow through because it was obvious that Diane was not processing any of their verbal interactions in the way he expected given what he knew of her excellent academic record. Instead of involving he police, the school agreed to have Diane work to repay the students whose tickets she had given away. This intervention lasted longer than Diane's lecture from a police officer would have and meant more to her than the threat of a juvenile record.

Diane's very limited sense of interpersonal and body boundaries made it very difficult for her to tolerate any invasive medical procedures. During her first trip to the dentist after returning home, Diane tolerated the administration of novocaine injections but panicked at the thought of the dentist drilling her teeth. Her panic was so intense that, in spite of considerable reassurance from a fairly supportive dentist, she was unable to allow the dentist to proceed.

During her next play session, Diane told her therapist that the idea of someone injecting things into her body did not bother her at all. She did not like the pain, but it did not particularly scare her. The idea, however, of someone taking something out of her body, like part of a tooth, was overwhelming. She claimed that before the dentist even started drilling it felt like her whole head began to tingle and that her blood started moving toward the hole. She knew it did not make sense, but she said that it scared her so much that she could not let the dentist proceed.

Armed with this information, Diane's mother spoke to the dentist, and between the two they talked Diane into trying again, this time with a dental dam in place. For some reason the dam, which covered her entire mouth, leaving only the target tooth exposed, made Diane feel as if nothing could escape from her body. The dentist was able to successfully fill the tooth.

Transference and Countertransference Issues

Because of Diane's poorly developed sense of her individual boundaries, transference problems tended to occur almost continuously. For quite some time the therapist was the good parent who was seen as having the power to make Diane's mother comply with Diane's wishes. At other times the therapist was the bad parent who was confrontive and demanding and would not let topics drop. Diane's perception of the therapist's capacity to influence others in her ecosystem vacillated between the grandiose and the impotent. In each case the perception was managed through constant interpretation of Diane's emotions, needs, and motives and through the use of experiences that disrupted her belief system. Most of these experiences involved bringing others into the interaction between Diane and her therapist so that each person's role could be clarified and operationally defined.

Diane was one of those children whose progress was so slow and whose regressions were so dramatic that it was easy for everyone involved with her to become frustrated and depressed. In sessions these reactions were addressed by varying the technique and content of the sessions periodically. There were also periodic meetings of the school and mental health personnel with Diane's parents and therapist, which helped to make everyone feel that they were involved in a team effort rather than trying to alter a very difficult situation on their own.

PART IV

Ecosystemic Play Therapy
for Groups

The model of group play therapy presented in Chapter Fifteen was derived in much the same way as the Ecosystemic Theory of individual play therapy presented thus far. That is, several different intervention strategies were integrated into a single model using developmental theory as a frame and an ecological perspective as a filter. The organization and structure of the group are geared to the developmental level of the participants, as are the activities and verbal interventions implemented within the group sessions. Similarly, the conceptualization of child pathology presented in Chapter Four does not change as group work is planned and implemented. The focus of course does shift to emphasize the interpersonal rather than intrapersonal aspects of children's psychopathology. However, as with individual play therapy, the goal of group work is to bring the child to a level of functional development consistent with the child's biologic endowment. Group play therapy is particularly oriented to fostering the generalization of the child's individual capacities to interactions with peers.

The group play therapy model presented herein is very structured, especially at the outset of the intervention, and is designed for use with Level II, III, and IV children who exhibit significant difficulties with respect to their peer interactions.

CHAPTER FIFTEEN

Group Play Therapy

So far in this text the application of Ecosystemic Theory to the practice of play therapy with individual children, parent-child dyads, and families has been discussed in more or less detail. In this chapter Ecosystemic Theory is applied to the practice of Ecosystemic Group Play Therapy for which it is particularly well suited. Play groups are, in fact, the best place to remediate and practice peer social skills. Two meta-analyses have revealed some of the strengths and weaknesses of group work. Bielman, Pfingsten, and Lösel (1994) found, in a review of 56 outcome studies completed between 1974 and 1997 that: (1) group treatment is effective; (2) middle socioeconomic children do better than low SES children; (3) treatment offered in clinical settings are more effective than that offered in schools; and (4) groups with a treatment focus produced more change than those that were psychoeducational in nature. Hoag and Burlingame (1997) in a review of 49 studies completed between 1981 and 1990 found that children changed the most on those dimension that were directly addressed in the group. They also found that children in these social-cognitive skills training groups showed poor generalization and long-term maintenance of positive changes in their behavior. This problem of poor generalization is specifically addressed in the description of Ecosystemic Group Play Therapy.

The history of group play therapy roughly parallels the evolution of individual play therapy. Group therapy for children was being conducted as early as 1936 (Bender & Woltman). Group work expanded slowly through the 1940s with Slavson's (1947, 1964) work being widely cited. In the 1960s and 1970s the focus of group work and research tended to be on social and sociocultural variables. Since that time group play therapy has been widely used to address an array of problems from peer social skills deficits to specific content areas such as divorce or chronic illness (Kymissis & Halperin, 1996; Sweeney & Homeyer, 1999). For a more complete history see Kraft (1996).

Almost irrespective of the theoretical frame used for the practice of group play therapy, group work is seen as having some inherent benefits not necessarily available in individual work:

1. Groups tend to promote more spontaneity than the child might show when alone with the therapist.
2. The group modality provides the opportunity to address both intrapsychic and interpersonal issues.
3. Vicarious learning and catharsis take place in the group.
4. Children have the opportunity to receive and reflect on feedback from their peers.
5. The presence of peers tends to more solidly anchor the session in reality. The child is less likely to engage in repetitive behavior or to withdraw into fantasy.
6. The pattern of the child's interaction in group provides the therapist an opportunity to observe a sample of the child's "real life" behavior.
7. Children have the opportunity to practice new behaviors and social skills.
8. The presence of other children may facilitate the child in developing a therapeutic relationship.

(Based on information from Axline, 1947; Ginnott, 1994; Landreth & Sweeney, 1999; Schiffler, 1969; Slavson, 1964; Sweeney, 1997; Sweeney & Homeyer, 1999.)

CONCEPTUAL MODEL

The structure that has become the foundation of Ecosystemic Group Play Therapy was originally developed by the author and Maria Nardone (Nardone, Tryon, & O'Connor, 1986) as part of a research project aimed at reducing the aggressive behavior of boys aged 9 to 12 who were in residential treatment. The original group model was designed to target two types of problems. One set of problems targeted were the specific skills viewed as essential to effective interpersonal interactions. They include the ability to:

1. Select and attend to relevant stimuli.
2. Remember those stimuli.
3. Sequence stimuli or events as well as the ability to predict a logical sequence.
4. Anticipate the consequences of one's own or another's actions.
5. Appreciate one's own or another's feelings.
6. Manage one's frustration regardless of its origins.

7. Inhibit one's tendency toward action, especially to delay one's initial (gut level) response by at least a few seconds.
8. Relax with only a minimum of external assistance or cueing.

(Adapted from *Teaching Children Self-Control,* Fagen, Long, & Stevens, 1975, p. 38.)

Based on this list, the Ecosystemic Group Play Therapy model presented here incorporates a variety of techniques to address three aspects of children's functioning in a group setting. First, the group seems to enhance children's self-control skills. Second, the social context of the group allows the children to build these skills while directly applying them to their social interactions with their peers and the group leader. Third, the structure of the group lets the children feel safe enough that they are often able to address content, which they might not be able to address in the context of individual play therapy.

The other type of problem specifically targeted by Ecosystemic Group Play Therapy is children's not infrequent failure to generalize the improvements they make in group to other settings. Ecosystemic Group Play Therapy aims to maximize generalization of behavioral improvement by incorporating cognitive, motor, behavioral, social, and emotional training components in discussions and tasks typical of a wide variety of the child's daily living situations. Related to this the basis for the format of this group is developed in the next few pages. The remainder of the chapter focuses on the types of clients best suited for Ecosystemic Group Play Therapy, the training needed to conduct such groups, and the nature of the group process.

BASIC ASSUMPTIONS

Ecosystemic Group Play Therapy Clients

Developmental Level

Level I children (0 to 2 years) are not suitable for group work because they are largely invested in their primary caretaker, in having their basic needs met, and in processing their own experience. They perceive their peers as competitors for limited resources rather than allies. This does not mean that one never brings together a group of Level I children; after all, nursery schools do it all the time. Rather, you should be aware that Level I children have little interest in, and even fewer of the requisite skills for, group interactions.

Group work can be conducted with children who have reached Level II development or above. Level II children (2 to 6 years) are still primarily oriented to the acquisition of individual skills (Wood et al., 1996), but they are interested in their peers as potential sources of information and supplies. Over the course of this developmental phase, their play behavior makes the transition from parallel to interactive play.

Level III children (6 to 12 years) are ideally suited for activity-oriented group therapy of the type described in the remainder of this chapter. Level III children develop strong attachments to their peers and are now able to view their peers as an important source of emotional supplies. They spend most of this developmental period learning to apply their individual skills to the group's work (Wood et al., 1996). They can see themselves as a part of a group without losing a sense of their individuality and will work to define their particular role.

As children enter Level IV (12 years and older), they become less interested in a highly structured group because they find it to be too much like school; this attitude limits their participation. To maximize the interaction of the group members, you might have a list of possible activities or discussion topics available, and you might want to impose no more than a few basic rules. Beyond this limited structure, you would want to turn the group over to the children as much as possible. In this less structured context, Level IV children tend to become progressively more interested in verbal interactions and the content of the sessions. During this developmental level, there is a valuing of the group that goes beyond what the individual members feel they can get from each other. Groups of Level IV children often develop an identity of their own that may be overtly noted when the children choose to name their group. For children who have attained at least Level II functioning, group work can be a very important part of their overall treatment plan.

Pathology

Ecosystemic Group Play Therapy is designed to address the interpersonal sequelae of each child's pathology. The individual children in a group may exhibit pathology that derives from similar or different biologic, environmental, or traumatic bases. However, what each child will have in common with the rest is the fact that his pathology manifests itself in interpersonal problems.

Aside from children exhibiting a specific pathology or even specific interpersonal problems, you might want to consider offering a short-term group to children who are new to a given setting, for example, offering a group for children recently admitted to the hospital (either medical or psychiatric), a group for new children in school (newcomers or for all children entering the lowest grade in a new school setting, such as those entering junior high school), or even those entering a summer camp. In this context, the group can serve as a ready-made peer system, facilitating each child's transition to the new setting and larger peer group. When children are to be included in such a group, it is imperative that you do good public relations work with both the other children and the adults in the setting so that group participation actually facilitates the child's adjustment rather than inhibiting it by stigmatizing him.

Group Composition

Children may be placed together in a group for one of several reasons. Each child may have a similar pattern of psychopathology. That is, all the children may have problems with self-control, they may all be depressed, or they may all be overly aggressive. All the children may have a common problem that is not psychological in nature but that affects their behavior and interpersonal adjustment. For example, all the children in a given group may have a specific medical illness such as asthma or diabetes, they may all be new arrivals to a particular school or residential program, or they may all be learning-disabled. Or the children may have certain experiences in common that have affected their interpersonal functioning, as is the case when all the children in a group have been abused, have experienced a recent parental divorce, or have suffered some other trauma. The reason for grouping the children should be known to the group members because it provides the initial basis for the development of a sense of cohesion.

Although it is important that the children share some common pathology or experience, the members of a given group should display some range of intra- and inter-personal functioning. If the children's needs are too similar, they will compete excessively for similar types of attention from the therapist. Additionally, one advantage of group work is the children's potential to model each other's behavior. If their behavior is almost identical, then the opportunity for modeling is virtually eliminated.

The following guidelines are also of value in determining the makeup of the group:

1. There should be no more than four to six children in a group run by one adult, and no more than six to ten children in a group with two adults.
2. There should be no more than a 3-year age spread among the group members, especially among younger children.
3. The socioeconomic status and/or the children's ethnic background should be somewhat similar. This may be one of the least important variables unless the differences between the children are very dramatic, in which case the group may become focused on these issues and unable to address other content or behavioral areas.
4. The children should all be within 15 IQ points of one another.
5. The ability to mix boys and girls within a group varies with the age of the children, the type of group, and the goals of the intervention. There is no fixed rule, but it is a dimension you should consider.

Exceptions to the degree of homogeneity needed to run a successful group abound. If your goal is to facilitate the group members' acceptance of individual differences, then you will certainly want to include more heterogeneity. At an extreme, however, heterogeneity makes it virtually impossible for the group to develop an identity separate from that of its individual members. Generally, the more distinct the problem the children have in common, the more the children may differ from one another and still do well in group. One therapist conducted a very successful group in spite of the fact that he violated virtually every rule just mentioned. The children ranged in age from 6 to 12. They represented four different racial groups: African American, Cambodian American, Anglo-American, and Hispanic American. There were six boys and two girls in the group. And the children's IQ scores ranged from 85 to 140. The bond created by the fact that all the children were trying to cope with life-threatening asthma overcame all the other differences between the group members and created a powerful level of empathy and cohesion.

PLAY GROUP THERAPISTS

Training

The training required to effectively conduct Ecosystemic Group Play Therapy varies somewhat from that required to conduct individual play sessions, depending on the type of group to be conducted. Because the group format to be described is so structured, it is possible to have training that is limited to conducting groups and does not include complete training in all aspects of psychotherapy. Group play therapy has been successfully conducted by teachers and paraprofessionals following a 6- to 15-week training period. Further, group play therapy may be successful even if you make only very limited interpretations of the group process or content, which also reduces the need for extensive training in psychotherapy techniques. You should, however, have a good background in the effect of development on children's peer interactions and in the area of group dynamics.

Role

In addition to those elements of your role delineated in Chapter Five, you are responsible for facilitating the individual group member's development of appropriate social skills in peer interactions when conducting Ecosystemic Group Play Therapy.

NATURE OF THE PROCESS

Role of Play

The role of play in group work does not differ from its role in individual play therapy as described in Chapter Five.

Curative Elements

As with individual Ecosystemic Play Therapy, it is the corrective developmental experiences created for the child within the group that are seen as having the primary curative effect. These experiences consist of the child's interactions with both you and his peers in the safety of the group. The verbal overlay that you can provide in the form of various levels of interpretation will greatly facilitate the child's internalization and ability to generalize the behavior changes made during the group, but they are not a substitute for direct experience. For a child to try a new behavior and be reinforced by peers is a more powerful and curative experience than any amount of discussion in which he might engage with you as either an individual therapist or even as the group leader.

PHASES OF ECOSYSTEMIC GROUP PLAY THERAPY

Intake

The intake procedure for children to be seen in group is identical to that described in Chapter Six. Note that several problems accompany accepting direct referrals of children to group therapy. Adults' (parents, teachers, nurses, therapists, and so on) nominations of children are a relatively reliable way of identifying children with fairly overt self-control problems in the setting over which the adult has control. Typically, however, the children who are acting out negatively are referred, while children who are moderately to severely withdrawn may not be referred. Parent referral is usually a possibility only if the parents are very familiar with the program being offered or have had their child or children in a group previously. Self-referral, especially with older children, assures you of a motivated group but usually fails to identify those children who are social isolates or who act out in antisocial ways. For these reasons, it may be best to encourage referrals to treatment in general and to reserve the decision as to the most suitable form of treatment for yourself.

Assessment

Any of the assessment methods described in Chapter Seven may be used to assess a given child's need for group therapy. If you have access to some subgroup in which the child is involved, you might consider using a data-based method such as a sociogram for identifying children having interpersonal difficulties.

Beginning

Scheduling group sessions is often one of the major stumbling blocks in establishing even a short-term group. The frequency of the sessions is the first problem. For older children, once a week or even once every other week may be sufficient to provide continuity. With younger children, the group must meet at least once or twice a week in order to remain stable and provide the continuity necessary for them to maintain and generalize their newly acquired behaviors. In an inpatient setting, frequent sessions present little difficulty other than that of trying to get everyone involved in the same place at the same times. In an outpatient setting, more frequent sessions often mean more cancellations and no-shows, so continuity is reduced below that which might be obtained via a less frequent schedule. In school settings, the question arises as to which class or classes each child can most afford to miss. To appease both students and teachers, it may be useful to change the group's meeting time at regular intervals (6, 8, 10 weeks) so that the children are not always missing the same class.

The other scheduling problem arises when the group is long-running as opposed to time-limited. In a time-limited group, the children and their caretakers agree to a set number of sessions, which allows all the children to start and finish as a group, greatly facilitating both the initial warm-up process and termination. When you conduct a long-running group, the problem of trying to introduce new children to the group and terminate children from the group at various intervals arises, which can be very disruptive to the group process, especially if several children enter or leave the group in close succession. To reap the benefits of long-term work without encountering all the concomitant problems, it may be useful to plan the group based on an interval schedule.

In conducting a long-term group using an interval schedule, you will plan, for example, to have the group "end" every 9 weeks. You then contract with the child and her caretakers to have the child enter the group only during the first session of any given 9-week interval and to have her leave only when the interval ends. In this case you would meet with the caretakers of all the children in the group after the eighth session of each interval and determine whether their child should terminate or continue for another 9-week interval. The ninth session of every interval is a termination session for those children who are leaving. The first session of each interval is a welcoming and orientation for new members, to allow for a maximum sense of continuity while regularly incorporating or terminating members.

Three other logistical issues bear mentioning. One issue is obtaining parental permission. When working with children who have already been labeled as in need of psychotherapeutic intervention, this usually presents few problems. When the children have not been previously identified, as might be the case in a school or medical hospital setting, then it may help to have someone other than the mental health professional, such as a teacher or nurse, make the first contact with the parent to explain the nature and goals of the group and the reasons for wanting the child to attend. If the teacher says to a parent, "I would like your son to attend a special 'friendship group' where he can learn how to make friends with his class-mates more easily," it may sound better than if the school psychologist says, "Your son is having trouble in Mrs. X's class. He fights often and has been referred to our socialization group for elementary students." In other words, the parent's frame of reference can be crucial.

Second is the issue of choosing a meeting place. Ideally, the room should be large, relatively free of furniture, and indestructible. (An optimum playroom arrangement was described in Chapter Eight.) It is nice to have a cushion for each child to sit on because cushions help create boundaries and a sense of personal space.

Other arrangements are certainly workable; the primary concern is not to try to fit too many children in too small a space because crowding, in and of itself, creates aberrant behavior. There is a definite advantage to using the same room every session so you do not lose time while the children explore and are distracted by the new environment.

Third is the problem of what to tell the children with regard to the group. Usually some simple explanation as to the nature of the group with some examples of the kind of things the group will be doing are sufficient to engage the children. If the group is to be conducted in a school setting, mentioning the fact that they will be missing one class may not hurt either. It may be necessary to insist that the child attend the first few times. If you are still facing considerable resistance after that point, you may need to re-assess the value of including that child in group at that time and consider an alternate intervention.

Working

The Experiential and Verbal Components

This group format combines activities and verbal interactions in each of the following five modalities: cognitive, motor, behavioral, social, and emotional. The inclusion of a cognitive component in the intervention provides a format in which to do some actual teaching. One way to do this is to use a formal problem-solving strategy to work out solutions to problems arising in the group. First, have the children describe the problem in concrete, behavioral terms. "We can't decide which game to play." "Jim and Bill are fighting." Second, have them generate possible solutions and encourage creativity; any solution should be worth considering. "We could each play something different." "We could flip a coin." Third, have the children select and implement one of the solutions based on some estimate of its possible effectiveness. Fourth, have them assess the impact and effectiveness of their solution. Teaching the group a key word for each step such as, "problem" (What is the exact problem?), "plan" (What are some plans which might solve the problem?), "action" (Put the best plan into action.), and "answer" (How did the plan work?) can help make the process sufficiently concrete. This strategy can be applied to both hypothetical and real problems and should be used at least once every time the group meets.

Children can be taught a progressive, deep muscle relaxation exercise to decrease their anxiety, focus their attention, improve their impulse control, and enhance their physical and emotional self-awareness. Younger children most easily learn exercises that require alternate muscle contraction and relaxation. If the group room is carpeted and each child has a seating cushion, then the children can lie on the floor and perform the following sequence: curl/relax toes, press knees together/relax, press hips to ground/relax, pull in stomach/relax, raise shoulders to ears/relax, make a fist/relax, wrinkle up face/relax. Each muscle group should be contracted/relaxed at least twice before moving on, and the entire exercise should end with some slow, deep breathing. Encourage the children to be quiet and to move only the target muscles. Once they have learned the exercise, the children can take turns being the leader who verbalizes the cue statements. With older children, a more sophisticated exercise, which may include some guided imagery, should be used. Although the exercise often does not trigger a significant degree of relaxation, it does help slow the children's motor behavior, stimulate their self-awareness, and focus their attention.

The behavioral component of the group process may involve replacing certain negative behaviors with positive ones by using some type of reinforcement system. Specifically, you may want to directly reinforce attention, frustration tolerance, and the ability to inhibit an initial, antisocial response to negative situations. A specific behavioral system is discussed in the section describing a sample group format.

The socialization component of the group is the most important because it is the reason for doing group rather than individual treatment. The focus of the cognitive problem solving and the group discussions can stress the significance of appropriate interpersonal behavior and social skills. By including discussions of interpersonal situations that arise outside of group, while using the same problem-solving strategy, generalization of the skills the children learn can be promoted.

The most direct way to incorporate an emotional component into the group process is to make it a relevant part of the interpersonal problem-solving strategy. In other words, children's understanding of their own and others' emotions should be made an integral part of defining interpersonal problems, identifying potential solutions, and evaluating the outcome of their behavior. This helps children draw a connection between their cognitions and affects and differentiate between the two. Emotions may be discussed on both a hypothetical and real level in order to cover a broad spectrum of situations and emotions within the time constraints of the group.

Besides incorporating these various components into the group's activities it is important that the group leader be attuned to both the individual and group processes that take place. Tracking individual processes in group is essentially the same as in individual work. The therapist can bring these to the child's attention using interpretation. It should be noted that individual interpretive work in group is usually not as deep as that which might be completed in individual play therapy. That is, highly volatile individual issues and processes are not usually opened up for group inspection and discussion. The primary advantage of group work is the opportunity to make the child aware of the pattern of her interactions with others. VanFleet (1998) suggests that the therapist consider the following when attempting to understand or debrief group interactions and activities:

1. *Leadership:* Who took a leadership role and how did leadership develop in the group?
2. *Emotional reactions:* How did members feel and how were their feelings handled?
3. *Communication:* How was it established and how effective was it?
4. *Decision making/Problem solving.*
5. *Supportiveness.*
6. *Peer pressure:* How was it manifested and how was it managed?
7. *Cooperation.*
8. *Competition.*
9. *Diversity issues.*
10. *Safety:* How were both emotional and physical safety established and maintained?
11. *Continuous learning:* Did the group learn from its own mistakes and processes as it proceeded?

Sample Format

The group format presented here is suitable for most school-age children and some early adolescents. It incorporates each of the five modalities previously discussed in a way that manages to remain fun for the participants.

Each session is approximately 1 hour long and divided as follows:

1. *Relaxation time (5 to 15 minutes).* Sets the tone for the group. Helps focus children's attention. Enhances learning. Increases body awareness.
2. *Discussion time (10 to 30 minutes).* Therapist leads a discussion of situations relevant to the children in the group while attempting to incorporate as many of the self-control skills as possible. For younger children, the therapist may read a story; for older ones, she might have a more open-ended discussion. This is a good time to do direct training in problem solving.

3. *Structured activity (10 to 30 minutes).* During this time, the therapist should engage the children in an activity that reinforces the self-control subskills or issues highlighted during the discussion. Example: One group of 4- and 5-year-old children read a story about a friendly ghost and then discussed things they were afraid of and ways of conquering their fears. During the activity they made finger puppet ghosts and "scared" one another.

4. *Free-play time (10 to 20 minutes).* This time allows the therapist to observe carryover and the children to practice their newly learned skills.

The sequence of activities planned for each session is very important because children's skills in many areas appear to be acquired hierarchically. The developmental therapy program (Wood, Combs, Gunn, & Weller, 1986) provides suggestions for the types of schedules, materials, and activities appropriate for children at various developmental levels.

Sample Treatment Plan

Table 15.1 shows a 12-session sequence designed to maximize children's social interaction. It begins with parallel play and proceeds rapidly to age-appropriate competitive games. It is probably best suited to the needs of Level III and early Level IV children.

Each session includes a discussion pertinent to the activity for the day. One way to facilitate such discussions is to present hypothetical situations in picture form. Liner, Maurer, and Detwyler (1975) created a set of cards that depict many situations children face everyday, along with questions to stimulate discussion. For example, one card depicts an obviously angry boy who appears to be pouting. The story beneath the picture says, "My little sister called me a name. I hit her. My mother saw me and punished me. . . ." The children are then invited to finish the story, preferably in a discussion that uses the problem, plan, action, and answer problem-solving strategy.

The activity planned for each session should be chosen for its capacity to enhance skills or concepts presented during the discussion. A list of therapeutic techniques and activities that might be used successfully is presented later in this chapter. Additional ideas for activities are in the following texts:

Allen, J., & Klein, R. (1996). *Ready, set, relax.* Watertown, WI: Inner Coaching.

LeFevre, D. (1988). *New games for the whole family.* New York: Perigee Books.

Jackson, T. (1993). *Activities that teach.* Cedar City, UT: Red Rock.

Table 15.1

Session	Discussion/Activity	Behavior Modification Stage
1	Introduction: present rules and point system, teach relaxation/ Kinetic Family Drawing (Burns & Kaufman, 1972).	Individual daily rewards
2	Teach a problem-solving strategy/ "Mother May I?"*	
3	Teach children affect terms/ Color-Your-Life Technique (O'Connor, 1983).	
4	Frustration tolerance/"Mastermind"*	Choice of daily or long-term rewards
5	Coping with anger/"Circle Game"*	
6	Sharing/"Pair Pictures"*	
7	Noncompetitive games/ "Snakes-in-the-Grass"*	
8	Competitive games/(Any game selected by group)	
9	Group vs. individual goals/ "Clay Therapy"*	Group rewards
10	Cooperation and planning/ (Cooperative activity selected by group)	
11	Plan final party/(Group selects activity)	
12	Farewell party and activity	

* Each activity followed by an asterisk is described in the "Specific Activities" section later in this chapter.

Jackson, T. (1994). *More activities that teach.* Cedar City, UT: Red Rock.

Rohnke, K., & Butler, S. (1995). *Quicksilver.* Dubuque, IA: Kendall-Hunt.

In addition to these texts containing various specific activities, the following are texts that suggest ways to facilitate multicultural understanding in school age children.

Cartledge, G., & Millburn, J. (1996). *Cultural diversity and social skills instruction: Understanding ethnic and gender differences.* Champaign, IL: Research Press.

Pasternak, M. (1979). *Helping kids learn multicultural concepts: A handbook of strategies.* Champaign, IL: Research Press.

Within the context of the group, the use of behavior modification may be indicated to either control the behavior of the children prone to negative acting out or to strengthen or weaken certain target behaviors. With respect to setting limits on the children's behavior, it is best to establish as few rules for the group as possible. Three rules that seem virtually all-inclusive are:

1. Don't hurt others, either physically or verbally.
2. Don't hurt yourself.
3. Don't damage any property.

Depending on the developmental level of the children, these rules may be worded in a more or less elaborate fashion. To prevent the institution of too many rules, it is important that any other rules, necessitated by the behavior of a certain group, be derived from these three. It is also useful if the children can be involved in the development of the additional rules. One group of children instituted a rule requiring that no shoes be worn during group meetings. At the time, heavy boots were popular footwear among Level III and IV boys and tended to be used as weapons when tempers flared. The boys accepted the new rule because it derived directly from rule 2 and because they had helped develop it. Some groups decide that foul language is not acceptable because it hurts others, while other groups decide that such language is all right as long as it is not used in name calling. In any event, the imposition of very limited and concrete rules makes behavior management much easier.

To reinforce these rules, use of a point system is very helpful. For example, children might earn 1 point for each phase of the group session in which they participate. They could also earn a point for each of the rules they followed for the whole session. Figure 15.1 is a sample sheet for recording the children's points.

Whatever reinforcement system is used, it should be faded over time. If the reinforcement system remains constant over the course of the group, then the children come to depend on it for their motivation. Many children develop a belief that they do not have to engage in the targeted behaviors if the reinforcement system is not in operation; this belief interferes with the generalization of the targeted behavior. Fading the reinforcement system prevents such dependency. Fading occurs in three phases:

1. *Initial phase:* Rewards should be relatively immediate. For example: Points are traded at the end of the session for such items as food or small toys.
2. *Middle phase:* Children are given a choice of trading in points at the end of the session as per previous meetings or saving up points over a limited period of time to earn a larger reward.

Name	Present	Relaxation	Talk Time	Activity	Don't Hurt Self	Don't Hurt Others	Don't Damage Property	Extra Points

Figure 15.1 A sample point record sheet.

3. *Final phase:* Children must save points as a group working toward a group reward over a limited period of time. One group saved for a party with cake and favors. The more points the group saved, the more elaborate the party.

Although the point system may be very useful in gaining both individual and group compliance, it is often more therapeutic if you can make use of peer pressure. This works well when most of the group is being compliant and only one or two children are acting out. Instead of setting limits on the offenders' behavior, you simply point out the fact that they are not being compliant and that they are interfering with the group process. And then you stop the group and wait until the acting-out children begin to comply. As the group waits, it is best for you to keep silent and let the children do the talking. If it becomes apparent that the acting-out child will trigger acting out on the part of the group before she relinquishes her own behavior, then you can move in to set limits in the usual way. At least eight out of ten times, however, simply labeling and waiting will bring about compliance with a minimum of hostility.

If the children are particularly hard to manage, some sort of time-out procedure may need to be implemented to firmly establish the children's adherence to the rules. One possible time-out procedure is as follows:

1. One violation of a rule results in a verbal warning.
2. The second violation of a rule results in a time-out during which the child must apply a problem-solving strategy to her own behavior. When she has generated some viable solution to her behavior problem, she may return to the group.
3. A third violation of a rule results in a second time-out similar to the first and the child's loss of the point she could have earned for following the particular rule for the duration of that session.

Before continuing with a discussion of specific corrective experiences that can be used in group sessions, it is important to note how the verbal component of the therapeutic work is accomplished in play group sessions. You will be interpreting the content of the group in the same way that you would interpret the content of a child's individual sessions. Interpretations at all five levels are appropriate for use in a group session. The focus of your interpretations, however, will generally be somewhat different than when conducting individual work. Specifically, you will want to focus more on interpreting the behavior and dynamics of the group than of its individual members.

At times it will be important for you to present your understanding of an individual child's thoughts, feelings, and motivations as they affect her behavior withing the session. However, the unique benefits of the use of a group format are best realized when you interpret the group process. At this level you might interpret how the group is responding to one of its members or to you, as the group leader. You might also interpret the group's emotions, characteristic patterns of behavior, and their unique beliefs. In other words, the material available for interpretation includes not just that of each member of the group but of the group as an entity in and of itself.

Specific Activities

Mother May I? In this game the players move toward the finish line as instructed by the "mother." In turn, each child asks the child playing the mother how far she may advance and then must remember to say, "May I?" before advancing. Should she forget to ask permission, she must return to the starting point. The first child to the finish line wins. This game reinforces the self-control skills of memory, sequencing, anticipating consequences, managing frustration, and inhibiting one's first response.

Circle Game. The children stand in a circle, with one child who is "it" in the center. The children on the circle are instructed to do anything, short of physical contact, they can try to make the child in the center laugh. If the child in the center can go 1 minute without laughing, she "wins." Later, the group is encouraged to do anything they can, again short of physical contact, to make the child in the center angry. The game reinforces the self-control skills of managing frustration and inhibiting one's first response.

Simon Says. Children follow the directions the game leader gives only if they are preceded by her saying, "Simon says . . ." If a child follows any other direction, she is out of the game. The last child in the game wins. The game reinforces selection and attention, memory, managing frustration, and inhibiting one's first response.

Frozen Tag. This game is played as other tag games in that the child who is "it" pursues and tries to touch the other players. Once touched, a player must stand motionless until she is rescued by another player. The game ends when all the players are frozen. This game reinforces several self-control skills, including the anticipation of consequences, managing frustration, and, most of all, inhibiting one's tendency toward action.

Mastermind. This is a commercial game produced by Invicta, in which the child has to reproduce a series of two to six color-coded pegs that her opponent has hidden behind a screen. The opponent gives feedback on the number of pegs that are the correct color and those that are correctly place in the sequence. The goal of the game is to reproduce the target sequence in as few trials as possible. The game fosters selecting and attending, memory, sequencing, anticipating consequences, and managing frustration.

Some more unusual games can be found in the *New Games Book* (Fleugelman, 1976); most of these games stress gross motor movement and the development of social skills. The following three games were selected from this book and have been found to appeal to Level II, III, and IV children:

Hunker Hauser. This is a two-player game. Both children stand about 12 feet apart on small platforms 6 to 18 inches high, such as old crates. Each child is given the opposite end of a rope about 30 feet long. The game is then played just like tug-of-war, the object being to pull your opponent off her platform. This is an excellent game for helping children learn to anticipate the consequences of the actions as well as requiring them to inhibit gross motor movement.

Snakes in the Grass. A playing field or floor at least 20 × 20 feet is required. One child is selected as the snake. She must lie in the center of the playing area on her stomach while the other players gather round and place one hand somewhere on her body. At "go," the players run away from the snake, who tries to touch them with her hands while keeping her stomach on the ground. Once a player is touched, she also becomes a snake and must help catch the rest of the children. The game can be made more or less difficult by varying the size of the playing field. Once all players are turned into snakes, the last one caught becomes the "it" snake for the next game. In addition to building memory, management of frustration, and anticipation of consequences, this game encourages extensive cooperation among the players.

Catch the Dragon's Tail. This is a game that an unlimited number of children can play but generally requires at least eight to work well. The children stand in a line, and each child holds the waist of the child in front of her, thereby forming the dragon. A handkerchief is placed hanging out of the back pocket of the last child in the line; this is the dragon's tail. The object is for the dragon's head, the first child in the row, to catch the "tail" without breaking up the dragon's body. While the goals for the first few children and the last few children in the line are clear, the children in the middle must decide whether to help the head or the tail. As with Snakes in the Grass, this game builds the skills of anticipating consequences and managing frustration while stressing cooperation among the players.

Aside from games, children can engage in a virtually unending number of art or creative activities such as painting a group mural, building a clubhouse, planning an outing, and writing and then enacting a play or television program. The key to making good choices with regard to the activity is to choose things that are fun. In fact, the critical determinant in the success of the group itself will be the therapist's ability to enforce the structure only as necessary to the optimal functioning of the group while maintaining an emphasis on the group's need to play and have fun:

Pair Pictures. Divide the children in the group into pairs. Provide each pair with a large sheet of paper and a box of crayons or felt pens. The only instructions are that the pair must complete a picture on the piece of paper. They may divide the work however they choose short of tearing the paper in half. The task fosters the children's ability to anticipate consequences, to appreciate other's feelings, and the ability to manage frustration.

Clay Therapy. This is a technique the author designed as a way of promoting self-expression and interaction within the context of a therapy group. It requires children to use clay to, in turn, add to a fantasy construction the therapist has begun. As with any form of play, the primary goal is for the children to have fun. The clay therapy technique is a nonproduct-oriented task in which the whole group can participate. The technique is particularly well suited to use with Level II children because it promotes their contributing their individual skills to a group effort.

The materials required are enough clay so that each group member has a fair-sized piece (at least baseball-sized) and a work surface. You might have the children sit at a table and build the group's project on a small board so that it can be passed from one child to another. You might also want to have a camera with self-developing "instant" film so that you can photograph the group's final project before you disassemble it and return it to the clay bucket, thus preventing arguments over ownership of the completed project.

Have the children sit around a table; give each child a lump of clay. Then tell the children that you will begin building something with your clay and that each of them will get a change to add to the initial shape using their clay. You should encourage the children to build whatever they like while assuring them that it does not have to be real or representational. The only rule you will need to make is to require that each child add to the original work. This is necessary to prevent certain, very needy, children from hoarding the clay they received in their turn and passing on only a small amount. Often children will ask if they may destroy the work of those who went before them; you should respond that this is up to them. You then mold a rather nondescript shape from your clay and pass it on to one of the children next to you. That child adds to the construction and then passes it to one of the children next to her. This child adds to the construction and then passes it on until everyone has had a turn. As the children are working, encourage them to discuss each other's work, to anticipate what they may do during their turn, and so forth. You may also choose to interpret as needed. It is important that the tone of the session remain light and fun and that it move quickly so as to maintain the interest of all the children. To this end, you might want to impose a time limit for each individual or to move the construction along if the group appears to losing interest.

Group A consisted of seven boys and two girls, aged 7 to 9 and at Level III developmentally. They had been having some difficulty becoming invested in one another as a group, and many engaged in moderately hostile acting out. They took to clay therapy with great interest. The therapist built a simple cube that was passed on and, after additions by several children, became a rather elaborate castle. At this point it was passed to a boy, David, who tended to be an isolate in the group, prone to rather hostile, antisocial actions. He promptly squashed the castle while looking around for reactions. The other children were outraged and immediately sought support from the therapist in ostracizing David. Initially the therapist reminded the group that they were each allowed to alter the construction in any way they saw fit. He then turned to David and offered this interpretation, "You must have really wanted to make something that was only yours, so much so that it was worth having everyone mad at you." At this point the boy was rapidly building something of his own that the other children were criticizing. They were again reminded of the rules, which prompted the remaining children to say that they would squash David's work when it was their turn. This resolution quieted everyone down again while David continued to work creating a fairly elaborate boat upon which the therapist commented favorably while reiterating David's apparent need to build something that was all his own. By the time David was finished with his boat, it was so interesting that the group encouraged the next child to add to, rather than destroy, David's work.

After a short break, clay therapy was used with this group a second time. Initially they wanted David to go first so that he could not destroy anyone else's work; however, they finally relented and let him take his turn after the children who were seated between him and the therapist. As the project, a giant, was handed to David, the group cringed, relaxing only when David proceeded to add a dog on a leash to the giant's right hand rather than destroying the work. All the children approved, and David was able to integrate his need for a personal product with the group's need for a unified outcome.

Group B consisted of 10 boys, aged 9 to 12. They had already developed some sense of being a group and took to clay therapy with interest and creativity. Their most creative project involved the creation of a giant with two heads, three legs, breasts, and a penis. By adding the "extra" body parts, each child was able to sublimate his need for a personal product, to make his mark, to the group's desire to create a single fantasy figure. This particular construction also allowed the boys to begin to discuss sexual issues in a relatively light, open way. Although there was considerable nervous giggling while the giant received his sex organs, they were extremely proud of the end product, which they asked to have displayed for the rest of the camp in which they were enrolled.

Other groups created a wide range of products, most of which included human figures of some type. The ability level of the individual group members rarely caused any problems because even the most artistically limited child could find something she could add, even if it were a hat or a base for the figure. Also, the ability of the group as a whole seemed to make little difference in the value of the sessions because even the groups of mildly retarded children were able to generate some product and have fun.

The clay therapy technique, for all its simplicity, has proved to be a valuable strategy in the author's repertoire. It provides an excellent opportunity to ease a group from parallel activities to group activities in a relatively nonthreatening way. For groups who already have some skill at working together, it is a forum for initiating affective expression and related group discussions. And, best of all, both you and the children can have fun.

Termination

The manner in which termination is effected in play group therapy varies, depending on whether or not all the members are terminating simultaneously or one at a time. The termination process does not differ from that discussed in Chapter Thirteen.

The child or children who will be terminating should be notified well in advance and some recapitulation of the treatment history expected. When just one or several children are leaving the group, this can be quite disruptive because the rest of the group is not experiencing the same regressive pull. Fortunately, the group's press toward further development will often modulate the regression displayed by the child who is terminating. When the entire group is terminating, the recapitulation may be quite marked.

Once the recapitulation process has run its course, you should review the progress each individual and the group as a whole made, regardless of the number of children who are terminating. There should also be an emphasis on celebrating the progress made.

If the entire group is terminating, then you should plan a full-session group party that allows the children to say their goodbyes. Children may or may not choose to have one of their peers from the community attend to facilitate the generalization of the gains they have made. If only one or two children are terminating, then it is best to plan to have the party last only for the first half of the session and to have the children who are terminating leave at that point. The remainder of the session can be used to process the children's reactions to losing a member of their group and to shift their focus on planning for the future of their group. All these problems are easily avoided if both the children and parents contract for a set number of sessions as described in the section on beginning group work.

The discussion of the termination of Ecosystemic Group Play Therapy brings us to the close of this volume. You now should have a significant repertoire of strategies for use in both the individual and group work you conduct with children. The potential value of your work, especially when you allow yourself to become fully attuned to the child's ecosystem, cannot be overestimated. However, you must always remember that the goal of any play therapy intervention is the development of the child's ability to play, to engage in behavior that is fun, intrinsically complete, person-oriented, variable/flexible, noninstrumental, and characterized by a natural flow. As a final word of caution: It is very unlikely that any play therapy you conduct will be effective unless you have learned to engage in just such play behavior for yourself.

Collateral Work

Whenever you conduct play groups for children, the need for collateral work is extensive. Each child's progress in group will be enhanced by your communication with those in her ecosystem, including her parents, teachers, and so forth. If you have eight to ten children in a group, you are faced with the problem of how, logistically, to communicate with the necessary people on a regular basis. One strategy is to arrange for the people involved in the children's lives to meet in a group at some interval. If the group is being conducted in a school (hospital) setting, the teachers (medical staff) of the children involved might meet with you once every 6 to 8 weeks. The caretakers of the children involved can meet as a group regardless of the setting in which the children are being treated. One therapist ran a successful outpatient group in which the caretakers and children contracted at the outset to have the child attend eight group sessions on a weekly basis. At the end of the 8 weeks, the caretakers of all the children met as a group and discussed their children's progress. They also reviewed what had happened in the group and the therapist's treatment plans for the coming 8 weeks. At the end of the meeting, the therapist met briefly with each caretaker to determine if their child should continue for an additional 8 weeks or should terminate over the next two sessions. The caretakers were thus intimately involved in both their child's and the group's progress and treatment planning.

References

Abikoff, H. (1979). Cognitive training intervention in children: Review of a new approach. *Journal of Learning Disabilities, 12*(2), 65–77.

Achenback, T. (1969). Cue learning, associative responding and school performance in children. *Developmental Psychology, 1,* 717–725.

Adebimpe, V. (1981). Overview: White norms and psychiatric diagnosis of Black patients. *American Journal of Psychiatry, 138,* 279–285.

Adelman, H., Kaser-Boyd, N., & Taylor, L. (1984). Children's participation in consent for psychotherapy and their subsequent response to treatment. *Journal of Clinical Child Psychology, 18,* 170–178.

Adler, A. (1927). *Understanding human nature.* New York: Greenberg.

Adler, A. (1963). *The problem child.* New York: Putnam. (Original work published 1930)

Allen, F. (1942). *Psychotherapy with children.* New York: Norton.

Allen, J., & Klein, R. (1996). *Ready, set, relax.* Watertown, WI: Inner Coaching.

American Psychiatric Association. (1987). *Diagnostic and statistical manual of mental disorders* (3rd ed., rev.). Washington, DC: Author.

Andronico, M., Fidler, J., Guerney, G., & Guerney, L. (1967). The combination of didactic and dynamic elements in filial therapy. *International Journal of Group Psychotherapy, 17,* 10–17.

Arieti, S., & Bemporad, J. (1978). *Severe and mild depression: The psychotherapeutic approach.* New York: Basic Books.

Arnold, S. (1977). Effects of cognitive training response cost procedure with impulsive preschool children (Doctoral dissertation, University of Georgia, 1977). *Dissertation Abstracts International, 38,* 5553B–5554B.

Association for Advanced Training in the Behavioral Sciences. (1988). *Cross cultural counseling.* Santa Monica, CA: Prepatory Course for the Psychology Oral Examination Training Materials.

Association for Play Therapy. (1997). A definition of play therapy. *The Association for Play Therapy Newsletter, 16*(1), 7.

Atkinson, D., Morton, G., & Sue, D. (1983). *Counseling American minorities: A cross-cultural approach* (2nd ed.). Dubuque, IA: Brown.

Axline, V. (1947). *Play therapy.* Boston: Houghton Mifflin.

Baldwin, J. (1992). Relational schemas and the processing of social information. *Psychological Bulletin, 112,* 461–484.

Bandura, A. (1977). *Social learning theory.* Englewood Cliffs, NJ: Prentice-Hall.

Barabash, C. (1978). A comparison of self-instruction training, token fading procedures and a combined self-instruction: Token fading treatment in modifying children's impulsive behaviors (Doctoral dissertation, New York University, 1978). *Dissertation Abstracts International, 39,* 2135A–2136A.

Barasch, D. (1999, April). The value of play. *Family Life,* 25–42.

Barnard, K., & Brazelton, T. (1990). *Touch: The foundation of experience.* Madison, CT: International Universities Press.

Baruch, D. (1949). *New ways in discipline.* New York: McGraw-Hill.

Beach, F. (1945). Current concepts of play in animals. *American Naturalist, 79,* 523–541.

Beck, A. (1967). *Depression: Clinical, experimental and theoretical aspects.* New York: Harper & Row.

Beck, A. (1972). *Depression: Causes and treatment.* Philadelphia: University of Pennsylvania Press.

Beck, A. (1976). *Cognitive therapy and the emotional disorders.* New York: International Universities Press.

Beck, A., & Emery, G. (1985). *Anxiety disorders and phobias: A cognitive perspective.* New York: Basic Books.

Bender L., & Woltman, A.(1936). The use of puppet shows as a psychotherapeutic measure for behavior problem children. *American Journal of Orthopsychiatry, 6,* 341–354.

Berlyne, D. (1960). *Conflict, arousal and curiosity.* New York: McGraw-Hill.

Bernstein, D., & Borkovec, T. (1973). *Progressive relaxation training: A manual for the helping professions.* Champaign, IL: Research Press.

Bettleheim, B. (1972). Play and education. *School Review, 81,* 1–13.

Bibring, E. (1954). Psychoanalysis and the dynamic psychotherapies. *Journal of the American Psychiatric Association, 2,* 745–770.

Bielman, A., Pfingsten, U., & Lösel, F. (1994). Effects of training social competence in children: A meta-analysis of recent evaluation studies. *Journal of Clinical Child Psychology, 23*(3), 260–271.

Bixler, R. (1949). Limits are therapy. *Journal of Consulting Psychology, 13,* 1–11.

Boll, E. (1957). The role of preschool playmates: A situational approach. *Child Development, 28,* 327–342.

Bornstein, B. (1945). Clinical notes on child analysis. *The Psychoanalytic Study of the Child, 1,* 151–166.

Bornstein, P., & Quevillon, R. (1976). The effects of a self-instructional package on overactive preschool boys. *Journal of Applied Behavior Analysis, 9,* 179–188.

Bowlby, J. (1973). *Attachment and loss: Vol. 2. Separation anxiety.* New York: Basic Books.

Bowlby, J. (1982). *Attachment and loss: Vol. 1. Attachment.* New York: Basic Books.

Bowlby, J. (1988). *A secure base: Parent-child attachment and healthy human development.* New York: Basic Books.

Bratton, S., & Landreth, G. (1995). Filial therapy with single parents: Effects of parental acceptance, empathy and stress. *International Journal of Play Therapy, 4*(1), 61–80.

Brems, C. (1994). *The child therapist: Personal traits and markers of effectiveness.* Boston: Allyn & Bacon.

Brody, V. (1978). Developmental play: A relationship focused program for children. *Journal of Child Welfare, 57*(9), 591–599.

Brody, V. (1992). The dialogue of touch: Developmental play therapy. *International Journal of Play Therapy, 1* 22–30.

Brody, V. (1997). Developmental play therapy. In K. O'Connor & L. Braverman (Eds.), *Play therapy theory and practice: A comparative presentation.* New York: Wiley.

Brown, R.H. (1977). An evaluation of the effectiveness of relaxation training as a treatment modality for the hyperkinetic child (Doctoral dissertation, Texas Technology University, 1977). *Dissertation Abstracts International, 38,* 2847B.

Burke, A., Crenshaw, D., Green, J., Schlosser, M., & Strocchia-Rivera, L. (1989). Influence of verbal ability on the expression of aggression in physically abused children. *Journal of the American Academy of Child and Adolescent Psychiatry, 28,* 215–218.

Burks, H. (1978). *Imagine.* Huntington Beach, CA: Arden Press.

Burns, R., & Kaufman, S.H. (1972). *Actions, styles, and symbols in kinetic family drawings (KFD): An interpretive manual.* New York: Brunner/Mazel.

Camp, B., Blom, G., Herbert, F., & Van Doornick, W.J. (1977). "Think aloud": A program for developing self-control in young aggressive boys. *Journal of Abnormal Child Psychology, 5,* 157–169.

Cantwell, D., & Baker, L. (1987). *Developmental speech and language disorders.* New York: Guilford Press.

Cartledge, G., & Millburn, J. (1996). *Cultural diversity and social skills instruction.* Champaign, IL: Research Press.

Chandler, M. (1973). Egocentrism and anti-social behavior: The assessment and training of social perspective taking skills. *Developmental Psychology, 9,* 326–332.

Chandler, M., Greenspan, S., & Barenboim, C. (1974). Assessment and training of role-taking and referential communication skills in institutionalized emotionally disturbed children. *Developmental Psychology, 10,* 546–553.

Chateau, J. (1954). *L'enfant et le jeu.* Paris: Editions du Scarabee.

Chethik, M. (1989). *Techniques of child therapy: Psychodynamic strategies.* New York: Guilford Press.

Chused, J. (1988). The transference neurosis in child analysis. *Psychoanalytic Study of the Child, 43,* 51–81.

Cole, P.M., & Hartley, D.G. (1978). The effects of reinforcement and strategy training on impulsive responding. *Child Development, 49,* 381–384.

Coleman, V., & Barker, S. (1991). Barriers to the career development of multicultural populations. *Educational and Vocational Guidance, 52,* 25–29.

Coleman, V., Parmer, T., & Barker, S. (1993). Play therapy for multicultural populations: Guidelines for mental health professionals. *International Journal of Play Therapy, 2*(1), 63–74.

Comas-Diaz, L., & Griffith, E.E.H. (Eds.). (1988). *Clinical guidelines in cross-cultural mental health.* New York: Wiley.

Cooper, S., & Wanerman, L. (1977). *Children in treatment: A primer for beginning psychotherapists.* New York: Brunner/Mazel.

Cramer, P. (1975). The development of play and fantasy in boys and girls: Empirical studies. *Psychoanalysis and Contemporary Science, 4,* 529–567.

Csikszentmihalyi, M. (1975). Play and intrinsic rewards. *Journal of Humanistic Psychology, 15*(3), 41–63.

Csikszentmihalyi, M. (1976). What play says about behavior. *Ontario Psychologist, 8*(2), 5–11.

Cullinan, D., Epstein, M.H., & Silver, I. (1977). Modification of impulsive tempo on learning disabled pupils. *Journal of Abnormal Child Psychology, 5,* 437–444.

Davis, A., Singer, D., & Morris-Friehe, M. (1991). Language skills of delinquent and nondelinquent adolescent males. *Journal of Communicative Disorders, 24,* 251–266.

Dennison, S., & Glassman, K. (1987). *Activities for children in therapy: A guide for planning and facilitating therapy with troubled children.* Springfield, IL: Thomas.

Des Lauries, A. (1962). *The experience of reality in childhood schizophrenia.* New York: International Universities Press.

Devereaux, G. (1951). Some criteria for the timing of confrontations and interpretations. *International Journal of Psychoanalysis, 32,* 19–24.

Dinkmeyer, D., & McKay, G. (1982). *Parent's handbook: Systematic training for effective parenting.* Circle Pines, MN: American Guidance Service.

Dohlinow, P., & Bishop, N. (1970). The development of motor skills and social relationship among primates through play. In J. Hill (Ed.), *Minnesota*

Symposia on Child Psychology (Vol. 4). Minneapolis: University of Minnesota Press.

Douglas, V. (1972). Stop, look, and listen: The problem of sustained attention and impulse control in hyperactive and normal children. *Canadian Journal of Behavioral Science,* 259–282.

Douglas, V., Parry, P., Marton, P., & Garson, C. (1976). Assessment of a cognitive training program for hyperactive children. *Journal of Abnormal Child Psychology, 4,* 389–410.

Dreikurs, R., & Cassel, P. (1972). *Discipline without tears.* Toronto: Alfred Adler Institute of Ontario.

Druker, J. (1975). Self-instructional training: An approach to disruptive classroom behavior (Doctoral dissertation, University of Oregon, 1974). *Dissertation Abstracts International, 35,* 4167B–4168B.

D'Zurilla, T., & Goldfried, M. (1971). Problem solving and behavior modification. *Journal of Abnormal Psychology, 78,* 107–126.

Elliott, R. (1984). A discovery-oriented approach to significant change events in psychotherapy: Interpersonal process recall and comprehensive process analysis. In L. Rich & L. Greenberg (Eds.), *Patterns of change: Intensive analysis of psychotherapy process.* New York: Guilford Press.

Ellis, D.E. (1976). *The assessment of self-instructional training in developing self-control of aggressive behavior in impulse-aggressive boys.* Unpublished doctoral dissertation, University of North Carolina at Raleigh.

Erikson, A. (1940). Studies in the interpretation of play: Clinical observation of play disruption in young children. *Genetic Psychology Monographs, 22,* 557–671.

Erikson, E. (1950). *Childhood and society.* New York: Norton.

Esman, A. (1983). Psychoanalytic play therapy. In C. Schaefer & K. O'Connor (Eds.), *Handbook of play therapy.* New York: Wiley.

Evans, M. (1987). Discourse characteristics of reticent children. *Applied Psycholinguistics, 16,* 319–324.

Fagen, S.A., Long, N.J., & Stevens, D.J. (1975). *Teaching children self-control.* Columbus, OH: Merrill.

Fall, M. (1997). From stages and categories: A study of children's play in play therapy sessions. *International Journal of Play Therapy, 6*(1), 1–21.

Fenson, L. (1986). The developmental progression play. In A. Gottfried & C. Brown (Eds.), *Play interactions: The contribution of play materials and parental involvement to children's development.* Lexington, MA: Heath.

Fenson, L., & Ramsey, D. (1980). Decentration and integration of play in the second year of life. *Child Development, 51,* 171–178.

Finch, A., & Nelson, W. (1976). Reflection-impulsivity and behavior problems in emotionally disturbed boys. *Journal of Genetic Psychology, 128,* 271–274.

Fleugelman, A. (Ed.). (1976). *The new games book.* Garden City, NY: Headlands Press.

Ford, D., & Lerner, R. (1992). *Development systems theory.* Newbury Park, CA: Sage.

Frank, L. (1955). Play in personality development. *American Journal of Orthopsychiatry, 25,* 576–590.

Frank, L. (1968). Play is valid. *Childhood Education, 32,* 433–440.

Frank, M., & Zilbach, J. (1968). Current trends in group therapy with children. *International Journal of Group Psychotherapy, 18,* 447–460.

Freud, A. (1928). *Introduction to the technique of child analysis* (L.P. Clark, Trans.). New York: Nervous and Mental Disease Publishing.

Freud, A. (1965). *Normality and Pathology in childhood.* New York: International Universities Press.

Freud, S. (1933). *Collected papers.* London: Hogarth Press.

Freud, S. (1955). *Analysis of a phobia in a five-year-old boy.* (standard ed., Vol. 10). London: Hogarth Press. (Original work published 1909)

Freud, S. (1957a). *Introductory lectures on psychoanalysis.* (standard ed., Vol. 16). London: Hogarth Press. (Original work published 1917)

Freud, S. (1957b). *Three essays on the theory of sexuality.* (standard ed., Vol. 7). London: Hogarth Press. (Original work published 1905)

Fromm, E. (1947). *Man for himself.* New York: Holt, Rinehart and Winston.

Fry, P. (1978). Resistance to temptation as a function of the duration of self-verbalization. *British Journal of Social and Clinical Psychology, 17,* 111–116.

Fuller, G., & Fuller, D. (1999). Reality therapy approaches. In H Prout and D. Brown (Eds.), *Counseling and psychotherapy with children and adolescents* (3rd ed.). New York: Wiley.

Garb, H. (1997). Race bias, social class bias and gender bias in clinical judgment. *Clinical Psychology: Science and Practice, 4*(2), 99–120.

Garber, J., Braafladt, N., & Zeman, J. (1991). The regulation of sad affect: An information processing perspective. In J. Garber & K. Dodge (Eds.), *The development of emotion regulation and dysregulation.* New York: Cambridge University Press.

Gardner, R. (1973). *The talking, feeling and doing game.* Cresskill, NJ: Creative Therapeutics.

Gelb, P. (1982). The experience of nonerotic contact in traditional psychotherapy: A critical investigation of the taboo against touch. *Dissertation Abstracts, 43.*

Gergen, K., Gulerce, A., Lock, A., & Misra, G. (1996). Psychological science in cultural context. *American Psychologist, 51*(5), 496–503.

Gil, E. (1991). *The healing power of play.* New York: Guilford Press.

Gilbert, J. (1986). Logical consequences: A new classification. *Individual Psychology, 42,* 243–254.

Gilroy, B. (1997). Building rapport: It's magic. *Association for Play Therapy Newsletter, 16*(4), 3–5.

Ginnott, H. (1959). The theory and practice of therapeutic intervention in child treatment. *Journal of Consulting Psychology, 23,* 160–166.

Ginnott, H. (1961). *Group psychotherapy with children.* New York: McGraw-Hill.

Ginnott, H. (1994). *Group psychotherapy with children: The theory and practice of play therapy.* Northvale, NJ: Aronson.

Gitlin-Weiner, K., & Schaefer, C. (Eds.). (1999). *Play diagnosis and assessment.* New York: Wiley.

Glasser, W. (1969). *Schools without failure.* New York: Harper & Row.

Glasser, W. (1972). *The identity society.* New York: Harper & Row.

Glasser, W. (1975). *Reality therapy.* New York: Harper & Row.

Glasser, W. (1986). *Control theory in the classroom.* New York: Harper & Row.

Glenn, J. (1978). General principles of child analysis. In J. Glenn (Ed.), *Child analysis and therapy.* New York: Aronson.

Glenwick, D., Barocas, R., & Burka, A. (1976). Some interpersonal correlates of cognitive impulsivity in fourth graders. *Journal of School Psychology, 14,* 212–221.

Goldberg, S., & Lewis, M. (1969). Play behavior in the year-old infant: Early sex differences. *Child Development, 40,* 21–31.

Goldfried, M. (1998). A comment on psychotherapy integration in the treatment of children. *Journal of Clinical Child Psychology, 27*(1), 49–53.

Goldfried, M., & Davison, G. (1976). *Problem solving in clinical behavior therapy.* New York: Holt, Rinehart and Winston.

Goldstein, J., Solnit, A., Goldstein, S., & Freud, A. (1996). *The best interests of the child.* New York: The Free Press.

Gordon, T. (1970). *Parent effectiveness training.* New York: Wyden.

Graham, P. (1974). Depression in prepubertal children. *Developmental Medicine and Child Neurology, 16,* 340–349.

Greenspan, S., & Greenspan, N. (1991). *The clinical interview of the child* (2nd ed.). Washington, DC: American Psychiatric Press.

Guerney, B. (1964a). Filial therapy: Description and rationale. *Journal of Consulting Psychology, 28*(4), 304–310.

Guerney, B. (1964b). *Psychotherapeutic agents: New roles for nonprofessionals, parents and teachers.* New York: Holt, Rinehart and Winston.

Guerney, L. (1983). Introduction to Filial therapy. In P. Keller & L. Ritt (Eds.), *Innovations in clinical practice: A sourcebook* (Vol. 2, pp. 26–39). Sarasota, FL: Professional Resource Exchange.

Guerney, L. (1991). Parents as partners in treating behavior problems in early childhood settings. *Topics in Early Childhood Special Education, 11*(2), 74–90.

Guerney, L. (1997). Filial therapy. In K. O'Connor & L. Braverman (Eds.), *Play therapy theory and practice: A comparative presentation.* New York: Wiley.

Hambridge, G. (1955). Structured play therapy. *American Journal of Orthopsychiatry, 25,* 601–617.

Harley, M. (1986). Child analysis, 1947–1984: A retrospective. *Psychoanalytic Study of the Child, 4,* 129–153.

Harley, M., & Sabot, L. (1980). Conceptualizing the nature of the therapeutic action of the child analysis: Scientific proceedings: Panel reports. *Journal of the American Psychoanalytic Association, 28,* 161–179.

Harter, S. (1983). Cognitive-developmental considerations in the conduct of play therapy. In C. Schaefer & K. O'Connor (Eds.), *The handbook of play therapy.* New York: Wiley.

Hermans, H., & Kenipen, H. (1998). Moving cultures: The perilous problems of cultural dichotomies in a globalizing society. *American Psychologist, 53*(10), 1111–1120.

Hersen, M., Kazdin, A., & Bellack, A. (Eds.). (1991). *The clinical psychology handbook.* New York: Pergamon Press.

Hindshaw, S. (1992). Externalizing behavior problems and academic underachievement in childhood and adolescence: Causal relationships and underlying mechanisms. *Psychological Bulletin, 111,* 127–155.

Hoag, M., & Burlingame, G. (1997). Evaluating the effectiveness of child and adolescent group treatment: A meta-analytic review. *Journal of Clinical Child Psychology, 26*(3), 234–246.

Horney, K. (1937). *The neurotic personality of our time.* New York: Norton.

Horton, J., Clance, P., Sterk-Elifson, C., & Emshoff, J. (1995). Touch in psychotherapy: A survey of patient's experiences. *Psychotherapy, 32*(3), 443–457.

Hug-Hellmuth, H. (1921). On the technique of child-analysis. *International Journal of Psycho-Analysis, 2,* 287–305.

Hughes, F. (1994). *Children, play, and development.* Boston: Allyn & Bacon.

Huizinga, J. (1950). *Homo ludens: A study of the play element in culture.* New York: Roy.

Hutt, C. (1970). Specific and diverse exploration. In H. Reese & L. Lipsitt (Eds.), *Advances in child development and behavior* (Vol. 5). New York: Academic Press.

Jackson, T. (1993). *Activities that teach.* Cedar City, UT: Red Rock.

Jackson, T. (1995). *More activities that teach.* Cedar City, UT: Red Rock.

Jacobson, E. (1938). *Progressive relaxation: A physiological and clinical investigation of muscular states and their significance in psychology and medical practice* (2nd ed.). Chicago: University of Chicago Press.

James, B. (1994). *Handbook for the treatment of attachment-trauma problems.* New York: The Free Press.

Jernberg, A. (1973). Theraplay technique. In C. Schaefer (Ed.), *The therapeutic use of child's play.* New York: Aronson.

Jernberg, A. (1979). *Theraplay.* San Francisco: Jossey-Bass.

Jernberg, A., & Booth, P. (1999). *Theraplay: Helping parents and children build better relationships through attachment based play* (2nd ed.). San Francisco: Jossey-Bass.

Jernberg, J., Booth, P., Koller, T., & Albert, A. (1980). *Manual for the administration and the clinical interpretation of the Marschak interaction method (MIM).* Chicago: Theraplay Institute.

Johnson, J., Rasbury, W., & Siegel, L. (1986). *Approaches to child treatment.* New York: Pergamon Press.

Johnson-Powell, G., & Yamamoto, J. (1997). *Transcultural child development: Psychological assessment and treatment.* New York: Wiley.

Kadushin, A. (1972). The racial factor in the interview. In A. Kadushin (Ed.), *The social work interview.* New York: Columbia University Press.

Kaduson, H., & Schaefer, C. (Eds.). (1997). *101 favorite play therapy techniques.* Northvale, NJ: Aronson.

Kagan, J., Pearson, L., & Welch, L. (1966). Modifiability of an impulsive tempo. *Journal of Educational Psychology, 57,* 359–365.

Kazdin, A. (1988). *Child psychotherapy: Developing and identifying effective treatments.* New York: Pergamon Press.

Kazdin, A. (1995). Bridging child, adolescent and adult psychotherapy: Directions for research. *Psychotherapy Research, 5,* 258–277.

Kazdin, A. (1996). Combined and multimodal treatments in child and adolescent psychotherapy: Issues, challenges and research directions. *Clinical Psychology: Science and Practice, 3*(1), 69–100.

Kelly, F. (1999). Adlerian approaches to counseling with children and adolescents. In H. Prout & D. Brown (Eds.), *Counseling and psychotherapy with children and adolescents* (3rd ed.). New York: Wiley.

Kendall, P.C., & Finch, A.J. (1976). A cognitive-behavioral treatment for impulse control: A case study. *Journal of Consulting and Clinical Psychology, 44,* 852–857.

Kerl, S. (1998). Working with Latino/a clients: Five common mistakes. *Association for Play Therapy Newsletter, 17*(4), 1–3.

Kiesler, D. (1988). *Therapeutic metacommunication: Therapist impact disclosure as feedback in psychotherapy.* Palo Alto, CA: Consulting Psychologists Press.

Klein, M. (1932). *The psycho-analysis of children.* London: Hogarth Press.

Klein, S.A., & Deffenbacher, J.L. (1977). Relaxation and exercise for hyperactive impulsive children. *Perceptual Motor Skills, 45,* 1159–1162.

Knell, S. (1993). *Cognitive-behavioral play therapy.* Northvale, NJ: Aronson.

Knell, S. (1994). Cognitive-behavioral play therapy. In K. O'Connor & C. Schaefer (Eds.). *Handbook of play therapy: Advances and Innovations* (Vol. 2). New York: Wiley.

Knell, S. (1997). Cognitive-behavioral play therapy. In K. O'Connor & L. Braverman (Eds.), *Play therapy theory and practice: A comparative presentation*. New York: Wiley.

Knell, S. (1998). Cognitive behavioral play therapy. *Journal of Clinical Child Psychology, 27*(1), 28–33.

Kohlberg, L. (1976). Moral stages and moralization: The cognitive developmental approach. In T. Lickona (Ed.), *Moral development and behavior: Theory, research and social issues*. New York: Holt, Rinehart and Winston.

Kohlberg, L. (1984). *The psychology of moral development*. San Francisco: Harper.

Kohlberg, L., Hewer, A., & Levine, C. (1983). *Moral stages: A current formulation and a response to critics*. Farmington: S-Karger AG.

Kottman, T. (1994). Adlerian play therapy. In K. O'Connor & C. Schaefer (Eds.), *Handbook of play therapy: Advances and Innovations* (Vol. 2). New York: Wiley.

Kottman, T. (1995). *Partners in play: An Adlerian approach to play therapy*. Alexandria, VA: American Counseling Association.

Kottman, T. (1997). Adlerian play therapy. In K. O'Connor & L. Braverman (Eds.), *Play therapy theory and practice: A comparative presentation*. New York: Wiley.

Kottman, T., & Johnson, V. (1993). Adlerian play therapy: A tool for school counselors. *Elementary School Guidance and Counseling, 28,* 42–51.

Kraft, I. (1996). History (of group therapy). In P. Kymissis & D. Halperin (Eds.), *Group therapy with children and adolescents*. Washington, DC: American Psychiatric Press.

Kramer, S., & Byerly, L. (1978). Technique of psychoanalysis of the latency child. In J. Glenn (Ed.), *Child analysis and therapy*. New York: Aronson.

Krasner, W. (1976). *Children's play and social speech*. Department of Health, Education and Welfare: National Institute of Mental Health, Maryland.

Kymissis, P., & Halperin, D. (Eds.). (1996). *Group therapy with children and adolescents*. Washington, DC: American Psychiatric Press.

La Greca, A. (1983). Interviewing and behavioral observation. In E. Walker & M. Roberts (Eds.), *Handbook of clinical child psychology*. New York: Wiley.

Landreth, G. (1991). *Play therapy: The art of the relationship*. Muncie, IN: Accelerated Development.

Landreth, G., & Sweeney, D. (1997). Child-centered play therapy. In K. O'Connor & L. Braverman (Eds.), *Play therapy theory and practice: A comparative presentation*. New York: Wiley.

Landreth, G., & Sweeney, D. (1999). The freedom to be: Child-centered group play therapy. In D. Sweeney & L. Homeyer (Eds.), *The handbook of group play therapy*. San Francisco: Jossey-Bass.

Landreth, G., & Wright, C. (1997). Limit setting practices of play therapists in training and experienced play therapists. *International Journal of Play Therapy, 6*(1), 41–62.

Lee, A. (1997). Psychoanalytic play therapy. In K. O'Connor & L. Braverman (Eds.), *Play therapy theory and practice: A comparative presentation.* New York: Wiley.

LeFevre, D. (1988). *New games for the whole family.* New York: Perigee Books.

Leland, H. (1983). Play therapy for mentally retarded and developmentally disabled children. In C. Schaefer & K. O'Connor (Eds.), *Handbook of play therapy.* New York: Wiley.

Levin, D. (1985). *Developmental experiences: Treatment of developmental disorders in children.* New York: Aronson.

Levy, D. (1938). Release therapy for young children. *Psychiatry, 1,* 387–389.

Lewis, M. (1974). Interpretation in child analysis: Development considerations. *Journal of the American Academy of Child Psychiatry, 13,* 32–53.

Liner, M. (Writer), Maurer, I. (Ed.), & Detwyler, R. (Ill.). (1975). *I have feelings: Self-awareness.* Los Angeles: Wise Owl.

Locke, D. (1992). *Increasing multicultural understanding: A comprehensive model.* Newbury Park, CA: Sage.

Lowenfeld, M. (1939). The world pictures of children: A method of recording and studying them. *British Journal of Medical Psychology, 18,* 65–101.

Lowenfeld, M. (1950). The problem of interpretation. *Psychoanalytic Quarterly, 20,* 1–14.

Lowenstein, R. (1951). The problem of interpretation. *Psychoanalytic Quarterly, 20,* 1–14.

Lowenstein, R. (1957). Some thoughts on interpretation in the theory and practice of psychoanalysis. *The Psychoanalytic Study of the child, 12,* 127–150.

Lubar, J., & Shouse, M. (1977). Use of biofeedback in the treatment of seizure disorders and hyperactivity. In B. Lahey & A. Kazdin (Eds.), *Advances in clinical child psychology.* New York: Plenum Press.

Lunt, I., & Poortinga, Y. (1996). Internationalizing psychology: The case of Europe. *American Psychologist, 5*(1), 504–508.

Luria, A. (1961). *The role of speech in the regulation of normal and abnormal behaviors.* New York: Liveright.

Mahler, M. (1967). On human symbiosis and the vicissitudes of individuation. *Journal of the American Psychoanalytic Association, 25,* 740–763.

Mahler, M. (1972). On the first three subphases of the separation-individuation process. *International Journal of Psycho-Analysis, 53,* 333–338.

Main, M., Kaplan, N., & Cassidy, J. (1985). Security in infancy, childhood and adulthood: A move to the level of representation. In I. Bretherton

& E. Waters (Eds.), *Growing points of attachment theory and research: Monographs of the Society for Research in Child Development, 50* (1–2, Serial No. 209).

Marsella, A. (1998). Toward a "global-community" psychology: Meeting the needs of a changing world. *American Psychologist, 53*(12), 1282–1291.

Marsella, A., & Pedersen, P. (Eds.). (1981). *Cross-cultural counseling and psychotherapy.* New York: Pergamon Press.

Mason, W. (1965). The social development of monkeys and apes. In I. DeVore (Ed.), *Primate behavior: Field studies of monkeys and apes.* New York: Holt, Rinehart and Winston.

Meichenbaum, D. (1977). *Cognitive-behavior modification: An integrative approach.* New York: Plenum Press.

Meichenbaum, D., & Goodman, J. (1971). Training impulsive children to talk to themselves: A means of developing self-control. *Journal of Abnormal Psychology, 77,* 115–126.

Miller, A. (1981). *The drama of the gifted child.* New York: Basic Books.

Mook, B. (1982). Analyses of therapist variables in a series of psychotherapy sessions with two child clients. *Journal of Clinical Child Psychology, 38,* 63–76.

Moore, S., & Cole, S. (1978). Cognitive self-meditation training with hyperkinetic children. *Bulletin of the Psychonomic Society, 12*(1), 18–20.

Morris, R., & Kratochwill, T. (Eds.). (1983). *The practice of child therapy.* New York: Pergamon Press.

Moustakas, C. (1959). *Psychotherapy with children.* New York: Harper & Row.

Nardone, M., Tryon, W., & O'Connor, K. (1986). The effectiveness and generalization of a cognitive-behavioral group treatment to reduce impulsive/aggressive behavior for boys in a residential setting. *Behavioral and Residential Treatment, 1*(2), 93–103.

Nemiroff, M., & Annunziata, J. (1990). *A Child's first book about play therapy.* Washington, DC: American Psychological Association.

Nowicki, S., & Duke, M. (1992). *Helping the child who doesn't fit in: Clinical psychologist decipher the hidden dimensions of social rejection.* Atlanta: Peachtree.

O'Connor, K. (1983). The color-your-life technique. In C. Schaefer & K. O'Connor (Eds.), *Handbook of play therapy.* New York: Wiley.

O'Connor, K. (1991). *The play therapy primer: An integration of theories and techniques.* New York: Wiley.

O'Connor, K., & Ammen, S. (1997). *Play therapy treatment planning and interventions: The ecosystemic model and workbook.* San Diego: Academic Press.

O'Connor, K., & Braverman, L. (1997). *Play therapy theory and practice: A comparative presentation.* New York: Wiley.

O'Connor, K., Ewart, K., & Wolheim, I. (in press). Advances in psychodynamic psychotherapy with children. In V. VanHasselt & M. Hersen (Eds.), *Advanced abnormal psychology*. New York: Plenum Press.

O'Connor, K., & Lee, A. (1991). Advances in psychoanalytic psychotherapy with children. In M. Hersen, A. Kazdin, & A. Bellack (Eds.), *The clinical psychology handbook*. New York: Pergamon Press.

O'Connor, K., Lee, A., & Schaefer, C. (1983). Psychoanalytic psychotherapy with children. In M. Hersen, A. Kazdin, & A. Bellack (Eds.), *The clinical psychology handbook*. New York: Pergamon Press.

O'Connor, K., & Schaefer, C. (1994). *The handbook of play therapy* (Vol. 2). New York: Wiley.

O'Connor, K., & Wolheim, I. (1994). Psychodynamic psychotherapy with children. In V. VanHasselt & M. Hersen (Eds.), *Advanced abnormal psychology* (pp. 403–417). New York: Plenum Press.

Paniagua, F. (1994). *Assessing and treating culturally diverse clients: A practical guide*. Thousand Oaks, CA: Sage.

Pasternak, M. (1979). *Helping kids learn multi-cultural concepts: A handbook of strategies*. Champaign, IL: Research Press.

Patterson, C. (1974). *Relationship counseling in psychotherapy*. New York: Harper & Row.

Patterson, G. (1971). *Families: Applications of social learning theory to family life*. Champaign, IL: Research Press.

Pelham, W., Bryan, B., & Paluchowski, C. (1978). Social skills training with hyperactive children: A preliminary evaluation of a coaching procedure and a reward system. Paper presented at the Annual Meeting of the Association for the Advancement of Behavior Therapy.

Pfeffer, C. (1986). *The suicidal child*. New York: Guilford Press.

Piaget, J. (1932). *The moral judgment of the child*. New York: Harcourt Brace.

Piaget, J. (1952). *The origins of intelligence in children*. New York: International Universities Press.

Piaget, J. (1959). *The language and thought of the child*. London: Routledge & Kegan Paul.

Piaget, J. (1962). *Play, dreams and imitation in childhood*. New York: Norton.

Piaget, J. (1963). *The psychology of intelligence*. Patterson, NJ: Littlefield-Adams.

Piaget, J. (1967). *Six psychological studies*. New York: Vintage.

Piaget, J., & Inhelder, B. (1969). *The psychology of the child*. New York: Basic Books.

Piel, J. (1990). Unmasking sex and social class differences in childhood aggression: The case for language maturity. *Journal of Educational Research, 84*(2), 100–106.

Pilowsky, D., & Chambers, W. (Eds). (1986). *Hallucinations in children*. Washington, DC: American Psychiatric Press.

Plant, E. (1979). Play and adaptation. *The Psychoanalytic Study of the Child, 34,* 217–232.

Poal, P., & Wiesz, J. (1989). Therapist's own childhood problems as predictors of their effectiveness in child psychotherapy. *Journal of Clinical Child Psychology, 18*(3), 202–205.

Popkin, M. (1983). *Active parenting handbook*. Atlanta: Active Parenting.

Portela, J. (1971). Social aspects of transference and countertransference in the patient-psychiatrist relationship in an underdeveloped country: Brazil. *International Journal of Social Psychiatry, 4,* 254–263.

Prout, H., & Brown, D. (1999). *Counseling and psychotherapy with children and adolescents* (3rd ed.). New York: Wiley.

Pulaski, M. (1974). The importance of ludic symbolism in cognitive development. In J. Magary, M. Poulson, & G. Lubin (Eds.), *Proceedings of the Third Annual UAP Conference: Piagetian Theory and the Helping Professions*. Los Angeles: University of Southern California Press.

Rank, O. (1936). *Will therapy*. New York: Knopf.

Rappoport, A. (1996). The structure of psychotherapy: Control-mastery theory's diagnostic plan formulation. *Psychotherapy, 33*(1), 1–10.

Raskin, D., & Esplin, P. (1991). Statement validity assessment: Interview procedures and content analysis of children's statements of sexual abuse. *Behavioral Assessment, 13*(3), 265–291.

Rivera, E. (1978). An investigation of the effects of relaxation training on attention to task and impulsivity among male hyperactive children (Doctoral dissertation, University of Southern California, 1978). *Dissertation Abstracts International, 39,* 2841A.

Robertiello, R. (1975). *Hold them very close, then let them go*. New York: Dial Press.

Robinson, R., Kaltner, D., Ward, A., & Ross, L. (1995). Actual versus assumed differences in construal: "Naïve Realism" in intergroup perception and conflict. *Journal of Personality and Social Psychology, 68,* 404–417.

Rogers, C. (1942). *Counseling and psychotherapy*. Boston: Houghton Mifflin.

Rogers, C. (1951). *Client-centered therapy*. Boston: Houghton Mifflin.

Rogers, C. (1957). The necessary and sufficient conditions of therapeutic personality change. *Journal of Consulting Psychology, 21,* 95–103.

Rogers, C. (1959). A theory of therapy, personality and interpersonal relationships as developed in the client-centered framework. In S. Koch (Ed.), *Psychology: A study of science* (Vol. 3). New York: McGraw-Hill.

Rogers, C. (1961). *On becoming a person*. Boston: Houghton Mifflin.

Rogoff, B., & Chavajay, P. (1995). What's become of research on the cultural basis of cognitive development? *American Psychologist, 50*(10), 859–877.

Rohnke, K., & Butler, S. (1995). *Quicksilver*. Dubuque, IA: Kendall-Hunt.

Roopnarine, J., Johnson, J., & Hooper, F. (1994). *Children's play in diverse cultures*. Albany, NY: State University of New York Press.

Rotter, J. (1954). *Social learning and clinical psychology*. Englewood Cliffs, NJ: Prentice-Hall.

Russ, S. (1998). Special section on developmentally based integrated psychotherapy with children: Emerging models. *Journal of Child Clinical Psychology, 27*(2), 2–3.

Safran, J. (1990a). Towards a refinement of cognitive therapy in light of interpersonal theory: Practice. *Clinical Psychology Review, 10,* 107–121.

Safran, J. (1990b). Towards a refinement of cognitive therapy in light of interpersonal theory: Theory. *Clinical Psychology Review, 10,* 87–105.

Safran, J., & Messer, S. (1997). Psychotherapy integration: A post modern critique. *Clinical Psychology: Science and Practice, 4*(2), 140–152.

Sander, L. (1983). Polarity, paradox, and the organizing process in development. In J.D. Call, E. Galenson, & R.L. Tyson (Eds.), *Frontiers of infant research*. New York: Basic Books.

Sandler, J., & Joffe, W. (1965). Notes on childhood depression. *International Journal of Psychoanalysis, 46,* 88–96.

Sandler, J., Kennedy, H., & Tyson, R. (1980). *The technique of child analysis*. Cambridge, MA: Harvard University Press.

Sandler, J., & Nagera, H. (1963). Aspects of the metapsychology of fantasy. *The Psychoanalytic Study of the Child, 18,* 159–194.

Scarlett, W. (1994). Play, cure and development: A developmental perspective on the psychoanalytic treatment of young children. In A. Slade & D. Wolf (Eds.), *Children at play: Clinical and developmental approaches to meaning and representation*. New York: Oxford Universities Press.

Schaefer, C. (1979). *Therapeutic use of child's play*. New York: Aronson.

Schaefer, C., Gitlin, K., & Sandgrund, A. (Eds.). (1991). *Play diagnosis and assessment*. New York: Wiley.

Schaefer, C., & Kottman, T. (Eds.). (1993). *Play therapy in action a casebook for practitioners*. Northvale, NJ: Aronson.

Schaefer, C., & Millman, H. (Eds.). (1977). *Therapies for children*. San Francisco: Jossey-Bass.

Schaefer, C., & O'Connor, K. (Eds.). (1983). *Handbook of play therapy*. New York: Wiley.

Schaefer, C., & Reid, S. (Eds.). (1986). *Game play: Therapeutic use of childhood games*. New York: Wiley.

Schiffler, M. (1969). *The therapeutic play group*. New York: Grune & Stratton.

Schiller, F. (1875). *Essays, aesthetical and philosophical*. London: Bell.

Shirk, S. (1998). Interpersonal schemata in child psychotherapy: A cognitive interpersonal perspective. *Journal of Clinical Child Psychology, 27*(1), 4–16.

Shirk, S., & Russell, R. (1996). *Change processes in child psychotherapy: Revitalizing treatment and research.* New York: Guilford Press.

Shirk, S., & Saiz, C. (1992). Clinical, empirical-developmental perspectives on the therapeutic relationship in child psychotherapy. *Development and Psychopathology, 4,* 713–728.

Shuval, J., Antonovsky, A., & Davies, D. (1967). The doctor-patient relationship in an ethnically heterogeneous society. *Social Science and Medicine, 1,* 141–154.

Simpson, D., & Nelson, A. (1974). Attention training through breathing control to modify hyperactivity. *Journal of Learning Disabilities, 7,* 274–283.

Singer, D., & Revenson, T. (1996). *A Piaget primer: How a child thinks.* New York: Penguin.

Sjolund, M. (1983). A "new" Swedish technique for play diagnosis and therapy: The Erica method. *Association for Play Therapy Newsletter, 2*(1), 3–5.

Skinner, B.F. (1972). *Cumulative record: A selection of papers.* New York: Appleton-Century-Crofts.

Skinner, B.F. (1974). *About behaviorism.* New York: Random House.

Slade, A. (1994). Making meaning and making believe: Their role in the clinical process. In A. Slade & D. Wolf (Eds.), *Children at play: Clinical and developmental approaches to meaning and representation.* New York: Oxford Universities Press.

Slade, A., & Wolf, D. (Eds.). (1994). *Children at play: Clinical and developmental approaches to meaning and representation.* New York: Oxford Universities Press.

Slavson, S. (1947). *The practice of group therapy.* New York: International Universities Press.

Slavson, S. (1948). Play group therapy for young children. *Nervous Child, 7,* 318–327.

Slobin, D. (1964). The fruits of the first season: A discussion of the role of play in childhood. *Journal of Humanistic Psychology, 4,* 59–79.

Sloves, R., & Peterlin, K. (1993). Where in the world is . . . my father: A time limited play therapy. In C. Schaefer & T. Kottman (Eds.), *Play therapy in action a casebook for practitioners.* Northvale, NJ: Aronson.

Solomon, J. (1938). Active play therapy. *American Journal of Orthopsychiatry, 8,* 479–498.

Sparrow, S., Balla, D., & Cicchetti, D. (1984). *Vineland adaptive behavior scales. Interview edition, expanded form.* Circle Pines, MN: American Guidance Service.

Spiegel, J. (1976). Cultural aspects of transference and countertransference revisited. *Journal of the American Academy of Psychoanalysis, 4,* 447–467.

Spitz, R. (1946). Anaclitic depression. *Psychoanalytic Study of the Child, 2,* 313–342.

Spivak, G., Platt, J., & Shure, M. (1976). *The problem-solving approach to adjustment.* San Francisco: Jossey-Bass.

Spivak, G., & Shure, M. (1982). The cognition of social adjustment: Interpersonal cognitive problem solving training. In B. Lahey & A. Kazdin (Eds.), *Advances in clinical child psychology* (Vol. 5). New York: Plenum Press.

Sroufe, L. (1979). The coherence of individual development: Early care, attachment and subsequent issues. *American Psychologist 34*(10), 834–841.

Steinmetz, M. (1995). Interviewing children: Balancing forensic and therapeutic techniques. *National Resource Center on Child Sexual Abuse News, 4*(3), 1–5.

Stevenson, J., Richman, N., & Graham, P. (1985). Behavior problems and language abilities at three years and behavioral deviance at eight year. *Journal of Child Psychology and Psychiatry, 26,* 215–230.

Sue, D.W., & Sue, D. (1977). Barriers to effective cross-cultural counseling. *Journal of Counseling Psychology, 24,* 420–429.

Sue, D.W., & Sue, D. (1990). *Counseling the cultural different: Theory and practice* (2nd ed.). New York: Wiley.

Sue, S. (1998). In search of cultural competence in psychotherapy and counseling. *American Psychologist, 53*(4), 440–448.

Sullivan, H. (1953). *The interpersonal theory of psychiatry.* New York: Norton.

Sutherland, S. (1989). *The international dictionary of psychology.* New York: Continuum.

Sweeney, D. (1997). *Counseling children through the world of play.* Wheaton, IL: Tyndale House.

Sweeney, D., & Homeyer, L. (1999). Group play therapy. In D. Sweeney & L. Homeyer (Eds.), *The handbook of group play therapy: How to do it. How it works. Whom it works best for.* San Francisco: Jossey-Bass.

Switsky, H., Haywood, H., & Isett, R. (1974). Exploration, curiosity and play in young children: Effects of stimulus complexity. *Development Psychology, 10,* 321–329.

Taft, J. (1933). *The dynamics of therapy in a controlled relationship.* New York: Macmillan.

Teasdale, J., Taylor, M., Cooper, Z., Hahurst, H., & Paykel, E. (1995). Depressive thinking: Shifts in construct accessibility or in schematic mental models? *Journal of Abnormal Psychology, 104,* 500–507.

Terr, L. (1983). Play therapy and psychic trauma: A preliminary report. In C. Schaefer & K. O'Connor (Eds.), *Handbook of play therapy.* New York: Wiley.

Thomas, A., & Cobb, H. (1999). Culturally responsive counseling and psychotherapy with children and adolescents. In H.T. Prout & D. Brown

(Eds.), *Counseling and psychotherapy with children and adolescents* (3rd ed.). New York: Wiley.

Tolan, P., Guerra, N., & Kendall, P. (1995). A developmental-ecological perspective on antisocial behavior in children and adolescents.: Toward a unified risk and intervention framework. *Journal of Consulting and Clinical Psychology 63*(4), 579–584.

Triandis, H. (1996). The psychological measurement of cultural syndromes. *American Psychologist, 51*(4), 407–415.

Truax, C., & Carkhuff, R. (1967). *Toward effective counseling and psychotherapy.* Chicago: Aldine.

Tuma, J., & Sobotka, K. (1983). Traditional therapies with children. In T. Ollendick & M. Hersen (Eds.), *Handbook of child psychopathology.* New York: Plenum Press.

Tyson, R., & Tyson, P. (1986). The concept of transference in child psychoanalysis. *Journal of the American Academy of Child Psychiatry, 25,* 30–39.

Valsiner, J. (1997). *Culture and the development of children's action: A theory of human development.* New York: Wiley.

VanFleet, R. (1994). *Filial therapy: Strengthening parent-child relationships through play.* Sarasota, FL: Professional Resource Press.

VanFleet, R. (1998). *Debriefing group activities.* Boiling Springs, PA: Play Therapy Press.

Vygotsky, L. (1962). *Thought and language.* New York: Wiley.

Wadsworth, B. (1971). *Piaget's theory of cognitive development.* New York: McKay.

Walder, R. (1933). The psychoanalytic theory of play. *Psychoanalytic Quarterly, 2,* 208–224.

Walker, C. (1979). Treatment of children's disorders by relaxation training: The poor man's biofeedback. *Journal of Clinical Child Psychology, 8,* 22–25.

Watson, J., & Raynor, R. (1920). Conditioned emotional reactions. *Journal of Experimental Psychology, 3,* 1–14.

Wechsler, D. (1991). *Wechsler Intelligence Scale for Children* (3rd ed.). San Antonio, TX: Psychological Corporation.

Weisler, A., & McCall, R. (1976). Exploration and play: Resume and redirection. *American Psychologist, 32*(7), 492–508.

Weiss, J., Sampson, H., & the Mt. Zion Psychotherapy Research Group (1986). *The psychoanalytic process: Theory, clinical observations and empirical research.* New York: Guilford Press.

Weisz, J. (1986). Contingency and control beliefs as predictors of psychotherapy outcomes among children and adolescents. *Journal of Consulting and Clinical Psychology, 54,* 789–795.

Weithorn, L. (1980). Competency to render informed treatment decisions: A comparison of certain minors and adults (Doctoral dissertation, University of Pittsburgh). *Doctoral Abstracts International,* 8202375.

Westermeyer, J. (1979). Sex roles at the Indian-majority interface in Minnesota. *International Journal of Social Psychiatry, 24,* 189–194.

Westermeyer, J. (1987). Cultural factors in clinical assessment. *Journal of Consulting and Clinical Psychology, 55*(4), 471–478.

Wolberg, L. (1954). *The technique of psychotherapy.* New York: Grune & Stratton.

Wood, M. (1979). *The developmental therapy objectives: A self-instructional workbook.* Austin, TX: ProEd.

Wood, M., Combs, C., Gunn, A., & Weller, D. (1986). *Developmental therapy in the classroom* (2nd ed.). Austin, TX: ProEd.

Wood, M., Davis, K., Swindle, F., & Quirk, C. (1996). *Developmental therapy-developmental teaching* (3rd ed.). Austin, TX: ProEd.

Wood, M., & Long, N. (1991). *Life space intervention: Talking with children and youth in crisis.* Austin, TX: ProEd.

Wubbolding, R. (1988). *Using reality therapy.* New York: Harper & Row.

Zakich, R. (1975). *The ungame.* Anaheim, CA: Ungame Company.

Zakich, R., & Monroe, S. (1979). *Reunion.* Anaheim, CA: Ungame Company.

Author Index

A

Abikoff, H., 435
Achenback, T., 435
Adebimpe, V., 78
Adelman, H., 186
Adler, A., 13, 54
Albert, A., 47
Allen, F., 14
Allen, J., 424
Ammen, S., vi, 90, 171, 180, 278
Andronico, M., 339
Annunziata, J., 337
Antonovsky, A., 78
Arieti, S., 130
Arnold, S., 435
Atkinson, D., 83
Axline, V., 14, 29, 31, 61, 146, 147, 153, 414

B

Baker, L., 278
Baldwin, J., 145
Balla, D., 196
Bandura, A., 34
Barabash, C., 436
Barasch, D., 142
Barenboim, C., 35
Barker, S., 75, 80, 82
Barnard, K., 275

Barocas, R., 440
Baruch, D., 49
Beach, F., 3, 5
Beck, A., 33, 35
Bellack, A., 441
Bemporad, J., 130
Bender L., 413
Berlyne, D., 4, 5
Bernstein, D., 436
Bettleheim, B., 4
Bibring, E., 288
Bielman, A., 413
Bishop, N., 3, 7
Bixler, R., 15
Blom, G., 437
Boll, E., 7
Booth, P., 19, 40, 41, 42, 43, 45, 47, 48, 49, 143, 237, 252, 255, 262, 275, 276, 352
Borkovec, T., 436
Bornstein, B., 25
Bornstein, P., 436
Bowlby, J., 20
Braafladt, N., 279
Bratton, S., 50
Braverman, L., vi, 16, 18, 90
Brazelton, T., 275
Brems, C., 80, 138, 139, 329
Brody, V., 15, 39, 275
Brown, D., 446

Subject Index

LINCOLN CHRISTIAN COLLEGE AND SEMINARY